Proceedings
of the
International Society for Music Education
30th World Conference
on Music Education,
Thessaloniki, Greece,
15-20 July 2012

Wendy Sims
Editor

Proceedings of the International Society for Music Education 30th World Conference on Music Education, Thessaloniki, Greece, 15-20 July 2012

Edited by Wendy Sims

ISBN13: 978-0-9873511-0-4

© 2012 International Society for Music Education (ISME)

Published in Australia in 2012
International Society for Music Education (ISME)
P.O. Box 909
Nedlands, WA 6909
Australia

Designed & set in Caslon & Myriad by
Sonustech Digital Solutions, London, UK

copy requests:
isme@isme.org

National Library of Australia Cataloguing-in-Publication Data
A CIP record is available from the National Library of Australia

Dewey Number: 780.7

All rights reserved. Except for the quotation of short passages for the purposes of criticism or review, no part of this publication may be reproduced, stored in a retrieval system, or transmitted, in any form or by any means, electronic, mechanical, photocopying, recording or otherwise, without prior permission from the publisher.

All presentations given at the 30th International Society for Music Education World Conference on Music Education were selected via a full peer review process, by a committee of international experts and authorities in music education. Additionally, all papers included in these Proceedings were fully refereed by members of this distinguished panel, and thus this is a highly selective group of papers, chosen to represent the best of the full papers submitted for consideration. The names and professional affiliations of the distinguished members of the editorial committees are provided, below.

Editor-in-Chief and Conference Program Co-Chair
Chair, ISME Publications Standing Committee

Wendy Sims	University of Missouri-Columbia, USA

Conference Program Co-Chair
Chair, Conference Organizing Committee

Polyvios Androutsos	Technological Educational Institute of Thessaloniki, Greece

Editor, Abstracts & Proceedings

Lindsey Williams	University of Missouri-Kansas City, USA

Associate Editors *(*ISME Publications Standing Committee members)*

*Victor Fung	University of South Florida, USA
Sondra Howe	Independent Scholar, USA
*Regina Murphy	St Patrick's College, Dublin City University, Ireland

Editorial Board	*(*ISME Publications Standing Committee Members; **Conference Organizing Committee Members; ^Commission Host)*
**Polyvios Androutsos	Technological Educational Institute of Thessaloniki, Greece
Diana Blom	University of Western Sydney, Australia
Bryan Burton	West Chester University of Pennsylvania, USA
^Smaragda Chrysostomou	National and Kapodistrian University of Athens, Greece
Gordon Cox	University of Reading (retired), England
^Zoe Dionyssiou	Ionian University, Greece

Natassa Economidou-Stavrou	University of Nicosia, Cyprus
*David Forrest	RMIT University, Australia
Andrea Giráldez	Universidad de Valladolid, Spain
Dina Grätzer	Collegium Musicum de Buenos Aire, Argentina
*Wilfried Gruhn	University of Music Freiburg, Germany
Panagiotis A. Kanellopoulos	University of Thessaly, Greece
**May Kokkidou	University of Western Macedonia, Greece
Eleni Lapidaki	Aristotle University of Thessaloniki, Greece
*Samuel Leong	Hong Kong Institute of Education, China
*Chee Hoo Lum	National Institute of Education, Nanyang Technological University, Singapore
Marie McCarthy	University of Michigan, USA
Graça Mota	College of Education, Polytechnic Institute, Portugal
Glenn Nierman	University of Nebraska-Lincoln, USA
*Alda de Jesus Oliveira	Universidade Federal da Bahia, Brazil
*Christian Onyeji	University of Nigeria
Ioulia Papageorgi	University of Nicosia, Cyprus
Dora Psaltopoulou-Kamini	Aristotle University of Thessaloniki, Greece
Theocharis Raptis	University of Ioannina, Greece
Deirdre Russell-Bowie	University of Western Sydney, Australia
^Lelouda Stamou	University of Macedonia, Greece
**Nikos Theodoridis	Aristotle University of Thessaloniki, Greece
^Angeliki Triantafyllaki	National and Kapodistrian University of Athens, Greece
**Costas Tsougras	Aristotle University of Thessaloniki, Greece
**Petros Vouvaris	University of Macedonia, Greece
Yiying Wang	Beijing Normal University, China
Heidi Westerlund	Sibelius Academy, Finland

Reviewers: Forum for Instrumental & Vocal Music Teaching and Special Interest Groups

(*Convener)

Forum for Instrumental and Vocal Teaching

*Helena Gaunt	Guildhall School of Music & Drama, England
Graham Bartle	ISME Honorary Life Member, Australia
Dawn Bennett	Curtin University, Australia
Gail Berenson	Ohio University, USA
Geoff Coates	Guildhall School of Music & Drama, England
Gareth Dylan Smith	Institute of Contemporary Music Performance, England

Special Interest Groups

Active Music Making

*Susie Davies-Splitter	Welcome to Music, Australia
Daniel Johnson	University of North Carolina Wilmington, USA
Jarka Kotulkova	International School of Prague, Czech Republic

Assessment, Measurement, and Evaluation (AME)

*Timothy S. Brophy	University of Florida, USA
Ming-Jen Chuang	National Taichung University of Education, Taiwan
Andreas Lehmann-Wermser	University of Bremen, Germany

El Sistema

*Theodora Stathopoulos	Formation Artistique au Coeur de l'Éducation, Canada
Richard Hallam	Hallam Creative Enterprises Ltd, England
Graça Mota	College of Education, Polytechnic Institute, Portugal

Jazz

*Kimberly McCord	Illinois State University, USA
Greg Carroll	American Jazz Museum, Kansas City, Missouri, USA

Musician's Health and Well Being

*Gail Berenson	Ohio University, USA
	Graham Bartle ISME Honorary Life Member, Australia
Helena Gaunt	Guildhall School of Music & Drama, England
Sylvia Schwarzenbach	ISME Honorary Life Member, Australia

New Professionals

*Alex Ruthmann	University of Massachusetts Lowell, USA
Dafu Lai	China University of Petroleum in Beijing, China
Benon Kigozi	Makerere University, Kampala, Uganda

Practice and Research in Integrated Music Education (PRIME)

*Markus Cslovjecsek	University of Applied Sciences Northwestern Switzerland (FHNW)
Daniel Hug	School for Applied Sciences Northwestern Switzerland

Spirituality in Music Education (SAME)

*Giorgos Tsiris	Nordoff Robbins, City University, London, England
Arvydas Girdzijauskas	Klaipeda University, Lithuania
	Diana Harris Open University, UK
	Emilija Sakadolskis Lithuanian University of Educational Sciences, Vilnius, Lithuania

Technology

*Samuel Leong	Hong Kong Institute of Education, China
*Fred Joseph Rees	Indiana University, Purdue University, USA
Matti Ruipo	Tampere University of Applied Sciences, Finland

Lauri Väkevä   Sibelius Academy, Finland

Editorial Assistants

Christopher M. Baumgartner   University of Missouri-Columbia, USA
Jennifer A. Moder   University of Missouri-Kansas City, USA
Daniel Keown   University of Missouri-Kansas City, USA

Table of Contents

CONFERENCE PROCEEDINGS	13
Incorporating Traditional *Choro* Music Experiences into Brazilian University Music Curricula through Class Instruction Using Comprehensive Musicianship Concepts Sergio Luis de Almeida Alvares	15
The Effect of Curriculum Reforms of 2002 on the Teaching of Music in Primary Schools in Sunga Sub-location, Maseno Division, Kenya Hellen Atieno	25
Fully Online Learning in a Pre-service Teacher Music Education Unit in Australia: Student Perspectives Bill Baker	43
Considering Cultural Plurality in Band Method Books Joel Luis da Silva Barbosa	51
Nurturing Students in a School Music Program through a Natural Disaster Judith Bell Tim Bell	57
Assessing Undergraduate Jazz and Rock Group Music-making: Adding to the Classic(al) Recipe Diana Blom John Encarnacao	63
Unleashing the Imagination: Creating Collectively Conceived Music through Improvisation Anthony Branker	71
Finding Flow in Collaborative Music Performance: Essential Music Reading Skills for a Piano Accompanist Judith Elizabeth Brown	79
The Multiple Layers of Culture and the Multiple Layers of Society Peter Douskalis	89
Praxial Music in Schools: A Clash of Cultures? John Drummond	101
Instrument Teaching in South African Higher Education Institutions: At the Center or on the Periphery? Marc Duby	107
Music Education and ePortfolios: New Thinking for the Preparation of Music Teachers Peter Dunbar-Hall Jennifer Rowley Madeleine Bell John Taylor	115
The role of music teaching and learning in an environment of cultural fragility: Case studies from Bali, Indonesia Peter Dunbar-Hall	123

Perspectives on music teaching in basic education in Brazil ... 129
Sergio Figueiredo

Practices and conceptions involving electric guitar classes in private music schools ... 135
Marcos da Rosa Garcia

Doctoral-level Artistic Research in the Field of Music: Issues and Case Studies ... 143
Michael Hannan

The Right to Play: A Children's Composition Project in Timor-Leste (East Timor) ... 149
Gillian Howell

Educational reforms and the professionalization of teaching: The mention in music education ... 157
Julio Hurtado Llopis

The Effectiveness of Loosening up Exercises Accompanied by Turkish Music on Adult Beginner Piano Students ... 163
Birsen Jelen
Burçin Uçaner

Place and Space: Celebrating South African Music across Two Continents ... 171
Dawn Joseph
Rene Human

Surgery or Studio: Music Teaching-learning in a Regional Conservatorium, NSW, Australia ... 179
Christopher Klopper
Bianca Power

Humor in Western Art Music and in Music Education: Literature Review and Research Findings ... 187
May Kokkidou

Using Music Technology with Young Children with Autism: Two Case Studies ... 195
Ling-Yu Liza Lee
Kimberly McCord

Mimesis as a Tool for Musical Learning and Performance, Maieutics, and the Stone of Heraclea ... 213
Anders Ljungar-Chapelon

Rhythm for Reading: A Rhythm-based Approach to Reading Intervention ... 221
Marion Long
Susan Hallam

Music Education and the Post-modern Condition: Challenges and Perspectives ... 233
Maria K. Magaliou

Learning Together Online: An Investigation of Collaborative Instruction on Students' Demonstrated Levels of Cognition in an Online Music Appreciation Course ... 241
Melissa McCabe

Scared to Share: Studio Teachers and an Asynchronous Web Forum for Pedagogical Learning ... 251
Eleanor McPhee

Ontology Theories of the Musical Work and the Meaning of Creation ... 259
Chrysoula Mischou

Evaluative Performances as a Contributor to Music Learning: Conditions for Positive Evaluation Experiences for Beginning and Intermediate Piano Students 265
Nancy Mitchell

Ethical Dimensions of 21st-Century Challenges to the Philosophy of Music Education at the Tertiary Level 273
David R. Montaño

Toward a Model for Assessing Music Teacher Effectiveness 281
Glenn E. Nierman

Colonial Legacy of Functional Art Music in Nigeria: Its Influence on Compositional Preferences of Music Students (The Nsukka Example) 289
Christian Onyeji
Elizabeth Onyeji

Informal Music Learning Experiences: The Role of the Musician in Creating a Successful Musical Performance in a Hospital Setting 299
Costanza Preti

"Make Music and Work at It:" The Ontological Foundation of Plato's Music Educational Proposals 305
Theocharis Raptis

Plato's Conceptions on Music 311
Gerasimos Rentifis

Using Affect Valence and Emotion Valence to Understand Musical Experience and Response: The Case of Hated Music 317
Emery Schubert

Teaching the Malay Gamelan within the Framework of Traditional Conventions in Malaysian Schools 325
Shahanum Mohamad Shah

Composing Atonal Music as a Child's Play: Coherence of Serial Musical Work While Creating Melodies 331
Angeliki Skandali

Music Student Teacher´s Experiences of Initial Teacher Preparation in Brazil: A Broad Perspective 339
Jose Soares
Sérgio Figueiredo

Transforming the Practice of Music Composition Teaching under Technological Environment 345
Pan-hang B. Tang

Effectiveness of Integrated Study in Teacher Training: A Communicative Group Activity Involving Music, Culture, and Physical Expression 353
Noriko Tokie

Undergraduate Music Students' Perceptions on their Preparation for the Teaching Profession 361
Angeliki Triantafyllaki
Smaragda Chrysostomou

5000 Languages, 5000 Ways to Sing? 369
Valerie L. Trollinger

Mentoring the Muse: Best Help for Generalist Educators in Kwa-Zulu Natal, South Africa   377
   Caroline van Niekerk
   Jansen van Vuuren

Music Materials in the Early Childhood Education   385
   Rosa Mª Vicente Álvarez

Defining Music Teacher Identity for Effective Research in Music Education   399
   Cynthia Wagoner

A Study of Children's Spontaneous Singing in the Minority Regions of China: Analyzing with the Standpoint of Researcher as Relative Outsider   411
   Yiying Wang
   Yanjie Yang

The Independent Music Teacher as Researcher: A case study   417
   Lorna Wanzel

An Examination of the Perceptions of Undergraduate Music Education Students in Pre-Service Conducting Experiences with University Choral Ensembles   423
   Jeffrey Ward

PHILOSOPHY PANEL PAPERS   433
   Reflection and Critical Considerations on the Conference Theme "Music Pædeia: From Ancient Greek Philosophers Towards Global Music Communities"

Music as Ethical Practice: The Contemporary Significance of Ancient Greek Insights   435
   Wayne D. Bowman

And Still I Wander… Deconstructing Western Music education through Greek Mythology   443
   June Boyce-Tillman

Personhood and Music Education   455
   David J. Elliott

Music Education and/as Artistic Activism: Music, *Pædeia*, and the Politics of Aesthetics   465
   Panagiotis A. Kanellopoulos

Music Paedeia for Today's World   481
   Paul R. Lehman

CONFERENCE PROCEEDINGS

Incorporating Traditional *Choro* Music Experiences into Brazilian University Music Curricula through Class Instruction Using Comprehensive Musicianship Concepts

Sergio Luis de Almeida Alvares
Universidade Federal do Rio de Janeiro (Brazil)

salvaresbr@gmail.com

Abstract
The purpose of the study was to foster the processes that underlie the environment of teaching and learning traditional Brazilian *Choro* music through class instruction in one specific Brazilian university music setting. The theoretical and pedagogical foundations for the development of the study relied upon concepts of comprehensive musicianship, educational objectives and practices, modes of musical knowledge, and aesthetic cultural meaning and relevance of *Choro* music to Brazilian music students. Research methodology was designed using a qualitative phenomenological approach with descriptive method techniques and procedures. Data were collected through participant-observational and action research practices for a period of three years from mid-2008 to mid-2011. Results focused mainly on student's experiences but indirectly also addressed university faculty and administrative perspectives and touched on some institutional and educational issues. Conclusions of the study supported the inclusion of *Choro* experiences into Brazilian university music curricula with recommendations for further research in other institutions.

Keywords
Choro, class instruction, comprehensive musicianship

Introduction
The article describes the process of incorporating traditional *Choro* music experiences into one particular Brazilian university music curricula through class instruction using comprehensive musicianship concepts.

Theoretical and Pedagogical Background
This section presents the foundations of the study and is divided into six segments: (a) traditional Brazilian *Choro* music; (b) comprehensive musicianship; (c) educational objectives; (d) educational practices; (e) knowledge; and (f) music and culture.

Traditional Brazilian Choro Music

Several musicologists regard the *Choro* as the earliest independent style of Brazilian music developed during the last quarter of the 19th century (Alvarenga, 1982; Andrade, 1962; Béhague, 1980; Hodel, 1988; Stigberg, 1986). It has been incorporated into both art music and popular genres, and it reflects the virtuosic, contrapuntal, and improvisatory character of contemporary Brazilian music. Its survival in the hot-house musical environment of Brazil is a case of unity in diversity nationwide. Furthermore, Cabral (1995) states that the greatest Brazilian instrumentalists of all time are *Choro* musicians; therefore, Brazilian music education must seriously consider incorporating *Choro* training formally.

Álvares (1999) surveyed opinions of three populations (students, faculty, and specialists) regarding the inclusion of *Choro* experiences into Brazilian university music curricula. Most respondents acknowledged that *Choro* is culturally relevant and technically beneficial to the training of Brazilian music students. Based on data provided by respondents, the following *Choro* experiences were identified as meaningful: (a) history and literature; (b) performance, solo and ensemble; and (c) theory and improvisation. Nevertheless, the author indicated a need for better development of training programs for musicians and music educators linked with contemporary Brazilian musical scenario.

Comprehensive Musicianship

The comprehensive musicianship approach has been influential in instrumental music education with positive effects since its development during the 1960's in the United States of America. It promotes "the development of competencies in creating music, performing music, and critical listening and analysis" (Willoughby, 1990, p. 39).

Several music educators have emphasized the importance of comprehensive musicianship in educational programs (Adler, 1968; Ball, 1969; Mitchell, 1969; Schwadron, 1965; Trotter, 1967). Comprehensive musicianship premises addresses important issues such as: (a) student oriented *versus* teacher oriented; (b) discovery learning (heuristics) *versus* receptive learning (algorithms); (c) Gestalt psychology (historical antecedent of cognitive psychology) *versus* behaviorist psychology; (d) cyclical sequence and spiral curriculum; (e) self actualization and humanistic motivation; and (f) process *versus* product.

In traditional music curricula, courses such as history, theory and performance are taught separately and often by different instructors. Because they are studied as distinct areas of music, the integration of knowledge from one course to another is often rare. Therefore, students tend to have a fragmented knowledge of music that prevents them from developing a comprehensive musical understanding (Mark, 1986). Findings from research support the inclusion of the comprehensive approach in the music curricula from lower to higher educational levels (Costanza & Russell, 1992; Garofalo & Whaley, 1979; Madhosingh, 1984; Parker, 1974; Whitener, 1983; Woods, 1973).

The concept of comprehensive musicianship as it applied to the study of music from elementary schools through the university […] assumed the role of a catalyst for reassessment regarding the nature of music and the use of musical processes in teaching and learning (Willoughby, 1990, p. 44).

Educational Objectives

In mid-20th century, Bloom (1956) and his associates recognized that learning is not a simple unitary process. Three domains of educational activities were then identified: (a) cognitive, emphasizing thinking and other intellectual processes; (b) psychomotor, focusing on physical skills and techniques; and (c) affective, concerning feelings, attitude and appreciation. Each of these domains were structured from simplest to most complex and called the taxonomy of educational objectives.

Classifying different types of learning into separated domains may facilitate analysis, study, and lesson planning. Nevertheless, this separation appears somewhat artificial, and none of these taxonomies seems to reach the true essence of learning when isolated from each other. With this caution in mind, the study intends to promote an interrelationship among these three kinds of learning experiences as proposed by Labuta (1974, p. 48) and illustrated in figure 1.

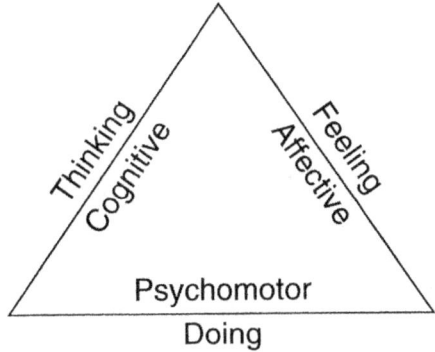

Figure 1. Interrelated domains of learning.

Educational Practices

By the end of the military dictatorship period in Brazil (1964-1985), works of post-Freire (1967) Brazilian scholars reflected upon social issues in Brazilian educational system (Cury, 1979; Libâneo, 1984; Mello, 1982; Saviani, 1980). These reflections brought up the concept that educational practices are not restricted to school or family. They do occur under various contexts of human existence, whether individual or social, whether institutionalized or not.

Libâneo (1998) identified three types of educational practices: (a) informal; (b) non-formal; and (c) formal. Informal education occurs in a diffuse and scattered manner, where the process of knowledge acquisition is not intentional and not institutionalized. Non-formal education is undertaken with some level of intentional and systematic procedures, taking place at non-conventional institutions such as professional organizations, media venues, or trainings agencies. Formal education occurs with high degrees of intentionality and organization, taking place in schools, colleges, universities, or other educational institution.

The current study explores the possibilities of incorporating informal and non-formal educational practices related to traditional Brazilian *Choro* music experience into formal Brazilian university music curricula, promoting a combined setting of educational practices available.

Knowledge

According to Fenstermacher (1986), education, regardless of its practice, relies on two principal foundations: accumulation and transmission of knowledge. Different conceptions of knowledge and how humans come to know affect the way educational practices are approached. Reimer et al. (1985) and Rideout (1987) suggest the importance of developing a comprehensive understanding of what knowledge is, how it is acquired, and the ways in which music and knowledge may be connected. Music may be experienced from the perspectives of the listener, performer, and composer, considering either an isolated or an integrated approach.

Álvares (2006) distinguished two modes of knowledge: (a) propositional; and (b) non-propositional. From Ancient Greece to early-20th century, it was common to define Western knowledge by representing the possession of specific information that could be expressed through verbal or written words related to beliefs, thoughts, or deductions (rationalism). Another common definition was associated with the capacity of perform certain tasks either under defined circumstances (empiricism) or under mutating environments (pragmatism). These traditional modes, called propositional knowledge, are based upon consensual credibility and validity depending on time and place of a certain society.

Epistemological developments throughout the 20th century departed from concerning of knowing *what* towards a search for understanding the representations of knowledge made by human minds, emotions, and procedures (Berlyne, 1974; Durkin and Crowther, 1982; Eisner, 1979; Elliot, 1995; Heller and Campbell, 1976; Kant, 1951; Langer, 1942, 1953; Meyer; 1956, 1967; Nettl, 1983; Perkins, 1977; Scruton, 1983; Serafine, 1988; Wittgenstein, 1966). This non-propositional mode of knowledge gave birth to concepts such as constructivism, semiology, phenomenology, and expressionism. The current study takes into consideration all the available modes of knowledge as material to expand the possibilities for teaching and learning *Choro* in the dawning of the 21st century.

Music and Culture

Scholars regard music as an integral part or culture in society (Blacking, 1973; Farnsworth, 1954; Hamm, Nettl, & Byrnside, 1975; Lomax, 1969 Lundin, 1967). Cassirer (1944) stated that "art may be defined as a symbolic language" (p. 168), while Merriam (1964) writes that the symbolic meaning in music "cannot be derived from properties intrinsic in its physical form; rather, it is the human attribution of abstract meaning" (p. 231) and that "the product is the result of behavior which is shaped by the society and culture of men who produce it" (p. 25). Furthermore, Geertz (1977) affirms that culture "denotes an historically transmitted pattern of meanings embodied in symbols, a systems of inherited conceptions expressed in symbolic forms, by means of which men communicate, perpetuate, and develop their knowledge about and attitudes towards life" (p. 89).

Music is "significant form," and its significance is that of a symbol, a highly articulated, sensuous object, which by virtue of its dynamic structure can express the forms of vital experience which language is peculiarly unfit to convey. Feeling, life, motion and emotion constitute its import (Langer, 1953, p. 32).

The concepts above strengthen the potential of music to promote a non-propositional mode of knowledge development. According to Gaston (1968), if we as humans are less exposed to stimuli we would be less complete in terms of human development. Incorporating traditional *Choro* music experiences into Brazilian university music curricula could broaden the scope of learning experiences for students mingling informal educational practices into a highly formal institutional setting. "To each musical experience is brought the sum of an individual's attitudes, beliefs, prejudices, conditionings in terms of time and place in which he has lived" (Gaston, 1957, p. 26).

Choro is culturally relevant and technically beneficial to the training of Brazilian music students [...] If music is an artistic product of the society in which it is created, then those who teach music must keep pace with significant current trends in that society (Alvares, 1999, p. 8).

Purpose of the Study

The purpose of the study was to foster the processes that underlie the environment of teaching and learning *Choro* through class instruction in one specific Brazilian university, using concepts of comprehensive musicianship and launching a transdisciplinary[1] approach in disciplines related to: (a) performance; (b) theory and improvisation; and (c) history, literature, and socio-cultural issues inherent to Brazilian music.

Methodology Approaches

The study used a qualitative phenomenological approach with the purpose to describe a *lived experience* of a phenomenon (Goetz & LcCompte, 1984). In the current case, the traditional Brazilian *Choro* music is the phenomenon, and the incorporation of *Choro* experiences through class instruction into one specific Brazilian university music curricula is the *lived experience*, which was undertaken by the students and, in some degree, by the author who served as instructor. According to Bresler and Stake (1992), "the aim of qualitative research is not to discover reality, for by phenomenological reasoning this is impossible. The aim is to construct a clearer experiential memory and try to help people obtain a more sophisticated account of things" (p. 76). Experience is:

> the source of all knowing and the basis of behavior. Experience, what we are aware of at any point in time, is the foundation of our knowledge of ourselves, of other people, and the world in general. Without human experience there would be no human world. (Becker, 1992, p. 11)

According to Gonzo (1992), "descriptive research is devoted to collecting information about prevailing conditions or situations for the purpose of description and interpretation" (p. 220). Following this concept, the author designed a descriptive research model underlying two major modes: (a) an observational research, "characterized by data gathering through observation of the behaviors of others" (Casey, 1992, p. 120); and (b) an action research, characterized by "doing research and working on solving a problem at the same time" (Cormack, 1991, p. 155). In the former, the author served as participant and observer, taking a double role as teacher and researcher in his own classroom. In the latter, the author proposed an action or a planned activity, which was the incorporation of *Choro* experiences in the curricula.

---

[1] *Transdisciplinarity* is a term used to signify a unity of knowledge beyond disciplines (Nicolescu, 1996).

Since August of 2008, *Choro* experience classes have been offered as elective courses available for undergraduate music students, including degrees in instruments, composition, and music education. Since March 2011, classes for graduate students have become available as well. Classes meet once a week for two-hour block period, are worth one academic credit, and last two consecutive semesters, named *Choro* I and II. Since March 2011, teaching assistantships have been granted, upon selection criteria, for students who have successfully completed both semesters.

Data gathering inside the classroom used some concepts from works of Erbes[2] (1972) and Reynolds[3] (1974), including: (a) behavior sampling; (b) checklist observation forms; and (c) class frequency and participation logs. Data gathering outside the classroom included: (a) videotaping; (b) web blogging and posting; and (c) community services such as (i) recitals, (ii) workshops, and (iii) participation in scientific events including local seminars, congresses and symposiums.

Results

The study explored the incorporation of *Choro* music experiences into one specific Brazilian university music curricula through class instruction using comprehensive musicianship concepts. Data analysis was based upon the following considerations from Bresler and Stake (1992): "the choice of what to report is subjective, evolving, emphasizing more what contributes to the understanding of the particulars observed [...] the usual reporting procedure is to present a long or short summary" (p. 85). The results were identified as follows:

1. From administrative perspectives, the study received full support, from the beginning developments of course syllabus to current grants for teaching assistantship, including further opportunities for public presentations inside and outside the campus facilities.
2. From faculty perspectives, the study received collaborative aids from professors, especially the instrumentalists.
3. From student perspectives, the main focus of the study, results revealed a successful experienced process reflected upon:

    a) increasing class enrollment;
    b) research and independent studies on:
      i) repertoire and style;
      ii) transcriptions;
      iii) social and historical literature;
      iv) past and present composers and performers;
    c) volunteer and collaborative peer tutoring;
    d) development of musical skills and instrumental technique;
    e) arranging and original compositions;
    f) workshops and presentations in community venues;
    g) academic paper submissions;
    h) development of virtual sites;
    i) positive attitudes for music production initiatives;
    j) exchanging experiences with *Choro* specialists outside the campus;

---

[2] *RIOS - Rehearsal Interaction Observation System*, suitable for large ensembles.
[3] Modified version of *OSIA - Observational System for Instructional Analysis* (Hough and Duncan, 1972), suitable for small ensembles.

k) after two semesters, some kept attending classes as auditing students.
4. From institutional perspectives, the study uncovered possibilities for successful experiences in mixing informal and formal educational practices in the classroom at a university level.
5. From educational perspectives, the study confirmed the premises of positive effects of comprehensive musicianship approach on instrumental music education.
6. From epistemological perspectives, the study signalized an alternative field to further explore potential combinations of propositional and non-propositional modes of knowledge researching.
7. From musicological perspectives, the study confirms the premises of *Choro* as a highly significant music to serve an aesthetic educational experience pathway to Brazilian university music students.

Conclusions

The incorporation of *Choro* experiences into Brazilian university music curricula through class instruction using comprehensive musicianship concepts has showed evidence to be doable and seemly successful in one particular institution for a period of three years of implementation, mainly in the scope of undergraduate degrees as illustrated by Figure 2. Regarding graduate programs, data is not enough to draw conclusions. It is recommended to further undertake research in other institutions to broaden knowledge of the current phenomenon explored.

Figure 2. Choro Ensemble

References

Adler, S. (1968). The contemporary music project institutes and curriculum change. *Music Educators Journal, 55*(1), 36-38, 123.

Alvarenga, O. (1982). *Música popular brasileira* (2nd ed.). São Paulo, Brazil: Livraria Duas Cidades. (Original work published 1947)

Álvares, S. (1999). A needs assessment and proposed curriculum for incorporating traditional Choro music experiences into Brazilian university music curricula. *International Journal of Music Education, 34*, 3–13.

Alvares, S. (2006). Vertentes do saber musical: Precedentes e consequentes epistemológicos rumo a uma fundamentação filosófica abrangente para uma educação musical contemporânea. In B. Ilari (Ed.), *Em busca da mente musical: Ensaios sobre os processos cognitivos em música – da percepção à produção* (pp. 429–452). Curitiba, Brazil: Editora UFPR.

Andrade, M. (1962). Ensaio sobre a música brasileira (2nd ed.). São Paulo, Brazil: Livraria Martins. (Original work published in 1936)

Ball, C. (1969). The answer lies in improved teaching. *Music Educators Journal, 56*(2), 58–59.

Béhague, G. (1980). Latin America. In S. Sadie (Ed.), *The new Grove dictionary of music and musicians* (6th ed.) (Vol. 10, pp. 505–534). London, England: MacMillan.

Becker, C. (1992). *Living and relating: An introduction to phenomenology*. Thousand Oaks, CA: Sage.

Berlyne, D. E. (Ed.). (1974). *Studies in the new experimental aesthetics: Steps towards an objective psychology of aesthetic appreciation*. Washington, DC: Hemisphere.

Blacking, J. (1973). *How musical is man?* Seattle, WA: University of Washington Press.

Bloom, B. S. (1956). *Taxonomy of educational objectives: The classification of educational goals*. New York: David McKay Company.

Bresler, L., & Stake, R. E. (1992). Qualitative research methodology in music education. In R. Colwell (Ed.), *Handbook of research on music teaching and learning* (pp. 75–90). New York, NY: Schirmer Books.

Cabral, S. (1995). A música dos craques: O chorinho. *Veja Rio, 5*(43), 78.

Casey, D. (1992). Descriptive research: Techniques and procedures. In R. Colwell (Ed.), *Handbook of research on music teaching and learning* (pp. 115–123). New York, NY: Schirmer Books.

Cassirer, E. (1944). *An essay on man*. New Haven, CT: Yale University Press.

Costanza, P., & Russell, T. (1992). Methodologies in music education. In R. Colwell (Ed.), *Handbook of research on music teaching and learning* (pp. 498–508). New York, NY: Schirmer Books.

Cormack, D.S. (1991). *The research process*. Oxford, England: Blackwell Scientific Publications.

Cury, C. R. J. (1979). *Educação e contradição: Elementos metodológicos para uma teoria-crítica do fenômeno educativo* (Unpublished doctoral dissertation). Pontifícia Universidade Católica, São Paulo, Brazil.

Durkin, K. K., & Crowther, R. D. (1982). Language in music education: Research overview. *Psychology of Music, 10*, 59–61.

Erbes, R. L. (1972). *The development of an observational system for the analysis of interaction in the rehearsal of musical organizations* (Unpublished doctoral dissertation). University of Illinois, Urbana.

Eisner, E. (1979). *The educational imagination*. New York, NY: MacMillan.

Elliot, D. J. (1995). *Music matters: A new philosophy of music education.* Oxford, England: Oxford University Press.

Farnsworth, P. R. (1954). *The social psychology of music.* Ames, IA: The Iowa State University Press.

Fenstermacher, G. D. (1986). Philosophy of research on teaching: three aspects. In M. Wittrock (Ed.), *Handbook of research on teaching* (3rd ed.) (pp. 37–39). New York, NY: Macmillan.

Freire, P. (1967). *Educação como prática da liberdade.* Rio de Janeiro, Brazil: Paz e Terra.

Garofalo, R. J., & Whaley, G. (1979). Comparison of the unit study and traditional approaches to teaching music through school band performance. *Journal of research in Music Education, 27,* 137–142.

Gaston, E. T. (1957). Factors contributing to responses in music. In E.T. Gaston (Ed.), *Music Therapy.* Lawrence, KS: The Allen Press.

Gaston, E.T. (1968). Man and music. In E.T. Gaston (Ed.), *Music in therapy.* London, England: Collier-Macmillan.

Geertz, C. (1977). *The interpretation of cultures.* New York, NY: Basic Books.

Goetz, J. P., & LeCompte, M. D. (1984). *Ethnography and qualitative design in educational research.* San Francisco, CA: Academic Press.

Gonzo, C. (1992). Towards a rational critical process. In R. Colwell (Ed.), *Handbook of research on music teaching and learning* (pp. 218–226). New York, NY: Schirmer Books.

Hamm, C., Nettl, B., & Byrnside, R. (1975). *Contemporary music and music cultures.* Englewood Cliffs, NJ: Prentice-Hall.

Heller, J., & Campbell, W. (1976). Models of language and intellect in music research. In A. Motycka (Ed.), *Music education for tomorrow's society: Selected topics* (pp. 40-49). Jamestown, RI: GAMT Music Press.

Hodel, B. (1988, Spring). The choro. *Guitar Review, 73,* 31–35.

Hough, J. B., & Duncan, J. K. (1972). *Revised observational system for instructional analysis.* Unpublished manuscript, The Ohio State University, Columbus.

Kant, I. (1951). *Critique of pure reason.* New York, NY: Hafner Publishing.

Labuta, J. A. (1974). Guide to accountability in music instruction. West Nyack, NY: Parker Publishing.

Langer, S. (1942). *Philosophy in a new key.* Cambridge, MA: Harvard University.

Langer, S. (1953). *Felling and form.* New York, NY: Scribner's.

Libâneo, J. C. (1985). *A democratização da escola pública: A pedagogia crítico-social dos conteúdos.* São Paulo, Brazil: Loyola.

Libâneo, J. C. (1998). *Pedagogia e pedagogos, para quê?* São Paulo, Brazil: Cortez.

Lomax, A. (1969). *Folk song style and culture.* Washington, DC: American Association for the Advancement of Science.

Lundin, R. W. (1967). *An objective psychology of music* (2nd ed.). New York, NY: Ronald Press.

Madhosingh, D. F. (1984). *An approach to developing comprehensive musicianship in the intermediate grades using the voice and the ukulele* (Unpublished doctoral dissertation). University of British Columbia, Vancouver, Canada.

Mark, M. (1986). *Contemporary music education* (2nd ed.). New York, NY: Schirmer Books.

Mello, G. N. (1982). Pesquisa em educação: Questões teóricas e questões de método. *Cadernos de Pesquisa, 40*, 6–10.

Merriam, A. P. (1964). *The anthropology on music*. Evanston, IL: Northwestern University Press.

Meyer, L. B. (1956). *Emotion and meaning*. Chicago, IL: University of Chicago Press.

Meyer, L. B. (1967). *Music, the arts, and ideas: Patterns and predictions in twentieth-century culture*. Chicago, IL: University of Chicago Press.

Mitchell, W. (1969). Under the comprehensive musicianship umbrella. *Music Educators National Conference, 55*(7), 71–75.

Nettl, B. (1983). *Twenty-nine issues in ethnomusicology*. Urbana, IL: University of Illinois Press.

Nicolescu, B. (1996). *La Transdisciplinarité*. Paris, France: Rocher.

Parker, R. (1974). *Comparative study of two methods of band instruction at the middle school level* (Unpublished doctoral dissertation). The Ohio State University, Columbus.

Perkins, D. (1977). Talk about art. *Journal of Aesthetic Education, 11*, 87–116.

Reimer, B., Heller, G., Heller, J., Campbell, W., & Webster, P. (1985). Toward a more scientific approach to music education research. *Bulletin of the Council for Research in Music Education, 83*, 1–40.

Reynolds, K. (1974). *Modification of the observational system for instructional analysis focusing on appraisal behaviors of music teachers in small performance classes* (Unpublished doctoral dissertation). The Ohio State University, Columbus.

Rideout, R. (1987). Old wines and new bottles: More thoughts on Reimer. *Bulletin of the Council for Research in Music Education, 92*, 42–55.

Saviani, D. (1980). *Educação: Do senso comum à consciência filosófica*. São Paulo, Brazil: Cortez.

Schwadron, A. (1965). *Comprehensive musicianship: The foundation for college education in music*. Reston, VA: Music Educators National Conference.

Scruton, R. (1983). *The aesthetic understanding: Essays in the philosophy of art and culture*. New York, NY: Methuen.

Serafine, M. L. (1988). *Music as cognitive*. New York, NY: Columbia University Press.

Stigberg, D. (1986). Choro. In D. M. Randel (Ed.), *The new Harvard dictionary of music* (p. 162). Cambridge, MA: Harvard University Press.

Trotter, R. (1967). Teaching musicianship in today's schools. *Music Educators National Conference, 54*(2), 34–41, 107–109.

Whitener, W. T. (1983). Comparison of two approaches to teaching beginning band. *Journal of Research in Music Education, 31*, 229-235.

Willoughby, D. (1990). Comprehensive musicianship. *The Quarterly, 1*(3), 39–44.

Wittgenstein, L. (1966). *Lectures and conversation on aesthetics, psychology, and religion beliefs*. Oxford, England: Blackwell.

Woods, D. G. (1973). *The development and evaluation of an independent school music curriculum stressing comprehensive musicianship at each level, preschool to senior high school*. (Unpublished doctoral dissertation). Univesity of California, Los Angeles.

The Effect of Curriculum Reforms of 2002 on the Teaching of Music in Primary Schools in Sunga Sub-location, Maseno Division, Kenya

Hellen Atieno
Maseno University (Kenya)
atieno.hellen@yahoo.com

Abstract

The 2002 curriculum reforms in Kenya recommended the merging of all creative arts subjects into one. Music and subjects like painting, drawing, pattern and print making, mosaic and collage, modeling, metalwork and basketry now form the content of the creative arts subject in primary schools. This was done on the assumption that a primary school teacher is trained to teach all subjects. The reform led to a rapid action by Kenya Institute of Education (KIE) to produce books on creative arts. With the merger also came the policy that made creative arts a non-examinable subject. Apparently no study has been carried out to ascertain whether the merging of creative arts subjects has enhanced the teaching of these subjects or not. This study specifically sought to find out if the merger has affected the teaching of music in primary schools and if so how has it been affected. This study was carried out in primary schools in Sunga sub-location, North West Kisumu location, Maseno division. Qualitative data was collected from the heads of four (4 in number) schools in Sunga sub-location and the Assistant Education Officer (AEO) of the area. Data collected was analyzed qualitatively and reported in prose form. The study revealed that there is a syllabus for the creative arts and that the government has set out a policy that should be a timetable for teaching; however, the subject is not taught in primary schools because teachers would like to concentrate on examinable subjects. Lessons for creative arts are used for teaching subjects like mathematics, English etc. Singing is done once in a while or ignored altogether, except for the annual Kenya Music Festivals. Data also revealed that teachers would wish to have music taught because of the many benefits it offers to pupils, especially pupils who are musically talented. Data also revealed that there is a move by the Kenya Institute of Education, to have songs integrated in the teaching and learning of other subjects. Further, data reveals that teachers trained to teach music are wasted and individual talents of both pupils and teachers are lost in the process. Informants wish to have music examined, even if it is through continuous assessment in the classroom so teachers can see the importance of the subject.

Keywords
Curriculum, reform, primary schools, music, Kenya

Introduction

Reforms in curricula have been a subject of many studies. Norman (2005) carried a comparative study on the impact of primary school curriculum reforms on diploma, bachelor, masters and PhD programs at Madang Teachers College or Divine Word University in Papua New Guinea. The author goes on to define the curriculum and spells out changes in the new curriculum that was under study. The author mentions elements like creation of some new subjects, change of names of some subjects, changes in weekly time allocations for subjects, etc. This has implications for timetabling and programming as well. The reformed curriculum uses new terms to replace the old, i.e. outcomes instead of objectives, and the structure of the reformed curriculum ought to be different. This study is yet to spell out the reforms of the new curriculum of 2002, especially for music. The study by Norman (2005) found that the curriculum reforms have impacted teacher education programs as evident in the planning of units of study, collation of student learning materials, the use of ideas and terminology in teaching, the assessment tasks set for students, and the professional reading done by lecturers. From the data gathered, it was found that the support for the curriculum reforms was more strongly evident in programs at Madang Teachers College than at Divine Word University.

Mutuku and Odwar (2010) conducted a study to determine if there is continuity in the school curriculum at upper primary level of education in Kenya. The study reveals that the music curriculum at the upper primary level lacks continuity in the content material. Pokana (2005) carried out an action research study to address significant impacts relating to the planning, implementation, and professional support for the reformed curriculum for elementary and primary schools in Papua New Guinea. The specific purpose of the research was to examine positive and negative impacts the new reformed curriculum had on teachers in the planning and implementation from Grades 3 to 8 Curriculum (the Upper and Lower Primary). In addition, it also assessed and evaluated the effectiveness and appropriateness of the professional support provided for teachers in the implementation by the Olsh Teachers' College Kabaleo. The study found out that the impact was minimal at the stage of evaluation when the study was taken.

UNESCO (2001) provides a summary of seminar papers presented at the International Seminar on "Case studies in curriculum development: Contributions to the Kosovo education reform." The summary of the paper by Budiene (2001) about reforms in Lithuania, stated that textbook production is an important aspect in a curriculum reform, which must also include the provision of textbooks in minority languages. Furthermore, Budiene pointed out that it is essential to have a clear, national philosophy on how the system should be, in order to avoid fragmentation and the risk of a "donor-driven" reform. Concerning reforms in Estonia, UNESCO reports that there was a consensus that students should be given more freedom to choose subjects that they want to learn, and parents can also be given a chance to decide which subjects they wanted their children to learn. The paper on curriculum reform on Romania as contained in the report states that there are several issues that need to be taken into account when carrying out curriculum reforms. First, there is a need to foster a *curriculum culture* and to reach a common understanding of what a curriculum is and what it should contain. Secondly, there is a need for broad consultation and shared vision between the political parties, the Ministry of Education and other social sectors. Thirdly, a curriculum reform needs time and resources, and a clear legal basis. Fourthly, there is also a need to inform the public about the changes made to the curriculum. Finally, there is a need for a development of a critical mass of professional curriculum developers. Several curricular reforms have been undertaken in Kenya since Independence. These reforms are undertaken to improve or make better the existing curricula. This study will concentrate on curricula reforms directly affecting Music.

A History of Music Curriculum in Kenya

Formal education in Kenya began with the missionary activities in Kenya as far back as 1911 before Kenya achieved her independence in 1963. This section will present the music curricula before and after independence.

The pre-independence Music Curriculum

This is the missionary era. We cannot trace any given curriculum of study however. Churches served as schools in the villages. School music was basically singing hymns (King, 1971; Weman 1960) and learning of European songs as evidenced in the Phelps-Stokes Commission report of 1923-24 on bush or village school curricula quoted here below (King, 1971).

> The music you hear will not be a native song but the parody of a familiar European hymn...The chorus of unintelligible sounds is the sing-song of the syllables as they follow one another in a meaningless succession. (p. 150)

This agrees with Kirby's view quoted in Weman (1960) stating the two fundamental reasons why and how music was to be taught in Africa: first is the habitual use of music for religious purposes. That is why singing of hymns was the content of School Music. Second is the traditional European method of training in School Music: the sing-song of the syllables. Evidence points to that fact that the syllables were solfa. As early as 1958, Gagg (1958) writing on the techniques of teaching music in West African schools strongly recommended that music teachers get acquainted with the tonic solfa system in order for them to get pupils to learn tuneful sounds. Rowley (1977), agrees with this and states that the wide range of the impact that solfa has had is because of its extensive use by the missionaries. In South African (black) schools, for example, the method used for teaching music up to 1960, when Weman wrote his book *African music and the church in Africa*, has been based purely on the Curwen system of tonic solfa [...] the exclusive use of the system shut out the African from contact with instrumental music" [...] and thus "instrumental tuition was never part of the general African school curriculum" (p. 117). The result of this system is that "music education consisted of an altogether one-sided cultivation of vocal music" (Weman 1960, p. 116). Consequently, school music became completely dominated by singing, and this according to Weman (1960) was the standard form practically everywhere. From 1911 to independence in 1963, the colonial government ruled, but the administration and provision of education was largely under the missionaries throughout the colonial era (Eshiwani, 1993). Education in colonial Kenya was segregated along racial lines. Each race, whites, Asians and Arabs, and Africans had separate schools and different curricula. The whites had the best schools, well equipped and staffed with trained personnel. Next in rank were Asian and Arab schools and then African schools. With segregated schools and curriculum, a similar music course was not possible. The discussion that follows will look at music in African elementary schools.

Music in Elementary African schools

Elementary schools for the Africans were sub-divided into primary or village schools and intermediate schools (Education Department of the Colony and Protectorate of Kenya, 1922). Village schools were the simplest unit of education in the 1920s. These schools could offer education up to Standard II. Intermediate schools could further education up to Standard IV. Music that was offered at the primary level was basically singing. It is during this period that one meets the first curriculum reform through the Jeanes experimental school started in October 1925 at Kabete. The Jeanes School hoped to reform the village school curriculum and methods of teaching. The curriculum reform included the reintroduction of African culture. This was to be realized by reviving the African [Kenyan] past and preparing its students to reintroduce the old games, folk tales and African [Kenyan] music as a central part of early schooling. By the 1940s, the Jeanes school program and other ideas about African education according to Sifuna (1980) had been abandoned in favor of the western literacy education. As he argues, several reasons contributed to this. One reason which directly affected the newly Africanized school music according to Sifuna is the attitude about African music, song and dance as it was taught in the mission schools. Thus Jeanes school teachers and students who were involved in the Jeanes school program refused to study their own folk songs and dances because "they had been taught for most of their educational life that their own songs, dances and customs were unchristian, uncivilized and therefore unacceptable" (p. 101).

Despite this attitude, the African Education commission recommended music to be one of the methods of education in recreation (African Education Commission, 1923-24)

> The instruction in music will draw upon the best of the native folklore and songs as well as upon the simple forms of western music, and may one day utilize the inspiring musical achievements of civilization. Pupils will be taught to sing at work and at play. Songs of service, faith, victory and joy should be selected. The natural outburst of the native in innocent and playful folk dances should be encouraged. (p. 33)

Even though attempts were made to set songs and hymns to African [Kenyan] tunes as reflected in one of the speech day programs at Jeanes school (King, 1971) presented below, the reform only verified the nature of the songs by adding the Kenyan ones. School Music remained as mere singing.

Jeanes School Speech Day

Tuesday Aug. 6th 1929, 4.45 p.m. in the School Hall

1. African Tribal Songs.
    a) Kikuyu Rattle song.
        The song centers around the rattle (Gichandi) and its ornaments. The singers ask riddles in turn.
    b) Luo Wedding song. The bridegroom's age-equals gather together and sing in praise of him, his work, his skill, his shield etc. The 8 stringed instrument (thom) [sic] is used. Gor, the man mentioned at the end was a famous old Chief of South Kavirondo.

c) Abananda (Bantu Kavirondo)
   i. K'arimiwa. According to a tradition of the tribe a weakly hunch-back saved people from the cannibals by cunning. They now sing in praise of him.
   ii. Mishere ulule. The singer recites the names of people and tribes and says what they each do, making puns on their names.
   iii. Lubenzu. The song of the bird and the beautiful maiden. She begs the feathers and is enticed far away from her own home. The bird represents the young man who will one day come and woo her.
   iv. The War Horn sounds and all rush to the call.
2. Presentation of Permanent and Provincial Jeanes Certificates by the Hon'ble the Director of Education.
3. Jeanes School Hymns (Swahili).
   1. God of our Fathers – African Tune
   2. Praise the Lord – African Tune
   3. Nobody Knows the trouble I've seen – Negro Spiritual
   4. Speech: Chief Koinange
4. Recreational Games and Drill.
5. Show of Handwork.
   1. Men's carpentry.
   2. Women's sewing.

Up to the 1950s, music was still treated as a recreational subject. Singing games formed part of the physical training syllabus: "It was generally agreed that present singing games which form part of the physical training syllabus in all schools were a contribution to physical education and happiness of the child" (Kenya, 1950, p. 13). The 1953 primary syllabus for African schools (Colony and Protectorate of Kenya Department of Education, 1953a) had a section entitled music (Appendix A). However, the syllabus emphasized singing. Surprisingly enough, it encouraged learning of African songs and African instruments plus good vocal training. A section on music in the tentative syllabus for intermediate schools (Colony and Protectorate of Kenya Department of Education, 1953b) however, shows that music was not included in the curriculum for African schools at the intermediate level. It reads: "Although Music is not included in the curriculum of the intermediate school, there may be many schools where there are opportunities for teaching music and schools should be encouraged to include music whenever possible" (p. 2).

Post independence Music Curriculum
Through the efforts of several commission surveys, reports and advises (e.g., Ominde Commission of 1964, Commission of inquiry the Ndegwa commission of 1971, etc.), many educational reforms were made both at primary and secondary levels of education (Odwar, 2005). This section will present and discuss these reports in relation to music teaching at primary level of education.

The recommendations of the Ominde commission with regards to primary and secondary education included among others the integration of racially separate schools. The report recommended that curriculum should be reformed to make it relevant to the post-colonial situation. A 7-4-2-3 system of education. Seven years of primary education, four years of secondary education, and two years of advanced education and three years of tertiary education was established (Republic of Kenya, 1964). These recommendations led to radical changes in curricula for primary and secondary schools. There were three primary school syllabus reforms, namely The New Primary Approach (NPA), The Unified Primary School Syllabus (UPSS) of 1967, and The Primary Education Project (PEP) of 1978. These reforms did not make any big changes in school music. The subject content remained singing. Only one hour was allocated for music in the timetable per week. The 1967 primary syllabus spells it out and writes that "Pure enjoyment is the sole aim of the lower primary music lesson" (p. 1); hence a continuation of the recreational concept of school music inculcated in the teachers in the early mission schools and later on continued by colonial teachers (Odwar, 2005).

According to the Bessey Report of 1972 (Ministry of Education, 1972), the Music section in the 1967 syllabus for upper primary School needed to be revised. The report states:

> The section on music in the 1967 syllabus needs revision. On the whole we found that schools were doing well in singing despite limitations of the present syllabus. Our impression is that singing has been very much stimulated by a countrywide network of music festivals at district, provincial and national levels. The children very quickly respond when they were asked to sing and individuals would take the lead without hesitation. They respond vividly when performing African traditional songs with dance and movement. We especially remember the singing and dancing in Mandera. A very high quality of singing was also attained in the schools for the blind. English songs were given great purity of sound and it was a pleasure to observe the response of the younger blind children to the rhythm of their African songs. In these schools a variety of instruments were used. These include the recorder, accordions and various percussion instruments. Experience with a wider variety of instruments and more music making will stimulate the development of African music. Children taking part in the local or national festivals looked forward to the journey and experience; in some schools children went to considerable trouble in personal preparations for what was obviously quite an event in their school lives. (p. 31)

Singing, as evident in this report, is the dominant musical activity. The particular instruments mentioned in the quote above were used to accompany songs and dances for the music festivals. Based on the recommendations of the Bessey report, a new syllabus came into being in 1975. The major component of this syllabus like the previous ones was singing, though the Western music literacy component is included though not taught due to lack of qualified personnel. Music, however, was not given prominence with some other subjects. This is evident as music, along with other subjects like arts, crafts, physical education, home science and agriculture were not examined at the end of Primary Education (Eshiwani, 1993).

It did not take long before Kenya saw the need to set up another committee to look into issues of education, since the previous curriculum had various problems. The National

Committee on Education Objectives and Policies (NCEOP) in 1975, chaired by Gachathi, was set up to review educational objectives and policies (Republic of Kenya, 1976). The committee made several recommendations. As a direct consequence of the committee's recommendations, the Government decided to undertake far-reaching changes in Kenya's primary and secondary education. The most important of these changes according to (Ogula, n.d.) was the development of reformed curricula and curriculum materials. To undertake the above task, PEP was established at Kenya Institute of Education (KIE) in 1978. While the curriculum for primary schools was still under development, the President in January 1981 appointed a Presidential Working Party chaired by Mackey on the Establishment of a Second University in Kenya (Presidential Working Party, 1981). The Working Party completed its work in September of the same year. One of its recommendations was that the 7-4-2-3 system of education be replaced by an 8-4-4 system of education; i.e. 8 years of primary education, 4 years of secondary education, and 4 years of minimum university education. The first year of university education should be spent on foundation courses (Republic of Kenya, 1981). The education system was restructured accordingly in 1985 (Kenya Institute of Education, 1984) and launched in 1986. This gave rise to the 1986 Music curriculum. In 1986 the new materials were implemented.

It is the 8-4-4 system of education that made music an important subject. The study of music became compulsory from primary schools up to University. It was allocated three hrs per week in the time table. This necessitated the creation of a second music department at one more public University (Maseno), besides Kenyatta, to offer music at degree level. The syllabus states that 8-4-4 primary music curriculum is no longer mere singing as has been the practice in the past (Ministry of Education, Science & Technology, 1984). The syllabus is intended to prepare learners for a National Examination at the end of standard eight. The principle objective of this syllabus is to produce learners who can read music and interpret the conventional signs and terms which are internationally used for writing music. The content covers singing, basic western music theory, collecting making and playing of traditional instruments, aural skills, etc. One wonders why such a curriculum had to go through another reform in 2002.

The 2002 Curriculum Reforms

The reform in the Curriculum was undertaken on the claim that the 8-4-4 syllabus was overloaded. Kiptoon (n.d.) citing several authors (e.g., Amutabi, 2003; King & McGrath, 2002; Owino, 1997) stated that the new policy curriculum for primary school also claimed to be overcrowded or overstretched. Therefore it was an obstacle for effective learning because the pupils worked under great pressure. Pupils were taught thirteen subjects, nine of which were examined at the end of standard 8. The author further cites Abagi (1997a) as cited in Bedi et al. (2002) and wrote:

> [T]o cover an extended curriculum in the same period increased pressure to students and staff and thus reduced students performance (lower test scores). For instance the pupils stayed in school from 7 am to 5 or 6 pm and also have short holidays. (p. 10)

The pressure negatively affected the children's motivation to learn resulting in the rise in drop-outs (Owino, 1997). According to Ogula (n.d), there were too many subjects in the primary school curriculum. Practical skills subjects, namely music, art and craft, agriculture, home science, and business education were not taught effectively in many schools because of lack of materials and equipment and qualified teachers. Most primary schools lacked adequate facilities such as workshops and special rooms for practical subjects and instructional materials such as textbooks, exercise books apparatus, and tools. Teachers complained of too much content in the primary school curriculum in all subjects. They wished to see the number of subjects retained, but recommended that the content in each be reduced. Thus, in the bid to reduce the number of subjects, the Ministry of Education in the 2002 curriculum reforms merged all the creative arts subjects into one block with the possibility of teaching each sub section. Secondly the subject creative arts was made non examinable at the end of eight years of primary education.

Methodology

The study was carried out in Sunga Sub-location, North West Kisumu location Maseno division. The study was carried out with four primary school head teachers in Sunga. Permission was sought from the Assistant Education Officer (AEO) who also willing provided information upon getting to know the subject of the research. This increased the number of informants to five. The AEO informed the concerned heads of schools about my intended visit after which the researcher visited the schools and conducted oral interviews with the head teachers about the teaching of music and how the 2002 reforms has affected the teaching of music in schools. Data was recorded in a notebook. Data was coded and analyzed qualitatively. Being qualitative in nature, the results are in word form. These are discussed as they are presented.

Results of Data Analysis and Discussion of Findings

Data shows that music was taught and examined at the end of primary education until the new curriculum reforms of 2002 that merged music, painting, drawing, pattern making, print making, mosaic and collage, modeling, metalwork, and basketry into one subject called creative arts. Data further shows that the syllabus requires that creative art, of which music is a component, be taught in schools. Although creative arts is in the timetable for teaching, it is not taught because it is not examinable at the end of primary education, not even as part of the general paper at Kenya Certificate of Primary Education (KCPE) laments the Head teacher of Eliobe Primary School (Personal interview, 2011). All the informants agree that time allocated for creative arts is used for teaching mathematics, languages, and sciences. The head teachers of every school emphasize the teaching of all subjects, but teachers get their way out because of the examination orientation of Kenyan education system. This behavior does not exclude the head teachers when they are the ones assigned to teach creative arts classes, explained the head teacher of the Maseno Mixed Primary School. This is further supported by the fact that parents and the AEO are also interested in good performance (as measured by letter grades) attained in the national examination of at the end of primary education (KCPE) of their children in the examinable subjects. Hence, emphasis is placed on examinable subjects. The head teacher Sunga primary School stated that "If pupils fail in the examinable subjects then the AEO, parents and the some head teachers are up on arms against the subjects teachers" (Sunga, 2011). This encourages teachers all the more to use the time allocated for creative arts subjects for teaching subjects, which are examined at the end of primary education.

Data also reveals that Kenya Institute of Education (KIE) has published books for teaching creative arts, inclusive of music. Creative arts, however, does not get full financial support from the government that is given to other subjects. In support of this, head teacher Sunga primary schools (personal interview, 2011) said, "Creative Art which include drawing ball game, athletics, music, art exhibition, Home science, Art & craft" is allocated very little money from government for free primary education". Further, data reveals that voiced-choir-singing and choral verses are the musical activities that schools participate in mainly for competition at the annual Kenya Music Festival (KMF). This they do according to the headmaster at Eliobe Primary Schools, for entertainment and to enable students to tour the country. This is what some schools currently describe as music. Data also reveals that teachers end up singing instead of teaching music whenever they occasionally attempt to teach music. The head teacher at the Maseno Mixed Primary School (personal interview, 2011) contradicts this statement by saying that even mere singing is not practiced in schools. The informant however recommends the use of Early Childhood (ECD) songs in introducing and ending a lesson in other subject areas. This is what KIE is now recommending for primary schools. It appears that to a large extent, she said, that Kenya is taking music back to its cultural traditional form of singing. Sadly the head, Maseno boarding, reckons that pupils cannot even sing the first verse of the national anthem and that teachers have even forgotten it.

According to the AEO of Sunga sub-location, the 8-4-4 had good objectives to produce self-reliant students. Thus a music student could acquire skills that he/she would later build on. Some learned practical playing skills as playing of *Orutu*, a single stringed instrument, and this could enable them earn a living by performing for money or in a band. This is now not possible because the subject is not examinable. This is supported by head teacher Sunga who said that pupils who studied music at the primary level and continued with the study of music at secondary schools had made good progress in the subject. This implies that learners interested in studying music must start learning the basics at secondary level. The four years of secondary education may not give them enough content and practical skills to enable them study music at University.

Our experience at Maseno University with students admitted to study music show that they do not have enough content at the time they are admitted to study music. Lecturers have to do a lot of remedial work in theory and practical music to cover up for what they missed at the lower levels of education. The AEO continues to explain how the merger assumed that teachers who are assigned creative arts classes at primary schools passed these subjects during their training. The head teacher at Sunga made it clear when he stated that before the merger, different creative arts subjects were assigned to different teachers however, with the merger one teacher is assigned to teach creative arts with its many components. This is another reason why music and many other creative arts subjects are not being taught.

The head teacher Maseno Boarding in agreement with the AEO laments how the music lessons under the 8-4-4 system of education were better in contrast to the current umbrella called creative arts, which encourages mainly singing. The informant further states that music lessons are useful for teaching other subjects like mathematics etc. The informant in agreement with the AEO explains how in the 8-4-4 music, pupils could come with percussive instruments and special artists could be invited to train the pupils how to play the instruments; hence pupils could use music to climb the academic ladder or earn a living. According to the head of Sunga, even the reformed curriculum is too congested and this is yet other reason why teachers ignore teaching non-examinable subject such as creative arts. The intrinsic motivation for teachers is examination, hence teachers do not prepare enough to teach creative arts according to the head at Maseno boarding because they are not motivated. The informant further says that the new system will not allow us (education system) to produce talented pupils because we (teacher/the system) cannot identify the talents in music and other arts. This is supported by the head of Sunga when he stated that creativity in the kids is annihilated; they cannot even say what a crotchet is. He believes that creative art is inborn in people. Hence learners who are not born academicians, i.e. those who are not good at hardcore subjects and are again denied education in their relevant subjects like music, are wasted. This leads to school dropout or choosing subjects to please teachers and parents or to pass examination just to get promoted to the next higher level of education. When creative arts subjects are ignored, the country losses the creative arts talented learners because they do not get to study their rightful subjects to get them in their rightful careers.

The reform has not only affected the teaching of music but also the music teacher. What on earth do trained music teachers do in schools when music is not taught? The music teacher at Eliobe according to the head, now trains choirs for KMF. In support of this, the head at Maseno mixed says that school music teachers of today cannot even compose songs, even the simplest praise songs, not because they can not, but maybe because they are not motivated. It is therefore correct to conclude that music teachers are also losing their theoretical music knowledge.

All the five informants (heads of the schools) wish to have music examined at the end of primary education. The head teacher Eiobe said "It were good music be given a general paper so long as it is examinable." Head of Sunga added that curriculum developers can make it examinable and if this is not possible then he recommends that a change of examination system so that music is graded by teachers on a continuous assessment (CAT) basis. This can be used as a measure for entry into higher (secondary) studies in music. This is important, he adds, because learning of music boasts the learning of other subjects. Head teacher, Maseno Boarding, is concerned with cultural retention through music. She said, "Culture is renewed and perpetuated through creative arts of which music form part hence without music there is distortion of culture".

Beside music, the informants lament the making optional or total removal of some subjects from primary curriculum; for example, the head of Maseno mixed laments that the subjects home science, agriculture should have not been removed. The removal of these subjects is due to the fact that KIE have the wrong persons in the curriculum making panels. She said "The ministry does not consider teachers on the ground while developing curriculum." The head teacher Sunga more or less concluded with "we could have a more productive society if the education did not lay so much emphasis on examination but also taken into consideration practical subjects like music, home science, agriculture, etc."

In summary, music as creative arts is not prioritized in schools. The actual teaching of music is neglected, hence development of music talent in pupils is impaired, and the career of the music teacher is endangered. The reform did not only affect the teaching of music but also the teaching of other creative arts subjects. Head teachers, wish to have the subject examined so that teachers can take the teaching of the subject seriously.

References

African Education Commission. (1923-1924). *Education in East Africa: A study of East, Central and Southern Africa by the second African Education Commission under the auspices of the Phelps-Stokes Fund, in cooperation with the International Education Board*. London, UK: Edinburgh House Press.

Budiene, V. (2001). *Luthuania's curriculum development reform: Lessons learnt*. Paper presented at International seminar on *"Case studies in curriculum development: contributions to the Kosovo education reform" by UNESCO International Bureau of Education* (May 2001).

Colony and Protectorate of Kenya Department of Education. (1953a). *Syllabus for African primary schools*. Nairobi, Kenya: The Eagle Press.

Colony and Protectorate of Kenya Education Department. (1953b). *Tentative syllabus for African intermediate school*. Nairobi, Kenya: The Eagle Press.

Education Department of the Colony and Protectorate of Kenya. (1922). *Departmental instruction governing native education in assisted schools*. Nairobi, Kenya: Government Printers.

Eshiwani, G. S. (1993). *Education in Kenya since independence*. Nairobi, Kenya: East African Educational Publishers.

Gagg, J. C. (1958). *Modern teaching in African schools*. London, UK: Evan Brothers.

Kenya (1950). *Colony and protectorate of Kenya. Conference of women Education 15th -16th August. To consider the Beecher Report in relation to the Education of the African Girls*. Nairobi: Government Printers.

Kenya Institute of Education. (1984), *Secondary education project: Guidelines on the development of the secondary education curriculum*. Nairobi, Kenya: K.I.E.

King, K. J. (1971). *Pan-Africanism and education*. Oxford, UK: Clarendon Press.

Kiptoon, J. (n.d). Education reform: Kenya. Retrieved from http/www.ibe.unesco.org/curriculum/AfricaPdf/nairKenya.pdf

Makori, A. (2005, May-June). *The Kenya's educational policy: Exploring some of the major impediments to redesigning pedagogy*. Paper presented at the International conference Nanyang Technological University, Singapore.

Ministry of Education. (1972). *A study of curriculum development in Kenya*. Nairobi, Kenya: Government Printers.

Ministry of Education, Science & Technology. (1984). *The 8-4-4 system of education*. Nairobi, Kenya: Government Printers.

Mutuku, J. M & Odwar, H. A. (2010). Continuity in the music curriculum in upper primary schools in Vihiga District, Western Province – Kenya. *Problems in Music Pedagogy, 7*, 67-75.

Ndegwa Report (1971). *Report of the commission of enquiry*. Nairobi: Government Printers.

Norman, P. A. (2005, September). *Impact of curriculum reforms on some teacher education programs*. Paper presented at the 2005 National Curriculum Reform Conference. Port Moresby, Papua New Guniea.

Odwar, H. A. (2005). *Music education in Kenya: A historical perspective*. Eldoret, Kenya: Zapf Chancery.

Ogula, P. A. (n.d). The Evaluation experience of primary and secondary education projects in Kenya. *Eastern Africa Journal of Humanities & Sciences*. Retrieved from http://www.fiuc.org/iaup/esap/publications/cuea/cueapub.php

Ominde Report (1964). *The Kenya education commission report part 1*. Nairobi: Government.

Pokana, J. S. (2005, September). *The impact of the reform curriculum on the basic education sector – the OLSH Kabaleo Teachers College Approach*. Paper presented at the 2005 National Curriculum Reform Conference. Port Moseby, Papua New Guniea.

Presidential Working Party. (1981). *Report on the second university in Kenya*. Nairobi, Kenya: Presidential Working Party.

Republic of Kenya. (1964). *The Kenya education commission report*. Nairobi, Kenya: Government Printer.

Republic of Kenya. (1976). *Report of the national committee on national objectives and policies*. Nairobi, Kenya: Government Printer.

Republic of Kenya. (1981). *Report of the presidential working party on the establishment of the secondary university*. Nairobi, Kenya: Government Printer.

Rowley, G. (Ed.). (1977). *The book of music*. London, UK: MacDonald Educational and QED.

Sifuna, D. N. (1980). *Short essays on education in Kenya*. Nairobi, Kenya: Kenya Literature Bureau.

UNESCO International Bureau of Education (2001, October). *International seminar on "Case studies in curriculum development: Contributions to the Kosovo education reform."* Seminar organized by UNESCO International Bureau of Education (IBE), UNICEF/Kosovo and the Department of Education and Sciences, United Nations Mission in Kosovo (DOES/UNMIK).

Weman, H. (1960). *African music and the church in Africa* (E. J. Sharpe, Trans.). Uppsala, Sweden: Appelbergs Boktryckeri.

Appendix A

Primary School Music Syllabus for African Schools 1953

Music

The aim of the Primary school music syllabus is to impart to children a love of their own music. The syllabus therefore gives suggestions to teachers for the teaching of African songs to children. Since a school is a place where we learn, the standard of singing in a school should be higher than the standard of singing of those who have not been to school. Attention will therefore be paid to voice production, diction, intonation, rhythm and choir training. The teacher should arrange occasional concerts to which parents or children from other schools are invited.

Every tribal group has its own songs. It is therefore necessary for the teachers in each district to make a collection of songs suitable for children to sing. A teachers' refresher course provides a good opportunity for teachers to compile a collection of vernacular songs and exchange new songs with each other. The songs should be selected with due regard to the morality of their words and actions and to their general suitability for children. The collection of songs should never be regarded as complete; each teacher should add it to any suitable songs that he hears. Some of the songs will be traditional, and some will be modern compositions. Some suitable topics for songs are suggested below; these should help teachers to know what kind of traditional songs to look for and give them ideas for composing new songs.

Some topics for traditional Songs
Hunting; songs of war and victory; songs in praise of famous men; songs about agricultural activity (digging, harvesting grinding etc.); songs which tell stories of the past; songs of mourning; songs of encouragement; songs about cattle, and songs about wild animals and birds.

Some topics for new songs
(To be sung with actions)

Lullabies, songs about smiths, carpenters, shoemakers, drivers, policemen, animal songs, imitating the noise which the animal makes and the way in which it walks; songs in which children can shoot imaginary arrows, throw spears, cut down trees, saw logs, drive teams of oxen, ride bicycles, pump up tires, wash and iron clothes, paddle canoes, haul ropes, etc.

Tonic Sol-fa
Tonic Sol-fa may be used in schools where children are of mixed tribes; but it should be borne in mind that the notes of European scales are not always the same as the notes of African scales, and that if Tonic Sol-fa (I.e. the European scale) is taught exclusively from the beginning, African music will suffer.

Pitch
Every choirmaster should have some instrument to give him correct pitch: a bamboo pipe, a descant recorder, or a tuning folk will suffice.

Gramophone Records
The use of Gramophone records is strongly recommended. "Gallotone" and "Trek" records of the music of many Kenya tribes may be purchased through Gallo (Africa) Ltd., P.O. Box 3695, Nairobi, or from most music dealers.

Hymns
An occasional music period may be devoted to the learning of hymns, although this syllabus will make it clear that hymn singing is not the main purpose of music in the Primary School.

STANDARD I
1. The best type of song for small children is a singing game which gives them an opportunity for imitative rhythmic activity and dancing.
2. Children should go outside for singing if possible.
3. There should be very little difference in standard I between a singing lesson and a P.T, lesson. Both should consist of rhythmic activity, which is often best performed in a cir-

cle formation. For songs with vigorous actions, the class might be divided into two groups: one group performing actions while the other are singing.
4. Boys must be taught to sing in their unbroken treble voices.
5. All singing should be in unison.
6. The lessons should consist partly of singing and acting familiar songs and partly of learning a new song and its actions. Remember that children enjoy variety as well as activity.
7. End each lesson with a breathing exercise.

STANDARD II

In Standard I, the main emphasis has been on rhythm and activity. From Standard II onwards, aim at a higher standard of singing. This can be achieved by the following types of training, some of which should be included in every lesson.

a. Voice production exercises

Singing is not shouting, and the teacher must try to make children realize the difference between the two, and to develop a preference for singing and a dislike of shouting songs. Before singing a song, make the children sings a few notes as sweetly as they can, getting louder and softer. Voice production exercises not only improve the tone of the voice; they also improve its range and its flexibility. While singing a song, listen constantly to the quality of the tone, and be especially careful to avoid forcing the voice in the louder passages or on the high notes.

b. Ear training

This teaches children to 'listen' to a note in their head before they sing it. If they have good ear training they will sing it in tune. The teacher is teaching children to listen and imitate whenever he teachers them a new song, but he may find that it is necessary to give ear training exercises if the children are singing out of tune. These exercises consist of a note or phrase sung by the teacher and imitated exactly by the children either collectively or individually.

c. Clear enunciation of vowels and consonants

The words should be sung so clearly that they can be understood by a person unfamiliar with the song.

d. Breathing and phrasing

The purpose of breathing exercises is to develop the lungs and thus enable the singer to control the emission of air through his throat. Only by doing this can he produce a smooth and regular note, and sing loudly or softly at will. Breathing exercises also help us to sing a long time without taking breath. Make the children breathe in through the nose, filling their lungs from the bottom, keeping the abdomen firm, and without hunching shoulders or tightening the throat. They should breathe out 'slowly' through the mouth with throat and chest relaxed. (Do not let them push out all their breath with one big puff!) Sometimes they may sing a note while they are exhaling. Music is written in phrase, and before a teacher teaches a new song he should decide where the phrases begin and end. Children should breathe only at the beginning of a phrase.

e. Choir training

A good choir has a good attack; the singers begin and end together. To achieve a good attack needs practice, but it does not necessarily require a conductor. If the singing is accompanied by dancing or rhythmic activity the singers can keep together by following the leader. Even if there are no actions accompanying the song, get one of the children to act as a leader rather than trying to conduct them yourself.

It is difficult for the children to concentrate on a high standard of singing if they are moving about vigorously. The teacher therefore has to find songs in which there is only a little movement, or songs in which only a few children move while the rest sing, or songs are not accompanied by movement. It is necessary to group the children in different ways according to the type of song that is being sung:

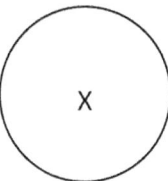

Here the leader (x) turns round while he is singing. A circle is a good formation for songs with imitative actions

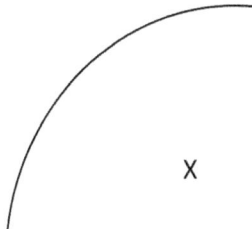

This formation is suitable for the "Question and Answer" type of songs. If there is an audience, both the choir and audience can see the leaders face

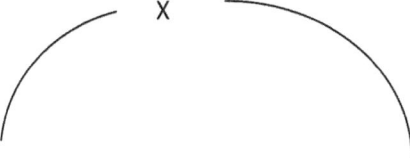

This formation is especially suitable for songs with stories. The choir sits on the ground, and the leader (story teller) on a stool.

Types of song

In Standard II, singing should still be in unison, but more use can be made of the type of song, which has a soloist and a chorus answering him. Try to get children to take it in turns to be the soloist.

Writing songs down

During writing lessons, children can write down the words of songs that they have learnt. Make sure that they write the title, keep the song in its lines of equal length, number and verses and indicate which part are to be sung by a soloist and which by the choir.

STANDARD III

Continue to improve the standard of singing. Try to get the children to express the mood of the song they are singing. A listener should feel sad during a sad song, and happy during a joyful one. Do not let the children sing loud all the time: practice singing softly and loudly, changing from one to the other gradually (Crescendo and Dimineundo).

Continue to teach some songs that have limitations in them and some of the solo-chorus type of songs that the children have learnt in standard II. Introduce some simple rounds or canons.

You will probably have to conduct rounds and canons so that you can show the children when to join in the singing. For a two part canon divide he choir into two groups ,and for a three-part canon divide them into three groups: [the figures below need to be reformatted to fit within a standard US letter-sized page.]

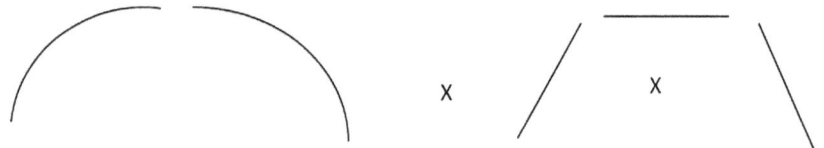

Encourage children to make up songs to sing and give them an opportunity to teach their own songs to other children.

By inviting a local minstrel to the school to play to the children, many children will be interested in making their own instruments and in learning how to play them. It is not usually possible to teach these instruments in class, but children should be encouraged to learn them out of school. An occasional music period might be devoted to instrumental concerts given by the children.

Here are some of the instruments, which the children might learn and use while they are singing:

Luyia: Litungu, inangoli, bukhana, shimuka, lukhuchi, ludulere, isuguti, eshitsiriba, im-
    bumi, tsindeche.
Luo: thum, orutu, nyatiti, orere, ajawa, abu tung', bul, gara
Nandi:
Kipsigis: kibugandet, chepkongo, chepkesem, kitubet, ndurerut, sugutit.
Nyika: mabumbumbu, mushondo, bung'o, voti, kitoli, mwangoloto, kidaba, bombombo,
    chapuo, kayamba.

Kikuyu: kihembe, mututriru, wandinidi, kiigamba, njingiri.
Kamba: mbebe, uta, ndumali, mutulilu, kyaa, kithembe, mukanda, iamba, maleve.
Drums and rattles can be used to accompany singing games from Standard I onwards.

Rhythm notation
Teach children how to recognize and read simple rhythms involving quavers, crochets, and minims. The best way to do this is to have a percussion band. The following "instruments" are suggested: drums, ankle bells, camel or cowbell, triangle (or iron bar), blocks (two blocks of wood) gourd rattles, (dried peas in a calabash), coconut clappers.

STANDARD IV
Continue to improve the standard of singing and choir drill and continue to encourage original compositions and the playing of local instruments. Let each child have a special exercise book in which he copies suitable songs that he likes. This collection of songs can be started during writing lessons, but children should be encouraged to compile their own collections. A prize might be offered for the best and neatest collection.

Types of song
Some more difficult types of songs can be added to types learnt in Standard I and III: songs with overlapping questions and answers, and songs with harmony. If you sing in harmony be careful that you do not make children with unbroken voices sing in their chest voices.

Rhythm notation
Continue with the percussion band. Introduce the rests for the quavers, crochets, minims, semibreves. Occasionally give the children "musical dictation" to see if they can write down simple rhythms which they hear.

Teachers' books
The Music Makers by A.M. Jones, Longmans.

Chiriku, by Gerold, Macmillan & Co.

Reference book
Ngoma, by Hugh Tracey, Longman

Fully Online Learning in a Pre-service Teacher Music Education Unit in Australia: Student Perspectives

Bill Baker
University of Tasmania (Australia)
Bill.Baker@utas.edu.au

Abstract

With the continued expansion of online learning environments the growth of e-learning in the education of teachers, and hence music teachers, is inevitable, and research into the ways in which students learn music education in this environment is important in order to develop appropriate pedagogies for the future, and to inform new practical approaches to music teacher education. This paper, part of a three-year ongoing research project, focused on data collected from seven pre-service teachers regarding their perceptions of the experience of learning music education online. This research project used a multi-method approach within constructivist ontology, and this paper focused on data collected using semi-structured interviews and analyzed using inductive category construction. Results revealed the importance of peer to peer, and of peer to tutor interaction to the subjects and has highlighted that these interactions are acknowledged by them to be significantly different from interactions that occur in face-to-face environments. This paper has also highlighted the value placed by students on the synchronous practical application of learning whilst studying music education online. Both of these findings are significant in respect of the education of pre-service teachers in music education.

Keywords
E-learning, music, music education, pre-service teachers.

The impact of e-learning on higher education has continued to increase exponentially since its inception (Boettcher & Conrad, 2010; Cleveland-Innes & Garrison, 2010; Commonwealth of Australia, 2002; Drummond, 2008; Epstein, 2006; Guri-Rosenblit, 2005; Herbert, 2007; Jones & O'Shea, 2004; Kerr, Rynearson, & Kerr, 2006; Nagel & Kotze, 2010; Paechter & Maier, 2010; Riddiford, 2009; Rovai, 2004; Sherbon & Kish, 2005; Song, Singleton, Hill, & Koh, 2004; Young & Norgard, 2006). The Organisation for Economic Co-operation and Development (OECD) states that "it has been estimated that there will be between 30 and 80 million online students in the world by 2025" (Commonwealth of Australia, 2002, p. 3). Digolo, Andang'o, and Katuli (2011) maintained that "in 2006, the number of students in the United States alone...was estimated at over 3.5 million...It is fast becoming a universal educational trend that must be adopted by all institutions of higher learning" (p. 138).

In Australia, Riddiford (2009) reported that the "analyst IBIS World expects online education to be the fastest growing industry in Australia this financial year" (p. 7). Universities have responded to the challenges of e-learning in different ways ranging from a minimal response to thoroughly embracing fully online learning (Boettcher & Conrad, 2010; Cleveland-Innes & Garrison, 2010; Drummond, 2008; Epstein, 2006; Guri-Rosenblit, 2005; Jones & O'Shea, 2004; Paechter & Maier, 2010). Throughout the world, through the facilities of e-learning, the delivery of higher education has shifted appreciably, resulting in the potential for increased participation and for geographically disparate yet synchronous participation in higher education, yet rigorous study of this approach in relation to music education has not occurred.

With the impact of e-learning in higher education continuing to grow, research into the application of e-learning pedagogy to music education, a traditionally face-to-face domain, will serve to inform the discourse in this area. This paper, part of a three-year ongoing research project, explored the application of e-learning to a pre-service teacher unit in music education in one Australian university. This paper focused upon data collected from seven pre-service teachers regarding their perceptions of the experience of learning music education online, and highlights the importance of this research to the education of teachers in music education.

It is important to note that the terminology surrounding e-learning and the differences between interpretations of e-learning is somewhat complex, with authors variously referring to it as: distance learning, e-learning, distributed learning, internet-based learning, blended learning and online learning to name some. Fully online learning is defined by the Commonwealth of Australia (2002) as an approach in which "all interactions with staff and students, education content, learning activities, assessment and support services are integrated and delivered on line" (p. 14). For the purposes of this research project e-learning refers to this approach in which all interactions take place in an online environment.

Aim of the Project

In 2009, the university of which I am a member decided to restructure education degrees and units and to offer all degrees in a fully online environment from the commencement of 2010. From 2010 face-to-face teaching of degrees continued for those students who elected an on campus mode of study, however students who selected the fully online learning mode were able to complete the coursework components of any degree without any on-campus attendance requirements. This restructuring effectively created two student cohorts distinguished by their mode of study, completing the same units for the same degrees. This research project investigates one unit in music education that is part of the restructured four year Bachelor of Education degree. This first year unit is the only unit in the degree where students study music education, and it is therefore introductory in nature. In 2010, 640 students were enrolled in the unit at census with 271 (42%) of these enrolled as fully online students. This paper, resulting from an ongoing three-year research project, builds on research into the perceptions of pre-service teachers of their participation in e-learning in music education in this unit (Baker, 2011a, 2011b). Baker (2011a, 2011b) analysed data from a survey of students who completed the 2010 iteration of the unit, and this paper explores data from seven interview subjects collected following the analysis of survey data. The research question underpinning this project asks "What is necessary to enable effective and efficient learning in music education for pre-service primary generalist teachers in a fully online environment?" Effective learning refers to that which encourages "deep" learning as defined by Biggs (2003), and efficient learning refers to that which enables students to engage meaningfully with key music education concepts and processes.

Baker (2011a) found that students highly valued interactivity and particularly contact with their tutor. If this is the case then it is the engagement in online discussions and the structure of learning that become significant in successfully adapting teaching and learning to this environment. Baker (2011b) explored data regarding student use of instructional videos designed for their use in the unit. These videos were highly valued by students, but were used in different ways to support their learning, ranging from passive use such as only viewing the videos and taking notes to an active use, using the videos actively by working along to them in some way.

Method

This research project uses a multi method approach within constructivist ontology (Blaikie, 1993; Burns, 1997; Denzin & Lincoln, 1994; Patton, 1990; Sarantakos, 2005). The use of more than one method of data collection is referred to as a multiple method approach. Denzin and Lincoln (1994) refer to qualitative research as being inherently "multimethod" in focus (p. 2) and for Patton (1990) the use of multiple methods of data collection is to be regarded as a source of methodological strength within the qualitative paradigm. Denzin and Lincoln (1994) acknowledge the strength of multiple methods of data collection when stating the "use of multiple methods, or triangulation, reflects an attempt to secure an in-depth understanding of the phenomenon in question" (p. 2). These multiple methods of data collection from the participant groups provide significant methodological strength to the research design and contribute to data validity.

Following the collection of survey data students were invited to participate in semi-structured interviews, with seven students electing to participate in this stage. Because interview subjects were not located in proximity to the researcher, including one student based in Hong Kong, all interviews were conducted by teleconference and recorded for transcription purposes. All subjects were sent copies of their transcripts and asked to check these for accuracy and intention before returning them to the researcher. Interview data were analyzed through an approach that uses "inductive category construction" (Sarantakos, 2005, p. 306). The inductive process involves identifying and coding domains of data and searches for themes across domains. According to Hatch (2002), the inductive approach "proceeds from the specific to the general. Understandings are generated by starting with specific elements and finding connections among them" (p. 161). Hatch (2002) stated that "inductive data analysis is a search for patterns of meaning in data so that general statements about phenomena under investigation can be made" (p. 161). Data were entered into charts or "matrices" (Miles & Huberman, 1984) that provided the framework for analysing themes and the relationships between them. For this paper all subject names have been replaced with pseudonyms.

Results

Interview data aligned with data collected via the survey, adding depth to those data and elaborating upon the themes evident therein. One area in particular arose from the interview data in relation to the online experience in music education that was not evident in the survey data. These related to subject perceptions of the equity of their experience when compared to that of face-to-face students. All subjects were asked if they thought that they had the same opportunities to learn as those completing the unit in a face-to-face mode. Of the seven subjects three suggested that learning online did not present the same opportunities for them, and four stated that they felt they had the same opportunity as face-to-face students, or that it was just a different way of learning without placing any value judgement on this difference.

For Jane learning online was different because it lacked the immediacy of face-to-face learning, she states that:

I don't think it was the same… I think that's impossible…like, just being able to talk to your lecturer at the end of a session, or whatever, for me, far outweighs writing something on an email and sending it to the lecturer, or getting someone else to listen and sending it back.

For Marie however, with the online resources supplied there was no significant difference to learning in a face-to-face context, stating that "I got just as much out of them, sitting here in my study, as I would have there [in a classroom]". Alice considered face-to-face feedback from peers a key element that was missing from her online learning experience, stating that "I think we do miss out on feedback from our peers. As well as that general discussion time that you just have over coffee just talking together with other students". However she goes on to state that she thinks "in some ways, I think that we've got it better, because it's a much more flexible environment and you don't have to be anywhere, at any particular time, it's up to me". This is an interesting conundrum; Alice misses informal contact with her peers but appreciates the flexibility of online learning.

Tracy had an earlier experience of a face-to-face environment but prefers online learning, stating that:

I think that this is a much better way for me to learn. I am in schools – so, it's a different opportunity, because although we don't have the same sort of interaction as people going to a tutorial, there's less timetabling, and, because we're in a classroom, it's probably got more relevance to what it is I'm learning.

This brings into relief the perspective of those subjects who were also simultaneously working in a school. Five out of the seven subjects were working in schools as teacher aides whilst studying the unit, or had access to contexts where they could apply the learning in music education directly, and they all report this as a key factor in their learning experience. Tracy continued, stating:

It gave me a confidence boost. I'm probably not as confident in the arts subjects- music, drama, dance, as the traditional subjects and actually being able to use information from the unit with my children and their friends, all kids that I get along well with was fun and helped to build my confidence.

Sally reinforces the importance of a practical context for the application of skills and understandings in the school where she works as an integration aide with students with disabilities, stating that:

[d]uring the course, I was lucky enough, that, because – the teacher I had – we only had 12 children in the class, last year, and because of the teacher, who was a relatively new to teaching, a mature-aged student - she said, 'oh – would you like to take music lessons every

week'. So, I said, 'yeah'. So I did music lessons, and art lessons, for the whole semester that I was doing music and art.

For Erica her experience of the unit was very positive but she missed face-to-face contact with peers and tutors, stating that:

I think that the unit was very successful, but my preference would be face-to- face, where you can work with other people, and bounce ideas off other people… It's a lot harder to have a discussion on a discussion board than it is face-to-face with other people.

Julie refers to lack of immediacy in using discussion boards to interact, stating:

I think that face-to-face, you can go up and approach the lecturer, or tutor, without necessarily having to organise a meeting beforehand – you can sort of catch them on the fly, or you can talk with other peers. So, those smaller issues can be cleared up more quickly. Whereas, if you have to wait, or if no one on the discussion forum knows the answer to your question, then it can slow you down.

For both of these subjects discussion boards did not enable the same sort of exchange with peers or tutors as is available in a face-to-face environment.

For Marie the discussion boards were "sort of like your online study group". But Marie also used a peer support group to her advantage in the unit. As a final year student Marie had built up a support network of peers over the years, through attending summer school face-to-face sessions and through discussion boards. For her this network was central to her success in this unit. Marie states that "none of us live close together, we just do it over phone, or Skype, or whatever we need to do, and we just meet every couple of months, and catch up, or have a study day or something".

Conclusions and Implications for Music Education

This paper has reinforced the importance of peer to peer, and of peer to tutor interaction in the online music education experience (Baker, 2011a). Peer-to-peer and peer-to-tutor interaction in an online environment has been revealed to be important to subjects and acknowledged by them to be significantly different from face-to-face environments. The use of discussion boards was acknowledged by all of the participants as generally useful but nonetheless certainly not a replacement for face-to-face interaction. Synchronous interaction technology does exist, such as web conferences, and these are used to effect in other units with smaller student enrolments, however these are not necessarily a replacement for face-to-face interaction either. This paper has highlighted the need for further research into the use of discussion boards in music education, and particularly into the ways in which peer to peer and peer to tutor interaction can be facilitated whilst acknowledging the fundamental difference between such interactions and genuine face-to-face communication.

This paper has also highlighted the value placed by students on the synchronous practical application of learning whilst studying music education online. This finding is a little confounding because online and face-to-face students both participate in periodic professional placements in schools, yet the online cohort with many students already working in schools also had the opportunity to apply their learning in music education on a daily basis. The importance of this practical context was highlighted by all subjects in this study. Further investigation of these findings may focus on ways to encourage students to develop such opportunities for themselves as part of studying music education online.

Both of these findings are significant in respect of the education of pre-service teachers in music education. These findings provide a focus for the next stages of this research project being the collection of data using survey and interview tools with the 2011 online cohort. With the continued expansion of online learning environments the growth of this mode of learning in the education of teachers, and hence music teachers, is inevitable, and research into the ways in which students learn music education in this environment is important in order to develop appropriate pedagogies for the future, and to inform new practical approaches to music teacher education.

References

Baker, W. J. (2011a). Fully online teaching and learning in a pre-service teacher unit in music education. In E. Mackinlay & D. Forrest (Eds.), *Making Sound Waves: Diversity, Unity, Equity Proceedings of the Australian Society for Music Education XVIII National Conference, Broadbeach, QLD, 2nd-5th July, 2011* (pp. 69-73). Parkville, VIC: Australian Society for Music Education.

Baker, W. J. (2011b). Using video to cross the boundary between Arts education and online learning in a preservice teacher education degree: Student perspectives. In J. Wright (Ed.), *Researching across boundaries. Proceedings of the Australian Association for Research in Education National Conference, Hobart, TAS, 27th November-1 December, 2011* (pp. 1-13). Deakin, ACT: Australian Association for Research in Education.

Biggs, J. (2003). *Teaching for quality learning at university.* Great Britain: The Society for Research into Higher Education & Open University Press.

Blaikie, N. (1993). *Approaches to social enquiry.* Cambridge, England: Polity Press.

Boettcher, J. V., & Conrad, R. (2010). *The online teaching survival guide: Simple and practical pedagogy.* Hoboken, NJ: Jossey-Bass.

Burns, R. (1997). *Introduction to research methods.* (3rd ed.). South Melbourne, VIC: Addison Wesley Longman.

Cleveland-Innes, M., & Garrison, D. R. (Eds.). (2010). *An introduction to distance education: Understanding teaching and learning in a new era.* New York, NY: Routledge.

Commonwealth of Australia. (2002). *Universities online: A survey of online education and services in Australia.* Canberra, ACT: Department of Education, Science and Technology.

Denzin, N., & Lincoln, Y. (Eds.). (1994). *Handbook of qualitative research.* Thousand Oaks, CA: Sage.

Digolo, B. E., Andang'o, E. A., & Katuli, J. (2011). E- Learning as a strategy for enhancing access to music education. *International Journal of Business and Social Science* 2(11), 135–139.

Drummond, G. (2008). Success in online education: Creating a roadmap for student success. *Distance Learning* 5(4), 43–48.

Epstein, P. (2006). Online, campus or blended learning: What do consumers prefer and why? *Distance Learning, 3*(3), 35–37.

Guri-Rosenblit, S. (2005). 'Distance education' and 'E-learning': Not the same thing. *Higher Education 49*, 467–493.

Hatch, J. (2002). *Doing qualitative research in education settings.* Albany, NY: State University of New York Press.

Hebert, D. G. (2007). Five challenges and solutions in online music teacher education. *Research and Issues in Music Teacher Education*, 5. Retrieved from http://www.stthomas.edu/rimeonline/vol5/hebert.htm

Jones, N., & O'Shea, J. (2004). Challenging hierarchies: The impact of E-learning. *Higher Education, 48*, 379-395.

Kerr, M. S., Rynearson, K., & Kerr, M. C. (2006). Student characteristics for online learning success. *Internet and Higher Education, 9*, 91–105.

Miles, M. B., & Huberman, M. A. (1984). *Qualitative data analysis: A sourcebook of new methods.* Newbury Park, London: Sage.

Nagel, L., & Kotze, T. G. (2010). Supersizing e-learning: What a CoI survey reveals about teaching presence in a large online class. *Internet and Higher Education, 13*, 45–51.

Paechter, M., & Maier, B. (2010). Online or face-to-face? Students' experiences and preferences in e-learning. *Internet and Higher Education 13*, 292–297.

Patton, M. (1990). *Qualitative evaluation and research methods.* (2nd ed.). Newbury Park, CA: Sage.

Riddiford, M. (2009, September 5). Online learning a $2.7bn industry. *The Australian*, pp. 7-7, 1. Retrieved from http://www.theaustralian.com.au/

Rovai, A. P. (2004). A constructivist approach to online college learning. *Internet and Higher Education 7*, 79–93.

Sarantakos, S. (2005). *Social research.* (3rd ed.). Houndmills, Hampshire: Palgrave MacMillan.

Sherbon, J. W., and King, J. L. (2005). Distance learning and the music teacher. *Music Educators Journal 92* (2), 36–41.

Song, L., Singleton, E. S., Hill, J. R., & Koh, M. H. (2004). Improving online learning: Student perceptions of useful and challenging characteristics. *Internet and Higher Education, 7*, 59–70.

Young, A., & Norgard, C. (2006). Assessing the quality of online courses from students' perspective. *Internet and Higher Education, 9*, 107–115.

Considering Cultural Plurality in Band Method Books

Joel Luis da Silva Barbosa
Universidade Federal da Bahia (Brazil)
jlsbarbosa@hotmail.com

Abstract

This paper addresses the teaching and learning processes of cultural plurality in band method books for collective instruction. It considers the topic within the context of the Brazilian music education. After decades of lethargic music activities in the school, Brazilian educators have the challenge of creating new and efficient music programs to consolidate music in this educational context. This is due to the approval of new educational laws. They stated that music and cultural plurality are obligatory contents in the curriculum. One means of providing music education in the Brazilian schools is to introduce wind bands in these contexts as they constitute an important music tradition of the country's culture. But how can a school band practice really fulfil the laws requirements regarding cultural plurality in a country with a so great diversity of music cultures? Band method books for collective instruction have been an efficient tool for creating and maintaining bands in schools in the USA, Australia, Singapore, and Japan. They hold a methodological knowledge that has been developed for more than 90 years with an efficacious pedagogy, which makes the activity financially affordable. Nevertheless, their manner of bringing the cultural plurality content and their didactic approach to it may not be enough to meet the law requirements. In the case of the Brazilian music education, it is urgent to define sensible criterions to choose what music cultures to include in method books for school bands and how to study them in this music practice.

Keywords
Wind band, method, multiculturalism, collective instruction

Introduction

In a world where the access to information is transforming lives, distances and societies, it is very important to understand different cultures, our own and the others. Culture has become an obligatory discipline in many curriculums. This paper discusses the limits of learning cultural plurality in band method books for collective instruction. It considers this issue within the current context of the music education in Brazil.

Historic context

In fact, music has not been fully present in the Brazilian regular schools since 1970. The Lei de Diretrizes e Bases (LDB) 9394-96, the main educational law in the country, established art as an obligatory content in 1996. It abolished the artistic education discipline and the art-education actions that were taken place in the schools. But it did not bring music effectively into the school activities. The last legal action to introduce music effectively in the schools was in August 18, 2008, when the National Congress sanctioned the 11.769 law and made music an obligatory content in the curriculum. The primary and secondary schools had three years to start fulfilling the educational requirements. The deadline was August 2011. Then, music is new in the school routine. It has not been part of the school culture nationwide, even though it is in the students' lives currently.

Besides the law for music, the Congress approved also the 11.645 law in 2008. It turns obligatory the history and culture of the Afro-Brazilians and of the Brazilian indians to the school curriculum. In order to fulfil the LDB 9394-96 law, it was written separate National Curriculum Standards for art and for cultural plurality (Ministério da Educação, 1997a). Both of them agree on the demand of including contents of the local and foreign cultural plurality.

In the last four years, many music teachers and researchers have discussed and written about what to do in the schools. This is an important question because for approximately 40 years there have been very few music programs in these educational environments. But the period was not completely bad. There were real music *warriors* facing adversities while trying to maintain music in the schools. One of the main music bearers were marching band directors. During this period, they built a strong music practice across the nation with *fanfarras*, including regular state and national festivals. *Fanfarra* is a kind of marching band with percussion and natural or one-valved brass instruments. Though many of them have no legal title to teach music at the school, they deserve a room in the presently music education scenario of the schools. Furthermore, the music graduate courses do not offer formation on this music tradition. The Ministry of Education included *fanfarra* in a recent program for comprehensive education called *Mais Educação*, More Education (Brazil, 2011).

The Proposal

Among the music programs that may do well in the schools are the wind bands, more precisely the concert and marching bands with woodwind, brass and percussion instruments. It may be so for three reasons at least. Firstly, *fanfarras* have played a significant role in the schools (Bertunes, 2005; Campos, 2008; Cislaghi, 2009). Secondly, the country holds a large band tradition in which the youth are the majority of the participants (Barbosa, 2011; Benedito, 2011). At last, even though there are only few cases of wind bands in schools, they are solid music education program (Silva, 2010). The schools have maintained them for long time, even decades, and they are located in culturally contrasting areas of the nation (Salles, 1985).

The Problem

But, as it may occur with the introduction of any music program in the Brazilian schools nowadays, it is necessary to invent a wind band practice for schools. On one hand, none of the different practices of the civil, religious or military bands would work entirely in the schools. They have particular aspects, including artistic ones, which are related specifically with their social and cultural communities that they cannot be reproduced in the schools. Their repertoire or some other aspects may work in the school band practice. On the other hand, the existing school band programs are few and individual experiences that do not constitute a real practice. Their experiences can guide the make up of this new school music practice, or new band practice. Nevertheless, they work with individually instrumental classes, which are too expensive to the regular schools, and they were built before 2008 so that their practices are not consistent with the new educational laws. They need to be updated.

The diversity of school band programs as a whole would constitute a consistent school band practice. In order to facilitate the introduction of band programs in schools, it is necessary to develop pedagogical materials. Band method book for collective instruction is the main material used to form school bands. They have been utilized in the schools of the U.S. since the 1920s and in Australia, Japan and Singapore in the recent decades. According to Colwell and Goolsby (1992), "band as a subject was offered in more schools than any other subject, save English, being available in 93 percent of American high schools" during the 1990s (p. 8). They used to be in three volumes and the content of each one is for a school year.

Discussion

Due to the scope of this paper, it will consider only the issue of introducing traditional music cultures from Brazil in a band method book for the Brazilian music education. Regarding cultural plurality, the main objective of the Brazilian NCS for the fifth to the eighth grades is "To know, to appreciate, and to acquire attitudes of respect before the musical manifestation diversity, and to analyze the combinations that occur among them currently, pondering their aesthetic and values"[1] (Ministério da Educação, 1997b, p. 81). In addition, the content's standard related to it states that the curriculum should include:

Interpretation, accompaniment, re-creation and arrangements of musics from the social, cultural environment and from the musical patrimony, built by the humanity in different geographic places, epochs, people, cultures and ethnic groups, through playing and/or singing individually and/or in group (band, choir and others), and building relations of respect and dialogue[2] (Ministério da Educação, 1997b, p. 83).

In order to have a significant music education in a band practice, the pupil needs to study his instrument more than a year, and attend enough band rehearsals weekly. This is so due to the instruments´ technique difficulties. Then, considering the law requirements, the very short period of time reserved to the music course, and the difficulties of the instruments, the band classes would have to take all music classes of the week. Consequently, they would have to meet the law's requirements.

Concerning the inclusion of cultural plurality in band method books, most of the current American ones declare to be multicultural. They contain traditional melodies from different countries of the world, including the U.S., and from composers of the concert music. Some of them add also historical and geographical information related to them. Most of the traditional tunes seem to belong to the childhood culture of these nations, but they come with no lyrics. They are chosen as means to know other cultures, develop instrument

---

[1] "Conhecer, apreciar e adotar atitudes de respeito diante da variedade de manifestações musicais e analisar as interpenetrações que se dão contemporaneamente entre elas, refletindo sobre suas respectivas estéticas e valores."
[2] "Interpretação, acompanhamento, recriação, arranjos de músicas do meio sociocultural, e do patrimônio musical construído pela humanidade nos diferentes espaços geográficos, épocas, povos, culturas e etnias, tocando e/ou cantando individualmente e/ou em grupo (banda, canto coral e outros), construindo relações de respeito e diálogo."

technique and acquire music reading skills so that the melodies of the first volume have simple rhythm and short range. Examples of these method books are: *Accent on Achievement*, *Essential Elements*, *Standard of Excellence*, *Sound Innovations*, *Belwin 21st Century* and *Best in Class*. Can this approach effectively help the student to comprehend the other's culture?

Let us reason on the use of melodies from the Brazilian cultural plurality in the band method book. The Brazilian music culture comprises national, regional and local music practices and traditions, besides international ones, such as orchestras, wind bands, and jazz bands. As examples, some of the national ones are related to the genres of *samba*, *choro*, *baião*; to the manifestations of the *boi*, *maculelê*, *capoeira* and *marujada*; and to the musics of work, childhood, and of the Brazilian Indians. They are spread throughout the country with some differences in each region. Some of the regionals are the *carimbó*, *maracatu*, *caboblinhos*, *coco*, *cururu*, *siriri*, *fandango*, *chamamé*, *vaneirão*, *jongo*, *aboio*, *frevo* and the *pífano* flute bands. We will not consider the religious traditions such as *toré* and *reisado*. Most of them are unknown to the students. Thus, the method book would have to be multicultural within the cultural diversity of the country.

The NCS point out several motives to include cultural plurality in the curriculum. We would like to add that it may: (a) awake the young to the importance of the country cultural diversity; (b) to counterbalance the mass media culture that emphasizes only few music practices in detriment of others, and (c) collaborate with the pupil's process of comprehending herself better. The point is not if it is relevant to know other music cultures, but if it is possible to comprehend them trough a beginning band practice, how, and what are the limits of it.

There are many limitations to comprehend a music tradition through a band practice. When a band plays melodies from any music practice or tradition mentioned above, for instance, the student may grasp part of its sounding structure, but its culture values and meanings. We say part of it because they are usually to be sung and, with the exception of the *frevo*, the band instrumental formation is not part of them. They have their own kind of instrumental group, using different combinations of accordion and instruments of wind, string, and percussion. They have even unique instruments made by their own musicians such as the *rabeca*, a bowed string instrument, and the *viola de cocho* and the traditional banjo, plucked string instruments.

Another point is that the musicians of these music traditions have their own manner of executing these melodies, the musical expressions. They hold this specific knowledge that is not taught in the graduate courses. It is impossible for a band director to specialize in all these practices. When the band plays these tunes, it sounds as an outsider of the music practice playing with "accent". The band cannot obtain the same musical expression as the original groups do so that the soundly universe of the band is very different from these music groups. When the band plays melodies from other music practice, it is still a band. Its music practice does not become similar to the other. It is just a group of a music practice playing the tunes of another music practice.

Most of those melodies have very simple compositional structure. Their main values are cultural and social. They belong to cultural traditions that are, mostly, rooted in communities. They are played and sung in events where music is just one part of the whole. These are manifestations that occur, generally, in the open air with dance, colorful outfits, stories, feasts, fireworks, drama and/or, in some cases, with religious relations. For this reason, to teach them may mean dealing with social, cultural and religious prejudices. In the band class, the students will play them completely out of their contexts. So, how deeply can one understand a culture, which is unfamiliar or even depreciated by him, in a classroom by separating a "combination of notes" of its music practice from its context and people? To focus on the tunes of a music culture, in order to grasp it, means to understand it more as repertoire than a human activity.

Considering the above points, the students may end up getting a distorted comprehension of the cultural plurality. It can even take them away from what they are expected to get close to. Texts, recordings and videos may help them, but would that be enough? In order to build "relations of respect and dialogue" (Ministério da Educação, 1997b, p. 83) with a music practice or tradition, one has to fully comprehend its values, concepts, and meanings for its makers and communities. But, how deeply can an outsider fully penetrate the music-making universe of the other, even when making music with him within his environment?

The music makers of a music culture carry the culture on their way of making it. Thus, the human contact of the students with the people of an unfamiliar music culture is a very strong means to understand it. When watching its activities, the real presence of the people, the ritual and the environment's atmosphere may increase their senses and sensibility. The body gestures, facial expressions, and manner of talking are part of the process. In this situation, the music sounding is just one of the means that the culture expresses itself. The experience of knowing something different may give pleasure or not. After that, the pupils will be a little more prepared to appreciate or not this music culture.

Final Consideration

It is necessary to have very sensible criterions to select what music culture can be included in the band method book and how it should be studied. The students must be conscious of the study process limitations. The book should not only give information on the history and region from where the tunes come from, but also to discourse about the music tradition to which they belong to. In order to fulfill the National Curriculum Standards (NCS) with propriety, the band activities on cultural plurality could be part of a bigger program of the school and of the Federal Brazilian Government, which includes interchange activities between the school and the cultural groups and its communities.

References

Barbosa, J. L. (2011). Educação musical com/ensino coletivo de instrumentos de sopro e percussão. In L. Marina (Ed.), *Abrangências da música na educação contemporânea: Conceituações, problematizações e experiências* (pp. 19-26). Goiânia, GO: Ciranda da Arte.

Benedito, Celso. (2011). *O Mestre de Filarmônica da Bahia: Um Educador Musical* (Unpublished doctoral dissertation). Universidade Federal da Bahia, Salvador, BA.

Bertunes, Carina. (2005). *Estudo da influência das bandas na formação musical: dois estudos de caso em Goiânia-GO* (Unpublished masters thesis). Universidade Federal de Goiás, Goiania, GO.

Campos, N. P. (2008). O aspecto das bandas e fanfarras escolares: O aprendizado musical e outros aprendizados. *Revista da ABEM, 19*, 103–111.

Cislaghi, M. (2009). *Concepções e ações de educação musical no projeto de bandas e fanfarras de São José-SC: Três estudos de caso* (Unpublished masters thesis). Universidade Estadual de Santa Catarina, Florianópolis, SC.

Colwell, R., & Goolsby, T. (1992). *The teaching of instrumental music*. Englewood Cliffs, NJ: Prentice Hall.

Ministério da Educação. (1997a). *Parâmetros curriculares nacionais: Pluralidade cultural*. Brasília, DF: Ministério da Educação/Secretaria de Educação Fundamental.

Ministério da Educação. (1997b). *Parâmetros curriculares nacionais: Terceiro e quarto ciclos do ensino fundamental: Arte*. Brasília, DF: Ministério da Educação/Secretaria de Educação Fundamental.

Ministério da Educação. (2011, September 31). *Educação: Mais educação*. Retrieved from http://portal.mec.gov.br/index.php?Itemid=586&id=12372&option=com_content&vie w=article

Salles, V. (1985). *Sociedades de euterpe*. Brasília: Author´s edition.

Silva, L. E. A. (2010). *"Musicalização através da Banda de Música: Uma proposta de metodologia de ensaio fundamentada na análise do desenvolvimento musical dos seus integrantes e na atuação dos "mestres de banda"* (Unpublished doctoral dissertation). Universidade Federal do Rio de Janeiro, Rio de Janeiro.

Nurturing Students in a School Music Program through a Natural Disaster

Judith Bell
Chisnallwood Intermediate School
Christchurch, New Zealand
bell.judith@gmail.com

Tim Bell
University of Canterbury
Christchurch, New Zealand

Abstract

The city of Christchurch, New Zealand, experienced three major earthquakes in September 2010, February 2011, and June 2011. Each caused substantial damage, and the February earthquake resulted in significant loss of life. Under such circumstances one might expect that music programs in schools would be a low priority; however, at Chisnallwood Intermediate school, in one of the worst affected areas of town, the music program received strong support from students and parents, and students worked harder and achieved more than in previous years. This was counterintuitive, since students had severe damage to their homes, the earthquake damage has caused financial hardship, and the school itself was closed for several weeks resulting in a significant loss of tuition time. It became apparent that participation in the music programs provided the students with routine and motivation in the midst of a lot of change and uncertainty in other aspects of their lives. Consequently they showed more commitment to their music than might have been expected, and through that commitment ended up achieving well. For example, the jazz big band and small combo group won prizes in national competitions despite being significantly younger than other groups in the competitions.

A key factor that enabled the program to continue was that the music department was already making considerable use of online cloud computing rather than local servers for communication with families. This included widely available services such as Wikispaces and Gmail, which are located overseas and were unaffected by the earthquake. Furthermore, the Wikispaces web pages could be updated and emails sent from any computer with Internet access, even though the school was closed down for safety reasons. After the first earthquake the music department started making heavy use of forms on Google docs so that parents could communicate back conveniently; this proved so successful that it has now replaced the paper-based systems that had been used previously, while greatly improving communication with students and their families. This experience has important implications for music departments. First, with appropriate preparation it is possible to keep communication with students and parents going using cloud computing technologies even if the school system is damaged; second, the music program itself can provide routine and security for students; and finally, under difficult circumstances it is possible for a music program to not only survive, but even thrive as the power of music to nurture the spirit becomes especially evident.

Keywords
Natural disaster, earthquake, student welfare, competitions

Introduction
This paper reports on the experience of a music department that became a focal point for a number of students who experienced considerable disruption and personal loss through three major earthquakes in Christchurch, New Zealand during 2010–2011.

We focus on the school of Chisnallwood Intermediate, which is located in the centre of some of the most heavily affected suburbs of Christchurch. In New Zealand an "intermediate" school takes students for just two years, from Year 7 and 8 (the students are about 11 to 13 years old). Chisnallwood had about 830 students in September 2010, and of those about 350 were learning an instrument out of class, and many were performing in one of the groups (orchestra, jazz band, choir, percussion, chamber etc.). Chisnallwood is one of the larger intermediate schools in New Zealand, and the city of Christchurch is the second largest city in New Zealand, with a population of around 376,000.

We describe how the events unfolded, recount the remarkable reaction from students when they returned to school after the events, and give advice on simple ideas that can be implemented to make the music program resilient in the face of such natural disasters as well as improve efficiency in normal circumstances.

Timeline of events
On Saturday 4 September 2010, a 7.1 magnitude earthquake shook Christchurch with no warning. The shake lasted for about 40 seconds, and resulted in significant damage to the city's infrastructure (particularly power, water, sewerage and roads). Remarkably there was no loss of life despite several buildings collapsing. In the east side of Christchurch the ground was vulnerable to liquefaction, and this resulted in many tons of silt being ejected from the ground, accompanied by widespread flooding. Because of the damage to infrastructure, all schools were closed for a week while checks were made. Because the school year in NZ runs from February to December, the disruption was late in the year. For the music department it led to the cancellation of some concerts, although a major tour went ahead because it was out of town, and in fact provided a break for the students.

Nearly six months later, at 12:51pm on 22 February 2011, there was a magnitude 6.3 aftershock centered closer to the central city. Sadly this caused substantially more damage, and resulted in the loss of 185 lives, the majority in two downtown buildings that collapsed. The impact on the community was much more significant because some students lost a family member, most knew of someone who had died, many houses had been rendered irreparable (about 16% of students' families had to abandon their houses immediately, and more later), and the damage to infrastructure was much more severe.

Because this quake occurred during a school day many students were stranded at school waiting for parents to navigate streets that had been severely damaged. Many parents arrived on foot having abandoned cars and waded through knee-deep flooding and silt, some arriving after midnight after a trek across town.

The February quake occurred just a few weeks after the start of the school year. At this point many students had signed up for music lessons and groups, but were only just beginning. The school was closed for about four weeks, and so a large amount of teaching time was lost. Considerable effort was put into getting the school opened quickly, as students in the area were stuck at home, often in difficult circumstances due to the damage to the area. Not only did damaged grounds need to be repaired and some walls need to be braced, but it was important to make sure that water and sewage were available; this was achieved by placing two large tanks on site – the sewage waste tank was placed right outside the performing arts centre, but it was a small inconvenience to be able to have students back at school.

A consequence of the earthquake was that itinerant music teachers who worked on a per-lesson basis lost a lot of work, and one quit music teaching and went into the now-lucrative building industry! Fortunately nearly all the teachers returned, and the music program began in full force as soon as students were back at school.

After the disruption teachers noted that in general students were better behaved when they returned. Because students in the area had spent weeks without a reliable water supply, and most local shops had been closed, they appeared to have realized that they can't take simple things like a drink of water or flushing toilets for granted, and were appreciative of even basic facilities. Teachers also reported improved academic performance. There are several possible explanations for this: improved behavior enables better learning; students were taking more responsibility for themselves; fewer activities outside of school; and class sizes were slightly smaller due to some people leaving the city.

A further 6.3 magnitude aftershock in June closed schools for a few days. The physical impact was less severe and more localized because most vulnerable buildings had already been cordoned, and the population had a much higher level of preparedness, although the stress on the community from the continued interruptions was severe.

Music as a focal point

The February quake occurred early in the school year. At that point 249 students had enrolled in the out-of-class music lessons, and most had just been issued with instruments and had taken just one or two lessons. After the quake it wasn't clear if all students would consider music a priority since they might wish to focus on core subjects after losing so much of their school time, and finances would be an issue for many families. An online survey was sent to parents asking if their children planned to continue with lessons, to plan staffing. Not all would have had internet access, or even power, although some had internet access through mobile phones. Fifty-nine out of the 249 responded, and of those, 85% said they would like to start lessons "as soon as possible", 13.5% wanted to resume at a later date, and just 1 student indicated that they wouldn't be continuing.

One parent commented in their response to the February survey: "We will be only too pleased for [student] to continue his guitar as we have heard 'smoke on the water' far too many times since the earthquake! :)". Another response endorsed the value of music in the midst of the crisis: "[Student] is really looking forward to returning to school and to her music activities – music is certainly a great healer – we are so pleased that our piano stood up to the horrific shaking".

At the time of the February quake the school roll was 830; when students returned to school it had dropped to 766, and by September had declined to 746, mainly due to families leaving the area. Interestingly the music roll had 65 *more* students at the end of that period – even some families that had to move to a new house out of the area still brought their students to the school to participate in the music program. Rather than being distracted from music by the events around them, it became apparent that students were throwing themselves wholeheartedly into the program, seizing opportunities for rehearsal and performance. Outside of school the community was dealing with stress due to damaged houses and job losses, with concerns about family breakups, increased use of alcohol, and increased domestic violence; in contrast to this students were enjoying pursuing their passion for music which provided security and was personally rewarding.

As an example, the music department's jazz program includes a big band and a jazz combo group, which is unusual for their age group. In August/September 2011 these groups competed in two national jazz competitions, the NZSM competition in Wellington, and the CPIT Jazzquest in Christchurch. In both cases they were the only intermediate school in the competitions, competing against high school big bands with students up to 5 years older. In the Wellington competition they received four prizes, including two top instrumentalist awards, and in the Christchurch competition the Big Band received a silver medal, and the combo received a gold medal (only 4 gold medals were awarded in the competition). These exceptional results were achieved with less time available for preparation, and are a strong reflection of the increased motivation and effort of the students. A consequence of the high standard that the students achieved was that they were given many opportunities to perform in the community, and this in turn is increased their motivation and confidence. Audience sizes for all types of concerts seem to have increased, apparently because they are a welcome break for the community from the pressures of recovering from the earthquakes.

One of the consequences of the earthquakes was that many of the main performance and music venues in town were out of action, and some key venues will take years to be repaired or replaced. Many improvised venues have been found to replace them, including churches, tents, portable buildings and open spaces. Some professional musicians left town during this period because of the lack of venues. The school music block became sought after for after-hours use by music groups who had lost their normal practice/tuition venues, including a pipe band and a ukulele group, and the hall has been heavily used for community meetings. There seemed to be more interest than usual from the community in choirs, which apparently provided an excellent way to nurture people's spirits in a time of great stress. At the school, several students wrote music to express their feelings about the events, which is another healthy outlet.

Many instruments at school and around the city were damaged or became inaccessible due to the earthquakes. Pianos seemed particularly vulnerable – some uprights fell over, sometimes breaking the pedals, or landing on the piano stool and sustaining damage. Some orchestras and music centers lost access to instruments and music that were in storage because the buildings they were in were too dangerous to enter. One student at Chisnallwood had her cello broken, not during a quake, but because several children had to share a room after their house was damaged, and the cello suffered from being in a confined space with her siblings! Fortunately the community rallied around by sharing instruments and fundraising to overcome the loss of resources.

Managing risk

Much of the on-line presence of Chisnallwood school is based on servers that are "in the cloud" e.g. using Wikispaces, Gmail and Google sites. This proved to be a significant advantage after the school was closed; staff weren't allowed on-site for safety reasons, and in some schools where their web pages and email were served from a computer on the school site, their main communication methods were knocked out for some weeks, just at a time when it was most needed (Harré, 2011).

The "cloud" storage for the Chisnallwood music web information is based overseas, so the web presence and communication were able to continue with no significant impact from the disaster. Because updates to the web pages are done via the web, they were able to be edited anywhere that Internet access was available. The east side of the city where the school is had lost power for one to two weeks, but websites could be updated through mobile phones (cellphone towers were running on backup generators), and teachers could drive to the west side of the city and use Internet connections at the homes of friends and family (and since water was off in the east side, it was usually accompanied by a welcome hot shower and a refill of water containers) In addition, social networking sites and text messaging (SMS) were used extensively to maintain communication.

Using online systems for getting feedback from families was valuable. Before September the school would normally send information about performances home with students and parents would sign and return it. In September, a music trip was scheduled to take place a week after the earthquake, so out of necessity a Google doc online form (see docs.google.com) was set up that enabled parents to "return" their form even though the school was closed; this included details for the trip like medical and dietary requirements, as well as giving permission. Because parents provided an email address and phone number, the permission could be verified by calling back, and the details verified by checking the school database (which was also stored in a different city by an online service provider).

The value of this robust form of communication was apparent in feedback from families. One parent wrote:

> *Thank you to all the wonderful staff at Chisnallwood, your support and constant information at an awful time like this is amazing! [Student] can't wait to get back to school and as parents I know that she will be well looked after. Arohanui*

A further advantage of using cloud-based systems for the music department's web presence is that it can be updated anywhere – during the June quake one of the music teachers was at a conference in South Korea and was able to edit online information based on text messages from colleagues at the school, even though they weren't able to get online. During the trip to the Wellington competition a significant snowfall meant that the schedule was being changed almost by the hour; the music teachers were able to update the online schedule even while on the road travelling to the competition using mobile Internet access.

Using online forms proved so effective that they have now been adopted for all enrolments and permission feedback. Not only has it removed dependence on students being able to physically deliver slips, but it has removed the need to enter the data as it comes in, and consequently has given music teachers significantly more time for doing music and less time typing up administrative information.

Various online systems are now readily available; the particular ones in use at the moment are the spreadsheet and associated forms in Google docs (docs.google.com) for collecting information from students and parents, the easily edited wikis from Wikispaces.com for publishing rapidly changing information, and the Gmail mail system (gmail.com) used by the whole school for email.

Information about concerts and events is posted on a public Wikispaces page, and a separate private wiki (called the "backstage" wiki) provides non-public information for students, such as rehearsal schedules and recordings of the music that is being rehearsed.

Conclusion

After a natural disaster, the top priorities are obviously the necessities of life such as food and water, but once they are addressed, music can play a valuable role in the lives of students. In fact, the temptation to give it a lower priority should be resisted, as maintaining a core program can provide valuable routines and opportunities for expression when students have had their world turned upside down. Our experience has shown that not only do students and parents appreciate those opportunities, but they can embrace them and perform even better than might be expected under normal circumstances.

References

Harré, D. (2011). How the cloud is proving its worth in Christchurch. *New Zealand Interface, 32*. Retrieved from http://bit.ly/N9rYD1

Assessing Undergraduate Jazz and Rock Group Music-making: Adding to the Classic(al) Recipe

Diana Blom
University of Western Sydney (Australia)
d.blom@uws.edu.au

John Encarnacao
University of Western Sydney (Australia)

Abstract

As the teaching of a broad range of musics has entered the academy over recent decades, default settings inherited from classical music are increasingly questioned. In particular, approaches to music performance – in a classical context focused on the individual, on technical facility, and on performance outcome – are often inappropriate for the assessment of popular music styles. Undergraduate music performance teaching at the University of Western Sydney has long included a consideration of the quality of collaboration, not only in the performance event, but the rehearsal process. An experiment with students choosing parameters for self and peer assessment of group music-making has underlined the importance of 'non-musical' (personal, interpersonal, and organizational) skills. Rather than suggest that modes of assessment inherited from classical models have no place in the assessment of rock and jazz groups, this paper argues that a synthesis of traditional (technique and expression oriented) and new approaches will best prepare young musicians for "real world" contexts, while also reflecting the process musicians partake in to bring any collaborative project to fruition.

Keywords
Group assessment, jazz, rock, undergraduate music education, rehearsal, performance

This paper introduces skills relevant to the assessment of classical, jazz, rock and world music groups. The "classic(al) recipe" of the paper's title refers to a comprehensive literature review undertaken to determine what is important when assessing group performance (Blom & Encarnacao, 2012). The literature is largely concerned with the performance of classical music. These skills are joined by others drawn from recent literature about jazz, rock and world music group assessment, and further augmented by skills identified by undergraduate students playing in jazz and rock groups at the University of Western Sydney over one semester. This list of potential assessment criteria prompts two research questions: What skills/criteria are considered relevant, by staff and students, to undergraduate group music assessment? and How can these areas be assessed? This discussion builds on findings from previous papers by the authors about assessing popular music groups.

Literature review

The literature suggests that the assessment of classical performance has concentrated largely on musical skills rather than non-musical skills (McPherson & Thompson, 1998). Birkett's skills taxonomy[1] (in Coll & Zegwaard, 2006) identifies within 'hard' or musical skills, technical, analytical and appreciative skills, which can serve to group the musical issues. Technical skills include playing technique, accuracy of playing notation, intonation, playing in time, articulation, phrasing, dynamic and timbral variation, tone quality, projection, balance/blend, expressive qualities, and emotional impact. Analytical skills include awareness of style/performance practice, interpretative qualities and having an understanding of the work. Appreciative skills include repertoire choice and cohesion of ensemble playing (Blom & Encarnacao, 2012). All are relevant to popular music group performance with accuracy of playing notation less relevant to playing in a rock group and some jazz group playing.

Skills associated with on-stage performing often combine musical and non-musical skill-sets (Blom & Encarnacao, 2012). These include confidence/stage presence, musical communication to the audience, musical communication within the group (aural, visual, and movement) for musical coherence and social unity. In rehearsal, warming up together, approaches to individual pieces, balancing rehearsal focus, integrating run-throughs, working sequentially and non-sequentially, and personal practice (and its effect in rehearsal), also combined musical and non-musical skill-sets.

More recent literature on issues in student rock and jazz performance highlight a range of non-musical skills particular to general group interaction, skills also raised, but to a lesser extent, in relation to classical ensembles. For Young and Colman (1979), the classical string quartet is "a special kind of small group which...might reasonably be assumed to manifest some of the established social psychological processes of small groups in a particularly striking way" (p. 17). Blom and Encarnacao (2012) group these non-musical skills under the headings personal, interpersonal and organizational, terms again borrowed from Birkett's taxonomy. Personal skills include punctuality, attendance, remembering equipment, sense of involvement and sense of individual personality. Interpersonal skills include sharing of decision-making, social factors, cooperative skills, equal involvement, negotiation of shared musical goals, trust and respect, confrontation and compromise, and each individual feeling he/she is contributing artistically. And organizational skills include allocating time for practicing and rehearsing, regulating the ensemble, operational principles of the ensemble, and leadership/roles. Investigating the rehearsal process of undergraduate rock students, Pulman (2009) places emphasis on the interpersonal relationships between people in a group, rather than their technical and/or musical skills: "(b) rehearsing... is a highly collaborative activity... [where] individuals' contributions themselves will, in part, be communicated through the interpersonal skills and attributes of each participant" (p. 121). He notes that non-musical skills were often those identified when students chose the assessment criteria.

Assessing jazz group performance raises the issue of whether individual assessments, an approach inherited from assessing Western classical music, provides a fair and effective

---

[1] Birkett's skills taxonomy was designed for professional accounting standards; Coll and Zegwaard (2006) introduce the terms "hard" and "soft" skills when applying Birkett's thinking to competency standards of science and technology graduates; and the idea of "hard" and "soft" skills is applied to group music assessment (Blom & Encarnacao, 2012).

measure of a jazz musician's achievement (Barratt & Moore, 2005). This approach saw students losing "the natural group interactions, the improvisatory flair, and the democratic contrapuntalism necessary for most fine jazz performance" (p. 303). New criteria determined between staff and students sought to encourage group interaction, including "risk taking", "level of communication," and "interaction," (Barratt & Moore, p. 307) all associated with group playing. For Kerr and Knight (2010), assessing student jazz performers in "public performance activities" (p. 302) within a resort environment was an important transfer of skills into the "real world" outside of the academy. This resulted in engagement with the performance skills of reading an audience, encouraging an awareness of the performers' own body language and physical gestures balance within a group, the overall volume of the group in relation to the variety of environments experienced as performers, and consideration of appropriate repertoire for various contexts. Interactive skills such as "the musical expression of 'fellow feeling,' respect for each band member's musical 'space,' and the ability to respond spontaneously and sensitively to other musicians' ideas" (Beale, 2001, as cited in Barratt & Moore 2005, p. 305) are all required in jazz group performance. Undergraduate jazz performers were found to have six modes of communication within two main categories, verbal and non-verbal, each containing three distinct modes: instruction, cooperation and collaboration (Seddon, 2005, pp. 52-53). In verbal instruction, "musicians are told what and when to play in pre-composed sections (the heads)" (p. 53) while in non-verbal instruction, "musicians learn pre-composed part(s) by ear or read from music notation" (p. 53). Through verbal cooperation, "musicians discuss and plan the organization of the piece prior to performance in order to achieve a cohesive performance" (p. 53) and through non-verbal cooperation, "musicians achieve sympathetic attunement and exchange stocks of musical knowledge, producing cohesive performance employing: body language, facial expression, eye contact, musical cues and gesticulation" (p. 53). In verbal collaboration, "musicians discuss and evaluate their performance of the music in order to develop the content and/or style of the piece" and through non-verbal collaboration, "musicians achieve empathetic attunement, tak[ing] creative risks which can result in spontaneous musical utterances. When they do, this signals empathetic creativity" (Seddon, p. 53).

To familiar musical technical skills, Boyce-Tillman (2003) adds the criteria of presentation of the musical event including "visual elements (dress, stage demeanor), stage management, communication with the audience, announcing the program, acknowledging applause, eye contact, confidence and ability to generate audience response" (p. 46) when assessing World Music performance. This plethora of group music-making skills/criteria provides a basis to compare with the responses of tertiary rock and jazz group student performers and staff.

Methodology

The paper discusses the responses of thirteen participants playing in three jazz groups, and fifteen participants playing in four rock groups, all part of a second-year undergraduate cohort in the music program at the University of Western Sydney. Students were asked to choose three criteria for self and peer assessment of their group's rehearsal process and three criteria for the assessment of their performance outcome by peers in another group. The staff selected two criteria for the rehearsal and two for the performance assessment, and these were also to be used by the students. Students were asked to explain the meaning of all criteria, including those given by staff. The criteria and student explanations were coded in relation to whether they were musical or non-musical skills, part of the rehearsal process or for the performance outcome. Musical skills were further subdivided into Birkett's categories of technical, analytical and appreciative, and non-musical skills were further subdivided into personal, interpersonal and organizational, as outlined above (as in Coll & Zegwaard, 2006). Because of the similarities between many of the criteria and explanations, responses were compared "over and over again with codings and classification that have already been made'" (Flick, 2002, p. 231) to determine to which category they belonged so that existing and new issues could be identified. Written consent was sought from all participants whose responses form part of this paper.

The task was designed as an exercise in understanding group music-making and assessment, and was assessed as a written component but not included in the marking of the rehearsal process or performance outcomes of the unit. Lectures on peer assessment, stagecraft, group dynamics and concert production were given to introduce students to a range of terms and group music-making issues. Students learnt the songs through visual and aural means. Rock and jazz students were given lead sheets (melody and chords) to work with, plus lyric sheets where appropriate. Recordings of the songs were available on the university teaching web site for listening.

Findings

The jazz students' contributions to the existing list of skills/criteria outlined above were threefold: confirmation of many of the issues raised by previous researchers; specific details of existing issues from students experiencing and seeing things from a new angle; and new skills/criteria. Both musical and non-musical previously identified skills were considered important. Musical technical issues such as playing technique, intonation, playing in time, and expressive qualities were raised, as were appreciative skills of cohesion of ensemble playing, on-stage performing skills of musical communication to the audience, musical communication within the group, especially non-verbal cooperation, the rehearsal issues of practice, punctuality, attendance, and remembering equipment. Non-musical interpersonal issues included sharing of decision-making, an individual's interpersonal skills, trust and respect, confidence, and each individual feeling they are contributing artistically; and the organizational skills of making time for practicing and rehearsing, as well as general organization. Improvisatory flair, risk taking and interaction, plus awareness of the performer's own body language, balance within a group and the interactive skills of respect for each band member's musical space were raised. From the six modes of communication, verbal instruction and non-verbal cooperation were identified.

Because students were playing in groups intensively for one semester, rather than over a three-year program, their insights offer new angles on, and detail about, previously identified issues. *Creativity* is a broader view of improvisatory flair. *Begin and end together* is a detail of cohesion of ensemble playing, and appearing as if they are engaged is an issue requires, which one student stated "applying themselves in a positive manner (not acting like a jerk)" and having an "attitude which is involved in the spirit of the music." These are likely to arise when students are placed in groups, as they were in this context, rather than choosing their fellow performers for group music-making. From this preliminary jazz group music-making also comes "helping each other set up," a new view of equal involvement, and "being prepared to attend extra rehearsals," part of the organizational skill of time for practicing and rehearsing yet with a personal willingness aspect drawn in.

New skills identified by the students specifically were "fluidity of arrangement" which goes beyond the analytical skill of awareness of style to include a flexible yet unified quality to the arrangement. Part of this is "engagement within others' solos", a detail of interaction and part of Barratt and Moore's (2005) "democratic contrapuntalism of jazz" but which focuses attention on the role of those not soloing at a given time. Student reference to "Overall quality of sound" includes balance, intonation and timbre yet embraces a holistic quality of all of these and "energy produced and conveyed in performance" and "attitude and positivity" goes beyond encouraging an awareness of the performers' own body language to the effect on the group as a whole.

Because of the short-term group music-making, the rock students' contributions reflected many of those of the jazz students in relation to musical technical issues, on-stage performing and non-musical interpersonal skills. The rehearsal environment introduced some new views of existing skills. One student indicated "attitude to the rehearsal" gives an inside detail of the rehearsal process within sense of involvement, as does "attitude to the musical contributions of others", a detail of trust and respect. Finally, participant suggested having "ideas ready" is an important preliminary stage when developing the improvisatory flair in jazz and rock music.

Conclusions

The list of skills considered relevant by students and staff for consideration as assessment criteria for group music-making is long and wide and, it could be argued, all are important. All group playing requires technical mastery, analytical and appreciative skills in rehearsal and on-stage, an understanding of stage presence, and all require reliable personal, interpersonal and organizational skills. However, each musical style has particular skill requirements and these become the starting focus for selecting criteria. Ensemble performance of classical music needs accurate and expressive notation reading and interpretation. Jazz improvisation requires each group member to develop technical and creative skills as individuals and as a group. Rock performance requires a different kind of improvisation to jazz and a keen understanding of on-stage performance persona. Yet contemporary classical chamber music may require improvisation skills, many styles of jazz and rock music require keen notation reading skills and all require consideration of on-stage dress and presentation.

Other factors to be considered are the level at which the student group performers are playing, and whether the students are studying one musical style over a three or four year intensive period, or over one semester. Also, whether or not the students have selected their fellow performers (each scenario offering "real world" modelling in its own way) will result in different group performance processes and outcomes and insights into the rehearsal room itself. While the finely focused issues raised by the students of this study only make the potential criteria list longer, they do offer a window into both staff and student understanding of the processes of group interaction and group music-making. Many of these, in turn, suggest an addition to Seddon's (2005) six modes of communication, of a preliminary mode in which attitude and preparation are basic but key factors.

While all areas discussed in the paper cannot be assessed, a combination of musical and non-musical issues can be drawn into the evaluation of performance in the performance program by adopting more than one approach within a semester, engaging both staff and students. Boyce-Tillman (2003) used a "performing diary" (p. 47) for world music students to document and evaluate their practice, instrumental lessons and performing experiences. In the project of this paper, the second year group performance students selected relevant issues as criteria for self- and peer-assessment of their rehearsal process and performance outcome. As has been seen, students engaged with issues well beyond the most frequently chosen musical technical issues of classical solo performance. Within a study examining students' ability to self-evaluate their recorded performances, Bergee and Cecconi-Roberts (2002) established small groups of peers who informally discussed performances and shared feedback with one another. While there was no strong effect on the students' ability to self-evaluate, the model of recording and/or videoing student performance with peer group discussion offers another way to include a wide range of assessment issues. As was noted earlier, different stages of a student's group music-making experience and expertise require consideration of different assessment criteria and different approaches to the discussion of assessment issues. Another approach is to give each semester a different focus: for example, group dynamics and interpersonal skills, rehearsal process and expectations, or Kerr and Knight's (2010) practice of a final performance outside the university environment in the "real world". Any of these approaches moves assessment beyond the *classic recipe* and has the potential to enable the assessment of music performance of any musical style to more closely reflect the experiences of musicians working in group, and in conditions beyond the university environment.

References

Barrett, E., & Moore, H. (2005). Research group assessment: Jazz in the conservatoire. *British Journal of Music Education, 22*(3), 299-314.

Bergee, M. J., & Cecconi-Roberts, L. (2002). Effects of small-group peer interaction on self- evaluation of music performance. *Journal of Research in Music Education, 50,* 256-268.

Blom, D., & Encarnacao, E. (2012). Student-chosen criteria for peer assessment of tertiary rock groups in rehearsal and performance: What's important?. *British Journal of Music Education, 29*(1), 25-43.

Boyce-Tillman, J. (2003). Assessing diversity. *Arts and Humanities in Higher Education 2*(1), 41-62.

Coll, R. K., & Zegwaard, K. E. (2006). Perceptions of desirable graduate competencies for science and technology new graduates. *Research in Science & Technological Education, 24*(1), 29-58.

Flick, U. (2002). *An introduction to qualitative research* (2nd ed.). London, UK: Sage.

Kerr, D., & Knight, B. A. (2010). Exploring an industry-based jazz education performance training programme. *International Journal of Music Education, 28*(4), 301-312.

McPherson, G. E., & Thompson, W. F. (1998). Assessing music performance: Issues and influences. *Research Studies in Music Education, 10*(1), 12-24.

Pulman, M. (2009). Seeing yourself as others see you: Developing personal attributes in the group rehearsal. *British Journal of Musical Education, 26*(2), 117-135.

Seddon, F. A. (2005). Modes of communication during jazz improvisation. *British Journal of Music Education, 22*(1), 47-61.

Young, V. M., & Colman, A. M. (1979). Some psychological processes in string quartets. *Psychology of Music, 7*(1), 12-18.

Unleashing the Imagination: Creating Collectively Conceived Music through Improvisation

Anthony Branker
Princeton University (USA)

branker@princeton.edu

Abstract

The purpose of this study was to examine the effectiveness of utilizing collaborative-based improvisational activities that make use of freer approaches to music-making as a pedagogical strategy to stimulate group interaction and improvisational music-making. Fourteen students from a college jazz program were divided into two small groups that worked together over a 10-week period. In addition to preparing for several public performances, they also engaged in a variety of collaborative music-making activities that included creating collectively conceived improvised and composed music. Resulting data were collected from observing and recording group rehearsal sessions and discussions, student responses to questions following each weekly session, student observations of recorded rehearsals and/or performances, field notes and informal jottings, and responses to post-study questions. When describing their perceptions of the impact of freer approaches to music-making on their development students recognized that: an openness to and gaining familiarity with these types of approaches to improvising and composing can "allow for ultimate freedom" when music-making; utilizing these kinds of approaches can expand upon one's musical palette and introduce new vocabulary; the use these concepts can increase one's awareness of musical relationships and the kind of conversational interplay that occurs within an improvising ensemble; and, this experience has enabled them to grow as listeners. Conversely, some students noted they: became more appreciative of structured music, which serves to provide direction; actually felt more constrained when playing freely improvised music; and, came to the realization that "striking out completely on [one's] own" in this way was not something they were entirely ready to do. When students make use of collaborative-based improvisational activities to create collectively conceived improvised and composed music, such a method can: promote cooperation, collaboration, and shared ownership; encourage a heightened sense of communicative interaction through dialogue within a group; facilitate the development of imaginative capacities as well as problem-solving and problem-finding skills; encourage risk-taking and the establishment of an environment of trust; and spotlight the importance of openness, unselfishness, and compromise. Findings from this study suggest that utilizing collaborative group activities that incorporate freer approaches to improvisation and composition as the conceptual basis for making music in the classroom not only has the potential to *stretch* students and their imaginations – thereby expanding upon the types of ideas they might normally come to create – but can also offer them the opportunity to re-imagine what it means to engage in creative music-making.

Keywords
Collaboration, self-directed learning, communication, freer approaches to music-making, improvisation, group process

Introduction
Music educators have long been charged with the mission of directing students through specific curricular structures in an attempt to develop predetermined proficiencies and fulfil educational objectives. Yet, many questions remain. Are the skills and proficiencies being acquired making an impactful contribution to the development of musical understanding and imaginative capacities of students? Are students receiving the kinds of classroom experiences that place considerable value on such notions as exploration, discovery, mutual exchange, and creative self-expression? What role can improvisation and collaborative music-making experiences play in all of this?

Improvisation and Music Education
When discussing the study of improvisation in jazz education, Sarath (2006) observed, "While jazz programs generally offer substantive training in improvisation, it is usually confined to mainstream jazz approaches and neglects important aspects of the jazz lineage, in addition to more varied approaches of the musical world" (p. 3). It is his belief that "the integrative and creative features of improvisation – its capacity to unite a wide array of musical skills, aptitudes and stylistic influences – points to its rightful place as a core aspect of musical understanding for all music students" (p. 3).

For Pogonowski (in press), "The purpose of music education is to use musical intuitions based on the musical knowledge and skills [students] are acquiring, at any stage of musical development, for communicating musical thoughts" (p. 17). When communicating these thoughts, intuition will inevitably seek to intermingle with the imagination in an effort to shape and guide the creative experience. This, in turn, can serve to inspire those working together by providing new points of departure for their explorations, ultimately enabling them to "move beyond the known" or that which they believed possible.

With the significance of these points well-noted, one could posit that music educators could provide students with a different kind of classroom experience if the study of the practice of improvisation were re-envisioned to be viewed, as Hickey (2009) states, "not as a product to be taught in a strict methodological or pedagogical manner, but as a process to be encouraged on the way to learning freedom and self-actualization" (p. 296). What can music educators do to place a greater emphasis on the *process* of improvisational music-making? How can they better cultivate the imaginations of their students and foster a disposition towards exploration?

Dialectics of Improvisation
While improvising, musicians are called upon to make music in-the-moment while also being confronted with the dialectical realities of the process, which involves "[creating] within a musical and social context, requiring both control and spontaneity, constraints and possibilities, innovation and tradition, leading and supporting" (Montouori, 2003, p. 239), all underpinning the larger dialectic of structure vs. freedom. Sawyer (2003) also noted, "In improvisational encounters, participants must balance the need to creatively

contribute with the need to maintain coherence with the current state of the emergent frame" (p. 4). In the dialogic sphere of *self* and *other* (Bakhtin, 1984; Holquist, 1981), we also find that the improvising musician is involved in an *intertextual* relationship with the tradition (Kristeva, 1980) as one converses or interacts with the past and all of the principles of language and vocabulary that enable them to express themselves in-the-moment.

While the concept of freedom is commonly associated with the metaphor of jazz, the improvising musician can still experience a sense of confinement or the need to conform to regulation. As Pressing (2002) explains, there will always be "a tension between the freedom of expression of the individual and the need to form coherent relations with other performers in the group" (p. 1). And, while there are often many choices, "Musicians" as Johnson-Laird (2002) observed, "do not have total freedom – at least in orthodox modern jazz. There are harmonic and rhythmic constraints on improvisations. Much of the hard work in learning to improvise consists of acquiring a tacit mastery of these constraints" (p. 420).

Free Improvisation

As Hickey (2009) noted, "Free improvisation is a form of improvisation that is ultimately the most open, non-rules bound, most learner directed" (p. 294). It can be said that the use of freer approaches to music-making, which focus on the aural and depart from the use of traditional notation, promote an *immediate* rather than *mediated* relationship with the music, thereby placing greater emphasis on feel, listening, and responsivity within the performance environment. In free improvisation, according to Bailey (1992), "Diversity is its most consistent characteristic. It has no stylistic or idiomatic commitment. It has no prescribed idiomatic sound. The characteristics of freely improvised music are established only by the sonic-musical identity of the person or persons playing it" (p. 83). As a result, this type of improvisational approach affords the performer the opportunity to redefine the soundscape while reimagining the ways in which melody, harmony, rhythm, texture, timbre, form can be attended to; all in an effort to provide the improviser with greater freedom of creative self-expression within a fluid and evolving framework. In this way, free improvisation addresses the structure vs. freedom dialectic that is often found in jazz improvisation. Here, the improvising musician has the chance to improvise freely and interact with a structure that is developing as it emerges.

Description of the Study

The focus of this study was to: 1. Gain a better understanding of what takes place when college jazz students come together to work in a self-directed manner in the jazz small group; and 2. Examine the potential effectiveness of utilizing collaborative-based improvisational activities that make use of freer approaches to music-making as a pedagogical strategy to stimulate group interaction and improvisational music-making.

Fourteen students from a college jazz program were divided into two small groups that worked together over a 10-week period. During this time, participants prepared for several public performances and engaged in a variety of collaborative music-making activities that included creating collectively conceived improvised and composed music. For the classroom activity involving the creation of group improvisations, students were given the freedom to establish their own way of communicating musical ideas and could develop their own approach to organizing a collectively improvised performance. The second collaborative activity under investigation involved developing collectively conceived group compositions inspired by extra-musical themes or sources (i.e. poetry, visual arts, movement, etc.). While no restrictions were placed on how to organize such a composition, it was shared that traditional music notation could not be utilized as a "mediated tool" (Vygotsky, 1978).

Resulting data were collected from observing and recording group rehearsal sessions and discussions, student responses to questions following each weekly session, student observations of recorded rehearsals and/or performances, field notes and informal jottings, and responses to post-study questions.

Findings
How do students describe their experience of creating collectively conceived group improvisations and group compositions?

Creating Group Improvisations
After their first attempt at creating freely improvised music as a group during week six, students in Group A shared a number of thoughts, including those related to the problematic nature of improvising in this way. Several alluded to certain preconceived notions that some students held based on their "philosophies, viewpoints, and musical predispositions" that kept them from being open to this experience and taking the exercise seriously. Others cited such problems as: skepticism, finding common ground, a reluctance to embrace the experience due to a "fear of freedom thrust upon them," as well as competing ideas within the group and a strong commitment to those ideas. As Michael observed:

It felt, at times, like members of the group had the preconception before we started playing that it wouldn't be impossible to make good music by free improvisation. With this attitude, it is impossible to have the trust, the confidence that you and your fellow musicians can make good music in any setting simply because you are perceptive and creative musicians…Discounting this possibility from the start presents a real hindrance to the collective creative process.

Students also shared a number of viewpoints on what they noticed about the music they created that week. It was observed that although the group "never really got on the same page" musically, there were some interesting moments that were experienced. As Jason recalls, "It was very creative in the sense that we were all trying things that we would not think to try in a conventional jazz setting." It was Leonard's belief that:

It had it's [sic] moments, I think. I don't really know. It could have been genius for all I know. I think free jazz is a pretty subjective business in general. Some things that we tried to do, like interact with each other, respond musically to other people's ideas definitely had good points, we made it happen a couple times, I think.

Creating Group Compositions
When asked what they noticed about the music that was created during their group composition activity in week nine, students in Group B shared a number of observations. For Jackson, the music created was not as crucial as the creative process. According to Eleanor, their collective creations "reverted back" to the more experimental group vibe they had adopted earlier in the study and in the semester prior:

This isn't necessarily good or bad, but I do think that it is interesting that that is what we defer to when presented with the challenge of creating our own group compositions. I think that it is largely because sound portraits are open enough so that they allow everyone to make a contribution to the overall sound of the piece.

Derek viewed this as an enjoyable experience and noted:

I laughed harder than I have in a long time. We were able to compose freely, relax, and laugh with each other. It was productive, we listened to each other, and I see nothing in the way of efficiency of the rehearsal or productivity, that needs to be improved upon.

For Derek, this sense of enjoyment, derived from the types of activities that utilized imaginative play, was central to the overall experience of creating in this setting, and was viewed as a positive feature.

For the 10th and final meeting for Group A, students were given an assignment to create a group composition in three movements that would be inspired by extra-musical sources. Understandably, students felt that the most difficult part of this activity was deciding how to start. As Leonard stated:

That's not something I think any of us have done before, and so we spent a lot of time discussing abstract principles to guide our choice, like should it be a texture, an object, should we be directly inspired in our sound by it or be more influenced in an impressionistic way? See I have no idea what I just said in terms of music, but we had that discussion nevertheless!

As far as identifying the successful parts of the activity or things that worked particularly well, students cited "the performance or music itself." Several were in agreement that using ideas generated from their initial free improvisation was a good idea and aided in the creation of the piece as well as a "good vibe" within the group; with the process viewed as being "democratic and engaging."

While George acknowledges that it was more difficult to compose as a group, he does share an interesting insight on the value of the group approach:

I would say that one advantage that a group composition has over an individual composition is that the final product already reflects many of the dynamics that would eventually go into a collaborative performance of an individual composition. In other words, musical clashes and concord that would first occur during a performance or rehearsal of an individual composition are simply one part of the process of a group composition: the music itself already contains the personality of the group. In theory, this could help unify the band in performance.

Developing as a Musician and Learner
How did students view their own evolution as musician and learner as a result of embracing the use of freer approaches to improvisation and composition?

When describing their perceptions of the impact of freer approaches to music-making on their development, students shared a number of realizations. These included the recognition that: an openness to and gaining familiarity with these types of approaches to improvising and composing can "allow for ultimate freedom" when music-making; utilizing these kinds of approaches can expand upon one's musical palette and introduce new vocabulary; the use these concepts can increase one's awareness of musical relationships and the kind of conversational interplay that occurs within an improvising ensemble; and, this experience has enabled them to grow as listeners. Conversely, some students noted they: became more appreciative of structured music, which serves to provide direction; actually felt more constrained when playing freely improvised music; and, came to the realization that "striking out completely on [one's] own" in this way was not something they were entirely ready to do.

A number of students from both groups shared that they were able to *feel creative* in this setting and cited a certain level of comfort that was experienced when interacting with other members, which facilitated this sensation. As one students noted, "The comfort that I had to risk and put myself out there without being judged liberated me, and it was that atmosphere that lent itself to experimentation and helped me *feel* creative." Others felt particularly creative when working on the conceptual compositions where individuals had the chance "to express themselves in unique ways within the group" and shared that having the chance to play in this kind of setting has "inspired [one] to compose and explore the limits of improvisational music."

There were also those who were not overly enthusiastic about what they experienced in this setting from a creative standpoint, noting: "At times, the frustration stemming from contrasting personalities, musical outlooks and communicative abilities led to a stifled creative impulse." One group member stated, "I felt creative at times, but for the most part, no…much of the time I felt blocked," while another admitted, "I did not feel that anything that we produced was particularly creative or inspired." Yet, it was also observed that while it "wasn't easy" at times, there were also those moments when they "overcame [themselves] and produced good creative music."

Conclusions and Implications

When students make use of collaborative-based improvisational activities to create collectively conceived improvised and composed music – such as those utilized in this study – such a method can: promote cooperation, collaboration, and shared ownership; encourage a heightened sense of communicative interaction through dialogue within a group; facilitate the development of imaginative capacities as well as problem-solving and problem-finding skills; encourage risk-taking and the establishment of an environment of trust; and spotlight the importance of openness, unselfishness, and compromise.

Utilizing collaborative group activities that incorporate freer approaches to improvisation and composition as the conceptual basis for making music in the classroom not only has the potential to *stretch* students and their imaginations – thereby expanding upon the types of ideas they might normally come to create – but can also offer them the opportunity to re-imagine what it means to engage in creative music-making.

References

Bakhtin, M. (1984). *Problems of Dostoevsky's poetics* (Ed. and translated by Emerson, C.). Minneapolis: University of Minnesota Press.

Bailey, D. (1992). *Improvisation: Its nature and practice in music*. New York, NY: Da Capo Press.

Holquist, M. (Ed.). (1981). *The dialogic imagination: Four essays by M.M. Bakhtin* (C. Emerson & M. Holquist, Trans.). Austin, TX: University of Texas Press.

Hickey, M. (2009). Can improvisation be 'taught'?: A call for free improvisation in our schools. *International Journal of Music Education, 24,* 285–299.

Johnson-Laird, P.N. (2002). How jazz musicians improvise. *Music Perception,* 19, 415–442.

Kristeva, J. (1980). *Desire in language: A semiotic approach to literature and art.* New York, NY: Columbia University Press.

Montuori, A. (2003). The complexity of improvisation and the improvisation of complexity: Social science, art and creativity. *Human Relations,* 56, 237- 255.

Pogonowski, L. (in press). *Movement III: Dialogue, collective musical cognition and reflection in group learning.*

Pressing, J. (2002. Free jazz and the avante-garde. In D. Horn & M. Cook (Eds.), *Cambridge companion to jazz.* Cambridge, UK: Cambridge University Press. Retrieved from http://www.psych.unimelb.edu.au/staff/jp/free-jazz.pdf

Sarath, E. (2006). Reclaiming the core of musical creativity: Philosophical perspective. *International society for improvised music.* Retrieved from http://www.isimprov.org/writings/Sarath-philo.html

Sawyer, R. K. (2003). *Improvised dialogues: Emergence and creativity in conversation.* Westport, CT: Ablex Publishing.

Vygotsky, L. S. (1978). *Mind in society: The development of higher psychological processes.* Cambridge, MA: Harvard University Press.

Finding Flow in Collaborative Music Performance: Essential Music Reading Skills for a Piano Accompanist

Judith Elizabeth Brown
Central Queensland Conservatorium of Music
Faculty of Arts, Business, Informatics and Education
j.e.brown@cqu.edu.au

Abstract

Piano accompaniment as a form of collaborative music performance is an activity undertaken in many settings, with participants bringing many levels of expertise to the activity. As a piano accompanist I have always been interested in exploring the characteristics of my collaborative performance experience that are particularly enjoyable and satisfying. This paper discusses some of the results of an autoethnographic study into the phenomenon of flow during collaborative music performance as a piano accompanist. Flow was first described by the American psychologist Csikszentmihalyi in the 1970s and is used to describe those best moments in our lives when everything seems to come together seamlessly. His research found that people could experience flow if the challenges they faced could be met with the right level of skill. The results of the autoethnographic study found that for a piano accompanist there were a number of specific challenges and skills that needed to be in balance so that flow could be experienced. This paper will discuss one of the concepts in the challenge-skills balance: the music reading skills that are of particular importance to meeting the challenges for a piano accompanist, and how the maintenance of the challenge-skills balance in this area can facilitate flow in collaborative music performance.

Keywords
Flow, autoethnography, collaborative music performance, piano accompaniment, music reading

Introduction

The American psychologist Mihalyi Csikszentmihalyi (1975) first defined the construct of flow after examining a group of artists who became so absorbed in their creation of a painting that they "persisted single-mindedly, disregarding hunger, fatigue and discomfort" (Nakamura & Csikszentmihalyi, 2002, p. 89). These artists were so focused on their work and found it so enjoyable that they described it as an "optimal experience". Furthermore, they continued to seek out further opportunities to engage in the activity, just for the sheer sake of doing it. Of interest to Csikszentmihalyi was the fact that these 'optimal experiences' did not occur during obvious pleasure-seeking activities but occurred when "a person's body or mind is stretched to its limits in a voluntary effort to accomplish something difficult and worthwhile" (Csikszentmihalyi, 2002, p. 70). A number of research studies have shown that music performance presents many opportunities for participants to experience the phenomenon of flow due to the specific skills that musicians need to meet the challenges inherent in many music activities (e.g. Bakker, 2005; Matthews, 2003; Sinnamon & Moran, 2006). In my autoethnographic study I created a narrative account of my most memorable experiences as a piano accompanist, and used an iterative analysis (Chang, 2008) to gain some understanding of the phenomenon of flow in collaborative music performance.

One of the key themes to emerge from this analysis of the autoethnographic narrative was the balance between the challenges I faced in my development as a piano accompanist and the skills that I needed to acquire to meet these challenges. Csikszentmihalyi's model for flow places a great importance on the balance between challenge and skill. This has been supported in various research studies in other areas of music study (Bakker, 2005; Bernard, 2009; Custodero, 2002, 2005; Jaros, 2008; Kraus, 2003; MacDonald, Byrne, & Carlton, 2006; Matthews, 2003; Preston, 2009; St. John, 2006; Steckel, 2006).

The method used for this study

As I began to explore the phenomenon of flow in my own experience as a piano accompanist, I came to realise that autoethnography offered a rich methodology that could allow me to dig below the surface of my own experience and help me to understand the phenomenon of flow in collaborative music performance. Autoethnography offers "a way of giving voice to personal experience to advance sociological understanding" (Wall, 2008, p. 39) and was an intriguing methodology to use to in my study. Bartleet and Ellis (2009) assert that autoethnography is especially useful for musicians as it can expand musician's awareness of their practice, values and beliefs. My research into the flow phenomenon in collaborative music performance resonates with this philosophical approach of autoethnography.

An autoethnography is by definition a case study of the self (Ellis, 2004). Consistent with a case study approach (Flyvbjerg, 2011), autoethnography "concentrates on experiential knowledge of the case" (Stake, 2005, p. 444). The type of experiential knowledge expounded in my study of the phenomenon of flow in music performance is subjective, and Stake acknowledges that this is common in case study research. "Case researchers greatly rely on subjective data, such as the testimony of participants and the judgement of witnesses. Many critical observations and interview data are subjective" (Stake, 2005, p. 454). With the rise of postmodern philosophy, there has been a gradual acceptance by qualitative researchers and those who review their work, that there are many ways of knowing and "no one way should be privileged" (Wall, 2006, p. 2). Autoethnography removes the risks inherent in the representation of others, and allows for the production of new knowledge by a unique and uniquely situated researcher, thus offering small-scale knowledge that can inform specific problems and specific situations (Denzin & Lincoln, 2003; Wall, 2006).

Collecting, disseminating and analysing the autoethnographic data

Just as many autoethnographers rely on the creation of an autobiographical narrative to represent their data (Bartleet, 2009; de Vries, 2006), my own research data on the phenomenon of flow in collaborative music performance was presented as a chronologically ordered series of autobiographical vignettes (Humphreys, 2005). The narrative makes use of creative writing devices such as direct speech and scenic description helping to create an evocative text "that is a powerful means of conveying complexity and ambiguity without rendering closure" (Sparkes, 2002, p. 11).

The analysis of this data took an iterative approach as suggested by Chang (2008). By reading and re-reading the data, Chang's approach has enabled me to compare and contrast my experiences of flow with other relevant literature in the field and gain a deeper understanding of the phenomenon. The subsequent analysis of the data enabled me to develop a theory to understand my experience of flow as a piano accompanist. Gregor (2002) described this as theory that "explains 'how' and 'why' something occurred" (p. 7). As with case study research, the theory that results from the analysis of this type of data can be used to inform practice (Bartleet & Ellis, 2009; Duncan, 2004) or provide new and interesting insights into a particular problem or phenomena (Matthews, 2003; Schindler, 2009; Wall, 2006, 2008). To assist the reader, in the following sections, where I discuss aspects of my autoethnographic analysis, excerpts from my narrative are shown in italics while quotes from other published sources are shown using a regular font.

The challenge-skills balance for a piano accompanist
One of the main pre-conditions for flow, according to Csikszentmihalyi (1996) is that "our abilities are well matched to the opportunities for action" (p. 111). He describes "challenges" as the circumstances one might face and "skills" as the ability to meet the demands of those challenges. He goes on to assert that the level of challenge and skill has to be finely balanced in order to achieve enjoyment and "optimal experience." Jackson and Csikszentmihalyi (1999) clarify this by stating that "to experience flow, it is not enough for challenges to equal skills; both factors need to be extending the person, stretching them to new levels" (p. 16). One of Csikszentmihalyi's (2002) earliest models of the phenomenon of flow identified that flow could occur even if the challenges and skills were quite modest and low-level, but the experience needed to be extending the person in both areas of challenges and skills, allowing them to be stretched beyond their present capabilities. Provided that the challenges could be balanced by the appropriate level of skill then the participant had the right pre-conditions to experience flow during that activity.

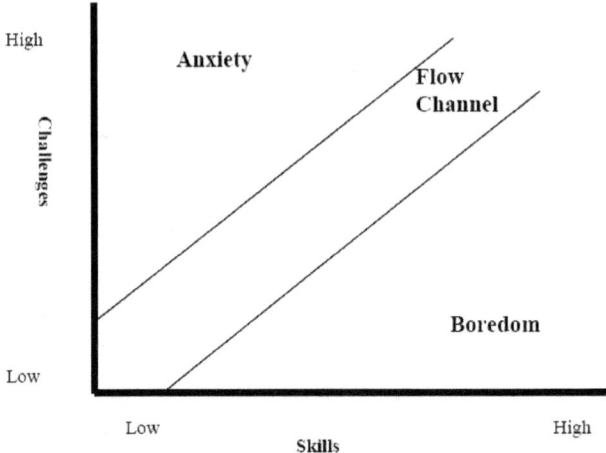

Figure 1. Flow model developed by Csikszentmihalyi (2002, p. 74)

Interestingly, these challenges and skills are different for each individual in each circumstance of life. My study, examining my experiences of flow as a piano accompanist and using data presented as autobiographical narrative vignettes, has also identified the effective balance between the challenges of the particular music collaboration and my skills as a pianist and accompanist, as an important theme in understanding the experience of flow. I will now focus on one of the concepts that contribute to this theme: the concept of the music-reading skills needed by a piano accompanist, and examine how this contributes to the notion of keeping the challenges and skills in balance during piano accompaniment to facilitate an experience of flow in collaborative performance.

Music reading challenges for a piano accompanist

I began to learn to read music at a young age. It was part of my development as a pianist and yet like many performers I did not think of it as a psychological process and was unaware of what was actually going on in my thoughts as I read the music score. "The notion that highly practiced perceptual skills are executed without the involvement of consciousness" (Sloboda, 2005, p. 11) resonates with my own experience of learning to read music. My music reading skills have now become automatic but, as postulated by Stewart, Walsh, and Frith (2004), "automaticity is not an all-or-none phenomenon and is better thought of as a continuum" (p. 194). Looking at the issue of the level of automaticity in a music performance, Chaffin, Lemieux, and Chen (2007) found that in a highly polished performance by a concert pianist there was considerable variability in the performance as she attended to the technical difficulties of the work as they arose in performance. Some aspects of the performance displayed elements of automaticity, and yet she was able to attend to specific problems as they occurred in performance. My narrative demonstrates the gradual development of my music reading skills leading to higher levels of automaticity when it comes to music reading in performance. Like the pianist in Chaffin, Lemieux, and Chen's study, my performances were never the same, yet as my music reading ability improved I was able to attend to other musical and technical elements in performance, including working with my collaborative musical partners.

Fluent reading
Early in the narrative I describe a rehearsal for the musical *Annie get Your Gun* where I was pushed into an extremely challenging music reading situation that involved my ability to read fluently and quickly. I had spent time preparing at home, at a much slower tempo, and suddenly I had to perform the accompaniment at a much faster tempo than I had planned. The challenge was presented at a moment's notice and yet I had the skills to meet this challenge. This part of the narrative provides a good example of the balance between challenge and skills that are a theme in my theory for understanding the phenomenon of flow for a piano accompanist.

Reading orchestral reductions
New challenges in the area of music-reading continue to manifest themselves, especially during collaborative performance, forcing me to develop specific skills to meet these challenges, thus facilitating many more opportunities to experience flow as I have to work hard to maintain the challenge-skills balance. As a piano accompanist I am often required to play music that was not specifically designed for performance on a piano including orchestral reductions of concertos and choral works. Playing this type of music is commonly required of an accompanist and over the years I have become more comfortable creating these performances from scores that were not initially composed as piano works. For instance, when accompanying an instrumental concerto for an examination, the pianist is expected to reduce any lengthy orchestral sections in a way that does not compromise the musical integrity of the work. These types of decisions rely on my understanding of musical style and harmony. Katz (2009) also provides insight into this issue for accompanists.

> *Since we cannot duplicate exactly what the orchestra plays, we are compelled to be inventive and highly creative in selecting what and how to play. Unlike a Schubert song where every note must be executed, comfortable or not, with orchestral transcriptions all is permitted and nothing is the 'real thing'. (p. 154).*

Reading music theater scores
Similarly, when playing accompaniments for music theatre songs, sometimes I am required to cut out chorus sections or dance segments, while retaining the solo vocal parts, creating a seamless transition from one section of a song to another, or even to join several songs together in one continuous medley of songs. An interesting turning point in my career as a piano accompanist came at a music theatre seminar where I had the opportunity to further refine some of these music reading and arrangement skills that I had been intuitively developing through my exposure to various styles of piano accompaniment.

> *"You know, you don't have to play all those dots on the page," he pointed out to me after one student's performance.*

> *He moved onto the piano and began the introduction to the song encouraging the singer to repeat their performance. The priority*

was not the exact notes but rather the rhythmic feel of the music – sometimes he added extra notes, sometimes he left notes out.

"How do you know what to play and what not to play?" I asked him after the session had finished.

He laughed.

"Some of these arrangements are just so terrible. They give no support to the singer at all. You have to go with your instincts" (Excerpt from narrative).

I found this conversation very liberating as an accompanist and later in the narrative I explain my mental wrestling with issues around the authenticity of my accompaniment. There are times as an accompanist where I need to be totally faithful to the score and perform every nuance that the composer has set out. This is certainly required whenever I play sonatas for a solo instrument and piano, such as those composed by Beethoven, Schubert, Hindemith, Meale and Brahms. However, in music theatre accompaniment, the vocal score, sometimes written in the form of a "short score" (McLamore, 2004), can be almost unplayable for it may include cues for the various orchestral instruments that would be normally playing in the orchestral arrangement for the show. As an accompanist in this genre, I had to learn which notes to omit while still maintaining the integrity of the music and realising the composer's intentions.

Reading Lead Sheets
Dealing with the challenges of playing the music scores for music theatre productions provided me with many opportunities to develop some specific technical skills pertinent to piano accompanists. One of the specific music reading challenges that was presented to me as an accompanist was learning to read a lead sheet (Levine, 1995). In this case the music is notated as a melody and the chord structure is shown for each bar, but the rest of the arrangement is left up to the pianist to create in a way that is appropriate for the style. As a classically trained pianist I needed a long time to develop the skills needed to both read and perform from these types of scores. As an accompanist, I am still required to perform from lead sheets in all types of situations, so the skills developed in these early years have been in frequent use. Of interest to my study, was the freedom lead sheets provided for me in collaborative situations: I was not tied down to playing an exact score but could create a performance that matched the intensity of my collaborative partners. The emotional possibilities of this type of performance provided many opportunities for flow. In my early years as an accompanist, my classical training provided me with a very strict approach to music reading, and much of my solo piano performance is based on interpretations of notated scores. However, when playing from lead sheets, once the skills of reading this new type of score are mastered, there are many opportunities to explore the emotional and aesthetic nuances of the music without the constrictions of the classical approach of an accurate rendition of a notated score.

Conclusion

This paper has outlined the characteristics of one the concepts pertaining to one of the important themes for flow in my experiences as a piano accompanist: the balance between the music-reading challenges and skills for a piano accompanist. The analysis of the data places this concept as an important part of my theory for understanding the phenomenon of flow for a piano accompanist. It also highlights a significant aspect of piano accompaniment: the transition from novice to skilled performance through deliberate practice (Ericsson, Krampe, & Tesch-Römer, 1993). As my motor skills and music reading skills were developed through deliberate practice and were refined by expert tuition from piano teachers, other teachers associated with my accompaniment partners, and the performance of challenging pieces such as orchestral reductions and music theatre scores, I was able to devote more of my attention to the other aspects of piano accompaniment that were less able to be practiced as they often occurred "in the moment" of performance.

Analyzing my autobiographical narrative, I have found four key concepts for the balance between challenge and skills in collaborative music performance. These concepts are: challenges and skills associated with the acquisition of motor skill development for a pianist; aural acuity; music reading; and sight-reading and quick learning. This paper has examined one of these concepts, the music-reading challenges for an accompanist, comparing their characteristics with the findings of other relevant literature in the field. This has enabled me to gain a deeper understanding the importance of this challenge-skills balance as a theme in my theory for understanding the phenomenon of flow during collaborative music performance.

References

Bakker, A. B. (2005). Flow among music teachers and their students: The crossover of peak experiences. *Journal of Vocational Behaviour, 66*, 26–44.

Bartleet, B.-L. (2009). Behind the baton: Exploring autoethnographic writing in a musical context. *Journal of Contemporary Ethnography, 38*, 713–733.

Bartleet, B.-L., & Ellis, C. (2009). Introduction. Making autoethnography sing/Making music personal. In B.-L. Bartleet & C. Ellis (Eds.), *Music autoethnographies: Making autoethnography sing/Making music personal* (pp. 1–20). Brisbane, Australia: Australian Academic Press.

Bernard, R. (2009). Music making, transcendence, flow, and music education. *International Journal of Education and the Arts, 10*(14), 1–22.

Chaffin, R., Lemieux, A. F., & Chen, C. (2007). "It is different each time I play": Variability in highly prepared musical performance. *Music Perception, 24*, 455–472.

Chang, H. (2008). *Autoethnography as method: Developing qualitative inquiry.* Walnut Creek, CA: Left Coast Press.

Csikszentmihalyi, M. (1975). *Beyond boredom and anxiety: The experience of play in work and games.* San Francisco, CA: Jossey-Bass Publishers.

Csikszentmihalyi, M. (1996). *Creativity: Flow and the psychology of discovery and invention.* New York, NY: Harper Collins.

Csikszentmihalyi, M. (2002). *Flow: The classic work on how to achieve happiness.* London, UK: Rider.

Custodero, L. A. (2002). Seeking challenge, finding skill: Flow experience and music education. *Arts Education Policy Review, 103*(3), 3–9.

Custodero, L. A. (2005). Observable indicators of flow experience: A developmental perspective on musical engagement in young children from infancy to school age. *Music Education Research, 7*, 185–209.

de Vries, P. (2006). Engaging in music to enhance self-study. *International Journal of Qualitative Studies in Education, 19*, 243 - 251.

Denzin, N. K., & Lincoln, Y. S. (2003). Introduction: The discipline and practice of qualitative research. In N. K. Denzin & Y. S. Lincoln (Eds.), *The landscape of qualitative research: Theories and issues* (2nd ed., pp. 1–46). Thousand Oaks, CA: Sage.

Duncan, M. (2004). Autoethnography: Critical appreciation of an emerging art. *International Journal of Qualitative Methods, 3*(4), 1–14.

Ellis, C. (2004). *The ethnographic I: A methodological novel about autoethnography*. Walnut Creek, CA: Alta Mira Press.

Ericsson, K. A., Krampe, R. T., & Tesch-Römer, C. (1993). The role of deliberate practice in the acquisition of expert performance. *Psychological Review, 100*, 363–406.

Flyvbjerg, B. (2011). Case study. In N. K. Denzin & Y. S. Lincoln (Eds.), *The Sage handbook of qualitative research* (4th ed., pp. 301–316). Thousand Oaks, CA: Sage.

Gregor, S. (2002). A theory of theories in information systems. In S. Gregor & D. Hart (Eds.), *Information systems foundations: Building the theoretical base* (pp. 1–20). Canberra, Australia: Australian National University.

Humphreys, M. (2005). Getting personal: Reflexivity and autoethnographic vignettes. *Qualitative Inquiry, 11*, 840–860.

Jackson, S. A., & Csikszentmihalyi, M. (1999). *Flow in sports: The keys to optimal experiences and performances*. USA: Human Kinetics.

Jaros, M. D. (2008). *Optimal experience in the choral rehearsal: A study of flow and affect among singers* (Unpublished doctoral dissertation). University of Minnesota, USA.

Katz, M. (2009). *The complete collaborator: The pianist as partner*. New York, NY: Oxford University Press.

Kraus, B. N. (2003). *Musicians in flow: Optimal experience in the wind ensemble rehearsal* (Unpublished doctoral dissertation). Arizona State University, USA.

Levine, M. (1995). *The jazz theory book*. Petaluma, CA: Sher Music.

MacDonald, R., Byrne, C., & Carlton, L. (2006). Creativity and flow in musical composition: An empirical investigation. *Psychology of Music, 34*, 292–306.

Matthews, W. E. (2003). *Teaching with improvisation: Three case studies of flow experience in beginning adult singers* (Unpublished doctoral dissertation). Columbia University Teachers College, New York, NY.

McLamore, A. (2004). *Musical theater: An appreciation*. New York, NY: Pearson Education.

Nakamura, J., & Csikszentmihalyi, M. (2002). The concept of flow. In C. R. Snyder & S. J. Lopez (Eds.), *Handbook of positive psychology* (pp. 89–105). Oxford, UK: Oxford University Press.

Preston, C. (2009). *The contribution of talk to generating flow experience in the music classroom*. Paper presented at the 7th Triennial Conference of European Society for the Cognitive Sciences of Music (ESCOM 2009), Jyväskylä, Finland.

Schindler, M. (2009). "Where was I when I needed me?" The role of storytelling in vocal pedagogy. In B.-L. Bartleet & C. Ellis (Eds.), *Music autoethnographies: Making autoethnography sing / making music personal* (pp. 181–196). Brisbane, Australia: Australian Academic Press.

Sinnamon, S., & Moran, A. (2006). *In the mood: Exploring flow states in musicians*. Paper presented at the 9th International Conference on Music Perception and Cognition, Bologna, Italy.

Sloboda, J. A. (2005). *Exploring the musical mind: Cognition, emotion, ability, function*. New York, NY: Oxford University Press.

Sparkes, A. C. (2002). Fictional representations: On difference, choice and risk. *Sociology of Sport Journal, 19*(1), 1–24.

St. John, P. A. (2006). *A community of learners: Young music-makers scaffolding flow experience*. Paper presented at the 9th International Conference on Music Perception and Cognition, pp. 1650–1657, Bologna, Italy.

Stake, R. E. (2005). Qualitative case studies. In N. K. Denzin & Y. S. Lincoln (Eds.), *The Sage handbook of qualitative research* (3rd ed., pp. 443–466). Thousand Oaks, CA: Sage.

Steckel, C. L. (2006). *An exploration of flow among collegiate marching band participants* (Unpublished doctoral dissertation). Oklahoma State University, USA.

Stewart, L., Walsh, V., & Frith, U. (2004). Reading music modifies spatial mapping in pianists. *Perception and Psychophysics, 66*, 183–195.

Wall, S. (2006). An autoethnography on learning about autoethnography. *International Journal of Qualitative Methods, 5*(2), 38–53.

Wall, S. (2008). Easier said than done: Writing an autoethnography. *International Journal of Qualitative Methods, 7*(1), 39–53.

The Multiple Layers of Culture and the Multiple Layers of Society

Peter Douskalis
New York University (USA)
peterdouskalis@gmail.com

Abstract

This article proposes a new process for the development of multicultural music curriculum. It examines the purpose of school, the purpose of music education, the student demographic, and what music they should learn. This article links these four questions together as a necessity for understanding in the thought process of multicultural music curriculum development. It is divided into four sections that support the basis of the proposal: 1. Societies within Societies; 2. Multiple Layers of Society; 3. Cultures within Cultures; and 4. Multiple Layers of Culture. These four sections investigate the multidimensional aspects of society and culture while also investigating the hierarchal levels in which they are designed. Through this investigation, I conclude that the process for multicultural music curriculum development needs to be more thoroughly developed to take into consideration these multiple dimensions. By doing so educators will be able to more thoroughly and comprehensively develop a well-rounded multicultural curriculum.

Keywords
Citizenship, curriculum, development, diversity, multiculturalism, society

The field of Music Education has such a rich literature that it would be impossible for me to do any justice to those in the field with this philosophical article. Narrowing down in the field, I have decided to explore our literature on multicultural curriculum. In this article, I explored a few of the writings of David J. Elliott, Scott Seifried, David Perkins, Andrew F. Smith, James A. Banks, Ellen J. Langer, Plato and Aristotle. In this article I will use specific writings from these authors, along with my own academic and teaching experience, to combine the thoughts of many to propose a new theory. I have taken and expanded the ideas of many and by doing so I wish to give something new to the field. The purpose of this study is to propose a new thought process for multicultural music curriculum development. The proposition is specifically targeted for, but not limited to, educators in largely populated areas with great ethnic diversity. The need for this study is to make educators aware of the multiple dimensions of culture and society so that a multicultural curriculum can be more thoughtfully and thoroughly developed.

Before beginning with my proposition, I will investigate the questions: Whom are we teaching? What music should we teach them? What is the purpose of school? And what is the purpose of music education? All of these questions are invariably linked together, for the answer to each question affects the next. Certainly, when one understands the demographics in their classroom, the question should be "what will I teach them?" This question then requires an answer from the next question of "What is the purpose of school?" And from the answer of that question, we proceed to evaluate the purpose of music education. If we agree that these questions need to be answered, then we can carry on with answering them.

This paper links the purpose of music education to the types of "musics" we are teaching our students, and by doing so; will investigate the ideas and layers of cultures and societies. Questions that may arise from this very statement are "whose culture?" and "whose society". It is only reasonable to expect that when trying to answer a set of questions, other questions will arise. I briefly answer these questions throughout while still maintaining my focus on the proposed subject. This will then set the stage for my proposition of what I will call the "Multiple Layers of Culture" and "Multiple Layers of Society" theories. The theories of this proposition are intended for use in elementary and secondary school education and may also be suitable, but not limited to, "general music", "music in our lives", or any course that covers world music. It is also applicable for performing arts ensembles.

This article does not address the repertoire and rehearsal techniques of concert band, symphonic band, jazz ensembles, choir, orchestra, or other performing arts ensembles at the elementary and secondary level. Although the theories I discuss are not intended for such courses, they could certainly be applied. In the true spirit of philosophy, I leave the content and suggestions of this paper open for discussion and encourage feedback, criticism and an expansion of these ideas through dialogue with experts in the field.

Questions
The four questions I will address to set up my propositions are: whom are we teaching? What music should we teach them? What is the purpose of school? And what is the purpose of music education? Banks (2004) stated, "The increasing ethnic, cultural, language, and religious diversity in nation-states throughout the world has raised new questions and possibilities about educating students for effective citizenship" (p. 299). It is this idea of citizenship that I will lean on to support my theories about the Multiple Layers of Culture and the Multiple Layers of Society.

Diversity is not a new concept in our globalized society and it is no new concept in the field of education. Banks (2004) also says, "Multicultural education was developed, in part, to respond to the concerns of ethnic, racial, and cultural groups that felt marginalized within their nation-states" and "A delicate balance of diversity and unity should be an essential goal of democratic nation-states and of teaching and learning in democratic societies" (p. 300). It is for this reason that I believe every educator has the responsibility to understand the demographics of their population. Ethnic and religious backgrounds, home and social culture are all important aspects of multicultural education. To effectively teach a multicultural curriculum, educators have the responsibility to understand the students in their classroom, not just to know musical content about several cultures. This of course means the subject and content matter will change per classroom, as the demographics of the population are likely to change. In the secondary school, the class demographic may change per "block," thus making the ability to understand the population in such depth more difficult. The fundamental idea should not be turned away because of this complication. Rather, it should be embraced in the same way music educators embrace teaching outside of their expertise. The way the field of music education currently functions in the United States, singers can teach concert band, trumpet players can teach orchestra, violin players can teach guitar and guitarists can teach choir. The common response to this hypothetical situation is to get a fingering chart or simply to learn the trade. After all, we are all musicians. It is this same logic that I wish to apply to population and demographic understanding. Educators should take the time to learn the musical culture of the population in each one of their classrooms. Music educators should undergo intense training and education for world music in order to become more adequately acquainted with the music and musical practices of multiple cultures. If we can agree to use this logic, we can continue to further develop this philosophy.

What music should we teach? Elliott (1996) says, "…no musical practice is innately better than any other" and "while no Music is innately superior to any other, some musical practices may be educationally more appropriate than others" (p. 8). Since no music is better than another, the process of choosing music in the multicultural curriculum for educational purposes in school should be made clear. I would like to apply this logic to my theory of the Multiple Layers of Culture. Because each student has their own culture, and each culture has its own music, the music we choose to teach should start with the corresponding musical cultures of the population in our classroom. As Langer (1997) suggested:

> *Perhaps the very notion of basics needs to be questioned. They are not useful, however, as first learned, for everyone across all situations. If they are mindlessly overlearned, they are not likely to be varied even when variation would be advantageous. Perhaps one could say that for everyone there are certain basics, but that there is no such thing as the basics. (p. 15)*

Let's apply this idea to the *certain* basics of music. Since every culture has its own basic music style and every style of music has its own set of basics, then each culture must have its own set of basics. This transitive relation is certainly valid, for since each culture has its own music with its own basics, educators should then take the task upon themselves to become more educated in these areas. This approach may in turn create a more encompassing atmosphere in the classroom, where students can educate their peers and the teacher about their own culture and music heritage. However, a point I will make later when discussing my Multiple Layers of Culture theory is, just because someone is of an ethnic background does not mean that the person is educated in their ethnic background or its musical practices. In the multicultural curriculum, you cannot just teach students music from any random culture without relevance and call it "multiculturalism". Taking the time to perform this classroom investigation will provide students with a more emotional attachment to their studies and will therefore give students motivation to further their own musical education. It is also my intention to challenge the "foundations" of music courses that choose Western classical music as the starting point for music education. Seifried (2006) quoted Cutietta (1991) as saying "popular music is typically used only for social ends or as a bait-and-switch technique to get the students involved in classical music" (p. 196). This is not the purpose of my proposition. In no way do I mean for educators to simply start with the students' backgrounds and interests and then use this knowledge to turn them to classical music. Why is it that the music curriculum avoids popular cultures? It is also not my intention to go in depth into this question, however it does need to be considered because the "popular culture" music in all cultures should be taken into account when pursing a fully developed multicultural curriculum. In fact, I address this idea later in this paper in order to suggest that classical music be placed farther in the scope of curriculum development, which brings me to my next question.

What is the purpose of school? Through this chain of questioning, we must understand *why* we are teaching our students before we can determine *what* we will teach them. However, this process is simultaneous and not necessarily linear. By educating the youth, we are preparing them to become adequate members of society, or as Banks earlier stated, effective citizens. Schools are not necessarily training people for specific jobs. That is the domain of a trade school. Schools, however are not training students for work and therefore, music educators are not training professional musicians. Just like in athletics, some students will pursue their interest to become professional athletes. However, this is not the goal, and as in music, the rest of the class cannot be left behind to tailor to the needs and desires of the few. If we agree that the purpose of school is to prepare our students to become effective citizens and members of society, we must then question, at what level of society? Is it the society of the community, the state, the nation, or some other abstraction? I will expand on this idea later, but first, if we are questioning the purpose of school, we must question our specific role as music educators.

What is the purpose of music education? In Book III of Plato's Republic (I. A. Richards, 1966), Socrates is in dialogue with Adeimantus and Glaucon. In this dialogue Socrates said:

> Good language and good harmony and rhythm are all dependent on a "good nature" or "good form" – not the sort of thing commonly named "good nature" or "good form", but a mind which is truly made in its inner being (p. 57).

Socrates later states that arts and music education are important for it will allow the citizens to be "in harmony with the beautiful measure of reason". Glaucon agreed and responded, "Such an education would be by far the best", which then incites Socrates' response: "That, Glaucon, is why music is so all-important in education. Because rhythm and harmony go down most deeply into the depths of the soul, and take the strongest grip upon it (p. 58)".

Aristotle wrote in Poetics (1967):

> Epic composition, then; the writing of tragedy, and of comedy also; the composing of dithyrambs; and the greater part of the making of music with flute and lyre: these are all in point of fact, taken collectively, in imitative processes (p. 15)…they all carry on their imitation through the media of rhythm, speech, and melody. (p. 16)

These two excerpts are both just small fragments of the philosophical ideas known as the Doctrine of Ethos and the Doctrine of Imitation, respectfully attributed to Plato and Aristotle. Combining these philosophies with the purpose of school, we must agree that our purpose as music educators, and the purpose of music education at the elementary and secondary level, is not to train professional musicians, but rather, to prepare our students to become adequate members of society. We must therefore ask the question, what is the music of "our" society? Is it Western classical music? It is not. However, the music from each individual students culture is not the music of our society, just as popular music is not the music of our society. Rather, they are *all collectively* the "musics" of our society. With this conclusion, we must take it upon ourselves to develop a curriculum that addresses all of these musics of "our" society and of each culture represented in our classroom. Society however, is subjective; for there are more layers than just the society "we" live in. What does it even mean to say, "our" society? It may be better to look at society in a multidimensional way.

Society within Society

The process of multicultural curriculum development needs to take into account multiple societies. Smith (2002) stated,

> *Rapid and widespread political, economic, and military changes after World War II gave rise to issues that were global in scope, and many people became aware of the impact that events outside U.S. borders had on domestic affairs. Yet the U.S. public education system remained largely unchanged. (p. 251)*

Because the demographic of the community or the demographic of the school changes, the curriculum should change as well. The educator needs to be able to evolve with the school and community population, not to appease the students and only teach them what they like, but to take the role as educator in better preparing students for the society in which they will take part; But which society? I suggest that there are more dimensions to society than taken into consideration when curriculum planning. Meaning, there exists societies *within* societies. The four layers of society I am proposing are: community, state/regional, national and the ultimate abstraction of the world society. I organize this purposefully from small to large because multicultural curriculum development should take into account the musical practices of each culture from the smallest layer to the largest layer of society. I specifically call these "layers" because music choices will overlap in each layer. Perkins (2004) wrote, "The knowledge arts include communicating strategically, insightfully, and effectively; thinking critically and creatively; and putting school knowledge to work out in what educators sometimes humbly call the 'real world'" (p. 33).

This "real world" idea is what I want to address, because this too has various factors that determine which real world? Or, better yet, whose real world? The "real world" will vary from student to student based on numerous factors including, but not limited to: race, ethnicity, social class, political affiliation, religion, and so on. To suggest that there always be one starting point in multicultural music education would do a huge injustice to the student population. Instead, I suggest an evolving curriculum that is based on taking into consideration the population of students based on the multiple layers of culture and multiple layers of society. This is to build off of the "dynamic multicultural curriculum" concept from Elliott (1995) who says, "*all* music education programs (general music and otherwise) ought to be organized and taught as reflective musical practicums. Of course, the precise details of each music curriculum-as-practicum will differ according to local circumstances" (p. 241). Lets examine the four layers of society I have proposed.

Multiple Layers of Society

At the community layer of society we must take into account the culture of each neighborhood. From where are your students coming? Inherently this idea immediately opens the way for world music curriculum, for if any students in the community population are of ethnic background then we also must consider world cultures in our curriculum development. To effectively perform this kind of curriculum development, the educator must be active in knowing and understanding the population of the community in which the school resides.

The state/regional layer will also determine the population of a school within a community. In this layer the educator should examine the culture of the city, county, community and all aspects of what makes up the region in which the school resides. By understanding the culture of the city/county and the communities within, the educator will have a better understanding of whom future students will be and from what backgrounds they come. Suburban band programs often have "feeder" programs. These feeder programs allow the teacher to know what students will be coming into the band and what instruments they play. With this knowledge the teacher can plan music choices and curriculum around the incoming population. This however, primarily takes into account instrumentation. Let's now use this logic for the regional layer of my proposition. If a teacher knows the makeup of the community, the culture of the area and the city/county, then the teacher can plan curriculum and musical choices around the population that will be entering the school.

At the community and state/regional levels we were specifically looking at the cultures of the students in the classroom and tailoring the curriculum to them. However, this is not 100% academically appropriate for numerous reasons that I will not go into here. It is the responsibility of the teacher to introduce new and unfamiliar material to the students with the conscious goal of making the society in which they will enter a better place. This concept is also subjective to any society in question. These first two stages may very well do that, for one student's culture may be unfamiliar to another student. This still takes into account world society even from the earliest stages; however, more branching out is needed into more unfamiliar music. The layer of national society will incorporate all aspects of the community and state/regional level. It is at this level that I propose the introduction of nationally appropriate and relevant music. This should include popular music and orchestral music. However, the factor of time is still an issue. So far, everything I have proposed is in the present tense. Meaning, when orchestral music is introduced at this stage of the curriculum, it should be newly composed orchestral music from living/breathing composers. I will propose a "spiral" to this layer theory that allows the concept of time to be a contributing factor.

The world layer will take into consideration the culture of each of the previous layers and all aspects there of. Because of the nature of culture, the world layer should exist from step one, taking into consideration the cultures of each of the students in the classroom first. To differ this layer from the rest, the world layer should then branch out to musics of cultures that are not represented in the overall population of the community layer. By doing this, a more general world music education can be achieved while still engaging the students emotional attachment to the material and content of the class. Elliott (1995) said, "music education is not a neutral enterprise. Music curricula can and do function socially and culturally in powerful ways" (p. 293).

It is important for educators to remember that we are first and foremost educators of people. Music is our trade, but most importantly we are educating the person. As students and teachers, we exist now, and therefore the order in which the curriculum is developed should be most relevant to who the people are *now*. To better understand who the people are in the classroom, I also propose a theory about the Multiple Layers of Culture and the concept of cultures *within* cultures.

Culture within Culture

What is culture? Elliott (1995) stated:

> *Culture is a term that various fields of inquiry apply in various ways. In addition to its use in biology and physical development, the term culture is often used by sociologists and anthropologists in the process-sense to mean a people's ongoing way of life, including the language, customs, and preferences of a particular social group. In this sense, most (if not all) people are "cultured" because everyone belongs to, or is inducted into, some human society. (p. 185)*

During the development of multicultural curriculum we must take into account the very people we are teaching and their cultures. Because many cultures are present in the classroom, it is necessary to understand how the students perceive information and how they hear music. Elliott (1995) also stated,

> *"Listening is mediated by cultural beliefs, associations, and values. We understand particular sounds as tones-for-us (or not) because we construct musical patterns in relation to culture-specific principles of musicing and listening" (p. 89).*

For this reason, we must look deeply as educators into the cultural values of our students and the musical practices of those cultures. Elliott (1990) described multiculturalism as referring to "the coexistence of unlike groups in a common social system. In this sense, 'multiculturalism' means 'culturally diverse'" (p. 151). When investigating the culture of a person, one will find that a person is not so simple. Multi-dimensional complexities exist within a culture. A culture can exist *within* a culture. For example, the Greek culture is different from the Greek-American culture. Although these two cultures are similar, because one comes from the other, the existence of the host nation (America) in Greek-American culture contributes to the development of cultural differences within the base culture. The more generations the base culture exists within the host nation, the more the culture shifts towards the host rather than the base. Often we see this idea in the foods of a culture. For example, Mexican food is always Mexican food, however, Mexican food in the United States is *different* from Mexican food in Mexico. It is this same logic that I am applying to the person and to music. From my first example, a Greek-American is *different* from a Greek. The culture is different because the understanding of "local" customs and traditions are not as present when a host nation is factored into the equation. Also, the idea of "local" customs is a changing factor since the presence of a host nation has changed the *location* of the base culture. Applying this logic to music, music within Greek culture will be different from music in Greek-American culture. Harmonic and melodic structures will vary. For example, in the Rembetika music (Greek blues) the bouzouki player often improvises. Due to the history of this music, which I do not have time or space to explain here, the improvisation usually utilizes Middle Eastern modes. With the host nation now as a factor, the improvising musician has more choices of scales. For example, commonly Greek-American bouzouki players will use pentatonic scales and include the "blue" note, which is traditional of American blues. This practice, however, is uncommon in the Rembetika music of Greece and therefore shows a difference in the musical practices of one culture and the musical practices of that same culture in a hosting nation. Elliott (1990) stated,

> Culture is generated by the *interplay* between a group's beliefs about their physical, social, and metaphysical circumstances and the linked bodies of skills and knowledge they develop, standardize, preserve, and modify to meet the intrinsic and extrinsic needs of the group. (p. 149)

The existence of the host nation with the base culture alters the culture and musical culture the more generations the base exists in the host nation. However, someone whose heritage is not of the base culture will not necessarily notice the existence of the host nation's cultural influence on the base culture. More likely, a person of the base culture from the base nation who is newly introduced to the culture of the hosting nation will notice the existence of these differences between base culture and base-host culture.

There is also the factor of mixed cultures. For example, a person of Brazilian decent that mixes with a person of Italian decent. The home culture is immediately fused between the two. Add a different hosting nation as a factor, for example the United States, and we have the fused culture interplaying with the culture of a society. Borrowing a concept from set theory in mathematics, if we think of this as a Venn diagram inside a circle it may become clearer. The circle on the left of the Venn diagram represents the Brazilian culture while the circle on the right represents the Italian culture. The middle connected section represents the interplay between the two cultures. The circle surrounding the Venn diagram represents the culture of the hosting nation, the United States. This picture creates an even more complex three-dimensional concept of culture that would be Brazilian-Italian-American. In terms of musical practice, a third dimension has been added to the equation as previously explained.

Elliott (1995) wrote, "different societies and different groups within societies tend to identify themselves with particular kinds of music" (p. 197). Lets now incorporate the idea that groups in a society within a society identify with particular kinds of music. Lets also incorporate the idea that cultures within a culture of a society within a society identify with particular kinds of music. If a cultural group identifies with a particular kind of music, does a cultural group within a culture identify with the same particular kind of music, a similar music, a different music, or a variation of all the types of music mentioned? The layers that I propose educators need to consider are divided into three groups: Group 1 consists of the layers: culture of the classroom, culture of each student and culture of school; Group 2: culture of neighborhood, culture of city/county and culture of state/region; and Group 3: culture of nation, culture of neighboring nations and culture of world. This is a coarse structure of the layers to maintain a tangible division. Establishing a coarse structure upon the layers is necessary such that the demarcation lines are better highlighted. The weight of this proposal requires way more explanation than I have time or space to write here, so I have grouped these individual pieces and only briefly explain each. This process should be executed in a multidimensional way, where looking at many layers at the same time is necessary. This is not to be treated as a linear process.

Multiple Layers of Culture

I purposefully list the considerations of cultural layers from smallest to largest, for it is more important to make sure we are educating the people in front of us, rather than a "national" or "world" ideal first. I start with the culture of the classroom over the culture of each student because we cannot begin to understand the culture of each student without examining the whole classroom first. Once the culture of the classroom is assessed the culture of each student should be looked at. This includes all of the previously mentioned ideas about cultures within cultures.

The culture of the school and the culture of the neighborhood should then be looked at as contributing factors to the culture of the classroom, which is all determined by the culture of the student and community society. What are the musics belonging to the overall makeup of the school and the neighborhood? Knowledge of the population of the neighborhood will contribute to knowledge of school, unless in areas where secondary students can choose and apply to which schools they attend. In this case, the culture of the city/county should be more carefully examined.

Knowledge of the culture of the city/county allows the educator to understand how the many cultural groups in the overall society interact and coexist. The cultural groups within the city/county makeup the societies within the larger society. This interplay then creates one overall culture, belonging to the city/county and is comprised of the mixture of all the cultural elements of the groups in coexistence. On a larger scale, this also exists for the culture of the state/region.Each state/region has its own general culture, which is comprised of all of the elements contributing to the composition of the culture of the city/county, neighborhoods, schools and population. The spiral effect here is that students begin learning about the society and culture right outside their door, rather than a culture in a country they have no connection to or previous knowledge of. By this time we begin to reach the culture at the national level.

The national level is often where "national standards" are applied. I will not refer or reflect in any way on the national standards of education or music education. Instead, I continue on the path outwards to broader multicultural curriculum development. Students should learn the music that is identified with the national culture. However, the culture of a nation is comprised of the cultures from each state/region, city/county, neighborhood and so on, including the factor of time. It is for this reason that I begin at the most specific place for multicultural curriculum: the classroom. The culture of the nation is defined by the societies and cultures within each state/region, city/county, all the way down to the classroom. It is here that the coexistence of all the represented groups forms one overall culture.

The final two layers of this multidimensional multicultural curriculum development theory are: culture of neighboring nations and culture of world. The cultures of neighboring nations and several world nations will be present in the classroom culture from the start.

Therefore, they will most likely have already been taken into consideration. Once incorporated into the curriculum, I suggest that not represented world cultures then be incorporated into the curriculum. By incorporating these cultures last, students will have already achieved a sufficient amount of information about the cultures around them, thus achieving the goal of better understanding the world and society around them. This process will allow students to become adequate citizens of *their* societies across *all* layers. Elliott (1995) wrote:

> Listeners come to hear musical patterns as tones-for-them-as musical patterns expressive of their social affiliations, homelands, beliefs, values, cultural convictions, and ideals. Hence a fundamental enjoyment for many listeners is the match that occurs between individual cultural-ideological beliefs or values and individually cognized musical expressions of these beliefs or values. This matching of knowledge and musical challenge not only results in self-knowledge and enjoyment, but tends to place or locate listeners in definite contexts of social-cultural communities. (p. 192)

Keeping students engaged and connected with the course material is necessary in creating a successful classroom environment. Elliott (1990) explained, "to 'live' a music culture…students must participate in or *make* a music culture" (p. 158). By making a music culture and learning of the social-cultural communities surrounding them, students have the ability to engage in an encompassing atmosphere in the classroom.

The Evolving Curriculum

Elliott (1995) tells us that:

> Practical curriculum making holds that the most important solutions to curriculum problems will not be found in highly specific written plans of the abstract conjuring of curriculum theorists. Solutions will be found, instead, in the professional reflections and judgments of individual teachers engaged in specific teaching learning situations. (p. 254)

The theory that I have provided certainly leaves room for wonder about the ability of implementation. The teacher in the specific situation needs to have the ability to manoeuvre through any set of curriculum standards in order to more highly tailor to the educational needs of the students. Things change over time. If societies change over time, and the students in the classroom change over time, then the curriculum should change over time as well. I propose that the curriculum be allowed to evolve with societies and cultures to better stay in touch and up to date with these changes. Since the theory I have proposed is meant to initially take all things considered in the present tense, this theory allows the curriculum to evolve with the societies in which it desires to be implemented. How long should it take for the students to cover all of the desired material that can be drawn from this theory? The answer is, however long the teacher has, needs, or wishes to implement a multicultural unit of study or curriculum. If the music class is a quarter or half a school year, then this theory should be condensed to only the most important musical aspects. This is something that should be left to the judgment of the teacher to decide. This theory merely provides a framework in which to manoeuvre when planning. In a performing arts course, this theory could be applied over several years, while in a general music course the theory would have to be more condensed if the time frame is more constricting.

Music is not just a present tense subject though. Music has a long history and that history is relevant to the understanding of music creations today. So how does time factor into the equation? The concept of time can then be applied to the Multiple Layers of Society and the Multiple Layers of Culture theories by going through each layer as previously explained in the present tense but in a backward spiral throughout history. This will allow the teacher to cover all relevant information while covering music throughout history.

Conclusion

Society, culture, and human beings are complex entities that cannot be summarized in a few words. All three together need to be looked at when developing a multicultural curriculum. However, these concepts are not simple, and therefore need to be examined fully before engaging in the educational process. Having students learn about each other's cultures and learn to perform each other's music allows students to engage in an encompassing environment in the classroom and truly prepares students to enter society with a better understanding of their environment. Understanding that society and culture are multidimensional concepts allows the educator to plan curriculum in a multi-layer way, which suits the purpose of the education we wish to provide our students.

References

Aristotle. (1967). 1-3 Basic Considerations, The differentiation according to medium, the objects of imitation. In G. F. Else, (Ed.), *Poetics* (pp. 15–18). Ann Arbor, MI: University of Michigan Press.

Banks, J. (2004). Teaching for social justice, diversity, and citizenship in a global world. *Educational Forum, 68*(4), 296–305.

Elliott, D. J. (1990). Music as culture: toward a multicultural concept of arts education. *Journal of Aesthetic Education, 24*(1), 147–166.

Elliott, D. J. (1995). *Music matters*. New York, NY: Oxford University Press.

Elliott, D. J. (1996). Consciousness, culture and curriculum. *International Journal of Music Education, 28*, 1–14.

Langer, E. J. (1997). *The power of mindful learning*. Cambridge, MA: Da Capo Press.

Perkins, D. (2004). Knowledge alive. *Educational Leadership, 62*(1), 14.

Seifried, S. (2006). Exploring the outcomes of rock and popular music instruction in high school guitar class: A case study. *International Journal of Music Education, 24*, 168–177.

Smith, A. (2002). How global is the curriculum? *Educational Leadership, 60*(2), 38–41.

Praxial Music in Schools: A Clash of Cultures?

John Drummond
University of Otago
Dunedin, New Zealand

john.drummond@otago.ac.nz

Abstract

High-school music education in English-speaking countries is addressing the challenge presented to traditional aesthetic music education by the philosophy of praxial music education, based on reflective musical activity. The aesthetic approach, in which music is studied as a phenomenon to be understood through classroom study, and with an emphasis on the canon of Western Classical Music, sits comfortably beside other subjects in the high-school curriculum. The praxial approach presents a challenge requiring different teaching skills, different resources, and a different relationship between teacher and learner. This might seem to be an argument for removing it from schools, and encouraging practical music education to be undertaken in the community. However, the Western formal education system is being challenged from other directions too, both by those who argue it is made out of date by contemporary technology, and by those who argue the value of alternative, non-Western, non-colonial epistemologies. In this context, praxial music education can be seen to reflect the ideas of educational reformers, and it has a place in formal schooling as a pathfinder.

Keywords
Aesthetic, praxial, epistemology

Stuart Wise, a teacher of high-school music teachers, tells the story of visiting a school in Christchurch, New Zealand, where he had heard there was an excellent program of musical creativity in contemporary popular music. The students were winning regional and national song contests, and hearing their songs performed by local bands. The music teacher welcomed Stuart and took him to the music studios. In one a group of early teenagers was composing on computers, while, in another, a band was working on a song one of them had created.

> *"Yes," said the teacher, "we do really well because of Marama: she's in Year 12 and she helps the younger students. She has an incredible musical talent, and she gives so much to them".* Stuart said he'd like to meet her.

> *"Ah," said the music teacher. "That's a problem. The principal has decided that she has discipline problems, and she's been told to leave the school. Yesterday was her last day"*

In his contribution to *Praxial Music Education: Reflections and Dialogues*, Tom Regelski (2005) draws attention to the term "discipline problems" (p. 225). He suggests it is a euphemism for student resistance to the perennialist, neoscholastic view of education, with its emphasis on uniform and prescribed subject-matter in a standardized curriculum, dominated by the teacher. "As a result, students need to be disciplined to study content and skills that often hold no intrinsic interest, no practical use, and no personal relevance for them" (p. 225) Marama's enthusiastic and effective work with the students was based on different principles, and she probably skipped other classes to do it. Music-making held intrinsic interest for her, and for those other students; it was personally relevant, and it might even have been of practical use if it enabled students to gain prestige, or even income, from the fruits of their music-making. It is important to note, however, that Marama was not operating independently. It wasn't her idea that the students should create songs and make music together. She was fulfilling the requirements of a praxial music education program. Any conflict between Marama and the School principal reflected a wider conflict between the demands of a praxial music education program and the prevailing view of education in the school.

Marama's story is not unique. Lucy Green (2008) revealed examples of many young people for whom music-making is the only school activity they find interesting, useful and relevant. The praxial *Musical Futures* program, now available in several countries, has been developed in response. Clearly a gap has developed between music study and the study of other subjects.

The praxial approach emerged in the 1990s to add to (or replace) the more passive activities associated with "aesthetic" music education (McCarthy & Goble, 2005). Music-making had been part of elementary music education for much longer, as, for example, the Orff system indicates, but at high-school level in most countries using European models of education, music-learning followed an approach which focused on "the development of sensitivity to the aesthetic qualities of things" (Reimer, 1970, p. 19). This meant studying about music rather than studying to make music. Music-making activities - choirs, orchestras, and, in the United States, the band program – were extra-curricular or co-curricular.

Aesthetic music education conforms to an eighteenth-century, Enlightenment definition of knowledge as, in Gilbert's words, "stuff" (2005, p. 69). Education is a process of accessing existing knowledge and exploring ways to understand it, under the guidance of an authoritative teacher. The institutions of formal learning are organized to suit this model, with the addition, in the late 19th and early 20th centuries, of mass production techniques. All pupils of the same age are placed in the same classroom. Knowledge is organized into disciplines, and learners must be disciplined to follow the rules and regulations for learning. The successful acquisition of knowledge is measured in formal examinations. The most suitable music to study using this approach is Western Classical Music, with its large available literature. Training music teachers can follow the same model used for the teachers of other subjects.

The praxial approach is based on a different epistemology. It takes the view that, in music at least, knowledge is based upon activity rather than study. Deep learning does not come from studying about, but from taking part. Its focus is on music not as 'stuff' but as an activity, one best understood through participation. Listening to music, the primary interaction in the aesthetic model, is only one form of participation, and a comparatively weak one. Elliott (1995) lists the activities of listening, performing, improvising, composing, arranging, and conducting. He further encourages awareness of the many different musical practices in the world. As Bowman (2005) points out, praxis as a concept lies "midway between the primarily executive sense of technique and the predominantly cerebral or contemplative sense of theory" (p. 53). It is reflective musical activity.

The consequences for formal learning of a praxial approach are challenging. The normal classroom is unlikely to be an appropriate venue for music making, except of the most regimented kind. The resources required to make music – instruments, acoustic spaces, and, in the contemporary world, high technology – are specialized. Training a praxial music educator requires a much greater focus on the teacher's musical versatility, and so requires more time. The particular talents and needs of individual students become more central, and group music-making becomes a matter not of uniformity but of negotiation. Learning may well be less linear than aleatoric. The liberation of creative thinking that results will inevitably seek to burst out of the normal frameworks of formal learning. What was once extra-curricular now becomes curricular, and staff workloads need to be rethought. And if pupils are allowed the self-direction offered by praxial learning in music, how will they behave when they study in other disciplines? This was, of course, Marama's problem.

In many European countries music-learning in school continues to follow the aesthetic model: praxial learning is undertaken in community music schools. In the Unites States, something similar occurs: bands, choirs and the 'glee club', like the football team, are extra-curricular activities. In schools in those English-speaking countries, which have moved towards a praxial approach to music education, an inevitable clash of cultures occurs, one whose tensions are evident but whose implications are rarely discussed. One simple solution would be to reject praxial music education. The European model of the community music school is the sensible location for making music; let music in the formal education system be merely of the aesthetic variety. It conforms to the traditional learning-models of the institutions, it causes less bother, the choirs and orchestras and bands can continue to work at lunchtimes and after school, and teacher-training can be achieved within the norms allowed. Let's pick the stone out of the shoe. Marama's problem is that she spent too much time in the music studio.

There is, however, another side to the story. Praxial music education is not alone in challenging the prevailing Western model of formal education, and the epistemology, which underlies it. Sir Ken Robinson argues, in his RSA Animate presentation on YouTube, that the traditional school learning system prepares young people poorly for the world they will inhabit. He argues that creativity is as important for adulthood as literacy and numeracy. Jane Gilbert (2005) suggests that "a paradigm shift is happening in the world outside education" and argues that "our education system needs redeveloping if it is to respond to the challenges posed by this paradigm shift" (p. 187). Like Robinson (n.d.), she argues for an education that allows for "different ways of being" (p. 190). Thomas and Brown (2011) advocate for learning systems that allow for the fluidity and evolving character of knowledge. Education Dean Charles Reigeluth argues, online, that education in the twenty-first century should focus on team rather than bureaucratic organization, shared rather than autocratic leadership, autonomy and accountability rather than centralized control, cooperative rather than adversarial relationships, customized rather than mass production, initiative rather than compliance, and diversity rather than conformity.

A different challenge to traditional Western education models is brought by writers like

Makere Stewart-Harawira (2005): "Despite having been devalued, marginalized, disenfranchised, and frequently submerged throughout the history of Western imperialism, traditional indigenous knowledge forms have a profound contribution to make towards an alternative ontology for a just global order" (p. 32). While Gilbert suggests that the paradigm shift is one from modern to post-modern, Linda Tuhiwai Smith (1999) responded that:

> Our colonial experience traps us in the project of modernity. There can be no post-modern for us until we have settled some business of the modern. This does not mean that we do not understand or employ multiple discourses or act in incredibly contradictory ways, or exercise power ourselves in multiple ways. It means that there is unfinished business, that we are still being colonised. (p. 34)

Dei and Kempf (2006) suggested that

> colonialism, read as imposition and domination, did not end with the return of political sovereignty to colonized people or nation states. Colonialism is not dead. Indeed, colonialism and re-colonizing projects today manifest themselves in variegated ways (e.g. the different ways knowledges get produced and receive validation within schools, the particular experiences of students that get counted as [in]valid and the identities that receive recognition and response from school authorities). (p. 2)

Deborah Bradley (2006) quotes this and suggested that

> Colonialism is alive and well, I fear, within many North American music education programs. Our music education curricula continue to validate and recognize particular (white) bodies, to give passing nods to a token few "others", and to invalidate many more through omission. The western musical canon predominates... Musical practices from around the world remain marginalized as curricular add-ons, if acknowledged at all. (p. 134)

It seems that we have two deeper culture-clashes in education: one a general mismatch between traditional Western models of learning and the changing nature – including the developing technologies - of the contemporary world, and the other between those models and the alternative epistemologies of indigenous peoples. This provides a context for the dissonance between formal school education paradigms and praxial music education. One aspect of the praxial approach, its greater inclusion of musical cultures beyond Western classical music, resonates with the challenge to accept alternative epistemologies; another, its acceptance of contemporary technology in creative music-making, resonates with the argument that this technology must lead to alternative modes of learning.

Rather than argue for the removal of praxial music education from the institutions of Western formal education, then, it may be more cogent to argue that it is a pathfinder, providing a gateway for wider changes to take place. Research at the University of Minnesota as far back as 1994 disclosed that students are engaged and learn when education takes place out of the school building (!); when students really want to do it (a school activity or task) and have a choice in what they pursue; when students have an opportunity to collaborate with others; when students produce something—there is a product and audience beyond the teacher; when students' efforts are useful to other people; and when students have an opportunity for reflection and refinement (Paradigm Shift). This is precisely what praxial music education offers: it is an educational alternative more suited to meeting contemporary challenges than is the traditional Western model of formal schooling. Thomas and Brown (2011) suggest that there is a need for a "new culture of learning" based on "peer-to-peer learning...amplified by the emerging technologies that shape the collective nature of participation". If traditional education is based on "listening", then Elliott's praxial list of listening, performing, improvising, composing, arranging, and conducting can be seen as a metaphorical description of what many consider to be the necessarily expanded condition of education as a whole in the contemporary world. For once, music education can be thought of as at the cutting edge of education reform, and not as a last-minute add-on to a busy curriculum. While, within the music education community, teachers and teacher-training institutions may struggle to make praxial music education work, given the shortcomings in training and the challenges of the school environment, the struggle may not be in vain. Perhaps, in the future, our schools might have more Maramas, and be better for it.

References

Bowman, W. D. (2005). The limits and grounds of musical praxialism. In D. Elliott (Ed.) *Praxial music education: reflections and dialogues* (pp. 52–78). Oxford, UK: Oxford University Press.

Bradley, D. The sounds of silence: Talking race in music education. *Action, criticism, and theory for music education*, 6(4), 132-62. Retrieved from http://act.maydaygroup.org/articles/Bradley6_4.pdf

Dei, G. J. S., & Kempf, A. (Eds.) (2006). *Anti-colonialism and education: The politics of resistance* (Vol. 7). Rotterdam, Netherlands: Sense Publishers.

Elliott, D. J. (1995). *Music matters: A new philosophy of music education*. Oxford, UK: Oxford University Press.

Gilbert, J. (2005). *Catching the knowledge wave? The knowledge society and the future of education*. Wellington, New Zealand: NZCER Press.

Green, L. (2008) *Music ,informal learning and the school: A new classroom pedagogy*. Farnham, U.K: Ashgate

Green, L. (2008). *Music, informal learning and the school: A new classroom pedagogy*. Farnham, UK: Ashgate.

McCarthy, M., & Goble, J. S. (2005). The praxial philosophy in historical perspective. In D. Elliott (Ed.) *Praxial music education: reflections and dialogues* (pp. 19–51). Oxford, UK: Oxford University Press.

Musical futures. http://www.musicalfutures.org

Paradigm shift: An example that works. Retrieved from http://neweducationparadigm.org/ShapingASolution%20.htm

Regelski, T. (2005). Aesthetic versus praxial philosophies. In D. Elliott (Ed.) *Praxial music education: reflections and dialogues* (pp. 219–248). Oxford, UK: Oxford University Press.

Reigeluth, C. (n.d.) *A new paradigm of learning and instruction*. Retrieved from http://www.indiana.edu/~iweb/reigeluth/dean.ppt

Reimer, B. (1970). *A philosophy of music education*. Englewood Cliffs, CA: Prentice-Hall.

Robinson, K. (n.d.). *Changing education paradigms*. RSA. Retrieved from http://www.youtube.com/watch?v=zDZFcDGpL4U

Smith, L. T. (1999). *Decolonising methodologies; Research and indigenous peoples*. Auckland, New Zealand: Zed Books.

Stewart-Harawira, M. (2005). *The new imperial order: Indigenous reponses to globalization*. London, UK: Zed Books

Thomas, D., & Brown, J. S. (2011). *A new culture of learning: Cultivating the imagination for a world of constant change*. Retrieved from https://www.createspace.com/

Instrument Teaching in South African Higher Education Institutions: At the Center or on the Periphery?

Marc Duby
University of South Africa (South Africa)
dubym@unisa.ac.za

Abstract

The situation of music departments within higher education institutions (HEIs) in South Africa (SA) seems to reflect an underlying tension within academia. While their high costs and low student numbers are to some degree offset by the relatively high visibility of student and staff concerts and other public activities, these cost factors tend to place them first in the firing line in terms of institutional economic realities. It seems plausible to state that academic planners in SA HEIs experience conceptual challenges in understanding what it is that musicians — and by extension, other performing artists — do, and how these activities integrate with a predominantly cognitive model of learning. With these thoughts in mind, one might say there are two levels of tension operating: one economic, and the other epistemological. My aim in this paper is to discuss some of the factors that fuel these tensions and suggest some alternative strategies for performing arts managers and planners that engage constructively with the managerial status quo.

> *A critique does not consist in saying that things aren't good the way they are. It consists in seeing on just what type of assumptions, of familiar notions, of established and unexamined ways of thinking the accepted practices are based...To do criticism is to make harder those acts which are now too easy.(Foucault, 1994, p. 160-161)*

In keeping with the conference sub-theme of musical environments, I begin by examining the place of expert instrumental teachers within HEIs, suggesting in the course of the discussion that some of the general imperatives that drive South African music academia (the improvement of qualifications and generation of research outputs) may well result in marginalizing this group of experts. In terms of another stated sub-theme (namely, constructing and deconstructing philosophies of music education), I go on to discuss what I perceive as an epistemological gap between practical music instruction and broader educational philosophies, in which a dominant "ideology of the cognitive", in which the acquisition and demonstration of intellectual knowledge are valued over other forms of pedagogy (for example, as typified by practical instrumental and vocal teaching and performance).

Related questions include how to account for the role of embodiment and neuroplasticity in the transmission of musical knowledge, and how and whether this alternative viewpoint on learning can be useful in elucidating what music practitioners do. Much as music departments defend the necessity of practical teaching as central to their activities, it seems that academic planners view this mode of engagement as economically untenable and outmoded. How then do we as music educators justify such a vital part of our teaching and bring it to the center of the field?

Keywords
Performing arts, instrument teaching, embodiment, neuroplasticity, epistemology, cognition

Economic Challenges for Practical Instrument Teaching

Practical instrument teaching[1], where the emphasis falls on the acquisition of practical skills, is a consistent problem area when budgetary matters come up for discussion in music departments. For students who wish to obtain a performance qualification, this traditional tuition model is based on what is construed as "uneconomic" one-on-one teaching; there is considerable resistance on the part of practitioners to changing a model that has operated for many years. This model, it might be argued, has something with the mediaeval guild system, in which learners are indentured as apprentices to a master. In India this teaching and learning strategy has operated for centuries in the form of the *guru-shishya* system, not only within music education but also in the area of spiritual advancement and religious devotion[2].

Very often, instrument teaching faculty in South African higher education institutions (HEIs) are appointed because they are skilled practitioners with significant performance expertise and a public profile. This is only fair insofar as instrument students are entitled to access to the best practitioners available. Under the current terms and conditions of academic employment in South Africa, however, such practitioners are required to demonstrate a high level of academic qualification or research skills or both.

In terms of public visibility, problems may well arise when the practitioner is so committed to outside performing that he or she is unable to maintain a regular teaching schedule, a somewhat ironic state of affairs given that this public profile is one of the motivating factors in hiring the teacher in the first place. It is not always easy to maintain a balance in such circumstances, especially when students are not getting full "value for money" due to practitioners taking part in more lucrative engagements and missing classes as a result.

With respect to directives regarding the improvement of academic qualifications and research outputs, these are clearly necessary so as to nurture and grow a new generation of academics in all disciplines. One might well ask, however, to what extent HEIs are prepared to take account of the specialized skills offered by musicians (and other performing artists, by extension) in reframing research policies to accommodate alternative ways of creative engagement. Further consideration needs to be given to develop strategies to make it possible for practitioners to improve their qualifications, with practice-led research in South Africa a promising option as a pathway to obtaining academic recognition.

---

[1] For the purposes of this discussion, I subsume the fields and practices of voice and instrumental music tuition under the heading of instrument teaching, understanding that playing an instrument is different in many ways from singing.
[2] Available from http://www.itcsra.org/sra_story/sra_story_guru/sra_story_guru_index.html, accessed 9 September 2011.

It seems to me that there is a need to engage with practitioners to empower them in these areas. New strategies for framing creative output as alternative modes of research are required to move beyond the current scenario where practitioners tend to be undervalued or denied access to opportunities for permanent employment because they do not comply with institutional requirements. Some practical suggestions in this regard include the formation of think tanks around the development of practice-based research and the recognition of creative outputs, ethnographic research and the archiving and documentation of artistic practice, collaborative encounters between academics and practitioners, and so on.

Towards an Epistemology of Artistic Endeavor

> *The radical learning that I have in mind is a process of becoming aware of the frame of reference within which we think, feel, and act. This frame of reference contains not only an individual life history but also the whole life-process of a given society. (Moisio, 2009, p. 63)*

In *The Artistic Turn*, in a section called "Deterritorializing the Research Space," Kathleen Coessens, Crispin, and Douglas (2009) describe a potentially fruitful strategy for revisiting artistic endeavor as follows: "To claim, or *re*claim, a territory for artistic research, we should first claim and reclaim recognition that they are different ways of knowing, of developing knowledge and new insights to be gained from the greater familiarity with knowledge traditions" (p. 79, emphasis in original). What Coessens and her colleagues are highlighting in this statement points to a more fundamental philosophical problem around the status of knowledge and the place of the practitioner in HEIs.

Coessens et al.'s manifesto points to the existence of an epistemological gap, whereby what is regarded as valid research for many South African HEIs operates according to the tenets of what Mark Johnson (1987) has characterized as an Objectivist framework. For Johnson, Objectivism is the dominant way of seeing, not only within HEIs but also in the world at large. Johnson sets the scene as follows:

> *In its nonsophisticated manifestation, as a set of shared commonplaces in our culture, [Objectivism] takes the following general form: The world consists of objects that have properties and stand in various relationships independent of human understanding. The world is as it is, no matter what any person happens to believe about it, and there is one correct "God's-Eye-View" about what the world really is like. In other words, there is a rational structure to reality, independent of the beliefs of any particular people, and correct reason mirrors this rational structure. (p. x)*

If it is the case that Objectivism is a particularly dominant *Weltanschauung*[3], as Johnson

---

[3] *(n.)* World view; a conception of the course of events in, and of the purpose of, the world as a whole, forming a philosophical view or apprehension of the universe; the general idea embodied in a cosmology (http://thinkexist.com/dictionary/meaning/weltanschauung/), accessed 9

argues, it seems a particularly inappropriate framework for assessing artistic processes and products, which often deal with ambiguous and polyvalent — in short, "irrational"— aspects of human existence. Certainly, creative activity does not seek to prove anything about the world in the same way as scientific endeavor does, and the different purposes and outcomes of these knowledge systems deserve to be acknowledged, as Coessens et al. (2009) suggest. It is a fact that artistic activity operates differently in many ways from — and implicitly challenges perhaps — the rigid ideology of Objectivism.

It seems to me that some South African HEIs value, and even prioritize, a model of learning that is based on the progressive development of a set of cognitive skills. This model, in very general terms, allows for methods of delivery and assessment through traditional approaches to teaching and learning: "chalk and talk" lecturing, essays, question-based examinations, and so on. Using these delivery methods makes it possible to accommodate large classes in keeping with imperatives to "massify" education.

Economic considerations aside, this emphasis on a particular cognitive and epistemological model tends to place the performing arts in general, and music in particular, in an institutional no man's land. One-on-one instruction is not regarded as economically viable, and, perhaps more crucially, requires assessment methods that account for learning activities outside the domain of the purely cognitive. As Marko Punkanen (2011) observed: "Improvisation is an integrative experience where bodily, emotional and cognitive levels of experience are present at the same time. In musical improvisation the whole body is used to express intentions, emotions and thoughts" (p. 29).

While Punkanen is referring to improvisation in the specific context of his experience as a music therapist, it seems to me that his insights can be extended to musical performance (the stated outcome and assessment context of instrument teaching) with minimal distortion of his line of argument.

Instrumental Music Studies and the "ideology of the cognitive"

A syllabus requirement for Instrumental Music Studies IIIA (a major subject in three-year degree offerings like BA and BSocSci, henceforth IMS) is a 40% essay component, substantially different from IMS III as part of the BMus curriculum. IMS III requires a small (10%) written component by comparison, implying thereby that IMS IIIA as an exit-level subject calls for demonstrable proof that music students at this level are capable of writing essays demonstrating the same degree of intellectual engagement as other major subjects.

This particular requirement (once again, evaluating students' cognitive skills) effectively decreases the amount of time and energy students in this course can devote to practicing a sufficiently demanding instrumental or vocal repertoire. The quandary assessors face in this regard is the lack of congruency between IMS IIIA (as a non-BMus subject) and IMS III as part of a 4 year BMus curriculum, summarized in this practical dilemma: Do IMS IIIA students perform a shorter program or do they perform technically less demanding music so as to account for less available time spent practicing?

While the literature component of IMS does provide an opportunity for students to demonstrate knowledge of the pieces they perform as well as insights into the historical and stylistic milieu from which their repertoire springs, in performance there are other skills based on alternative taxonomies that are under evaluation: for instance, psychomotor and affective competencies. It seems in principle that in the case of IMS, these different taxonomic areas need to be taken into account, and the fact that these are presented in tandem is a complicating factor for the assessors' task, as well as the fact that ensemble performance requires the assessment of not one, but two strata of performance: individual and ensemble.

Whether in the classroom or the examination, traditional essay-based student learning is in line with typical academic offerings in the humanities. Where this "ideology of the cognitive" (in other words, what facts or theories are recalled, analyzed, or evaluated at increasing levels of complexity as the learner progresses through the degree program) places practical music studies is the immediate question. While there is no doubt a cognitive component in instrumental or vocal performance (one thinks most immediately of memorization, for argument's sake), this is not the only kind of knowledge that is being assessed here, as Punkanen (2011) suggests.

Neuroplasticity and Embodied Learning

Nicholas Carr (2010) provides experimental evidence indicating how occupational engagement actually modifies brain structure arguments according to contemporary theories of neuroplasticity. Drawing on the work of Edward Taub, Carr concludes that: "Playing a violin, a musical tool, [had] resulted in substantial physical changes in the brain" (p. 32), and in connection with research done into the brain structure of London taxi drivers, he states:

> In the late 1990s, a group of British researchers scanned the brains of sixteen London cab drivers who had between two and forty-two years of experience behind the wheel. When they compared the scans with those of a control group, they found that the taxi drivers' posterior hippocampus, a part of the brain that plays a key role in storing and manipulating spatial representations of a person's surroundings, was much larger than normal. Moreover, the longer a cab driver had been on the job, the larger his posterior hippocampus tended to be. (p. 22–33)

Carr further described an experiment conducted by Alvaro Pascual-Leone et al. (1995) wherein changes in brain organization came about through "purely mental activity" (p. 32). The experiment demonstrates that the acts of physical practicing and its purely mental counterpart led to similar changes in brain structure: the test group, given the task of learning to play a simple melody on a digital piano, exhibited the same development as the control group, who merely imagined practicing the same melody. Carr concluded by observing that: "[Pascual-Leone, et al.] found that the people who had only imagined playing the notes exhibited precisely the same changes in their brains as those who had actually pressed the keys. (p. 33)."

What Carr does not mention is the difference in acquired motor skills exhibited by the two groups, as stated by Pascual-Leone et al. (1995): "…The mental group's performance was at the level of that occurring with only 3 days physical practice. After a single 2-h[our] physical practice session, the mental group's performance improved to the level of 5 days' physical practice" (p. 1041). The experimental data, which highlights the difference in acquired skills between the two groups, bears out the necessity of time spent engaged in physical practicing to develop and cement the motor skills required for musical competence.

It seems that there is proof that learning to play an instrument has a measurable effect on the structure of the musician's brain. This implies that this type of learning is embodied at the most fundamental level, and that there is therefore a definite need to consider other types of assessment that account for an emergent view of learning as an integrated activity. The traditional view of learning as the acquisition of more and more complex collections of facts, demonstrated by powers of reasoning and assessed by means of traditional paper and pencil testing, does not adequately account for how musicians' learning and development processes actually take place.

With reference to John Dewey's theories, Mark Johnson (2011) highlights the inherently dualistic implications of this traditional understanding of learning in stating:

> Dewey's view of knowing requires us to give up any rigid dichotomy between what has traditionally been thought of as modes of conceiving and knowing versus modes of perceiving and doing. The rejection of this form of dualism has recently been supported by research in the cognitive sciences that challenges any such rigid distinction between the conceptual and the perceptual, and even between the perceptual and the motor dimensions of cognition. (p. 148)

It is my belief that a more nuanced understanding of artistic practices both inside and outside the institution is valuable for calling into question traditional perspectives on learning processes. Playing musical instruments, singing, acting, or dancing are simply different ways of producing knowledge, and their mysterious opacity to non-practitioners should not diminish their potential as alternatives to established epistemological frameworks. At the same time, one should not valorise these activities at the cost of more conventional learning pathways, but consider them as different, and equally valuable, ways of acquiring and developing knowledge.

Communicating these ideas to the "powers that be" in HEIs clearly is a challenging task for arts educators. Nonetheless, these discussions become of vital importance when performing arts departments are threatened with economic sanctions, and it is hoped that these lines of argument may be of some assistance in framing responses to academic planning divisions.

Acknowledgments

This research is carried out with financial assistance from the National Research Foundation, and any opinions or findings therein are expressly the author's responsibility, for which the NRF accepts no liability.

References

Carr, N. (2010). The shallows: How the Internet is changing the way we think, read and remember. London, UK: Atlantic Books.

Coessens, K., Crispin, D., & Douglas, A. (2009). The artistic turn: A manifesto. Ghent, Belgium: Leuven University Press.

Foucault, M. (1994). "So is it important to think?" in J. D. Faubion. (Ed.). *Michel Foucault: The essential works*,3. Power. London, UK: Penguin.

Johnson, M. (1987). The Body in the mind: The bodily basis of meaning, imagination, and reason. Chicago, IL: University of Chicago Press.

Johnson, M. (2011). Embodied knowing through art. In M. Biggs and H. Karlsson (Eds.). The routledge companion to research in the arts. Abingdon, UK: Routledge.

Moisio, O. (2009). Essays on radical educational philosophy. Jyväskylä studies in education, psychology and social research (unpublished doctoral dissertation, Jyväskylä: University of Jyväskylä.

Pascual-Leone, A., Dang N., Leonardo, G., Cohen, L. G., Brasil-Neto, J. P., Cammarota, A., & Hallett, M. (1995). Modulation of muscle responses evoked by transcranial magnetic stimulation during the acquisition of new fine motor skills. Journal of Neurophysiology, 74, 1037–45.

Punkanen, M. (2011). Improvisational music therapy and perception of emotions in music by people with depression. Jyväskylä Studies in Humanities. (unpublished doctoral dissertation, Jyväskylä: University of Jyväskylä.

Music Education and ePortfolios: New Thinking for the Preparation of Music Teachers

Peter Dunbar-Hall
University of Sydney (Australia)
peter.dunbar-hall@sydney.edu.au

Jennifer Rowley
University of Sydney (Australia)

Madeleine Bell
University of Sydney (Australia)

John Taylor
University of Sydney (Australia)

Abstract

This paper explains and analyses a project to implement ePortfolios into a Music Education degree at an Australian university. The project began in 2009 and concluded in 2011. The background, history and multiple intentions of the project are described, especially how its aim was to address university expectations, music education proficiencies, and official government teacher accreditation criteria. The research reported here relied on action research in which each stage of the project was used to generate the next stage. Interviews with students were held regularly, students were trained in the technological aspects of ePortfolios, and student ePortfolios were analyzed for their content, mode of delivery, and usefulness.

During implementation of the project a number of issues, often unforeseen, emerged. Six of these are discussed in this paper: 1. student perceptions of ePortfolios; 2. students' identities as "digital natives"; 3. the role of ePortfolios in representing students' multiple musical and pedagogic identities; 4. mapping of ePortfolios across the subjects of the degree program; 5. assessment in relation to ePortfolios; and 6. ePortfolios as sites of learning.

Through raising these issues, and requiring active responses to them, the project became a form of curriculum evaluation, a pathway to reinterpretation of the degree program involved, and a new way to ensure that future music educators are comprehensively prepared for their profession.

Keywords
ePortfolio, teacher preparation, information and communication technology (ICT)

Introduction: Background and Aims of the Project

At the 2010 ISME conference, we presented our work on the early stages of the introduction of ePortfolios into a Music Education degree program at an Australian university (Dunbar-Hall, Rowley, Webb, & Bell, 2010). At that time, our research reflected the problems that had arisen in addressing expectations of ePortfolios from a range of directions. These were: 1. to reflect the incremental nature of the four year degree program involved; 2. to provide a way for students to demonstrate their abilities as teachers and musicians, through composition, performance, research, and teaching practices; 3.) to utilize a range of digital artefacts to show students' musical and pedagogical abilities, and simultaneously demonstrate their proficiency in information and communication technology (ICT); 4. to think of ePortfolio use as a process to learning, rather than as a product of studies; 5. to address University expectations that students have mastered generic attributes of tertiary study; and 6. to utilize ePortfolios as proof that students could fulfill the legal requirements of teacher accreditation as expressed by a government authority. So many unconnected areas meant that the project needed to be multi-faceted. It also meant that it uncovered unexpected results. In this paper, we report on the outcomes of these issues at the conclusion of the project, investigate the viability of ePortfolios to act as an agent of change in the preparation of future music educators, and position ICT-based work as a new partner in music education.

Before discussing the outcomes of the project, a brief outline of its progress and research methodology explain how it was implemented. The project began in 2009 and was completed in 2011 (see Dunbar-Hall et al, 2010; Rowley, in press; Rowley & Dunbar-Hall, 2009; Rowley & Dunbar-Hall, 2010; Rowley & Dunbar-Hall, in press). It was implemented in stages through which the contribution of students, input of staff, delivery of technological training, design of ePortfolio tasks, evaluation of student products, consideration of assessment, and the process of curriculum mapping are positioned as steps in an action research method through which each stage of the process was used to design and implement the next stage until the project reached its conclusion:

Stage 1

- Introduction of the idea of ePortfolios as a student task
- Review of literature on ePortfolios in professional degree training, and specifically in the preparation of music educators
- Discussion with students about what they saw as the purpose of ePortfolios, and ideal inclusions
- Listing different expectations of ePortfolios and planning how to address these

Stage 2

- Adding simple ePortfolio tasks into a small number of subjects
- Focus group interviews with students on their developing perceptions of ePortfolios, their problems and advantages
- Provision to students of one-to-one training in technological aspects of ePortfolio work (e.g. uploading materials; producing and editing audio and video files; design considerations; personalizing ePortfolios)

Stage 3
- Design and implementation of more complex ePortfolio tasks
- Adaptation of existing assessment tasks into ePortfolio assets
- Collaboration with Music Education staff
- Assessment of student ePortfolios to date
- Mapping of ePortfolios across the complete four year degree program.

Throughout, a number of issues emerged which represent the pedagogical implications of the project. These are: students' growing perceptions of ePortfolios; whether students were able to utilize their abilities as 'digital natives' in an ICT environment focused on educational activities and outcomes: the role of ePortfolios in student identity formation, especially in the representation of their multiple identities as musicians/educators; mapping ePortfolio work throughout the subjects of this degree program; links between ePortfolios and assessment of student work; how, for students, producing ePortfolios became processes for learning, rather than an outcome of their studies. These issues represent how we perceive ePortfolios as a new and significant way to further the preparation of music educators.

Student Perceptions of ePortfolios

When interviewed, students were clear that an ePortfolio was a good way to show the range of abilities expected of a music educator. They especially commented on its position as a place to express personal beliefs about teaching music, and that it would become a preferred way to apply for a job. Showing technological skills was also seen as a role of ePortfolios, especially as students are about to enter a profession in which, as one student commented, classrooms are changing to be more technological.

After working on an ePortfolio, another student commented on its ability to help categorise information, as it required separation of sets of information to demonstrate specific learning outcomes. This student was clear that putting together an ePortfolio, however, was a matter of critical reflection, that not everything undertaken in a degree needed to be included, and that "I used it to pick things out that I think are important." Her ownership of the medium is also obvious in this comment. The ability of an ePortfolio to present information that was not possible "in a paper format," especially through inclusion of hyperlinks, was another way students saw them, and the possibility of including materials from activities outside their university studies, such as participation in community music groups, was another advantage of them. One student had a different use of an ePortfolio. She had been using one as a site of reflection - a place where she could record her work and her interpretations of it.

Students as "Digital Natives"

These student perceptions of ePortfolios indicate how some students had adopted this ICT medium to benefit their presentation of themselves and contribute beneficially to their studies. Current research into learning methods often identifies students as "digital natives" (Bennett, Maton, & Kervin, 2008) - the generation of young people whose lives rely on technological skills, equipment and ethos. How would students' uses of ePortfolios confirm or contradict the impression of current students as automatically technologically astute and expecting their studies to be technologically delivered/supported?

Some students adapted to ePortfolio use quickly, transferring their existing skills onto its platform. Other students were not so confident, and for some it presented challenges. Clearly the term 'digital natives' does not apply to all students. In response to students' reactions to working in this electronic environment, the project employed an expert who taught students requisite skills (such as film editing) in one-to-one situations. The project, therefore, acted as a site of teaching and learning for students who needed to learn/improve ICT skills that could increase their professional prospects.

Student identity and ePortfolios

A major outcome of ePortfolio engagement was for students who agreed that through designing and producing one they had moved from thinking of themselves as students, to adopting personae as teachers. They explained that as ePortfolio tasks required them to focus on many aspects of learning and teaching, they began to see the range of tasks required of music educators, and how their emergent identities as educators were being influenced and formed. They commented on the following areas of pedagogy they had been thinking about during ePortfolio construction: classroom technology; transfer of learning; professional experience; philosophy of teaching; pedagogy; reflective teaching and/or learning; planning teaching; designing units of work/topics; practice teaching in schools; educational objectives; evidence of teaching ability; assessment; the longitudinal nature of learning;

Making assets for an ePortfolio also led to student realizations and self-assessment of themselves as teachers, as they needed to watch footage of themselves working with learners. One student explained this as: "I guess it makes you become a better teacher…I was recording my students…I was watching (and) "oh, is that how I teach?"…I've got to change a few things, change a few methods, teaching techniques…it made me think."

Mapping ePortfolios throughout the Degree Program

An important stage of the project was mapping ePortfolio work across the Music Education subjects of the four years of this degree. This followed a plan in which simple ePortfolio tasks were introduced into the first two years of the degree, and more complex tasks were assigned to its later years. In this way student ePortfolios were designed as both sequential, to reflect students' developing understandings of music education, and incremental. Growth in conceptual and musical complexity of tasks was mirrored in expectations of increased technological awareness, and involvement and skill development, by moving from text-based documents to recorded audio and video files which needed to be edited and uploaded within the technical constraints of the specific ePortfolio software used in the project. These constraints include; the upload limit per file; online viewing of file types; and organization of materials within the ePortfolio software framework.

Mapping ePortfolio tasks across this degree ensured that student workloads were planned, and that tasks were regularly positioned. Another aspect of mapping was to confirm that each student's final ePortfolio could demonstrate the ability to respond to the complete list of teacher attributes required of beginning teachers by the New South Wales Institute of Teachers (2011), the government authority that controls teaching accreditation. These seven rubrics were used as the guidelines for checking that ePortfolios would address teacher preparation comprehensively:

1. Teachers know their subject content and how to teach that content
2. Teachers know their students and how they learn
3. Teachers plan, assess and report for effective learning
4. Teachers communicate effectively with their students
5. Teachers create and maintain safe and challenging learning environments through the use of classroom management skills
6. Teachers continually improve their professional knowledge and practice
7. Teachers are actively engaged members of their profession and the wider community

Assessment and ePortfolios

As the tasks that would make up an ePortfolio were listed, it became clear that they were being drawn from the assessable assignments of subjects. This meant that assignments were being re-theorized and extended in purpose. They became not only demonstration of learning, but also response to teacher accreditation criteria, and a way of showing technological skills. This meant that as ePortfolio work was introduced into subjects, the role of assessment began to shift. This shift affects both students - in the changed expectations of and the amount and types of work for assignments - and staff - in their setting of assignments and assessment of them.

Whether their ePortfolios should be assessed as a final product was raised with students as the project developed. This is an important consideration, as completed ePortfolios were conceptualized at the outset of the project as capstone artifacts that would summarize students' learning journeys over the four years of the degree. While opinions on holistic, summative assessment varied, the consensus among students was that as the individual tasks which made up their eProtfolios had already been assessed when they had been set as assignments in the subjects of the degree, to re-assess them as part of an ePortfolio was not a valid educational position.

ePortfolios for reflection

Perhaps the most significant advantage of ePortfolios is their ability to influence the ways students see their studies and themselves during their development into music educators. One student noted how making an ePortfolio enabled understanding of degree content and processes, and "how to divide up what I've done to make it understandable to somebody else." Other comments on the personal advantages of ePortfolios regularly use words such as "reflect," "realize," "think," and "philosophy of teaching." For example:

> *"it's made me realize all the different things you can do"*

> *"it's good if it makes you think"*

> *"its pedagogical value ... mostly would come from questions we've had to reflect on"*

> *"(it was good because it got) us to reflect on why it is we want to do this"*

> *"it made me think"*

"I found it was great for reflecting on parts of my teaching... I found that my philosophy of teaching actually changed."

Conclusion: ePortfolios and New Perspectives of Music Educator Preparation

"There's little doubt technology is not only changing the way we teach and learn, it is also challenging centuries-old academic structures and practices..." (Williams, 2011, p. 33).

Because an ePortfolio sums up the work of this four-year degree program, it draws attention to the aims of the degree as a whole, its officially accredited professional status, and the range of skills it develops. Its implementation makes explicit many issues often left implicit in music teacher preparation. For staff, introduction of ePortfolios acts as a form of curriculum evaluation and leads to rethinking ways of delivering teaching. For students it provides demonstration of abilities, utilization of technology, and thinking about job application and placement. For them it also acts as a site for learning, for clarifying what their studies are about, for thinking about identity, and for reflection and self-evaluation. In these ways we position ePortfolios as an advantageous new undertaking in the preparation of future music educators.

References

Bennett, S., Maton, K., & Kervin, L. (2008). The 'digital natives' debate: A critical review of the evidence. *British Journal of Educational Technology, 39*, 775–786.

Dunbar-Hall, P., Rowley, J., Webb, M., & Bell, M. (2010). ePortfolios for music educators: Parameters, problems and possibilities. *Proceedings of the 29th Conference of the International Society for Music Education*, Beijing, China, pp 61–64.

New South Wales Institute of Teachers. (2011). *Professional teacher standards*. Retrieved from http://www.nswteachers.nsw.edu.au

Rowley, J. (in press). Technology, innovation and student learning: ePortfolios for music education. In *Beyond transmission: Innovations in university teaching*. Farrington, UK: Libri Press.

Rowley, J., & Dunbar-Hall, P. (in press). Uncovering the meanings of ePortfolios: Action research, students, and music teacher preparation. *Proceedings of the XVIIIth Conference of the Australian Society for Music Education*, Perth: Australian Society for Music Education.

Rowley, J., & Dunbar-Hall, P. (2009). Integrating ePortfolios: Putting the pedagogy in its place. *Proceedings of the 2009 Conference of the Australasian Society for Computers in Learning in Tertiary Education (ASCILITE)*, Auckland, New Zealand: ASCILITE.

Rowley, J., & Dunbar-Hall, P. (2010). Integrating ePortfolios for music teachers: A creative and pedagogic undertaking. In D. Gibson & B. Dodge (Eds.), *Proceedings of the 2010 International Conference of the Society for Information Technology & Teacher Education* (pp. 213–2:15). Chesapeake, VA: AACE.

Williams, L. (2011, June 1). University of the future is here. *The Australian – Higher Education Supplement*, p 33.

The role of music teaching and learning in an environment of cultural fragility: Case studies from Bali, Indonesia

Peter Dunbar-Hall
University of Sydney (Australia)
peter.dunbar-hall@sydney.edu.au

Abstract

This paper investigates three contexts of teaching and learning music and dance in Bali, Indonesia, and positions them as ways in which music and dance under threat of decline or loss are being proactively reclaimed and maintained. The three contexts are: (1) the teaching of children in village settings, (2) the work of formalized institutions, and (3) the use of *seniman tua* (senior artists) in passing on both repertoires of the past and the pedagogies associated with them. These three contexts of teaching and learning also reveal strategies teachers use to transmit repertoire, and provide numerous means through which different sectors of the music and dance community in Bali provide different perspectives on and methods for researching and passing on knowledge of music and dance which Balinese people see as endangered. Apart from the ways these three contexts function, the paper also considers how learning music and dance are implicated in observance of religious events, in local village pride, in constructions of Balinese identity, and in challenging received notions of gender roles in the performing arts. The use of early recordings, as a source of repertoires from the past, and ways in which musicians act as 'carriers' of music and dance across generations are also investigated. Through these vignettes, the importance of teaching and learning music and dance in a setting of cultural fragility is emphasized.

Keywords
Cultural maintenance, pedagogy, children, institutions, senior artists

Introduction

In a world where some cultural traditions are in decline or at risk of passing out of existence, the teaching and learning of music take on relevances beyond those where music and dance are robust, strongly supported, and continually developing. Rather than purely imparting musical skills, in locations of cultural frailty, teaching and learning become important agents in cultural maintenance and revival, and can be investigated in relation to agendas of local identity formation and representation. The Indonesian island of Bali presents examples of this. Developments in tourism, globalization, changes to Bali's economic and social identity from mostly agrarian to increasingly urbanized, and the results of Balinese people's needs to stay abreast of educational and socio-economical levels and expectations outside of Bali, mean that knowledge and performance of many aspects of Balinese cultural representation - in this case, music and dance - are declining. This situation, and that it needs addressing, is recognized by both non-Balinese and Balinese people. For example, the priest, Mangku Widia, from the village of Tenganan Pegeringsingan in eastern Bali, noted that:

> we elders...want to and have to do something in order that our young develop a feeling and an understanding for the unique community and culture again. They ought to know why they do what they do. So we have to dig out, compile our knowledge about our history and culture, put it into archives and make it publicly accessible...That's the only way we can give our young a direction and show them what they can do... (Ramseyer, 2009, p. 195)

This paper investigates ways in which Balinese people who are aware of this situation proactively work to counter the effects of decline of knowledge and performance of music and dance. It is presented as three case studies, and is based on fieldwork carried out in Bali, especially research into teaching and learning, the effects of tourism, and the contexts of performance. The first case study is in the teaching of children, at village level. Second is the role of formally established teaching institutions, and third the utilization of *seniman tua* (Indonesian - senior artist/s) as a resource in transmitting music and dance. Through these contexts, the aims of teaching and ways it is carried out, and the importance of learning to play an instrument or to dance are shown as important to Balinese people as significant means to keep music and dance alive in the face of cultural fragility.

Teaching of children

It is important for children in Bali to learn to dance to some level of ability. This is partly because dance, like music, is an important part of religious events; being able to participate in a religious event as a performer is one means of achieving personal and community *dharma* (spiritual balance and well-being). For this reason, some schools teach music and dance - but this is not general. The majority of music and dance teaching occurs in *sanggar* (Indonesian - studios), based in villages (Dunbar-Hall, 2006, 2011; McIntosh, 2006).

At these *sanggar* it is usual for girls to learn various 'welcome dances', used to greet deities present during religious rites. Dances choreographed from the characteristic movements of animals are also popular, for example, *Tarian Kelinci* ('Rabbit Dance'). It is common for boys to learn some form of *baris* (stylised warrior dance), most often *Baris Tunggal* ('Solo Warrior Dance'). The teaching of dance is usually carried out by groups of instructors, who can move around among the children to correct movements and stance. A series of recorded dance accompaniments on cassette is often used. These present multiple performances of a dance without the need to rewind a tape to its beginning. This allows the intense repetition used in the teaching of Balinese music and dance. *Gamelan* is taught in much the same way - with groups of instructors and with many repetitions of pieces.

It is usual for all girls to dance, and for some boys to play *gamelan* and/or dance. But in the recent decade, this gender protocol has been challenged. The growth in popularity of women's *gamelan* groups is flowing down into children's learning situations, so that now it is becoming more common to see girls' *gamelan* groups as well as boys' ones. This is an example of change that is occurring in Balinese performance aesthetics, but one that contributes to knowledge of music and dance being widely disseminated among children.

These learning situations are based in villages, and it is usual for contests between villages, or between different *sanggar*, to fuel the need to learn and practice; local pride in children's performances is strong. Among many parents, a desire to keep Balinese cultural representation and associated religious ideas alive in the face of Indonesian nationalist policies and identity is also a significant force in furthering the teaching of Balinese music and dance to children.

Teaching institutions
Children who become expert performers often continue to learn music and/or dance in formal teaching institutions. These are of two kinds: government run schools/colleges, and privately run music schools.

KOKAR (a secondary school specializing in performing arts) and ISI (Institut Seni Indonesia - Indonesian Institute of Arts) provide training across many forms of performance - dance, different types of *gamelan*, *wayang kulit* (puppet theatre), etc. ISI produces recordings and VCDs, many of which are fed into the tourist market. Its four-year degree programs include research projects in which students are required to conduct fieldwork in a village to research local traditions of music and dance. In this way, performance traditions are documented, and hopefully archived for future use (Institut Seni Indonesia, 2006). Research is also carried out by staff (e.g. Rai, 2001), and appears in ISI's own academic journal, *Mudra: journal of art and culture*. For example, in a 2009 issue of this journal, articles on traditional dance in eastern Bali, touristic performances of music and dance, puppetry, *gamelan luang*, and performing arts and their religious implications appeared alongside articles on literature and painting.

Privately run music institutions can be exemplified by the group Mekar Bhuana, a performing and teaching organization that specializes in reviving and documenting old repertoires. This group performs on historical instruments, thus ensuring they replicate the sounds of older ways of playing music, and pays much attention to differentiating between regional styles of performance. The result of this research and teaching can be heard on their recording of music learnt from recordings made in the early 20th century, *Semara pagulingan: antique Balinese court gamelan* (Bhuana, 2009). Among this group's processes for learning is the use of *seniman tua*.

Seniman tua
The practice of locating a senior artist and employing her or him to teach is long established in Bali. Partly, their use is the result of the fact that Balinese music and dance are not notated - to learn them relies on having them transmitted in real time by someone who can perform them (Dunbar-Hall, 2000). In addition to this, they represent ways that music and dance were performed in the past, with nuances of stylistic difference that continually move away from their origins. *Seniman tua* are regularly used as teachers, and are greatly respected. They are awarded government prizes; they are invited to perform at the annual *Pesta Kesenian Bali* (Bali Arts Festival), and they are honored at special commemo-

rative events, where films and recordings from the past are played, and exhibitions of photographs of the artists' lives and careers are mounted.

Their use not only helps keep repertoires and playing styles from the past alive, it helps perpetuate Balinese teaching practices, and in response, perpetuates learning styles. This means that a distinctive system of pedagogy is transmitted alongside the music and dance it is being used to pass on. Thus Colin McPhee's (1944) description of the teaching of a *seniman tua*, Nengah, he employed in the 1930s to teach *gamelan angklung* to a group of children, remains a description of how a *seniman tua* would work today, especially in its lack of verbal interaction and way in which the children learnt not only by hearing the music played, but by watching the movements of the teacher's hands:

> Nengah's method was strange. He said nothing to the children, but began to play through the melody gazing out into the dusk. He played it again. He then played the first phrase and told the children to begin. (Two of the children) commenced, following him and watching every movement of his hands. A third child joined in, and then others . . . while Nengah said nothing at all and continued to stare into space. (p. 198-199)

Two examples of the work of *seniman tua* can demonstrate their importance in Balinese musical life. The first concerns the work of the late I Wayan Gandra (c.1930 - 2002). Gandra, son of another famous Balinese musician, I Made Lebah (1905? - 1996) was a composer, performer and teacher. He was taken to the USA in the 1960s by Mantle Hood to teach Balinese music at UCLA, and taught in Bali and Australia. He, like many *seniman tua*, was well known for his ability to memorize lengthy pieces of music. Shortly before his death in 2002, he taught a dance piece in *kebyar* style (the most prevalent style of modern Balinese music), *Truna Gandrung*, to members of the group Cudamani (Cudamani, no date; Cudamani, 2011). He had learnt this piece from north Balinese musician, Pan Wandres, who created it around 1920. Gandra had not taught this piece for at least twenty years. Within a few months of his teaching of the piece, it was learnt by other groups in the same region of Bali, and, under the tile *Kebyar Gandrung*, was being regularly performed.

This example of a *seniman tua* at work shows a number of aspects of how music and dance are maintained in Bali. First, Gandra's pedigree, from the family of a famous musician father, and the implications of this - credibility, and personal and family acknowledgement; his ability to 'carry' music across decades and teach it to younger musicians, thus ensure that this piece was not lost; the fact that through two musicians in succession (Wandres - Gandra) this piece was transmitted through the *seniman tua* process across a period of approximately 80 years; and the learning of this piece by other groups of performers and its subsequent popularization.

The second example concerns the teaching of *legong* (stylized court entertainment from pre-colonial/19th century Bali). *Legong* is a popular tourist performance genre (Dunbar-Hall, 2001). It is often performed in shortened versions of dances, or with a cut-down *gamelan* (to save on payments to musicians), or with an inappropriate *gamelan* (*legong* should be accompanied by *gamelan pelegongan*, but is often performed with *gamelan gong kebyar*, with a different timbral character and style of playing). The influence of *kebyar* dances, is also felt in changes to the style of *legong* dancing. While *legong* is still taught and learnt, often a generalised style emanates from filmed versions of only one style used as the source, and this dilutes the tradition and its distinctive regional differences. Through these adaptations to it and general loss of knowledge about it, there is a threat of *legong* suffering further decline, or, as has already happened to approximately a third of its repertoire, being forgotten (Davies, 2009).

To counteract these damaging influences, and to keep *legong* traditions alive, some performing groups bring in *seniman tua* to teach. One such case of this is by Yayasan Polosseni, in southern Bali. This arts organisation teaches *legong*, using Sang Ayu Ketut Muklin (b. 1926) as teacher. In a similar way that Gandra passed on repertoire he had learnt from a musician of the early twentieth century, this *legong* teacher teaches as she was taught as a child by Nyoman Camplung (Myers, 2009). In this way this performance organization can utilize "an unbroken lineage of *legong* teachers (that) preserves contact between the present and the dancer's origins" (Myers, 2009, p. 22), so that problems of loss of knowledge and performance technique can be resisted.

Conclusion

Among Balinese people there is recognition that their performing arts are moving through a period of rapid change. Pressures, both from within and outside Bali, are leading to declines in traditional knowledges of music and dance, at the same time that developments in new forms of performing arts are bringing their own outcomes into recognition. In this context, the teaching of music and dance from the past and the stylistic awareness of how music and dance were performed previously, becomes a major means of reviving repertoires and of documenting them for the future. Through the example of the teaching of music and dance to children, with implications of religious participation, village pride, and local Balinese identity, continuity in instruction in performance can be seen. In teaching institutions, formalised study of music and dance, and research that investigates tradition and Balinese culture indicates the role of educational institutions in this. Alongside repertoires, ways of teaching, and learning, are also implicated. The use of *seniman tua* as a regular occurrence in transmission of repertoires acts to pass on distinctive Balinese pedagogies for teaching music and dance. These three case studies can be used to emphasize how teaching and learning music and dance have roles to play in contexts of cultural fragility.

Recordings

Odalan Bali: Gamelan Cudamani. Cudamani, no date

Semara pagulingan: antique Balinese court gamelan. Sanggar Mekar Bhuana, 2009.

References

Cudamani. (2011). *CAL Performance presents Cudamani*. Retrieved from calperfs.berkeley.edu/learn/program-notes/2004/pn-cudamani

Davies, S. (2009). The history. In D. Myers (Ed.), *Legong* (pp. 20–25). Kedewatan, Indonesia: Amandari.

Dunbar-Hall, P. (2000). Concept or context? Teaching and learning Balinese *gamelan* and the universalist-pluralist debate. *Music Education Research, 2*, 127–140.

Dunbar-Hall, P. (2001). Culture, tourism and cultural tourism: Boundaries and frontiers in performance of Balinese music and dance. *Journal of Intercultural Studies, 22*, 173–188.

Dunbar-Hall, P. (2006). Reading performance: The case of Balinese *Baris. Context, 31*, 81–94.

Dunbar-Hall, P. (2011). Children's learning of music and dance in Bali: An ethnomusicological view of the cultural psychology of music education. In M. Barrett (Ed.), *The cultural psychology of music education* (pp. 17–40). Oxford, UK: Oxford University Press.

Institut Seni Indonesia, (2006). *Panduan studi*. Denpasar, Bali: Institut Seni Indonesia.

McIntosh, J. (2006). *Moving through tradition: Children's practice and performance of dance, music and song in south-central Bali* (Doctoral dissertation). The Queen's University Belfast, Northern Ireland, UK.

McPhee, C. (1944). *A house in Bali*. Oxford, UK: Oxford University Press.

Myers, D. (2009). *Legong*. Kedewatan, Indonesia: Amandari.

Rai, I. W., (2001). *Gong: antologi pemikiran*. Denpasar, Bali: Bali Mangsi.

Ramseyer, U. (2009). *The theatre of the universe: Ritual and art in Tenganan Pegeringsingan, Bali*. Basel, Switzerland: Museum der Kulturen, Basel.

Perspectives on music teaching in basic education in Brazil

Sergio Figueiredo
State University of Santa Catarina (Brazil)
sergio.figueiredo@udesc.br

Abstract
Recent Brazilian educational legislation regarding music in schools as a result of the enactment of Law 11769/2008 represents an advance in terms of the inclusion of music in basic education (ages 0 to 18). This advance means that the new legislation establishes the possibility of including music education for all students in basic education. Despite such an unquestionable advance for music education in Brazil, the challenges are many for diverse reasons. Although the new legislation establishes that music is compulsory curricular content in schools, different approaches to arts teaching in general have been applied in different educational contexts. In the recent past, music education was a part of "artistic education", and in that period one only teacher was responsible for all the arts contents. Different legislation changed this idea of one teacher for all the arts, but such a practice is strongly attached to diverse educational systems. The new legislation enabled the establishment of a new scenario for music in Brazilian schools. Considering the current situation for music in Brazilian schools, this work presents a discussion about the Brazilian educational legislation. The discussion comprises an analysis of educational legislation, music teachers' formation in Brazil, as well as objectives and contents that could be applied in school musical education. The text is built from: Brazilian educational documents – laws and complementary orientation and guidelines for basic and higher education; and bibliographic studies published in Brazil - music education, teacher preparation and curricular proposals.

The literature presents several discussions in terms of music education in Brazil and could offer possible ways to improve this area in schools today. The possibilities are multiple and should constitute a permanent exercise for music educators to define consistent and coherent contents for music in schools, whilst respecting the complexity and variety of the musical phenomena at all times. This paper concludes that, although music education in Brazil is facing several challenges, significant progress has been made in terms of the inclusion of music in schools following the approval of the new legislation.

Keywords
Brazilian music education, basic education, music teacher education, educational policies

Music Teaching from Current Educational Legislation
Since 1996, the Law of Guidelines and Bases of the National Education (Law 9.394) regulates the Brazilian education at the different levels through a series of guidelines. Table 1 summarizes the levels of the Brazilian education:

Table 1. Brazilian education.

Basic education				Higher education	
Early-childhood education	Fundamental teaching (initial years)	Fundamental teaching (final years)	Middle teaching	Under-graduate courses	Post-graduate courses
(ages 0 to 5)	(ages 6 to 10)	(ages 11 to 15)	(ages 16 to 18)	(ages 18 on)	

The compulsory education period today is Fundamental Teaching (ages 6-15). However, the extension of compulsory education to include early years and middle teaching is one of the targets of the Ministry of Education in Brazil.

Arts teaching was established by the 9394/96 Act as "compulsory curricular content in the several levels of basic education" (Brasil, 1996, art. 26), which represents an advance of the previous legislation. Legislation passed between 1971 and 1996 established the practice of the *artistic education* comprising the teaching of scenic arts, visual arts, geometric drawing and music. In that perspective, a single teacher was responsible for the teaching of all of the artistic areas. The outcomes of the *artistic education* were not satisfactory. Among the criticisms was the superficiality of approaches for each one of the artistic languages delivered in schools (Hentschke & Oliveira, 1999; Penna, 2002; Tourinho, 1993).

Arts teaching as compulsory curricular content allowed different interpretations. For some, the law of 1996 proposed a change in the arts teaching model that necessitated the teaching of each artistic language by specific professionals. But for others, the Law of 1996 just modified the name of the discipline, substituting *artistic education* for *arts*, thus reiterating the former model where a teacher would be responsible for all of the artistic areas.

Complementary documents to the Law 9394/96 (e.g., Brasil, 1997, 1998) provide various examples of arts teaching, including visual arts, dance, music and theater. However, these documents are not compulsory and educational systems use such references freely. The result of different practices regarding the teaching of the arts in Brazilian schools has been a diversity of approaches, which also includes the maintenance of the *artistic education* model in several schools until the present, even after 15 years of the establishment of Law 9394 in 1996. An important consequence of this period—1971 to 1996—was the gradual decrease of music as a part of the curriculum for the arts in schools, and in many Brazilian schools, music has never been offered during basic education.

Considering the necessity of a clear orientation in the legislation to guarantee the presence of music in the school curriculum, a national movement was established in Brazil to change the text of the law, including the teaching of music as compulsory curricular content. As a result of such movement, the Law (11769) that established music as "compulsory curricular content" (Brasil, 2008) was finally approved.

Since the enactment of the new law, the expectation and demand that emerged after this process increased. However, Brazilian music education is still facing several challenges today. Some of the challenges that remain outstanding are: 1. *Qualified music teachers to teach in basic education*: in agreement with the Brazilian legislation, to be a teacher in basic education it is necessary to have a specific university degree that prepares teachers – called *Licenciatura*. Consequently, to be a music teacher in Brazilian schools it is necessary to have a certificate/diploma from a *Licenciatura* in music; 2. *Appropriate infrastructure for music activities in schools*: it is necessary to reorganize physical spaces and to make available suitable equipment to assist in the formative specificities of the music area, so as to ensure that music teachers have appropriate resources and alternatives for the development of their work in schools; 3. *Places for music teachers in basic education*: considering the recent change of the legislation, many schools need qualified music teachers. It is necessary that more music teachers are recruited across many educational systems in Brazil to guarantee that music will be consistently delivered in Brazilian education; 4. *Review of the pedagogic proposals in schools*: it is necessary to review the concepts and functions of music teaching in schools, and create and adapt a suitable workload for the development of significant musical activities in the students' formation; and 5. *Production of appropriate didactic material for the different school levels*: it is necessary to develop elaborate printed and audio-visual materials that aid teachers in their pedagogic practice; these materials must consider regional aspects and offer adequate proposals to the different educational systems.

Music Teacher Preparation

Teacher preparation has been the focus of debates, reflections and actions in different knowledge areas, with the objective of finding and establishing concrete ways to invigorate educational performance in basic education. Such a perspective has generated a wide range of policies to improve and (re)define teachers' professional formation, including, fundamentally, two levels: 1. Initial education – encompasses the students' formation in the university degree, preparing new teachers for the Brazilian basic education; and 2. Continuing education – relates to a permanent process of upskilling or renewal of those teachers who already are active in schools.

Licenciatura in music courses (i.e. courses that prepare music teachers for basic education) are offered by public and private universities in all Brazilian geographic regions. At present, 80 courses assist more than 2000 students all over the country. One of the big challenges regarding this formation in the courses that prepare music teachers is the perceived lack of students' motivation for teaching in basic education. Research data shows that only about 25% of students demonstrate interest in teaching music in basic education, which represents a small number of music teachers to assist the demand of the Brazilian education today (Figueiredo, Soares, & Welch, 2010).

The Ministry of Education in Brazil has established several programs and actions that seek to integrate the graduating students' formation with the teaching reality in schools (Figueiredo & Queiroz, 2010). From these initiatives, students in their initial formation are stimulated to learn and to deepen their teaching perspectives and experiences in schools. For instance, programs such as PIBID (Brasil, 2009a) – that offers scholarships for undergraduate students to develop initial teaching in schools – and PRODOCÊNCIA (Brasil, 2009b) – that offers undergraduate programs for teachers in schools represent a real alternative to motivate students to teach in basic education in the future, thus contributing to the presence of music education in Brazilian schools.

Parallel to the formation in universities, other governmental programs including continuing education and professional qualification have been relevant in addressing the educational policies in Brazil. Such programs seek to contribute to the constant improvement of national education. ProExt (Brasil, 2011a) and Plano Nacional de Formação De Professores (Brasil, 2011b) are part of the governmental policies to assist teachers at different teaching levels and knowledge areas in developing methodologies, activities and other aspects that have a direct impact in the school practice.

In the Brazilian context, universities have been responsible for many of the programs of initial and continuing education. With regard to music, several universities have assumed the responsibility for the preparation of more music teachers by offering new courses in new contexts. Regarding music, several actions are currently being developed by universities that concur with governmental policies and align with the various social and cultural contexts of the country. These proposals assist the professional qualification of music teachers and the students of basic education, both of whom benefit from the actions.

Objectives and Contents for Music Teaching in Brazilian Schools

The Brazilian legislation established that the education systems (at federal, state and city levels) have freedom and autonomy to organize their pedagogical projects whilst still respecting a common national base. The music area is included in this legislation, which means that different proposals could be developed in different Brazilian schools.

Assuming that several forms of teaching music in schools could be applied, it is possible to suggest objectives that could contribute in the establishment of proposals for Brazilian music education whilst respecting both legislative and recent music education perspectives. Such objectives might be stated as: 1. To enable the student to develop basic knowledge and abilities in music through offering experiences that allow for the development of musical understanding as a form of human, artistic and cultural expression; 2. To develop the student technically, intellectually and cognitively, offering support for musical expression and for the development of both formal and informal musical knowledge; 3. To facilitate access and experience with music as cultural and artistic expression so as to foster appreciation of the cultures of the world; 4. To prepare students to deal with the diversity of their social universe, participating critically in the selection, practice and musical values that characterize their cultural environment; and 5. To facilitate understanding of music as a wide field of knowing that contributes both to subject knowledge formation as well as towards the individual's professionalism.

Regarding content matter, it is possible to identify elements of musical knowledge that could form the building blocks of music teaching in Brazilian schools. Among several possibilities that would work in music education proposals are the following suggestions:

1. Musical activities that enhance perception of the fundamental elements that characterize musical phenomena: sound, with its parameters and forms of organization;
2. Listening, performance and creation of diversified musical expressions, encompassing different styles and periods that represent music as a cultural expression of different societies;
3. Practices of music that include the immaterial cultural patrimony of Brazil, according to the particularities of regions, states and cities of the country;
4. Practices of music related to students' cultural universe and of the society in which they live;
5. Definition of activities and musical repertoires that dialogue and intersect with educational themes, as indicated in the official documents, such as: ethics, health, environment, sexual orientation, cultural plurality, work and local themes;
6. Strategies of sound discovery and construction and exploration of several musical materials;

7. Practices that integrate the use of traditional resources of music with other alternatives and possibilities of musical performance; and
8. Conception and elaboration of different ways of representing music visually and of reading music.

Undoubtedly many other possibilities could comprise these wide points presented, but these starting points could be useful in the definition of strategies for music education in schools. The possibilities are multiple and should constitute a permanent exercise for music educators to define consistent and coherent contents for music in schools, whilst continually respecting the complexity and variety of the musical phenomena.

Final Considerations
The new vista for Brazilian music education considers music as obligatory curricular content in schools. It thus represents progress for the music area, and also brings big challenges to be faced by the education systems. However, the one issue that stands apart from others is that, irrespective of the difficulties, this new perspective can provide students of basic education with significant musical experiences that contribute to their formation process.

Among the many issues and challenges for ensuring the inclusion of music in all Brazilian schools, dialogue with public policies is the most essential. That dialogue could make possible the establishment of alternatives for the improvement of the professional teaching qualification for existing teachers in schools. Such dialogue could also aid in the process of new teachers' formation in their preparation for teaching music in schools.

Considering the objectives and contents for music teaching, we can assert that some parameters can be established to orientate the practices of music education in schools, whilst respecting the freedom and autonomy of the educational systems within Brazil in the definition of their proposals. Based on the guidelines of the legislation and on the perspectives of contemporary musical education, we can consider some of the objectives and general contents that would guide the educational practice in schools. Clearly, the proposed definitions in this text do not include all of the possibilities, but they suggest some fundamental beginnings for the definition of curricular actions for music teaching in Brazilian schools.

Acknowledgement
I would like to acknowledge the collaboration of Dr. Luis Ricardo Silva Queiroz in the preparation of this text.

References
Brasil. (1996). *Lei 9394/96 - Lei de Diretrizes e Bases da Educação Nacional*. (Law of Guidelines and Bases of National Education). Retrieved from http://www.planalto.gov.br/ccivil_03/Leis/L9394.htm

Brasil. (1997). *Parâmetros Curriculares Nacionais:* Arte - 1º e 2º ciclos. (National Curricular Parameters: Arts – 1st and 2nd levels). Retrieved from http://www.pesquisamusicaufpb.com.br/images/stories/Documentos/musica_escola/pcnarte14.pdf

Brasil. (1998). *Parâmetros Curriculares Nacionais:* Arte - 3º e 4º ciclos. (National Curricular Parameters – Arts – 3rd and 4th levels). Retrieved from http://www.pesquisamusicaufpb.com.br/images/stories/Documentos/musica_escola/pcnarte58.pdf

Brasil. (2008). Lei 11.769/08. Altera a Lei nº 9.394, de 20 de dezembro de 1996, Lei de Diretrizes e Bases da Educação, para dispor sobre a obrigatoriedade do ensino da música na educação básica. (Modifies the Law 9394/96, to treat music as a compulsory teaching in Basic Education). Retrieved from http://www.planalto.gov.br/ccivil_03/_Ato2007-2010/2008/Lei/L11769.htm#art1

Brasil. (2009a). *PRODOCÊNCIA. – Programa de Consolidação das Licenciaturas.* (Teaching Preparation Improvement Program) Brasília: MEC. Retrieved from http://www.capes.gov.br/educacao-basica/prodocencia

Brasil. (2009b). *PIBID – Programa Institucional de Bolsa de Iniciação à Docência.* (Scholarship Institutional Program of Initial Teaching). Brasília: MEC. Retrieved from http://www.capes.gov.br/educacao-basica/capespibid

Brasil. (2011a). *PIBID – Programa Institucional de Bolsa de Iniciação à Docência.* (Scholarship Institutional Program of Initial Teaching). Brasília: MEC. Retrieved from http://www.capes.gov.br/educacao-basica/capespibid

Brasil. (2011b). *ProExt.* (University Community Program). Brasília: MEC. Retrieved from http://portal.mec.gov.br/index.php?option=com_content&view=article&id=12241&Itemid=487

Brasil. (2011c). *Plano nacional de formação de professores.* (Teacher Preparation National Plan). Retrieved from http://portal.mec.gov.br/index.php?option=com_content&view=article&id=13583&Itemid=970

Figueiredo, S., & Queiroz, L. (2010). *Educational policies and practices in the preparation of music teachers in Brazil.* Proceedings from the 29th World Conference on Music Education, Beijing, China.

Figueiredo, S., Soares, J., & Welch, G. (2010). *Music teacher education in Brazil and the UK: Challenges and perspectives.* Unpublished paper, Institute of Education – University of London, United Kingdom.

Hentschke, L., & Oliveira, A. (1999). Music curriculum development and evaluation based on Swanwick's theory. *International Journal of Music Education, 34,* 14-29.

Penna, M. (2002). Professores de música nas escolas públicas de ensino fundamental e médio: Uma ausência significativa. (Music teachers in public schools: A significant absence). *Revista da ABEM, 7,* 7-19.

Tourinho, I. (1993). Usos e funções da música na escola pública de 1o grau. (Uses and functions of music in school). *Fundamentos da Educação Musical, ABEM, 1,* 91-113.

Practices and conceptions involving electric guitar classes in private music schools

Marcos da Rosa Garcia
Federal University of Paraíba (Brazil)
marcosrosa2408@yahoo.com

Abstract

This article discusses issues related to teaching the electric guitar in a private music school that offers free courses in the city of João Pessoa, Paraíba, Brazil. This work aims to present and reflect on the processes that characterize the teaching of the electric guitar in the context mentioned, taking into consideration its educational and spatial dimensions and the profile of the students. Together, these aspects constitute an educational environment, its respective concepts and practices. This study is based on a extant literature in the field of music education and related areas, as well as on empirical data collected through interviews and questionnaires applied to students and a teacher working in this context. From the literature, it was evident the importance of the context for the formation of the guitar players interviewed, for the perspectives and contents proposed and for the performance difficulties of the educator, the musician-teacher, observed.

Keywords
Electric guitar, music school, musician-teacher

It is noticeable that the number of young people who became interested in the electric guitar and thus want to learn how to play it has increased in the recent years. This interest emerges not only because of its unique sonority and specific music application, but it is also due to the image and the attitude of many musicians and performers, in addition to television advertisements and billboards that exploit the image of the electric guitar and the symbolism behind this pop culture icon. For many, playing the electric guitar has become a rite of passage in adolescence and, sometimes, what would be just a hobby becomes a profession.

In Brazil, private music schools offer individual and group classes to those interested in learning how to play an instrument. These schools are responsible for an active portion of the classes conducted in music-educational contexts of today and need to be recognized for their role in the musical formation of individuals. They are an alternative to other institutionalized courses that are traditionally recognized, such as the ones offered by conservatories and universities. For these schools, teachers do not need to be examined for their teaching expertise is legitimated by their role as musicians:

> *The musician-teacher is a professional whose formation was geared to the practice of artistic activities in the area of music. His*

> teaching activity is placed in the background, although it is often the most constant activity and the one that ensures a regular remuneration... In the perspective of students, the competence of the musician-teacher reveals itself in his artistic and musical performance, proven in performance situations. (Requião, 2001, p. 98)[1]

In private music schools, teachers are employed based on the indication of other teachers and by being recognized for their virtuosity. Thus, it is common the thought that a good musician will consequently be a good teacher. This is linked to the social status regarding both the *recruitment* of these teachers by schools and the choice of students to take classes in these contexts.

Perspectives on teaching the electric guitar

Each instrument has its trajectory outlined from a tangle of cultural aspects: its specific repertoire, its musical insertion, its sound characteristics and its social legitimacy, among others. The teaching and learning of the electric guitar today is directly related to these elements as well as to the relationships built between individuals (guitar players), understanding the context of their socio-cultural formation.

In this sense, there are two main perspectives with regard to methods and methodologies of teaching and learning of young guitar players. The first one is more related to learning a repertoire that often contemplates songs of genres like rock, pop and blues. This is also a process that is linked to several practices that characterize the self-training, especially the practice of listening and copying (Green, 2001).

The second perspective is the one of several private tutors and takes place in formal or non- formal schools. Generally speaking, it involves the application of theoretical knowledge to the instruments, emphasizing technical mastery aspects. In this regard, Filho (2002) stressed "the prevalence of a technical vision, especially in relation to the diagrammatic study of scales and modes" (p. 3). This kind of study is based on the representation of theoretical contents on the instrument neck and it is used in most of the books and methods published worldwide.

Borda (2005) emphasized a number of other elements that should be part of the formation of all guitar players:

> ...learning how to play chords according to the chord symbol represented, knowing scales and arpeggios to apply them to the harmonic progressions of a song or theme. In the study of the electric guitar, we tend to work with a survey of the possible applications of chords and scales in the songs. We work with the auditory, visual and tactile mapping by understanding the logic of the neck of the instrument. In addition to developing techniques of reading music, learning how to play melodies, coun-

---

[1] The original Portuguese quotations were all translated by the author.

> *ter melodies and accompaniments, the guitar player learns how to improvise, to create within (or out of) a predetermined harmonic progression. (p. 21)*

Therefore, we realized that presently some authors still differ when listing the most important, or fundamental, aspects in the formation of the guitar player. During the research, it was possible to perceive that the performance of the teacher observed, Felipe Grisi, is much closer to the second perspective aforementioned.

Context definition

The Studio Music School, were the classes were observed, is located on the second floor of the Studio Instrument Music Store. It has four acoustically isolated classrooms where there are classes of instrument and theory. Each room has individual chairs (in the theory room, there are classroom desks) and the specific materials necessary for each instrument class as guitars, basses, keyboards, amplifiers, drums, etc. (Figure 1). There is also the guidance office and a mini auditorium used especially for workshops and presentations.

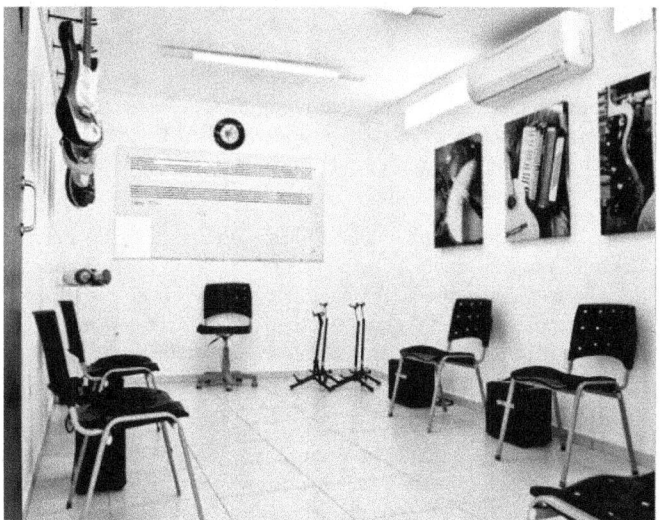

Figure 1. Electric guitar classroom

According to its website, the school has as its work goals the formation and expression of people through music, providing the development of social and instrumental skills, caring about the values of this profession and attitudes of the professionals:

> *Above all, the Studio School is concerned with education, while maintaining the professional attitude and believing that the best education is in a good example. More than music, we try to share experience and expertise, planting a seed that will later grow into*

> *respect, discipline and proper social conduct. (Studio School, 2011)*

According to the guitar teacher interviewed, the regularly enrolled students take part in "a music program that was set but is not strict" for he has the freedom to tailor "the program according to the profile of each student" (F. Grisi, interview, January 5, 2011). It has a length of three years (six semesters), during which, regardless their choice of instrument, students will have to attend theory, reading and perception classes, group practices and other meetings.

According to the secretary staff, during the period in which the observations were conducted, the school had a total of 187 students enrolled, from which 60% were electric guitar students and the other 40% studied other instruments such as guitar, drums, electric bass, keyboard, and vocal technique.

Eighteen electric guitar students answered our survey. They all studied with Teacher Grisi, were regularly enrolled and assiduous. In its majority, the respondents were male adolescents (fifteen males and three females) and fifteen of them were enrolled in a regular high school program. Two students had a higher education degree and only one had finished a post- graduation course.

Student responses emphasized that a major influence on their interest in studying music and then searching for a school was the live performances —shows— they had seen in different moments of life. The same relation appears when the question becomes more specific, for the shows have also aroused their interest in the study of the electric guitar, especially the performance of great guitar players, known as *guitar heroes*.

Seven out of the 18 students said they had studied with private tutors before seeking information or enrolling in this school. Most of them had taken private lessons and practiced by themselves, what is quite common among guitar players (Garcia, 2010, 2011). According to the data collected, 11% of the students had never taken lessons before, 22% had studied in other music schools in the city, 28% consider themselves self-taught and 39% had studied with private tutors.

This school attends a considerable number of students who seek to be professional musicians and another portion of students who want to learn how to play the electric guitar for fun or hobby. The following table shows the reasons why the students interviewed decided to learn how to play the electric guitar in this school.

Table 1. Main reasons why students take electric guitar classes

For fun, learning how to play the songs I like;	6 students
Learning how to play solos as other guitar players do;	3 students
Developing or improving musical knowledge;	2 students
Working professionally with music;	6 students
Other reasons;	1 student (religious reason)

The musical style preferred by 67% of the students is rock, a common taste to the vast majority of young and beginner guitar players. But not only the younger people prefer rock music, since older students who have experienced the boom of this musical style are very much influenced by it too. The musical preferences of the students reflect on their musical performance and many independent rock groups are formed among colleagues.

Teacher and school conceptions

Each group of students attended a one-hour instrument lesson (50 minutes) each week. Electric guitar lessons observed follow a pattern of about five minutes of waiting, while teachers and students await the arrival of the whole group in order to start the class and the discussion of subjects. This time is also used to arrange the room and/or to tune up the instruments. After that, 10 minutes of class are used to review the activities done in the previous meeting. Then, 15 minutes are spent developing new subjects and giving explanations and examples to the students, followed by twenty minutes of repetition and internalization of the activities by students, with or without direct guidance of the teacher.

After class, it is common that students stay in the room having fun with the instruments or just interacting socially.

The observed classes took place collectively, with groups ranging from two to four students. According to the teacher, "forming groups is another school ideology, for we believe that when the class is collective, a student can help the other; the information is not restricted to the interaction between teacher and student" (F. Grisi, interview, January 5, 2011). When asked if the students had to take any kind of leveling test, the answer was affirmative. This test consists of an interview that takes into consideration the musical experience of the student. However, according to the teacher, in order to arrange the students into groups, the main criterion used is the age group. Whenever possible, students with the same average age tend to study in the same group.

During the interview, Grisi (interview, January 5, 2011) said he planned each lesson based on the semiannual course plan of this school, which was developed collectively by its teachers and their coordinator. In this plan, both theoretical and practical elements to be worked out during the electric guitar lessons are highlighted. So, when a class starts with some kind of theoretical description, the time spent doing it does not exceed 15 minutes. This is a brief description and its unique purpose is that students understand what they are doing and do not simply repeat what the teacher does on the instrument.

According to the course plan available and especially to the interview with Grisi, on the first semester, classes are very much focused on scales, major and minor natural scales, because "a good share of the students who join the school already have a good knowledge of chords. We also work with chords; we are not that concerned about students who already know them, but for those who do not, it is also an important aspect of the first semester" (interview, January 5, 2011). During this semester, students start to develop some technical skills so they can get acquainted with the instrument specificities.

In the second semester, elements of the pentatonic scales, harmonic field, formation of chords, triads and intervals are discussed. According to Grisi (interview, January 5, 2011), the study is focused on these elements and they are applied to the instrument practice. Following that, in the third semester, they work with Greek modes and focus on tonal and modal improvisation. Still, they work with chords and their inversion. In the fourth semester, they learn other scales, like the harmonic minor and exotic scales (whole tones and diminished- dominant), and a little more complex harmonies of jazz, for example. Finally, during the last year, the fifth and sixth semesters, they work with the melodic minor, with harmonic analysis (cadence) and some alternative instrumental techniques.

We noticed that the school program gives emphasis to several theoretical concepts, such as scales, arpeggios and harmony, and their application to the instrument. It seems to be a consensus that electric guitar lessons are developed through the practical application of theoretical knowledge. Thus, little attention is given to the development of repertoire, phrasing, or even to the specific dynamic and articulation that constitute the unique and characteristic sonority of the electric guitar.

Still, we realized that this school does not set a pre-determined and specific repertoire to each student or class. As for the songs covered in class, the teacher commented that he listens to the suggestions and comments of students: "I always try to make students play everything, but there are always the tastes...so I'm not going to force them" (F. Grisi, interview, January 5, 2011).

Despite the school definitions, the teacher points out that there are two main difficulties of working in this context: 1. the need to adapt to group lessons, as before starting in this school Grisi had only taught private lessons, primarily individual ones in his own home; and 2. knowing how to work with students who do not study hard and have trouble keeping up with the classes.

Conclusions

Currently, the teaching of the electric guitar has been influenced by the history of the musical development of the instrument and its integration into different contexts, formal, non-formal or informal. Therefore, along with the increase in the number of formalized and legitimized electric guitar courses in the recent years, as well as the increase of musicians who give private classes in their homes and/or the houses of students, the demand of interested people in learning the instrument has raised. Music schools have played an important role in the formation of several guitar players. This can be seen from the number of students enrolled in the respective context and their answers to the questionnaire.

After analyzing the data collected and observing the classes, we realized that the students who attend classes with Professor Grisi have a very heterogeneous profile, as their influences, goals and musical tastes are quite different and plural. Such choices and preferences are directly or indirectly related to their contexts of life and the religious, educational, professional, familiar, emotional and/or psychological nature of them.

The formative experiences of the musician-teacher are prevalent in their practice as an educator, so the technical mastery of the instrument is predominant in their classes. Their difficulties in class are related to the relationship with (control of) students, more specifically a group of students. This is due to their exclusive artistic formation as guitar player and the lack of experience with other educational methods and methodologies, such as proposals for the collective teaching of an instrument.

References

Borda, R. (2005). Por uma proposta curricular de curso superior em guitarra elétrica. (Unpublished master's thesis). Universidade do Rio de Janeiro, Rio de Janeiro.

Filho, J. B. de M. (2002). Guitarra elétrica: Um método para o estudo do aspecto criativo de melodias aplicadas às escalas modais de improvisação jazzística. *Proceedings of the XI Encontro Anual da ABEM, Brazil*. Retrieved from http://www.abemeducacaomusical.org.br/Masters/anais2002/ABEM_2002.pdf

Garcia, M. da R. (2010). O ensino de guitarra elétrica no contexto de aulas particulares. *Proceedings of the XIX Congresso da ABEM, Brazil,* 1487-1496. Retrieved from http://bit.ly/N7Ks3p

Garcia, M. da R. (2011). Processos de auto-aprendizagem em guitarra e as aulas particulares de ensino do instrumento. *Revista da ABEM, 19*(25), 53-62.

Green, L. (2001). *How popular musicians learn: A way ahead for music education*. London, UK: Institute of Education.

Requião, L. (2001). Escolas de música alternativas e aulas particulares: uma opção para a formação profissional do músico. *Cadernos do colóquio*. Retrieved from http://www.seer.unirio.br/index.php/coloquio/article/viewFile/53/22

Studio School. (2011). *A escola*. Retrived from http://bit.ly/LZPYem

Doctoral-level Artistic Research in the Field of Music: Issues and Case Studies

Michael Hannan
Southern Cross University (Australia)
michael.hannan@scu.edu.au

Abstract

Degrees such as the Ph.D. and Masters by Research in creative and performing arts areas are typically undertaken either as standard research projects involving a written thesis or as artistic research projects, which focus on creative work or performance. In the field of music in Australia, the UK and other European countries, these artistic research projects usually involve a creative or performance component and a written component (often termed an "exegesis"). As the paradigm of artistic research is a relatively recent phenomenon, the range of approaches of both the creative/performance component and the written component are many and varied. Artistic research "theses" are not normally published and are not always available in the university library where the thesis was written. Thus academics involved in supervising or examining them often have little idea of the range of practices. It is timely, therefore, to outline the range of designs and methods, which may be used for artistic research projects in the field of music and to offer some case studies of doctoral artistic research projects as exempla.

Keywords
Artistic research, research training, exegesis

Artistic research is variously referred to as practice-based research and practice led-research. Candy (2006) makes a distinction between the two terms; while Smith and Dean (2009) have also distinguished between practice-led research and research-led practice. The term "artistic research" has currency with European artist/academics (Balkema & Slager, 2004) and has been adopted in ISME policy and planning discussions (Lundström, 2009). Artistic research is practiced by some artists in the academy but others artist/academics reject the idea or are reluctantly forced to couch their work in the language of artistic research in order to comply with institutional research policies, to qualify for research grants, or to strive for other expected research status goals.

Whereas artist/academics are usually able to navigate the requirements of higher education research expectations with minimal compliance to justify their artistic work as research or equivalent to research, the same cannot be said for postgraduate research students in the creative and performing arts. The format of their creative or performance research degree submissions typically consists of a body of creative and/or performance work accompanied by a thesis (which has come to be known as an "exegesis"), a substantial written document which is intended to contextualize the creative/performance work in its particular cultural and artistic field, document and explain the artistic process and make claims that the creative/performance work creates new knowledge and new understandings.

This format for research degree presentation derives from the notion that creative and performance work can be regarded as a form of research (or at least equivalent to research) but only if it is backed up by a written explanation of what is going on in the work and where it fits into the history of production in particular art-forms.

The model of the "exegesis" is instructive. Traditionally an exegesis was a critical explanation accompanying a canonical text (such as the Bible). Artist/academics such as Nigel Krauth who write extensively about artistic research, see the exegesis as attractive to the concerns of conservative institutions like universities and as central to the modernist project: if you don't have to explain it, it mustn't be culturally significant (Krauth, 2002).

Interestingly most of the artists/academics who write about artistic research and the associated phenomena of artistic research degrees are from creative writing (like Krauth), as well as visual arts and theater studies. Music artist academics have generally been reluctant to put their toes in the water. This is odd since there are several strong traditions in music that link research with practice. The first is historical performance practice where musicians research the way music was performed in previous eras and in different locations in order to inform their performances; and the second is computer-based music composition where research into the nature of sound and how to create new sounds and new sonic structures are the central concerns. It is no accident that the first PhD degrees involving creative production in any art form emerged in the 1960s from the computer music centers of university such as Columbia/Princeton and Stanford. Basically these artistic projects were accepted as research because they were intimately related to disciplines such as computer science, electronics and psychoacoustics.

Within the recent literature of artistic research however the humanities and cultural studies disciplines have driven the main methodological approaches. This is because visual, literary and dramatic arts are usually strongly based on cultural narratives whereas in music, particularly in instrumental and electronic media, the work may have no more cultural narrative content than what the composer or performer projects onto it as a way of making it accessible to potential audiences. Essentially these musical artists are working with new ways of creating and interpreting abstract musical sounds and structures. Unlike their visual, literary and theatrical compatriots, typically their work involves little critical engagement with social, cultural and political agendas.

While cultural theory provides the intellectual context for artistic research in many disciplines, a number of methodological strategies have emerged for the framing of the exegesis. The most widespread of these is reflective practice (Schön, 1983). Reflection on the arts practice as it evolves becomes a way of articulating understandings of the creative process. Reflection may take place before practice, during practice and after practice. Reflective writing is a critical and analytical process aimed at making sense of the experience of practice and aimed to improve practice. Ideally it is a cyclic process as in action research. In fact action research is another model that has been adopted by and adapted to artistic research (Candy, 2006)

To conduct reflection on practice some sort of collection of data is needed. In the case of music practice, making audio and/or video recordings of the progressive stages of the practice provides evidence that can be examined and analyzed in order to be able to write a reflective journal of the practice. In this way, the reflective methodology is somewhat like ethnography although the artist may be only studying his or her own creative culture rather than the culture of a wider community. In fact there is a relatively new discipline called auto-ethnography where the writer, the auto-ethnographer, critically examines his or her own private world to produce understandings of personal experiences situated in culture. In auto-ethnographical studies the community or communities of practice to which the artist belongs can also be examined through participant observation and reflective writing (Bartleet & Ellis, 2009).

Music is rich in inter-related disciplines that may be tapped into for artistic research. These include acoustics, aesthetics, analysis, audio electronics, biomusicology, composition, computer science (music programming languages), creativity theory, criticism, ethnomusicology (music anthropology), music cognition, musicology, music theory, music therapy, organology, performance practice, psychoacoustics, and sound theory (including audio-visual interaction).

Areas of research in the humanities and social sciences involve methods and techniques that may be useful in artistic research. These include action research, discourse analysis, ethnography, phenomenology, semiotics, statistics and survey (questionnaire, interviewing, focus groups).

Other relevant disciplines from which methods may be derived include experimental science (development of new materials and processes), business (market research, audience research), cultural studies, demography, education, history, law, linguistics, mathematics, media studies, medicine, other artform disciplines (visual arts, creative writing, drama, dance, screen, architecture, etc.), politics, psychology and sociology.

We have here an indicative list of disciplines that may be applied in artistic research, but it should be noted that artistic research is commonly interdisciplinary. For example a project involving music composition, may encompass approaches derived from fields such as aesthetics, music theory, computer science, acoustics and psychoacoustics, to name but a few disciplines.

Artistic research is also characterized by what Barrett (2007) refers to as "emergent approaches" (p. 6): The outcomes of creative research are necessarily unpredictable. Strategies are not pre-determined but emerge and operate according to specific demands of action and movement in time.

Case Studies

The author has supervised ten artistic research PhD projects to completion. Most of these were in contemporary music practice but two were in visual arts and one in new media. To provide some idea of the typical approaches used by his students three of these projects are outlined below.

Project 1. Fred Cole's (2001) Creative Practices in Australian Techno and Other Electronica: A folio of original compositions and supporting documentation.

Fred Cole is a musician with a background in performance in classical music, rock music and jazz. His artistic practice also includes composition in a variety of styles, mainly produced in his state-of-the-art home studio. He became interested in electronic dance music through friends who were professional DJs. Cole's project developed in the following way. He attended local dance parties and collected all the Australian commercial releases of electronic dance music he could find. He developed a set of interview questions and interviewed 87 of the electronic dance music composers or producers who had issued these recordings. The interviews all took place in the studios of the artists in Australian major cities. The interview questions were centered around creative practice issues including perceptions of genres, electronic equipment and software configurations, compositional and performance techniques, musical training, creative influences, compositional collaboration, DJing, marketing strategies and audience responses. The data collected was processed using a grounded theory methodology and became a major part of the exegesis.

The knowledge gained about the Australian electronic dance music scene also fed into Cole's own creative practice. The centerpiece of his project was the composition and production of two CDs of electronic dance music (8 works, 93 minutes duration). Cole documented and reflected on his composition and production methods in the exegesis. The exegesis also included an appendix of Cole's critical responses to the 90 CDs of Australian electronic dance music CDs he had collected.

Project 2. Melissa Carey's (2007) Intermedia Frottage: Visual Representations of Music and Aural Representations of Image.
Melissa Carey is a composer with a strong interest in multimedia technologies. Unlike many of the performance or composition students who undertake artistic research at doctoral level Carey had a strong interest in cultural and media theory.

The artistic production component of Carey's thesis involved "methodical experimentation with available sound/image and image/sound conversion software" (she used applications called Phonogramme and Metasynth) and documentation of, and critical reflection on, the results of this experimental process (in the exegesis). The final presentation of the work was more akin to a visual arts artistic research project, taking the form of a solo exhibition in an art gallery. Carey exhibited the computer graphical elements printed onto canvasses and the associated audio elements were available to the viewer/auditor through headphones.

The exegesis also contained an extensive researched account of the history of visual representations of music and sound, including "graphic notations, physical models, sound inscription and computer simulations" and well as a substantive documentation of "theories relating to sound, image, and sound/image combinations" drawn from film theory, aural and visual perception theory and design theory.

Project 3. Peter Martin's (2008) Writing for guitar groups, with and without orchestra.
Peter Martin is a composer and guitarist with a background in popular music, jazz and media music. He also studied classical guitar in Spain for several years. Martin formed a guitar trio with university lecturer colleagues performing original music especially written for the trio. His project grew out of this performance and composition experience. The creative centerpiece of his doctoral project was a three movement concerto for three guitars and orchestra, but also it included works written by Martin for the trio. These works were presented as scores and recordings. The recordings of the trios were from commercially available CD releases; and the recording of the concerto was a MIDI realization of the

orchestral parts with Martin playing all three guitar parts as overdubs.

Martin's exegesis provides a history of the phenomenon of guitar groups and guitar concerti. The main focus of the study is on the techniques of writing for guitar ensemble and for guitar and orchestra. Martin draws on his own solutions to problems of dynamic balance and timbral differentiation, and also analyses works in the group and concerto repertoires from these and other perspectives. Although the research is focused on composition technique, it is also strongly grounded in performance practice methodology. In addition to the explication of technique issues Martin also provides musicological analyses of the all works in the submission in conjunction with reflection on the compositional process.

Conclusion

This paper expresses the view that there has been little written about artistic research in the field of music compared to other artistic disciplines. As a result, it is contended, musicians are generally more concerned in their creative and performance endeavors with the materials of music rather than the broader cultural narratives that are the feature of creative writing, visual arts and theatre arts. Some suggestions are made about approaches to the artistic research project exegesis drawing on methods used in music research but also more generally from arts, social sciences and science research.

Three case studies of doctoral research projects in the area of music composition are presented to illustrate typical approaches to the exegesis. The methods involved include analysis and reflection on the creative and performance processes and techniques of the work being produced, investigations into the history and theory of the field and fieldwork to gain insights into the work of practitioners engaged in the same field of artistic activity.

References

Balkema, A., & Slager, H. (Eds.) (2004). *Artistic research*. Amsterdam, Netherlands: Lier en Boog.

Barrett, E. (2007). Introduction. In E. Barrett & B. Bolt (Eds.) *Practice as research: Approaches to creative arts enquiry*. London, UK: I. B. Tauris & Co.

Bartleet, B., & Ellis, C. (Eds.) (2009). *Music autoethnographies*. Bowen Hills, Australia: Australian Academic Press.

Candy, L. (2006). *Practice based research: A guide*. Sydney, Australia: Creativity and Cognition Studios, UTS. Retrieved from http://www.creativityandcognition.com/resources/PBR%20Guide-1.1-2006.pdf

Krauth, N. (2002). The preface as exegesis. *TEXT*, 6(1), XX–XX. http://www.textjournal.com.au/april02/krauth.htm

Lundström, H. (2009). Email communication, July 17.

Schön, D. (1983). *The reflective practitioner: How professionals think in action*. New York, NY: Basic Books.

Smith, H., & Dean, R. (Eds.) (2009). *Practice-led research: Research-led practice in the creative arts*. Edinburgh, Scotland: University of Edinburgh Press.

The Right to Play: A Children's Composition Project in Timor-Leste (East Timor)

Gillian Howell
University of Melbourne (Australia)
howellgm@yahoo.com.au

Abstract

This paper describes a children's community music project in Timor-Leste (East Timor) that explored aspects of children's rights through composition and songwriting. It considers some of the challenges and rewards that can arise in post-colonial, post-conflict, developing countries, and describes the creative processes used to develop the music with the child participants. Written within the autoethnographic domain, the author-practitioner both reports on and interprets the project in its context and considers the potential of cultural projects to encourage new understanding of wider civil and political issues among participants and observers. 'The Right to Play' music project took place as part of the author's 4-month artist residency in Timor-Leste and was part of the town of Baucau's celebrations to mark International Human Rights Day in December 2010.

Keywords
Composition, songwriting, Timor-Leste (East Timor), music workshops, community music, children's rights

Introduction - Timor-Leste in context

Timor-Leste (East Timor) is one of the world's newest nations. For several centuries it was a far-flung Portuguese colony, prized for its sandalwood. Indonesia invaded the country in 1975, and remained in occupation for the next 24 years, ruling in an atmosphere of fear and resistance. The people of Timor-Leste voted for their independence in a 1999 referendum, but the Indonesian forces retreated with tremendous violence, causing a wave of bloodshed and terror to sweep the country, and leaving the small half-island of Timor-Leste with 70% of its economic and physical infrastructure destroyed (Chomsky, 2003; East Timor Government, 2008). Roads, powerlines, and buildings were torn apart and burned, three-quarters of the population was displaced, and a UN peacekeeping presence, and transitional administration came in as a result.

Twelve years on, Timor-Leste is slowly rebuilding itself; however, many challenges remain. The country is ranked 120 out of 169 countries in the U.N. Human Development Index – a comparative measure of life expectancy, literacy, education and standards of living – and it is estimated that 41 percent of the million-strong population live below the poverty line (UNHR, 2011). Health standards are very low, with more than 50% of the population without access to safe drinking water, 60% without adequate sanitation, and high rates of infant mortality. Education opportunities are limited, with only 25% of the population completing primary school education (UNDP, 2006).

Human Rights in Timor-Leste

During the years of Indonesian occupation, more than a quarter of the population was killed or died as a direct result of the occupation. An estimated 10,000 civilians were imprisoned and often tortured during the period. That brutal era has a "uniformly appalling human rights record" (Kingsbury & Leach, 2007, p. 1). Today, Timor-Leste's formal justice system remains fragile and severely limited in its capacity to serve the population (International Crisis Group, 2011; UNMIT, 2010a). There is a strong lack of trust and confidence in local security forces and justice systems among the general population.

Human rights education in East Timor is greatly needed, but has a long way to go before awareness and understanding translates into actions and upholding of justice across the general population. The UN Human Rights and Transitional Justice Section documents alleged human rights violations in East Timor, but also has a strong education agenda, running outreach activities and capacity-building workshops to raise awareness about human rights. Every year it supports activities around International Human Rights Day (UNMIT, 2010b). Also working towards greater understanding of human rights in East Timor is the non-government organization Ba Futuru, which has developed a comprehensive human rights education training manual for use with young people (James, 2006).

The Right to Play – Aims and Intentions

"The Right To Play" was a songwriting and composition project that took place in Baucau, Timor-Leste in December 2010 to mark International Human Rights Day and engage local children and adults in a creative, collaborative music process. It was the result of a partnership between an Australian composer/musician and a local community arts center and employed a small team of Timorese and Australian artists. Twenty-three children ages 9 to 13 years took part in the four-day project, and together composed three songs, celebrating and describing children's rights. The Right to Play took its name from Article 31 of the United Nations Convention of the Rights of the Child [UNCRC][1].

The project's aims were both educational and social. Firstly, the project aimed to engage a group of local children and artists in participatory and creative music processes. Music in Timorese schools aligns with a transmission-based approach dominated by teacher-talk and little student input (Quinn, 2009), while music-making in communities is frequently the domain of older youth and beyond. The Right to Play project would model an alternative approach to music-making for children.

Similarly, the Right To Play project aimed to offer a professional learning opportunity to the Timorese artists involved. The arts center had a well-established program of visual arts and dance workshops, but its musical offerings were limited. They were keen to develop new skills in music workshop leadership.

The decision to focus the songwriting and composing on human rights and children's

---

[1] "State Parties recognize the right of the child to rest and leisure, to engage in play and recreation activities appropriate to the age of the child, and to participate freely in cultural life and the arts."
Article 31, United Nations Convention on the Rights of the Child (1989)

rights responded to an interest expressed by community members, and the local UN Human Rights office. Linking to International Human Rights Day events was also seen as a way of giving The Right To Play project additional status and interest in the community.

Lastly, the Right To Play aimed to be an opportunity for cultural exchange between the Timorese and Australian artists. In particular, the Australian artists were keen to incorporate local music traditions into the composition work.

Methodology

This paper is a descriptive, interpretative account of The Right To Play project, written within the autoethnographic domain. It draws upon the field notes of the project leader (the author), video, audio and photographic footage.

Autoethnography places me as both informant and investigator alongside my role as project leader. It enables me to report the events that took place and challenges me to interpret them as objectively as possible. There are strong ethical arguments for the use of autoethnography in reports of projects taking place in developing and post-colonial settings, where true "informed consent" is questionable, given that research itself, and the ethics that surround it are Western constructs and not necessarily well-understood or relevant in traditional or developing societies (Cunningham & Jones, 2005; Tuhiwai Smith, 1999).

Challenges encountered

East Timor's current cultural context is complex — the legacies of colonialism, war, and occupation are compounded by the pressures of ongoing trauma, poverty, religion and underdevelopment. These legacies result in common characteristics or responses that are not 'cultural' or uniquely Timorese, but are "the consequences of what international actors have brought to Timor-Leste for 500 years and are intrinsic to 'Timorese identity'" (La'o Hamutuk, 2011, p. 2). These factors, along with Timor's vastly inadequate infrastructure and the level of financial poverty that the majority of local people experience, combine to make Timor a particularly challenging place for outsiders to work.

Differences in communication style were a factor in many of the challenging situations I encountered. My Australian preference for a direct approach was in contrast with the Timorese preference for "face-saving" indirect styles and meant that misunderstandings could persist without being brought to my attention. I did not always know what was going wrong until long after the event in question had passed.

I will share three challenges that arose in The Right To Play project in response to the complex cultural context of Timor-Leste; however, I can only offer *my* interpretations of these events, derived from informal conversations, my online journal, and autoethnographic recollection. Others present – Timorese and Australian – would have drawn different conclusions, based on their different points of view and cultural knowledge.

Language

Language can be a symbol or expression of power. During colonial times, or times of occupation, the language of the occupying power takes on greater status than the local vernacular, and is the language of decision-making and access (Drummond, 2005; Taylor-Leech, 2007). In Timor-Leste, since the time of the UN administration and presence of a sizeable contingent of foreign "development specialists", English has taken on some of this status.

In The Right To Play workshops, I undertook to speak Tetun, the national language of Timor-Leste in which I had rudimentary but progressing skills, with the knowledge that a senior member of the local creative team was a strong English speaker, able to take on a role as translator as required. This had been part of the initial planning and I assumed that it would be acceptable.

My assumption proved incorrect. While initially happy to work in tandem with me and translate ideas when necessary for the group, I later learned my skilled colleague was unhappy to be cast in a role of translator and felt it to be demeaning, especially during stressful moments in the workshops, and undermined his role as a project leader. I later learned that many multilingual Timorese professionals refuse to act as translators for their foreign colleagues, due to the perceived lesser status of the role. A more acceptable solution would have been for me to hire someone to act in the translator role on my behalf.

Gender and participation

Timor-Leste is still a very traditional society, and opportunities to participate in education, youth organizations, workplaces and social activities are dramatically different for girls and boys, especially outside of the capital Dili. Girls' movements are closely regulated by their family members, and they are often expected to attend to domestic duties while their male siblings are free to engage in a range of activities (Wigglesworth, 2007).

With this in mind, the arts center coordinator and I determined to recruit equal numbers of male and female participants for The Right To Play. We invited three primary schools in the town to nominate ten students each (five boys, five girls) to take part, and for this reason girls were well represented among the project participants. In some of my more informal workshops in other parts of Timor-Leste, female participants were much fewer in number, so the decision to specify gender parity at the outset in Baucau was important.

Leadership, partnership and capacity

The decision for the arts center team and I to work together had been mutual, proposed first over email and then confirmed when I arrived in Baucau. However, did we feel a mutual sense of ownership and leadership? I approached the partnership with the arts center much as I would approach any project with a cultural organizations in Australia – I, as the visiting artist, was there to lead the project, to contribute my talents and experiences, and to work collaboratively with the group in the realization of the project. The arts center coordinator, an experienced project leader in visual arts, would work alongside me in similarly collaborative way. We would learn from each other, but this was an opportunity for the arts center team to get some professional expertise and input from an outsider into directing creative music activities.

However, in a developing country context like Timor-Leste, where the emphasis for more than a decade has been on capacity-building of local people and organizations, "partnership" may be interpreted as meaning the visiting artist is there to help the local people realize a project, taking on a supportive, scaffolding role rather than one of artistic direction and leadership. This difference in how the project intentions and roles were understood created confusion and doubt for me. Was I imposing a project on the local creative team that they didn't really want to do, but were unwilling to admit this directly? Was I undermining the local people by taking a leadership role, even though this was a music workshop and I was the only musician in the group?

Later, I learned from the arts center coordinator was that he did not feel equal in the partnership and that his arts center's profile was too low in the project. For personal reasons he was absent for different periods of the workshop days, which further lessened his role and input. In hindsight, a more explicit unpacking of the roles and intentions of the partnership was required.

This issue is complex, and reflects the post-colonial, post-conflict legacy of conflicting relationships with foreigners. On the one hand, foreigners might represent help, protection, and the opportunity to have stability return to a community. On the other, there will be a frustration with the foreigner as the holder of power, the decision-maker and even cultural imperialist. Foreigners may unthinkingly take on the more authoritative position when working with local people, assuming that they know best.

Ultimately, any foreigner coming to undertake work – artistic or otherwise – in a developing country does so of his or her own choice. The onus must be on them to be sensitive to the cultural expectations of their host society in the context of their work. Local people may not reveal or offer these expectations at the outset, as the learned lack of agency that results from extreme poverty, civil instability, and foreign entities holding all the power often complicates their discussion.

Composition strategies

The Right To Play resulted in the creation of three original songs, each exploring an aspect of human rights and children's rights. The creative strategies evolved in response to the participants' ideas, local music resources, children's music experiences in the playground, and group discussions about human rights, guided by the Transformative Arts and Human Rights Education handbook (Ba Futuru, 2004).

The first song of the project came through awareness that children's rights begin from the moment a child is born, asking, "What does a new-born baby need from others to survive?" Lyrics emerged from the discussion, and melodic material was derived from the notion of 'first breath' – the children blew into short bamboo pieces of differing lengths, flute-style, and melodies evolved from the different pitches.

> *When you are born your mother and father cuddle and care for you*
>
> *They take you for vaccinations, and give you milk*
>
> *Everybody loves you.*
>
> *Lyrics from 'Moris' [Birth]*

The second song began with a discussion about why an education is important in a child's life. The group chanted the written responses rhythmically and a melody emerged. Each verse was bridged with percussion riffs, played on hand-drums, buckets and bamboo sticks.

> *To discover your capacity, and share it with others...*
>
> *When you learn to sing, you can give inspiration*
>
> *You can learn languages, study arts, and study doctrine to find salvation!*
>
> From 'Direitu atu edukasaun' [The Right to Education]

The third song explored a child's right to play and know their own culture, and was inspired by Timorese children's playground games. It was a rhythmic montage of traditional chants and patterns, nominated by the group. A blues-style finale song framed the chants.

> *All children have rights*
>
> *The right to play, the right to education, to good health*
>
> *The right to seek their own freedom*
>
> From 'Direitu atu toka' [The Right to Play]

The four-day project concluded with a public performance of the songs by the children, attended by members of the local community and media. The educational and social aims of the project were realised, and despite cross-cultural challenges along the way, it was considered by the leadership team to be a very successful outcome.

Conclusion – Considering Cultural Projects and Social Change

How much impact can a four-day music project have on one group of children's understanding of human rights and children's rights, or on the community members who attended the concert for International Human Rights Day? At the start of the project, children's responses to initial questions about human rights suggested scant knowledge and understanding, or perhaps shyness. By the end of the project, answers to the same questions were far more confident and forthcoming. The group wrote three songs that made general assertions about children's rights without going into detail or analysis. Thus, a change in the participants' confidence to express their knowledge and understanding occurred.

The project also modeled a democratic creative learning process in which the voices and opinions of the participants were sought, valued and empowered. Despite cultural differences, the creative team of leaders worked together collaboratively (albeit in the absence of the arts center coordinator for the latter half of the project) and demonstrated the way those differences could lead to new positive outcomes. The project model could be considered a manifestation of the importance and value of diverse voices within a community.

However, the sustainability of change resulting from a four-day music experience is questionable. Will these principles be reinforced or contradicted through the children's other life experiences? As the country strives toward transparent and accountable public and civil life, there are still large gaps between children's everyday experiences and the Constitutional ideal that states, "All citizens are equal before the law, shall exercise the same rights and be subject to the same duties" (Constitution of Timor-Leste, cited in UNMIT, 2010a, p. 6). The institutions of state within a democratic society that ensure citizens grow up with certain expectations of rights and responsibilities are still being built in Timor-Leste.

Aid organizations, development organizations, and individuals and governments from around the world have been providing assistance to Timor-Leste since 1999. Arts projects with a social change intention or social justice agenda are an emerging part of this assistance, with theatre projects and visual arts groups offering avenues for expression and learning for young people. However, at this stage, no data is available about the success of these projects, in particular in relation to stated intended outcomes of social or behavioral changes.

Ultimately, change starts with individuals. A good foundation for change comes with an increase in awareness and understanding, and this can be developed through engaging participatory activities that activate children's imaginations. The real, sustainable shifts in community that stem from these understandings into attitudinal changes, increased civic participation, actions and decisions require greater time to take root. Thus, this one small project *may* have played a very small part in generating dialogue or awareness among a group of children and their families in one part of this small emerging nation. More certain, is that the participants shared a positive, collaborative, creative endeavor that valued each person's contributions, introduced them to new music-making processes and people and worked positively within the capacities and resources of the community.

Acknowledgments
Thanks, appreciation and respect to Mario da Costa and the skilled, supportive team of artists at Afalyca Arts; Erminia Oliveira; Lorraine McBride; and Tony Hicks. My host organization in Timor-Leste was Many Hands International.

References
Ba Futuru. (2004). Transformative arts and human rights education handbook (children's version) [Electronic Version]. Retrieved from http://bafuturu.homestead.com/Publications.html.

Chomsky, N. (2003). *Radical priorities* (3rd ed.). Oakland, CA: AK Press.

Cunningham, S. J., & Jones, M. (2005). *Autoethnography: A tool for practice and education.* Paper presented at the CHINZ'05 - 6th ACM SIGCHI New Zealand chapter's International Conference on Computer-Human Interaction, New Zealand.

Drummond, J. (2005). Cultural diversity in music education: Why bother? In P. Shehan-Campbell, J. Drummond, P. Dunbar-Hall, K. Howard, H. Schippers, & T. Wiggins (Eds.), *Cultural diversity in music education: Directions and challenges for the 21st century* (pp. 1-11). Brisbane, Australia: Australian Academic Press.

East Timor Government. (2008). *Economy.* Retrieved 21 April 2011, from http://www.easttimorgovernment.com/economy.htm

International Crisis Group. (2011). *Timor-Leste: Reconciliation and return from Indonesia.* Retrieved from http://www.crisisgroup.org/en/regions/asia/south-east-asia/timor-leste/B122-timor-leste-reconciliation-and-return-from-indonesia.aspx

James, S. (2006). *Human rights education and transformation through the arts* [Electronic Version]. Retrieved from http://www.hurights.or.jp/english/education/human-rights-education/country-experiences/east-timor/

Kingsbury, D., & Leach, M. (Eds.). (2007). *East Timor: Beyond independence*. Melbourne, Australia: Monash University Press.

La'o Hamutuk, (2011). *Comments from La'o Hamutuk on the draft country chapter for Timor-Leste: 2011 survey for monitoring implementation of the fragile states principles*. Dili, Timor-Leste: La'o Hamutuk.

Quinn, M. (2009). *Using talk in classrooms: Constructing meaning.* Paper presented at the Understanding Timor-Leste Conference, Dili, Timor-Leste.

Taylor-Leech, K. (2007). Sustaining language policy and language rights: Where to from here? In D. Kingsbury & M. Leach (Eds.), *East Timor: Beyond independence* (pp. 239-250). Clayton, Australian: Monash University Press.

Tuhiwai Smith, L. (1999). *Decolonizing methodologies: Research and indigenous peoples*. London, UK: Zed Books.

UNDP. (2006). *The path out of poverty: Timor-Leste human development report.* Retrieved from http://planipolis.iiep.unesco.org/format_liste1_en.php?Chp2=Timor-Leste

UNHR. (2011). *Report on the rights of persons with disabilities in Timor-Leste*. Retrieved from http://unmit.unmissions.org/Default.aspx?tabid=156&ctl=Details&mid=456&ItemID=15055

UNMIT. (2010a). *Facing the future: Periodic report on human rights developments in Timor-Leste*. Retrieved from http://unmit.unmissions.org/Default.aspx?tabid=182

UNMIT. (2010b). *Press release - Human Rights Day 2010 celebrated around Timor-Leste*. Retrieved from http://unmit.unmissions.org/Default.aspx?tabid=156&ctl=Details&mid=2149&ItemID=11178

Wigglesworth, A. (2007). Young people in rural development. In D. Kingsbury & M. Leach (Eds.), *East Timor: Beyond independence* (pp. 51-64). Clayton, Australia: Monash University Press.

Educational reforms and the professionalization of teaching: The mention in music education

Julio Hurtado Llopis
Universitat de València
Valencia, Spain

julio.hurtado@uv.es

Abstract

The reform of the curriculum in the European Higher Education Area, known as the Bologna Process, involves structural changes to university degrees. The proposed Degree in Primary Education allows the student to choose an area of specialization, including the mention in music education. The organization of itineraries that lead to obtaining the mention in music education has to be sufficiently broad and common to all the universities in order to be recognized as such by the Education Authorities. The universities have the autonomy to design and offer the content of this specialization. The *Agencia Nacional de Evaluación de la Calidad y Acreditación*, Spain's National Agency of Quality Evaluation and Accreditation, decides whether the proposed degree should be approved so that it can be introduced, or whether it needs further adaptation in order to comply with the implicit and explicit requirements of the Bologna Process. This article describes the most important aspects of the process of establishing the curriculum for the University of Valencia's new degree, with special reference to those aspects that relate to specialization in music. A description of the methodology used to reach a consensus and design the course content of the new subjects included in that mention is also given.

Keywords
Music education, Bologna process, curriculum.

Modern society needs well-trained professionals in the field of education; teachers who are capable of innovation and of adapting their teaching practices to the rapid changes that are occurring in an increasingly globalized world. Music education, which in Spain has been included in the compulsory education system since 1990, is not exempt from this urgent need to improve the training of teachers. For this reason the initial training currently given to music teachers needs to give students the skills to develop their real educational role so that it can contribute to improving the status of the subject in primary schools.

Music teachers in primary schools have to possess very specific knowledge that is distinguished by the teaching tools they use. They do not have to emulate the music teacher in the conservatory. Their purpose is different. In this respect research is extending scientific knowledge of the discipline by contributing to the establishment of sounder epistemological foundations that support the educational theories. For this reason, university lecturers are expected to offer their students the best possible training. Martínez Bonafé (2004) proposes that, together with the characteristics of the structure of the work, the spaces and strategies of training, knowing how to teach is one of the core values around which professionalism is constructed. It is something that is developed within a context of knowledge and beliefs related with teaching.

This is a time of changes to the curriculum and reforms in the higher education systems of Europe. A change in the law does not bring with it a change in teaching practices if those concerned do not make it happen. Particularly when there is no consensus amongst university teaching staff on a conceptualization of knowing how to teach that might act as a key element in the processes of professionalization. This is probably because concepts of the educational and the pedagogical have been constructed from the traditional curricular split between theory and practice; between training for teaching children and training in the specialization; between initial and continuous training, etc. All this contributes to lack of clarity and consensus on the core and indispensable components required for developing the training process and professionalizing teachers of music education in primary schools. According to Paolo Freire (1997), by recognizing that they are also part of the learning process, trainee teachers must, right from the beginning of their training, be fully convinced that teaching does not consist of transferring knowledge, but of creating the possibility for it to be produced or constructed. The University of Valencia, like the other Spanish universities, has had to adapt its curricula to the requirements for inclusion in the Bologna Process launched by the European Union. These include the design and development of the curriculum of the music education mention being discussed in this article.

The new model aims to facilitate the mobility and exchange of students and graduates within the European Higher Education Area (EHEA). It also aims to adapt course content to meet society's new demands, which have arisen as a result of the changes being experienced by the so-called knowledge society. For this purpose a common qualification referred to as the Undergraduate or Graduate Degree that uses a credit system known as the European Credit Transfer and Accumulation System (ECTS) has been introduced. This implies a very important change in the configuration of university courses since the *licenciaturas* that were studied for five years and the *diplomaturas* that were studied for three have now disappeared and have been replaced by the four-year undergraduate degree course consisting of 240 ECTS (European Credit Transfer System) of which, in the case of the degree in primary education, between 30 and 60 can be devoted to the specializations now called mentions.

The hours of teaching practice have been increased considerably and, although the time devoted to theory is approximately the same, the aim is that students should be actively involved in their learning. In order to achieve this, the time and work necessary to achieve the skills and the targets proposed in the subjects is estimated. In this way it is hoped that lecturers will guide and assist learning by introducing methodologies that offer an alternative to the master class. To achieve these targets, as university lecturers at teacher training colleges we have to rethink teaching by constructing a new academic culture that will bring about change through reflection, innovation and the introduction of new teaching methods (Angulo 1994).

Project Objectives

This article describes the most important aspects of the process of discussing and reaching a consensus on the content to be included in the subjects that make up the music education mention in the University of Valencia's Degree in Primary Education.

In order to define these aspects of the curriculum, the groundwork undertaken included: 1. participating in the drafting the white paper coordinated by the Conference of Deans and Heads of Faculties of Education Science and Teacher Training Colleges; 2. becoming acquainted with the process of creating the European Higher Education Area (EHEA) published in Royal Decree 1393/2007; 3. analyzing Order ECI/3857/2007, of 27 December, establishing the requirements for the ratification of official university degrees that qualify their holders to exercise the profession of Primary Teacher; 4. reaching a consensus on the subjects that would have to be included in the music education mention; 5. distributing the 30 credits awarded to the music education mention amongst the various subjects agreed on; 6. developing the syllabus for each subject; 7. including the mention in the curriculum of the degree to be submitted to ANECA for ratification; and 8. preparing the teaching guide and syllabus for each subject.

Methodology

Collaborative action-research (A-R) methodology was used to enable the department's lecturers to reach decisions and draw up the new curriculum. This methodology is very appropriate for encouraging reflection and discussion, giving a voice to all those taking part and respecting their opinions and beliefs for the purpose of improving teaching practices (Elliott, 1994). It is associated with various qualitative concepts, which give greater priority to the direct interpretation of events (Guba and Lincoln, 1989) and in our case it can be adapted to the needs and characteristics of the work. By using theoretical tools that permit the use of A-R it is possible to resolve or respond to the problems raised by organizing seminars and "focus groups" in which all the members of the group can participate and contribute their knowledge.

In the search for answers, methods are investigated and reflected on, new actions are planned and carried out to improve and evaluate the intended and unintended consequences of these actions. The data are questioned with the aim of ensuring that evaluations are based on evidence, being reflected on at each stage in order to generate new plans, thus commencing the cycle or spiral that is characteristic of this methodology. Latorre (2003) provides a useful summary of action-research with a synthesis of the methodological principles on which we have based our collegiate work.

One of the great advantages of working in this way is that the proposals adopted by the group are usually better and more readily accepted than those imposed from outside, because the members of the group are those best acquainted with the problem and its possible solutions. Given the intrinsic difficulties of implementing a new curriculum and teachers' tendency to revert to old ways in certain activities, this way of working helped provide us with the organization and, above all, the opportunity to reflect, guaranteeing motivation and predisposing teachers to change the academic culture.

Results

I will now discuss some of the most important ideas in the process of analyzing the documents and actions adopted by the team entrusted with designing and developing the content of the new music education mention for the degree in primary education. Resolutions were adopted in the process of working through which we reached a consensus on certain key actions so that a new model of teaching methods could be implemented. We participated in the network of Spanish universities created by the Conference of Deans and Heads of Faculties of Education Science and Teacher Training Colleges in order to draw up the guidelines that are proposed in the White Paper. This work was evaluated in 2005 by the *Agencia Nacional de Evaluación de la Calidad y Acreditación* (ANECA), the National Agency of Evaluation of Quality and Accreditation. It was produced, by consensus, by the members of the group with the external participation of teaching professionals, starting by carrying out studies and considering practical cases, useful for designing a degree course that would meet the EHEA criteria and lead to the professionalization of teaching. The itineraries or mentions are the elective subjects leading to specialization in certain areas of knowledge. In principle the Spanish universities have to offer those that correspond to the special subjects on the old curriculum, including music education.

As a starting point, according to the data collected in the White Paper on Primary Education concerning the selection of a model of Primary Education studies compatible with most of the European models, the following conclusions can be extracted: a/ all countries have a specific qualification for Primary teachers, which usually allows for different specializations or training itineraries; these are usually different in different countries due to the characteristics of their curricula; b/ in the case of physical education and music education, teachers study their specialties in different academic institutions from those that train teachers, except in Spain.

During the training period, students studying for a degree in primary education have to acquire an understanding of everything related with education, which will qualify them to design, implement and evaluate teaching syllabi and actions; graduates will be able to work in the classroom with pupils aged from six to twelve years. These studies also include training in all the areas of knowledge that are taught in primary schools, their organizational principles and school management, as well a knowledge of the physical, emotional and intellectual development of primary children. In the primary stage, teachers will be responsible for teaching the usual subjects taught by class teachers as well as having specific teaching skills in one of the following specific areas: Physical education, Music education, a foreign language or Attention to Special Educational Needs. These specific skills are acquired via the itineraries or mentions that are the elective subjects leading to specialization in specific areas of knowledge. The Spanish universities are obliged to offer at least the mentions that correspond to the specializations offered under the previous curriculum.

The content proposed for degrees in primary education is structured around a balance between educational psychology (30%), training in the different areas of knowledge (40%) and teaching practice (30%). There is also a consensus on the need to devote a percentage of time to the various specializations. An end of course project also has to be submitted. This covers aspects related with the music education mention that will to be evaluated by a qualified panel. The degree in primary education offered by the University of Valencia is made up of: 60 credits awarded for the basic subjects; 99 for compulsory subjects (training in teaching and discipline); 45 credits for teaching practice in schools; 30 credits for elective subjects (which includes the music education mention) and 6 credits for the end of course project (ECI 2007).

Conclusions

The training of teachers specializing in music education for primary schools is included in the Degree in Primary Education. This conclusion was reached via the various mechanisms used for the design and approval of harmonization within the EHEA. With regard to specialization, Spain, Estonia and Poland, and to some extent Sweden, have continued to provide specialized training in physical education, art and foreign languages in different educational institutions or faculties, such as faculties of sports science and/or physical education, art education or fine arts, and languages. In the rest of the countries specialization is in most cases provided by post-graduate options. In the case of Physical Education and Music education, educational institutions that specialize in providing this training do exist, but in general the subjects that relate to these areas are given in all institutions; that is, a basic knowledge of physical education, art education and, in the vast majority, a foreign language are parts of the core curriculum.

The music education mention is offered in the University of Valencia's new undergraduate degree courses in primary education. This option consists of six elective subjects that the students concerned have to choose when they enroll for the third and fourth year. In third year, they have to take four subjects worth 4.5 ECTS credits each: music and information and communication technologies; listening to music; music and movement and teaching a musical instrument. In the fourth year they have to pass two subjects worth six credits each: Teaching music and voice training. This mention qualifies the primary teacher to teach music education in primary schools. Students wishing to take the itinerary of Specialist in Music education have to take a proficiency test, from which those who hold an intermediate grade or equivalent in music are exempt.

References

Agencia Nacional de Evaluación de la Calidad y Acreditación. (2005). *Título de grado en magisterio: [libro blanco]*. Madrid, Spain: Agencia Nacional de Evaluación de la Calidad y Acreditación.

Elliott, J. (1994). *La investigación-acción en educación*. Madrid, Spain: Morata.

Freire, P. (1997). *Pedagogia da Autonomia - Saberes necessários à prática educativa*. São Paulo, Brazil: Paz e Terra.

Guba, E. G., & Lincoln, Y. S. (1989). *Fourth generation evaluation*. Newbury Park, CA: Sage.

Latorre, A. (2003) *La investigación-acción: Conocer y cambiar la práctica educativa*. Barcelona, Spain: Graó.

Official Bulletin of State (1990, October 10). Law 1/1990: The general organisation of education system. *Author, 238*, 28927–28942. Madrid, Spain.

Martínez Bonafé, J. (2004): La crisis de la identidad profesional docente. *Cuadernos de pedagogía, 332*, 127–145.

Orden ECI/3857/2007, de 27 de diciembre, por la que se establecen los requisitos para la verificación de los títulos universitarios oficiales que habiliten para el ejercicio de la profesión de Maestro en Educación Primaria.

Real Decreto 1389/2007, de 29 de octubre, por el que se modifica el Real Decreto 1412/2000, de 21 de julio, de creación del Consejo de Política Exterior.

The Effectiveness of Loosening up Exercises Accompanied by Turkish Music on Adult Beginner Piano Students

Birsen Jelen
Gazi University (Turkey)
birsenka@yahoo.com

Burçin Uçaner
Gazi University (Turkey)
burcinucaner@yahoo.com

Abstract

The aim of this study is exhibiting the effectiveness of Turkish music accompanied loosening exercises on adult beginner piano students who suffer from pain, aches and cramps, also known as playing related musculoskeletal disorders (PRMD). Studies show that after personal and physical growth is completed, beginning to play an instrument can cause various physical problems. This study was conducted on piano students at Gazi University's Music Education Department. A sample of 18 volunteering piano students, who suffer from PRMD, was selected by random sampling. The students were taught the posture and loosening-up exercises and they were given a written and illustrated program to follow. At the beginning of each of the lectures for duration of 14 weeks, the instructors had the students do the exercises accompanied by music pieces that are used in Turkish music therapy. To make sure that the students do the exercises outside the class, they were checked frequently via e-mail, phone calls and in-person conversations. After 14 weeks, a survey was given on the intensity of PRMD of the students and the data were evaluated. The majority of the students stated that Turkish music accompanied loosening and posture exercises had positive effect on reducing PRMD and that they felt tranquil, relieved, calm, relaxed, loosened and happier in general.

Keywords
Piano education, Turkish music, music therapy, posture exercises, progressive loosening exercises.

Introduction

Education on various musical instruments is offered in most of the Turkish universities that train music teachers. Taking piano lessons are mandatory for all these music education students. Piano lessons are given for only one hour a week and students are expected to gain the necessary technical and musical abilities in this limited time. Students who are registered in music education schools generally start their piano education as an adult. Beginning to learn an instrument at such an age, after personal and physical growth is completed, could cause psychological and physical problems. Such physical problems include muscle cramps, focal dystonia, overuse syndrome, misuse syndrome, and RSI-repetitive strain (Öztürk, 2006).

Body posture (shoulders, arms, hands and fingers) should be used in a natural position to play an instrument without causing physical problems. The teacher should take into account each student's personal and physical dissimilarities especially while working with adult piano beginners. In order to prevent musculoskeletal injuries, daily practice should start with warming up all muscles and organs by stretching and loosening up exercises without the instrument. Attention should be given to arms and shoulders (Çimen, 2003).

Musicians can experience physical discomfort foe a variety of reasons such as, playing with the wrong technique, changing technique, not giving importance to exercise techniques, playing etudes and pieces that are not convenient to the level of technique, physical distortions, changing instructors frequently, increasing individual study hours and the instruments and tools that are used not being useful and qualified enough (Gençel, 2005; Uçaner & Öztürk, 2010).

According to Mark (2003), when a muscle contracts while playing an instrument, the opposing muscle is released and lengthened to permit movement. If the opposing muscle remains tense, then both muscles contract simultaneously. This inhibits movement and can cause injuries; repetition, excessive forcing of the piano keys is potentially injurious to the muscles, tendons and other sensitive structures of the body.

A literature survey shows that piano players are at the top of the list of instrumentalists who are most likely to suffer from injuries at one point of their careers. There is a long list of injured famous pianists such as Clara Schumann, Alexander Scriabin, Sergey Rachmaninoff, Wanda Landowska, Arthur Schnabel, Gary Graffman, Leon Fleisher, Glen Gould, Michel Beroff and many others. At some point in their careers, these pianists had to either cancel some of their concerts or tours, or change their concert programs or restrict their repertoire because they suffered injuries (Mark, 2003).

Literature Survey

At professional levels of performance, playing the piano is analogous to athletic performance in the intense level of demand and practice, emphasis on speed and accuracy, and stress of competition (Quarrier 1993; Rozmaryn 1993). Such high physical loads predispose professional level pianists to musculoskeletal disorders, as reflected by Manchester and Cayea's research which has shown piano to be associated with high rates of upper-extremity injuries in university-level performers (Manchester & Cayea, 1998).

Numerous terms have been used to describe musicians' musculoskeletal disorders, including "overuse syndrome," "repetitive strain injury," and "cumulative trauma disorder." As "playing" is the "work" of musicians, "playing-related musculoskeletal disorder" (PRMD) is an appropriate music-specific derivative of work-related musculoskeletal disorder" (Bragge et al., 2006). Zaza, Charles, and Muszynski (1998) defined PRMD as "...pain, weakness, lack of control, numbness, tingling, or other symptom that interfere with musicians' ability to play the instrument at the level he/she is accustomed to..." (p. 2014).

Uçaner and Öztürk (2010) investigated the effects of relaxation exercises accompanied by Turkish music on eliminating pains of violin and flute students. It was found out that more than 50% of the students that attended the study were suffering from musculoskeletal disorders. As a result of the study it was found that the music that students listened effected students' physical disorders in a positive way and had a refreshing, relaxing, and calming effect while letting them concentrate on the exercises.

In the light of existing literature and dealing with piano students who have PRMD at university level music education schools in Turkey, this study aimed to exhibit the effectiveness of the loosening exercises accompanied by Turkish music on adult beginner piano students who suffer from pain, aches and cramps as their main PRMD.

Experimental Process

The experiment lasted for 14 weeks. Posture and loosening exercises have been done with the students before each lecture. During the planning of the exercises, help from a physiotherapist has been taken. Exercises have been planned to last for 15 minutes. The sample was chosen by random sampling method at Gazi University's Music Education Department, among 18 volunteering piano students who have long-term pain, aches and cramps as their main PRMD.

Posture Exercises

Posture exercises are devoted to increasing the length of the spine. During this exercise, the front lobe of the hip bone should be lifted and the back lobe should be lowered; in other words, one should sit as perpendicular as possible. In order to obtain this position, one should have strong abs, strong hip muscles and thigh muscles. These exercises play an important role in preventing future scoliosis and jaw joint aches (Uçaner & Öztürk 2010; Akçalı, 2006; Güreser, 2003; Savaş, 2003).

Progressive Loosening

This technique has been developed by Jacobson in 1920's and has proved its success in decreasing the tension of the muscles. The progressive loosening technique involves the stretching and loosening of the muscle groups in the human body (Akçalı, 2006). After doing the posture exercises with the students, this technique proceeds as follows:

- The exercises were done in a quiet and dim room with Turkish music used in the therapies.
- Students were asked to sit in a chair in a comfortable way and close their eyes.
- Students were asked to tense their forehead, eye, shoulder, arm, hand, chest, back, leg and foot muscles one by one, count to 5 and loosen them.
- Students were asked to inhale deeply after loosening each muscle and exhale slowly.
- This procedure was repeated for muscles that were tense.
- Finally, students were asked to relax and concentrate on the music for a few minutes.
- To have students do these exercises outside the class, they were checked frequently via e-mail, phone calls and in-person conversations.

Questionnaire

In this section, the questionnaire given to the students during the pre-experiment period is evaluated. At the end of the experimental period, views from an expert on educational sciences, an expert on statistics and a music education expert were taken in order to prepare the questionnaire. The questionnaire had 3 parts: 1. students' personal information; 2. Questionnaire itself; and 3. open-ended question.

Findings and Interpretation

A total of 18 students, 11 girls and 7 boys, have attended the study. Twelve of these students were between the ages of 18-21 and the remaining six are between 22-25. Six students were freshmen, two were sophomores, five were juniors, and five seniors. Most ($n = 14$) of the students started playing the piano during high school, while three during college and only one student during preschool. Three students have been playing the piano for 1-3 years, 12 students for 4-6 years, and three students for more than 6 years.

Table 1. PRMD that the students encountered.

Body Parts	Pain f	%	Ache f	%	Cramp f	%	Total F	%
Right Shoulder	11	61.1	1	5.6	0	0	12	66.7
Left Shoulder	12	66.7	1	5.6	1	5.6	14	77.8
Right Arm	8	44.4	3	16.7	0	0	11	61.1
Left Arm	3	16.7	4	22.2	1	5,6	8	44.4
Right Wrist	6	33.3	6	33.3	0	0	12	66.7
Left Wrist	4	22.2	4	22.2	1	5,6	9	50.0
Right Arm	6	33.3	2	11.1	0	0	8	44.4
Left Elbow	2	11.1	4	22.2	0	0	6	33.3
Right Elbow	1	5.6	5	27.8	1	5,6	7	38.9
Left Hand	1	5.6	4	22.2	1	5,6	6	33.3
Right Hand Finger	1	5.6	3	16.7	0	0	4	22.2
Left Hand Finger	0	0	4	22.2	0	0	4	22.2
Back	14	77.8	1	5.6	0	0	15	83.3
Neck	15	83.3	0	0	0	0	15	83.3
Waist	5	27.8	0	0	0	0	5	27.8
Head Ache	2	11.1	0	0	0	0	2	11.1

Nearly all of the students suffered from back and neck pain, majority had right-left shoulder and right wrist pain, half of the students had left arm, left wrist and right elbow pain and ache. One third of the students had left elbow, right and left hand pain and ache, one fourth suffered from right and left hand finger pain and ache and only a very little percentage had wrist and head ache. Shortly, general PRMD was measured mostly as pain and aches; little bit discomfort was measured as cramps. The most pain was measured in the neck area and the least pain was measured in the right-left hand and fingers. Most of the aches were measured in the right hand wrist. Only one student complained from left shoulder and arm, left wrist and right hand cramps.

Loosening and Posture Exercises on Decreasing the PRMD of Students

Identical results have been obtained for the loosening and posture exercises. Eight of the students described the effect of loosening and posture exercises to be highly effective, six students thought the exercises had a mid-level effect, while two students described the exercises to have a partial effect, and two described them as having no effect.

Turkish Music on Decreasing the PRMD of the Students
Nearly half of the students ($n = 8$) felt that Turkish music were highly effective on decreasing their physical discomforts, one third ($n = 5$) felt the music had a mid- level effect, one fourth ($n = 4$) were partially effected and only one student was not affected.

Qualitative Findings and Interpretation
At the third part of the questionnaire students were asked to explain the effect of Turkish music. In this part of the study the data were content analyzed.

Nearly all the students stated that, parallel to the exercises, the effect of the music that they listened had relaxing, refreshing, tranquility and calming effect. In this section, some examples of the students' statements are given. Students are coded with the letter S and also the number of the questionnaire was shown.

> S1: Music and the exercises reminded me of meditation. I felt relaxed and liked the music.

> S2: Before playing piano I wasn't doing any exercises and this was making me feel tired after practicing. Now, because I do the exercises, I feel much more relaxed and vigorous during and after the lesson. Listening to the music had a huge effect on me. Doing the exercises with music accompaniment, I dreamed the places that make me happy and I forgot about stress. So I'm starting to play piano more readily than normal. And this is making me feel more successful.

> S4: While I listen to the music I feel calm and this makes me feel comfortable, so I don't tighten myself while playing piano.

> S6: Music and the exercises made the exhaustion of my body and mind go away. I did the exercises with pleasure. I felt ready for the lecture.

> S7: Music was the reason to leave myself relieved, I imagined myself in nature and this made me feel relaxed psychologically.

> S9: Music gave me happiness and peace, I felt relaxed and loosened.

S10: Thanks to the music that I heard, I cooled down and didn't feel tight as I normally do during the piano lessons. My body was much more relaxed and my back pain was reduced.

S12: The relaxation, tranquility and quietness that music gave me affected my body so that I felt softer and lighter.

S16: I let myself go by listening to music and doing the exercises. My neck and my back pain disappeared and all my muscles relaxed.

S18: When I play piano I always felt so stressful that I thought that I was never going to be successful but, having the music and the exercise together made me feel more comfortable and relaxed for the first time during the piano lesson. I let myself go.

Results and Suggestions

After 14 weeks, the majority of the students stated that Turkish music accompanied loosening and posture exercises had a positive effect on reducing PRMD and that they felt tranquil, relieved, calm, relaxed, loosened and happier in general. Loosening and posture exercises should be performed before daily piano practices and should be made part of the routine and should be turned into a habit. Educators and students in institutions that offer education on health problems related to playing instruments should be made conscious about the topic, and courses and conferences should be organized. Consultation from a physical therapy expert should be received before selecting an instrument. As in abroad, departments focused on musicians' health should be set up within institutions of health.

References

Akçalı, C. (2006). *Musculoskeletal disorders of double bass players and prevention methods for those disorders.* (Unpublished masters thesis). Yıldız Teknik University, Sosyal Bilimler Institute, İstanbul.

Bragge, P. Bialocerkowski, A., & McMeeken J. (2006). A systematic review of prevalence and risk factors associated with playing-related musculoskeletal disorders in Pianists. *Occupational Medicine, 56,* 28–38.

Çimen, G. (2003, October). *Physical disorders related to instrumental playing.* Paper presented at the 80th Year Turkish Republic Music Symposium, İnönü University, Malatya, Turkey.

Gençel, Ö. (2005), *Physical inconveniences that occur during the flute education in associations which train music teacher and its effects to the student success* (Unpublished masters thesis). Uludağ University, Sosyal Bilimler Institute, Bursa.

Güreser, G. (2003). Temporomandibular joint diseases. *Journal of Physical Medicine, 6,* 37–45.

Manchester, R. A., & Cayea, D. (1998). Instrument-specific rates of upper-extremity injuries in music students. *Medical Problems of Performing Artists, 13,* 19–25.

Mark, T. (2003). *Pianist's injuries: Movement retraining is the key to the recovery*. Retrieved from http://bodymap.org/main/?p=271

Öztürk, B. (2006). *The effect of videotaped microteaching technique on piano student's success* (Unpublished doctoral thesis). Ankara University, Turkey.

Quarrier, N. F. (1993). Performing arts medicine: The musical athlete. *Journal of Orthopaedic and Sports Physical Therapy, 17*, 90–95.

Rozmaryn, L. M. (1993). Upper extremity disorders in performing artists. *Maryland Medical Journal, 42*, 255–260.

Savaş, S. (2003). Conservative treatment of Skolyoun. *Journal of Süleyman Demirel University, 10*, 33–38.

Uçaner, B., & Öztürk, F. (2010, July). *Keman ve Flüt Öğrencilerinde Çalgı Çalmaya Bağlı Ağrıların Giderilmesinde Türk Müziği Eşliğinde Yapılan Gevşeme Egzersizlerinin Etkisi*. Proceedings of the 29th World Conference of the International Society for Music Education, Beijing, China.

Zaza, C., Charles, C., & Muszynski, A. (1998). The meaning of playing related musculoskeletal disorders to classical musicians. *Social Science & Medicine, 47*, 2013–2023

Place and Space: Celebrating South African Music across Two Continents

Dawn Joseph
Deakin University (Australia)

djoseph@deakin.edu.au

Rene Human
University of Pretoria (South Africa)

africamusic@mweb.co.za

Abstract

In this paper, the authors consider the notion of African music as a rich part of their own "place" and "space", as one is based in South Africa (Johannesburg) and the other in Australia (Melbourne). The authors explore the notion of African music as a way forward to negotiate such a "space" and "place" in a contemporary society. The teaching of African music by both authors, stated as lived experience in their various settings, has initiated and created a space for celebrating South African music as a way to transcend the social and cultural boundaries of place. This paper is located within the historical framework of post-colonialism, and touches on issues of objectivity, hegemony, representation of a culture and universal values. By using narrative reflection both authors provide a snapshot of their own teaching and learning, making a contribution to understanding the challenges they face regarding issues of culture, difference, otherness, re-contextualizing and authenticating their space and place. They find that the re-contextualization of African music is largely brought about by means of cultural dialogue, in a neutral space within cultures and between cultures. Likewise, the concerns and issues raised in this paper may be similar to those experienced by others teaching traditional African music in different countries. The authors, in their ongoing research into the teaching and learning of traditional African music, find that the creative engagement of different music and culture can foster a way forward for a place and space to celebrate South African music across two continents. This paper also addresses the issues of cultural authenticity as a redefined and renegotiated space when teaching and learning African music. Culture and music form an on-going and ever-changing practice that does not only interact with a changing society but also reflects it. Both authors approach authentic re-contextualization as a given and are constantly responsive to it through recognition, anticipation and monitoring of the process, keeping it as close to the original as possible. The authors continue to appreciate and respect the rich array of cultural and musical diversity they encounter.

Keywords
Traditional African music, culture, difference, otherness, re-contextualization, authenticity

Background

This paper situates itself across South Africa and Australia where both authors teach African music in their local settings in new places. The authors were both born and educated in South Africa. Their Bachelor of Music degrees strongly emphasized western classical music and pedagogy. Dawn (of Indian background) since 2001 has taught music at Unnamed University (Melbourne) in undergraduate and postgraduate courses. René (of Afrikaner background) lives in Johannesburg and since 2004, teaches the music honors course at the University of Unnamed. As current tertiary music educators, teaching students from a range of cultures, languages and ethnicities, the authors strongly feel that their teaching and thinking has to be inclusive. Both authors grew up at a time when "apartheid established a value system where European cultural manifestations were not only regarded as the most valuable but also as the only accepted" system (Thorsén, 1997, p. 9). In a new democratic South Africa and in a multicultural Australia, using the lens of a different genre, they stimulate new thinking and development while creating a space and place for traditional African music in their respective settings. Dawn continues to share her South African identity and culture with her Australian tertiary students through music. The state of Victoria where she now lives has representatives from more than 230 countries, speaking more than 200 languages and dialects, and following more than 120 religious faiths (Victorian Multicultural Commission, 2010). Amongst this vast array of people, many are refugees and immigrants from Africa. The 2006 census reports that there are 104,130 South African born people in Australia (Australian Government Department of Immigration and Citizenship, 2010), making them one of the fastest-growing groups immigrating to Australia, 8 per cent a year on average (Migrants changing our population mix: ABS, 2006). Given these statistics and the increasing number of Africans, she includes African music in her teaching and her ongoing research has shown it opens up her students' minds, ears and eyes to value, appreciate and respect difference and celebrate similarities (Joseph, 2002, 2004, 2005, 2006, 2009). In South Africa, René is within a far larger population of 49.9 million people boasting 11 official languages, many cultures and religious beliefs of which 79. 8% of the population is Christian. Africans make up 79.4% of the population as opposed to whites, 9.2 % (The South Africa: Fast facts, 2010). As part of political change towards a democratic South Africa in the 1990's, René, as white Afrikaner, had to re-negotiate her white South African identity, considering her own space in relation to her "collective African heritage". She, like Dawn, has learnt that being part of Africa and living in Africa, her identity not only "lie[s] on the borderline between oneself [herself] and the other", but, whether by birth or place, her roots are already "half someone else's" (Bakhtin, 1981, p. 293). Both authors accept their implied identity and align their musical identity and sense of being to Ntuli's (2001) notion of the endogenous, which refers to indigenous knowledge that is received from other sources outside the original. This received knowledge has become part of what Ntuli (2001) refers to as a collective heritage, which the authors include as part of cross-cultural representation and teaching of traditional African music.

In their educational settings both authors, through reflection and narrative enquiry, make a contribution towards the teaching and learning of African music and open up dialogue with others who may find themselves in similar situations. Both authors situate their tales as "lived experience" (Chase, 2005, p. 658). According to Craig (2009) "it is through living and telling ... teachers express their personal practical knowledge to themselves and to others" (p. 602). René, as an early career academic, and Dawn, as mid-career academic, find it necessary and most useful across two continents to converse (email, SMS, telephone conversations and regular onsite visits to Unnamed University by Dawn and keep in touch as they reflect on their practice. Buckley (2000) points out "reflection cannot occur without conversation" (p. 143). Within university settings, especially in that of teacher education programs, this aspect is a common goal of the profession (Greiman & Covington, 2007) and an important element of professional preparation (Russell, 2005). By communicating with each other they think aloud and reflect on "what they are doing and why, and reason through their problems so that their pedagogy is more appropriate to the given situation" (Loughran, 1996, p. 50). It is through such processes that they are able to "create meaning around practice" as they learn and converse with each other as it "provides a starting point for adapting [their] practice" (Young, 2006, p. 1).

In this paper, Authors1 and 2 use the discourse of narrative to tell their story. Beattie (2000) argues by using this approach: "[T]he knower is connected to the known, and knowledge–making is recognized as an active creative, interpretative process, in which the telling and retelling of one's story provides a framework for the construction of professional knowledge in teaching" (p. 5). Hence, the use of narrative enquiry allows their voices to be heard "as they speak of their concerns, issues and ways in which they experience their learning and their lives" (Beattie, 2000, p. 3). Theoretical Perspectives This research is located within the historical framework of post-colonialism. In cultural studies it is often categorized as post-modernism, and touches on issues of objectivity, hegemony, representation of a culture and universal values (Williams, 2001). In the context of this paper, these notions are to be found in the idea of authenticity ("art proper" and "false art"), which is then interlinked with notions of blackness, otherness and difference in the form of power, power relationships and all forms of power (Williams & Chrisman, 1994). The teaching of African music by two non-indigenous academics does not preclude them from teaching African music. Both authors contend that their identity by "conscious intention" has evolved along an intercultural continuum over time. They have reached a phase of adaptation, moving into an area where category boundaries have become more flexible and permeable. It can be argued that "what we teach" and "how we teach" can be influenced by our own culture, race and nationality. In a previous paper they argue that as South Africans, they do present an authentic experience for their tertiary students and choral singers (Joseph & Human, 2009). Performing music within its "original" setting while staying close to its cultural roots, even when travelling "outside of its culture of origin", as experienced by both authors, is not only possible but acceptable. Music requires "no visa" *per se;* it will continue to travel and be shared in different contexts where pedagogical practice considers teacher, learner and knowledge. With regards to "re-contextualized authenticity", a cultural studies approach upholds the culturally autonomous meanings of the music as practiced in the original culture (Campbell, 2004; Dunbar-Hall, 2005). It also upholds an understanding of the culturally autonomous meanings of the host culture and the discrepancies that may arise in engagement with difference. The original culture as well as the host culture should be considered. In agreement with Bhabha's (1994) Third Space theory (1994), and with regards to the understanding, appreciation and performance of the original culture when re-contextualized into the host culture, the authors, from their experience, suggest that the process should take place through cultural dialogue in a neutral space found *between* differing cultures. This space should be devoid of bias, political and hegemonic issues. Values and differences should be clarified for the benefit of both cultures involved. Both authors approach authentic re-contextualization as a given and are constantly responsive to it through recognition, anticipation and monitoring of the process, keeping it as close to the original as possible.

In their various settings they provide a "space" for traditional African music *per se* to transcend social and cultural boundaries - "music knows no boundaries" (Pohjola, 1993, p. 112). To be able to move between different cultures, a person has to know exactly where he/she comes from. One must first negotiate one's own identity, understand what the boundaries in one's own culture are, and where these boundaries are located, before addressing difference in other cultures (Bhabha, 1994, p. 28). As music educators, we do not take an anthropological or an ethnomusicological approach, rather, we position our paper as a "music as culture approach" and as "a way of clarifying the relationship between music education and culture" (Dunbar-Hall, 2005, p. 1). A cultural approach towards music education implies that to teach different types of musics one also has to teach the historical, social and political contexts in which they exist. Like many cultures in the world, traditional South African choral music Lortat-Jacob (2006) confirms that one is not just "producing notes and melodies" (p. 91) but rather learning of people's lives and their history. In their music teaching they acknowledge that music is "both performance and story" (Frith, 2002, p. 109). Creating and teaching African music within a specific cultural framework of time and space plays an important part in its transmission.

From such a perspective, everything said should be understood in context: whatever one says implies how one is positioned (Hall, 1994). Taking into consideration both authors' positions and their current dilemma of contextualizing cultural identity in a globalized world where concepts of displacement, Diaspora and "perpetual wanderings" have become buzz words, Gupta (2010) argued that "one has to be comfortable with the notion that one has one's own cultural identity and doesn't necessarily have to be at home… we are forced to travel, just because of what is going on around us" (p. 25). As cultural identities have a history, it is a process that continues to be constituted from within and not outside our representation. Hence, culture and music form an on-going and ever-changing practice that does not only interact with a changing society but also reflects it. It is part of the global world in which we live and to which we must adapt. The authors strongly believe that, by teaching from a mono-cultural perspective within a western paradigm, "we do our students a disservice when we prepare them to live in a society that no longer exists" (Nieto, 1992, p. 281).

Dawn's Narrative in Australia
The demographics of classrooms have changed in Melbourne, and as a teacher educator Dawn needs to adapt as well as adopt "a more critical multicultural approach to their [her] practice to meet the challenges posed both by societal diversity and the system in which they [she] work[s]" (Hagan & McGlynn, 2004, p. 245). She, like Merton (2011), believes that "all identities and differences are seen as being worthy of affirmation" (p. 24) and the notion of being inclusive of other music like that of Africa can be seen as "celebratory and positive" (Fraser, 1997, p. 182). Dawn has widely written on her teaching of African music in previous papers (Joseph, 2003, 2004, 2006 & 2009) where she argues that African music can be seen as a pedagogy that can be participatory and inclusive. Working at a university

with increasing numbers of international students and students of migrant parents, the teaching of another music like that of Africa "will enable minority students to maintain their heritage culture" (Mansouri, Jenkins, Leach, & Walsh, 2009, p. 11). At her campus there is a large cohort of Zimbabwean students, which she has taught in her music elective unit: Discovering music A. This unit focuses on traditional and contemporary African music. Like her fellow African students, Joseph is a "minority" academic from Africa. Through the teaching and learning of African music she creates spaces for students to think of diverse ways to understand "others". The discourse of "we are all the same", denies the possibility that there are "different knowledge and values systems that stand in contrast to those held by the hegemonic cultural group" (Allard, 2006, p. 326). In the case of music, the hegemonic ideal is normally that of western classical music and Joseph, like Human, provides an inclusive curriculum where traditional African music is also celebrated.

René's Narrative in South Africa
René, like Dawn, is similarly confronted with the issues of cross-culturalism, intercultural understanding, acknowledgement of "other", re-contextualizing authenticity and negotiating across cultural borders. Although the Choral Direction Honours course she teaches is based on a western educational perspective, it is mostly taught within a cross-cultural context to black students from other African states (e.g. Botswana, Nigeria and Kenya) as well as black and white students from South Africa. In current Ph.D. research, René is formulating generic cross-cultural standards for African musical arts assessment, adhering to a global need for formalization of these structures, to make it accessible for international educational settings. The creation of new cross-cultural spaces, René strongly believes, is neutral: here no single hegemonic influence should be dominant, nor minority, cultures marginalized. In such spaces misunderstandings between different cultures are minimized as "each generation must renew the commitment to diversity" (Welch, 2010, p. 131). Both authors therefore accentuate the importance of creating neutral spaces in their environments where the practicing and teaching of traditional African music can take place. Rene finds in her teaching that different cultural, linguistic and ethnic voices are able to engage, explore and experience music making where meaning eventually finds a place. Dunbar-Hall (2005) confirmed that music's location and its original purpose may change and be reshaped through cultural interaction and the process of re-contextualization and that new meanings and/or aesthetic positions can be awarded. In such settings newness of musical meaning finds a place for both authors.

Concluding Remarks

Although René is a white Afrikaner and Dawn is Indian, they contradict Allard's (2006) finding that "so many teachers and teacher educators are 'white' and middle class, they are likely to have had few experiences working with people of different 'race' or cultural heritage" (p. 327). Their experience of African music, living and working amongst different cultural, racial and linguistic groups has strengthened the notion of being inclusive, moving away from traditionally hegemonic western perspectives on music education. Rather, they create a place and space for traditional African music to be celebrated as part of the rich and diverse cultures they interact with. The authors agree with Schippers (2005) that the "re-rooting" of musical traditions in new cultural settings challenges the idea that (particularly world) music should always be experienced in its original context. Many musics travel remarkably well from one context to another, and this should be taken into account when creating situations in which music is taught and learned.

As cross-cultural music education becomes a global phenomenon (Borg, 2007; McCarthy, 2009; Omolo-Ongati, 2005; Schippers, 2005), educators are charged to reconsider their response to the reality and existence of culturally diverse music. Notions of achieving cross-cultural learning and teaching, of understanding 'other' cultures and of developing universal approaches towards teaching, learning and assessment, are eminent. By celebrating South African (African) music across two continents, both authors have "an appreciation of and respect for cultural diversity; and a willingness to teach in ways that challenge existing inequalities" (Villegas & Lucas, 2002, p. 177).

References

Allard, A. (2006). 'A bit of a chameleon act': A case study of one teacher's understanding of diversity. *European Journal of Teacher Education, 29*(3), 319–340.

Australian Government Department of Immigration and Citizenship (2010): "Community Information Summary." Retrieved from http://bit.ly/LTSUmq

Bakhtin, M. M. (1981). *The dialogic imagination: Four essays by M. M. Bakhtin*. M. Holquist (Ed.). C. Emerson & M. Holquist (Translators). Austin, TX: University of Texas.

Beattie, M. (2000). Narratives of professional learning: Becoming a teacher and learning to teach. *Journal of Educational Enquiry, 1*(2), 1-23. Retrieved from http://www.literacy.unisa.edu.au/jee/Papers/JEEPaper6.pdf

Bhabha, H. (1994). The Location of Culture. London: Routledge.

Borg, K. (2007). Assessment for learning creative subjects. P. Ericxon & H. Örtegren (Special Issue Eds.). *Journal of Research in Teacher Education. 2*, 81–93. Umeå, Sweden: University of Umeå.

Buckley, A. (2000). Multicultural reflection. *Journal of Teacher Education, 51*, 143–148.

Campbell, P. S. (2004). *Teaching music globally: Experiencing music, expressing culture*. New York, NY: Oxford University Press.

Chase, S. E. (2005). Narrative inquiry: Multiple lenses, approaches, voices. In N. K. Denzin & Y.S. Lincoln (Eds), *The SAGE handbook of quantitative research* (pp. 651–679). New York, NY: Sage.

Craig, C. J. (2009). Research in the midst of organized school reform: Versions of teacher community in tension. *American Educational Research Journal, 46*, 598–619.

Dunbar-Hall, P. (2005). Training, community and systemic music education: The aesthetics of Balinese music in different pedagogic settings. In P. S. Campbell & J. Drummond (Eds.), *Cultural diversity in music education: Directions and challenges for the 21st century* (pp. 125- 132). Brisbane, Australia: Australian Academic Press.

Fraser, N. (1997). Justice Interrupts: Critical reflections on the "post socialist condition". New York, NY & London, UK: Routledge.

Frith, S. (2002). Music and identity. In S. Hall & P. Du Gay (Eds.), *Questions of cultural identity* (pp. 108–27). London, UK: Sage.

Greiman, B. C., & Covington, H. K. (2007). Reflective thinking and journal writing: Examining student teachers' perceptions of preferred reflective modality, journal writing outcomes, and journal structure. *Career and Technical Education Research*, 32(2). Retrieved from http://bit.ly/PasrHL

Gupta, S. (2010, May-June). An interview, a story and three poems. *Muse India: A Literary e-Journal, 31,* 25.

Hagan, M., & McGlynn, C. (2004). Moving barriers: Promoting learning for diversity in initial teacher education. *Journal of Intercultural Education, 15*(4), 243-252.

Hall, S. (1994). Cultural identity and diaspora. In P. Williams & L. Chrisman (Eds.), *Colonial discourse and post-colonial theory* (pp. 392–403). New York, NY: Columbia University Press.

Joseph, D. (2002). Umoja: Teaching African music to generalist teacher education students. In Callaghan, Jean and Rosevear, Jennifer (Eds), *Research Matters: Linking Outcomes with Practice. Proceedings of the XXIVth annual conference* (pp. 86-98), Melbourne: Australian Association for Research in Music Education (AARME)

Joseph, D. (2003). An African music odyssey: Introducing a cross-cultural music curriculum to Australian primary teacher education students. *Music Education International, 2,* 98–111.

Joseph, D. (2004). Smaller steps into longer journeys: experiencing African music and expressing culture. In Chaseling, Marilyn (Eds), *AARME 2004: Proceedings of the XXVIth Australian Association for Research in Music Education Annual Conference* (pp. 216-225), Melbourne: AARME.

Joseph, D. (2005). Travelling drum with different beats: experiencing African music and culture in Australian teacher education. *Teacher Development: An International Journal of Teachers' Professional Development, 9,* 287-300.

Joseph, D. (2006). Cross- and intercultural engagement: A case study in self- reflection and finding meaning. In P. Burnard & S. Hennessy (Eds.), *Reflective practice in arts education* (pp. 149–158). Netherlands: Springer.

Joseph, D. (2009). Masakhane: Musical understanding in African music. In W. Baker (Ed.), *ASME 2009: Proceedings of the XVIIth National Conference,* (pp. 96-102). Tasmania, Australia: ASME.

Joseph, D., & Human, R. (2009). African music: Negotiating a space in contemporary society. *Journal of International Intercultural Education, 20*(4), 359-370.

Lortat-Jacob, B. (2006). Concord and discord: Singing together in a Sardinian brotherhood. In K. Ahlquist (Ed.), *Chorus and Community* (pp. 87– 110). Urbana, Il & Chicago, IL: University of Illinois Press.

Loughran, J. J. (1996). Developing reflective practice: Learning about teaching and learning through modeling. London, UK: Falmer Press.

Mansouri, F., Jenkins, L., Leach, M., & Walsh, L. (2009). *Building bridges: Creating a culture of diversity.* Victoria, Australia: Melbourne University Publishing.

Merton, J. M. (2011). *Critical multicultural teacher education: Identity and difference in New Zealand* (Unpublished doctoral thesis). Deakin University, Melbourne, Australia.

McCarthy, M. (2009). Rethinking "music" in the context of education. In T.A. Regelski & T. J. Gates, (Eds.), *Music education for changing times: Guiding visions for practice* (pp. 29–37). New York, NY: Springer Publishers.

Migrants changing our population mix: ABS (2006). Retrieved 16, November 2006, from, http://bit.ly/MYkd2r

Nieto, S. (1992). *Affirming diversity: The sociopolitical context of multicultural education.* White Plains, NY: Longman.

Ntuli, P. (2001, August). *Cultural hegemony and the re-investigation of the indigenous knowledge systems.* A paper presented at the Apex Art Conference, Rio de Janiero, Brazil. Retrieved from http:// www.apexart.org/conference/ntuli.htm

Omolo-Ongati, R. (2005). Prospects and challenges of teaching and learning musics of the world's cultures: An African perspective. In P. Campbell, J. Drummond, P. Dunbar-Hall, K. Howard, H. Schippers & T. Wiggins (Eds.), *Cultural diversity in music education: Directions and challenges for the 21st Century* (pp. 59–68). Brisbane, Australia: Australian Academic Press.

Pohjola, E. (1993) *The Tapiola sound.* Fort Lauderdale, FL: Walton Press.

Russell, T. (2005). Can reflective practice be taught? *Reflective Practice, 6,* 199–204. Retrieved from http://www.metapress.com/media/2FA16892CG$QQVBA5J2Q/Co

Schippers, H. (2005). Taking distance and getting up close: The seven- continuum transmission model (SCTM). In P. S. Campbell, J. Drummond, P. Dunbar- Hall, K. Howard, H. Schippers & T. Wiggins (Eds.), *Cultural diversity in music education: Directions and challenges for the 21st century* (pp. 29–34). Brisbane, Australia: Australian Academic Press.

The South Africa: Fast facts (2010). Retrieved from http://bit.ly/ZB6z1

Thorsén, S.M. (1997). *Music education in South Africa: Striving for unity and diversity.* Retrieved from http://bit.ly/L0LCCn

Victorian Multicultural Commission (2010). *The education kit.* Retrieved from http://bit.ly/MV8bYQ

Villegas, A. M. & Lucas, T. (2002). Educating culturally responsive teachers: A coherent approach. Albany, New York: State University of New York Press.

Welch, A. (2010). Cultural difference and identity. In R. Connell, C. Campbell, M. Vickers, A. Welch, D. Foley, N. Bagnall, & D. Hays (Eds.), *Education, change and society* (pp. 130–167). South Melbourne, Australia: Oxford University Press.

Williams, A. (2001). *Constructing musicology.* Ashgate, UK: Aldershot. Williams, P., & Chrisman, L. (Eds.). (1994). *Colonial discourse/post-colonial theory: A reader.* Columbia, UK: Columbia University Press.

Young, R. (2006). Insights for programme leaders from a review of research into the use of 'reflective practice' on programmes for new academic staff. *The Higher Education Academy.* Retrieved May 31, 2010, from, http://bit.ly/LoQYsw

Surgery or Studio: Music Teaching-learning in a Regional Conservatorium, NSW, Australia

Christopher Klopper
Griffith University (Australia)
c.klopper@griffith.edu.au

Bianca Power
Charles Sturt University (Australia)
b.power@griffith.edu.au

Abstract

This study documents and analyzes the environment where music education happens in a regional Conservatorium in New South Wales, Australia. The study aimed to gain insight into the structure, nature and professional practice of a regional conservatorium, and identify innovative pedagogical possibilities. An ethnographic case study was undertaken over one year, with intensity ranging from weeklong immersion schedules to occasional short-term observation of activities. Schwab's (1969) commonplaces of schooling (Milieu, subject matter, students and teachers) were applied as *apriori* themes, providing a scaffold for preliminary classification and further exploration of the data. Empirical themes were identified as they emerged through data analysis, and subsequently applied. A dominant finding of the study underscores that relationship is at the heart of curriculum transfer in the music studio.

Keywords
Regional conservatorium, professional practice, teaching-learning music, commonplaces of schooling, ethnographic case study

Introduction

Regional Conservatoriums of Music New South Wales (NSW), Australia are unique in that they are not associated with a tertiary institution and are part-funded by The NSW Department of Education and Training. No other Australian state or territory funds or partially funds non-tertiary conservatoriums located in regional areas. Regional Conservatorium teach across wide geographical areas requiring specialist teachers to travel vast distances in order to provide students in outlying communities, villages and cities with access to them. Despite these continued efforts very little systematic inquiry has been directed toward music studios, especially those outside the auspices of a sheltering institution such as a university or metropolitan conservatorium. This study documented and analyzed the environment where music education happens in a regional Conservatorium in New South

Wales, Australia. The study aimed to: gain insight into the structure, nature and professional practice of a regional conservatorium; and identify innovative pedagogical possibilities.

Review of Literature

NSW Regional Conservatoriums are most often the principal provider of music education services for their region by servicing schools, individuals, and the wider community through specialist instrumental and vocal training with emphasis on the music education of school-aged students and curriculum support for schools. Music learning in studio contexts remains largely outside the realm of curricular review or pedagogical scrutiny (Montemayor, 2008). Discussing provision of music education in private studios, Thompson (1983) and Glaros (2006) assert the need for innovative and motivational methods to hold the interests of students, and the role of studio teachers in "keeping with the times."

The teacher-student relationship has been seen as crucial in determining the level of expertise a pupil is able to acquire (Hallam, 1998). Lierse (2007b) identified teacher-student relationship as an important factor in developing the whole student. The necessity of this relationship changing as students mature and move through the stages of learning has also been identified (Csikszentmihalyi, Rathmunde, & Whalen, 1993; Davidson, Moore, Sloboda, & Howe, 1998; Lierse, 2007b; Pitts, Davidson, & McPherson, 2000). Additionally, Creech and Hallam (2009) assert the potential of parent-teacher relationships to enhance the outcomes for students, teachers, and parents alike.

The music studio setting is often not perceived as a community due to the primarily individualized nature of instruction (Lierse, 2007b). Peer influence and interaction is a key factor in the sense of "community" in the music studio, particularly among adolescent students (Barr, 2007; Keeler, 2011; Lierse, 2007b; Montemayor, 2008). The importance of preparing students for musical life beyond the private studio through fundamental guidance on instrumental teaching; and opportunities for ensemble music making was confirmed in the literature (Ford, 2009; Keeler, 2011; Mahamuti, 2009).

Bridges (1988) conceptualized private studio teaching as the "backbone" of Australian music education, acknowledging "many children and older students owe their personal musical development primarily to studio teachers who give individual lessons" (p. 49). Despite its fundamentality to music education in the Australian culture, the private music studio environment is a neglected area of research in music education (Lierse, 2007a).

Method

This ethnographic case study relied heavily on fieldwork, with intensity ranging from weeklong immersion schedules to occasional short-term observation of activities. Observations, semi-structured interviews with the Executive Director and teaching and non-teaching staff ($n=5$), and informal interviews with students ($n=20$) and parents/caregivers ($n=5$) were conducted.

Schwab's (1969) commonplaces of schooling (Milieu, subject matter, students and teachers) were applied as *apriori* (deductive, pre-determined) themes, providing a scaffold for preliminary classification and further exploration of the data. Empirical (inductive) themes were identified as they emerged through data analysis, and subsequently applied.

Results and discussion

Milieu
Milieu refers to the context or setting in which the regional conservatorium exists. The components include:

Governance, Management, Finance and Partnerships
The Conservatorium is located in the West Wing of the Court House. The Court House is a grand architectural work built of sandstone and is strategically central and commanding in this regional city of NSW. There appeared to be a great sense of industry about the Conservatorium, which on closer examination revealed the happenings to be that of the Court House and not the West Wing where the Conservatorium is located. Attendance at the Conservatorium is with purpose. That is to receive tuition. People attend to gain a service for which they pay, and it appears that this dominates and overrides the sense of relationship and community. I later learned that there is no central place to congregate, to connect, which contributes to the perceived lack of relationship and community. "*There's also no room to loiter here. You know, the foyer… you see how big that is! You're lucky to get two people in there*" (Interviewee). Having spent numerous days and hours immersed in this community it reminded me of a doctors' surgery. There is an overall practice with individual practitioners utilizing the facilities. Their patients (students) come, present symptoms (rehearse), receive diagnosis (commentary) and are presented with a script (invoice). The General Practitioner, or in this case the Music Teacher, does not take responsibility for the administration of the practice. The administration office collects the fees and administers payments to the teachers.

Due to the large number of teaching staff teaching at various times during the day and week, and in a range of available venues within the West Wing, there is little opportunity for all staff to be together. This was particularly noticeable while sitting in the staff common room. I asked of the teachers: "*So there's no formal mechanisms at this institution to allow for collaboration and sharing of ideas between staff?*" and the repeated response was "*Not that I'm involved in, not that I know of*". One of the teachers commented: "*Well, I suppose we have to communicate with the administration staff here, even if it's only, you know, once a fortnight to get paid*" (Teacher), highlighting the surgery transaction mind-set and not one of relation.

Opportunities for music instruction and related activities
In the Strategic Plan 2006-2009 (Mitchell Conservatorium Inc., 2009b), the Conservatorium asserted to provide students with: "professional music teachers, early childhood music learning and enjoyment, other school age and adult music learning and enjoyment and lifetime opportunities for music development" (p. 2). On an information pamphlet (Mitchell Conservatorium Inc., 2009a), the following activities were listed: Individual tuition, group tuition (various ensembles have been listed), early childhood music, music therapy, Alexander technique and instrument hire.

The conservatorium offers a service to regional, rural and remote NSW schools that may not otherwise have access to music education through supporting music specialists to travel to the schools. This program is primarily music focused but affords the freedom to tailor the program to what the schools want, whether they want the dance, movement, or a bit of drama thrown in there as well. This is an illustration of the Conservatorium going to the community as opposed to the community coming in and becoming organically a sense of "community".

Parents
A few of the teachers encouraged parents being actively involved in their children's music. Parent involvement reinforces the child's music learning and concretizes the relationship, and the value of what they're doing. The relationship automatically changes, when parent and student are side-by-side in a classroom. Suddenly the child is not just practicing in isolation, and getting lost, but a musical interaction has been forged. This musical interaction is between a parent and a child and the teacher "*it's a …a pleasant social event and it helps to facilitate the situation*" (Teacher).

Subject matter
Subject matter constitutes the movements and ideas that focus on what is taught and learned in the regional conservatorium.

Standards
Currently there are no set standards, syllabus or curriculum followed. Pre-established curricula such as AMEB, Kodaly, Suzuki and NSW Creative Arts syllabus are currently used. This provides opportunity for these curricula to be adapted to meet the needs of the teacher and student, placing responsibility firmly on the teacher to establish and develop a curriculum based on his/her own knowledge and experiences.

Core knowledge
A significant theme was the perceived need to prepare students for a life beyond the conservatorium. Teachers spoke about "*trying to encourage people to play music for life, to keep playing*" (Teacher). Not just as a performer but for life: "*If you can cooperate during a piece of music you've probably got a good chance of being able to cooperate in other situations as well*" (Teacher).

Assessment
Formal assessment is only offered if a student elects to participate in grading systems (AMEB, Trinity, RSCM): "*I'm running along the lines of that grade system, so I know where they're up to as far as ability wise goes*" (Teacher*).*

The conservatorium requires all teachers to provide a progress report to parents biannually. There is no template for this report and it is up to the teacher to offer an assessment of the student's progress. When discussing the effectiveness of this reporting to parents a teacher commented: "*I think the reports are somewhat superfluous if you had a lot to do with the parents, but you still have to do the, the formality of it and all this kind of thing*".

Students
In considering Schwab's third commonplace of schooling, students, trends and issues are related to those for whom the regional conservatorium exists.

Recruitment of students
Two main modes of recruitment occur through either active recruitment or positive peer pressure. Not only is it challenging to find a medium that connects with all potential students, but also the same difficulty is experienced when advertising concerts that in turn would profile the organization.

A current strong mode of recruitment is the in-school-testing program. The format has changed over time to be more of a demonstration than a testing, followed by instrumental tryouts. The outcome is hoped to be the same, which is that students go home and say, "*Mummy, Mummy I want to learn the flute, send the form back in*".

Student expectations and engagement
Students expressed the importance of "keeping it fun" during lessons and the need for teachers to consider students' other obligations such as sport when offering ensemble performance opportunities. A further consideration is of children who live in rural areas and need to travel to get to town. This adds another dimension to be understood by the teacher and accommodated.

Child protection
For many of the teachers, the current physical environment they teach in does not comply with child protection requirements. One teacher felt strongly about this and described his practice: "*I leave my door open whenever I teach, or I have ... if I have a parent in there. When I teach I have my windows widely open or the blinds ... I don't teach behind blinds, that sort of thing*". Challenges of occupational health and safety, duty of care and child protection are underpinned by a Code of Conduct which aims to clarify the conduct expected in the performance of all duties and a guide to solving ethical issues.

Teachers
Teachers are central in the conversation about professional practice of pedagogic activities offered by the regional conservatorium.

Teacher preparation
At present there are a number of tertiary institutions in NSW that offer music related qualifications. It is beneficial to note that the majority of awards offered are performance based and not pedagogically oriented. This confirms the findings of Clinch (1983) that the majority of those said to be "qualified instrumental teachers" were trained by institutions whose main objective is to train them to be musicians, not teachers. The level of qualification however affects the rate of pay: "*So if you come in and you've been to a Conservatorium and you've done your four years, then you're on the full pay and if you come in and you haven't got a formal training you're on what we call an Associate rate*" (Executive Director). However, for teachers who are affected by the associate rate of pay, they felt confident that working at the Conservatorium offered them more than in a private studio as the Conservatorium provided administrative support to collect and process fees and insurance coverage.

Professional practice
Paramount to the professional practice is the teacher-student relationship through "knowing their students". The majority of teachers viewed themselves as performer first and then

teacher or mentor second. While this was a strong response of teachers, one teacher shared: "*essentially I view my role as an educator being different for every student. Primarily I'm employed as an instrumentalist teacher. I think that's very specific and if at the end of the day that's what the parents are willing to pay for and that's what they want, that's what I'll give them, but my role will change depending on the student*". Discussion followed and consensus found that the role of the teacher is multi-faceted, multi-dimensional and most importantly variable for each student. The different roles performed within each teacher-student relationship supports the belief that no one method of teaching could be adopted, but rather methods should be adapted to suit the needs of the student. The ability to adapt or change, for most, is learned over time. This professional evolution for some has resulted in a shift from performer towards teacher: "*I'm no longer a performer; I don't class myself as a performer, even though I thoroughly enjoyed performing. The opportunities to perform are very few and far between, particularly when I am a very busy teacher ... Most of the time I'm just a teacher.*"

Pedagogic activities

The pedagogical activities offered by the Conservatorium are essentially student-centered. It was expressed that while the student is central to the activities planned, the appropriate direction followed is negotiated between the student's needs and the teacher's experience. This dialogic negotiation is crucial in the maintenance of the student-teacher relationship: "*I draw on my own experience as a musician and performer and, no doubt, my own training*".

The Heart of Curriculum Transfer in the Music Studio is Relationship

For a curriculum to be student centered it is crucial that the teacher knows, hears and responds to the needs of the student. Using pre-established curricula might offer a framework and a starting point for a curriculum, but effective adaptation can only be achieved through careful consideration positioned on knowledge and experience.

Schwab (1969) advocated that the heart of curriculum transfer was in the classroom, however this investigation underscores that relationship is at the heart of curriculum transfer in the music studio. The triangulation of expertise (teacher, performer and musician) is paramount to the connection and interaction between teacher and student. It provides the opportunity for musical interaction and the necessary engagement for a master apprenticeship relationship to emerge. Parental involvement is crucial for success. It is advocated that their involvement be organic and not imposed. The organic nature of the involvement is relational and is worth trialing to support student success.

References

Barr, A. S. (2007). Reversing the pyramid. *American Music Teacher*, 57(1), 24–26.
Bridges, D. (1988). The private music teacher in Australia. *Australian Journal of Music Education*, 1(1), 49–55.
Clinch, P. (1983). Some aspects of instrumental tuition in Australia. *The Australian Journal of Music Education*, 2(1), 1–2.

Creech, A., & Hallam, S. (2009). Interaction in instrumental learning: The influence of interpersonal dynamics on parents. *International Journal of Music Education, 27*, 94–106.

Csikszentmihalyi, M., Rathmunde, K., & Whalen, S. (1993). *Talented teenagers: The roots of success and failure*. New York, NY: Cambridge University Press.

Davidson, J. W., Moore, D. G., Sloboda, J. A., & Howe, M. J. A. (1998). Characteristics of music teachers and the progress of young instrumentalists. *Journal of Research in Music Education, 46*, 141–160.

Ford, T. (2009). I just want to teach the flute! *Pan: The Flute Magazine, 28*(3), 39–43.

Glaros, P. (2006). Technology in the private studio: A never ending story. *Journal of Singing, 62*, 567–572.

Hallam, S. (1998). The predictors of achievement and dropout in instrumental tuition. *Psychology of Music, 26*(2), 116–132.

Keeler, S. (2011). Working the ensemble experience into the private piano studio. *Clavier Companion, 3*(1), 20–23.

Lierse, S. (2007a). Discussion of the national review of school music education. Deakin West ACT, Australia: Australian College of Educators.

Lierse, S. (2007b). *The private music studio: Celebrating a micro musical community*. Paper presented at Celebrating Musical Communities: Proceedings of the 40th Anniversary National Conference, Nedlands, WA.

Mahamuti, G. (2009). Professional development makes you recession-resistant. *Clavier Companion, 1*(5), 48–50.

Mitchell Conservatorium Inc. (2009a). *A guide to parents*. Bathurst, NSW:Author.

Mitchell Conservatorium Inc. (2009b). *Strategic Plan, 2006-2009*. Bathurst, NSW:Author.

Montemayor, M. (2008). Flauto: An ethnogrpahic study of a highly successful private studio. *International Journal of Music Education, 26*, 286–301.

Pitts, S. E., Davidson, J. W., & McPherson, G. E. (2000). Models of success and failure in instrumental learning: Case studies of young players in the first 20 months of learning. *Bulletin of the Council for Research in Music Education, 146*(1), 51–69.

Schwab, J. J. (1969). The practical: A language for curriculum. *School Review, 78*(1), 10–23.

Thompson, S. (1983). Studio teaching: Some present thoughts. *The Australian Journal of Music Education, 2*(1), 2–3.

Humor in Western Art Music and in Music Education: Literature Review and Research Findings

May Kokkidou
University of Western Macedonia (Greece)
ugenius@otenet.gr

Abstract

Humor and laughter are primarily social vocalizations that bind people together, a hidden language that we can all speak. They are both a learned reaction and an instinctive behavior programmed by our genes. The finest moments in life, those we always recall with pleasure and excitement, are moments of laughter, those when humor plays the leading role. By the same token, music too has a special strength; its nature and importance are, as Reimer puts it, self-evident. Laughing and listening to music are things that every human takes pleasure in doing; they are both therapeutic and good for the mind-brain.

But how have composers incorporated Humor into their works and how does musical Humor affect children's willingness to listen to music? How does musical Humor influence children's attitudes and activities? This study represents an attempt to answer the above questions by looking at the capacity of pre-school children to identify and interpret Humor in Western classical music and to express themselves on this subject, verbally, vocally and kinetically.

Keywords
Pre-school music education, western-art music, humor, musical humor

On humor and laughter

Since the time of Aristotle, philosophers and scholars have tried to understand and explain the origins and the functions of humor and laughter. In the literature, three theories on humor and laughter show up repeatedly: relief theory, superiority theory and incongruity theory (Buijzen & Valkenburg, 2004). From the perspective of relief theory, people laugh because they need to reduce physiological tension from time to time. According to superiority theory, people laugh because they feel some kind of triumph over others or feel superior to them. In incongruity theory, people laugh at things that are unexpected or surprising (McGhee, 1979; Meyer, 2000). In the 3WD model, a model of Humor in three dimensions, which was created in the early 1990s, humor must be examined as regards its structure, content, and response. A joke or other humorous thing can be put to the 3WD test to see what kind of humor it really is, and whether or not it is even funny (Martin, 2007).

McGhee (1979) focused on the combination of cognitive processes with mood alterations in the perception of humor, defining this as an experience that is both cognitive and emotional. He noted that it requires a high level of perception both of the stimulus and of the incongruent information. It is also claimed that a cheerful mood is an essential precondition for the perception of humor. According to Abraham Maslow (1968), humor is a supreme manifestation of the human spirit, a peak experience, a way of bringing delight to the heart; it is not driven by other needs but is linked to the disposition to play.

Humor in music and music education

Humor in music is closely linked to its parodic or comic elements. In the first case, parody is used by composers chiefly to distance themselves from past generations, as well as from their more conservative contemporaries. This kind of humor is comprehensible only by initiates of the field, those who are in a position to appreciate its wit and shrewdness. The second case, the comic, has to do with composers who deploy the unexpected and the exaggerated, who impose twists and distortions, in order to give their work a comic character.

A common argument against the existence of musical humor is that in most instances that provoke smiles or laughter, this does not appear to lie in the musical sounds themselves but in the associated ideas, that is in extra-musical factors. Lister (1994) questioned how the listeners hear and interpret music as humorous and discussed two kinds of Humor: absolute humor, that is, that which lies within the musical material itself, and referential humor, that is, when it is the extra-musical connotations and associations which let the music perceived as humorous.

It is a fact that several western composers have implied by the titles they gave to their works that music can express humor (Mull, 1949). Alfred Brendel, in 1976, remarked that in some cases music can be comical without verbal support, while making it clear that the possible formal peculiarities of a piece do not constitute evidence of its comic nature. One must take into account the listener's background knowledge. Brendel claimed that if the clearly musical oddities and inconsequentialities of a piece are to be perceived as amusing by a listener, this depends on the psychological mood of the piece as well as on the listener's disposition.

Humor as such appears officially neither among the aims of education nor in the details of curricula, perhaps because it is thought that it may cause unwelcome diversions from the steady routine of teaching-learning, as curriculum designers equate humor with silliness and importunity (Glasser, 1998). As for music education in particular, we studied the aims and content of 20 music curricula, from Europe and America, and found that not one of them made any reference to the perception of humor in music. By the same token, few are the studies that focus on humor in music; fewer still are those that concern themselves with the pre-school age group.

Helen Mull (1949) played three recordings to female college students (Strauss's *Till Eulenspiegel's Merry Pranks*, Strauss's *Staendchen* and Rameau's *La poule*) and asked them to make a judgment as to which of three compositions was the most humorous, regardless of any knowledge of the composition's title. Mull noticed that the subjects indicated as more humorous the passages that could be characterized in terms of the degree of contrast in timbre, intensity, pitch, rhythm and complexity and wrote that subjects gave most reports of humor to Strauss's *Till Eulenspiegel*.

David Huron (1992) examined live recordings of Peter Schickele's music and identified 629 instances of audience laughter. Each of the laughter-evoking moments was analyzed to determine possible reasons why listeners might have laughed. Huron noted that the musical devices used by Schickele involve violations of expectation. He concluded that in Schickele's music, all of the laughter-evoking events can be plausibly linked to a violation of listener expectations. Most of these violations involve schematic expectations.

LeBlanc, Sims, Malin, and Sherrill (1992) studied the relationship between humor perceived in music and the self-reported levels of preference for music, with subjects representing four different age levels (Grades 3, 7, 11 and college undergraduates). The researchers conclude, among other findings, that perception of musical Humor is largely a function of age, and that higher levels of perceived humor were significantly associated with higher levels of preference.

Randall Moore and David Johnson (2001) studied the effects of music experience on perception of Humor in western-art music. Following two marked examples of the task, 202 university students (106 music and 96 non-music majors at a state university) rated 14 excerpts on two seven-point Likert-type scales, non-humor/humor and dislike/like. Results indicated that there was a general agreement among subjects as to what was considered a humorous composition and what was not. Music majors showed significantly stronger perceptions of humor in music than non-majors did on 43% of the excerpts. On the basis of the above observations and research findings, we designed the present study.

Research on Humor Perception by Kindergarten Children: Methodology and Findings

We know that children in early childhood usually appreciate simple forms of humor. They have a strong preference for visual and physical humor (e.g., grimaces, visual surprises, clownish behavior) and they also laugh at other simple forms of humor such as unusual voices and sounds (Buijzen & Valkenburg, 2004; McGhee, 1971, 1979; Shultz, 1996). Still, can pre-school pupils appreciate humor in music? And, if so, how do they perceive and interpret music as humorous? Does the understanding of musical humor depend on prior experience?

These were the initial questions that informed the design of this study. The research sample was 25 children of pre-school age, four to six years old, who were attending a state pre-school in a suburban area in Northern Greece. All the children were taking part in a seven-month program of music education, with three 40-minute lessons per week.

The study was carried out during April and May 2011. The researcher conducted five weekly interview sessions with the pupils, presenting five pieces of music for listening and asking the children to express their impressions verbally, with an emphasis on the humorous dimensions of the pieces. Specifically, the pupils were asked two questions: "Is this music funny?" and "Why?" When the first question was answered negatively, explanatory information was provided on the extra-musical context of the composition. There followed a second listening before the questions were put again. At this stage most pupils were able to respond in ways that showed that they discerned the Humor in the music. Finally, with a third listening we returned to the music itself and discussed the elements of structure and expression that have to do with humor, that is, we sought the pupils' personal interpretations, as far as they were able to express them.

The pieces or passages presented for listening were: the opening of the first movement of Kodaly's *Háry János* suite; the first movement of *Eine Kleine Nichtsmusik* by P.D.Q.Bach (Peter Schickele) (The pupils were already familiar with W.A.Mozart's *Eine Kleine Nachtmusik.*); *People With Long Ears* from Camille Saint-Saëns's *Carnival of the Animals*; the first part of Richard Strauss's *Till Eugenspiel's Merry Pranks*; the third movement of Bizet's *Jeux d'enfants (The Spinning Top)*.

On first listening to Peter Schickele's *Eine Kleine Nichtsmusik,* pupils recognized the differences between Mozart's original and Schickele's parody, paying particular attention to the latter's use of a motif from Tchaikovsky's *Nutcracker Suite*. However, on a first listening the pupil's did not consider the *Nichtsmusik* to be funny, but asked the researcher why the music was different. When they had received the reply, "So that the composer can make us laugh and feel happy", they listened again and this time laughed spontaneously at most of the elements of parody.

The Hungarian composer Zoltan Kodály opens the first movement of his *Háry János* suite with a loud "sneeze" produced by the whole orchestra. The children did not find this music funny. When the researcher asked them what the opening of the work sounded like, giving as possible answers laughter, sobbing, sneezing and hiccoughs, pupils effortlessly chose the sneeze, and asked to listen to the piece again. The second listening was accompanied by laughter and vocal mimicry.

Pupils showed a similar reaction to Camille Saint-Saëns's *People With Long Ears*. At first they gave negative answers to the question, "Is this music funny?", while when, thanks to the educative method, they realized that the composer was putting across an animal noise, some children began spontaneously to mimic it while others laughed, though reservedly.

From *Till Eugenspiel's Merry Pranks* we listened to the theme "once upon a time", Till's theme on the French horn, the clarinet theme that indicates Till's laughter when he is preparing a prank, and Till's horse-ride through a market. The pupils did not at first find this music humorous. There followed a brief narration of the story, focusing on Till's character. The pupils showed increased interest during the second listening but did not laugh at any point during the music or narration. They just asked to hear the rest of the work, particularly the end, when Till is hanged. That is, they were more focused on the dramatic nature both of the story and of the music.

As for *The Spinning Top* from Bizet's *Jeux d'enfants*, during the first listening the pupils showed a clear disposition to physical movement. They did not find the music funny until they had learned that it presents a spinning top. They asked, of their own accord, that they might express themselves in movement, and laughed when "the top stops spinning" and "we wind the string" in order to set it spinning anew.

The pupils, then, did not react with laughter to any of the pieces on a first listening. Nevertheless, after hearing explanatory information they showed perception of the humor in the music, laughed spontaneously and even at such length as to prevent them from following the development of the work. The title of a work was one of two basic factors leading to perception of high spirits in music. The other factor was the content of the narration. It is notable that the pupils asked to listen to the music again whenever they could. In some such cases, their laughter was even louder and mostly infectious. No gender or age-related differences in reactions were noted, but the sample was small and we cannot consider this as being in any way a definitive finding.

Discussion

The conclusions which may be drawn from observation of the children's reactions and behavior and from the post-listening conversations are as follows: 1. laughter is not a spontaneous response to music: searching for and discovering the humorous dimension in music has to do with searching for and discovering analogies in real life; 2. perception of humor or its implications in music requires additional cognitive stimuli; 3. young pupils are able to appreciate humor in music, which demonstrates their ability to use metaphor and comparison in order to proceed to symbolic interpretations; 4. humorous element provides motivation for a closer relation with a work of music; and 5. existing knowledge and previous experience have a supplementary function, facilitating the perception of musical humor. As general observations, we noticed: 1. the pupils' increased interest in the works and their general demand to listen to them again; and 2. their spontaneous reactions in the form of kinetic and theatrical expressiveness, inspired by listening to the music.

In general terms, humor functions as a factor that increases pupils' interest and plays a role in the formation of their musical preferences. Therefore we can argue, as did Walton (1993), that there is analogy between understanding humor and understanding music for the purpose of musical analysis; both deepen the understanding of a musical piece and enrich the experience of the listener.

The findings of our research showed that children aged 4 to 6 can be aware of musical humor, though within a referential context. In addition, it seems that a close relation exists between a sense of humor in music and the amount of musical training. These findings are consistent with results from previous research (Lister, 1994; Mull, 1949; Walton, 1993).

To conclude, to achieve appreciation of Humor in music requires a frame of reference, through an intervention in the listening process that enriches listening with relevant information of an intellectual or cognitive nature. This contrasts with Brendel's (1976) view, which rejects informational background as a factor in the perception of humor in music. Rather, the results of the present study tend to confirm the position taken by Stuss, Gallup, and Alexander (2001), who regard humor as a metacognitive function. Many of the children's reactions to the music they heard reflect an ability to think relationally, metaphorically and metacognitively. Thus, the results of this study contradict the view that children up to 10 or 12 years of age cannot think metaphorically (Gibbs, 1994). It is clear that music brings forth metaphoric expression, which may include images, emotions and metaphor. Further, the children's verbal responses to the experience of listening to humor in music revealed the way in which they perceived and processed both the musical stimulus and the additional information (Rodriguez & Webster, 1997).

Finally, we should note that we observed that activities using humorous music had a generally positive effect on the general atmosphere in class. As we know, when learning takes place in an attractive and happy ambiance, this has a positive effect on learners' development in all sectors, social-emotional, cognitive, moral (Cohen, 2006; Fontana, 1995 Glasser, 1998; Zins, Weissberg, Wang, & Walberg, 2004), so we can claim beneficial effects for "musical Humor activities" from a wider standpoint. Musical humor is an important tool that music educators can use in order to achieve educational goals. Music teachers should therefore encourage young listeners to appreciate Humor in music. This may also have a complementary function in increasing students' interest in music, motivating them to enjoy music by listening to it more than once.

References

Brendel, A. (1976). *Musical thoughts and afterthoughts*. London, UK: Robson Books.

Buijzen, M., & Valkenburg, P. M. (2004). Developing a typology of humor in audiovisual media. *Media Psychology, 6*, 147–167.

Cohen, J. (2006). Social, emotional, ethical, and academic education: Creating a climate for learning, participation in democracy, and well-being. *Harvard Educational Review, 76*(2), 201–237.

Fontana, D. (1995). *Psychology for teachers* (3rd ed.). London, UK: Macmillan Press.

Gibbs, R. W. (1994). *The poetics of mind*. Cambridge, UK: University Press.

Glasser, W. (1998). *Choice theory: A new psychology of personal freedom*. New York, NY: Harper Collins.

Huron, D. (1992). Music-engendered laughter: An analysis of humor devices in PDQ BACH. In S. D. Lipscomb, R. Ashley, R. O. Gjerdingen, & P. Webster (Eds.) Proceedings of the 8th International Conference on Music Perception & Cognition (pp. 700–704). Adelaide, Australia: Causal Productions. Retrieved from http://musicog.ohio-state.edu/Huron/Publications/MP040049.PDF

LeBlanc, A., Sims, W. L., Malin, S. A., & Sherrill, C. (1992). Relationship between humor perceived in music and preferences of different-age listeners. *Journal of Research in Music Education, 40*, 269–282.

Lister, L. J. (1994). Humor as a concept in music: A theoretical study of expression in music, the concept of humor and humor in music with an analytical example, W.A. Mozart, Ein musikalischer Spass, KV 522. Frankfurt, Germany: Peter Lang.

McGhee, P. E. (1971). Cognitive development and children's comprehension of humor. *Child Development, 42*, 123–138.

McGhee, P. E. (1979). *Humor: Its origin and development*. San Francisco, CA: Freeman.

Martin, R. (2007). *The Psychology of Humor*. Amsterdam, Netherlands: Elsevier Academic Press.

Maslow, A. (1968). *Toward a psychology of being* (2nd ed.). New York, NY: D. Van Nostrand.

Meyer, J. C. (2000). Humor as a double edged sword: Four functions of humor in communication. *Communication Theory, 10*, 310–331.

Moore, R., & Johnson, D. (2001). Effects of musical experience on perception of and preference for humor in Western art music. *Bulletin of the Council for Research in Music Education. 149*, 31–37.

Mull, H. K. (1949). A study of humor in music. *The American Journal of Psychology, 62*, 560–566.

Rodriguez, C. X., & Webster, P. R. (1997). Development of children's verbal interpretative responses to music listening. *Bulletin of the Council for Research in Music Education, 134*, 9–30.

Shultz, T. R. (1996). A cognitive developmental analysis of humor. In A. J. Chapman & H. C. Foot (Eds.), *Humor and laughter: Theory, research, and applications* (pp. 11–36). New Brunswick, NJ: Transaction Publishers.

Stuss, D. T., Gallup G., & Alexander, M. P. (2001). The frontal lobes are necessary for "theory of mind." *Brain, 124,* 279–286.

Walton, K. L. (1993). Understanding humor and understanding music. *The Journal of Musicology, 11*(1), 32-44.

Zins, J., Weissberg, R. W., Wang, M. C., & Walberg, H. J. (2004). *Building school success on social-emotional learning: What does the research say?* New York, NY: Teachers College Press.

Using Music Technology with Young Children with Autism: Two Case Studies

Ling-Yu Liza Lee
Chaoyang University of Technology (Taiwan)
Liza.lylee@gmail.com

Kimberly McCord
Illinois State University (USA)
kamccor@ilstu.edu

Abstract

This study investigated two approaches toward engaging young children with autism in music using music technology. A case study approach was used to describe strategies used to engage two children in music that otherwise show a lack of interest in participating in musical activities. Both male children, one age four and the other age five have clinical diagnosis of autism with communication disorders. Both have challenges with joint attention and are withdrawn socially. The four-year old child was seen individually over 22 weeks with 30-minute instructional sessions twice a week. The five-year old was a member of an inclusive kindergarten general music class. Data analysis involved a telephone interview as well as a personal interview with the parents and the music teacher in order to triangulate data, gather background and set guidelines for the study. The results showed the positive efficacy of using Soundbeam and iPad technology by increasing joint attention and socially withdrawn behavior to participate in musical activities.

Keywords
Soundbeam, iPad, Technology, Autistic Spectrum Disorder

Technology is becoming an increasingly important tool for professionals in Special Needs Education and Music Therapy. Children with ASD show increased social responsiveness when music interventions including recordings, acoustic instruments and electronic instruments are used (Finnigan & Starr, 2010; Lee, 2004, 2009). Electronic instruments that incorporate movement are multi-modal approaches toward engaging children with challenges in attention and engagement. One such example is the Soundbeam, an electronic instrument that uses an ultrasonic beam to translate movement into sound. The Soundbeam has been used to complement stories with improvised soundtracks created by the Soundbeam player (Lee, 2008) and studied in therapeutic situations with children with ASD to increase movement control, attention span, eye contact, vocalization, social interaction and positive emotions (Ellis, 1995; Lee, 2011). Improvisational music and movement has been a key intervention in children with ASD in music therapy and music education settings (McCord, 2004, 2009; Orff, 1974).

The recent introduction of the iPad to special education and inclusive classrooms has opened up a new level of accessibility for students on the autism spectrum. Many children with ASD are sensitive to sound and sometimes sensitive to touching instruments. Using a wireless speaker placed at a comfortable distance with volume control makes playing virtual instruments on an iPad more accessible. In addition, music software programs such as *Bloom* can be used to calm agitated children. Children can also be calmed through sensory-based interventions like the vibration cushion on which the sound can be felt as well as heard and seen.

Purpose and Research Questions

The aim of the study was to investigate the effectiveness of using the Soundbeam and the iPad in individual and inclusive music settings to increase joint attention and motivation. The research questions are:

1. Does the use of the Soundbeam and/or the iPad promote joint attention in children with autism?
2. Does the use of the Soundbeam and/or the iPad reduce disruptive and withdrawn behavior in children with autism?

Music therapy provides a non-threatening and soothing way of communication for the children with special needs, especially autistic children (Alvin & Warwick, 1992; Lee, 2006). Technology not only changes life but also has constantly evolved and developed our life. Combining music and technology in the field of special education has positive effects were documented.

The effects of music therapy for autistic children

Studies have shown that music therapy has a significant, positive influence when used to treat autistic individuals (Allgood, 2005; Brownell, 2002; Wager, 2000). Participating in music therapy allows autistic children the opportunity to experience non-threatening outside stimulation, as they do not engage in direct human contact. Music can be a communication channel for children with autism (Kissinger & Worley, 2008). The attraction of music to autistic children is due to a feeling of inclusion and being fully absorbed within a musical environment (Alvin & Warwick, 1992).

Music therapy uses music as a tool to support stronger speech skills, better eye contact and strengthen other areas in the life of a child with autism (Berger, 2002). Music promotes positive mood and calmness (Rahim & Hamzah, 2008). Brain research in music has demonstrated that music provides a soothing "blanket" for the listener that allows the system to relax, especially in individuals with autism (Berger, 2002). Neuoscientist Nina Kraus has studied brain activity in children with autism and has documented positive changes when engaged in musical activities. For example, children with ASD struggle with prosody, or communicating emotion and intention through acoustic cues such as pitch contour. Therefore, qualities drawn from music—pitch, voice inflection and expressivity may improve prosody in children with ASD and ultimately impact their ability to develop reading comprehension skills (Marmel, Parbery-Clark, Skoe, Nicol, & Kraus, 2011; Musacchia, Sams, Skoe, & Kraus, 2007; Strait & Kraus, 2011; Wong, Skoe, Russo, Dees, &

Kraus, 2007).

The effects of music technology for autistic children

Musical engagement is supported through active participation, enabled by a variety of adaptive technologies such as the MIDImate switch access system (Assistivex, 2003), and automatic movement technologies that convert movement to music, such as the Soundbeam (Soundbeam Project, 2003; Swingler, 2003). The use of these adaptive technologies has created a paradigm shift in which access to a musical instrument no longer requires physical strength, endurance and fine motor abilities (Ellis, 1995). As a result, participation in musical tasks and the subsequent emotional, psychosocial and therapeutic rewards are no longer restricted by physical barriers (Schwellnus et al., 2002).

Some children with ASD do not have the ability to communicate with language on their own. Due to the importance of communication, socialization and interacting with others, autistic children need researchers to develop new solutions for helping with speech. Research has shown that technology could be the new solution for them to improve their lives (Hailpern, 2007). The iPad is still too new for much published research but special educators are finding success with the devices in classrooms. They are being used as devices to speak for those with communication disorders, to help with daily routines and to play videos that model appropriate behavior and ways to socially interact with others.

Research shows that sound therapy combines the power of new technologies with an aesthetic response to sound. This non-interventionist approach can encourage users' interaction and development of their communicative skills (Ellis, 1995). Through sound therapy sessions, an autistic child made progress in a number of areas, such as movement control, attention span, eye contact, vocalization, social interaction and positive emotions (Ellis & Van Leeuwen, 2000). A study showed the benefits of developing an audiovisual immersive interactive environment to encourage creative interaction and expression for a 12-year-old male with Autistic Spectrum Disorder. Results indicated setting the increased engagement spans and vocal utterance while in the environment (Williams, 2008).

There is evidence that has positive impacts on the essential behaviors and building blocks required for learning complex skills. In fact, music therapy has been identified as an emerging treatment for children with ASD (National Autism Center, 2009). For example, results from a meta-analysis show greater improvements in gestural and verbal communication among children with ASD spectrum disorders who received short-term music therapy interventions as compared to control groups who received equivalent therapy without the musical component (Gold, Wigram, & Elefant, 2006). Similarly, in a recent creative movement study conducted with 38 young children (ages 3-7 years) diagnosed with autism, Hartshorn and colleagues found increased attentive behavior, most especially on-task passive behavior, and a decrease in stress behaviors including stereotypes, negative responding to touch and resisting the teacher following 30 minute sessions of creative movement held twice a week, (Hartshorn, et al., 2001). The Soundbeam uses movement as a means to create sound.

Methodology

Lincoln and Guba (1985) reported "For naturalistic inquirers, the reporting mode of choice is the case study" (Lincoln & Guba, 1985, p. 357). Studying children with disabilities is best achieved through qualitative methods because a researcher is unlikely to find two children alike enough to draw similarities. We chose the two students because they both had difficulty with joint attention and were not motivated to participate musically in more traditional ways. One student, Kuochien was unable to speak or sing and the other student, Xavier, had limited vocabulary and chose not to speak or sing in his inclusive music class.

Stake (1995) identified the most interesting cases in education are people and programs. "We are interested in them for both their uniqueness and commonality" (p. 1). The children in this study are different in abilities and interest in some ways but very similar in others. The approaches toward engaging them musically are different; individual therapeutic approach using the Soundbeam and inclusive music classroom setting using the iPad.

We collected data through field notes, journals, and video recordings of selected classes and sessions. We had many discussions with parents, teachers and staff to gain greater insight into the children and to support or disprove our observations. Trustworthiness of the data was established through my extended immersion in the field and through triangulation of the multiple data sources. Data were entered into a qualitative research program to aid in discovering patterns indicative of changes in children's musical experiences.

We hoped to enhance the life and development of these children in some of the ways described in the literature. O'Brien (1987) identified five outcomes for lifestyle enhancement that encourage students with severe disabilities to develop competence through skill acquisition in ways that enhance the person's community presence, respect, and choice. Special educators recognize the importance of promoting self-determination by having students participate in planning what they will do and learn (Browder, 2001). Friend and Bursuck (2006) stated that "students need to be aware of their strengths and weaknesses, the potential impact of these strengths and weaknesses on their performance, the support they need to succeed, and the skills required to communicate their needs positively and assertively (p. 357). We believe that breaking down barriers for children with autism by use of music technology can enhance their lives and social and musical development.

Participants

One participant was a 4 year-old male who had a clinical diagnosis of autism and profound and multiple learning disabilities. He was mute, not particularly interested in music, had a high sensitivity to touch, no eye contact and had serious disruptive behavioral problems. He was enrolled in a special kindergarten in Taichung, central Taiwan, and was selected by purposive sampling to participate in the study. The study took place at the "Soundbeam Technology Child Development Center" of Chaoyang University of Technology, Taiwan. This was a 22-week study, with half-hour sessions twice per week. The total number of interventions was 44 sessions.

Soundbeam Curriculum Design

A. Hypothetical curriculum design
The initial hypothetical curriculum design was through four stages based on previous research: free exploration stage, instructional learning stage including: sound guidance, image guidance with sounds and purposive guidance. The target goals are:

a. Free exploration phase
   At this stage, the Kuochien would explore sounds freely through physical movement. Through sound exploration, the sounds will motivate the child's curiosity, attention and learning.
b. Sound guidance phase
   The target sounds of Soundbeam would lead the Kuochien to imitate the target objectives, such as a flying bird.
c. Image guidance with sounds phase
   The target sounds of Soundbeam and target images of Arkaos VJ3.61FC1 and G-force would lead the Kuochien to imitate the target objectives' motions.
d. Purposive guidance phase
   The purposive guidance included sound vocalization, Soundbeam activities, image activities and relaxation time.

B. Revised alternative curriculum design

According to the Kuochien's responses, after implementing the study the researcher adjusted the curriculum phases in order to reach the study goals. The alternative curriculum phases were the following:

a. Sound guidance phase
b. Image guidance with sounds phase

The other participant was a 5-year old male with a clinical diagnosis of autism with an additional communication disorder. The words he was ever heard to say are yes and no. He is socially withdrawn and often sits with his hands over his ears during music class or hides under the teacher's desk. He was in an inclusive kindergarten music class in a Mid-western city in the United States. This was an 18-week study. The music class met twice a week but the iPad intervention was only used in one class per week. The iPad intervention was only used in classes where instruments were played or singing was a part of the lesson. Lessons that involved listening or movement were taught without using the iPad.

iPad Curriculum Design

A. Kindergarten Curriculum

The music teacher decided what activities and songs were taught based on her own curriculum, on days she planned activities or songs that the iPad could be used it was programmed for that particular activity. The student used an iPad in his special education classroom and at home so he was familiar with how to operate it. He had not used the applications we used at home or with his special education teacher. We were careful to select applications that did not require any extra training. In addition, typical students in the classroom also used the iPad at times so as not to stigmatize the student with autism.

a. Establishing comfort
   Ten sessions were spent just sitting next to the child in music class to get him used to and adult sitting next to him. In the first four sessions he was visibly distracted by me and often would turn his back to me. As he gradually relaxed and became used to me, he would sometimes share an instrument with me or let me sit next to him when he sat under the teacher's desk. He never made eye contact, sang or spoke any words other

than yes or no.
b. Participating with the class
The student was very sensory defensive. He did not like to be touched and he disliked most instruments, especially high pitched or sustaining instruments. He would cover his ears or move to the teacher's desk where it was dark and away from the class. He would sit under the desk often with his hands over his ears. Many children with autism will have tantrums and disrupt the class in these situations but this student would withdraw instead of being outwardly disruptive.
c. Using the iPad
The iPad had a wireless speaker with volume controls. I placed the speaker away from the student, first across the room and eventually next to the student or on top of the teacher's desk. He was shown how to adjust the volume but would not do it. He would hold his hands over his ears instead until I adjusted the volume. At first we used simple instruments like a triangle that appeared on the screen as an actual size triangle. The student tapped the screen and it would ring. With the speaker away from the student, he was able to tolerate the sound. Later, we used programs that were pre-recorded phrases sung by a child from our university lab school. Xavier could activate the phrases by tapping on the iPad and the device would sing his solo part when the music teacher prompted him.

Data analysis

Soundbeam case study

The assessment instruments included a pre-diagnosis and post-diagnosis of the Kuochien from a medical doctor at a local hospital, anecdotal observation forms to gather data on the Kuochien's changes of behavior and development from four observers who were trained graduate students, interview reports from the parents at home and teaching logs from the researcher. All intervention sessions were recorded on video and these were viewed and reported by four observers.

Coding
The following is the researcher's coding symbol:

Data Resource	Coding	Meaning
Observation form of music activities	O-1-2-08152008-3-2	The observation form of the second time of the week one on August 15, 2008 for the activity 3 by observer two
The parental interview	PI-09102008-1	The parental interview on September 10, 2008 by observer one
The parental observation form	PO-10112008	The parental observation form on October 11, 2008
The researcher's teaching log	RTL11222008	The researcher's teaching logs on November 22, 2008

The iPad case study
The student had a medical diagnosis of autism and had an Individual Education Plan that specified a self-contained classroom for all classes except music, physical education and art.

Some videotaping was done in the classroom but because I sat next to him and the music teacher was involved in teaching the class it was difficult to always capture everything on videotape. The music teacher and I would debrief after each class and I would type up all of our observations and impressions. In addition, every-other-week the special educator would come and observe the class and run the video camera. Many of the interventions were done under the teacher's desk and video did not capture how the student interacted with the iPad due to cramped space and inability to get the camera into the space.

The following is researcher two's coding symbols:

Data Resource	Coding	Meaning
Observation form of music activities	On task Off-task Hands over ears Under desk	A list of each activity planned by the music teacher was included with codes next to steps and behaviors observed.
iPad interactions	1-on task 2- off task 3 hands over ears 4- under desk	A list of each activity planned by the music teacher was included with codes next to steps and behaviors observed.
Music and special education interviews	What helps What doesn't work	Interviews and reviews on my observation forms
The researcher's teaching journal	What helps What doesn't work	Researcher Two journal

Results

Soundbeam Case Study
In order to increase the objectivity and reliability of the research results, a cross-comparison was conducted on the triangulated data. There are four stages to the results:

A. Accommodation stage: from week 1 to week 4
Due to the Kuochien's seriously disruptive behavior, the parents accompanied him to class for the first and the second week. Later, Kuochien attended sessions without his parents from week 3 to the end of the study. The curriculum design at this stage focused on free exploration. The sounds were changed every minute to test Kuochien's preferences. Initially, the sensor was placed behind and above Kuochien, but no matter what the position the instructor chose, Kuochien could not calm down and sit still in a chair. The distance range of sounds was set to be broader, between 0.20m and 5.00m.

The Kuochien's developmental areas of disruptive behavior, cognition, language, attention span and emotions made no improvement at this stage.

Disruptive behavior
Kuochien had serious disruptive behavioral problems, such as: biting, hitting, kicking, slapping and scratching people and hurting himself throughout the first stage.

Kuochien couldn't stop crying, screaming and slapping people for the whole session when he first came to the class. (O-1-1-08012008-1-1, O-1-1-08012008-1-2, RTL08012008)

When a drum sound was played, Kuochien suddenly turned to slap a teaching assistant. (O-1-2-08082008-3-2, O-1-1-08082008-3-4)

When a single note of piano sound was played, the instructor tried to motivate Kuochien to vocalize by singing "Aah~~~with a high tone. Kuochien started to slap the instructor's face. (O-2-1-08122008-3-1, O-2-1-08122008-3-4, RTL08122008)

During the Soundbeam activity session, Kuochien bit and scratched the instructor's arm while he was held to the soundbox. (O-2-2-08152008-3-2, O-2-2-08152008-3-3, RTL08152008)

Joint Attention
Kuochien's disruptive behavior affected his learning, so he could not focus on anything during this stage.

When the instructor sang "U~~~" with a sound effect, Kuochien stared at the instructor for a second, then ran around the room. (O-4-1-08262008-3-1, O-4-1-08262008-3-4)

While having Kuochien sit on the sound chair, the instructor sang "I" with sound effect tone to Kuochien. Kuochien tried to struggle from the chair. (O-4-2-08292008-3-1, O-4-2-08292008-3-2)

When the instructor sang "Aah~~~" with clapping hands, Kuochien tried to scratch the instructor's hands. (O-4-2-08292008-3-1, O-4-2-08292008-3-2, O-4-2-08292008-3-3, O-4-2-08292008-3-4)

The parents observed Kuochien's joint attention at home found that Kuochien still could not concentrate on anything they taught.

His attention is still poor and can't listen to parents. (PO-08262008)

He likes to start at something that he is interested, but dislikes to listen to whatever his parents taught him. (PO-08292008)

B. Vocalization stage: from week 5 to week 7
Kuochien has been mute since he was a baby, so his parents asked for help with his spoken language ability. The second stage was focused on vocalization. The curriculum contents included Soundbeam activities and relaxation time. The sounds were focused on one single note at a time to elicit Kuochien's vocalization. The sensor was placed depending on Kuochien's movement direction. The range of the sounds was between 0.20m and 2.00m. Kuochien's developmental areas of disruptive behavior, cognition, language, attention span and emotions were starting to show improvement.

Disruptive behavior
At the vocalization stage, Kuochien's disruptive behavior was improved slightly. There

were no violent behaviors recorded at week 5 *(O-5-1-09022008-1-2, O-5-2-09052008-1-3, RTL09022008)* and week 7 *(O-7-1-09162008-1-1, O-7-1-09192008-1-4, RTL09162008)*. At week 6, Kuochien acted inappropriate, when the assistant corrected his violent behavior, he starting kicking and beating people *(O-6-1-09092008-1-1, O-6-1-09092008-1-2, RTL09092008)*. Similarly, when the assistant turned off the lights during relaxation time, Kuochien was scared of the darkness; therefore, he started crying *(O-6-1-09092008-1-1, O-6-1-09092008-1-2, RTL09092008)*. After the instructor added relaxation time, Kuochien's resistance to taking lessons was decreased *(O-7-1-09192008-2-2, O-7-1-09192008-2-3, RTL09162008)*.

The parental observation form showed Kuochien had decreased violent behavior at home. He stopped biting his parents before going to bed as long as the parents played relaxation music from the class for him *(PO-09022008, PO-09092008, PO-09162008)*.

Joint Attention
At this stage, Kuochien attention lasted longer. He could focus on listening to the sounds from the Soundbeam and music for relaxation. The duration lasted from 5 seconds to 66 seconds *(O-7-1-09192008-1-2, O-7-1-09192008-1-4, RTL09192008)*. At week 5 and 6, he could look at the instructor from 5 to 10 seconds with the instructor's assistance *(O-5-1-09022008-1-2, O-5-1-09022008-1-3, O-6-1-09092008-1-1, O-6-1-09092008-1-2)*. At week 7, Kuochien looked at the instructor and target objectives for a few seconds without reminders and assistance *(O-7-1-09192008-1-1, O-7-1-09192008-1-2)*.

According to the parental observation form, Kuochien had no obvious differences at week 5 and 6 *(PO-09022008, PO-09092008)*. At week 7, he could watch a TV cartoon and was able to listen to relaxation music from the class by himself at home *(PO-09162008)*.

C. Shifting stage: from week 8 to week 13
Kuochien made greater changes at this stage. The curriculum contents included a "Hello Song," Soundbeam activities, relaxation time and "Goodbye Song." In order to know Kuochien's preference for pitched or un-pitched sound, the instructor adjusted the sound to a single note within one octave. The sensor was pointed at Kuochien's direction of movement. The pitch sequence that was chosen was the whole tone scale. The range of the sounds was set up between 0.20m and 2.00m. From week 12, the observers and I started documenting Kuochien's sounds and the pitch of those sounds. Kuochien's developmental areas of disruptive behavior and joint attention were improving more than in the previous stage.

Disruptive behavior
Kuochien did not display disruptive behavior at weeks 8, 9, 11 and 12 *(O-8-1-09232008-1-1, O-9-2-10032008-2-4, O-11-1-10142008-3-2, O-12-1-10212008-1-3)* but it reoccurred at weeks 10 and 13 due to illness. When Kuochien displayed violent behavior, the assistant played relaxation music and Kuochien was able to calm down *(O-10-1-10072008-1-2, O-10-1-10072008-3-4, O-13-1-10282008-2-1, O-13-1-10282008-3-3)*.

Joint Attention
Kuochien's attention was longer than in the previous stage. While listening to the sounds from Soundbeam and relaxation music, Kuochien's attention span could last from 10 se-

conds to 7 minutes *(O-10-1-10072008-1-1, O-11-1-10142008-2-4, O-12-1-10212008-2-1, O-13-1-10282008-3-4)*. When Kuochien listened to the music, he did not need the instructor's guidance. Kuochien's attention span could last for 7 minutes during relaxation time *(O-12-1-10212008-3-1, O-13-1-10282008-3-4, RTL10282008)*. From week 8 to 13, Kuochien was able to look at the instructor for 20 seconds *(O-8-1-09232008-1-3, O-9-2-10032008-2-1, O-10-1-10072008-2-3, O-11-1-10142008-2-2, O-12-1-10212008-2-3, O-13-1-10282008-2-4)*.

The parent observation form indicated that Kuochien focused more on the parents' directions. At week 9, Kuochien was able to look at picture books for a few seconds *(PO-09302008)*. At week 10, the teacher told the parents that Kuochien could sit and attend in class for a longer period of time *(PO-10072008)*. From week 11 to 13, the Kuochien's attention showed no improvement at home *(PO-10142008) (PO-10212008) (PO-10282008)*.

D. Stable stage: from week 14 to week 22

From week 14 to the end of the study, Kuochien was becoming much more stable. The curriculum contents included a "Hello Song," Soundbeam activities with visual aids of G-Force, relaxation time" and "Goodbye Song." The visual aids of G-Force played a crucial role for Kuochien to motivate him to improve his behavior and participation. The sensor was pointed at Kuochien's direction of movement. The sounds were focused on single shot. The range of the sounds was set between 0.20m and 2.00m. At this stage, Kuochien's learning performance became stable.

Disruptive behavior

Due to illness during week 14 and 18, Kuochien manifested violent behavior in class, but after I added the visual aid of G-Force, he stopped his disruptive behavior immediately and was able to stare at the pictures on the screen *(O-14-1-11042008-2-3, O-18-1-12022008-2-4)*. Except for two weeks of illness, Kuochien's violent behavior and other problems were clearly decreased *(O-15-1-11142008-2-1, O-16-1-11182008-4-3, O-17-1-11252008-2-2, O-19-1-12092008-3-4, O-21-1-12232008-3-3, RTL12302008)*.

The parental observation forms indicated that Kuochien only displayed violent behavior at week 14 and 15 at home. After, there was no disruptive behavior until the end of the study *(PO-11042008) (PO-11112008) (PO-12116008) (PO-12302008)*.

Joint Attention

After the instructor added the visual aid of G-Force, Kuochien's attention made dramatic changes. His attention increased by looking at the instructor, watching the visuals and listening to the relaxation music from 10 seconds to 10 minutes. At this stage, Kuochien did not need the instructor's assistance to attend in the class *(O-16-1-11182008-2-1, O-17-1-11252008-2-3, O-18-1-12022008-2-2, O-19-1-12092008-2-4, O-20-1-12162008-3-3, O-21-1-12232008-4-1, RTL12302008)*.

The iPad Case Study

Both the music teacher and myself observed Xavier during each session and every-other-week by the special educator. The three of us triangulated data. When possible we videotaped by it was difficult to videotape most sessions. Our work falls into three stages for the results:

A. Becoming Comfortable With Another Adult

My sitting next to him in class at first distracted Xavier. In the first few weeks instead of sitting side-by-side on the carpet, he turned and sat with his back to me. Often he would sit with his head down in his lap for long periods of time. Occasionally he would watch his peers as they answered questions or performed movement. When asked questions or asked to volunteer to participate in music activities he would most often shake his head no, except for group movement. He would participate in circle movements and would sometimes perform hand movements or keep a steady beat. He never sang or volunteered to play an instrument. If an instrument was given to him he would either hold it without making sound or put it down.

> *The music teacher chooses groups of six students to come to the front of the classroom and play their instrument for each special word in a song. Xavier is given a wood block and shown how to play it but he stands holding the block and the mallet watching the other students play. The teacher helps to coach him by pointing at him for his turn and he stares without expression holding the woodblock silent. (1)*

> *At the beginning of each music class a students is chosen to come to the front and to lead the class in body percussion to the steady beat of a recording. Xavier will stand up and try to imitate the movements. He watches the student leader from the corner of his eye and does not make eye contact however. (2)*

> *The music teacher teaches a song about clocks chiming with a part for triangles. As soon as the teacher demonstrates how to play the triangle Xavier puts his hands over his ears and puts his head down. (3)*

> *Another day the teacher accompanies the class performing movement on her recorder. Xavier quickly gets up and runs to the teacher desk and tucks himself away into a corner and covers his ears and begins rocking. He makes no sound but he is obviously very uncomfortable. (4)*

> *I would follow him over to the desk and sit patiently next to him on the floor watching him. On the times he went under the desk with the special educator in the room she would sometimes call to him and ask him to come out. He would not respond.*
> *Carol, (special educator): The only time I have seen him behave like this in my class is each month when they test the tornado si-*

> rens. I now try to prepare him for it ahead of time by giving him noise- canceling headphones.
> Kim (researcher) to Linda (music educator):I wonder if we could use those in music to see if that helps. Special educator agrees. (5)

> I learned quickly to not try to look at Xavier too much or to talk to him. It seemed to make him uneasy around me.
> Kim to Linda: Xavier didn't seem to like it when I tried to be his partner in the clapping game today. Is he better with the other kids or do you try to engage with him?
> Linda: No he refuses to participate if it involves touching or looking at another person. He prefers to stand to the side and watch. I used to try to encourage him to participate, it just seems like he should be able to tolerate that but it was one of the few times he said "no." I decided it was so unusual for him to speak that it must be really important for me to understand this was important to him. (6)

B. iPad Interventions

Eventually I introduced the iPad by playing instruments on it myself as I sat next to Xavier. He seemed more interested and watched me play it for as long as a minute with some songs. As soon as I would stop playing he would quickly look away. I carefully positioned the wireless speaker across the room. The first time I played the iPad I demonstrated it for the class because all of the kindergarten children were very curious about the iPad and what it could do. Many had never seen one and they wanted to try it. All children had a chance to try it and when it was Xavier's turn he shook his head no. We added it with a song and several students were chosen to play the triangle sound on the iPad and all of the children were delighted by it. Xavier only watched out of the corner of his eye. We asked him if he would like to play and he stood silent without responding. His special education teacher was there that day and coaxed him to try it by telling him he is a very good iPad user.

> When it came for Xavier's turn to play he paused for a few seconds trying to decide if he should and then quickly tapped the triangle on the screen and the sound played. The special educator praised him and asked if he wanted to try again, and he did. (1)

> Carol: Later that day Xavier seemed to be looking on the classroom iPad for the triangle. I asked him what he wanted to do on the iPad, it seemed like he was looking for something and he didn't seem to acknowledge my question, I wonder if he was looking for the triangle on our iPad. We later loaded that application and a few others on the classroom iPad to see if he would practice playing in the special education room where he felt more

comfortable. After three weeks he did find another application we were using. "Xylophone" and he played with it for almost fifteen minutes. (1, 5)

One day the music teacher introduced the Orff instruments to the class. The kindergarten students sat on the floor sharing an instrument between two students taking off the bars and putting them on and exploring the instruments. Many students were most interested in playing the instruments and quickly the sound became loud and chaotic. Xavier went under the teacher's desk with his hands over his ears and rocked. I offered him the headphones plugged into the iPad. On the iPad was a xylophone. I had adjusted the volume very low and selected a marimba so the sound would be a low pitch. He ignored me and rocked for ten minutes as the students in the classroom played the instruments. As the teacher instructed the students to put away the mallets and replace the bars in order it became quieter and he took his hands off his ears and relaxed a bit and noticed the headphones and the iPad. I told him these are his special headphones that won't hurt his ears and on the iPad was an instrument like the other kids played only this one was low and soft and I think he will like it better. I left him there. In the meantime the class left and the room was silent. There was twenty minutes before the next class came so the music teacher and I pretended to busy ourselves and ignore Xavier under her desk. I had my wireless speaker and I turned it down very low so we could check to see if he was doing anything. He was playing! Tentatively to be sure but he was carefully playing each note going up and down the marimba. (1,3,4,5)

In his special education classroom Xavier used his headphones with the iPad and played with the instruments. When he was with his class and there were many instruments playing he went under the desk and would quickly put his headphones on and play from there. On one day the music teacher was teaching a song that was punctuated with an instrument at the end of each phrase. Each student had a turn to play and instrument of their choice. Xavier went under the desk where I had the iPad and headphones set out for him. We also had the little speaker on and the teacher said, "It is Xavier's turn to play this time (looking under the desk) Xavier see if you can play your instrument with us! And he did! He had chosen a drum sound and played a bit delayed but after the phrase finished and as we all waited. The other students became fascinated about how there could be a sound but they couldn't see Xavier and we explained the little speaker. Xavier continued to participate, sometimes going under the desk immediately on entering the classroom and sitting with the iPad ready to play.

Kim to Linda and Carol: What do you think about taking the headphones away to see if he will play without them?

Carol: Let me work with him this week in my classroom without them and talk to him about doing this when he goes to music.

It took longer than a week, actually three weeks before Xavier would play the iPad without the instruments. His special education teacher had to model playing many times with low volume from the iPad before he trusted it enough to try it without his headphones. The next week we placed my iPad under the desk without the headphones and left him alone. The students were learning a chant that included playing a woodblock, 1,2,3 then passing it to the next person. Xavier was with the group and when the woodblock came to him he held it without playing it but passed it to the next student on cue. When the activity was finished he left the class and went under the desk and we heard him playing on a drum sound, 1,2,3.

C. Interviews with the music and special educator

Both Linda and Carol saw improvements in Xavier's joint attention and motivation. He participated musically now using the iPad and enjoyed playing the iPad both at home and in the special education classroom. He would not play the iPad in the music classroom except under the desk but he did play it in quiet places with few peers and adults in the room. All music applications we used were loaded on school iPads and his home iPad. We also used a singing application called SingingFingers. I recorded a child from another school singing a song in phrases onto the iPad. To play the song back Xavier only needed to run his fingers across a colorful line. He never seemed interested in this and only wanted to play the instruments. We were never able to get him to use other programs that would speak short phrases for him that he tapped on. He does use this program in other places but refused to use it in music. He would say "no."

In summary, by the end of the study Xavier was participating in music class by playing instruments from under the teacher's desk using an iPad without noise cancelling headphones. He would play the same instruments in his classroom and at home without hiding but he was not willing to do so in class, nor was he willing to use traditional instruments with the class or under the desk. He also was not interested in speaking or using a speech program or a singing program with the class or under the desk.

Conclusion

The teachers, parents and observers all confirmed the positive effects of using the Soundbeam and iPad technology along with music activities on changing the Kuochien's and Xavier's disruptive or withdrawn behavior, joint attention. The conclusion of the changes of the subject's disruptive behaviors and other areas of development is shown in the table 2.

Table 2. The changes of the Kuochien's disruptive behaviors and joint attention.

	Stage I Accommodation Stage (Week 1 to 4)	Stage II Vocalization Stage (Week 5 to 7)	Stage III Shifting Stage (Week 8 to 13)	Stage IV Stable Stage (Week 14 to 22)
Disruptive Behavior	Serious disruptive behavioral problems, such as: biting, hitting, kicking, slapping and scratching people and hurting himself	Improved slightly.	Improved more	Behaviors of violent and other problem were decreased obviously
Joint Attention	Could not focus on anything	Lasted few seconds	Lasted from 10 seconds to 7 minutes	Lasted from 10 seconds to 10 minutes

Table 3. Xavier's changes in withdrawn behavior and joint attention.

	Stage 1 Being comfortable with another adult	Stage 2 iPad interventions	Stage 3 Teacher interviews
Withdrawn Behavior	Began with turning his back and eventually sat side-by-side	Ignored iPad when students in the classroom, then would play by himself, eventually played with class from under the teacher's desk	The music and special educators noticed gradual improvement and participation.
Joint Attention	Little attention paid to adults or music activities. Does participate in movement and will follow what peers do. Often sits with his head down with hands over his ears.	Will only make sound if he is hidden under the teacher's desk away from peers. Does participate with the class and plays instruments on iPads outside of music class.	The music teacher is pleased with his progress and hopes he can continue to make progress in the following year.

Recommendations

In this study, the children with autism demonstrated dramatic positive changes in behavior and joint attention by using technology. Although these case studies provided an initial positive result, they are two cases representing a limited number of sessions. Engaging disruptive and socially withdrawn children with autism can be challenging, particularly those with communication disorders. Music technology can provide a method for equalizing the curriculum so that all children can participate.

References

Alvin, J., & Warwick, A. (1992). *Music therapy for the autistic child* (2nd ed.). New York, NY: Oxford University Press.

Allgood, N. (2005). Parents' perception of family-based group music therapy for children with autism spectrum disorders. *Music Therapy Perspectives*, 23(2), 92–99.

Assistivex (2003). Web link: www.assistivex.com/Public/category

Browder, D. M. (2001). *Curriculum and assessment for students with moderate and severe disabilities*. New York: The Guilford Press.

Brownell, M. (2002). Musically adapted social stories to modify behaviors in students with autism: Four case studies. *Journal of Music Therapy*, 39(2), 117–144.

Berger, D. S. (2002). *Music therapy, sensory integration and the autistic child.* London, UK: Jessica Kingsley Publishers.

Ellis, P. (1995). Incidental music: A case study in the development of sound therapy. *British Journal of Music Education, 12*, 59–70.

Ellis, P., & Van Leeuwen, L. (2000). *Living sound: Human interaction and children with autism.* Paper presented at ISME Commission on Music in Special Education, Music Therapy and Music Medicine, Regina, Canada.

Finnigan, E., & Starr, E. (2010). Increasing social responsiveness in a child with autism. *Autism, 14*, 321-348.

Friend, M., & Bursuck, W. D. (2006). *Including students with special needs.* Boston, MA: Pearson Education Company.

Gold, C., Wigram, T., & Elefant, C. (2006). Music therapy for autistic spectrum disorder. *Cochrane Database of Systematic Reviews 2006, 2.* DOI: 10.1002/14651858.CD004381.pub2

Hailpern, J. (2007). Encouraging speech and vocalization in children with autistic spectrum disorder. *Accessibility and Computing, 89*, 47–52.

Hartshorn, K., Olds, L., Field, T., Delage, J., Cullen, C. & Escalona, A. (2001). Creative movement therapy benefits children with autism. *Early Child Development and Care, 166*, 1-5.

Kissinger, L., & Worley, D. W. (2008). Using the harp as a communication channel with children with autism. *International Journal of Special Education, 23*(3), 149-156.

Lee, L. (2004). *Using musical improvisation to effect linguistic and behavioral changes in a cohort of Taiwanese autistic children.* Paper presented at the Sixth Annual American Music Therapy Association (AMTA) Conference. Austin, TX.

Lee, L. (2006). Music education in the facilitation of social and behavioral changes in a cohort of autistic children. In M. Prause-Weber (ed.), *Proceedings of the ISME Commission Seminar on Music in Special Education, Music Therapy, and Music Medicine* (pp. 29–36).

Lee, L. (2008). The use of musical instruments and supplemental materials to enhance spoken language acquisition by children with autism: A case study. *Proceedings of the 2008 International Society for Music Education Commission on Music in Special Education, Music Therapy and Music Medicine* (pp. 83-94).

Lee, L. (2009). *A case study on integrating Soundbeam Technology and music activities to enhance a special needs child's development of motor skills and attention span.* Paper presented for EAPRIL conference/4th European Conference on Practice-based and Practitioner Research on Learning and Instruction, Trier, Germany.

Lee, L. (2011). *A Study on the use of technology of sounds and music activities on developing children with visually impaired physical movement.* Paper presented at The 8th Asia-Pacific Symposium on Music Education Research, ISME Asia-Pacific Regional Conference. Taipei Municipal University of Education, Taipei, Taiwan.

Lincoln, Y. M., & Guba, E. G. (1985). *Naturalistic inquiry* (7th ed.). Newberry Park, CA: Sage.

Marmel, F., Parbery-Clark, A., Skoe, E., Nicol, T., & Kraus, N. (2011). Harmonic relationships influence auditory brainstem encoding of chords. *NeuroReport 22*, 504–508.

Magee, W. L. (2011). Music technology for health and well-being: The bridge between the arts and science. *Music and Medicine, 3*(3), 131-133.

McCord, K. A. (2004). Moving beyond "That's all I can do:" Encouraging musical creativity in children with learning disabilities. *Bulletin of the Council for Research in Music Education,159*, 23–32.

McCord, K. A. (2009). Improvisatory musical experiences in the lives of children with severe disabilities. In C. Abril & J. Kerchner (Eds.), *Music experience in our lives* (pp. 127-143). Lanham, MD: Rowan & Littlefield.

Musacchia, G., Sams, M., Skoe, E., & Kraus, N. (2007). Musicians have enhanced subcortical auditory and audiovisual processing of speech and music. *Hearing Research. 104*(40), 15894–15898.

O'Brien, J. (1987). A guide to life-style planning. In B. Wilcox & G. T. Bellamy (Eds.), *A comprehensive guide to the activities catalog: An alternative curriculum for youth and adults with severe disabilities* (pp. 175-189). Baltimore, MD: Paul H. Brookes.

Orff, G. (1974). *The Orff music therapy.* (M. Murray, Trans.). New York: Schott Music.

Rahim, N. A., & Hamzah, Z. A. (2008). Music therapy: Storytelling with special needs children. Paper presented at Third International Conference on Interdisciplinary Social Sciences, Monash University Center, Prato, Tuscany, Italy.

Schwellnus, H., Tam, C., Chau, T., Knox, R., Johnson, P., & Hamdani, Y. (2002, July). Using movement-to-music technology for play with children with special needs, *OT Now.*

Soundbeam Project (2003). Soundbeam 2®. Web link: www.soundbeam.co.uk/

Strait, D. L., & Kraus, N. (2011). Can you hear me now? Musical training shapes functional brain networks for selective auditory attention and hearing speech in noise. *Frontiers in Psychology, 2*, 1–10.

Stake, R. (1995). *The art of case study research.* Thousand Oaks, CA: Sage Publications.

Swingler, T. (2003). Electronic music interfaces for people with disabilities: Do they lead anywhere? In G. Craddock et al. (Eds.), *Proceedings of the AAATE Conference: Assistive Technology - Shaping the Future* (pp. 247–252). Dublin: IOS Press.

Wager, K. (2000). The effects of music therapy upon an adult male with autism and mental retardation: A four year case study. *Music Therapy, 18*(2), 131-140.

Williams, C. (2008). Creative engagement in interactive immersive environments. *Digital Creativity, 19*(3), 203–211.

Wong, P. C. M., Skoe, E., Russo, N. M., Dees, T., & Kraus, N. (2007). Musical experience shapes human brainstem encoding of linguistic pitch patterns. *Nature Neuroscience, 10*(4), 420–422.

Mimesis as a Tool for Musical Learning and Performance, Maieutics, and the Stone of Heraclea

Anders Ljungar-Chapelon
Lund University (Sweden)
Royal Northern College of Music (England)
anders.ljungar-chapelon@mhm.lu.se

Abstract

The concept of *imitation* and to *imitate* has relations to the old Greek concepts *mi'mēsis* and *mime'omai*. These are concepts, which since the antiquity has been used explaining learning in a general sense as to artistic activity. It is of importance while discussing mimesis to make a distinction between *making a copy* and *imitation*. The process of mimesis could be misunderstood in relation to learning and artistic expression and be equaled to a soulless copying of a model. The use of mimesis for learning implies a learning style often based on having no teacher, but that the learning person becomes his own teacher, which can be described as *automaieutics* (Ljungar-Chapelon, 2008). This concept is based on *maieutics* (Plato, 1992) and the idea that teaching has similarities with the task of a mid-wife. Processes related to mimesis and automaieutics establish platforms for artistic creation, and links to the concept of the *Stone of Heraclea* (Plato, 2001) and magnetism originated from the creator of art, how it magnetizes performers and audience. Further the concept of mimesis relates to *te'chne* (craftsmanship) and *poiēsis* (creation), and its symbiotic relations to musical learning, artistic creation and performance.

Keywords
Automaieutics, maieutics, mimesis, musical expression and learning, poiesis, techne.

> ... to see science under the lens of the artist, but art under the lens of life. (Nietzsche, 1886/1993, p. 5)

The concept of *imitation* and to *imitate* has relations to the old Greek concepts *mi'mēsis* and *mime'omai*. These concepts has since antiquity been used to explain actions in relation to artistic activity as to learning in a general sense. The use of mimesis for learning implies learning styles often based on having no teacher, and that the learning person – a child or adult – becomes his own teacher. In other words: mimesis creates foundations for self-teaching, and is related to processes which could be described as *automaieutics* (Ljungar-Chapelon, 2008). This is a concept based on *maieutics* (Plato, 1992), and ideas that teaching has similarities with the task of a mid-wife, with the addition that automaieutics is a process whereby the learner himself becomes the mid-wife/teacher (Ljungar-Chapelon, 2008). The processes of mimesis and automaieutics in combination with Plato/Socrates idea about artistic expression and the concept of the *Stone of Heraclea* (Plato, 2001) regarding the magnetism originated from the creator of art, which magnetises the performer and audience, establishes platforms for artistic creation.

German philosopher Gadamer (1960/2001) pointed on *te'chne* and *poiēsis* as aspects of mimesis in relation to the arts. Techne relates to craftsmanship, and poiesis to creation. Both concepts have a symbiotic relation to learning the craft of a given art (e.g. how to play a musical instrument), and at the same time *how* the craft is used. Within performing arts this includes music, dance and theatre and has been discussed in the *Poetics* by Aristotle (1996):

> Similarly in the case of the arts I have mentioned: in all of them the medium of imitation is rhythm, language and melody...For example, music for pipe or lyre (and any other arts which have a similar effect e.g. music for pan-pipes) uses melody and rhythm only...(p. 3-4)

It is of importance while discussing mimesis to distinguish between *making a copy* and *imitation*. The process of mimesis could be misunderstood and equalled to a soulless copying of a model. Such an inexpressive formula is however not included in a discussion of mimesis based on Aristotle and Gadamer.

In 18th century France a distinction was articulated in relation to the terms *imitation* and *copying*. Both expressions were described as "Termes qui désignent en général l'action de faire ressembler" (Girard, 1769, II: p. 14), and both concepts includes a "resembling", but with the difference that copying is understood as "... on copie par stérilité... servilement" (1769, II: p. 14), and imitation as "... on imite par estime... en embellissant" (1769, II: p. 14). Girard compares the process of copying with when a printer prints the text from a manuscript "Copie ne se dit qu'en fait d'impression, & du manuscrit de l'auteur sur lequel l'imprimeur travaille" (1769, I: p. 213). These examples include that imitation can be associated with a *free recreation of a model*, and stands in opposition to copying which aims for an *exact reproduction of the model*. A similar opinion was expressed by Baillot (1834/2001) – violin virtuoso and professor – at the *Conservatoire* in Paris. He explained the difference between copying and imitation as "... imiter n'est pas copier, ne vous y tromper pas! se choisir un modèle n'est pas, matériellement parlant, copier ce modèle; c'est suivre la marche du maître qu'on préfère et s'éclairer de son experience" (p. 8). In other words: imitation should not be confused with copying, and choosing a model is in Balliot's perspective not based on copying but to follow a master's path, and while doing so learning from the master's experiences and skills.

While using an enlarged concept of language based on Dilthey (1905/1924), it is possible to compare how a graphic artist works with woodblocks and copper plates using different tools, colors and qualities of paper, with how a musician works with and interprets a score in relation to specific instruments, acoustics of concert halls, co-musicians and the audience. Woodblocks and copper plates in principle have the same structure and form for each new printing, but the graphic artist can strongly influence these parameters in choices of colors and paper qualities. In a similar way a score can be said having the same kind of given structure comparable with the structure and form of woodblocks and copper plates, which directly will be influenced by the musicians interpretation, choice of instruments and its connected aesthetics. This could be described as an analogy between printing plates and scores concerning interpretation and flexibility in relation to mimesis, imitation and artistic expression.

To use models for learning is probably as old as mankind. The dialect we speak our mother tongue, how we learned to walk, are examples of a universal learning based on imitation. Of course, there are countless examples of how imitation has been used as a learning tool. Within language teaching imitation has often had a major importance. An example is French language teacher and author Adam and his *La vraie manière d'apprendre…* (1787). Here he explains that four year old children often speak there mother tongue surprisingly well. His conclusion is that children learn through imitation – without teachers – in combination with using their mother tongue in every day life. Adam recommends this method for adults wanting to learn foreign languages.

A 16th century example using imitation as a tool for learning is found in *Il libro del Cortegiano* (1528/1978) by Castiglione, an Italian courtier, diplomat, soldier and prominent Renaissance author. He became influential within aristocratic circles concerning education, and one tool for training a courtier was imitation:

> *Therefore anyone who wants to be a good pupil must not only do things well but must also make a constant effort to imitate and, if possible, exactly reproduce his master. And when he feels he has made some progress it is very profitable for him to observe different kinds of courtiers and, ruled by the good judgment that must always be his guide, take various qualities now from one man and now from another. (p. 66)*

Using imitation within musical learning and education is an often-used method within the tradition of European music, and has been so since hundreds of years in ways similar to Castiglione's method with reference to the courtier (Ljungar-Chapelon, 2008). This includes that young musicians today often during their final years of studies travel to master classes, and take contact with outstanding virtuoso players for the sake of developing virtuosity and getting new impulses with regards to development of virtuosity and musical interpretation.

An example how imitation was used in a musical context in the 18th century with an outspoken weight on techne is found in Quantz (1752/1975). He describes when a student plays second flute in a duet the process of learning can be defined as an act of imitation. The student follows his teacher's playing, expressions, sound qualities, rhythm and intonation while all the time adapt to the act of playing together. In other words: the teacher becomes a role model in action. This procedure has connections to how French language teacher Pluche (1751), highlights that an eminent tool for learning foreign languages is "… par la très-constante habitude d'entendre puis de répéter des choses bien dites" (p. 40). He concludes that the process of intellectualization should be introduced as a second step, and in a similar way Bach (1753/1981) insists on the importance of listening to outstanding musicians as models, as being the strongest tool for musical learning. A comparable description regarding musical learning is found in the first ever-printed Swedish musical dictionary by Envallsson (1802). Here is described that students should study virtuoso players, their skills, art, taste and musical expression, and with his talent (automaieutics) use these findings as inspiration and tools.

Rampal (1989) – one of the 20th century most influential flute virtuosos – has described how listening and imitation were powerful methods while learning the flautistic craft as a boy:

> When I started out, I tried to imitate exactly the way my father played. It's a part of a family's musical heritage; I suppose I had his sound in my genes. As I progressed, though, I changed and developed my own style. (p. 16)

When Rampal points on how he as a beginner tried to copy his father's flute playing (Joseph Rampal was a distinguished flute virtuoso), and gradually while making progress could anticipate from his father's playing, can be understood as an example of the above described distinctions between copying and imitation.

As a conclusion mimesis and imitation in combination can be considered as powerful tools with a universal dimension concerning human learning, with and without teachers. Within a musical context these tools has been used since long as a strong method developing instrumental craftsmanship and techne. Using mimesis and imitation as tools gives these processes strong elements of realness, which can be explained while associating to when a child learns how to speak its mother tongue: children learn how to speak with the help of mimesis in everyday life because the language is an essential and existential necessity in life.

Reflections around musical performance, its preparation and practicing related to interpretation and its artistic dimensions (mimesis and poiesis) raise the question: What happens within the framework of an artistic performance in its unforeseeable, explosive instant of the moment? Plato/Socrates discuss closely related questions in the dialog *Ion* (Plato, 2001), while analyzing the craft and performance by a rhapsode. A raphsode was in old Greece a professional singer reciting Homer and the *Iliad* (1711) and *Odyssey* (1716). Maybe we could make a "transcript" of the crafts and arts of a rhapsode to a musician of today and the past, and then ask questions concerning *what* musicians *does* and *expresses* in the unforeseen moment and instant of performance?

In the dialogue *Ion* (2001) Plato/Socrates describe two elements, which connects to the above-mentioned questions: 1. The rhapsode is in the moment of performance influenced and "possessed" by the muses or gods, and is consequently not fully aware of how the performance gets its final shape; and 2. A discussion around the *magnetism* and how an artwork leads trough Homer, to the rhapsode, and finally to each person in the audience. Plato/Socrates describe this magnetism as:

> … there is a divinity moving you, just as in the stone which Euripides calls a magnet, but which is commonly known as the stone of Heraclea. This stone not only attracts iron rings, but it also imparts to them the same power of attracting other rings, and sometimes you will see a number of pieces of iron and rings suspended from one another so that they form a very long chain: and all of them derive the power of suspension from the original stone. Similarly, the Muse herself first makes some men inspired;

> then from these inspired people a chain is suspended as still other
> people receive the inspiration. For all good poets, epic as well as
> lyric, compose their beautiful poems not by art, but because they
> are inspired and possessed. (p. 10-11)

A significant aspect based on Plato/Socrates is that the *Iliad* or *Odyssey* – the "scores" for the rhapsode – go through a metamorphosis in the instant of performance, which includes elements of *improvisation* (from Latin *improvisus,* unforeseen), and has energy caused by the rhapsode being magnetized by Homer's text. These elements are transformed by the rhapsode to the audience, which in its turn is "possessed" and magnetized by the performance of Homer's text. This idea from Plato/Socrates has a relation to when Rameau (1754/2004) wrote that musicians should not think during the act of performing music, but be "taken away" by the emotion which inspires the music "... don't think but let the emotion be your judgments compass" (p. 62/259). Such an opinion leads our thoughts to Proust (1913-1927/1987) and aesthetics concerning *intuitive processes,* the emotional *involuntary memory,* and the famous metaphor of the *Madeleine cake.*

Philosopher Ast (1805) claimed that music is the art of inner emotion. Musical expression is created when the inner center and emotion of man is brought into vibration, as when a bell brought into vibration creates sound. Baillot (1834/2001) thought that the essence of musical expression – *L'expression* – were human emotions, and that the musicians task was to reshape them into musical expressions. This metamorphosis was the key while developing artistry within the frame of music and musicians. Altès (1880/1906) – flute virtuoso and professor at the *Conservatoire* in Paris – quoted Baillot and concluded "... his [the musicians] soul must possess that expansive force, that warmth of feeling which radiates beyond him, which magnetizes, penetrates, burns" (p. 286). This characterization of musical expression and its performance leads back to *Ion,* the magnetizing stone and its possessive character (Plato, 2001). A Swedish example of this idea is to be found in Cronhamn's *Flute Method* (1858-1860) "... this poetic spirit, this rich fantasy which always possesses, fascinates and charms" (p. x). A possibility while discussing emotional aspects of musical performance and expression is to interpret them as processes of mimesis regarding human emotions. This is linked to when Schopenhauer (1818/1960) describes that the final intention for music is to express the essence of *Happiness, Sorrow, Melancholia,* the *Heroic* and so forth (§ 52, p. 374-375). Probably many musicians are familiar to, and use processes concerning mimesis for creating emotional expression. An example of this did I experience some years ago in a rehearsal of the aria *Aus Liebe will mein Heiland sterben* from *St Matthew Passion* by Bach (1727/1989), when the conductor Dan-Olof Stenlund asked me to "Play the flute part so everybody understands that Jesus is innocent."

A radical alternative would be to understand artistic processes of performance and their emotional dimensions as how Diderot describes this in *Paradoxe sur le Comédien* (1770/1981). Diderot argues that actors should never feel the emotions included in the role, but in principle should stay unmoved in relation to the emotions of the role character. This would be a contrary opinion compared with how Bach (1753/1981) discusses that the performing musician *has* to be moved emotionally by the emotions in the score for *making it possible* for the audience to be moved by his performance, or as to speak with Plato/Socrates: to magnetize the audience.

Maybe, in reality musicians are "taken away" during the act of performance, and become "possessed" by the music in similar ways as when Plato/Socrates described the magnetism from the Stone of Heraclea. To this can be added that Heidegger (1961) explains the essence of the arts as mimesis processes of human life, an opinion with roots in the Antiquity. In a master class (February, 2011) at the Royal Northern College of Music (Manchester, England) British composer Ferneyhough insisted that his *Cassandra's Dream Song* (1970) for solo flute can be understood as the Greek heroin's despair, with her visions of how Troy and her civilization would be destroyed. This would be to interpret music and the arts with the lenses of life.

References

Adam, N. (1787). *La vraie manière d'apprendre une langue quelconque, vivante ou morte, par le moyen de la langue françoise; ou démonstration et pratique de la nouvelle méthode d'enseignement*. Paris, France: Benoit Morin & Laporte.

Altès, H. (1880/1906). *Grand method for flute*. Paris, France: Millerau.

Aristole. (1996). *Poetics*. London, UK: Penguin Classics.

Ast, F. (1805). *System der Kunstlehre oder Lehr- und Handbuch der Aesthetik*. Leipzig, Germany: J. C. Heinrichs.

Bach, C. P. E. (1753/1981). *Versuch über die wahre Art, das Clavier zu spielen*. Wiesbaden: Breitkopf & Härtel. (Facsimile)

Bach, J. S. (1727/1989). *Matthäus-Passion*. BWV 244. Kassel: Bärenreiter.

Baillot, P. M. (1834/2001). *L'Art du Violon*. Courlay: Fuzeau. (Facsimile)

Castiglione, B. (1528/1978). *The Courtier*. London, UK: Penguin Classics.

Cronhamn, J. P. & Fürstenau, A. B. (1858-1860). *Flöjt-skola af A. B. Fürstenau öfversatt och omarbetad af J. P. Cronhamn. Andra Upplagan utökad med Th. Böhms tabeller öfver Flöjtens nya construction*. Stockholm, Sweden: Abraham Hirsch.

Diderot, D. (1770/1981). *Paradoxe sur le Comédien*. Paris, France: Flammarion.

Dilthey, W. (1905/1924). *Die Entstehung der Hermeneutik*. Leipzig und Berlin, Germany: Verlag B. G. Teubner.

Envallsson, C. (1802). *Svenskt musikaliskt lexikon, efter grekiska, latinska, italienska och franska språken*. Stockholm, Sweden: Carl F. Marquard.

Ferneyhough, B. (1970). *Cassandra's Dream Song for solo flute*. London, UK: Edition Peters No. 7197.

Gadamer, H.-G. (1960/1990). *Wahrheit und Methode. Grundzüge einer philosophischen Hermeneutik*. Gesammelte Werke Band 1 & 2. Tübingen: J. C. B. Mohr (Paul Siebeck).

Girard, G. (1769). *Synonymes François, leurs Différentes significations et le choix qu'il en faut faire pour parler avec justesse*. Paris, France: Le Breton.

Heidegger, M. (1961). *Nietzsche*. Band I. Pfullingen: Verlag Günther Neske.

Homer. (1711). *L'Iliade*. (Madame Dacier, Trans.). Paris, France: Rigaud.

Homer. (1716). *L'Odyssée*. (Madame Dacier, Trans.). Paris, France: Rigaud.

Ljungar-Chapelon, A. (2008). *Le respect de la tradition. Om den franska flöjtkonsten: dess lärande, hantverk och estetik i ett hermeneutiskt perspektiv*. Malmö: Lund University, Malmö Academy of Music, Sweden.

Nietzsche, F. (1886/1993). *The Birth of Tragedy*. London, UK: Penguin Classics.

Plato. (1992). *Theaetetus*. Indianapolis/Cambridge: Hackett Publishing Company.

Plato. (2001). *Ion*. New York, NY: The Modern Library.

Pluche, N.-A., Abbé. (1751). *La mécanique des langues et l'art de les enseigner & Supplement à La mécanique des langues*. Paris, France: Chez Veuve Estienne & Fils.

Proust, M. (1913-1927/1987). *À la recherche du temps perdu*. Paris, France: Gallimard, La Pleiade.

Quantz, J. J. (1752/1975). *Essai d'une methode pour apprendre à jouer de la flûte traversière avec plusieurs remarques pour servir au bon gout dans la musique*. Paris, France: Zurfluh. (Facsimile)

Rameau, J.-P. (1754/2004). *Observations sur notre instinct pour la musique*. Courlay: Fuzeau. (Facsimile)

Rampal, J.-P. (1989). *Music, My Love*. New York, NY: Random House.

Schopenhauer, A. (1818/1960). *Die Welt als Wille und Vorstellung*. Frankfurt am Main: Cotta-Insel Verlag.

Rhythm for Reading: A Rhythm-based Approach to Reading Intervention

Marion Long
University of London (UK)
m.long@ioe.ac.uk

Susan Hallam
University of London (UK)

Abstract

This paper illustrates how the process of putting psychological theory into classroom practice in the primary context can involve a move away from new technologies and personalized learning to a highly energetic and multi-sensory approach that emphasizes social cohesion. The rhythm-based music intervention is an entrainment strategy in which groups of children rapidly develop music notation reading skills while synchronizing stamping, clapping and chanting actions in time with a musical accompaniment for 10 minutes per week.

The theoretical framework draws on multi-disciplinary areas of literature and converges on meter as the underlying organizational feature common to music and language. The investigation was carried out in a primary school and employed a mixed design experiment, involving a randomly selected sample of children, 8-10 years of age. Intervention groups received the rhythm-based music intervention for 10 minutes each week for 6 weeks. The effects of training in rhythm were measured before and after the intervention, examining reading behavior and rhythmic performance. Controls were matched on their abilities in reading comprehension and rhythmic performance. Statistically significant effects occurred in reading comprehension scores for the children with lower attainment in reading. One implication of this approach is that children with reading difficulties benefit from holistic teaching, promoting an overlap rather than a distinction between curriculum areas.

Keywords
Scaffold, entrainment, reading comprehension, rhythm, attention, regulation

Introduction

According to theories of learning, cognitive scaffolding is a metaphor that describes an approach to teaching young children founded on observed interaction between parent and child (Urquart, 2000). Teachers position themselves as parents involved in developing the child's control of their cognitive attention by providing verbal instruction, questions, guiding the child's responses and directing the child's focus (Bruner, 1983), but maintaining the complexity of the task all the while, until a practical or conceptual process has been internalized (Bruner, 1983; Urquart, 2000). So although the level of task complexity remains unmodified, it can be stratified and segmented into a sequence of smaller tasks that match and nurture the needs of the learner (Wood, Bruner, & Ross, 1976). One limitation of this approach is that individual tailoring of the task to meet every child's needs cannot realistically be expected of teachers in the classroom setting (Mercer & Fisher, 1998). Described as an information processing model of learning, scaffolding regards language as the principle form of social interaction; Bruner coined the term "tool of thought" because the use of language preceded flexible thinking while imparting cultural values and beliefs (Bruner, 1996).

Arguably, music in everyday life plays an important role in the transmission of knowledge and imparts cultural values and beliefs. Marsh (2008) studied children's playground games and observed among the children an untaught readiness to master the games and to pass these down from older to younger children. She suggested that music with action provides an alternative means of channeling the child's cognitive attention. Her comprehensive cross-cultural ethnographic approach showed that children's clapping games are complex in terms of the demands of cognition, physical coordination and musicianship. Further, the children learned the games without prior modification of their rhythmical complexity, though the co-ordination of the clapping actions was simplified when older children taught a game or song to younger children.

Predating Marsh's work, Blacking was among the first ethnomusicologists to point out that the human body behaves as an instrument by transmitting, receiving and engaging in social and cultural exchanges (Juntunen & Westerlund, 2001). In studies of Venda children's singing he, like Marsh, found that children adopted scaffolding techniques in teaching songs to younger children (Blacking, 1995). Complex rather than simple songs were preferred. Perhaps these songs carried greater social-cultural value or were simply more appealing, but Marsh (2008) noted that accurate knowledge of playground songs was considered to be socially advantageous by children.

The social-cultural value of songs in childhood may be explained by examining mother-infant dyads and studies of early cultural behavior. Scholars suggest that conditions in the Pleistocene era required individuals to engage in high levels of mutuality and within group dependency as "a society of intimates." Strong group cohesion was necessary for survival and entrainment as a means of achieving the integration of information through group singing, is thought to have played an important role in social fitness and bonding (Merker, Madison, & Eckerdal, 2009). Thus, early societies practiced bonding behaviors, but Dissanyake (2006) proposed that socially cohesive behavior followed a social interaction proto-type established between infant and mother in the first months of life. This dyadic interaction appears to function principally for emotional regulation, but also scaffolds the distribution of the infant's attention. For example, researchers have found that infants prefer fast rhythmic patterns, though slower more elongated patterns of words, phrases, contours, exaggerated actions, and gestures and facial expressions are typically provided by mothers as an entrained form of interaction (Dissanyake, 2006; Phillips-Silver, Aktipis, & Bryant, 2010). Furthermore, mothers, having habituated and entrained their infant's attention to the predictability and regularity of certain patterns, will in subsequent interaction subvert and manipulate these patterns by surprising their infant with visual, vocal or kinesic novel experiences. So, mothers actively scaffold the assimilation and accommodation of *new* information upon infants' prior experience (Dissanyake, 2006).

The supply of a stream of predictable and familiar patterns in mother-infant interactions is of high importance because these provide a necessary framework or structure against which new information can be assimilated. It is argued here, that assimilation is most efficient if the invariant (consistent) framework has optimal stability and resilience. Historically, Gibson (1969) identified rhythm and tempo to be invariants, abstracted by infants. This means that they quickly learn to discern and identify what is consistent in their auditory environment and then habituate to this. At seven months of age, infants discriminated changes in both tempo and rhythm, and detected an invariant pattern amid rhythmic change (Pickens & Bahrick, 1997). Further, evidence for perception of temporal invariants as embodied was suggested by a study showing that the infants habituated more readily to duple and triple meters after being bounced up and down while keeping time with the rhythmic structure (Phillips-Silver & Trainor, 2005). These findings suggest that infants' discernment of temporality in the auditory stream involves analysis of rhythmic structures as a multi-layered system, as proposed by Bregman (1990, 1993).

The development of infants' rhythmic awareness is relevant to the development of speech imitation. Vocal learning relies on coupling between auditory input and motor output (Patel, 2006). Researchers have found that both motor synchronization and syntax are temporally related, information processing being based on predictions of future events (Schmidt-Kassow & Kotz, 2008). This research lends support firstly to "prosodic bootstrapping theory" (Gleitman & Wanner, 1982) in which reading behavior is attuned to grouping of words as phrases which imitate the contours of natural speech and secondly, to research investigating the deliberate scaffolding of attentional cognitive structures in infants through infant-mother communication (Drake, Jones, & Baruch, 2000).

Theoretical work on the dynamics of attending has accounted for the perception and abstraction of invariants as an inferred hierarchy of ratio-based subdivisions (Jones, 1976). An "ideal hierarchy" of time value subdivisions in duple meter (Jones & Boltz, 1989) is consistent with children's preferred time ratio of 2:1 (Drake & Betrand, 2003) such as in counting songs and nursery rhymes (Goswami, 1990, 2003; Schmidt-Kassow & Kotz, 2008) and playground songs (Marsh, 2008), where invariants, as individual focal points are inferred as distributed regularly in time.

Moreover, studies of rhythmic performance showed that a duple meter enabled the individual to optimally divide their attention between different levels of rhythmic output simultaneously, demonstrating a natural capacity to assimilate multiple layers of rhythm linked by the ratios governing the subdivision of beats (Klein & Jones, 1996). Many studies have found that individuals prefer tapping to music that has a simple, stable metrical structure, consisting of simple time ratios and structures which would facilitate straightforward divisions of attention as reviewed by Large (2000). London (2004) noted that this process occurred without conscious effort, arguing for a subliminal process of metrical entrainment in which meter, as an invariant, functions as the perceptual ground against which rhythmic figures are positioned.

A recent study of children's ability to entrain to an external timekeeper showed evidence of individual differences in rhythmic development at 2.5 years of age (Kirschner & Tomasello, 2009). Historically, systematic observations of children's rhythmic development by Jaques-Dalcroze (1905) showed that varying levels of rhythmic organization do exist.

Individual differences in children's rhythmic capacity, in expressing rhythms and in measuring time were proposed to relate to an irregularity of gait that could be corrected under "the control of the eye and muscular senses", thereby advocating an embodied pedagogic approach to rhythm (Jaques-Dalcroze, 1905, p. 31-32). Through rhythmic training, Jaques-Dalcroze developed a systematic approach for regulating the natural rhythms of the body (see Bachmann, 1993), viewing the influence of rhythm at three levels. Firstly, like Jones (1976) and Large (2000) (who later also described rhythmic perception at the mechanical physical level), he stated that in moving a body in space and time in continuous repetition, responses would pass beyond the conscious control of the brain and become automatic (Jacques-Dalcroze, 1973). He also referred to manifestation of rhythmic processing at the perceptual level and metaphysical level. In describing the effort required to master movement and consistent with Dissanyake's (2006) stance, he noted that emotional regulation and integration were fundamental to rhythmic control in human expression: "Rhythm is the very image of the soul, reproduced in the inflections in the voice, the successive variations of passages of a speech" (Dalcroze, 1973, p. 31).

In spite of the systematic efforts of Jaques-Dalcroze to interpret and account for impairments in rhythmic awareness, this remains a relatively neglected area of pedagogic research. However, a growing body of evidence suggests that a difficulty with processing rhythmic information impacts deleteriously on reading behavior (Anvari, Trainor, Woodside, & Levi, 2002; Corriveau & Goswami, 2009; Douglas & Willats, 1994; Overy, 2000, 2008; Tallal & Gaab, 2006; Wolff, Michel, Ovrut, & Drake, 1990; Wolff, 2002). Nonetheless, the emerging link between rhythmic awareness and development of reading was first proposed by music educators. Similar to the pedagogy of Jacques-Dalcroze, the Kodaly method recognizes that rhythmic control is fundamental to the development of the individual (Simpson, 1973). The Kodaly approach was investigated in a study by Hurwitz, Wolff, Bortnick, and Kokas (1975). They hypothesized that the initial emphasis on rhythm-based actions would influence several areas of learning: sequencing, spatial reasoning and reading behavior. They found that after one year of training in rhythmic movement, children from the Kodaly trained group had made significant gains in their reading behavior.

Overall, the studies reviewed here suggest that entrainment to and abstraction of a metrical pulse (an invariant) has its roots in inherent responses initially manifesting in human infancy. Music pedagogues such as Jaques-Dalcroze and Kodaly have argued that our natural rhythmical responses remain imprecise and approximate in early childhood and that training in rhythm benefits child development in terms of information processing with greater responsiveness, flexibility, clarity and precision (Simpson, 1973). The observations of Jaques-Dalroze suggested that rhythmic training improved behavior consistent with information processing. So, following the line of enquiry developed by Hurwitz and colleagues and the theoretical models of the distribution of cognitive attention by M. R. Jones and her co-workers, the effects of a rhythm-based music intervention on children's reading behavior were investigated.

Method

Recruitment and sample

The study was located in a junior mixed-infant schools (for children aged 4-11 years), in a small market town. Class teachers randomly selected 25 mixed ability children, aged between eight and nine years.

Design

A mixed design was used. The children were tested on abilities in reading and rhythm at the beginning and end of each investigation. Previous findings showed that Kodaly method training enhanced reading comprehension in boys (Hurwitz et al., 1975). Therefore the children were matched as pairs according to baseline scores in reading comprehension, gender and rhythmic ability and the children from each matched pair were randomly assigned to the intervention or control group of each experiment. Thus, the intervention and control groups were comparable on baseline scores. The intervention group took part in a 10 minute rhythm-based music intervention each week for six weeks. The controls remained in their usual classroom music lesson.

The rhythm-based music intervention

The rhythm-based music intervention was shown to the children in three stages. First, the researcher demonstrated marching 'on the spot', keeping time with the beat of a musical accompaniment. The intervention involved mental anticipation of the lifting of one foot while striking the other foot against the floor in synchrony with the strong beat of the musical accompaniment and the actions of the other children in the room. This activity applies theoretical modeling of entrainment through maintenance of normal anti-synchrony, as 'one foot comes up the other goes down' (Clayton, Sager, & Will, 2004), consistent with a stable hierarchical distribution of cognitive attention (see Clayton, Sager & Will, 2004; Jones & Boltz, 1989).

Second, clapping actions were synchronized with the marching action which divided the organization of attention (Jones & Yee, 1993), between upper and lower limbs. Cognitively, the children were required to plan ahead, synchronize, monitor and integrate multi-level physical coordination with the musical accompaniment and the invariant impulses of other participants in the room.

Lastly, the children read simple staff notation, chanting on a monotone the alphabet letter names of four notes in time with the self-regulated control of marching and clapping actions. During the course of the intervention the same four pitches were read, but the durations were occasionally varied (see Table 1).

Table 1: Possible combinations of actions and utterances in the music intervention.

	Alternating left/right foot strikes floor	Hands clap	Each utterance synchronizes with a foot striking the floor.
One beat note 'D'	1	1	'D!'
One beat rest	1	0	'Shh!'
Two beat note 'D'	2	1	'D! Wait!'
Two beat rest	2	0	'Shh! Wait!'

Note: four note names were used – C,G,D,A

Measuring abilities in reading behavior and rhythmic performance

(i) Reading behavior
The Neale Analysis of Reading Ability (NARA) (Neale, 1989) measures oral reading ability and comprehension of the text. This reading test is a more sensitive and ecologically valid tool than single word reading or forced choice reading comprehension tests. It measures integration of text with other context driven features of reading behavior such as vocabulary, schematic and general knowledge.

Scoring of reading accuracy was achieved by miscue analysis: recording the number of omitted, added, mispronounced, reversed or substituted words in the reading. Reading comprehension was scored by recording the number of correct responses to questions demanding literal and inferential responses, posed immediately after the child had read the passage of text. Literal responses required the child to simply retrieve information directly from the text, whereas inferential responses required assimilation and accommodation of the text to schematic and general knowledge.

The reading comprehension scores were recorded as a percentage of correct comprehension responses given. Rate of reading scores were recorded as words per minute (wpm). Reading accuracy raw scores were calculated by deducting the number of incorrect scores from a maximum score of 16 as directed in the manual. The raw scores for reading accuracy were then converted to a percentage. Practical time constraints on individual testing limited each child to reading two or three passages of text and answering comprehension questions on these. This form of testing formed an adequate basis for before and after comparisons to be made. The manual allows for retesting after six weeks.

(ii) Rhythmic performance
In previous research, readers with a learning disability were able to discriminate rhythmic patterns similarly to age matched controls, but were unable to perform the same patterns (Atterbury, 1985). A clapping-in-time test was included in this investigation. The children clapped in time with the beat of the music in small groups (of two or three), and then each child was required to maintain the beat independently. This test categorized each child as having a strong or weak sense of meter. A strong sense of meter was scored when the child maintained their clapping in time with the musical stimulus without the support of others in the group. The song used, "Moreno O Ba Etelle" is a lively Gospel music chorus with a strong regular metrical beat at a moderate tempo, pre-recorded by "Holy Spirits Choir" of South Africa.

Results
Having met the assumption for equality of error variance, a multivariate analysis of variance revealed a significant multivariate main effect for ability in reading: Wilksλ = .508 (F (4, 14) = 3.389, p = .039, ηp^2 = .492). Using ηp^2 as the measure of association, the main multivariate effect of the independent variable of above or below mean level in reading ability on the system of dependent variables accounted for 49% of the total variation in scores and associated error in the mean change scores. This was exceeded by the multivariate main effect of the independent variable of group: Wilksλ = .442 (F (4, 14) = 4.420, p = .016, ηp^2 = .558), which accounted for 56% of the total variation in scores and associated error. The main multivariate effect for the independent variable of rhythmic production

was not significant: Wilksλ = .654 (F (4, 14) = 1.848, $p > .05$, $\eta p^2 = .346$).

Between subjects significant main effect

The critical value for F reached significance in change in reading comprehension, (F (1, 17) = 3.434, $p = .012$, $\eta p^2 = .610$). A main effect occurred for group on change scores in reading comprehension: (F (1, 17) = 14.526, $p = .001$, $\eta p^2 = .461$). Gains occurred in the intervention group ($n = 13$, M = 21.15, SD = 35.86), but not the control group ($n = 12$, M = -1.04, SD = 19.55). There was a medium effect size, with 46% of the proportion of total variation in scores and associated error being attributable to the main effect of group on the change in reading comprehension. There were no main effects for change in reading accuracy or change in rate of reading.

Significant Interaction Effect

An interaction effect occurred between group and ability to clap in time on change scores in reading accuracy: (F (1, 17) = 7.539, $p = .014$, $\eta p^2 = .307$). The children of the intervention group with a weak response in the clapping in time test ($n = 4$, M = 15.63, SD = 20.45) improved in reading accuracy more than controls of commensurate rhythmic ability ($n = 5$, M = -16.5, SD = 49.45) and more than the rhythmically competent children in the intervention group ($n = 9$, M = 6.96, SD = 21.90) and rhythmically competent controls ($n = 7$, M = 13.10, SD = 20.37). A small effect size was recorded. This finding demonstrated that reading accuracy mean change scores for intervention group children with a weak clapping response showed greater improvement than those of controls. Furthermore, children in the intervention group with a weak clapping response made greater gains than children in the same group with a strong clapping response (see Table 2).

Table 2. Mean change scores and standard deviations.

Experimental Group	n	Reading Comprehension		Reading Accuracy		Reading Rate	
		Int.	Ctrl	Int.	Ctrl	Int.	Ctrl
Overall Sample	13:12	21.15 (35.86)	-1.04 (19.55)	9.62 (21.02)	0.76 (36.71)	0.37 (13.27)	-6.0 (16.24)
Above mean reading score sample	8:5	10.94 (29.46)	-17.5 (18.96)	4.39 (11.97)	-4.5 (39.86)	0.21 (16.19)	-13.9 (18.97)
Below mean reading score sample	5:7	37.50 (42.39)	10.71 (8.63)	18.00 (30.52)	4.46 (37.05)	0.63 (8.35)	-0.4 (12.48)
Above threshold rhythm score sample	9:7	18.06 (29.39)	-8.93 (21.30)	6.96 (21.90)	13.10 (20.37)	-2.61 (14.91)	-6.2 (19.98)
Below threshold rhythm score sample	4:5	28.13 (52.42)	10.00 (10.46)	15.63 (20.45)	-16.5 (49.45)	7.07 (5.03)	-5.8 (11.26)

Discussion

This investigation reported a significant effect of group on gains in change in reading comprehension and a significant interaction effect of ability in clapping in time on reading accuracy, favoring the children in the intervention group that had a weak clapping response in baseline tests. Although the participants' reading comprehension skills had not been directly targeted during the rhythm-based music intervention, the empirical evidence strongly indicated that significant gains in reading comprehension occurred following participation in the intervention.

An embodied cognitive scaffold

The music intervention impacted on the children's reading comprehension without improving reading accuracy or rate of reading. This is intriguing, but may be explained by referring to social constructivist theory, where it is reasoned that learning consists of the internalization of social interactional processes; development proceeds when interpsychological regulation is transformed into intrapsychological regulation (Vygotsky, 1978). As a social interactional process, the rhythm-based music intervention demanded interpsychological regulation and intrapsychological regulation in social, physical and mental behavior. After participating in the intervention, the below average reading ability children read the NARA stories with improved expression and answered reading comprehension questions accurately, which implied that intrapsychological regulation had occurred.

The established view of cognitive scaffolding asserts that although the level of task complexity remains unmodified, the child is taught to tackle a challenging task by breaking it down into a series of manageable sub-tasks which are later reassembled in their more challenging composite form (Wood et al., 1976). By contrast the embodied cognitive scaffold proposed here, maintains its congruent multi-level form; consistent with observations of children instructing peers (Marsh, 2008; Blacking, 1995).

One advantage of using music rather than language as "a tool of thought" (Bruner, 1996) is that scaffolding can take place as a group activity. Thus the limitations of conventional language-based scaffolding, employed at an individual level in the classroom (Mercer & Fisher, 1998), can be complemented by a collaborative activity that benefits children through group level interaction. These findings show that reading comprehension was improved through cognitive scaffolding of attention, using the rhythm-based music intervention as a tool of thought (Bruner, 1996).

The findings of the present study suggested that participation in a rhythm-based intervention improved reading behavior when rhythmic awareness was weak. Substantial weakness was systematically observed in some young children's natural rhythmic response by Jaques-Dalcroze and Zoltan Kodaly (Simpson, 1973) and also among very young children (Kirschner & Tomasello, 2009). The gains in reading behavior shown by rhythmically weak children in the present study suggest that engaging the children in structured rhythmic activity has positive implications for the development of their reading. Therefore, the rhythm-based music intervention as a multi-level enactive approach provided a useful method for scaffolding the orchestrated processes that mediate multi-level cognitive tasks such as reading.

Temporal Organization
Following research by Clayton et al. (2004) and M. R. Jones and colleagues, the abstraction of an invariant (the beat) and maintenance of an anti-synchrony pattern (of lifting and striking alternate feet) is consistent with a stable organization of modeled distributions of cognitive attention (e.g., Jones & Boltz, 1989). The rhythm-based music intervention involved marching 'on the spot' with clapping actions, and following Jones and Yee (1993) subdivided the inferred temporal organization of attention. In this way the rhythm-based music intervention is an embodied cognitive scaffold.

Arguably, a lack of rhythmic stability in the weaker children's reading behavior would obscure rhythmic perception of the natural stress patterns of the language in reading. The effect of the intervention appears to have addressed unevenly distributed cognitive attention and through training in rhythm the organization of children's reading behavior appeared to improve. To date, there is little empirical evidence suggesting that language processing is organized by the perception of invariants in the same way that music and dance are (Phillips-Silver, Aktipis & Bryant, 2010). However, these findings suggest that unifying principles may indeed underlie the production of meter in the generative processing of language, music and dance.

Theory of affordances and bi-pedal locomotion
Maintaining anti-synchrony in time with the others in the room was more difficult for particular children, clearly illustrating individual differences in the production of a regular rhythmic pulse. Studies of infants showed that in developing sufficient physical and mental control to transfer from crawling on four limbs to bipedal locomotion, imposes a redistribution of cognitive attention. Researchers, Palmer, Jungers, and Jusczyk (2001) reported the assimilation of temporal invariants in music at this stage in development, suggesting greater discrimination across all the senses. Ecological theories of Gibson, Riccio, Schmuckler, Stiffregen, Roseberg, and Taormina (1987) showed that infants plan paths and judge the traversability of surfaces primarily using vision, describing the maintenance of balance and mental focus as a conscious process, "every stagger or waver produces optical flow patterns that control activities essential to maintaining balance while engaged in locomotion, especially on a compliant surface" (Gibson et al., 1987, p. 543). So it is interesting that the rhythm-based music intervention subverts normal human gait. By marching "on the spot" rather than through space, the usual optic-flow patterns that would normally provide visual sensory information to the vestibular system were absent due to the relatively static nature of the task. Indeed, the usual optic-flow patterns were replaced by a reading task – through which, parallel horizontal lines of music staff notation arguably provided sufficient visual sensory information to stabilize physical balance and set parameters for the distribution of cognitive attention. It is suggested here that difficulties with reading comprehension are associated with weak production of meter and were resolved through cognitive scaffolding using entrainment.

Conclusion
Previous research has identified a temporal deficit in poor readers. These findings justify consideration of weak production of meter in future research on reading behavior. This research was exploratory and involved only a small sample, yet cautious interpretation of the significant effects suggested that training in rhythm produced gains in reading com-

prehension among weaker readers. Future research should measure the prosodic qualities of reading behavior to establish an empirical basis for explaining gains in reading comprehension in relation to spatial-temporal processing. These findings suggest that future applications of entrainment studies may incur positive educational outcomes.

References

Anvari, S. H., Trainor, L. J., Woodside, J. & Levy, B. A. (2002). Relations among musical skills, phonological processing and early reading ability in preschool children. *Journal of Experimental Child Psychology, 83*, 111-130.

Atterbury, B. W. (1985). Musical differences in learning disabled and normal achieving readers, aged seven, eight and nine. *Psychology of Music, 13*(2), 114–123.

Bachmann, M. L. (1993). *Dalcroze today: An education through and into music.* Oxford, UK: Oxford University Press.

Blacking, J. (1995). Expressing human experience through music. In R. Byron (ed.). *Music Culture and Experience: Selected Papers of John Blacking.* Chicago: University of Chicago Press.

Bregman, A. S. (1990). *Auditory scene analysis: The perceptual organization of sound.* Cambridge, MA: MIT.

Bregman, A. S. (1993). Auditory scene analysis: Hearing in complex environments. In S. McAdams & E. Bigand (Eds), *Thinking in sound, the cognitive psychology of human audition* (pp. 10-36). Oxford, UK: Oxford University Press.

Bruner, J. S. (1983). *Child's talk: Learning to use language.* New York, NY: Norton.

Bruner, J. S. (1996). *The culture of education.* Cambridge, MA: Harvard University Press.

Clayton, M., Sager, R., & Will, U. (2004). In time with the music: The concept of entrainment and its significance for ethnomusicology. *Eur. Meet. Ethnomusicol. 11*, 3–75.

Corriveau, K. H., & Goswami, U. (2009). Rhythmic motor entrainment in children with speech and language impairments: Tapping to the beat. *Cortex, 45*(1), 115-130.

Dissanyake, E. (2006). In the beginning: Pleistocene and infant aesthetics and twenty-first century education in the arts. In L. Bresler (Ed.), *International handbook of research in arts education* (pp.783-797). Dordrecht, The Netherlands: Springer.

Douglas, S., & Willats, P. (1994). The relationship between musical ability and literacy skills. *Journal of Research in Reading, 17*(8), 99-107.

Drake, C., & Betrand, D. (2003). The quest for universals in temporal processing in music. In I. Peretz & R. Zatorre (Eds.), *The cognitive neuroscience of music* (pp. 21-31). Oxford, UK: Oxford University Press.

Drake, C., Jones, M. R., & Baruch, C. (2000).The development of rhythmic attending in auditory sequences: Attunement, referent period and focal attending. *Cognition, 77*, 251-288.

Gleitman, L. R., & Wanner, E. (1982). Language acquisition: The state of the art. In E. Wanner & R. L. Gleitman (Eds.), *Language acquisition: The state of the art (*pp. 3–48). New York, NY: Cambridge Books.

Gibson, E. J. (1969). *Principles of perceptual learning and development.* New York, NY: Appleton-Century-Crofts.

Gibson, E. J., Riccio, G., Schmuckler, M. A., Stoffregen, T. A., Roseberg, D., & Taormina, J. (1987). Detection of the traversability of surfaces by crawling and walking infants. *Journal of Experimental Psychology: Human Perception and Performance, 13*(4), 533-544.

Goswami, U. (1990). Phonological priming and orthographical analogies in reading. *Journal of Experimental Psychology, 49*, 323-340.

Goswami, U. (2003). How to beat dyslexia: The Broadbent lecture 2003. *The Psychologist, 16*(9), 462-465.

Hurwitz, I., Wolff, P. H., Bortnick, B. D., & Kokas, K. (1975). Non-musical effects of the Kodaly music curriculum in primary grade children. *Journal of Learning Disabilities, 8*, 45–52.

Jaques-Dalcroze, E. (1905 / 1966). An essay in the reform of music teaching in schools. In E. Jaques-Dalcroze (Ed.), *Rhythm and music education*. London, UK: The Dalcroze Society.

Jaques-Dalcroze, E. (1921). *Rhythm, music and education*. London: Riverside Press, new edition, 1967, paperback edition, 1973.

Jones, M. R. (1976). Time, our lost dimension: Towards a new theory of perception, attention and memory. *Psychological Review, 83*, 323-355.

Jones, M. R., & Boltz, M. (1989). Dynamic attending and responses to time. *Psychological Review, 96*, 459–491.

Jones, M. R., & Yee, W. (1993). Attending to auditory events: The role of temporal organization. In S. McAdams & E. Bigand (Eds.), *Thinking in sound: The cognitive psychology of human audiation* (pp 68–112). Oxford, UK: Oxford University Press.

Juntunen, M. L., & Westerlund, H. (2001). Digging Dalcroze, or, dissolving the mind-body dualism: Philosophical and practical remarks on the musical body in action. *Music Education Research, 3*(2), 203-214.

Kirschner, S., & Tomasello, M. (2009). Joint drumming: Social context facilitates synchronization in pre-school children. *Journal of Experimental Child Psychology, 102*, 299-314.

Klein, J. M., & Jones, M. R. (1996). Effects of attentional set and rhythmic complexity on attending. *Perception and Psychophysics, 58*, 34-46.

Large, E. W. (2000). On synchronising movements to music. *Human Movement Science, 19*, 527-566.

London, J. (2004). *Hearing in time: Psychological aspects of musical meter*. Oxford, UK: OUP.

Marsh, K. (2008). *The musical playground*. Oxford, UK: Oxford University Press.

Mercer, N., & Fisher, E. (1998). How do teachers help children to learn? In D. Faulkner, K. Littleton, & M. Woodhead (Eds), *Learning relationships in the classroom* (pp.111-130). London, UK & New York, NY: Routledge.

Merker, B., Madison, G., & Eckerdal, P. (2009). On the role and origin of isochrony in human rhythmic entrainment. *Cortex, 45*, 1-17.

Neale, M. D. (1989). *Neale analysis of reading ability* (Revized British Edition). Windsor: NFER-Nelson.

Overy, K. (2000). Dyslexia, temporal processing and music: The potential of music as an early learning aid for dyslexic children. *Psychology of Music, 28*, 218–229.

Overy, K. (2008). Classroom rhythm games for literacy support. In T. Miles, J. Westcombe, & D. Ditchfield (Eds.). *Music and dyslexia: A positive approach* (pp. 26-44). Chichester, England: John Wiley & Sons.

Palmer, C., Jungers, M. K., & Jusczyk, P. W. (2001). Episodic memory for musical prosody. *Journal of Memory and Language, 45*, 526–545.

Patel, A. D. (2006). Musical rhythm, linguistic rhythm, and human evolution. *Music Perception, 24*, 99-104.

Phillips-Silver, J., Aktipis, C. A., & Bryant, G.A. (2010). The ecology of entrainment: Foundations of coordinated rhythmic movement. *Music Perception, 28*(1), 3-14.

Phillips-Silver, J., & Trainor, L. (2005). Feeling the beat: Movement influences infant rhythm perception. *Science, 308*, 1430.

Pickens, J.E. & Bahrick, L.E. (1995). Infants' discrimination of events on the basis of rhythm and tempo. *British Journal of Developmental Psychology, 13*, 223-236.

Schmahmann, J. D., & Pandya, D.N. (1997). The cerebrocerebellar system. In R. T. Bradley, R. A. Harris, & P. Jenner (Eds.), *International Review of Neurobiology, 41*, 613-636, Academic Press.

Schmidt-Kassow, M., & Kotz, S.A. (2008). Entrainment of syntactic processing? ERP-responses to predictable time intervals during syntactic reanalysis. *Brain Research, 1226*, 144-155.

Simpson, K. (1973). *Some great music educators.* London, UK: Novello.

Tallal, P. & Gaab, N. (2006). Dynamic auditory processing, musical experience and language development. *Trends in Neurosciences, 29*(7), 382-390.

Urquart, I. (2000). Communicating well with children. In D. Whitebread (Ed.), *The psychology of teaching and learning in the primary school* (pp. 57-77). Oxford, UK: Routledge.

Vygotsky, L. S. (1978). *Mind in society: The development of higher psychological processes.* London, UK: Harvard University Press.

Wolff, P. H., Michel, G. F., Ovrut, M., & Drake, C. (1990). Rate and Timing precision of motor coordination in developmental dyslexia, *Developmental Psychology, 26*, 349-59.

Wolff, P. H. (2002). Timing precision and rhythm in developmental dyslexia. *Reading and Writing, 15*, 179-206.

Wood, D., Bruner, J., & Ross, G. (1976). The role of tutoring in problem-solving. *Journal of Child Psychology and Child Psychiatry, 17*, 89–100.

Music Education and the Post-modern Condition: Challenges and Perspectives

Maria K. Magaliou
Third Directorate of Primary Education
Athens, Greece
marmagaliou@gmail.com

Abstract

Education faces a crisis globally. New conditions of the postmodern world have altered the way knowledge is processed and distributed and have caused a dramatical change in the essence of the term "knowledge" and consequently on the role and the priorities of education worldwide. Although music plays an important and indisputable role in our everyday lives, music education has been critisized for not meeting young people's needs and for remaining "frozen" and untouched by today's societal and educational change. The present article examines what postmodern philosophy claims about the current state of knowledge and education and explores ways in which music education can meet the demands of postmodern pedagogy and promote the adjustment of the individual and societies in the current social condition. A re-definition of the priorities of music education and a critical reflection on its past omissions and failures is also discussed as a presupposition for it to "reconnect with society" and to become a tool for democracy.

Keywords
Music education, postmodernity, globalization

Theoretical background

In the 1980s French philosopher Francois Lyotard adopted the term "post-modern" (Lyotard, 1984) and since then an international conversation has begun on postmodernity in various fields, like art, history, sociology and education. Lyotard (1984) was interested in the changing state of knowledge and education in advanced societies, where technology, globalization and capitalism have radically transformed the emergence, transference, delivery, and even the presumed nature of knowledge (Locke, 2008). The ambiguity of the term, the absolute affirmation of pluralism, the sensibility to any kind of meta-theory, the co-existence of different and often contradictory approaches in every field of knowledge are recognised as the basic characteristics of postmodernity.

Modern philosophy was based on the notion that individuals and systems consist of given structures and are ruled by laws of a determinist nature, that man can prove and use these laws through the use of rationalism, and that the liberalization of man from the commitments of ignorance would deterministically be succeeded through science. According to these philosophical grounds, a better school would be created, that would respect children's nature and would prepare new generations for the constant progress of societies (Matsaggouras, 2001). Human knowledge was thought to be based on grand narratives, which were supposed to entail absolute certainty. But this is not the case for today's advanced societies, which don't have absolute, all-guiding, or all-knowing insights, capable of dictating a definitive account of human knowledge (Locke, 2008). Post-modernity, according to Lyotard (1984), is simply an acknowledgement that the grand narratives supported by modernism no longer warrant the claims to certainty on which they have based their persuasive and educative power and can no longer reveal the deep, inner meanings of society. As human rights catastrophes of recent decades make evident, there is no longer any justification for the belief that human kind will "naturally" progress towards freedom and peace as a matter of course.

Modern philosophy has considered knowledge as an end in itself. In the post modern perception knowledge is taking an operational character, as great importance is attributed to the relationship between the suppliers and the users of knowledge, in analogy to the relationship between the suppliers and the consumers of material goods (Lyotard, 1984). Lyotard considers digital technology a decisive parameter for the new nature of knowledge in postmodern society, as the quantity of knowledge is defined by the processing and consumption of information in the cyberspace. The consumption of information ruins the legitimization of knowledge as truth and diverts it to an instrument. What determines knowledge is not its usefulness, but the way it is distributed, stored and delivered. According to the postmodern notion, anything that cannot be recognized and stored by a computer will not constitute knowledge anymore. The opposite of knowledge will not be ignorance, but what Lyotard calls "parasite", meaning, whatever cannot be recognised by the digital system (1984).

Post –modern philosophy has inevitably affected current educational thought. Although educational sciences have critisized postmodern views, they have adopted some of their positive elements like: 1. the acceptance and recognition of pluralism, which resulted in the growth of multicultural education; 2. the questioning about the boundaries of education and the rejection of modernity dogmatisms about the omnipotence of education; and 3. the dispute of rationalism and scientific orientation, which resulted in the recognition of the importance of emotional intelligence, the education of the imagination and feelings, as well as the broadening of pedagogical speculation about current social issues (Delikonstantis, 2001). Based on the above elements, postmodern pedagogy has emerged, aiming at the production of operational/functional knowledge as well as on the holistic, interdisciplinary study of the natural, as well as the social reality (Matsaggouras, 2001).

Aim of the paper

The present article discusses the contribution of music education in meeting the demands of post-modern pedagogy about the cultivation of emotional intelligence and the education of feelings, the acceptance and recognition of pluralism and future citizens' sensitization about current social issues. It also discusses changes that are necessary in the established philosophy and practices of music education worldwide, so that music education accomplishes the above mission.

The success of music education in accomplishing its mission has been seriously questioned by the educational community and society in recent years. As Elliott (2007) claims, this mission "has been too narrowly conceived" (p. 19). The emphasis has been on developing musical skills alone, or "educating feeling", without a deeper insight on how music education could contribute to enabling students' adaptation to the rapidly changing ways people live, learn, interact, work and create self-identity and self-respect in today's world. In addition, there has been criticism about whether there has been any compelling empirical evidence that young people's "musical lives, habits, dispositions and tastes have been benefited in tangible or lasting ways" by music education (Regelski, 2006, p. 5).

It has been claimed that "unless each of today's professions can maintain its integrity, redevelop its mission, strengthen its internal alignment and persuade society that it is a valuable and trustworthy domain, it will be marginalized socially, morally, financially and in global terms" (Gardner, Csikszentmihalyi, & Damon, 2001, p. 24,). If we accept this statement, we should be really skeptic about the future of music education. If music education is to survive as an integral part of today's education it should redefine its philosophy and practices, so that they are in line with the demands of general education in the era of post modernity. It should help future citizens find ways to face the challenges of the new global condition.

Summary of main ideas

A challenge future citizens will have to face is that they should be able to adjust in rapidly and constantly changing conditions. This means that they will encounter difficulties in defining their identity and these difficulties could affect their social and emotional well-being. Arts education in general and music education more precisely can play a crucial role in helping people to assert their identity and succeed an emotional balance in their life. Throughout history, singing, playing music and dancing have been ways for people to fight against violence, to explore their identity and their emotions and have functioned as tools that help them survive through the tensions and troubles of the world (Denac, 2009).

Music as a form of art has the potential to afford intrinsic value to those who hear or perform it. If that potential is realized, "music has a significant contribution to make to the personal development of students: to the broadening of their interests and the development of their skills" (Arnstine, 2000, p. 6) as well as to the definition of their identity and the maintenance of their emotional and intellectual balance in a rapidly changing world, characterized by uncertainty and instability. But this potential can only be accomplished through meaningful and intrinsically worthwhile activities that enhance the quality of students' immediate experience and contribute to their individual development "in ways that make their lives richer, more varied, and more rewarding" (Arnstine, 2000, p. 5).

Another challenge future citizens will have to face is the increasing connectivity and interdependence between different cultures, caused by "the collapse of many geographical and cultural borders, an enormous increase in new migratory populations, … and a mass back-and-forth transfer of media images" (Bloom, 2004, cited in Elliott, 2007, p. 15). As Tomlinson (1999) noted, "culture can no longer be conceived as having inevitable ties to meanings in one location;" but is generated "by people on the move and in the flows and connections between cultures" (p. 2). Without understanding and respecting other people and acquiring the attitudes and skills needed to interact effectively with them, young people cannot function as responsible citizens in today's world.

The connectivity and interdependence between different cultures, often described as globalization, inevitably affects our relationship with music. During the process of musical enculturation, people construct a musical identity, which is tied with both the regional and the international context. Our musical identities, often described as hybrids (Forari, 2007), are a mixture of different musical cultures and musical elements (Gilroy, 1993). Furthermore, our musical identities are not static, as the social factors determining them constantly change and shape them accordingly (Forari, 2007). Music education should aim at helping young people realize that our musical world consists of various different musical cultures and develop a respect for this diversity, regarding it as a wealth for humanity and as a tool for democracy. When musics are kept separate "so are values and attitudes and broad outlooks on life" (Arnstine, 2000, p. 12). A music education that values and stresses musical diversity can help people realize that "music of other times and places sounds different because people's values and beliefs were different ..." (Arnstine, 2000, p. 12). Let's not forget that diversity is the essence of democracy, while uniformity constitutes a kind of dogmatism (Forari, 2007).

Furthermore, music opens great opportunities for the promotion of co-operation and co-ordination of efforts, an element that is necessary in order for citizens of a globalized world to interact effectively with each other. As Christopher Small (1997) points out the meaning of the act of musicking lies "not only in the relationships between the humanly organized sounds which are conventionally thought of as the stuff of music, but also in the relationships which are established between person and person within the performance space" (p. 3-4). Music is a group activity in which "the interactions between individuals are as precisely timed and orchestrated as those within a single brain. The individuals are physically separate but temporally integrated" (Benzon, 2001, as cited in Regelski, 2006, p. 10). It has also been maintained that music has a unique capacity to enhance and deepen the solidarity of human groups and the sense of belonging of those involved (Arnstine, 2000).

A way music education can cultivate co-operation and group cohesion is through the connection of school music with community music. Music education has been criticized for being isolated from musicking in the adult life and outside school. A way to bridge this gap could be found in collaborative projects between schools and community music. As Elliott points out "school-music must redevelop its ends and means by integrating and/or merging with various forms of community music education to serve a wider spectrum of people and personal needs" (Elliott, 2007, p.19). Such collaborations could stress the social dimensions of music making and offer the framework in which "connections between community needs and the needs of individual students can be celebrated and strengthened" (Bates, 2004, p. 10).

It has also been maintained that music has the power to enable people to acquire an independent and fulfilling existence in order for them to contribute their part to a free and democratic community. Our musical identities as socio-political products determine who we are and function as means of self-determination and attribution of social meaning. Music can "tell us who we are" (Arnstine, 2000, p. 12) and help us understand how our identities, ideologies and life attitudes are shaped and change.

According to Woodford (in Locke, 2008) music's power lies in "its capacity to function as society's conscience, as a powerful democratic tool" (p. 76). Through music education, students can realize the interaction between changes in the arts and changes in society, as each exerts influence on the other. As Arnstine (2000) very felicitously notes:

> Changes in our music are usually heard long before changes in
> our values are understood or even perceived. Thus changes in our
> music are among the first and most powerful indicators of
> changing values and a changing society. People without an edu-
> cation in music are not aware of changes in it at all; they are
> aware only of what's happening in the present, and this is not a
> condition conducive to social responsibility. (p. 12)

Music education can help people realize that there are many forms of music that can be enjoyed by everyone, whatever their origin. But when people realize this fact, it is possible for them to realize also that the current balkanization of culture is not accidental, but it favors a small group of people, who may profit be keeping the constituent groups of society separate, so that they find it hard to recognize their common interests and nearly impossible to act in concert to achieve them (Arnstine, 2000).

Elliott (2007) has recommended the term "critical pedagogy" as a term that can describe what music education can offer in terms of helping students in their search for personal and musical identities. As he points out "critical pedagogy approaches the classroom as an opportunity for doing political and social work with and for students, teachers and the communities in which they live" (p. 20). Within such a framework, schools can nurture the abilities of critical reflection and empower the potential for democratic engagement and social transformation. If music educators adopt this view, the music-teaching situation can become a site for questioning and investigation, an arena of socio-political change.

But the adoption of this view requires a complete rethinking of the why, what and how of music teaching. It requires curricula that promote authentic music learning, serve the needs of the great majority of students and help students gain the deepest satisfactions music can offer (Reimer, 2005). It also requires devoted and professional music educators, who can decide what courses of action are appropriate in light of local circumstances, present needs and resources and the current socio-political framework (Bowman, 2005). With no definitive pedagogical approach or political doctrine and without a definitive account of what counts as music in the post-modern context, "ethical judgment" on the part of music educators is needed in our days more than ever (Locke, 2008, p. 81).

Conclusions and implications for music education

Music education can cultivate empathy with the physical and social environment and a heightened awareness of the human condition (Palmer, 2004). It can also make a contribution to "the ongoing search for an understanding of ourselves and each other" (Palmer, 2004, p. 129). But this contribution can only be accomplished by a school curriculum of music education that is founded on genuine music learning, is intrinsically motivating and used in life (Regelski, 2006). If music education reconnects with the social roots of all musicking, it can reconnect with today's society (Regelski, 2006). This reconnection presupposes a conversion from traditional aesthetic premises to "an expanded philosophy of music that considers music a central praxis of humankind, a vital part of our individual and social 'being'..." (Regelski, 2006, p. 11). Based on such an expanded philosophy and a critical examination and reform of curricula, music education can have "an effect on the general well being of local, national, and ultimately world community" (Palmer, 2004, p.

129). The position and function of music education in contemporary society should be reconsidered, through fruitful dialogue. This dialogue has only just begun and has the power to offer new visions and challenges to the music educators' profession.

References

Arnstine, D. (2000). Teaching what's dangerous: Ethical practice in music education. *Philosophy of Music Education Review, 8*(1), 3-13.

Bates, V. (2004). Where should we start? Indications of a nurturant ethic for music education. *Action, Critisism and Theory for Music Education, 3*(3). Retrieved from http://act.maydaygroup.org/articles/Bates3_3.pdf

Bowman, W. (2005). To what question(s) is music education advocacy the answer? *International Journal of Music Education, 23*, 125-129.

Delikonstantis, K. (2001). Metamonterna pedagogiki (in greek) (Post-modern Pedagogy). In D. Chatzidimou (Ed.), *Pedagogiki kai ekpedefsi, timitikos tomos gia ta exintapentachrona tou kathigiti Panagioti Xocheli. (Pedagogy and education, volume in honor of Professor's Panagiotis Xochelis sixty-five years)* (pp. 207-218). Thessaloniki, Greece: Kiriakidis Brothers.

Denac, O. (2009). The pedagogical value of art and music in the past and the present. *US-China Education Review 6*(10), 54-60.

Elliott, D. J. (2007). Critical pedagogy for culturally responsive music education. Keynote Address. In P. Symeonidis (Ed.), *Mousiki Pedia ke anazitisi politismikis taftotitas. (Music Paideia and search of cultural identity). Proceedings of the 5th Conference of the Greek Society of Music Education.* Thessaloniki, Greece: Greek Society of Music Education.

Forari, A. (2007). Moussikes taftotites ke ekpedefsi (in greek) (Musical identities and education). In P. Symeonidis (Ed.), *Mousiki Pedia ke anazitisi politismikis taftotitas. (Music Paideia and search of cultural identity). Proceedings of the 5th Conference of the Greek Society of Music Education.* Thessaloniki, Greece: Greek Society of Music Education.

Gardner, H., Csikszentmihalyi, M., & Damon, W. (2001). *Good work: When excellence and ethics meet.* New York, NY: Basic Books.

Gilroy, P. (1993). *The black Atlantic: Modernity and double consciousness.* London, UK: Verso.

Lyotard, J. F. (1984). *The postmodern condition: a report on knowledge* (G. Bennington & B. Massumi, Trans.). Manchester, UK: Manchester University Press.

Matsaggouras, H. (2001). Poria pros mia meta-proodeftiki pedagogiki: I anadisi enos neou pedagogikou pradigmatos (in greek) (Course towards a meta-progressive pedagogy: the emergence of a new pedagogic paradigm). In D. Chatzidimou (Ed.), *Pedagogiki ke ekpedefsi, timitikos tomos gia ta exintapentachrona tou kathigiti Panagioti Xocheli. (Pedagogy and education, volume in honor of Professor's Panagiotis Xochelis sixty-five years)* (pp. 445-448). Thessaloniki, Greece: Kiriakidis Brothers.

Locke, K. A. (2008). Music education and ethical judgement in the postmodern condition. *Action, Criticism & Theory of Music Education, 7*(1), 74-87.

Palmer, A. J. (2004). Music education for the twenty-first century: A philosophical view of the general education core. *Philosophy of Music Education Review 12*(2), 126-138.

Regelski, T. A. (2006). Reconnecting music education with society. *Action, Criticism & Theory for Music Education 5*(2), 2-20.

Reimer, B. (2005). The danger of music education advocacy. *International Journal of Music Education, 23*, 139-142.

Small, C. (1997). Musicking: A ritual in social space. In R. Rideout (Ed.), *On the sociology of music education*, (pp. 3–4). Norman, OK: The School of Music, University of Oklahoma.

Tomlinson, J. (1999). Globalization and culture. In J. Tomlinson (Ed.), *Globalization and culture* (pp. 1-31). Chicago, IL: University of Chicago Press.

Learning Together Online: An Investigation of Collaborative Instruction on Students' Demonstrated Levels of Cognition in an Online Music Appreciation Course

Melissa McCabe
Towson University
Towson, MD (USA)
melissamccabe@comcast.net

Abstract

The primary purpose of this study was to investigate the effect of collaborative instruction on students' demonstrated levels of cognition in an online undergraduate music appreciation course. Undergraduate students (N = 91) enrolled in an online music appreciation class were recruited as volunteer participants for this study. Data were collected using online surveys and online discussion transcripts. Discussion transcripts were analyzed and rated for cognition level by trained judges using a system based on the principles of Bloom's Taxonomy of Learning. Results from the discussion transcripts analysis were used to compare types of instruction, levels of cognition and levels of student satisfaction for each course assignment. A one-way ANOVA indicated a significant difference ($p < .05$) between the types of instruction (collaborative versus non-collaborative) and students' demonstrated levels of cognition. Data indicated that collaborative small group assignments that foster high levels of discussion and interaction may encourage the use of higher order critical thinking skills. A Friedman Two-Way ANOVA found significant differences among student preference rankings indicating preference for a variety of instructional strategies implemented throughout the course.

Keywords
Cognition, distance learning, collaboration, online

With approximately half of the households in the United States or 150 million people connected to the Internet, an estimated 2 million students are taking post-secondary courses that are fully delivered online (Picciano, 2002). An early indication of the widespread popularity of online courses can be found in a survey conducted by the U.S. Department of Education, which revealed that more than 54,000 online courses were being offered in 1998, with over 1.6 million student's enrolled (Lewis, Snow, Farris, & Levin, 1999). Moreover, Allen and Seaman (2003) reported that: (a) over 1.6 million students took at least one online course during the Fall of 2002, (b) over one-third of these students took all of their courses online, (c) among all U.S. higher education students in Fall 2002, 11% took at least one online course, and (d) among those students at institutions where online courses were offered, 13% took at least one online course.

As the number of online distance learning courses increases and the popularity of distance education programs keeps growing, educators will continue to raise important questions about the quality of these courses and programs (Muirhead, 2000). One of the most common criticisms of distance learning courses is the perception of inferior interaction between the instructor and the students. Some researchers suggest courses taken at a distance can be impersonal, superficial, misdirected, and potentially dehumanizing and depressing, and that they disrupt the interactions that create a productive learning community (Merisotis & Phipps, 1999; Nissenbaum & Walker, 1998). Although the question of sufficient interaction is just as valid in a traditional classroom setting, the isolated nature of distance learning compounds the problem (Purcell-Robertson & Purcell, 2000). In a regular college course there is unity of space, time, and sequential actions (Spiceland & Hawkins, 2002). A distance education class lacks all of these (Edelson, 1998). Many educators worry that without classroom discussion and student interaction, instructors cannot provide real guidance and feedback (Edelson, 1998; Jaffe, 1997).

On the contrary, online learning has been advocated by hundreds of institutions of higher learning as an effective mode of distance course delivery (Bullen, 1998; Duderstadt, 1999; Schrum, 1998). Many researchers believe that the course delivery medium is rarely the determining factor for a variety of educational outcomes, including student satisfaction and learning (Russell, 1999) and that strong feelings of community can be developed in distance learning environments (Rovai, 2001). Verduin and Clark (1991) suggested that teaching and learning at a distance can be as effective as traditional instruction provided: (a) the methods and technologies used are appropriate to the instructional tasks, (b) there is student-student interaction, and (c) there is timely teacher-to-student feedback. Although there remains some debate, many experts in distance education are convinced that learning at a distance can be as effective as traditional programs (Rovai & Barnum, 2003).

Although the number of online courses continues to soar, the pedagogy of developing successful online learning environments and expectations for groups working online is not well documented at present (Gabriel, 2004). Researchers have come to focus on how collaborative learning contributes to educational effectiveness at the cognitive and social levels. Findings indicate that collaboration facilitates higher developmental levels in learners than by the same individuals working alone (Johnson, Maruyama, Johnson, Nelson, & Skon, 1981; Stodolsky, 1984; Webb, 1989).

Currently, the majority of empirical studies on distance education focus on the use of asynchronous learning technologies in the teaching and learning process. The potential benefits of asynchronous learning technologies include: providing access to information; enabling student interaction and collaboration; allowing for active and self-paced learning; and fostering student reflection and critical thinking are just some of the benefits identified by educational researchers (e.g. Bonk & Reynolds, 1997; Dede, 2000; Doherty, 1998). However, the needed articulation from theory and research to course design guidelines and impact research has not taken place (Roblyer & Wiencke, 2003).

Continued study of the effects of collaborative instruction on students' level of cognition may provide insight to guide appropriate inclusion of collaborative learning techniques in an online learning environment. The purpose of this study was to investigate the possible relationship between collaborative instruction and the levels of cognition exhibited by students in an online undergraduate music appreciation course.

Methodology

Participants
Undergraduate college students (N = 91) enrolled in an online music appreciation course for non-music majors at a mid-west university volunteered to serve as participants for this study. Participants were members of a larger class (N = 115) and were chosen as an accessible population. The participants represented a diverse sample that consisted of a wide range of ages, life and musical backgrounds, and academic degree specialties.

Method
This study compared three types of instructional learning strategies in an online music appreciation course: (a) collaborative learning assignments in small groups of five, (b) large group discussions, and (c) independent learning assignments. Using existing course curriculum, goals and objectives as a guide, three independent assignments, three large group discussions and three collaborative small group assignments were developed and systematically implemented throughout the semester.

Description of the Course Assignments

Independent Assignments (I)
Introductions- self-portrait. Students created a self-portrait collage to share with their instructor and classmates. Artistic ability was not essential. Students could use crayons, markers, computer graphics, or pictures from magazines that best portrayed who they were at this point in their life. Once the collage was complete, the student transmitted a digital image of his/her artistic endeavor as an attachment. Additionally, students explained why they included certain elements and what influenced their decisions in creating their portrait collage.

Concert reflection or CD listening journal. Students attended a university music event or an approved live concert. After the performance, students prepared a one page reflection discussing the music performed: genre, form, and how the experience personally affected them. If a student was unable to attend a musical performance, he/she could choose to do the listening journal assignment instead. Students listened to one musical selection from each of the five time periods covered in class and prepared a listening journal based on the following criteria: (a) accurate use of terms showed understanding of concepts; (b) considered many different elements of music (melody, meter, harmony, form, dynamics, tempo, instrumentation); showed understanding that elements changed as a piece progresses; (c) narrative style made clear which piece/movement was being discussed; (d) some information about work from lecture or book was included; and (e) attempted to describe the music in his/her own terms, with genuine reaction.

Reflection essay. Students were given a reading assignment comparing the social influences of jazz and rock and roll. Students wrote a reflection essay and posted their ideas, impressions, and observations on the main discussion board.

Large Group Discussions (D)
Students participated in three class discussions. Students were required to post their ideas, impressions, and observations as well as respond to at least two other student's postings. Responses to these questions were graded. Students were encouraged to respond as many times as possible.

Collaborative Small Group Assignments (C)
Online debate. Students were divided into pro and con positions to debate a topic relevant to the course content via the online threaded discussion board. Each group created a position statement related to their assigned position on the debate and posted it to their group discussion board. A position statement presented the facts for each side of the issue. In part two of the debate the students were free to discuss how they really felt about the issues of the debate. This area was more focused on personal opinion whereas the position statement was primarily based on facts. This part of the debate occurred during a synchronous chat session located within the small group pages.

Host and moderate a discussion topic. Each group was assigned to create a discussion topic to host at a specific time during the semester. Each group researched and composed a discussion question on a topic of their choice. The group was responsible for facilitating the discussion throughout the week by responding to classmates' postings and fostering dialogue. Additionally, the group posted a summary of the discussion at the end of the week.

Group project: virtual field trip. Each group selected a topic related to the course content that they wanted to explore further in depth. The group created a presentation through exploring and incorporating at least five different websites. This field trip was presented in various different creative formats: PowerPoint, a fictional newspaper, creative writing, photographs, a slide show, multi-media, etc.

Procedures

Surveys
Students were asked to complete a set of surveys evaluating each of the nine course assignments at various times during the semester. Each survey asked students to evaluate the nine researcher-designed assignments based on the level of perceived interaction, level of knowledge gained, and the level of satisfaction. Open-ended questions were also provided in order to gain insight on student's perceptions of collaborative instruction. Upon completion of all nine assignments, students were asked to rank the nine assignments in order of preference.

All students enrolled in the course, regardless of participation in this research study, completed these surveys as part of the regular course. Surveys were administered online through the password protected BlackBoard™ Course Site, and students were able to submit surveys at any time during the semester.

Discussion Analysis
Prior to formal analysis, participants' names were deleted and replaced with an identifica-

tion code. The use of an identification code allowed me to link data from each survey to the level of cognition analysis that was conducted on the discussion transcripts. A frequency number was calculated by counting the total number of message posts generated for each assignment. These frequency numbers were used to gauge the level of activity that occurred during each individual assignment.

Discussion transcripts were analyzed and rated for cognition level by two trained judges. Judges were trained (using definitions, examples, practice, and feedback) and assessed before the formal data analysis. A cycle of training, rating, and reliability analysis continued until reliability correlations exceeded a .80 acceptable limit for affective instruments (Gable, 1986). The rating system was based on the principles of Bloom's (1956) Taxonomy of Learning. Bloom's (1956) Taxonomy of Learning is a hierarchical representation that characterizes a student's depth of knowledge: (a) Level 1: Knowledge, knowing facts with little or no understanding of the meaning; (b) Level 2: Comprehension, understanding the meaning of the facts; (c) Level 3: Application, applying the understanding to new problems; (d) Level 4: Analysis, breaking a complex problem down into smaller parts; (e) Level 5: Synthesis, building a complex solution from separate areas of knowledge; and (f) Level 6: Evaluation, evaluating the suitability of facts for use in a problem domain.

It is important to realize that the divisions outlined above are not universally accepted and other systems or hierarchies have been devised. However, Bloom's taxonomy was chosen because it is easily understood and widely applied. Results from the discussion analysis were used to compare the type of instruction, the students' demonstrated levels of cognition and the levels of students' self-reported course satisfaction for each assignment. The transcripts were rated and entered into a N6 database. Paragraphs were chosen as the unit of analysis.

Results

Upon reviewing the discussion transcripts containing the nine different assignments, two judges independently rated each message post for level of cognition. The six-level scoring rubric was applied to each message post to indicate the extent to which a cognitive process was used. There were a total of 2,424 message posts created by participants in this study. Independent assignments generated a total of 394 posts, the large group discussions generated a total of 886 posts, and the collaborative small group assignments generated a total of 1,144 posts. To check the reliability of the judge's scoring, 20% of the participant's discussion transcripts rated independently by each judge were compared. A percent agreement statistic using the formula agreements divided by agreements plus disagreements indicated satisfactorily high reliability between judges, PA = 0.95.

Results from the discussion analysis were used to compare the type of instruction, the students' demonstrated levels of cognition and the levels of students' self-reported course satisfaction for each assignment. Level of cognition ratings ranged from 1-6 for each of the three types of instruction: (a) independent assignments, (b) large group discussions, and (c) collaborative small group assignments. Independent assignments level of cognition means were: (a) concert reflection M = 2.41, (b) self portrait M = 2.78, and (c) reflection essay M = 2.82. Large group discussions level of cognition means were: (a) class discussion two M = 2.87, (b) class discussion one M = 2.93, and (c) class discussion three M = 3.3. Collaborative small group assignments level of cognition means were: (a) virtual field trip M = 2.42, (b) online debate M = 3.54, and (c) hosting a discussion M = 3.86. A one-way Analysis of

Variance (ANOVA) was applied to examine participants' cognition level ratings across the nine assignments. Results indicated that there was a significant difference in levels of cognition as a function of the type of instruction, $F (9, 900) = 21.49, p < .05$.

A *post hoc* analysis was conducted. The Newman-Keuls Multiple Comparison Procedure revealed that collaborative small group assignments, such as hosting a discussion and the online debate, resulted in significantly higher levels of cognition than any of the other assignments. In addition, large group discussions and independent assignments, such as the reflection essay and the self-portrait, resulted in moderate levels of cognition that were significantly higher than the independent concert reflection assignment (M = 2.41) and the collaborative virtual field trip assignment (M = 2.42). These results seem to indicate that collaborative small group assignments that foster high levels of discussion and interaction may encourage the use of higher order critical thinking skills.

A Friedman Two-way ANOVA was conducted comparing mean student preference rankings assigned to each of the nine course assignments. Students ranked the nine assignments in order of preference (1 = liked the best; 9 = liked the least). A summary of assignment rankings in order of preference include: self-portrait (M = 2.97), virtual field trip (M = 4.58), class discussion one (M = 4.82), concert reflection (M = 4.98), class discussion three (M = 5.29), reflection essay (M = 5.29), class discussion two (M = 5.44), online debate (M = 5.57), and hosting a discussion (M = 6.06). A significant difference was found among mean preference rankings of the nine assignments, $\chi^2 (9) = 80.79, p < .05$. These results seemed to indicate that students prefer a variety of instructional strategies implemented throughout the course. This variety was apparent in the top three ranked assignments, which represented an assignment from each of the three instructional strategies: (a) independent assignments, (b) large group discussions and (c) collaborative small group assignments.

Discussion

Collaborative small group assignments appeared to encourage the use of higher order critical thinking skills. In particular, collaborative assignments which required students to work together to create an assignment and then follow-up with a discussion generated the highest levels of cognition when compared to large group discussions and independent assignments. By working collaboratively in small groups, students had frequent opportunities to create new ideas, share those ideas with others, and receive feedback. The resulting group analysis, debate, and shared perspectives helped to develop conceptual learning and higher order thinking skills (Alexander, 1995; Bruner, 1960; Rosie, 2002). Data from this study is consistent with research indicating that collaboration facilitates higher developmental levels in learners than by the same individuals working alone (Johnson et al., 1981; Stodolsky, 1984; Webb, 1989).

The use of the Bloom's Taxonomy framework revealed several insights regarding the three types of instruction presented in this study. First, 41% of the posts generated from collaborative assignments were classified as analysis or higher indicating that most of the discussions were geared toward the understanding and justification of ones ideas. Only 24% of the large group discussion posts and 15% of the independent assignment posts were classified as analysis or higher indicating that most of these discussions were oriented toward comprehension and application of the course content (see Table 1).

Table 1

Summary of Cognition Levels by Type of Instruction

Cognition Level	Percent of Total Posts		
	Independent	Discussions	Collaborative
1	3	2	5
2	48	26	24
3	34	48	30
4	10	17	22
5	4	4	15
6	1	3	4

Second, the postings are spread out across the different levels, with all levels being represented. This may indicate that in most discussions students needed to recall knowledge, comprehend information, and apply the information as well as synthesizing and evaluating the information-although these levels were done less frequently. Lastly, 83% of the higher-level postings (those classified as synthesis or evaluation) occurred in discussions that specifically asked students to solve a problem presented in the question. In other words, the nature of the question influenced the level of response from the students.

It is apparent that large group discussions and collaborative small group assignments generated higher levels of student-student interaction. Data indicated that all students contributed to the online discussions and appeared to be using at least a minimal level of critical thinking. The viewpoint from many of the students was that their experience in the online music appreciation course was a more interactive and engaging learning experience than many face-to-face courses they had previously taken. Some students indicated difficulties contacting members of the group due to lack of participation by fellow group members.

Conclusion

Although further research is needed in order to resolve issues concerning the effectiveness of collaborative learning in the online classroom, there are some conclusions that can be drawn from the existing study. First, online participation has to be seen by students as something integral to their success in the course. If it is viewed as busy work that they do only to get a participation grade, then it is unlikely that meaningful discussions will result. Having students work collaboratively online to complete one or more assignments and then participate in an online discussion, or having students moderate a discussion, are suggestions for making online activity integral to the course.

Secondly, many students are accustomed to what Sternberg (1987) describes as the didactic approach to teaching in which the instructor lectures; students listen and take notes; and there is limited student-student and student-instructor interaction during class. This online music appreciation course placed tremendous demands on the students. Unlike the traditional face-to-face classroom where a student's presence may be considered their participation, students suddenly found themselves in a situation where they were required to actively participate by making written contributions to discussions and collaborate with other students online to complete assignments where they were given the freedom to choose when to participate, from where to participate, how frequently to participate and how substantially to participate. Although course expectations were laid out in the course outline, many students only had a vague idea of what an online course was and what they were expected to do.

Future research could build on the results of this study by focusing on one or more of the factors identified in this study. For example, it would be useful to know what impact different styles of instructor participation have on student participation. At what point does an instructor get too involved, meaning that the instructors presence actually hinders student-student interaction and limits discussion possibilities?

Another issue that emerged from this study was the lack of student experience with online classes and students' difficulty integrating online courses with the rest of their face-to-face class loads. These issues could serve as the basis for a future study that compares participation of full-time distance education students with those taking only one online course as part of a campus-based program.

References

Alexander, S. (1995). *Teaching and learning on the world wide web*. Paper presented at the First Australian World Wide Web Conference, Southern Cross University, Lismore, NSW, Australia.

Allen, I. E., & Seaman, J. (2003). *Sizing the opportunity: The quality and extent of online education in the United States, 2002 and 2003*. Needham, MA: Sloan-C.

Bloom, B. S. (Ed.). (1956). *Taxonomy of educational objectives*. New York, NY: Longmans, Green and Company.

Bonk, C. J., & Reynolds, T. H. (1997). Learner-centered web instruction for higher-order thinking, teamwork, and apprenticeship. In B. H. Khan (Ed.), *Web-based instruction* (pp. 167-178). Englewood Cliffs, NJ: Educational Technology Publications.

Bruner, J. (1960). *The process of education*. Cambridge, MA: Harvard University Press.

Bullen, M. (1998). Participation and critical thinking in online university distance education. *Journal of Distance Education, 13*(2), 1-32.

Dede, C. (2000, June). *Implications of emerging information technologies for education policies*. Paper presented at the Congressional Web-based Education Commission Proceedings, Washington, DC.

Doherty, P. B. (1998). Learner control in asynchronous learning. *Asynchronous Learning Networks, 2*(2), article 4.

Duderstadt, J. (1999). Can colleges and universities survive in the information age? In R. Katz & Associates (Eds.), *Dancing with the devil: Information technology and the new competition in higher education* (pp. 1-25). San Francisco, CA: Jossey-Bass.

Edelson, P. (1998, February). *The organization of courses via the internet, academic aspects, interaction, evaluation, and accreditation*. Paper presented at the National Autonomous University of Mexico, Mexico City.

Gable, R. K. (1986). *Instrument development in the affective domain.* Boston, MA: Kluwer Academic.

Gabriel, M. (2004). Learning together: Exploring group interactions online. *Journal of Distance Education, 19*(1), 54-72.

Jaffe, D. (1997). Asynchronous learning: Technology and pedagogical strategy in a distance learning course. *Teaching Sociology, 25*(3), 262-277.

Johnson, D., Maruyama, G., Johnson, R., Nelson, D., & Skon, L. (1981). The effects of cooperative, competitive and individualistic goal structures on achievement: A meta-analysis. *Psychological Bulletin, 89*(1), 47-62.

Lewis, L., Snow, K., Farris, E., & Levin, D. (1999). *Distance education at postsecondary education institutions: 1997-98.* Washington, DC: U.S. Department of Education, National Center for Educational Statistics.

Merisotis, J., & Phipps, R. (1999). What's the difference? Outcomes of distance vs. traditional classroom-based learning. *Change, 31*(3), 13-17.

Muirhead, B. (2000). Interactivity in a graduate distance education school. *Educational Technology and Society, 3*(1), 93-96.

Nissenbaum, H., & Walker, D. (1998). A grounded approach to social and ethical concerns about technology and education. *Journal of Educational Computing Research, 19*(4), 411-432.

Picciano, A. (2002). Beyond student perceptions: Issues of interaction, presence and performance in an online course. *Journal of Asynchronous Learning Networks, 6*(1), 21-40.

Purcell-Robertson, R., & Purcell, D. (2000). Interactive distance learning. In L. Lau (Ed.), *Distance learning technologies: Issues, trends and opportunities* (pp. 16-21). Hershey, PA: Idea Group.

Roblyer, M., & Wiencke, W. (2003). Design and use of a rubric to assess and encourage interactive qualities in distance courses. *The American Journal of Distance Education, 17*(2), 77-98.

Rosie, A. (2002). Online pedagogies and the promotion of "deep learning." *Information Services and Use, 20*(2/3), 109-116.

Rovai, A. P. (2001). Building classroom community at a distance: A case study. *Educational Technology Research and Development, 49*(4), 33-48.

Rovai, A. P., & Barnum, K. T. (2003). On-line course effectiveness: An analysis of student interactions and perceptions of learning. *Journal of Distance Education, 18*(1), 57-73.

Russell, T. L. (1999). *No significant difference phenomenon.* Raleigh, NC: North Carolina State University.

Schrum, L. (1998). Online education in the information age: A study of emerging pedagogy. In B. Cahoon (Ed.), *Adult learning and the Internet* (pp. 53-61). San Francisco, CA: Jossey-Bass.

Spiceland, J., & Hawkins, C. (2002). The impact on learning of an asynchronous active learning course format. *Journal of Asynchronous Learning Networks, 6*(1), 68-75.

Sternberg, R. J. (1987). Five ways to think about thinking skills. *Instructor, Special Issue,* 32-33.

Stodolsky, S. (1984). Frameworks for studying instructional processes in peer-work-groups. In P. L. Peterson, L. C. Wilkinson, & M. Hallinan (Eds.), *The social context of education* (pp. 107-124). New York, NY: Academic Press.

Verduin, J. R., & Clark, T. A. (1991). *Distance education: The foundations of effective practice*. San Francisco, CA: Jossey-Bass.

Webb, N. (1989). Peer interaction and learning in small groups. *International Journal of Education Research, 13*(1), 21-29.

Scared to Share: Studio Teachers and an Asynchronous Web Forum for Pedagogical Learning

Eleanor McPhee
University of Western Sydney (Australia)
emcphee@iinet.net.au

Abstract

Studio music teachers in Australia are generally accomplished musicians who are self-taught teachers and the solitary nature of the profession means that opportunities for peer discussion/collaboration are difficult to attain. This paper investigates a seven-month collaboration between forty-nine studio music teachers using an online asynchronous discussion forum. This online forum represents part of a larger study that included an earlier forum (stage 1), twenty interviews and a focus group. The purpose of this online component was to analyse the contents of this forum to determine the key musical/pedagogical issues for its participants and to ascertain whether the forum was an effective medium for reflective collaboration based on the posting patterns of the participants. Although the forum questions received a large number of responses (200), results suggested that participants were scared to share with each other, based on the lack of discussion on the forum coupled with the high rate of non-participating observers (lurkers).

Keywords

Studio music teaching, asynchronous online forum, instrumental pedagogy, music teacher development

Introduction

There is little incentive for instrumental teachers to gain a qualification for studio teaching, despite the existence of a few relevant courses in Australia, as they have historically tended to be short-term offerings, most often closing due to lack of students. As studio music teachers in Australia are generally accomplished musicians but self-taught teachers, who lack pedagogical training specifically targeted to studio teachers, this paper aimed to determine whether an asynchronous online web forum might prove to be an effective means by which studio teachers could raise significant issues and develop their practice through informal and collaborative means. The paper investigated the posting habits of 49 studio music teachers, most teaching high school aged students, on a seven month long asynchronous web forum. It aimed to ascertain the issues of significance for studio music teachers who teach school aged students and to determine whether the participants' posting patterns demonstrated shared problem solving.

This paper represents the second stage of a larger study and responds to the following questions about learning via an asynchronous online web forum:

1. What are the key musical/pedagogical issues raised by the online studio music teachers?
2. What issues do the posting patterns of participants raise?

Background

The professional development of school music teachers has been a focus of much research (Conkling, 2007; Conway, 2002, 2006; McCotter, 2001), which generally concentrates on pre-service and early career teachers. In contrast, the professional development of studio teachers who generally embark on a teaching career without the benefit of formal teacher training (Baker, 2006; Haddon, 2009; McPhail, 2010) has received little attention. Studio music teachers, due to the nature of the one-one-teaching context, are often isolated from pedagogical theory and the critique of practice that is fundamental to formal teacher training (McPhail, 2010) however much of the formal teacher education available in Australia is aimed at classroom music teachers and therefore is not always relevant to the studio teaching scenario (Watson, 2010).

Key issues raised in literature in relation to studio music teachers can be divided into issues of effective teaching as it pertains to the student/teacher relationship and issues of pedagogy. The characteristics of effective teaching was seen to be enthusiasm, clear communication, the ability to inspire, flexibility and being able to develop a student's musical independence (Gaunt, 2007, 2010; Mills, 2002; Mills & Smith, 2003; Persson, 1996; Purser, 2005). Issues of pedagogy were technique, musical expression, modeling and repertoire (Haddon, 2009; McPhee, 2011, in press; Mills, 2002; Mills & Smith, 2003; Purser, 2005). Teachers develop their own solutions to key issues by drawing on models of past or current learning to inform their work (Haddon, 2009) and therefore rely on personal biography to teach effectively in the preliminary years (Baker, 2006; Knowles & Holt-Reynolds, 1994). Narratives of personal biography then become powerful tools for negotiating meaning (Jonassen & Hernandez-Serrano, 2002).

While professional development can take many forms, advances in technology have opened up new avenues for learning (Bauer, 2007; Bauer & Moehle, 2008; Irwin & Hramiak, 2010). Computer-mediated communication (CMC) represents a way in which instrumental teachers can share knowledge given the relative isolation of their profession as CMC presents an effective way to support collaborative learning (Hirsch, 2005). The pedagogical potential of CMC in music education has been explored previously (Ballantyne, Barrett, Temmerman, Harrison, & Meissner, 2009; Bauer, 2001; Chong, 2008; Thompson, 1999; Woody & Fredrickson, 2000) however not often in a studio music situation. Asynchronous online discussion is a particularly useful forum for studio music teachers because its lack of time constraints allows participants to respond to discussion at a time of convenience to them and this factor encourages reflective learning, in-depth thinking and meaningful processing of information (Black, 2005; Dixson, Kuhlhorst, & Reiff, 2006; Gilbert & Dabbagh, 2005; Hara, Bonk, & Angeli, 2000; Lang, 2000).

Method

Participants

Forty-nine studio music teachers took part in this asynchronous online discussion forum that followed on from a smaller forum (stage 1) of ten participants, which was designed to test the web-based discussion format. The 49 were drawn from a large pool of potential participants including every Australian university with a music or music education undergraduate course, all Australian music teachers' associations and the top ten community music schools that appeared in a Google search for each state, following a logical assumption that a school with a large web presence would be more likely to be interested in research on online learning.

The study was also advertised extensively through paid Facebook advertising, a Facebook group and Twitter posts using Twitter hashtags targeting existing music education communities. Participants were invited to respond to questions posted on a weekly basis on the web forum that was hosted on the wordpress.com platform. They were advised that they could take part in the forum for as long or as little time as they wished and that they could respond to any of the questions that were meaningful for them. As participants tended to drop in and out of the study, a continual advertising strategy was implemented which ran from March until September and email newsletters were sent to non-subscribing participants on a monthly basis which participants could opt out of by return of email with 'unsubscribe' in the subject header.

These recruitment processes supplied forty-nine instrumental and vocal teachers who work in universities, secondary schools, primary schools, private music schools and in their own studios. Forty-two participants taught in Australia and a further seven joined the forum from outside Australia as a result of Twitter, Facebook and email advertising.

Table 1. Origins of participants

Australian state or country of origin	Number of participants
New South Wales, Australia	23
Queensland, Australia	6
Victoria, Australia	3
South Australia, Australia	2
Western Australia, Australia	1
*Australia	4
United States of America	3
Argentina	1
Poland	1
Switzerland	1
Dubai	1

* Participants who didn't provide a state of origin

It was hoped that participants would be a representative sample in terms of instruments and gender, however, due to the small return rate on the recruitment processes, this couldn't be satisfactorily achieved resulting in a large gender bias of 33 women and 13 men.

Of the 49 participants, piano teachers and wind teachers were well represented with 14 participants from each group. String teachers were 6 in number followed by guitars, percussion and voice with 4 participants representing each.

Data Collection and Analysis

Individual questions were posted on a weekly basis within an asynchronous online discussion forum using a free, cloud-hosted weblog publishing tool. Participants could respond to any of the questions by way of a comment button on every post and these responses would appear in chronological order. Only the researcher/moderator, me, could post questions to the forum wall, however participants were encouraged to raise their own issues which were used as topics for next week's post.

In this way the weekly questions formed discussion threads and were drawn from the literature, issues raised in the stage 1 forum, and issues raised by the stage 2 participants during the course of the study. The questions were based around issues of personal history, teaching philosophy, teacher effectiveness, pedagogical strategies and lesson planning strategies.

Thematic analysis was used to code and organize the forum data into musical and pedagogical themes and the metadata of the web forum itself was used to categorize themes to allow patterns to emerge. The researcher's previous experience as a music educator provided a foundation by which to interpret the data. The participant responses were similarly coded using each individual response as a unit of analysis (see Table 2).

Table 2. Codes, posting rates of participants and key issues

Codes	Teacher Effectiveness	Teacher Philosophy	History informs Practice	Teaching Strategies	Planning Strategies	Co-curricular Issues
Researcher Questions	9 questions	8 questions	4 questions	5 questions	3 questions	1 questions
Participant Responses	49 responses	43 responses	36 responses	35 responses	20 responses	2 responses

Findings

This forum had thirty discussion threads that included 221 comments from 49 participants. Participants chose to respond to any and all of the questions raised, however only two participants chose to ask me, as researcher/moderator to post questions of their own to the forum wall and one response raised a further issue that allowed me to use it to post a new question.

Proportionally, the personal histories questions had the highest number of responses and these paint a picture of a participant group who were mentored to teach either by their own teacher or by their own music-teaching parent. These mentors either actively encouraged and provided feedback on participants' early teaching or simply provided an inspirational example by which participants could measure their own teaching and attempt to emulate. Although participants cited the flexibility of studio teaching as a reason that they began to teach, overwhelmingly, teachers fell into studio teaching by chance when they were asked to teach someone connected to them, a family member or friend for example, and used these early experiences to build a larger teaching practice.

Only nine had any sort of formal teaching qualifications with most learning to teach through analysing the model that their early teachers had provided, both positive and negative, and through experimentation. Of the nine teachers who had had formal teacher training, two had undertaken an instrumental pedagogy course and had found that this gave them the confidence to tailor avenues of informal learning to their own specialities. The other seven had classroom music teaching qualifications and found that, for the most part, this did not prepare them for studio teaching and the most effective learning they gained from this was the mentoring and supervision received in school placement opportunities.

Descriptions of excellent early teaching both received and observed, paint a picture of an ideal teacher who engenders a trustful relationship with his/her students in order to foster self-expression and creativity. This teacher is flexible, patient, tolerant, and understanding, is an expert at his/her instrument and yet is prepared to learn from his/her students. This participant group have drawn heavily from their past experiences to develop their own teaching practice, and it is therefore unsurprising that they believe that the most important attribute for the ideal teacher is to be someone who is willing to share stories from his/her own life to inspire their students and to provided a role model both musically and personally.

Although all the forum responses provide an insight into instrumental teaching practice, the forum proved not to be particularly effective as a means to promote collaborative learning. I expected that, as in the stage 1 forum, participants would post comments based on personal history and experience and would then revisit the threads to reflect on and discuss the questions further in light of the responses of others. Instead, this participant group tended to view the forum as a data-gathering tool rather than a tool for reflective discussion. The response rates of participants fitted into three distinct profiles and could therefore be categorized into high-range, middle-range and low-range groups. Of the 49 participants, 20 posted on the forum only once and a further 12 posted two or three times and thus didn't engage with the other participants on the forum. Of this large low-range group who responded between one and three times, one was a follower of the Facebook updates, five were receiving the Twitter feed and one was a email subscriber to the forum itself so it is possible that these participants were following the forum and only responding to questions that were meaningful to them however, one can only hypothesize this although the large number of weekly hits that the site received is suggestive. One participant who fits into this group is notable because she was a follower of the Facebook page and emailed me to specifically state that she was following the questions and responses with interest however would only respond to any questions that were particularly meaningful to her. This participant left a detailed response to the question "Does a student's cultural background affect the ways in which you teach?" which related to the participant's practice as a Spanish language choral director, a highly specialized vocation in predominantly English speaking Sydney.

Of the middle-range group - participants who posted between 4 and 10 times - posting patterns indicated that all but two of these participants were answering a number of questions in a block as a direct response to a prompt from the researcher/moderator in the form of an email update. Of the high-range group, only 6 participants of the 49 posted in patterns that suggested that they were reading, reflecting on and responding to, not only the questions posted by the researcher/moderator, but also the comments posted by other participants. These six participants posted between 6 and 30 times over periods of 6 weeks to 30 weeks and during this time engaged with the forum at a rate of between one and three posts per session. The site also received an average of 12 hits per day and 2,660 hits overall which suggests that a substantial number of invited participants were observing without posting.

Because of these patterns of posting, one cannot determine from this study whether any of the issues raised were of more importance to the participants because there appeared to be little selectivity when engaging with the questions. Participants posted responses to whichever question appeared at the top of the forum wall for the week that they participated and they either only answered that one question or worked systematically back through a small number (3-9) of previous questions, showing no preference to one question over another.

Discussion

The low number of participants in light of the extensive advertising used to promote this study and yet the paradoxically high hit rates that the site received coupled with the lack of discussion on the forum suggests that participants seemed reluctant to share their experiences and beliefs on a web-based forum. The high number of responses on personal history/background questions seems to support this because this style of questioning allows people to share their beliefs and opinions under the guise of personal storytelling (Jonassen & Hernandez-Serrano, 2002) and, thereby avoiding the potential confrontation of holding one's present teaching practice up for scrutiny. If, as Purser (2005) suggested, self-taught studio teachers are afraid to "air in public what has been developed in private" (p. 297), perhaps personal histories could be used to scaffold teaching practice and an exploration of the themes and beliefs present in these histories could provoke discussion and reflection in a non-confrontational way.

Although the discussion forum received a good deal of use between March and October of 2011, it would be difficult to deem this process a successful tool to facilitate shared discussion and problem solving between participants as more than half the participants posted only once or twice and only as a direct response to a prompt from the researcher/moderator. When investigating the posting habits of participants, it was possible to determine whether participants were engaging with, and reflecting on, the responses of others by the dates and times that posts were left and also by the number of responses which were left as a direct response/reply to another contributor. The six participants that did actively engage with the forum and reflect on their own and other's responses did not provide enough of a pool of participation to achieve much meaningful discussion. This leaves me with more unanswered questions than when I started including: what are the issues that stop participants engaging in discussion in this way? Is anonymity a factor? What are the issues that they would have liked to have seen discussed?

References

Baker, D. (2006). Life histories of music service teachers: The past in inductees' present. *British Journal of Music Education, 23*(1), 39-50.

Ballantyne, J., Barrett, M., Temmerman, N., Harrison, S., & Meissner, E. (2009). Music teachers Oz online: A new approach to school-university collaboration in teacher education. *International Journal of Education & the Arts, 10*(6). Retrieved from http://www.ijea.org/v10n6/

Bauer, W. I. (2001). Enriching the traditional music classroom through Internet-based technologies. *The Technology Source.* Retrieved from http://technologysource.org/?view=article&id=116

Bauer, W. I. (2007). Research on professional development for experienced music teachers. *Journal of Music Teacher Education, 17*(1), 12-21.

Bauer, W. I., & Moehle, M. R. (2008). A content analysis of the MENC discussion forums. *Bulletin of the Council for Research in Music Education, 175*, 71-84.

Black, A. (2005). The use of asynchronous discussion: Creating a text of talk. *Contemporary Issues in Technology and Teacher Education, 5*(1), 5-24.

Chong, E. K. M. (2008). Harnessing distributed musical expertise through edublogging. *Australasian Journal of Educational Technology, 24*(2), 181-194.

Conkling, S. W. (2007). The possibilities of situated learning for teacher preparation: The professional development partnership. *Music Educators Journal, 93*(3), 44-48.

Conway, C. (2002). Perceptions of beginning teachers, their mentors, and administrators regarding preservice music teacher preparation. *Journal of Research in Music Education, 50*, 20-36.

Conway, C. M. (2006). Navigating through induction: How a mentor can help. *Music Educators Journal, 92*(5), 56-60.

Dixson, M., Kuhlhorst, M., & Reiff, A. (2006). Creating effective online discussions: Optimal instructor and student roles. *Journal of Asynchronous Learning Networks, 10*(4), Retrieved from http://bit.ly/MK3C4x

Gaunt, H. (2007). One-to-one tuition in a conservatoire: The perceptions of instrumental and vocal teachers. *Psychology of Music, 36*(2), 215-245.

Gaunt, H. (2010). One-to-one tuition in a conservatoire: The perceptions of instrumental and vocal students. *Psychology of Music, 38*(2), 178-208.

Gilbert, P. K., & Dabbagh, N. (2005). How to structure online discussions for meaningful discourse: A case study. *British Journal of Educational Technology, 36*(1), 5-18.

Haddon, E. (2009). Instrumental and vocal teaching: how do music students learn to teach? *British Journal of Music Education, 26*(1), 57-70.

Hara, N., Bonk, C. J., & Angeli, C. (2000). Content analysis of online discussion in an applied educational psychology course. *Instructional Science, 38*(2), 115-152.

Hirsch, J. (2005). Learning collaboratively with technology. *The School Administrator, 62*(7). 10-15.

Irwin, B., & Hramiak, A. (2010). A discourse analysis of trainee teacher identity in online discussion forums. *Technology Pedagogy and Education, 19*(3), 361-377.

Jonassen, D. H., & Hernandez-Serrano, J. (2002). Case-based reasoning and instructional design: Using stories to support problem solving. *Educational Technology Research and Development, 50*(2), 65-77.

Knowles, J. G., & Holt-Reynolds, D. (1994). An introduction: Personal histories as medium, method, and milieu for gaining insights into teacher development. *Teacher Education Quarterly, 21*(1), 5-12.

Lang, D. (2000). Critical thinking in web courses: An oxymoron? *Syllabus, 14*(2), 20-24.

McCotter, S. S. (2001). Collaborative groups as professional development. *Teaching and Teacher Education, 17*, 685-704.

McPhail, G. (2010). Crossing boundaries: Sharing concepts of music teaching from classroom to studio. *Music Education Research, 12*(1), 33-45.

McPhee, E. (in press). Finding the Muse: Teaching musical expression to adolescents in the one-to-one studio environment. *International Journal of Music Education*.

McPhee, E. (2011). Shared concerns: Investigating instrumental teachers' discussions in an asynchronous web forum. Paper presented at the Australian Society for Music Education Conference, Gold Coast, Australia.

Mills, J. (2002). Conservatoire students' perceptions of the characteristics of effective instrumental and vocal tuition. *Bulletin of the Council for Research in Music Education, 153/154,* 78-82.

Mills, J., & Smith, J. (2003). Teachers' beliefs about effective instrumental teaching in schools and higher education. *British Journal of Music Education, 20*(1), 5-27.

Persson, R. (1996). Brilliant performers as teachers: A case study of commonsense teaching in a conservatoire setting. *International Journal of Music Education, 28,* 25-36.

Purser, D. (2005). Performers as teachers: Exploring the teaching approaches of instrumental teachers in conservatoires. *British Journal of Music Education, 22*(3), 287-298.

Thompson, K. (1999). Internet resources for general music. *Music Educators Journal, 86*(3), 30-36.

Watson, A. (2010). Musicians as instrumental music teachers: Issues from an Australian perspective. *International Journal of Music Education, 28,* 193-203.

Woody, R. H., & Fredrickson, J. M. (2000). A partnership project: Integrating computer technology and Orff-Schulwerk. *General Music Today, 13*(2), 8-11.

Ontology Theories of the Musical Work and the Meaning of Creation

Chrysoula Mischou
Secondary Education (Music School)
Kavala, Greece
chrymischou@hotmail.com

Abstract

The present project presents the Ontology theories of the musical work with the Platonic theory further presented as we believe it gives the aptest answers to the questions about musical ontology. We also examine the attempt of an ontological definition of the composing process. Some philosophers think of it as a creation, in the sense of "bringing into life" something non existing before. Others think of it more of a discovering process, in the sense of bringing to the surface something always existing. Examining the nature of musical work and its perpetual or not reference in its very first appearance, we face important and interesting questions like Is there a creation? Are musical works eternal? Is a composer a creator or just creative? Does a composer give a birth or he just discovers? Which is the procedure a composer follows? The aim of this project was a macroscopic journey into the abstract meaning of music and the familiarity with the Ontology theories of music. These are issues that everybody, related to music, faces, consciously or not, especially the music educator who uses musical work and its abstract nature as a tool in the educational process, where he has to explain and introduce it to the students.

Keywords
Philosophy, ontology, musical work, creation, Platonism, Aristotelian view

Musical work has an *abstract* existence and is encountered directly only through the mediation of performances or scores (Davies, 2003). As an abstraction, musical work has been described both as "universal" and "particular" (Davies, 2004, p. 37). Platonism and Aristotelian view are two options of the first case (universal).

According to *Platonism*, musical works are universals, consisting of sound structures. [of course we have to make clear that Plato never spoke about Ontology of music. The theory just borrows his name because it is structured on his philosophy. We can say the same about Aristotelian view] Musical works are "Platonic universals", patterns or structures existing in the realm of the Forms (Davies, 2003, p. 31). "They don't have spatiotemporally properties and always exist, even if they are never performed, even if score is never written" (Goehr, 2005, p. 35).

According to Platonists, composing a work means more to discover than to create a kind (Goehr, 2005). Musical works are normal kinds that are not created because all possible works of music pre-exist their notation. So, all that a composer does is to recognize a work. A composer does not create and nobody ever creates anything. The gifted poet, scientist, or philosopher is merely good at recognizing propositions whose existence is prior and independent (Sharpe, 2000). Composers make works by discovering such structures. These structures become their creation, as they define the context of the performance of the works (Davies, 2004).

There is also an alternative Platonic view. Musical works is quasi-Platonic universals, as they can be created. This happens because they are encountered directly through performances and in this way they are spatiotemporally specific, since they depend on compositional activity and on properties of their particular characteristics (performances/scores) (Goehr, 2005).

According to *Aristotelian view*, musical work is "universal" as happens in Platonism too, but the difference is that it can be created as it can be destroyed too (Davies, 2003, p. 32). Specifically, a universal comes into existence with its first instance and goes out of existence when its last instance disappears (Davies, 2004, p. 38). [We could interpret the word *instance* as appearance of a token. This means that musical work takes shape and can be found as a performance or a score]

The main alternative view to *universal* is *particular* and is expressed through *Nominalism*, *Type-token* theory and *Idealism*. According to *Nominalism*, musical works are specific and defined as classes of performances, since there are specific performances and score copies (Goehr, 2005). Here, instead of the vertical relationship between work and performances i.e. the relationship between an abstract idea and its specific instances, we are interested in "horizontal relationships between performances and scores" (Goehr, 2005, p. 40). The notation system can provide the answers to questions of musical Ontology so, musical works are classes of performances "perfectly compliant with the scores" (Scruton, 1997/2009, p. 111).

Type – token theory suggests that the work and its names (the way composer defines it) are called types and the performance of the musical work is called a token (Kivy, 1993, p. 48). When a composer creates a type, creates at the same time a token of the type or the tool for the production of a token of the type (i.e. a music score) (Goehr, 2005, p. 40).

Idealism suggests that musical works are identified with ideas formed in the mind of composers. As soon as these ideas are formed, they are expressed into score copies or performances, so that they can be publicly accessible. Musical works are not identified with the way they are performed, as one would expect, but through the ideas themselves.

Speaking extensively of the *Platonic view* (which expresses us), it is worth mentioning Jerrold Levinson, a representative of Platonism, that professes one of the most convincing theories have arisen to date. He believes that musical works are abstract entities that since they are created, are integrated and always existent, immutable and permanent. He disagrees with the concept of musical work as just a sound structure. He argues that the work is identical to the sound structure and the structure of the performance means (i.e. orchestration), but also is characterized by the creation of a specific moment, a specific composer, in a specific music-historical context (Goehr, 2005, p. 36).

All these, consisting an attempt of a definition of the musical work, are summarized below:

> MW = Musical Work
> S/PM structure = sound structure / performing-means structure
> X = a particular person - composer
> t = the time of composition

So, we have the type of musical work:

> (MW) = S/PM structure – as – indicated –by – X – at – t

Levinson insists on the concept of creation and has many supporters but also critics (they don't accept *creation* and replace it with *discovery*). The fact that such a difference of thinking is developed under the same theory, that of Platonism, is worthy of interest and study.

The main reason for holding to the idea that composers truly create their compositions is that it is one of our firm beliefs concerning art. According to Levinson, "there is probably no idea more central to thought about art than that it is an activity in which participants create things – these things being artworks". The whole tradition of art assumes art is creative in the strict sense and it is a godlike activity where the artist brings into life something non-existing before (Levinson, 2005, p. 5).

A second, related reason to preserve *creation* is that some of the status, significance and value we attach to musical composition derives from our belief in this. He supposes that a small part of the glory surrounding Beethoven's Symphony No. 5 seems to be removed if we conceive of it as existing before Beethoven's compositional act. "There is a special glow, as Levinson notes, that envelops composers, as well as other artists, because we think of them as true creators" (Levinson, 2005, p. 5).

Supporters of *creation* mainly argue that: 1. the number of elements and possible combinations that are available to the composer is endless and contains infinite possibilities; 2. sound structures have new and different meaning in different historical contexts; and 3. the style of a musical work is a result of human action and is usually quite personal.

Critics of *creation* think of it more of a discovering procedure and warn about the danger of confusing creation with creativity. While it is true that a denial of *creation* entails that composition is a kind of selection, it is wrong to suppose that the composing process lacks in creativity and composition is an unimaginative tracing of an abstract pattern. They continue that if we are to make sense of composition, we must acknowledge its creativity. And this can be done while denying that composers create the works which they compose (Dodd, 2005).

It would be helpful for us to distinguish creativity from creation, if we consider an analogy between musical works and thoughts. Thoughts are eternal entities and a thinker does not create them but must take them as they are. The fact that we do not literally create the entities that we think and say does not entail that we do not have intelligence (Dodd, 2005). And this happens because the fact that one thinks creatively is determined, not by whether one brings any thoughts into existence, but by the nature of the thoughts one thinks. To think creatively is to grasp propositions that few others can grasp, and to be able to see connections between propositions that others cannot see. Something similar goes for creativity in the field of musical composition. A composer is creative, not through bringing works into existence, but by having to exercise imagination in composing these works. "A creative thinker possesses the imagination to have thoughts beyond the reach of most people. A creative composer possesses the imagination to compose works of music that others don't have the capacity to compose. Indeed, composition is a form of discovery, but discoveries can be creative" (Dodd, 2005, p. 28). Levinson (2005) agrees that discoveries can be creative but insists that creatability is demanded and not just creativity for a satisfactory discussion on the nature of musical composition.

Critics of *creation* argue that the deep-rooted idea there is about the worth of composer / writer / scientist is not in danger because it doesn't matter whether or not the composer is credited with bringing an abstract entity into being. "Our opinion of Einstein's genius would not be any greater if we were to regard the facts stated by his Special Theory of Relativity as created by him rather than discovered by him" (Dodd, 2005, p. 33). What impresses us is how someone could have the creativity, imagination and intelligence to make such a discovery. The same can be said about a music composition, where "we may marvel at a great piece of music, not because its composer brought it into existence, but because only someone extremely gifted could have come across it" (Dodd, p. 33). "There is indeed a special aura that envelops composers, but there is no anti-Platonistic message into this. Aura exists, not because composers are true creators, but because they are truly creative" (Dodd, p. 33). What matters, when it comes to the status of a scientist, writer or composer, is originality, importance and value of their work.

Finally the operative word here is not *creator* but *creative* (Kivy, 1993). "An original, creative discovery is not, in the literal sense, the bringing into being of what has never before existed. It is the revealing of what has always been there, but which no one has yet had the genius and creative imagination to see" (Kivy, 1993, p. 43). If music were a mere created artifact, for example a kaleidoscope, it would become lower in the estimation of most of its practitioners, as well as its audiences (Kivy, 1993). The composer wishes to be known as a discoverer and transmitter of truths about the world. "He doesn't wishes just discovering sound structures, but sound structures that are revelatory of something beyond themselves: metaphysical will, emotive life, harmony of the spheres" (Kivy, 1993, p. 45).

To summarize, we came across musical work as an eternal entity, abstract and universal, consisting of sound structures, floating in the universe and in the Realm of possible, waiting for being discovered (Platonism). We also encountered it as an abstract universal that has a beginning and an end (Aristotelian view). We also came across it as a particular, perfectly compliant with the score (Nominalism) and as a particular individualized through its performances (Type-token theory). Also as a particular identified with ideas formed in the mind of composers (Idealism). We also encountered musical works as quasi-Platonic universals that can be created and are encountered directly through performances (alternative Platonic view).

In addition, we saw *creation* being supported under the point that specific actions of the composer, like making of decisions and choices in forming sound structures, have as a result to bring into life something non existing before. We also saw it being rejected and replaced by *discovery*, which doesn't contain less the meaning of creativity than creation contains it.

We *agree* with Platonic view that musical works are eternal entities, abstract and universal, consisting of sound structures that are not created but exist and wait for someone to bring them to the surface, and so we agree with the justification of the use of *discovery*, which also contains all the arguments about creativity we came across above.

We *disagree* with the rejection of *creation* because such an Ontological reference in the very first appearance of each artwork and such compliance to Platonic Ideas, should bring radical changes to our life and the use of words, if it was to follow a tactic of consistency and precision. In such a context, one by one most of the words / meanings, if not all of them, should be abolished, since their use would be prohibited. We could say that the Idea of Creation, references for the very first time to Big Bang (we will never be sure about the starting point of the reference). The meaning of creation and creativity will always enclose reference (perpetual or not). So, it will always be unfounded and avoidable, which is unjust to the human nature that aims high towards Divinity.

All of these considerations towards the attempt to give a definition of the musical work through Philosophy and especially through Ontology, are issues we can face, consciously or not, in everyday reality and practice especially in the field of Music Education and Pedagogy. The abstract nature of music, is what gives to it its non proof nature, its non spatio-temporally character and maybe its metaphysical dimension, things that lead to the need for refuge in Philosophy, looking for answers.

References

Davies, S. (2003). *Themes in the philosophy of music*. New York, NY: Oxford University Press.

Davies, S. (2004). *Musical works and performances: A philosophical exploration*. New York, NY: Oxford University Press.

Dodd, J. (2005). Musical Works as Eternal Types. In J. Young (Ed.), *Aesthetics: Critical concepts in philosophy, III* (pp. 24-41). London, UK: Routledge.

Goehr, L. (2005). *The imaginary museum of musical works* (Korompili, Trans.). Athens, Greece: Ekkremes.

Kivy, P. (1993). *The fine art of repetition: Essays in the philosophy of music*. Cambridge: Cambridge University Press.

Levinson, J. (2005). What a musical work is. In J. Young (Ed.), *Aesthetics: Critical concepts in philosophy, III* (pp. 3-23). London, UK: Routledge.

Scruton, R. (1997/2009). *The aesthetics of music*. New York, NY: Oxford University Press.

Sharpe, R. A. (2000). *Music and humanism. An essay in the aesthetics of music*. New York, NY: Oxford University Press.

Evaluative Performances as a Contributor to Music Learning: Conditions for Positive Evaluation Experiences for Beginning and Intermediate Piano Students

Nancy Mitchell
University of Toronto (Canada)
n.mitchell@utoronto.ca

Abstract
Evaluative performances, such as competitions and conservatory examinations, are often used as a way to structure piano students' learning and to provide concrete evidence of achievement. However, assumptions that students will work harder and learn more as a result of participating in these evaluations are not necessarily true in all cases. Using qualitative data collected from current and former piano students as well as teachers and parents, this study examines the conditions under which evaluative performances contribute to meaningful music learning, which is characterized by positive emotions and the development of relevant skills. Several factors contribute to establishing a good fit between the student and the demands of the evaluation: musical preferences, goal orientation, and ability to manage performance anxiety. In addition, the student's participation in evaluative performances must take place within the context of supportive relationships with parents and teachers.

Keywords
Piano instruction, examinations, music competitions, motivation

Introduction
Evaluative performances, such as competitions and conservatory examinations, are often used as a way to structure piano students' learning and to provide concrete evidence of achievement. Echoing the sentiments of proponents of standardized academic testing (Phelps, 2005), many teachers and parents believe that students who participate in these kinds of performances will be more motivated, will work harder, and as a result, will learn more than students who do not participate. However, just as researchers in the broader field of education have called into question assumptions regarding the benefits of standardized testing (Broadfoot, 1996; Kohn, 2000; Moll, 2004), so too should those concerned with music education examine whether long-standing beliefs and practices surrounding evaluation in piano study serve the best interest of the student.

Previous research has examined various aspects of music examinations and competitions. Researchers interested in exams have found that most examination systems use similar, although not identical, curriculum content (Babin, 2005), that emphasizing participation in exams can have a negative impact on pedagogical practice (Tye, 2004), that, with the right guidance from the teacher, exams can be used to help students achieve larger learning goals (Davidson & Scutt, 1999), and that self-efficacy is the best predictor of success in an examination (McCormick & McPherson, 2003). The issue of competition in music education is highly controversial. Some research indicates that competition enhances motivation and creativity (Eisenburg & Thompson, 2011), while other studies indicate the opposite effect (Austin, 1990; Miller,1994). Another important issue related to competitions is the potential for teachers to neglect the needs of struggling students in favour of those who are more likely to win (Dill Bruenger, 2004).

Taken together, these studies present a conflicting picture of the potential benefits of student participation in evaluative performances. It would appear that for some students, exams and competitions provide a sense of accomplishment and contribute to a deeper level of learning. However, for others, these same evaluations result in decreased interest in learning music. The question remains: what accounts for the difference in students' experiences?

Purpose

The purpose of the present research is to better understand how beginning and intermediate piano students experience the process of being evaluated and specifically, what factors contribute to constructive experiences with evaluative performances. In this study, an evaluation experience will be considered constructive if it contributes to student learning and results in positive emotional outcomes. Because so many teachers are trained to assume that competitions and exams are a necessary part of high quality music instruction, it is important for teachers to be able to assess whether participation in an evaluative performance will contribute to meaningful learning outcomes for a particular student rather than simply relying on tradition to guide their pedagogical practice (Tye, 2004).

Design of the Study

This qualitative study was conducted using grounded theory methodology (Strauss & Corbin, 1998), starting with the broad question "How do beginning and intermediate piano students experience the process of participating in an evaluative performance?" Participants were selected based on theoretical sampling to include a variety of perspectives on the issues of evaluation. Twenty-four participants were involved in this study: five current students, eleven former students, three teachers (one of whom taught the five current students), and five parents (corresponding with the five current students). The current students were preparing for either a competition or a conservatory examination or both during the data collection period. They were interviewed twice before the performance and once after, and also had five lessons video-taped leading up to the evaluation. All other participants were interviewed once, with the exception of six of the former students who submitted their responses through an online survey. Data was coded manually and using a trial version of NVivo9. This analysis revealed several important themes, two of which are discussed below.

Findings and Discussion

The findings of this research indicate two important areas which must be considered when deciding whether an evaluative performance is likely to benefit a particular student. The first is the fit between the characteristics of the student and the demands of the evaluation. The other is the context in which the student's learning takes place, specifically the relationships between the student and significant adults, such as parents and teachers.

Several factors must be present in order for there to be a good fit between the demands of the evaluative performance and the characteristics of the student. The first issue to be considered is students' musical tastes, as the syllabus requirements are not necessarily relevant or engaging for all students (Bartel, 2004; Regelski, 2006). Students who spoke positively about their experiences with competitions and examinations enjoyed the music they had been required to learn. One of the current students described her personal connections to her repertoire:

> And then I'm playing "Sixteenth Century March" in here and I love this song 'cause I love history and I'm playing "Lady Moon" and I just like it. And this, too – I'm playing "Leap Frog". I'm big about animals so I wrote, like, little things about each frog. I'm playing the "Clockwork Ballerina" and I just love playing this song.

Her enthusiasm for this music was palpable and inspired dedicated practicing followed by a successful performance in a competition. The former students tended to have less positive opinions on the music they had been required to learn. One gave as her reason for quitting: "I wasn't interested in the music". This particular student had gone on to play the guitar and saxophone and was enjoying the music she was learning on these instruments, but the repertoire she had been required to learn during her piano studies left her uninspired.

If students enjoy the music they are learning, they will be more motivated to work hard so that they can learn to play it well. Students who had positive experiences with evaluative performances showed evidence of a combination of performance and mastery goals (Lacaille, Koestner, & Gaudreau, 2007). They valued the formal recognition of achievement that was afforded by participating in competitions and exams and had goals related to the marks or ranks they hoped to achieve, but also had specific musical goals, such as playing expressively or playing from memory. The word "accomplishment" was used by several students to describe success in both areas (e.g., passing a grade or playing a piece well).

The presence of both types of goals appears to be important, as students who were not interested in learning music or who did not value the pursuit of certificates and awards had less positive views on evaluative performances. One former student described her involvement as follows:

> I never felt that it [participating in evaluative performances] was that important for my musical studies. It seemed like an extraneous pursuit, a rite of passage — something that I had to get done, but that it didn't really matter in the long run.

This student ended up pursuing advanced-level music studies, but always felt that her personal connection to music was much more important than any external recognition she might receive for performance. She still loved music, but resented having been forced to participate in evaluations. Another former student, who was less interested in learning the piano, resented the amount of work that was required to prepare for exams. For her, the reward of earning a certificate did not justify the investment of time and energy in practicing music she did not enjoy.

Parents also valued the way in which evaluative performances contributed to mastery and performance goals for their children. One parent, whose daughter had recently begun working toward an exam with a new teacher after a period without evaluation, described her views on exams as follows:

> [I]t always seemed like piano was, you were working towards something, and now it seems like, you're not really working towards anything. ... I feel like, why am I paying all this money, when I don't know how serious [my daughter is in her studies]

This parent viewed exams as a way to structure the lessons and to ensure that her daughter was pursuing her piano studies diligently, which she considered to be a good return on her investment in her daughter's education. Other parents echoed her statement of evaluative performances being an indication that the student was engaged in serious study, citing an increase in systematic practicing leading up to evaluations. This attention to detail was valued as an indication of deeper learning. Some of the parents also appreciated the certificates of achievement that their children received, as these were viewed as credentials that could be beneficial additions to their children's resumes later in life.

The teachers also expressed the importance of evaluative performances as goals. One described her approach in this way: "I strongly encourage competitions and exams. I find when students don't have those goals, I find we don't progress as much and there's a sense of drifting and it kind of gets on my nerves". For this teacher, maintaining forward momentum was important not only for students' learning, but also for her own enjoyment in teaching. The other two teachers shared similar views; however, they expressed concern that the extensive demands of the exam curriculum were too rigorous for many students. For this reason, these two teachers preferred to enter the majority of their students in local competitions, which required that students prepare fewer musical selections, thus leaving more time to pursue other musical interests (Zenker, 2004). In addition to being concerned with their students' mastery of musical skills, all of the teachers felt personally invested in the marks their students received, and viewed their students' successes as evidence that they were doing well as teachers.

All the students reported some level of nervousness either leading up to or during performance, but the ones who had positive views on evaluation felt that they were able to control the anxiety rather than being controlled by it (Sinden, 1999). One parent described her daughter as having "just the right amount" of anxiety in that it helped motivate her to practice diligently, but didn't interfere with the quality of the performance. However, not all students were able to manage their anxiety levels so effectively. One former student described in vivid detail the overwhelming terror she felt as she entered her first (and last) conservatory exam:

> I basically, looking back on it, had a panic attack, a full-blown panic attack. ... I felt like I was going to be sick to my stomach. I

> *remember the sight reading piece of music — I couldn't see the sheet music because it was like I could only see red, it was like blood in front of my eyes. I froze ... I made tons of mistakes ... I could barely breathe. I knew that my mom and my best friend were sitting out [in the waiting room]. The combination of them hearing me fail and ... the examiner asking me things that I just couldn't do — it was horrendous. And I walked out of there and said "I am never touching the piano again."*

This experience had a profound impact on this student's future engagement with music-making, as she still cannot play the piano in front of anyone other than her immediate family.

Even if a student's interests, motivation, and anxiety level work well with the demands of a competition or exam, the experience cannot be positive unless the learning takes place within the context of supportive relationships with parents and teachers (MacArthur, 2008). Students who had constructive experiences with evaluative performances had parents who offered encouragement and practical support without being overbearing. This research also confirmed Davidson and Scutt's (1999) findings that the relationship with the teacher is of great importance. The current students and their parents described their teacher as being warm, knowledgeable, and having good pedagogical skills. In the words of one of the parents, "X [teacher] has been an amazing teacher. Very tuned into the kids' temperaments and keeping them on task." All of the teachers who were interviewed obviously enjoyed working with their students and expressed a desire to have nurturing relationships with them.

Unfortunately, some of the former students had had extremely difficult relationships with their teachers and felt that they lacked the necessary support from their parents. One described a teacher who was intimidating and physically abusive. This student expressed regret that her parents had not stood up to the teacher and protected her. The student mentioned above who had experienced a panic attack and subsequent failure in her exam held her teacher and parents accountable: "All those irresponsible adults! What were they thinking?" She felt that she had been abandoned when she should have been counselled not to enter an exam for which she was inadequately prepared.

Conclusion

This research reinforces the idea that evaluative performances have the potential to contribute to students' engagement in music learning. However, the findings also draw attention to the possible negative results when evaluations are misused. In cases in which the student's musical preferences are a good match for the syllabus requirements, the student holds both performance and mastery goals, and the student does not experience debilitating performance anxiety, participating in an evaluative performance can be considered an option. The student's relationships with his or her parents and teacher are also crucial pieces of this puzzle, as the support offered by these important adults establishes the emotional context in which the student's learning takes place (Cameron & Carlisle, 2004). When all of these criteria are met, the evaluation can provide a helpful structure to learning, an incentive to work hard, and a reward for dedicated practicing. However, care must be taken to ensure that students do not become bored, frustrated, overly anxious, or otherwise disengaged from meaningful learning in the pursuit of certificates and awards.

Reference

Austin, J. R. (1990). Competition: Is music education the loser? *Music Educators Journal, 76*(6), 21-25.

Babin, A. (2005). *Music conservatories in Canada and the piano examination system for the preparatory student: A historical survey and comparative analysis* (Unpublished master's thesis). University of Ottawa, Ontario, Canada.

Bartel, L. (2004). Music making for everyone. In L. Bartel (Ed.), *Questioning the music education paradigm*, (pp. 228-243). Waterloo, Ontario: Canadian Music Educators Association.

Broadfoot, P. M. (1996). *Assessing assessment: Education, assessment and society*. Buckingham: Open University Press.

Cameron, L., & Carlisle, K. (2004). What kind of social climate do we create in our music classrooms? In L. Bartel (Ed.) *Questioning the music education paradigm*, (pp. 21-38). Waterloo, ON: Canadian Music Educators Association.

Davidson, J., & Scutt, S. (1999). Instrumental teaching with exams in mind: A case study investigating teacher, student and parent interactions before, during and after a music examination. *British Journal of Music Education, 16* (1), 79-95.

Dill Bruenger, S. (2004). Teaching the masses or coaching the elite: A comparison of the challenges facing high school music and sports educators. In L. Bartel (Ed.) *Questioning the music education paradigm*, (pp. 191-209). Waterloo: Canadian Music Educators' Association.

Eisenburg, J., & Thompson, W. F. (2011). The effects of competition on improvisers' motivation, stress, and creative performance. *Creativity Research Journal, 23*(2), 129-136.

Kohn, A. (2000). *The case against standardized testing*. Portsmouth, NH: Heinemann.

Lacaille, N., Koestner, R., & Gaudreau, P. (2007). On the value of intrinsic rather than traditional achievement goals: A short-term prospective study. *International Journal of Music Education, 25*, 245-257.

MacArthur, L. J. (2008). *The drive to strive: Exploring the experiences of elite-level adolescent artistic performers* (Unpublished doctoral dissertation). University of Toronto, Canada.

McCormick, J., & McPherson, G. (2003). The role of self-efficacy in a musical performance examination: An exploratory structural equation analysis. *Psychology of Music, 31*(1), 37-51.

Miller, R. E. (1994). A dysfunctional culture: Competition in music. *Music Educators Journal, 81*(3), 29-33.

Moll, M. (2004). *Passing the test: The false promises of standardized testing*. Ottawa, ON: Canadian Centre for Policy Alternatives.

Phelps, R. P. (2005). *Defending standardized testing*. Mahwah, NJ: Lawrence Erlbaum Associates.

Regelski, T. (2006). *Reconnecting music education with society. Action, Criticism, and Theory for Music Education, 5*(2). Retrieved from http://act.maydaygroup.org/articles/Regelski5_2.pdf

Sinden, L. M. (1999). *Music performance anxiety: Contributions of perfectionism, coping style, self-efficacy, and self esteem* (Unpublished doctoral dissertation). University of Arizona, Tuscon, AZ.

Strauss, A., & Corbin, J. (1998). *Basics of qualitative research: Techniques and procedures for developing grounded theory* (2nd ed.). Thousand Oaks, CA: Sage.

Tye, J. K.-C. (2004). *A survey of the current status and practices of piano teachers in Penang, Malaysia: Preparation for the practical piano examinations of the Associated Board of the Royal Schools of Music, London* (Unpublished doctoral dissertation). University of South Carolina, Columbia, SC.

Zenker, R. (2004). Music as a lifelong pursuit: Educating for a musical life. In L. Bartel, *Questioning the Music Education Paradigm* (pp. 121-135). Waterloo: Canadian Music Educators Association.

Ethical Dimensions of 21st-Century Challenges to the Philosophy of Music Education at the Tertiary Level

David R. Montaño
University of Denver
Denver, CO (USA)
dmontano@du.edu

Abstract

Exponentially increasing forces of globalization, and of global destabilizations of biophysical, economic and socio-political systems, are now presenting profound challenges to research in the philosophy of music education at all levels. The specifically ethical dimensions of those challenges, with respect to the ethical development of students and the ethics of curricula and their relationships to society, are increasingly global in scope and depth. Emblematic of the position in which American music education finds itself is that, as recent work in the sociology of music education has substantiated, at least secondary-level music education in the United States now remains a disproportionately white, middle-to-upper-class endeavor that is musically exclusionary and probably largely understood by students' parents as a means toward social class reproduction and upward social mobility. This is in turn part of a self-perpetuating cycle in that it feeds, and is in turn fed by, tertiary music-major education as it remains disproportionately oriented. Social contract theory, ethics of principles, virtue ethics, and deontological theory, including understandings about beneficence, justice, and autonomy, can contribute to a philosophy that might articulate a better compact than currently seems to exist between schools of music and both their students and society at large.

Keywords
Philosophy of music education, schools of music, ethics

Introduction

Exponentially increasing forces of globalization, and of global destabilizations of biophysical, economic and socio-political systems, are now presenting profound challenges to research in the philosophy of music education at all levels (Montaño, 2010). The specifically ethical dimensions of those challenges, with respect to the ethical development of students and the ethics of curricula and their relationships to society, are increasingly global in scope and depth. Emblematic of the position in which American music education finds itself is that, as recent work in the sociology of music education has substantiated, at least secondary-level music education in the United States now remains a disproportionately white, middle-to-upper-class endeavor (Elpus, 2010; Elpus & Abril, 2011) that is musically exclusionary and probably largely understood by students' parents as a means toward social class reproduction and upward social mobility (Elpus, 2010). This is in turn part of a self-perpetuating cycle in that it feeds, and is in turn fed by, tertiary music-major education as it remains disproportionately oriented. Multifaceted issues surrounding what it means to offer "professional" music degree programs, or referring to at least some of them as such, are closely related.

Relevant Statements by NASM in its *Handbook 2010-11*

It can be argued that the purposes and characteristics of baccalaureate programs in music as articulated by the National Association of Schools of Music (NASM) in the standards for accreditation in its *Handbook 2010-11* (NASM, 2010) are incomplete and skewed in certain crucial respects that bear on notions about responsibility to both students and society, and therefore raise profound ethical questions. First, NASM states that it "recognizes two generic types of undergraduate degrees in music. To be consistent with general academic practice, these degrees are labeled (1) liberal arts degrees and (2) professional degrees" (p. 75). However, other than stating that "[t]he professional degree focuses on intensive work in music supported by a program in general studies" (p. 75), the *Handbook* offers no definitional commentary or discussion regarding the term *professional*. A number of observations are pertinent to make in response: 1. Professional degrees are commonly understood in the American economic and employment landscape as preparing their holders for entry, typically after becoming licensed by a governmental or government-approved body, into a specific profession; 2. Typically, research and mechanisms of economic supply and demand, as well as students' and potential students' cognizance of them, keep industries and higher-education institutions in a continuous process of dynamic mutual influence and re-alignment so that there is an intent that a balance of professional jobs and professionally prepared graduates is roughly maintained; and 3. Though professional degrees in music therapy and public school music education are aligned with such practices in definition and dynamic balance, those in music performance and composition generally are not.

Regarding admission to undergraduate study in music, NASM (2010) states that the required backgrounds that should be common among applicants for all baccalaureate specialties include performance background, but backgrounds in composition or scholarship skills need only be reviewed for entrance into those specialties themselves.

Other relevant observations can be made about many of NASM's (2010) statements related to curriculum. "Basic criteria for membership" of degree-granting institutions" in the Association include that "[t]he institution shall offer regular classes in such areas as theory, history, and appropriate repertoires of music, as well as instruction in performance" (p. 45). It is true that the words "such as" are used here, but it remains striking that no mention is made of composition or of any ethnomusicological, social scientific, or philosophical perspectives on music, all of which are crucial to any holistic understanding of human musical activity that can inform efforts to enable music making by as many human beings as possible and preserve the musical lives of cultures.

Regarding undergraduate musicianship studies as a music program component, NASM (2010) states, "Musicianship is the body of knowledge, skills, practices, and insights that enables music-making at any level. To some extent, every musician functions regularly as performer, listener, historian, composer, theorist, and teacher" (p. 73). If every musician functions as a historian and theorist, each also functions, or should function, to some extent as musical ethnographer and sociologist, cultural analyst, and philosopher, none of which is mentioned.

Describing the liberal arts degree with a major in music, NASM (2010) states, "The degree focus is breadth of general studies combined with studies in musicianship and an area of emphasis in music such as performance, theory, music history and literature, music industry, and so forth" (p. 83). It is true that the words "and so forth" are used here, but here it again remains striking that no mention is made of composition or of any ethnomusicological, social scientific, or philosophical perspectives on music.

Regarding the curricular structure for liberal arts degrees, NASM (2010) specifies performance to be among the sets of requirements, but not composition and improvisation. Regarding the common body of knowledge and skills that should be included in all professional baccalaureate degrees, NASM (2010) states that "[s]tudents must acquire . . . [t]echnical skills requisite for artistic self-expression in at least one major performance area at a level appropriate for the particular music concentration," but only a "rudimentary capacity to create original or derivative music" (p. 87). "History and Literature" are also included as a category (p. 88), but not ethnomusicological, social scientific, or philosophical perspectives.

The specializations that NASM (2010) describes for baccalaureates in public-school music education include "General Music," "Vocal/Choral Music," and "Instrumental Music" (p. 99), but not "Compositional/Improvisational Music". Even "General Music" has attached to it "[t]he ability to lead performance-based instruction" (p. 99) but not a similar ability to lead composition/improvisation-based instruction. Composition is mentioned within a category labeled "Specific Music Fields or Combinations" (p. 100), but this sublimates it to performance in such a way as to imply that it does not deserve a category at the same hierarchical level.

Though NASM (2010) does make some statements that reflect what can be described as broader, more encompassing thinking about music professionalism and the baccalaureate curriculum, they are found as recommendations in an appendix titled "Music in General Education and the Training of the Professional Musician" (pp. 174-175). The full implications of those recommendations do not yet appear to have found reflection in the standards in the main body of this latest edition of the *Handbook*.

Previous Philosophical Investigations

Montaño (2000, 2002, 2008, 2010) has presented a number of arguments regarding certain issues in the philosophy of music education at the tertiary level that he has proposed need greater attention than they now appear to be receiving. Those issues are about relevant curricula and their relationship to society—the need to incorporate philosophical and social scientific studies of music into undergraduate music-major core curricula (Montaño, 2002); the need "to view and treat students throughout music education as not only potential creators, recreators, and consumers of the sounded results of musical activity but as potential enablers of musical activity in the broadest possible set of ways" (p. 284); that the still exceedingly influential European conservatory model represents an essentially closed rather than open-ended system that profoundly skews students' understandings of human musicality (Montaño, 2008); that research relating to the survival value of music-making as it developed in human evolution is important to an understanding of the efforts needed for humanity to meet the challenges of global biophysical, economic, and socio-political destabilizations that in this century threaten the survival of humanity and of the planet in the form in which we know it (Montaño, 2010); and that "[a]long with many other ways in which humanity has veered far from principles of conservation and sustainability, it can be argued that we have done so with respect to the human resources of arts-making" (p. 155). With respect to the relationships between tertiary schools of music and both their students and the public good, these issues are profoundly ethical in nature.

Perspectives from the Philosophy of Ethics

Ethics, known also as the philosophy of morality, critically examines principles for how to determine right from wrong and about value systems regarding right and wrong (Wall, 2001). I posit that there are questions implicated by the educational practices I have referred to here that are ethical in nature. More specifically, these questions involve the ethics of how those practices affect students, potential students, and the society they have a responsibility to serve. This includes whether some music-major students are in effect being used by their schools of music for those schools' own purposes.

Beneficence is a term used in ethics that refers to doing good and avoiding evil, or what is wrong. This can be considered a fundamental starting point, but it does not in itself offer methods for determining what is right or what is wrong, or for what to do when an action or policy would produce both good and bad results for different persons in a social group (Wall, 2001, p. 410).

Consequentialist theories of obligation include utilitarian ethics, which, rather than appealing to abstract reason, promotes the use of a calculus based on pleasure and pain. Ethics, in this view, is a matter of calculating "how to produce the greatest balance of pleasure over suffering" (Waller, 2008, "Utilitarian Ethics," para. 1). Particularly well-known versions of utilitarianism that were initially formulated by Jeremy Bentham (1748-1832) and John Stuart Mill (1806-1873) make clear that all persons affected by consequences must be considered, that only actions or policies that produce the greatest good for the greatest number of people can be considered right (Wall, 2001, p. 360). As difficult as the relevant values are to quantify in such a calculus, there is further difficulty and even danger in any attempts to quantify them in terms of quality (Waller, 2008, "Mill and the Qualities of Pleasure," para. 1). So, for example, attempts to claim a higher value in one set of musical practices, such as those typically labeled as from "Western art music," than in other musical practices are exceedingly difficult to quantify and defend.

The great rationalist philosopher Emmanuel Kant (1724-1804) arrived at a fundamental ethical principle known as the *categorical imperative*, which asserts that persons should act in such a way that they could will their acts to be made universal laws (Waller, 2008, "Kant's Categorical Imperative," para. 1) and, in so doing, that they should treat other persons as ends in themselves rather than ever as means toward their own ends (Waller, 2008, "Kant's Categorical Imperative," para. 3). This imperative is an example of deontological theories of obligation, in which the rightness of acts are measured by more than the consequences of them or even regardless of them. Kant saw universal principles, arrived at through reason, as fulfilling that role (Wall, 2001, p. 363).

> *The interest of virtue ethics is not only on rightness of acts but also on rightness of the motives behind those acts. As Waller (2008) describes the social implications of this view, We humans are social beings, who live best in cooperative relations, exercising our distinctive rational capacities. Virtuous acts and virtuous characters are those that contribute to a good, healthy, flourishing life for ourselves, our families, our communities, and our species.*
> *(Waller, 2008, "What Counts as Virtue," para. 3)*

Wall (2001) posits a definition of right action: "*An action is right if it follows a rule that conforms to the principles of beneficence, justice, and autonomy*" (p. 413). Thus, beneficence, discussed above, can be combined with the other two principles toward an effective whole.

Social justice, often referred to as distributive justice, is an area of ethics in which the concern is for how fairly the goods of any social group or society are distributed. It is based in turn on theories of justice, for which Wall (2001) gives three meanings: (1) "The most basic meaning of justice is that *all human beings are of equal intrinsic value*. (2) "[M]oral rights should be the same for all". (3) "[People] must be treated with respect" and "*may not be used exclusively for the good of others*" (p. 411).

As Wall (2001) describes it, autonomy is the principle that "[r]ational beings may do what they want to, as long as their actions harm no one else," and that "our freedom must be compatible with the freedom of others" (pp. 412-413).

Perhaps the most complex approach to ethics is embodied by constructivist, social-contract theories of justice, which examine political, social, and ethical systems constructed by social groups for the mutual benefit of their members (Waller, 2008, "Social Contract Ethics," para. 1). The fundamental question always is: In terms of their ultimate justice and fairness, does any of those examined systems represent what can be considered in effect a contract that members of the affected group would sign if given the opportunity (Waller, 2008, "Social Contracts and Human Nature," para. 1)? The great social-contract theorist John Rawls formulated what he refers to as "the veil of ignorance" to play a crucial part in making such determinations. In the relevant thought experiment, members of a group are to consider themselves behind this "veil of ignorance" in that each is to know nothing about himself/herself, about his/her abilities, or about what advantages or disadvantages with which he/she will be born (Waller, 2008, "Fairness and Social Contract Theory: John Rawls," para. 1). More particularly, the contractarians know nothing of (1) their physical and mental assets or their psychology, (2) their place in society, (3) what they value or their conception of the good (4) the economic and political state of their society, or (4) the generation to which they belong (Voice, 2011, "The Veil of Ignorance," para. 1). As Waller (2008) describes Rawls's offered perspective, "If we look at a rule of law or a principle of ethics or a social policy in our society, and we can honestly say we would adopt that policy from behind the veil of ignorance, then it is reasonable to conclude that the policy in question is *fair*. If we wouldn't adopt it, then perhaps the policy should be modified" ("Justice as Fairness," para. 1).

An ultimate purpose of Rawls's thought experiment is the formulation of principles of political justice and distributive justice in terms of the goods of society. The result is what he referred to as "justice as fairness". If members of a society find themselves in an original position that is fair—that is, behind a veil of ignorance—they will necessarily agree to fair principles in defining a just society (Voice, 2011, "The Idea of Imaginative Identification," paras. 6-7).

The contractarians' lack of information about their values behind the veil of ignorance, presumably including cultural conceptions of what is good music or whether one might derive more fulfillment as a composer or a musical ethnographer, for example, is of special significance to us here. This ignorance leads them to respect all values and formulate principles of justice that will not provide unfair advantages to any particular conceptions of the good (Voice, 2011, "The Veil of Ignorance," para. 6). Rawls sees community as an outcome of this process. In what he refers to as the idea of "private society," persons conceive of their pursuits as individual, private, and competing, with the institutions of society and society itself merely understood as efficient facilitators of those pursuits. What he refers to as the "social nature of mankind" leads the contractarians to form principles of justice based on social unions that pursue conceptions of the good, including, for example, families, friendships, and (of particular interest to us here) universities (Voice, 2011, "Community," para. 2), surely because of the modern university's historic dedication to "soft" boundaries and diversity in liberal learning.

Perspectives from Research in Ethical Development

If the ethical questions implicated here should be crucial to schools of music in their continuous policy and curricular thinking, they are crucial as well to the ethical development of their students with respect to their relationships with the musical communities within society. Such ethical questions, therefore, should be infused integrally into the music-major curriculum itself.

Lawrence Kohlberg (1969, 1980) formulated a model of developmental stages for morality. A "Preconventional" level 1 includes stages 1 ("Punishment and obedience orientation") and 2 ("Naive instrumental hedonism"); a "Conventional" level 2 includes stages 3 ("Good-boy, nice-girl" morality that includes the importance of others' reactions and acts' effects on social relationships) and 4 ("Law-and-order orientation"); and a "Postconventional" level 3 includes stages 5 ("Morality of social contract") and 6 ("Universal ethical principles") (Lefrançois, 1996, p. 336). Later work (Colby & Kohlberg, 1984) has indicated that late adolescents and early adults (the typical ages of college undergraduates) are primarily still at the third stage and that as few as 12.5% of adults think at the postconventional level, which encompasses abilities in the higher levels of ethical thought, including social-contract theory (Lefrançois, 1996, p. 337).

Peery (1999) formulated a model of ethical development specific to the undergraduate years of college-age students. Consisting of nine "Positions," it describes a sequence from a "dualistic absolutism" to a central point (Position 5) characterized by perception of human knowledge and values as "relative, contingent, and contextual," and then toward self-orientation "in a relativistic world through the activity of personal Commitment" (Peery, 1999, p. 64). As Peery describes the model more explicitly:

> In Positions 1, 2, and 3, a person modifies an absolutistic right-wrong outlook to make room, in some minimal way, for that simple pluralism we have called Multiplicity. In Positions 4, 5, and

> 6, a person accords the diversity of human outlook its full problematic stature, next transmutes the simple pluralism of Multiplicity into contextual Relativism, and then comes to foresee the necessity of personal Commitment in a relativistic world. Positions 7, 8, and 9 then trace the development of Commitments in the person's actual experience. (pp. 64-65)

Conclusion

With respect to tertiary music-major education, it seems that theories of collegiate-age intellectual and ethical development, and—within the larger philosophical discipline of ethics—social contract theory, ethics of principles, virtue ethics, and deontological theory, including understandings about beneficence, justice, and autonomy, can contribute to a philosophy that might articulate a better compact than currently seems to exist between schools of music and both their students and society at large. Ethics, then, should play a crucial role in continuing efforts in the philosophy of music education at the tertiary level.

References

Colby, A., & Kohlberg, L. (1984). Invariant sequence and internal consistency in moral judgment stages. In W. M. Kertines & J. L. Gewirtz (Eds.), *Morality, moral behavior, and moral development* (pp. 41-51). New York: John Wiley.

Elpus, K. (2010). Sociological issues confronting music education in North America. In L. Williams (Ed.), *Abstracts, 29th World Conference of the Society for Music Education* (pp. 184-185). Perth, Western Australia: International Society for Music Education.

Elpus, K., & Abril, C. R. (2011). High school music ensemble students in the United States: A demographic. *Journal of Research in Music Education, 59*, 128-145.

Kohlberg, L. A. (1969). Stage and sequence: The cognitive developmental approach to socialization. In D. Gosslin (Ed.), *Handbook of socialization theory and research*. Chicago, IL: Rand McNally.

Kohlberg, L. A. (1980). *The meaning and measurement of moral development*. Worcester, MA: Clark University Press.

Lefrançois, G. R. (1996). *The lifespan* (5th ed.). Belmont, CA: Wadsworth Publishing.

Montaño, D. R. (2000). Musicians as enablers and the valuing of music education: A historic opportunity in the twenty-first century. In M. Taylor & B. Gregory (Eds.), *Proceedings of "Music of the Spheres," the 24th World Conference of the International Society for Music Education* (pp. 271-289). Regina, SK, Canada: University of Regina.

Montaño, D. R. (2002). Toward a more comprehensive preparation of professional musicians: The need for the study of music as a human behavior in the core curriculum for all college music majors. In H. Lundstrom (Ed.), *Perspectives in music and music education no. 3: The ISME Commission for the Education of the Professional Musician, 1998 Seminar in Harare, Zimbabwe—The Musician in New and Changing Contexts* (pp. 77-81). Lund, Sweden: Lund University.

Montaño, D. R. (2008). Keeping pace with the new paradigm of the "engaged" university dedicated to the public good: Twenty-first-century imperatives for schools of music. In W. Sims (Ed.), *Proceedings of the 28th World Conference of the International Society for Music Education* (pp. 189-195). Perth, Western Australia: International Society for Music Education.

Montaño, D. R. (2010). Global destabilizations, sustainable solutions, and schools of music: Challenges and potentials in a perilous time. In W. L. Sims (Ed.), *Proceedings of the 29th world conference of the International Society for Music Education* (pp. 155-61). Perth, Western Australia: International Society for Music Education.

National Association of Schools of Music (NASM) (2010). *Handbook 2010-11*. Reston, Virginia: National Association of Schools of Music.

Peery, W. G. (1999). *Forms of ethical and intellectual development in the college years: A scheme*. San Francisco, CA: Jossey-Bass.

Voice, P. (2011). *Rawls explained: From fairness to utopia*. Chicago, IL: Open Court [Amazon Kindle version]. Retrieved from http://www.amazon.com

Wall, T. F. (2001). *Thinking critically about philosophical problems: A modern introduction*. Belmont, CA: Wadsworth/Thomson Learning.

Waller, B. N. (2008). *Consider ethics: Theory, readings, and contemporary issues* (2nd ed.). New York, NY: Pearson Longman [Amazon Kindle version]. Retrieved from http://www.amazon.com

Toward a Model for Assessing Music Teacher Effectiveness

Glenn E. Nierman
The University of Nebraska-Lincoln
Lincoln, NE (USA)

gnierman@unl.edu

Abstract

The increased attention to teacher effectiveness in the United States today is driven by language defining core subjects in the pending reauthorization of the Elementary and Secondary Education Act and Race to the Top regulations. The purpose of this paper is to propose a framework specifying particular dimensions of a teacher evaluation system that would provide a valid assessment of music educators' contribution to students' musical and personal growth. The paper identifies four major content areas—student achievement, teacher skills, teacher knowledge, and teacher dispositions—to be assessed. It recommends that student achievement (most heavily weighted at 40%) be assessed by applying a value-added standard to students' growth in their abilities to perform, to create, and to respond to music. Further, teachers' skills, knowledge, and dispositions could be evaluated by standardized tests, peer observations, and student evaluations respectively, using a group standard and an equal weighting of 20% each. It seems reasonable to conclude that music teacher evaluation will become a "high stakes" assessment; and ultimately, its validity and reliability will be tested in the courts. Therefore, the design of the system demands the utmost attention of the profession.

Keywords
Assessment, teacher effectiveness, measurement, evaluation

Like the wildfires that exploded across part of the Midwestern United States this fall consumed acres of land, so the debate about how to evaluate teaching effectiveness has consumed hours of Internet reading and pages of legislative policy manuals. Everybody has joined in the debate—parents, administrators, politicians, and teachers themselves. It's not an exaggeration to say that some pursue this debate with the fervor of a politician about to be ousted from office. And why not? Everyone is an expert in the teacher evaluation. After all, we have all had years of practice in at least a "pick-up version" of this game as we went through our years of formal schooling.

Historically, classroom observations were the primary measurement tool for teacher effectiveness. As the Standards Movement of the 1990s gained momentum, however, Mari Pearlman (2002) reported that these observation practices came under fire, and since that time, "numerous alternative evaluative practices have been developed or reborn" (par. 12). It is in this climate of searching for "alternative evaluative practices" for teacher effectiveness that we find ourselves today. The criteria for evaluating teacher pre-service candidates championed by the Interstate Teacher Assessment and Support Consortium (Council of Chief State School Officers, 2011) and teacher accrediting institutions such as National Council for the Accreditation of Teacher Education (NCATE) (National Council for the Accreditation of Teacher Education, 2008)—skills, knowledge, and dispositions—are spilling over into the discussion about how to assess practicing teachers in the United States. State, district and local education leaders are currently mulling over various kinds of measures for estimating the impact of teachers on student learning.

Why, specifically though, at the start of the 2011–12 school year in the United States, is there such an emphasis on teacher evaluation systems in general, and why now are music educators being drawn into the discussion? According to the National Association for Music Education (National Association for Music Education, 2011), "The issue is being brought to the front burner by talk of the reauthorization of the Elementary and Secondary Education Act and Race to the Top Requirements" (par. 1). In brief, music educators in the United States would like these evaluations of their teaching to be based on the individual student's music learning, an area in which they can document achievement, not on learning in the STEM (Science, Technology, Engineering, and Math) subjects as is the practice in some states.

In the United States, education is the primary responsibility of the individual states and the school districts within the states rather than the federal government. The music education profession is thus currently engaged in a sprint to influence the development of laws and policies for the teacher evaluation systems before their enactment could institutionalize systems that are not valid for music educators.

In designing individual measurement tools, educators often utilize a "table of specifications" in which questions such as the following are considered: 1. What content will be tested? 2. What measurement tools will be used to assess the content? 3. By what standard will the content area be assessed? and 4. What weight will be given to the measurement? It is these same four questions that will be used as the framework for proposing a model for assessing music teacher effectiveness in this paper.

What Areas will be Measured?

The assessment of music teacher effectiveness could be conceptualized as consisting of four areas: student achievement, i.e., student learning; teaching skills; teaching knowledge; and teaching dispositions.

Student Achievement

It is evident that part of the content of a music teacher evaluation system should involve the extent to which students demonstrate what they know and are able to do—student achievement. This is due in part to increasing evidence from the research literature that suggests that teacher efficacy plays a large role in student achievement (Hanushek & Rivkin, 2010), but primarily from the fact that RTTP fund regulations stipulate that student achievement must be a "significant" part of teacher evaluation systems (United States Department of Education, 2010).

Music and the arts have the unique ability to integrate the cognitive, affective, and psychomotor domains in helping the student learn. The content most relevant to music students' learning would seem to be broadly captured in three arts processes used as the framework for the 1997 National Assessment of Educational Progress (NAEP)—performing, creating, and responding (Persky, Sandene, & Askew, 1998, p. i).

Performing, the ability of the student to make music using a musical instrument (traditional or non-traditional) or his/her voice, is at the core of learning in music. Music is a skills-based subject. Students learn best the cognitive aspects of the discipline when encountering the elements of music in the authentic context of producing sound. The physical properties of a tone (pitch, loudness, timbre, duration, etc.) and the factors that influence those dimensions (e.g., the effects of length, thickness, and tension of a string on pitch) are best comprehended through the authentic experience of making music on a string instrument, for example. The ability of the arts to help the student experience the affective/aesthetic dimension of what it is like to be a "feelingful" human being and to understand and use those feelings to enhance the quality of life and interactions with others is heightened by performing alone or with others.

Just as performing constitutes an important dimension of musical learning, so too developing creative potential and processes is an essential part of what it means to be musical. Webster (2002) argues that it is plausible to think of creative experience in music as a central focus of music education. Creativity, as conceptualized here, would include the musical behaviors of composing, arranging, and improvising. In terms of the creative process, creativity would include both convergent and divergent thinking.

Further, the student's ability to respond to music is critical to life-long learning in the discipline. Responding to music is focused in the musical behavior of listening and refers to perceiving, describing, analyzing, and evaluating musical works.

Teaching Skills
There is an expanding research base that links student achievement to teacher quality. Good teachers demonstrate certain teaching skills. A skill, according to Simpson (1966) is a psychomotor behavior; it involves both the mind (knowing) and "muscle" (doing). Teaching skills include mastery of various instructional strategies—questioning and modeling. Modeling, for example, is very important for music educators who are going to help students grow in their ability to make music. Other teaching skills include mastering classroom management techniques, observing, and planning.

Teaching Knowledge
Examining what knowledge is required of pre-service music educators is perhaps a good barometer of teaching knowledge valued by the profession. In most traditional music teacher education programs, four general domains of knowledge are typically addressed: general education (knowing across the liberal arts); content knowledge (aural skills, theory, analysis, music history, conducting, etc.); pedagogical knowledge (learning theories, assessment strategies, philosophical frameworks, multicultural issues); and pedagogical content knowledge (knowledge constructed as a result of attempts to incorporate theory into practice during field experiences, for example), a concept proposed by Shulman (1987). An evaluation of music educators should include assessment of what knowledge they bring to the classroom.

Teaching Dispositions
In the US, NCATE influences greatly what teachers should know and be able to do. Just as teaching skills and teaching knowledge are a part of NCATE's Standard 1 (NCATE, 2008, par. 2), so teacher preparation institutions are asked to demonstrate that their students are developing professional teaching dispositions. NCATE's Online Glossary (n.d.) defines professional dispositions as "professional attitudes, values, and beliefs demonstrated through both verbal and non–verbal behaviors as educators interact with students, families, colleagues, and communities." Two professional dispositions required by NCATE are fairness and the belief that all students can learn. In addition to these two dispositions, other important dispositions may include intellectual curiosity, sensitivity to diversity, personal diplomacy, empathy, and an appreciation of the value of music making and events in the related arts (Olson et al., 1987).

What Measurement Tools will be Used?
Once the content of the music teacher evaluation system has been selected, how will these areas be measured? To assess students' achievements in music, particularly in the areas of performing and creating, is particularly challenging. The measurement tasks must be administered within a reasonable amount of time, and yet maintain a sense of validity, authenticity, and integrity to the art form. The assessment of students' ability to perform music with others, for example, could be accomplished with digital recordings using sophisticated microphones strategically placed to allow assessment of the individual while hearing the group's music making in the background. The assessment of creating in music should include composing, improvising, and arranging activities. Designing measurements for this area is quite a challenging task. Not all musical creators use traditional notation. The discipline has a wide array of mediums and genres for musical expression. The student's ability to respond could be measured by asking students to analyze and describe aspects of music listening examples they hear, to critique musical performances, to demonstrate their knowledge of music notation, and to describe music's role in society.

A model for assessing student achievement in music as described above—the 1997 NAEP tasks (Persky, Sandene, & Askew, 1998)—already exists in the United States. With some refinement and the funds to administer the authentic performing and creating tasks, student achievement in music could be validly assessed at varying grade levels.

Measurement tools, such as observation schemata for assessing teachers' skills (both for observations in real time and video recorded teaching vignettes (National Board for Professional Teaching Standards, 2011) and multiple choice tests for assessing teacher content knowledge (Educational Testing Service, n.d.) have been in use in the profession for a number of years. These measurement tools could be an excellent model for skills and knowledge assessment.

By contrast, the measurement of teaching dispositions is a relatively new and daunting task. Some of these beliefs involve moral and ethical issues. The line between correct and incorrect answers might be very thin. Among the findings of the Gates Foundation's $45 million dollar Measure of Effective Teaching study is support for the notion that student perceptions are useful in predicting teacher effectiveness. In a study of 2,519 classrooms, Kane and Cantrell (2010, p. 9) and their group of researchers found that students gave high ratings to teachers whose classes consistently made learning gains; and the perceptions were generally consistent across the teacher's classes. Perhaps students using a rating scale might be the most valid and reliable way to measure teacher dispositions such as fairness, compassion, and respect for diversity. There is no one who observes the teacher in action more frequently than the students themselves.

By What Standard will the Content Area be Assessed?

The term standard has different meanings, but in this context, standards refer to the rules or bases for evaluating the extent to which mastery of a content area has been demonstrated. There are at least three common standards on which the measurements for music teacher effectiveness might be judged: individual standards—growth (using the student's own skills, knowledge or abilities as the benchmark for comparison); group standards (individual achievement compared with that of the group as a whole); and arbitrary, fixed standards (e.g., determining that a score of 90% correct constitutes an exemplary teacher; 80% correct, a good teacher; 70% correct, a developing teacher; etc., rather arbitrarily).

Student achievement might be most effectively evaluated using an individual standard so that gains might be assessed on the basis of student growth. The literature currently refers to what is improved about what students know and are able to do as a consequence of their study with a particular teacher as "value added." Music, as a "non–tested" subject (a subject other than reading or math), does not already have a battery of tests at its disposal; and therefore, a potential solution is to create a new pre and post–test model based on the 1997 NAEP tools in order to measure student growth in music.

Teachers' skills, knowledge, and dispositions, on the other hand, might be more effectively evaluated using a group standard. If teacher knowledge in particular is to be measured using standardized, multiple–choice tests, then it would be quite easy and appropriate to evaluate teachers on these tests using a norm–referenced standard. Dispositions, on the other hand, might be more problematic using this standard because of their highly affective nature. Nevertheless, using the group standard for dispositions seems to be the "lesser of the evils" when considering the other standards, unless an arbitrary, fixed standard (greater than 80% of the dispositions being rated as "acceptable," for example) could find support.

What Weight will be Assigned?

The final decision about what weight will be assigned to the content measurements seems to revolve around the area of student achievement. A stipulation of RTTP funding is that student achievement must be a "significant" part of teacher evaluation systems, but what has been operationalized as a "significant" proportion varies from a weight of 20% for student performance in tested subjects in Delaware to 51% for teachers in tested grades in Rhode Island (Marion & Buckley, 2011, p. 8).

The following weights could be used for a music teacher evaluation system: 40% for student achievement and 20% each for teacher skills, knowledge, and dispositions. The rationale for these weightings is that student learning as a measure of effective teaching has gained voice in the United States because there is a body of literature that shows that the quality of teaching is directly related to student performance and because student gain scores are then one important measure of accountability. Therefore, the assignment of 40% of the summative score to be based on student performance (twice the weight of an other variable and almost half the total weight) seems to meet the spirit of "significant." Further, if the belief that effective teaching is not taking place unless learning occurs strikes philosophical resonance, a weight of 40% seems appropriate for student achievement.

On the other hand, student achievement is an area that is influenced by many factors outside the school and beyond the teacher's control. These factors are difficult to control statistically. It seems equally important that factors such as teachers' skills, knowledge, and dispositions—factors that could be measured more traditionally and perhaps more validly and reliably by observation and standardized tests—collectively receive somewhat more weight than student achievement.

Epilogue

A music teacher evaluation system must address the dimension of accountability required by society and must display the dimensions of validity and reliability required to maintain the integrity of the discipline. Regardless of the content assessed by selected measurement tools, which are then evaluated by some standard and given a particular weight, music teacher evaluation seems destined to become a "high stakes" assessment in the United States. Teachers will be fired or retained, tenured or placed on probation, and given increases in salary based on these evaluations. The efficacy of the system will ultimately be tested in the courts on the basis of its validity and reliability; and therefore, the design of the system demands the utmost attention of the profession.

References

Author, (2011). *Interstate teacher assessment and support consortium model core teaching standards: A resource for state dialogue.* Washington, DC: Council of Chief State School Officers.

Educational Testing Service. (n.d.). *Praxis II music content knowledge preparation materials.* Retrieved from http://www.ets.org/praxis/prepare/materials/0113

Hanushek, E., & Rivkin, S. (2010). Generalizations about using value–added measures of teacher quality. *American Economic Review, 100*(2), 267–271.

Kane, T., & Cantrell, S. (2010). *Learning about teaching: Initial findings from the measures of effective teaching project.* Retrieved from http://www.gatesfoundation.org

Marion, S., & Buckley, K. (2011). *A survey of approaches used to evaluate educators in non–tested grades and subjects.* Retrieved from http://www.nciea.org

National Association for Music Education. (2011). *NAfME recommendations for music teachers: Teacher evaluation.* Retrieved from http://www.menc.org/resources/view/music–education–advocacy–central

National Board for Professional Teaching Standards (2011). *The portfolio.* Retrieved from http://www.nbpts.org/for_candidates/the_portfolio

National Council for the Accreditation of Teacher Education. (2008). *Unit standards in effect 2008.* Retrieved from http://bit.ly/LoZHuA

National Council for the Accreditation of Teacher Education. (n.d.) *NCATE glossary.* Retrieved from http://bit.ly/N7L7Si

Olson, G., Buckner, R., Collins, I., Costanza, A. P., Gonzo, C., Haack, P., & Willman, F. (1987). *Music teacher education: Partnership and process.* Reston, VA: Music Educators National Conference.

Pearlman, M. (2002). Overview of teacher evaluation. In J. W. Guthrie (Ed.), *Gale Encyclopedia of Education*. Retrieved from http://www.answers.com/topic/overview-of-teacher-evaluation

Persky, H., Sandene, B., & Askew, J. (1998). *The NAEP 1997 arts report card, NCES 1999–486*. Washington, DC: U.S. Department of Education, Office of Educational Research and Improvement, National Center for Education Statistics.

Shulman, L. S. (1987). Knowledge and teaching: Foundations of the new reform. *Harvard Educational Review*, 57(1), 1–22.

Simpson, E. (1966). *The classification of educational objectives, psychomotor domain, OE5–85–104*. Washington, DC: United States Office of Education.

United States Department of Education. (2010). *Race to the top executive summary*. Retrieved from http://www2.ed.gov/programs/racetothetop/executive-summary.pdf

Webster, P. (2002). Creative thinking in music: Advancing a model. In T. Sullivan & L. Willingham, (Eds.), *Creativity and music education* (pp. 16–33). Edmonton, AB: Canadian Music Educators' Association.

Colonial Legacy of Functional Art Music in Nigeria: Its Influence on Compositional Preferences of Music Students (The Nsukka Example)

Christian Onyeji
University of Nigeria (Nigeria)

Elizabeth Onyeji
University of Nigeria (Nigeria)

Abstract

The consistency in the preference for choral music composition among composition students in Nigerian universities against instrumental music composition motivated this enquiry with the objective to ascertain the possible cause and solution. The dearth, if not near extinction of instrumental works in Nigeria is quite problematic. A significant reversal of the trend is perforce to this study. An overview of compositional output in the country within and outside the university system linked the compositional preferences to the colonial legacy of what we describe as the notion of "functional art music." A 20-year period of teaching and supervision of composition in the department of music formed the backdrop for this study, during which consistency in the preference for vocal music compositions by students in their project works against instrumental music was noted. An output analysis of compositions from other institutions was directly and indirectly done through colleagues who provided evidence that supports the conclusion in this study. A historical background of art music in Nigeria is presented, constructing a bridge from there to the present music scene that clarifies the compositional preferences of students in music departments in the 21st century. It also highlights and clarifies the stifling of instrumental compositions as well as lack of diversity in creativity and output in the country for the benefit of learners and student composers. Department of Music, University of Nigeria, Nsukka is used as the focus study location owing to its strategic position as the first indigenous department, producing the highest number of manpower in art music composition and teachers for the country. Qualitative and quantitative research methods were employed in data gathering.

Keywords
Functional art, composition, preferences, missionary, choral, colonial

Introduction and Background

Persistent preference for vocal music compositions by student-composers as well as the dearth of instrumental works in Nigeria, within and outside departments of music owing to such preference, constrained this enquiry to ascertain the root cause of such preference. Having been engaged in the teaching of composition in the University of Nigeria for more than 15 years, and in music education respectively, it was possible to note the worrisome development in which instrumental music composition is isolated by student-composers under the guise of choice/preference, relevance/functionality, and performability. A cursory glance at the composition projects within the libraries of departments of music in Nigeria show very high number of vocal (primarily choral) compositions which do not present evidence of balanced exposure to creative possibilities in music by the students. Such situation raises many questions such as why the students prefer vocal compositions in their project work, whether they have no requisite training in instrumental music composition, etc. It was also important to trace the lead to such preference as well as bring to the fore the possible effect of the dearth of instrumental compositions and the imbalance such dearth portends in the creative output of Nigeria composers. In order to address these issues it was significant to go back to history and trace the possibility of dominant formative influences as well as pioneering effects on art music composition, performance and education reflecting on the students' preferences.

A Historical Perspective on Art Music in Nigeria

Most African countries south of the Sahara share similar political history marked by Western colonization, education, religion and social influences. The West established European music education in Africa. This coerced new mode of musical expression, documentation and communication (see Agawu, 2003; Herbst, Rudolph, & Onyeji, 2003). In the schools and churches, Africans acquired some level of musical training in piano and organ playing, classical singing and choral directing. "It was in this religious Western-oriented educative milieu that the African art composers emerged to compose sacred and secular choral works based on the western hymn and/or madrigal. Music teaching in schools was rooted in choral singing and teacher training emphasized choral work" (Herbst, Rudolph, & Onyeji, 2003, p. 146).

More specifically, "the history of art music in Nigeria dates back to the first half of nineteenth century, when Christian missionaries set their feet on Nigerian soil. The Anglican came in 1842, the Methodist in 1845 and the Baptist in 1850" (Adegbite, 2001, p. 78) Following on the heels of the missionaries is the British colonial government. According to Idolor (2001),

> By 1958, Ukeje (1979) records that the first day school established by the C.M.S. missionaries in Onitsha and post-primary schools like Baptist Teachers College, Ogbomosho, Wesley College, Ibadan and Zik Grammar School, Sapele founded in 1897, 1905 and 1943 respectively had music literally taught in their program of studies. (p. 136)

"Music literacy (then) (solfa notation in particular) became expedient for the Missionary as well as the Colonial educational objectives and content. It served for producing church choirs and recreational school music" (Nzewi, 1999, p. 4). The overriding influence and dominance of school and church choral music compositions and performances is noticeable in the history of art music development in Nigeria as in other countries in Africa.

The earliest forms of literary musical expressions in Nigeria are those choral music compositions and performances in church choirs for church services and school choral competitions and performances. Functionality or utilitarian value attached to the choral music as well as availability of performers and listeners have since then been argued as the significant reason for the proliferation of choral music in Nigeria. This scenario is replicated in many African countries where Western cultures exist. Andoh (2009/2010) affirmed that "the bulk of Ghanaian art compositions are choral" (p. 124). According to him, "the history of the introduction of certain types of European music to Ghana, especially choral music, is closely tied with the history of the Christian mission" (p. 124). "The churches raised choirs and singing bands out of which arose choirmasters and organists who were themselves creative composers" (Andoh, 2008, p. 1). "Many of the composers of the early Ghanaian era, from about 1890s to 1950s, began to compose in the style of the Western idioms they were familiar with, with the bulk of their output being made up of choral works" (Andoh, 2007, p. 163).

The platform provided by the Christian missionary and school activities in Nigeria enabled the construction of an unending bridge from the choral music "nursery" of the missionary era to the present times. The church, choir, recreational musical outlook and background of musical compositions targeted at immediate consumers during the missionary era gave a functional undertone to art music composition. To appreciate the argument advanced here, it would be necessary to frame what we call "functional art music compositions."

Framing functional art music composition
Functionality, as applied to music, describes the value placed on musical product beyond the music itself as an artistic expression. Except in the descriptions of harmonic processes in tonal music in which functionality applies to chords, and the general sound/tonal structures in Western diatonic music, the notion of functionality in music has been exclusively applied to the description of music of African and some non-Western musical cultures such as the Aborigines of Australia, the Red Indians in American and some Latin American music.

Nketia (1982), Akpabot (1986), Coplan (1980), and, indeed, most writers and researchers on African music have described it as a functional art tied to the social and religious lives of the people. According to Akpabot, "one of the chief characteristics of African traditional music is its association with social and ritual ceremonies" (p. 1). As such "the arts, [music in particular] are employed and implicated in the life rites, work, religion, ceremonies, games and festivals, the mechanisms of social order and in social activities' (Oehrle & Emeka, 2003, p. 41). Functionality in music seeks to identify and define the ends to which music is put starting from its conception to its composition and consumption. Functionality in a musical tradition is its attachment to, definition of, marking of and signifying of other social considerations that gave rise to the composition and performance of the music.

Though contestable on the basis that Western art music is also a social art, bringing people together for the appreciation of music and life, proponents of Western art music would have people believe it's a non-functional art. The question is how would one describe a church hymn or a Mass written for Catholic liturgy if it does not lead to the ends of spiritual growth of worshipers? Western art music could be described as functional when one considers the creative intentions. To argue therefore that a church anthem is functional art music of the church is stating the obvious. Church music falls under the category of functional art when valued as works that have spiritual and social growth as their creative intentions.

Functional Art Music in Nigeria

It does appear that the art music tradition bequeathed to Africa and Nigeria in particular is essentially functional. Though valued in Nigeria, being in consonance with the musical foundation of the people, the puzzle however is why the progress of art music development in the country seems to have stagnated and become choral oriented. Composition of instrumental works seems almost extinct or disappearing.

A large number of trained musicians and composers are products of church choirs, or choral music enthusiasts and church organists. Many of the composers operate from the platform of church choral music while some attempt operatic works still from the choral music perspective. According to Ekwueme (2001), "Contemporary musical practice in Africa, in spite of acculturation and incorporation of features resulting from various forces of external influence, has tended to maintain the same predominance of group and vocal activity" (p. 16). The choral influence is also noticeable in the few attempts by these composers to write solo art songs as observed by one of Nigeria's foremost soloists. According to her "most solo songs by Nigerian composers…have always presented limitations for singers because the writers themselves are still quite limited in their expressive techniques for solo voice having written always for choruses" (Nwosu-LoBamijoko, 2001, p. 71). The limitation raised by Nwosu-LoBamijoko is quite significant in understanding the lack of creative development of Nigerian solo art songs on the one part but also illuminates the reasons why instrumental works have been isolated by composers and music students in Nigeria. Quite predominantly therefore, one finds "choral setting of biblical verses, psalms or Christian stories, native airs belonging to a choral genre that resulted from composers' attempting to fuse elements of Nigerian traditional music with Western choral idiom" (Herbst, Rudolph, & Onyeji, 2003, p. 151-152).

The need to satisfy the church and the choirs, the need to be relevant to the immediate society (the church inclusive), the need for immediate performance of composed works and the general orientation and formative influences have altogether been advanced to direct the preference for vocal music compositions. The value of a composition as a product for church consumption, the obligation to compose for the church, the sheer desire to provide social commentaries on happenings in the country, the assumed greater appreciation by the public and, indeed, the misconception that vocal music composition is easier are some reasons student-composers have advanced for their preference. It is summed up that the functional art music heritage, a legacy of colonization in Nigeria, that laid emphasis on vocal music for church and school use has driven the preferences of student-composers in Nigeria.

Curriculum Provisions

Music studies in Nigeria provide bi-cultural program in which students learn music from Western and African cultures on equal footing enabling a graduate "to take his place alongside music graduates from other part of the world" (Ekwueme, 2004, p. 155). More specifically "all students are expected to be proficient in performance on at least one instrument or in solo singing (Ekwueme, 2004, p. 156). With the level platform for the study, composition and performance of both vocal and instrumental works, it becomes quite worrisome that the preference of student-composers lies consistently on vocal music. With the obvious and robust enjoyment of instrumental works in Nigerian traditional music, the feverish pitch with which such music is performed as well as the proficiency and high-level skills of instrumental music players in Nigeria, it is quite problematic that student-composers coming from such cultural background would preferentially compose vocal works.

Evidence from the Department of Music, University of Nigeria, Nsukka

A statistics of the available students' projects in the Department of Music was taken. Table 1 below shows the number and preferences of student-composers in their composition projects in the holding of the department as far back as 1979. It is evident from the statistics below that there is a general leaning toward vocal music composition.

Table 1. List of available students' composition projects in the department of music library at the University of Nigeria, Nsukka showing their preferences.

S/N	Name of Student	Year of composition	Type of composition
1	Onwuka Ugochukwu	1979	Vocal
2	Joel Akubuokwuoma	1979	Vocal
3	Fueshiangha Michael Forchu	1982	Vocal
4	Ekpa, Aniedi Edet	1984	Vocal
5	Uquah Samuel Edoho	1984	Instrumental
6	Udegbe, Esmond-Ralph T.	1984	Instrumental
7	Uwheru, Amos Eriurhoro	1985	Vocal
8	Opara, Theophilus A.	1986	Vocal
9	Odediran Adjai .O.	1984	Instrumental
10	Nwosu Uzoma	1988	Vocal
11	Idowu J. Odewale	1988	Vocal
12	Babajide Bayo	1988	Vocal
13	Aminu, Yekinni Philip	1988	Vocal
14	Onwuchekwa Chigbu P.	1990	Vocal
15	Obong, Ime Tom	1990	Instrumental
16	Onyeji, Christian	1990	Instrumental
17	Alade Olabode Adebayo	1990	Vocal
18	Esimagbele, Godwin E	1991	Vocal
19	Loko, Olugbenga	1991	Instrumental
20	Festus, Ife Olisaeke	1991	Vocal
21	Chinedu Michael Chukwudi	1991	Vocal
22	Nwosu Gary Augustine Onwurah	1991	Instrumental
23	Aminu, Yekinni Philip	1992	Vocal
24	Bassey Etukudoh Udoh	1992	Instrumental
25	Ojobor Wilfred Mascaras	1992	Vocal
26	Olujimi Babatunde Olunfunso	1992	Vocal
27	Adelani, Akuchukwu S.	1992	Instrumental
28	Anya, Bertha Ifeyinwa	1992	Vocal
29	Bassey, Ernest R.	1992	Vocal
30	Echezona Gloria O.	1992	Vocal
31	Okoro, Benjamin D.	1992	Vocal
32	Nnam, Jude Chika	1993	Vocal
33	Yekini I. Adeniyi	1993	Vocal

34	Kumuyi/Adesoji H.	1994	Vocal
35	Ofsun, Mana Koranteng	1995	Vocal
36	Akubuiroh Juliana Ijeoma	1995	Vocal
37	Ikeogwu Michael	1995	Vocal
38	Ogunbona, Ohubayo Simeon	1995	Vocal
39	Akanle, Oyewole Isaac	1995	Vocal
40	Eyeniyan Godwin Utieyin E.	1996	Instrumental
41	Nwamara/Alva-Ikoku O.	1998	Vocal
42	Ubaka, Johnbull Mathew	1988	Vocal
43	Akai Malachi Pius U.	1998	Instrumental
44	Authority, Olunole Albert Uzodimma	2001	Vocal
45	Udor, Isaac Essie	2002	Instrumental
46	Omoyele Orioye Emmanuel	2003	Instrumental
47	Sylvanus Emaeyak Peter	2004	Instrumental
48	Omodiale Godwin Usiabulu	2004	Vocal
49	Ofuani Sunday	2005	Vocal
50	Ewulu, John Izuchukwu	2005	Vocal
51	Akpakpan, Johnson James	2005	Instrumental
52	Ohwofasa, Justina Enoh	2006	Instrumental
53	Olisaeke, Festus Ife	2006	Instrumental
54	Adelabu Emmanuel Tosin	2006	Vocal
55	Ofosu, Osborne	2006	Vocal
56	Ofosu, Joana	2006	Vocal
57	Agbo, Benedict	2009	Vocal
58	Ugwu, Blessing Onyinyechi	2007	Vocal
59	Ikumapayi A. Abayomi	2007	Vocal
60	Aghware Hosea Ogheneruemu	2007	Vocal
61	Ugwuja, Edmund Paul	2007	Vocal
62	Adebowale, Z. Ademor. N.	2008	Vocal
63	Nwankwo, Jude .O.	2008	Vocal
64	Akan, Joseph Abiodun	2008	Vocal
65	Odo, Vitus Okonkwo	2010	Vocal
66	Ojo, Shade Emmanuel	2010	Instrumental
67	Adeyemi Abidemi Adebayo	2010	Instrumental
68	Jayeola, Folorunso David	2010	Instrumental
69	Ahiaba, Goodness	2010	Vocal
70	Nnam, Jude	2010	Vocal
71	Oguntade, Kayode	In Progress	Vocal
72	Sam-Adikiapiri, Prisca	In Progress	Vocal
73	Anukam, Franklin	In Progress	Vocal
74	Adelabu, Emmanuel Tosin	In progress	Vocal

Out of the available 74 composition projects, 20 are instrumental works from which at least five resulted through persuasion from their supervisors including one of the writers. The total number of instrumental compositions is less than 28% of the total compositions. This gives an unbalanced preference for vocal music composition.

Various reasons were presented by student-composers, which all revolve around the need for the composition of church music arising from their formative period and need for church music as highly valued. A fair numbers (26%) of the respondents also added the preference for choral music by audiences arising from the import of textual messages. Difficulty in handling instrumental composition judged to be too abstract was expressed. Two of such responses from student-staff members are given below.

> *1. My first encounter with a musical ensemble was with my primary school choir. My interest in choral music led to my joining many choral groups in Lagos including the Laz Ekwueme Chorale. With this background, I developed interest in composing choral music. I also prefer to compose for the voice because I began my music career as a singer. (Nwankwo, Jude, 1st August 2011).*

> *2. The reason behind my preference to compose predominantly vocal music is simply born out of need and purpose. I function as a church musician and here in Nigeria most of our performances in the church are thematic oriented in terms of worship. The words are often necessary (Rev. Fr. Ben Agbo, 3rd August 2011).*

These responses evidence the points being made and reflect the general situation in the country as already argued.

Discussion

It may seem improbable that the dominance and preference for vocal music compositions could be linked to the colonial music practice in Nigeria or that music output could be linked to functionalism of art music in churches and schools. It was significantly noted that much of the current educational, creative and performance activities in music are comfortably situated on the foundations and platforms established in the colonial time. Many composers still grapple with the effects of their formative years, which generally rely on Western norms. In this also is the continuous hegemony of the church in Nigeria where most musical works are performed or targeted. To this end, very little amount of creative works are composed for the sheer celebrations of creativity in sound. This, very well, is in consonance with the African philosophy of creativity in which music generally addresses other ends than music itself. Functionalism is deeply rooted in African arts creativity. Text being a strong parameter for realising the socio-philosophical gains of the arts, particularly in music, is considered very significant in creative works in music. As such, composers place higher value on music for the human voice. To some degree also, instrumental works operate from the principles of vocal music, being sometimes direct "translations" of vocal works for the instruments or incorporating text-based instrumental patterns. Identifying the primacy of text in indigenous music in Nigeria, Ekwueme (2004) was unequivocal in affirming "words are of primary importance in Igbo music making" (p. 17). As such text is a pervading phenomenon in music making among most Nigerian societies, reflecting in art music compositions.

The church, being the ubiquitous context for the performance of art music in Nigeria, attracts almost all the composers, performers. The direct consequence is the near extinction of instrumental music, its composition and performance. While not arguing against the need to "stress the importance of permitting and encouraging students, in consultation with their lecturers, to develop their own purposes and goals within their fields of study" (Oehrle & Emeka, 2003, p. 47), it seems such student-determined choice in composition is working against the very same foundation it is intended to build upon, recommending some form of lecturers' enforcement to reverse the trend. The current situation presents the ugly impression of lack of proper exposure of composition students to instrumental music composition. The connecting bridge between the colonial music practices and the contemporary Nigerian art music scene has continued to elongate, almost unnoticed, determining the preferences made by student-composers. Whether the trend would be easily reversed is rather a mute point, going by the devotion attached to their creative preference by the composers.

Recommendations

Existing theories and expert prescriptions make it almost impossible for anyone to pontificate on the compositional preferences of student-composers, given the overwhelming suggestions that creativity is best left to the discretion of the creative personality to ensure the fledging of the creative endowment unique to each person. Be that as it may, the current tilted preference for vocal music composition recommends an exclusive action to ensure instrumental music composition in Nigeria does not run to extinction. The current situation recommends a lecturer-prescribed choice for students to not only counter the existing notions about instrumental cum vocal music composition but to also get them to practically engage in such compositions to balance the equation in some ways. It is the recommendation of the writers that composition lecturers and supervisors be actively involved in the selection of composition projects by students and, where necessary, have the students compose at least one instrumental and one choral work for their graduation. It is also critical for the lecturers to engage the students in motivational sessions to clarify the importance of composing in instrumental genres. Institutions offering music should introduce instrumental ensembles and motivate students to compose for them.

Conclusion

The foregoing brings us face to face with the challenge of keeping the status quo and running the risk of instrumental music extinction in order to allow the student-composers determine and develop along their individual interests and preferences. To change the status quo requires deliberate measure to "enforce" preference shift. This is tacitly recommended as it would require deliberate enforcement by teachers of composition. The study linked the prevalence of the vocal compositions to the choral music legacy of the colonial music era that have been perpetuated by the church. On the whole however, it would require concerted and deliberate efforts of all music composers, patrons and lovers to have more of instrumental compositions in Nigeria from Nigerian composers.

References

Adegbite, A. (2001). The present state of development of African art music in Nigeria. In M. A. Omibiyi (Ed.), *African art music in Nigeria: Fela Sowande memorial* (pp. 77-82). Lagos, Nigeria: Stirling-Horden.

Agawu, K. (2003). *Representing African music: Postcolonial notes, queries and positions.* New York, NY: Routledge.

Akpabot, S. (1986). *Foundation of Nigerian traditional music*. Ibadan, Nigeria: Spectrum Books.

Andoh, T. E. (2007). The nationalistic music of I. D. Riverson. *Legon journal of Humanitie, 48*, 159-177.

Andoh, T. E. (2008). I. D. Riverson's konyimdzi aben, na hom ndzi dew: A study of style and language behaviour in harmony. *International Journal of Multi-Disciplinary Scholarship, 2*(1), 1-12.

Andoh, T. E. (2009/2010). The growth and development of choral music in Ghana: The contributions and aspects of the choral styles of Ephraim Amu. *Journal of Performing Arts, 4*(1), 123-135.

Coplan, D. B. (1980). Marabi culture: Continuity and transformation in African music in Johannesburg, 1920-1980. *African Urban Studies 6*, 49-73.

Ekwueme, L. (2001). Composing contemporary African choral music: Problems and prospects. In M. Omibiyi-Obidike (Ed.), *African art music in Nigeria* (pp. 16-57). Lagos, Nigeria: Stirling-Horden.

Ekwueme, L. E. N. (2004). *Essays on African and African-American music and culture*. Lagos, Nigeria: Lenaus.

Herbst, A., Rudolph J., & Onyeji, C. (2003). Written composition in the African context. In A. Herbst et al., (Eds.), *Musical arts in Africa: Theory, practice and education* (pp. 142-178). Pretoria, South Africa: Unisa Press.

Idolor, G. E. (2001). Formal education and the development of African art music in Nigeria. In M. A. Omibiyi (Ed.), *African art music in Nigeria: Fela Sowande memorial* (pp. 135-149). Lagos, Nigeria: Stirling-Horden.

Nketia, K. (1982). *The music of Africa*. Sussex, UK: R J Acford.

Nwosu-LoBamijoko, J. (2001). Art singing in Nigeria: The composer and the performers. In M. A. Omibiyi (Ed.), *African art music in Nigeria: Fela Sowande memorial* (pp. 70-76). Lagos, Nigeria: Stirling-Horden.

Nzewi, M. (1999). *Modern art music in Nigeria: Whose modernism?* Unpublished seminar paper presented at the Department of Music University of Natal, Duban, RSA.

Oehrle, E., & Emeka, L. (2003). Thought systems informing the musical arts. In A. Herbst et al, (Eds.), *Musical arts in Africa: Theory, practice and education* (pp. 38-51). Pretoria, South Africa: Unisa Press.

Informal Music Learning Experiences: The Role of the Musician in Creating a Successful Musical Performance in a Hospital Setting

Costanza Preti
University of London (England)
costanza.preti@gmail.com

Abstract

This paper reports a study of the music performance techniques developed by a group of musicians taking part in a long term live music program in a pediatric hospital in Italy. It also examines how these techniques were effective in creating an engaging musical performance for the hospitalized children and their caregivers. The presence of professional musicians (not music therapists) performing in healthcare settings is an increasing phenomenon that is under researched at present. As part of a wider cross-cultural study, eight musicians playing in a pediatric hospital setting were observed across four weeks. The average length of a musical intervention observed was approximately 40 minutes. The observations were recorded on an observation schedule and simultaneously audio recorded. Overall, 36 hours and 40 minutes of musical interventions were observed. Results suggests that independently from the musician playing, all sessions observed had a common structure that formed the basis for each musician's own variations according to their experience, confidence, and type of instrument used. For the first time, short-term longitudinal data were gathered empirically for a group of musicians without a music therapy background playing in a pediatric hospital. These musicians were able to create a music routine informed by their craft knowledge and experiences as performers in the hospital. Implications for informal music education outcomes are discussed.

Keywords

Music in hospitals, informal learning, community music, music and health, music and well-being

Background

The use of live music has increasingly featured in hospitals in the last ten years, both in Europe and US (Clift et al., 2009; Dileo & Bradt, 2009). Although there are no specific data on the number of healthcare settings using live music (e.g. nor survey type of data on the nature of the musical interventions), in recent years, three systematic reviews on the use of music in pediatric settings have been published (Mrázová & Celec, 2010; Naylor, Kingsnorth, Lamont, McKeever, & Macarthur, 2010; Robb & Carpenter, 2009). Even though both reviews are inconclusive, they arise from the need to summarise increasing research and music programs in pediatric settings.

In addition to the reported benefits of using music for the reduction of stress and anxiety (Longhi & Pickett, 2008), live music in hospitals can often be an educational experience for the children involved in it (Bunt, 1997). Even involuntarily, children may learn songs sung by visiting musicians and/or they can improve their rhythmic skills by practicing during group improvisational sessions. All these experiences could be defined as informal ways of learning. As Green (2001, 2008) suggests "music learning can occur without music teaching" (2001, p. 104) and there are a number of features that contribute to define this particular way of learning.

For most hospitalized children music programs in hospitals represent the first occasion to experience a close encounter with live music, different musical instruments and the chance to play unusual percussion instruments within a group. As Ockelford (2000) observes, music sessions can be a "unique and secure framework" (p. 212) providing children with an opportunity to listen and respond to sounds. Music listening and playing engage cognitive skills such as concentration and memory, as well as co-ordination (Schellenberg, 2005). Accordingly, in this context, although music can be considered as an informal and relatively unstructured form of education, it can be powerful and long lasting (Welch et al., 2009).

Aim

The aim of the study was to investigate the music performance techniques developed by a group of musicians (N = 8) taking part in a long-term live music program in a pediatric hospital, in Italy.

Method

As part of a wider, cross-cultural study, eight musicians were observed during their sessions in the hospital over four weeks. The hospital was selected because of its unique long-term live music program, with 45 hours of music a week, extended across the hospital. The music program scheduled each day consisted of an average of six hours of music a day, across different wards. The average length of a music session observed was approximately 40 minutes. The observations were recorded on an observation schedule and simultaneously audio and video recorded. Overall, 36 hours and 40 minutes of musical interventions were observed.

The observation schedule aimed to: 1. record the number and the quality of interactions happening between musicians, child and caregivers; and 2. to determine what kind of musical event/action triggered a particular response in any of the groups involved in the session. The observation schedule was adapted from the schedule adopted by the Structured Observation System (SOS), a data collection method developed to document changes in the communication behavior of children identified with speech and language delays which takes the shape of an observation schedule with a built-in rating scale (Preti & Welch, 2011).

The use of observations were considered a suitable method in so far as data were collected on non-verbal behavior and the case study observations took place over an extended period of time so that the researcher was able to develop more intimate and informal relationships with the group of participants observed (Cohen & Manion, 1995). Thematic analysis informed by grounded theory (Strauss & Corbin, 1990) was performed on the observations data with the support of Atlas.ti software (Atlas.ti, 2005).

With regard to ethical procedures it was made clear to all participants involved in the study that the researcher adhered to the code of ethics approved by The British Educational Research Association (BERA). A standard form supplied by the hospital—guaranteeing confidentiality and anonymity in the data processing—was used to provide written consent from the participants.

Results

Analysis of the observation data showed that the musicians operated on the basis of two simple techniques which they alternated during their sessions playing for someone and playing with someone. The former was generally employed at the beginning and at the end of a session, while the latter was most commonly used during the middle part of the session. Musical interactions occurred with single children and their caregivers and, more often, within a group that the musicians were bringing together during their session. Occasionally some of the musicians also played for staff, generally nurses and in some cases for/with doctors (Preti & Welch, 2012). From the observation data appeared that, overall, the musicians did not have specific items of repertoire associated with a type of location. The music was selected according to the physical and psychological condition of the child/patient, irrespective of the hospital spaces where they happened to be.

The performance space, however, impacted on the musicians' playing styles such as requiring more or less dynamic changes, which was also reflected in the choice of little percussion instruments handed out to the children and their families. For example, if the situation in the ward, or waiting room, was quiet and the child was perceived to be willing to improvise with the musicians, they were more likely to use louder percussion instruments, such as a tambourine, and sing lively tunes. On the contrary, if the child was in pain and rather distressed, musicians were more likely to adopt a "soft" approach and extract instruments such as an ocean drum, a kalimba or a rain stick.

Independently from the musician playing, all sessions appeared to have a common structure that formed the basis for each musician's own variations according to their: 1. Experience; 2. Confidence; and 3. type of instrument used. The structure remained broadly the same, regardless of the different spaces in which they were playing, or the different health conditions of the young patients involved in the music making.

Each intervention appeared to be organized according to the following stages:

1. Entrance in the ward, playing a "signature" piece;
2. Musical introduction to a familiar song (while physically moving towards one of the children);
3. Performance the song;
4. While singing, demonstrating to the child how to use a little percussion instrument;
5. Handing out the percussion instrument to the child;
6. Playing the same song with variations, while the child was playing the percussion instrument;
7. Introducing new songs (following the actions from 4-6); and
8. Closing the session by playing the "signature" piece from the entrance, or a "goodbye" song.

Typically, the observed details of these stages were as follows:

Stage 1. Musicians walked into the designated space playing their "signature" song, which was often a well-known piece of music. The musical introduction served three purposes, namely: 1. for musicians to announce themselves to their "audience" and to signal the beginning of the musical activity; 2. to attract the attention of the children; 3. to take a few moments for a mental snapshot of the current mood in the different spaces of the hospital where they were scheduled to perform (e.g., wards, waiting rooms, corridors) including observing the age and the children that would have likely to be involved in the session (e.g. health conditions; ethnicities, their body language in response to music). Overall, this stage allowed the musicians to prepare mentally for the coming interactions.

Stages 2 and 3. The musician began to sing or to just play, focusing on the child that they had selected after their initial "musical walk." Such choice appeared to be made on the basis of which child was perceived to be more curious or responsive to the music. There were variations in this approach, depending on the kind of instrument played. Musicians that played the guitar and the violin tended to accompany themselves throughout the session while singing; musicians that played the saxophone and the flute were observed to be more flexible with the use of their instruments and to make more use of solo voice with rhythmic accompaniments, alternating this approach to an instrumental one. Their posture was typically lowered, such as on their knees, in order to establish eye contact with the child while singing. The first direct interaction was generally quite short (around a minute) but it became slightly longer when the musicians played at bedsides, within a ward.

Stage 4 to 5. While singing the song, the musician usually introduced further new instruments to either the child-patient (who was often seen to be slightly intimidated if new to the musical intervention) or to the care giver, in order to reassure the child within the framework of the collective musical activity. All these actions were non-verbal and were mediated by the use of facial expressions and body language. The aim was for all participants to have a little instrument to join in and feel part of the group. They all sung the song with the percussive accompaniment.

Stage 6. Musicians performed variations on the same song to give everyone the chance to memorize it. These techniques included mainly: 1. "leaving gaps in between lyrics" and letting the child complete the missing section(s) of the song; 2. "lyric substitution" when the musician's approach to a well-known song was to turn its lyrics into an absurd text waiting for a reaction from the child; and 3. musical riddles where the child had to "guess" what the song was about (generally an animal).

Stage 7. The session continued with new songs and rhythmic improvisations on the little percussion instruments, drawing on the same rules of engagement (Stage 4 to 6). Stage 8. Musicians often used the same song played at the beginning of the intervention to mark the closure of the session.

This structure have been developed by the musicians and consolidated through their experience in the hospital. Even though some of them performed small variations, the basic framework remained unchanged across the four weeks of observations, suggesting that it provided a secure and effective framework for the musicians.

Discussion and conclusions

From what has been observed in the Italian context there are at least two main educational outcomes from a regular musical intervention in a hospital setting: 1. Children learn how to play together by watching and imitating other children or the musicians leading the session; and 2. There is a process of skills and knowledge acquisition that is both conscious and other-than conscious. These results are supported by the findings of Green's (2001) research on informal ways of learning music.

Music sessions in a hospital setting appear to be an informal and relatively unstructured form of education, which provides children with an opportunity to engage with and through music. Music fosters social interactions between hospitalized children, their caregivers and the hospital staff (Preti & Welch, 2011). Music in hospitals appeared also to be a learning experience for some of the parents and caregivers, especially those with long-term hospitalized children. Parents were observed to learn the musical repertoire from the musicians, which they then sang to their child during stressful procedures, having experienced their positive reactions to certain songs. Improvisation on percussion instruments appeared also to be an occasion for informal learning experiences (Green, 2008) for both children and parents. Therefore, beside the distraction and relaxing impact that music exerted on the children, the live music program in this particular hospital constituted a learning experience (both in terms of music and of self) for most of the hospitalized children and their caregivers.

For the first time, short-term longitudinal data were gathered empirically for a group of musicians without a music therapy background playing in a paediatric hospital. These musicians were able to create a music routine informed by their craft knowledge and experiences as performers in the hospital.

Acknowledgments

This research was supported by a Research Studentship, PTA030200300938, from the Economic and Social Research Council, and by a Wingate Scholarship. I am grateful to the participants and the musicians who took part in the study, and shared their experiences during some difficult situations.

References

Atlas.ti. (2005). ATLAS.ti scientific software development gmbH. [http://www.atlasti.de/]

Bunt, L. (1997). Clinical and therapeutic uses of music. In D. Hargreaves & A. North (Eds.), *The social psychology of music* (pp. 268-289). Oxford, UK: Oxford University Press.

Clift, S., Camic, P. M., Chapman, B., Clayton, G., Daykin, N., Eades, G., ...White, M. (2009). The state of arts and health in England. *Arts & Health, 1*(1), 6-35.

Cohen, L., & Manion, L. (1995). *Research methods in education*. London: Routledge.

Dileo, C., & Bradt, J. (2009). On creating the discipline, profession, and evidence in the field of arts and healthcare. *Arts & Health, 1*(2), 168-182.

Green, L. (2001). *How popular musicians learn: A way ahead for music education*. Aldershot, UK: Ashgate.

Green, L. (2008). *Music, informal learning and school: A new classroom pedagogy.* Aldershot, UK: Ashgate.

Longhi, E., & Pickett, N. (2008). Music and well-being in long-term hospitalized children. *Psychology of Music, 36*(2), 247-256.

Mrázová, M., & Celec, P. (2010). A systematic review of randomized controlled trials using music therapy for children. *Journal of Alternative & Complementary Medicine, 16*(10), 1089-1095.

Naylor, T. K., Kingsnorth, S., Lamont, A., McKeever, P., & Macarthur, C. (2010). The effectiveness of music in pediatric healthcare: A systematic review of randomized controlled trials. *Evidence-Based Complementary and Alternative Medicine, Sep 30 [Epub ahead of print].*

Ockelford, A. (2000). Music in the education of children with severe or profound learning difficulties: Issues in current UK provision. A new conceptual framework, and proposal for research. *Psychology of Music, 28*(2), 197-217.

Preti, C., & Welch, G. F. (2011). Music in a hospital: The impact of a live music program on pediatric patients and their caregivers. *Music and Medicine, 3*(4), 213-223.

Preti, C., & Welch, G. F. (2012). The incidental impact of music on hospital staff: An Italian case study. *Arts & Health: An International Journal for Research, Policy and Practice.* doi: 10.1080/17533015.2012.665371

Robb, S., & Carpenter, J. S. (2009). A review of music-based intervention reporting in pediatrics. *Journal of Health Psychology, 14*(4), 490-501.

Schellenberg, E. G. (2005). Music and cognitive abilities. *Current Directions in Psychological Science, 14*, 322-325.

Strauss, A., & Corbin, J. (1990). *Basics of qualitative research: Grounded theory procedures and techniques.* London: Sage.

Welch, G. F., Himonides, E., Saunders, J., Papageorgi, I., Vraka, M., Preti, C., & Stephens, C. (2009). *Researching the second year of the National Singing Programme in England: An ongoing impact evaluation of children's singing behaviour and identity.* London, UK: Institute of Education, University of London.

"Make Music and Work at It:" The Ontological Foundation of Plato's Music Educational Proposals

Theocharis Raptis
University of Ioannina, Greece
charisraptis@yahoo.com

Abstract

Plato is one of the most referred to philosophers in the literature of music education. The most interesting point in the reception of Plato's music in education is the diversity of the interpretations of his work. In this paper, I examined the platonic convictions about music and I drew a seeming inconsistency in Plato's theory. Music seems to be regarded as a thing of the senses, which is incapable of adhering to the essential platonic values (i.e., truth and moral). On the other side, music is an indispensable part of platonic educational proposals. The only way to overcome this problem is to examine platonic ontology and to determine how to understand this platonic dualism. This examination allows for the correct interpretation of platonic suggestions about music education and enables a better understanding of the significance of music in the educational proposals Plato's. At the same time this examination highlights the importance of the incorporation of the philosopher's suggestions into his wider philosophical vision. In this way music education can have a relationship to and with the realms of ethics, aesthetics, politics and logic, as examples, and can find an interrelated path in the future.

Keywords

Philosophy of music education, music education in ancient Greece, platonic music education, ontology, perception-conception

Introduction

"Make music and work at it" (Plato, 1971 p. 211) was Apollo's order to Socrates in his dreams in jail, as he was awaiting execution. The protagonist himself in Plato's dialogues interprets the term "music" in two ways, firstly, as music in the popular sense of the word and secondly, as philosophy. This interpretation of Apollo's music educational order could even be understood as an incitement to us to combine these two ideas of "music" and to always examine platonic music education framed within his philosophy.

Plato is one of the most referred to philosophers in the literature of music education. Certain passages of the platonic dialogues are often used to strengthen the arguments for the justification of music in public education (Alperson, 1994; Stamou, 2002) and function as the "Magna Charta" because of the authority of the philosopher's name (Antholz, 1980, p. 777). But at the same time many authors criticize Plato's views about music. They find them extremely conservative and restrictive and notice that the philosopher has a low opinion of music because he doesn't trust music's competence in the most important human effort, which is the approach of truth and the ethical life to which it is related.[1] From this point of view one could argue, that the most interesting feature in Plato's reception to music education literature is the immense diversity of views on Plato's music educational convictions, some of which seem to be poles apart (Anderson, 1966).

In this paper, I explored the reason for this peculiarity in Plato's reception in the literature of music education and focused on a seeming inconsistency in his thoughts about music. Therefore I have attempted to provide some answers to the charge of inconsistency and in so doing, I drew on platonic ontology. Finally, I have shown the results of my interpretation of Plato's reception in music education and also of the function of philosophy in music education generally.

Plato's Ambiguous Attitude Towards Music

I think that the dissension of Plato's reception in music education is grounded in a supposed inconsistency in how Plato perceived music. On the one hand Plato argued that the tangible world and its perception to the senses cannot guide a human to the truth. The senses guide a person to the realm of Becoming (gignesthai) and not to the realm of Being (einai). Because of this, the music we play and listen to, as something given to the senses, is not classified to the field of knowledge but to the field of opinion (doxa) (Bowman, 1998). And it should not be forgotten that, while the material world is mimesis from the real world of Forms, music is, as a mimetic art, mimesis from mimesis and appears consequently even one step more away from the realm of truth. On the other hand Plato recognizes the effectiveness of music practice on the human soul and therefore on the city. This formative power of music explains the recognition of music as an indispensable part in the platonic concept of education, in the *Republic* and the *Lows*. It should be pointed out that lyre playing, singing, dancing and listening to music, are forms of music making useful not only for children but also for adults, especially in the context of city festivals. At this point it is worth noting that Plato spoke not for the theoretical study of music — that is *harmonics*, a special mathematic study for adults which prepares them for dialectic (Plato, 1963) — but for music practice.

These two directions in Plato's thought about music seem to be absolutely contradictory which could be of crucial importance in our search for the cause of the diversity in Plato's reception to music education. If music is perceived as being part of the deceptive world then how can it be the base of an educational concept for a philosopher whose aim is the course from Becoming to Being and who seeks by means of reason the truth in the world of universals?

A first explanation could be that Plato made different suggestions for different ages in his educational program. Music as a thing given to the senses is more important in childhood, namely when reason cannot guide the life of man, while for adults' education the theoretical study of music constitutes the base. This could explain to some extent Plato's ambiguous positions on music education, but it has already been mentioned that musical practice

---

[1] As a typical example of Plato's stormy relation to music education one could mention Karl Popper's critic in his work *The open society and its enemies, Vol. 1, Plato*, who wonders why so many educationists (and musicians) are so enthusiastic about Plato's educational theories in the republic. Popper suggests that either they do not understand the republic, or they are simply flattered by Plato's emphasis upon the political power of music, or both of them. (Popper, 1966).

is also important for adults in Plato's city, especially in the context of festivals. A second explanation could be that Plato integrated into his work two main directions of thought about music at his time. The first direction takes music as a means of rational contemplation and assumes that mathematics is the suitable foundation to essentially understand the phenomenon of music. This rational direction was born and developed in the circle of Pythagoreans. As for the second, here emphasis is placed upon perceptible music. As such, music is associated with the emotions and consequently could be a powerful educational means, which affects, in a decisive way, human life. The butt of this direction was also found by the Pythagoreans and the most famous supporter of this direction in Athens was Damon (Schäfke, 1964). However, a satisfying answer to our question should primarily explain why and how these theoretical directions could find a place in Plato's philosophy (Erler, 2006). A third explanation was suggested by Dénes Zoltai, from a Marxist economic base, who explains the inconsistency in Plato's work because of Plato's rejection of democracy (Zoltai, 1970). However, with this suggestion our question gets a new form: if Plato refuses democracy, why does he accept the pedagogical power of music, this fruit of democracy, according to Zoltai?

Plato's Ontological Schema

I think that the most appropriate field to look at for an explanation to our problem is in platonic ontology and especially in the relation between the tangible world of particular things and the permanent world of Forms, certainly with a focus on music. Plato is known as a dualist but how can this dualism be understood? It is more generally thought that for Plato two worlds existed, the apparent world given to senses and the world of Forms given to intellect. These two worlds are thought to be separated and Aristotle was the first who claimed that his teacher envisioned two simultaneously existing worlds and that a radical separation (chōrismos) exists between these two worlds (Aristotle, 1961–1962). If this interpretation is right and an absolute gap exists between the two worlds then it is extremely difficult to see how music, as a thing given the senses, can contribute to a human's route towards the unchanging world of Forms. In our brief case study of platonic ontology we will examine two famous platonic paragraphs in the *Symposium* and in the *Republic*.

In the *Symposium* it can be seen how man can be guided by Eros' contribution, from the realm of appearances to the realm of Forms and particularly to the Form of beauty. In the upward course to the realm of Forms man passes through four levels of love to beauty namely, love to beautiful bodies, to beautiful souls, to the beauty of the sciences and finally, to beauty itself, to the absolute Form of beauty. The adverb *exaiphnēs* (suddenly), indicates an element of discontinuity between this last level and the previous. The most important point here is the capacity of communicating beauty in all other levels with the absolute Form of beauty. The keyword in this section is participation (methexis): "… all the multitude of beautiful things *partake* of it [form of Beauty]" (Plato, 1961, *Symposium*, 211b, p. 204–205). The term "participation" (methexis) describes the ontological connection between Forms and individuals. In *Phaedrus* there are even two terms with a similar ontological meaning, namely "presence" (parousia) or "communion" (koinōnia) (Plato, 1971 *Phaedrus*, 100 d, p. 344–345). Absolute beauty is present in every beautiful thing and there is communion between these two types of beauty. It must also be mentioned that the difference in these beauty-levels consists in the variation of the intensity of their participation in the absolute Form of beauty. In this way it can be understood, for example, that the beauty of sciences stays at a higher level than beautiful bodies, because the participation in absolute beauty in the sciences is more intensive.

The second platonic paragraph under discussion is the line-analogy from the *Republic*, where Plato draws briefly on his ontology and epistemology (Plato, 1963). Plato divides a vertical line in the upper, intelligible, and in the lower, visible section. The first is the level of knowledge and is based on abstract thinking, while the second and lowest is the level of opinion and is based on things given to the senses. Above all these sections, there is the ungrounded principal, which grounds everything. The mimetic arts stay in the lowest segment of the second level of perception because they are shadows even from the visible world. Elliott Eisner (2001) mentioned that "the values that it expresses are alive and well in American schools at least today" (p. 7) with regard to the hierarchy of subjects in the school curriculum and the low position of music. But the point is that in platonic educational proposals and in contrast to the school curriculum of today, music has a privileged position. The only way to explain this fact is to overcome the separation of the diverse levels and to emphasize the unity, which is symbolized with the line. Plato supposes that there is one world with diverse levels, which consist in varying presentations of the absolute Form or in more or less the intensity of community with the Form. The first and absolute principal could be understood as an order-principal (taxis), which guarantees the coherence of all levels of Being. There is an ideal order, which can be more or less applied to every level of Becoming, in the universe, in the human soul, in the polis. The ideal order guarantees the coherence of every level with each other. Also the crucial point here is that platonic ontology is based on a main Unity of Unity and Multiplicity, of Being and Becoming, or of Unity and Indefinite Duality, in terms of the unwritten doctrine, and this basic schema can even be found in Plato's later dialogues (Raptis, 2007).

In this light the platonic suggestions about music education can be better understood. For the Philosopher who looks for the truth in the realm of Forms, an absolute separation from the level of senses could signify the rejection of all sensuality. On the other hand it enables the ontological coherence of all levels of being, the participation of perceptible music on absolute Forms. Music in wide sense, as a combination of poetry, music in narrow sense and dance, with its mimetic nature can bring about the right behavior with the appropriate feelings and can help man and especially young people to live the right kind of life, a life which is grounded in reason and temperance. Music in a narrow sense — closer to the "music" term today — enables with its special elements, i.e., rhythms and modes and, because of the mathematic relations, which are their base, one of the best approaches to the world of forms. The special feature of music is that it allows a first presentiment of the ideal order and in this way can help the establishment of order in the human soul and in the polis. In this ontological schema music has a special "between" ontological status. As something sensual, it motivates the soul to move, but at the same time, the intensive presence from the ideal order within it, guides the soul to the world of forms. From this aspect the concrete platonic proposals about music can be understood. The criterion for the right music is the degree of intensity in which the absolute form is present in certain musical works. This music must be plain and simple, so that the ideal order, which is manifest in mathematical relations, is perceivable and can be best received.

Discussion

From all the above, it becomes clear that the only way to understand Plato's suggestions about music education is to study his philosophical and particularly ontological foundation.

Generally, the corpus of great philosophers should not function as a reservoir, isolated from contextual fragments, in order to give our argument prestige just because of the authority of the philosopher's names. Rather the suggestions and opinions about music and music education should be systematically placed within the whole philosophical universe of each philosopher, because only in this way do they gain consistency and legitimacy. Furthermore, it is with such placement that what a philosopher means can be understood and consequently we avoid the misinterpretations of his work. Especially for a philosopher from the remote past it is important to also take into account the historical distance. We cannot hope or expect to extrapolate concrete proposals about our music education today from philosophers of bygone eras but we can try to reveal what are the philosophical fundamentals, how the philosopher understands his historical and social situation, how he forms his convictions about music education and how we can use these structures of thinking to make the appropriate proposals in our time.

Finally, the essential contribution of a systematical approach to philosophy is that music education can be placed in a wide horizon and can converse substantially and systematically with realms like ethics, aesthetics, logic, politic etc. The philosophical frame enables the "big picture way of thinking" (Elliot, 1995, p. 8), or the "larger view" (Reimer, 2003, p. 4) in music educational thinking. That is the reason for the prosperity of the philosophy of music education in recent years. It investigates and conceptualizes the foundational principals and tendencies of music education and its specific feature is that it "creates necessary presuppositions for the exploration and improvement" (Panaiotidi, 2002, p. 247–248) of the music educational process. In this way, the platonic order "make music and work at it" (Plato, 1971) could be understood as an invitation to a permanent philosophical inquiry in our function as music educators, which places music education in a wider frame and thereby guarantees a well thought out, critical and always timely music educational practice.

References

Alperson, P. (1994). Music as philosophy. In P. Alperson (Ed.), *What is music: An introduction to the philosophy of music* (pp. 193-210). University Park, PA: The Pennsylvania State University Press.

Anderson, W. D. (1966). *Ethos and education in Greek music*. Harvard, MA: Harvard University Press.

Antholz, H. (1980). "Die schwankenden Pfeiler musischer Erziehung." Platon oder: die mühsame Versöhnung von Philosophie und Kunst. *Musik und Bildung, 12*, 776-779.

Aristotle. (1961–1962). *Metaphysics* (Vols. I-II). (H. Tredennick, Trans.). Cambridge, MA, Harvard University Press.

Bowman, W.D. (1998). *Philosophical Perspectives on Music*. New York, NY: Oxford University Press.

Eisner, E. (2001). Music education six months after the turn of the century. *International Journal of Music Education, 37*, 5-12.

Elliott, D. J. (1995). *Music matters. A new philosophy of music education*. New York, NY: Oxford University Press.

Erler, M. (2006). *Platon*. München, Germany: Beck.

Panaiotidi, E. (2002). What is philosophy of music education and do we really need it? *Studies in Philosophy and Education, 21,* 229-252.

Plato. (1971). *Euthyphro, Apology, Crito, Phaedo, Phaedrus.* (H. N. Fowler, Trans.). London, UK: William Heinemann.

Plato. (1961). *Lysis, Symposium, Gorgias.* (W. R. M. Lamb, Trans.). London, UK: William Heinemann.

Plato. (1963). *The republic* (Vols. 1 & 2). (P. Shorey, Trans.). London, UK: William Heinemann.

Popper, K. R. (1966). *The open society and its enemies* (6th ed., Vol. 1). London, UK: Routledge & Kegan Paul.

Raptis, T. (2007). *Den Logos willkommen heißen. Die Musikerziehung bei Platon und Aristoteles.* Frankfurt, Germany: Peter Lang Verlag.

Reimer, B. (2003). *A philosophy of music education: Advancing the vision* (3rd ed.). Upper Saddle River, NJ: Prentice Hall.

Schäfke, R. (1964). *Geschichte der Musikästhetik in Umrissen* (2nd ed.). Tutzing, Germany: H. Schneider.

Stamou, L. (2002). Plato and Aristotle on music and music education: Lessons from ancient Greece. *International Journal of Music Education, 39,* 3-16.

Zoltai, D. (1970). *Ethos und Affekt. Geschichte der philosophischen Musikästhetik von den Anfängen bis zu Hegel.* Berlin, Germany: Akademischer Verlag.

Plato's Conceptions on Music

Gerasimos Rentifis
University of Athens (Greece)
gerasimosrentifis@yahoo.gr

Abstract
In ancient Greek society, the music was prominent over the other arts, since it has a dominant position in the religious festivals, athletic contests, social events (e.g. marriage, work, death) and spiritual activities. The purpose of this paper is to present the ideas of Plato on music and its place in Plato's proposed educational system. Our effort will give incomplete conclusions, if we do not consider the moral-social context of his times, and the position of art in education and society. Watching graphically, these components and having in mind the basic theories of Plato for the state, the human soul and the Ideas, we will be able to evaluate accurately the perceptions of the Athenian philosopher relating to the moral-educational role of art. Plato, in his work and especially in the second book of the *Republic* refers to what should be the permissible content of harmony, melody and rhythm, to ensure the greatest utility of music and to avoid the risk posed to the morals of youth when listening to music. Specifically, we will attempt to present the Platonic conceptions about the ethical-shaping nature of art, namely music and how it contributes through the educational process to shape the morals of young people.

Keywords
Plato, education, ethos

Introductory Remarks
In ancient Greece, music constituted one of the major areas of social and educational life, and was part of any constituent expression of private and public life, like the marriage, funeral, harvest, feasts and festivals. Naturally, it was present in religious life as well, where no religious ceremony was celebrated without singing and musical instruments (West, 1922). Plato argued that art and music in particular, has a powerful influence in shaping the character of young people and the spiritual life of society in general. Specifically, Plato believed that good quality music coincides with the virtue of a good man (Warren, 1968) and realized the catalytic power of the way in which affects the human senses, vision and hearing, but also how it penetrates the soul to its depths, shaping attitudes and behaviors, fostering values and implanting principles. In the Laws Plato states that: "those who sing obscene songs or do movements that mimic corruption could be affected by that which they mimic" (p. 88). The Athenian philosopher disputed on the content and format of music and took under consideration the position that music should hold, as well as the level at which to place this whole idea in the Platonic Republic. His aim is to make the guards virtuous and morally abstemious and to happen this according to Plato, the arts should create such a high valued environment in which only artworks that will promote

harmony and pureness will have a position.

Political and Social Environment and the Experience of Plato as a Motivation in the Formation of Notions in Music

In the 5th century B.C. Athens was the prince city of Greece, with the greatest naval power, financial and commercial activities all over the known world. In Athenian society the highest ideal is the active participation of citizens in political activities and obedience to the laws, which ensure social cohesion and ensure the conditions of a sound ethical conduct. The cultivation of the arts and sciences, such as architecture, rhetoric and literature make Athens enviable, and many spiritual people flocked from every part of the land so as a result, during the time of Pericles, Athens is experiencing a golden age of economic, cultural and social life.

But the last quarter of 5th century BC, the year that Plato is born and grown, Athens was not presenting the same picture. The Peloponnesian War led to the collapse of power and economic decline. Moreover, the death of Pericles and the tyranny of the Thirty led to dissolution of the unity of the state and the devastation of democracy. In this negative environment the Sophistic movement emerged, which brought in the social surface, all those contradictions, which exist in society. The opposition to tradition, the question of law, the debate on natural law, the search for new educational processes burdened the already ailing social and political situation.

The ardent desire and therefore the continuing concern that tormented Plato's spirit throughout his turbulent life were the correction of "wrong", the proper organization of the state and the establishment of a fair social system, which would be able to respond to the values and principles of justice and happiness of people. All these firstly require the submission of disorder in order, the subjugation of arrhythmia in the rhythm, the subjugation of the imbalance in the balance which comes with the symmetrical, balanced and harmonious cultivation of physical and mental powers.

The treatment of man, conceived as a psychosomatic entity, namely the moral education and cultivation of the virtues of the soul and the development of a healthy body are thus the necessary conditions for the salvation of the state, the cancellation of the risks of falling and destruction. Essence of the Platonic position thus appears to be the brunt of the soul to the true, the critic control and eternal dialectical inquiry, which aims to divert man from the dark side of consciousness in the pure light of Reason.

To ensure treatment, Plato argues that one should pay attention to education. For this he suggests a proposal for treatment of diseased state, which through the man shaping power of education will shape moral personalities. Plato suggests a substantial improvement of the educational institution that was before him and was traditionally a private matter and makes the case of state education following the Greek culture of music and gymnastics. From this perspective, the concept of Plato may have a lifesaving side (Cushman, 1958) and furthermore the program of science and learning cannot be separated from what he calls the healing of body and soul.

Plato, therefore, organizes the educational system so rigid and fixed; the music has a key role in contributing to the shaping of young people. Moreover argues that there should be laws on education in the arts of the Muses, which is why the musicians will not be able to teach young people what they please on the beat, melody or words, without them caring whether they exhort them to virtue or vice (Plato, *Laws*, 2, 656 c). Their works will be checked by competent judges, who are righteous people and know the moral values of work (Plato, *Laws*, 2, 659 a-b).

Plato and the Pythagoreans

The ideas of Plato on music derive their influence on the Pythagorean mathematical theory of music. According to this, the harmonic movement of sounds through the sensory organs can lead the mind to the contemplation of the mathematical structure of the universe and the laws governing it. In the Republic, Plato distinguishes theorists of music into two categories, those experimenting with the tension of the strings trying to discover the minimum time unit of measurement based on the music sensation and confining the empirical research and the Pythagoreans, who attempt to establish the harmonious matching of musical sounds and search for numbers when they hear harmonies. Plato endorsed the concept of Pythagoreans that astronomy, and music are sister sciences, and he highlighted their common goal, which is to result in mental conception of the mathematical layout of the world. So as the astronomer will treat the stars as idols to detect patterns of virtual objects, in the same way the harmonic through numerical relations will become comprehensible to the agreements.

Plato was influenced by the ideas of Pythagoras and highlights in his work the special moral and educational role of music and allows in the ideal Platonic state only the Dorian and Phrygian harmony, the first as appropriate in wartime, because it expresses masculinity and the latter as appropriate in peacetime, because it mimics the morals to be held by the man when he is prosperous and depicts acts of sane people who have a free mind (Plato, *Republic*, 399 a 1-c 6). According to Anderson, Dorian refers to men who should be gallant in battle and the Phrygian to women, which should lead decent and prudent lives (Warren, 1968). Moreover, the Athenian philosopher argues that music education is particularly important for growing a personality, because rhythm and melody penetrate the human soul and they form it in such a way as to attach decency and beauty to it (Plato, *Republic*, 400 d 5- e1).

Art, Society, and Education

In all historical periods and in all cultures people consciously or unconsciously create art, channeling their thoughts in their artistic creations, feelings and concerns. In Athens in the 5th century BC there was no distinction between good and productive arts, but all were covered by the same term. So poetry, music, sculpture, shipbuilding, carpentry, etc., where considered to be arts, which during the Golden Age of Pericles gave top artistic creations to Athenian citizens. That is the stimuli that Plato has for the art, who will attempt to integrate it into an artistic ethic, aiming at an evaluation and deontology of art making and becoming. For the Athenian philosopher, art must have an entertaining mission and to lead the human soul from the illusory to the real from the perceptible to the virtual. The art as a mimetic image of reality affects the shaping of human nature and the effect can be positive or negative. So according to Plato, in order artwork to fulfill the purpose of creation, it should have a technical and moral superiority.

Education in Plato's political system has a central position and is the main concern of the state. With proper education people will be educated and those in turn, as interpreters of the law will govern the educational issues and guide the education of young people. Education for Plato is eminently a political act of philosophy while at the same time the main food of the soul. The best teacher is the philosopher, who leads his students to truth and good. The Platonic conception of education can not be separated from the teaching of virtue and his general Moral Theory. According to Plato, the true virtue can be acquired through education and the ideal state is the one in which such an education can be achieved.

Plato attempts to explain the nature of music and its use in educational processes (Lippman, 1964). Reason, harmony and rhythm are considered to be essential elements of music. For this reason Plato considers that it is necessary to use only those kinds of harmonies, which contribute to the stability of the masculine ethos. Moreover he argues that the human soul is like a stringed instrument, which education will have to wind up, by tightening or relaxing the strings, in order to become unified and not fragmented and have a life full of harmony rather than dispute (Nettleship, 1969). So Plato excludes mournful harmonies, as well as those considered soft because they do not fit at all in the character of the guards, who should be distinguished for bravery, perseverance and decency. Therefore, only the harmonies that are suitable for mounting heroic and military character are used. Plato incorporates music into all stages of treatment of the guards aiming to instill some of mental row models, so that later they will accept freely and consciously the highest knowledge, which will reveal the Philosophy (Jaeger, 1971).

Plato will apply the same criteria in the musical instruments as well, from which he will reject the complex and harmonious such as triangles, the piktis and flute and will accept the lyre and guitar. Specifically as far as the flute is concerned, Plato indicates that if young people surrender in its sweet and plaintive music, they will lose what impetuous and brave soul and will end up sybaritic warriors (Plato, *Republic*, 411 a-b). The musical instruments that are permitted are the lyre and the guitar, which are simple in playing but the music they produce is complex. Kaimakis (2005), when explaining the restrictions on musical instruments argues that, instruments that are prohibited require both skilled performers and advanced level of learning, which is not part of education the philosopher planned for young people. Therefore, Plato preferred simplicity over complexity, because he believes that simplicity in art sculpts a consistent and comprehensive personality (Cilbert, 1934).

Concluding Remarks

Plato has not devoted any work exclusively in music, but the references are so many to realize that this is a concept with a particular moralistic force. The music is both useful and dangerous. Music can help create wise citizens or destroy the ethos. It can instill values and ideals, or self-indulgence and cowardice. The standpoint of Plato is intensely moral and political, as it seeks to create a standard and well-organized state established in a humane educational system. In his effort, music is a major asset, which plays an important role in educating young children. What Plato really accomplishes, is nothing different from the modern reviews and criticism of images, which appear in the media and from the discussions on the harmful effects of these images in behavior, character and attitudes of the recipients. In the context of speculation over education, Plato argues that the most perfect piece of art is philosophy, which heals the man as a psychosomatic entity and saves the state from wrong.

References

Cilbert, K. (1934). The relation of the moral to the aesthetic standard in Plato. *The Philosophical Review, 43*(3), 279-294.

Cushman, R. E. (1958). *Therapeia: Plato's conception of philosophy.* Chapel Hill, NC: The University of North Carolina Press.

Jaeger, W. (1971). *Παιδεία, Η μόρφωσις του Έλληνος ανθρώπου, μτφρ.* Athens, Greece: Γ. Π. Βερροίου, εκδ. Παιδεία.

Καϊμάκη, Π. (2005). *Φιλοσοφία και μουσική*, εκδ. Athens, Greece: Μεταίχμιο.

Lippman, E. (Ed.). (1964). *Musical thought in ancient Greece.* New York: Columbia University Press.

Warren, A. (1968). *Ethos and education in Greek music.* Cambridge, MA: Harvard University Press.

West, M. L. (1922). *Ancient Greek music.* Oxford, UK: Clarendon Press.

Using Affect Valence and Emotion Valence to Understand Musical Experience and Response: The Case of Hated Music

Emery Schubert
University of New South Wales (Australia)
E.Schubert@unsw.edu.au

Abstract
This paper proposes a new approach for organizing emotional and affective descriptions of experiences in response to music. The need for this approach is justified by frequent confusion and inconsistent use of terminology. Much empirical literature examines this question by analysis of definitions and responses to music. However this produces an unbalanced picture of how music affect and emotion can be understood and described, especially when only positive or pleasurable musical experiences are sought. To remedy this, a study with 60 participants is reported in which open ended descriptions of a self-selected hated piece is described. A large number of negatively valenced words were used to describe hated pieces, and very few positive terms. This is asymmetric to literature on liked music, where both positive and negative terms are used to describe the music and the evoked feelings. Based on recent literature it was argued that affect valence terms are those which describe the attraction to (e.g. love, awe) or aversion from (e.g. hate, annoying) a piece of music, while emotion valence is reserved primarily for the contemplation of enjoyed (positive *affect*) music (that is, negative *emotions* such as sadness and grief, as well as positive *emotions* such as joy and peacefulness). This organization of musical experience has important implications for music research and education.

Keywords
Music experience, emotion in music, affect, valence, hated music, negative emotion

Introduction
Music educators and researchers need to communicate about powerful experiences resulting from music listening, and they frequently rely on verbal descriptions, and in particular emotions (Droe, 2006) to perform this communication. A piece of music may leave us with a sense of awe, or in rapture, or it may be ineffable—beyond verbal labeling. We might love a piece because of the powerful emotions it coveys. Indeed the emotion that music conveys is considered a key source of music's power. Considerable amounts of literature have been written about this power, the most important recent publication being an Oxford University Press volume by Juslin and Sloboda (2010). In the introduction they point to a fundamental issue regarding verbal communication:

> A major problem that has plagued the field of music and emotion is terminological confusion. Researchers have tended to use words such as affect, emotion, feeling, and mood in different ways, which has made communication and integration difficult. Sometimes, researchers have used the same term to refer to different things. At other times, researchers have used different terms to refer to the same thing. (p. 9)

They go on to present some definitions, which complement and develop previous attempts to hone in and stabilize the usage of these terms. A similar outcome was proposed a quarter of a century earlier by Price (1986). In this article I restrict the discussion of terminology to that pertaining to emotions, affect and preferences, focusing on the key terms as defined by Sloboda and Juslin (2010), and Price (1986), listed in Table 1.

Table 1. Definitions of key terms as used by Juslin and Sloboda (2010, 'JS') and Price (1986, 'P'), with proposed term based on Charland (2005).

Source	Original term and definition	Proposed term
JS	Affect - This is used as an umbrella term that covers all evaluative—or "valenced" (positive/negative)—states (e.g. emotion, mood, preference). The term denotes such phenomena in general. If that is not intended, a more precise term (e.g. mood, emotion, preference) is used instead.	Affect in the broad sense (including affect valence and emotion valence)
P	Affective response - Reaction involving feelings and emotions. Learned behavior resulting from a life history of interactions with musical stimuli; encompassing mood-emotional, preference, and taste responses.	
P	Emotion - A general affective reaction encompassing the feeling states. Affective experience.	
P	Behavioral preference - Differential response for one stimulus as op-posed to another. Demonstrated choice through non-verbal actions, such as concert attendance, recording purchase, choosing to listen to specific music. Also called operant preference.	Affect Valence
P	Evaluation - To judge the relative worth, meaning, or significance.	
P	Hedonic value - Reward value as judged by the capacity of a stimulus to reinforce a response, and degree of preference or pleasure reflected in verbal evaluations. A consequence of arousal-raising and arousal-reducing stimulus properties; includes pleasantness-unpleasantness, reward-punishment, positive-negative feedback, attractiveness-repulsiveness, and positive-negative incentive value.	
JS	Preference - This term is used to refer to longer-term affective evaluations of objects or persons with a low intensity (e.g. liking of a particular type of music).	
P	Preference - An act of choosing, esteeming, or giving advantage to one thing over another. Propensity toward something (see also behavioral preference and verbal preference).	
P	Verbal preference - A choice; liking of something over something else. Demonstrated choice through verbal actions (spoken or written), based upon many musical and sociological factors, including musical contour, degree of symmetry, order, closeness to optimal level of complexity, societal pressures, and degree of enjoyment. Developed through training and familiarity	
JS	Emotion induction - This term is used to refer to all instances where music evokes an emotion in a listener—regardless of the nature of the process that evoked the emotion.	Emotion Valence
JS	Emotion perception - This term is used to refer to all instances where a listener perceives or recognizes emotions in music (e.g. 'a sad expression'), without necessarily feeling an emotion him- or herself.	
JS	Emotion - This term is used to refer to a quite brief but intense affective reaction that usually involves a number of sub-components—subjective feeling, physiological arousal, expression, action tendency, and regulation—that are more or	

	less 'synchronized'. Emotions focus on specific 'objects' and last minutes to a few hours (e.g. happiness, sadness).	
JS	Musical emotions - This term is used only as a short term for "emotions that were somehow induced by music", without any further implications about the precise nature of these emotions. (If an author believes that there are certain emotions that are 'unique' to music in some way, this is explicitly stated.)	

The aim of the present research is to propose a way of verifying and consolidating some of these definitions. In particular, I will argue that our understanding of these terms has been limited by failing to consider the variation of kinds of musical experiences. Many studies consider positive musical experiences (for reviews see Salimpoor, Benovoy, Longo, Cooperstock, & Zatorre, 2009; Schubert, 2003, 2010). For example, the study by Schubert (2010) reporting response to loved and hated excerpts demonstrated that a range of emotions can be enjoyed, including negative ones. However, the study used rating scales that recorded a range of emotional responses along various emotion dimensions (valence, arousal, dominance and emotional strength). Not reported in that study was whether disliked pieces were also rated with a variety of both positive and negative emotions. Further, the paper did not allow investigation of words that might be used to describe the music because of the forced-choice rating scale procedure used (as distinct from open-ended, verbal description). In this paper, I report a study that collects open-ended descriptions of music that is hated by the participants. This approach allows an examination of the nature of the language used for describing music in a way that is rarely reported in the literature. I will then argue that this approach will provide valuable information that will inform our understanding of affective responses to music. Specifically I will discuss how affect and emotion can be distinguished from the, at times vague, definitions provided in the research literature. As a consequence, the definitions provided in Table 1 will be revisited.

Method

Design and Procedure
An experimental paradigm similar to that used by Schubert (2010) was adopted, where participants were asked to self-select a piece of music that they loved and a piece that they hated. However, in contrast to Schubert (2010) who used rating scales to measure responses, open-ended self-reports are collected. In the present study, participants performed several tasks, including being asked to select a piece of music they hate, provide the details of the piece, and explain why they hate the piece. The participants did not explicitly play the piece, but were encouraged to imagine it. They were then asked what emotions the piece evoked (internal locus), and what emotions the music expressed (external locus) (Evans & Schubert, 2008; Gabrielsson, 2002; Juslin & Laukka, 2004; Salimpoor et al., 2009; Schubert, 2007). All items were completed online in the participants' own time. Ethics approval was obtained from the host University's Ethics Advisory Panel.

Participants
Sixty participants took part in the study. Their ages ranged from 18 to 42 years (mean = 22.3, SD = 4.6), with 33 males. They were enrolled either in an introductory music course, an undergraduate music course, or a postgraduate music course. The years of music lessons reported ranged from 0 to 15 years (M = 6.2, SD = 5.1, 17 participants reporting none). They received course credit for participating.

Results

Responses to the open ended questions were sorted into negative and positive emotion words, for both felt emotions and for expressed emotions. A summary of the most frequently reported negative valenced adjective words for the hated pieces are shown in Table 2. Positive valenced terms were rarely used —10 expressed (e.g. one mention of the music being "carefree") and 3 felt (e.g. one mention of feeling "happy") emotion words. In contrast 40 and 49 *negative* emotion words were reported for expressed and felt responses respectively—as show in Table 1. The most frequently reported word describing expressed emotion was "anger" with seven mentions. The most frequently reported felt emotion was annoyance, with 10 occurrences. Words used that had the same root were combined (e.g. annoyed, annoying and annoyance were all grouped into the tally of "annoyed/annoyance") – as shown in Table 2,

Table 2. Summary of negative emotion/affect words used to describe hated piece reported, displayed by locus.

	Locus	
	Expressed	Felt
Negative Emotions Reported	anger (7)	anger (4)
	depression (2)	annoyed/annoyance (10)
	hate/hatred (5)	cringe/cringing (3)
	sad/sadness (3)	frustrated/frustration (4)
		hate/hatred (3)
		irritated/irritation (4)
		pain (2)
Other	22	19
Total	40	49

Note. Only (non-repeated within participant) emotions reported at least twice overall are shown (with frequency in parentheses). Those reported once (overall) have count shown under "Other". Total is the number of adjectives used, including repeated terms across participants and non-repeated multiple terms within participant.

Discussion

The results can be contrasted with other studies that investigate emotional responses to liked music (e.g., Garrido & Schubert, 2011; Schubert, 2003). First, there is an asymmetry between positive and negative emotion words describing loved versus hated music: Whereas music that is enjoyed can express and evoke both positive (joy, calm, etc.) and negative (sadness, grief) emotions (Gabrielsson, 2010; Garrido & Schubert, 2011; Juslin & Laukka, 2004; Schubert, 1996), hated music only tends to evoke and portray negative emotions. In addition, felt emotions are generally of an evaluative kind, describing states of aversion or preparation for aversion/avoidance/aggressive behavior (frustration, irritation, anger), while expressed emotions are a mixture of more withdrawn and contemplative emotions (sadness, depression) and evaluative terms that were also felt (hated, anger), some terms fitting into both evaluation (feeling anger because the music is hated) and contemplation (feeling anger because the wonderful, angry sounding music created that emotion in me through a process of contagion — see Juslin & Västfjäll, 2008). These finding are discussed with respect to some recent literature that attempts to make a distinction between affect and emotion.

Charland (2005) makes the distinction between affect valence and emotion valence. In the context of the present study, emotion valence refers to the emotional character identified by the participant. These are akin to emotional states, or states of contemplation as discussed above. They do not require or consist of evaluation. They may, here, be thought of as, or to include, musical emotions (see Table 1). Affect valence experiences, on the other hand, refer to the individual's approach or withdrawal tendency: "they are designed or intended to preserve the well-being of the organism in some way" (Charland, 2005, p. 88) and as such involve or are defined by evaluation or appraisal. In the study, the emotions, actually *affect* valence, reported for the hated examples—annoyance, cringing, irritation—are distinct from *emotion* valence terms. The distinction is conceptualized in Figure 1, where sample words are taken from the present study and Schubert (2003).

Anger evoked by the hated piece *is* an affect valence quality – the action tendency would be to withdraw from (or perhaps to attack) the music/musicians/playing device, whether by stopping it/them or leaving it/them. However, in studies of enjoyed and loved music, sadness is construed as an *emotion* valence. In this case (regardless of the actual emotion) it is a mental state, and does not in itself negate the positive affective evaluation.

A theoretical explanation of this separation of affect and emotion is adapted from Schubert (1996, 2009-2010). The theory suggests that when listening to music the listener is in a state that produces cognitive activation which in itself is pleasurable (after Martindale, 1988), while inhibiting cognitive circuits that are otherwise activated during, or in preparation for, painful events. In that state, activation of any emotion (including sadness) adds to the pleasure—positive affect—of the listening experience. The findings of the present study suggest that this inhibition or "dissociation" does not occur when hated music is heard or thought about. At times, painful responses are reported (the word 'pain' itself was mentioned explicitly as being felt on two separate occasions in response to a hated piece of music), and it is this *affect* response that provides a stark distinction between emotion valence and affect valence. The abhorrent reactions to hated music are fundamentally negative affects and do not require any necessary activation of negative *emotions*. Negative emotions such as sadness and grief sometimes reported in response to loved music were very rarely encountered in response to hated music in the present study. The adjectives reported are more closely tied to an evaluative response commensurate with withdrawal and repulsion. Further, if emotions could be seen to be evoked, these would not be musical emotions of the kind that Juslin and Sloboda (2010) refer to as musical emotions (as defined in Table 1, see also Juslin & Laukka, 2004)

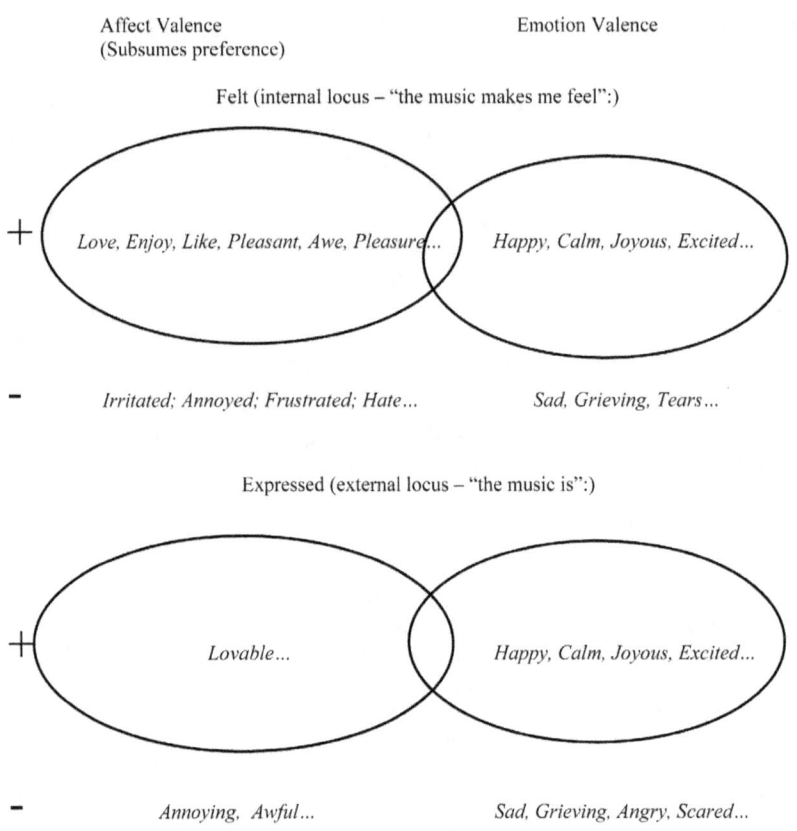

Figure 1. Proposed distinction between affect and emotion in music, by locus, using sample words.

This explanation provides a parsimonious account of how it can be that loved pieces of music can evoke negative emotions, and further, that they can evoke negative emotions that might appear to be connected with negative evaluations. The explanation is dependent on Charland (2005) and Colombetti's (2005) distinctions between affect and emotion valence. The distinction between emotion valence and affect valence explicitly helps to clarify some of the definitions that are commonly used in music literature. Take for example Price's definition of "emotion" (Table 1). It clearly encompasses both affect and emotion valence, and as such does not provide as helpful a definition as that proposed here. Rather, that and other definitions grouped near the top of Table 1 indicate affective response in a broad sense, encompassing both affect and emotion valence experiences. In addition, affect valence subsumes preference and pleasure experiences — thus preference related terms are grouped into affect valence in Table 1. A clearer conceptualization of affect and valence can be extracted by examining how some adjectives can be organized into affect and emotion, with affect *in the broad sense* encompassing all valenced adjective descriptions, with sample words shown in Figure 1.

Conclusions

By examining an infrequently studied aspect of musical response—namely, to music that is reported as being hated—we are in a position to provide a clearer distinction between affective and emotional responses to music. Responses to hated music primarily evoke *affect* valence responses, meaning that the experiences reported describe a withdrawal/avoidance/aggression tendency or action. This is distinct from *emotion* valence, which may, too, be negative, but allows for the possibility of contemplating and even enjoying the emotion without a necessary approach/avoidance/aggression tendency. Hence, sadness or grief is an emotional response to music, and is not likely to be a reason for avoiding or approaching a piece. Reported hatred, or anger, or annoyance, are, on the other hand, evaluative responses indicating a desire or enactment of aversion (moving away from or turning off the music). The results were explained in terms of Charland's (2005) distinction of emotion valence and affect valence, and from a cognitive theoretical perspective of activation of cognitive units (being responsible for affective responses), and activation of specific emotion nodes (being responsible for emotion valence responses).

Further research will expand the current study to compare directly self-selected loved and hated pieces, however the current study addresses a methodological imbalance in examining neutral, experimenter selected, and/or pleasant/enjoyable music, rather than explicitly investigating the other end of this continuum – strongly disliked music. The study has important implications in music education where improvements in defining affective (in the broad sense) experiences will help clarify communication in research and training. For example, when one is responding to music, or analyzing a reaction to it, it is instructive to classify the reaction as either emotional, or affective (or something else), so that the classes of experience are not confused. The affective experience generally pertains to the evaluative experience (liking, making me angry, annoying, and so forth) whereas the emotion is a range of experiences that can be used to describe the music and/or listening experience — for example answering the "why" question – "Why does it have this *affect*?" "Because it is sad", "Because it makes me feel happy", and so forth (emotion valenced reasons). Future research will continue to tease apart these distinctions and possibly allow further stratifications of the concepts that are an important part of the music researcher's toolkit in describing and understanding music experiences and perceptions.

Acknowledgements

This research was supported by an Australian Research Council grant (DP1094998).

References

Charland, L. (2005). The heat of emotion: Valence and the demarcation problem. *Journal of Consciousness Studies, 12*(8–10), 82-102.

Colombetti, G. (2005). Appraising valence. *Journal of Consciousness Studies,* 12(8–10), 103-126.

Droe, K. (2006). Music preference and music education: A review of literature. *Update: Applications of Research in Music Education, 24*(2), 23-32.

Evans, P., & Schubert, E. (2008). Relationships between expressed and felt emotions in music. *Musicae Scientiae, 12*(1), 75-99.

Gabrielsson, A. (2002). Perceived emotion and felt emotion: Same or different? [Special issue]. *Musicae Scientiae, 6*(1), 123-148.

Gabrielsson, A. (2010). Strong experiences with music. In P. N. Juslin & J. A. Sloboda (Eds.), *Handbook of music and emotion: Theory, research, applications.* (pp. 547-574). Oxford, UK: OUP.

Garrido, S., & Schubert, E. (2011). Individual differences in the enjoyment of negative emotion in music: A literature review and experiment. *Music Perception, 28*(3), 279–295.

Juslin, P. N., & Laukka, P. (2004). Expression, perception, and induction of musical emotions: A review and a questionnaire study of everyday listening. *Journal of New Music Research, 33*(3), 217-238.

Juslin, P. N., & Sloboda, J. A. (2010). Introduction, aims, organization, and terminology. In P. N. Juslin & J. A. Sloboda (Eds.), *Music and emotion: Theory, research, applications* (pp. 3-12). Oxford, UK: OUP.

Juslin, P. N., & Västfjäll, D. (2008). Emotional responses to music: The need to consider underlying mechanisms. *Behavioral and Brain Sciences, 31*(5), 559-575.

Martindale, C. (1988). Cognition, psychobiology, and aesthetics. In F. Farley & R. Neperud (Eds.), The foundations of aesthetics, art, and art education (pp. 7–42). New York: Praeger.

Price, H. E. (1986). A proposed glossary for use in affective response literature in music. *Journal of Research in Music Education, 34*, 151-159.

Salimpoor, V., Benovoy, M., Longo, G., Cooperstock, J., & Zatorre, R. (2009). The rewarding aspects of music listening are related to degree of emotional arousal. *PloS one, 4*(10), 29-49.

Schubert, E. (1996). Enjoyment of negative emotions in music: An associative network explanation. *Psychology of Music, 24*(1), 18-28.

Schubert, E. (2003). Update of the Hevner adjective checklist. *Perceptual and Motor Skills, 96*(3), 1117-1122.

Schubert, E. (2007). Locus of emotion: The effect of task order and age on emotion perceived and emotion felt in response to music. *Journal of Music Therapy, 44*, 344-368.

Schubert, E. (2009-2010). The fundamental function of music [Special issue]. *Musicae Scientiae, 13*(Special Issue), 63-81.

Schubert, E. (2010). Affective, evaluative and collative responses to hated and loved music. *Psychology of Aesthetics, Creativity, and the Arts, 4*(1), 36-46.

Teaching the Malay Gamelan within the Framework of Traditional Conventions in Malaysian Schools

Shahanum Mohamad Shah
Universiti Teknologi MARA, (Malaysia)
shahanum@yahoo.com

Abstract

The Malaysian secondary school music curriculum introduced in 1996 emphasized the promotion of national culture through the learning of Malaysian traditional music. The Malay gamelan was selected as one type of traditional music to be learned as it represents one of the major types of Malaysian traditional music and one that is more frequently performed. The gamelan is, by nature, an oral tradition. Learning the gamelan among court musicians was by non-formal education (i.e. by listening, observing and playing). When the Malay gamelan was taken out of the purview of the royal courts in the 1960s and made public, the repertoire was notated using cipher notation for preservation. With the advent of formal music education in schools and universities, notation is now being used in part to expedite the learning process. However, this raises the question of authenticity of the context of learning the gamelan and the development of necessary skills required in gamelan playing. Based on the researcher's own experience of learning the gamelan via the two methods and examining teaching methodologies employed in Indonesia and Malaysia, it was felt that there may be a need to reconsider how the teaching of the Malay gamelan should be approached and experienced in order to teach the real character of traditional music. This study sought to gauge any perceived differences when teaching the gamelan within the framework of traditional conventions. Two groups of eight students each were taught the gamelan using the framework of basic gamelan conventions. Results indicate that the most important skills perceived by the students is the development of aural sensitivity and ensemble awareness.

Keywords
Malay gamelan, music curriculum, traditional teaching method

Introduction

When music was introduced as an elective subject in the Malaysian secondary school curriculum in 1996, emphasis was placed on promoting national culture through the learning of Malaysian traditional music. Through the study of music, it was felt that students may better understand the cultures of Malaysia's different ethnic groups, thereby strengthening inter-racial communication, understanding and harmony. The Malay gamelan was selected to be included in the curriculum as it represents one of the major types of Malaysian traditional music and one that is more frequently performed.

As this component of the curriculum is aimed at preserving local music traditions, implications concerning the authenticity of the tradition when designing the teaching of local music traditions need to be considered. Like most, if not all other traditional forms of music, gamelan is, by nature, an oral tradition. Learning the gamelan among court musicians was by non-formal education, i.e., by listening, observing and playing. The transfer of skills and knowledge was carried out orally within the community of musicians. Subsequently, when the Malay gamelan was taken out of the purview of the royal courts in the 1960s and made public, the repertoire was notated using cipher notation for preservation. With the advent of formal music education in schools and universities, notation is now being used in part to expedite the learning process.

Establishing an accurate context for practical activities on the gamelan can provide not only a sound methodology but also allow for appropriate evaluation (Steptoe, 2005). Teaching gamelan using notation may not only be a misrepresentation of the authentic practice of this music but may also not give students the skills necessary in playing gamelan music as opposed to playing in western ensembles. According to Supanggah (2008), some of these differences include: 1. Emphasis on togetherness with no individual instrument dominating; 2. High level of sensitivity and depth of feeling are important as opposed to personal virtuosity; 3. Technique can be studied at the same time as studying the repertoire; 4. Aural sensitivity is very important in playing the gamelan where musical dialogue occurs through listening; and 5. Musical changes are marked or led by the gendang through aural signals. In modern day compositions, the characteristics are still maintained and as such, teaching methods that develop these characteristics need to be adopted.

Based on the researcher's own experience of learning the gamelan via the two methods and examining teaching methodologies employed in Indonesia and Malaysia, it was felt that there may be a need to reconsider how the teaching of the Malay gamelan should be approached and experienced in order to teach the real character of traditional music. The purpose of this study was to gauge any perceived differences when learning the gamelan within the framework of traditional conventions.

Method

As this study is exploratory in nature, the researcher's intention was to teach the gamelan using a different approach and to get students to reflect on the differences, if any, in learning the gamelan by rote and according to the basic conventions of gamelan music. Sixteen school and university students with experience learning the gamelan the way it is typically taught in schools served as subjects for this study. The method uses cipher notation to teach the gamelan and the syllabus also includes the introduction of the instruments within the ensemble and the playing technique of each instrument. There is usually no reference to the form of the *lagu* and the function of the instruments. The students were put into two groups of eight students each with one group comprising secondary school students and one group comprising university students. The university students that were selected were recent high school graduates who had studied the gamelan in school. The reason for including this group of students was to obtain the feedback of students who had more experience playing the gamelan than the school students did and to see if they perceived differences in their playing experience as well. The students were taught two pieces that they had never previously learned. A total of eight sessions of two hours each was held over a period of four weeks for each of the two groups.

As opposed to its Indonesian counterpart, the Malay gamelan is smaller in size. A basic gamelan ensemble used in Malaysia today and which was used in this study typically comprises eight instruments. The instruments are the bonang barung, saron peking, saron barung, saron demung, gambang, kenong, a pair of gongs and the gendang (drum). The Malay gamelan uses a five-tone pentatonic tuning system usually in the key of C or Bb Major. The traditional repertoire is basically heterophonic in texture as there is the main melody played simultaneously with ornamented versions of the melody in the melody part (Matusky, 2008).

In developing a structured method of teaching the gamelan in the traditional approach and to ensure that students have a foundation to understand gamelan music, it is very important for students to understand the characteristics which define the Malay gamelan, and learn traditional playing techniques and repertoire. Although there is a difference in repertoire with the Javanese gamelan, the same body of conventions used to describe the Indonesian gamelan (Hardjo, 2004; Perlman, 2004) can be used to describe the Malay gamelan repertoire:

1. Form-defining instruments – the gong acts as the punctuating instrument that marks the structure of a composition/demarcates the time cycles of the lagu, while the kenong defines the subunits;
2. Instruments that bear the melodic framework and include the saron family. The instruments play the same melody but in different octaves;
3. Elaborating parts – parts which are rhythmically more active as played by the bonang and gambang; and
4. The gendang, which is the rhythmic instrument and controls the tempo.

The researcher organized the lessons for each *lagu* in the steps listed below using the conventions mentioned above. As the students already know how to playing technique of the instruments, this step was not included in the lesson plan. Students were required to try each instrument in turn to gain a complete perspective of the materials being studied.

1. Students are first introduced to the melody line that is similar to the concept of balungan in Indonesian gamelan. Students are made to feel the stress of the beats that fall on beats 2 and 4, and to listen to the question and answer nature of the melody. The melody is taught in phrases and repeated until mastered (Figure 1).

-	5	5	2	3	2	3	5	-	3	5	6	5	3	2	5
-	5	5	2	3	2	3	5	-	3	5	6	5	3	2	3
-	3	2	1	1	2	3	1	3	2	1	1	5	6	1	2
-	2	2	3	5	3	2	1	3	2	1	1	5	5	3	5

Figure 1. Melodic framework

2. Once the melody is mastered, students are introduce to the structure of the *lagu* as determined by the gong cycle. The instruments that provide the underlying structural punctuation are the gong and kenong (Figure 2). Students will learn to direct their attention to the structural markers and observe their relationship to the melody thereby

allowing them to relate their own playing to those around them.

-	-	-	-	-	-	-	Kn	-	-	-	-	-	-	-	Kn
-	-	-	-	-	-	-	Kn	-	-	-	-	-	-	-	Kn
-	-	-	-	-	-	-	Kn	-	-	-	-	-	-	-	Kn
-	-	-	-	-	-	-	Kn/Sw	-	-	-	-	-	-	-	Kn/G

*Kn – Kenong; Sw – Suwuk; G – Gong

Figure 2. Punctuating instruments (64 beat pattern)

3. The instruments that have improvisatory function (i.e. the bonang and gambang) are then introduced. Once the part is mastered, students are taught to improvise.
4. Students are introduced to the rhythmic pattern of the gendang and how the pattern changes as it heads to the end of the *lagu* and the gong.

Analysis and Discussion

At the conclusion of the four weeks of lessons, the students were asked to reflect and write down their thoughts and experiences about learning the gamelan using the new approach. Their reflections were then analyzed for themes in their experiences. The feedback obtained from the students' reflection indicated that they did feel a difference between the two approaches as indicated by their responses in Table 1.

Table 1. Themes in students' responses as indicated in their reflections.

Comments related to	No. of Students
Developing listening skills	16
Increase ensemble skills	14
Understanding the structure and parts of the different instruments	15
Learn faster with notation but concentration is on individual parts	15
Understand individual part in relation to other parts	13
Some element of freedom is felt	5

Among some of the comments written are as follows:

- I learn faster with notes. But when I play with notes, I feel like I am only focusing on my part, counting to make sure I am correct. I tend not to listen to other parts.
- It forces me to listen, I feel like it helps develop my listening.
- I listen to others parts. I try to relate to other parts.
- When I understand the structure and melody it was easier to get back when I am lost. If I get totally lost, I know to wait for the gong…provided the gong is correct.
- I can also listen to the gendang and gong to know where we are.
- If the bonang improvises, I can still get a grasp of the melody.
- I know where I fit in relation to the other instruments.
- Not focusing on notes made me somewhat freed up.

From the responses provided, it appears that among the key difference perceived by the students is the development of aural sensitivity. This is an important factor as listening is considered a main element of music education. When students have an understanding of what is heard as opposed to what is seen, it can develop sensibility to listening to music, understanding of the musical language, and sensitivity in playing while listening. Although it appears that students learned their individual parts more quickly with notes, achieving ensemble sensitivity was more challenging as it also meant that they were concentrating on their parts. Students knew their parts but not their relationship with other instruments. When they made mistakes they did not know how to return to the ensemble. When learning without notation, students grasped the feeling of ensemble playing quickly. Even when concentrating upon their individual parts, students had ensemble awareness and were aware of others within the ensemble when playing without notation. This is important in gamelan playing as it emphasizes relationships, as musicians need to know how to interrelate with the other parts. As the parts all relate back to the melody (balungan) of the lagu,the potential for developing a sense of ensemble and group identity is greatly enhanced (Steptoe, 2005).

Conclusion

Given the nature of the art form and the semi-improvisatory style of the gamelan, it is suggested that the non-formal method of transmission actually be applied to teaching the gamelan as it will help students develop their listening and aural abilities as well as an awareness of playing in an ensemble. As Malay gamelan repertoire is more melodic in nature and not structurally complex, this may be possible given the time constraints of lessons in schools and universities. Notation can be used as a working guide that provides the framework of a piece. An understanding of the function of each instrument will allow the musicians to elaborate the line according to the instrument played. In this way, students not only learn to do, but also learn to think the way traditional musicians do. It can also allow students to learn to be reactive and flexible.

When designing the syllabus, it is also worth considering that the gamelan can be used to develop a wide variety of musical skills such as elements of music (i.e., pitch, duration, dynamics, tempo, timbre), texture, structure, listening, performing and it is also a very useful tool to instill creativity, teach improvisation and composition, all of which are components of the music curriculum. Learning activities that are important include listening complemented by sharing, discussing, and analyzing activities by the students themselves. The gamelan can also be used to encourage active participation in music making, emphasize musical knowing, foster intercultural acceptance and understanding that can help with the musical growth of children. In this way, students are directly involved in preserving and revitalizing their own music culture which is an important mission and vision of the music curriculum (Bramantyo, 2009).

References

Bramantyo, T. (2009, April). *Intercultural musicology in music education: In search for philosophy of music education in Malaysia*. Paper presented at the Colloquium for Music Research 2009, Universiti Putra, Malaysia.

Hardjo, S. (2004). *Enculturation and cross-cultural experiences in teaching Indonesian gamelan*. Retrieved 27 from
http://www.victoria.ac.nz/asianstudies.publications/occassion/03Gamelan.pdf

Matusky, P. Y. (2008, August). *Aspects of basic instrumentation and traditional form of repertoire of Malay Gamelan and the challenge of repertoire expansion*. Paper presented at the 2008 World Gamelan Symposium and Festival, Terengganu, Malaysia.

Perlman, M. (2004). *Unplayed melodies: Javanese gamelan and the genesis of music theory*. Berkeley, CA: University of California Press.

Steptoe, S. (2005). *Gamelan music in Britain*. Retrieved from http://bit.ly/LZSlOb

Supanggah, R. (2008, August). *Pengalaman mengurus, memperlengkap dan memperluas kaedah pengajaran seni di Sekolah Tinggi Kesenian Indonesian pengkhususan seni muzik dan tari gamelan*. Paper presented at the 2008 World Gamelan Symposium and Festival, Terengganu, Malaysia.

Composing Atonal Music as a Child's Play: Coherence of Serial Musical Work While Creating Melodies

Angeliki Skandali
Athens University (Greece)
skanasar@mus.auth.gr

Abstract

The paper reports on an atonal music composition experiment in school environment for children aged 12-15 years. Based on Schoenberg's view of atonal music, it explores children's music writing in the context of Piaget ideas, the Lerdahl and Jackendoff model of the experienced listener under the name of the Generative Theory of Tonal Music and the J.J. Natiez's critic tripartite semiological model. It is presented here how three analytic concepts are suggested as instrumental for a taxonomy of the children's understanding and practise of melody-making: introductiveness, serial polarism and schematisism are called to make the childen's poietic coherence. The inspiration is to put forward research when sought to discover theoretical propositions according to which perception and memory at early ages have to do with concepts. Examples of student compositions are provided.

Keywords
Introductiveness, polarism, schematisism

Introduction

Schoenberg's warning about "...writing a book on twelve-note composition was: 'Do not call it Twelve-Tone Theory, call it 'Composition with Twelve notes'. Personally it is on the word Composition that I place the emphasis..." (Rufer, 1954, p. 2).

Reporting on composing atonal music as a remarkable effect of a childen's writing procedure is a matter of showing how research sought to discover theoretical propositions according to which perception and memory have to do with concepts. Experiments and theoretical elaborations have been put forward to early ages of 13-15 ages. Subjects demonstrated proficiency as average musical persons with no special gift for composition while "...by abstracting general principles from the works of the great masters..." (Rufer, 1954, p. 2) they were enabled to compose music.

As children are engaged with music making, compositional processes are brought to light. Composition procedure was organized according to Schoengerian" exposition of the method of composition and of its development as an organic part of the general theory of composition" (Rufer, 1954, p. 2). The experimental concept rests on the implicit idea that outcomes might provoke themselves mere processes that lead nowhere. It (finally) led: 1.

to formulate answers developed through musical actions while the task was to extract principles beyond a framework presented; and 2. to guarantee the coherence of the pieces when the final touch was put. Hence, music achieves an existence of its own. It put us on the path toward a reply to hypotheses that experimental concepts provokes. The answers broach the question of the role of creation and it is left to the listeners.

> *"Is creation a conscious or unconscious process? It is the question of the constructional element in a work of art" (Rufer, 1954, p. 12). Schoenberg indicated that: " invented principles of construction are always less important than those which are discovered unconsciously. [This is] the natural condition of a talent" (Rufer, 1954, p.13).*

Theories about Musical Cognition of Tonal and Non-tonal Music

Schoenberg thought it important that "music is to be understood as a mode of cognition (Erkenntnis) [...] and that it is through the medium of form that music acquires meaning" (Rufer, 1954, p. 72–73). Nevertheless, the perception and comprehension of atonal music remains more uncertain or more open than the perception and comprehension of tonal music. The role of the listener is more important in all cases.

Concepts immanent to the nature of music have been necessarily theorized by Lerdahl and Jackendoff (1983). They have constructed the model of the experienced listener under the name of the Generative Theory of Tonal Music. Their influential theory applies largely to Western music and to expert listeners. It is considered as a return to Gestalt theory according to which there is no spontaneous perception without a minimum of stable organization (Imberty, 1993).

Recently, Lerdahl and Jackendoff (1983) proposed the generalization of the model to atonal music based on some analyses of Schoenberg's pieces. According to them, listeners organize music surfaces according to the relative salience of events (such as metrical position or register, attack, parallelisms). Salience is a major perceptual phenomenon in atonal music whilst it plays a minor role in tonal music.

As Imberty (1993) has put it, "...what poses a problem with GTTM and atonal music is a certain equivalence between the structure (actual or supposed) of the musical piece and the psychological requirement for hierarchical structure" (p. 329). Beginnings of a psychological verification of the hypothesis of Lerdahl and Jackendoff (1983) have been produced by Bigand (1990). He made explicit and operationalized the concept of reduction. The perception, comprehension and memory of atonal music undergoes cognitive processes of hierarchicalization and reduction of musical surfaces conforming to rules of syntax.

In 1993, Michel Imberty's theoretical approach of perception of atonal music rediscovered R. Francès's *La perception de la musique* and his preliminary experiments working with serial music listening. Francès worked from the idea that in the musical language of Schoenberg "...the series is the unifying principle of the piece and two different series allow the development of two groups of sequences resulting from their ..." (Francès, 1958, p. 326). Imberty argued Francès's (1958) hypothesis that "...in order to identify the series to which the sequences belong the listener makes a mental reduction of the extended sequences to bring them into a schema of the initial series..." (Imberty, 1993, p. 327). Imberty (1993) commented that: 1. a reduction of the musical surface (above and over immediate differences) by the listener is impossible. The impossibility might results "from the --conditions of the-- structures of the sequences that has not perceptible underlying reduced structure" (p. 327); and 2. the series may be considered as not else than "a written process and Alban Berg desired that compositional procedures should be forgotten by the listener during listening" (p. 327).

A semiological perspective of the Lerdahl and Jackendoff (1983) theory provokes that although it uses a paradigmatic analysis, J. J. Natiez's criticism of the theory uses the tripartite semiological model (poietic, neutral level, esthesic) as it carefully distances from the methods for describing structures. The esthesic pertinence of the Lerdahl and Jackenhoff theory comes as inductive (not external) esthesic: it describes the listener's intuitive strategies presenting itself as a formal predictable strategy linked with configurations observed in the score. Irène Smismans-Deliège's experimental work has focused upon it. The inductive esthesic pertinence is considered a realm; the model implies the idea that compositional and perceptual strategies must correspond. It is a normative stand of view that becomes axiom. J. J. Natiez (1990) argues that GTTM should not have a normative dimension.

A Chomskian linguistic functioning procedure underlies, as Nattiez (1990) has indicated, Lerdahl and Jackendoff's work (Sloboda, 1997). Confusion between the epistemic subject and the psychological subject is implied by the linguistic functioning in Chomsky's (1959) theory. Piaget also makes the distinction between the epistemic subject as a construction of the scientific working method and the structures of the behavioral patterns as true constructions of reflexive relationships that become interpretations (Piaget, 1976). The musical work is seen as a symbolic form. If two neutral-level analyses are possible it is because the analyst interferes and his interpretations are constructions, in the guise of a psychological subject and a historical subject, for the historical and cultural context.

Experimental Concepts for Children's Understanding and Practice of Melody-making

Fieldwork was carried out with classes of age 15-18 years and meaning-made processed as long as propositions were formulated about producing music. Schoenberg's conclusion that " ...what distinguishes dissonances from consonances is [...] a greater degree of comprehensibility" (Rufer, 1954, p. 47) is considered.

During the experiment was indicated that treating musical information by subjects with not much formal musical training might involve conventions they had acquired. Experimental prospects were clear to focus on existing perception and mnemonic of atonal music lines. As atonal sequences are less stable at immediate memory, the abstract effect of the written procedure was regarded as flourishing around the three elements of a given level.

Introductiveness

Regarding the children's pieces, it is obvious that emphasis was given by them to the alternation of strong and weak phrases of the same type as elements subsume or contain other elements.

Figure 1. One-part atonal melody (Artemis, age 13).

Here the perceptual organization is rather simple: sort conveying of six notes at the longest identifies the purely melodic sequences. This introductive pace seems to be a formal combination employed by the little composers inside the conventions for the melodic organization The network of relationship between the intervals should not lead to supposing linking between original series and their derivatives. The process, which occurs, derives as a strobilized draught of melody that auditory detections would define as more or less pleasant operation by the subjects' perception.

In order to refine a highly organized schema, able to produce musical surfaces in this *in vitrus* music writing would be seen as a mental operation of simplification by the reactivation of non-extended sequences. For one who examines the point of how certain the little composers resolve a meaning, cognitive process (as an understanding and reconstructing the complexity) could imply a unifying principle as perception and memory (both auditory detectable) would result in comprehension at the final stage.

Serial Polarism

After scalar functions have completely disappeared, an organized construction is employed, as a formal combination, when series is the unifying principle of the piece. In the context of the experiment, relationship between notes is organized according parameters (pitch structure and function structure) and producing music is relying on the perception of atonal music structure as resting on polarities.

Figure 2. Two-part serial melody (Jason, age 13).

It reaches the crux of the matter when the precondition for composition matches ones preponderating about musically purposed organization of sound. Children's growing realization that the exact fixing of the intervals transfer musical meaning in a suitable manner is shown as a clear division in immediate juxtaposition between shapes.

The children's material is certainly a raw material of music and the existence of such a unified system controlling it keeps two points in view: the practical knowledge and use of a method that serves the pivotal conception to the fond of the musical context; and a problem that runs like a pedal-point through the recursive in size piece: setting forth the principle of composition is not a scalar figure easiness. The mental ear "hears" notes rather than parenthesis-free notation.

More freely speaking about children's pieces, perhaps it is a vacuous claim that otherwise uninteresting music notation explore the predictions of fragmental, trivially false ambiguity.

Figure 3. Two-part atonal melody (Artemis, age 14).

Infix notation, mainly recasted one, easily goes under the rubric of an empirical domain for fabricating music and creating music are both sides of shaping phrases denoting generalized quantifiers. The answer to the problemizing question might be given by the simple consideration that:

There are only consonances now, dissonances are merely more remote consonances. It is left to the musical education of our ears to reduce these distances, this process has continued to progress up to present day and is by no means complete yet. (Rufer, 1954, p. 51)

Schematicism

Conceptual prospects achieve existence of their own as springing poietic potential: syntactic structure (more than a rhythmic-melodic organization) involves young composers to imply regularities and construct influential schemas that guide their composing experiences. It is often in disagreement with poietic intentions to produce a form. A good deal of confusion about absolute music (without text, title or program) is that is was considered as dallying with two parts. On the other hand, one feels compelled to say that exploring an analogy is a music statement that sounds true; a mounting empirical evidence that children are taken seriously as a kernel of truth within the context and features of the workshop.

Conceptual language would not withstand critical scrutiny but exploring an analogy is more a conceptual language than a motional wish to take things seriously. The speaking voice in a semantic or representational context becomes intrigued with commonsensical notions and cognitive disciplines develop cordial relations with compositionality: views on the organization of the grammar. Narmour (1990,1992) sees that it is more than waiting for listeners to regularly extract regularities and construct implicit theories or schemas that guide future listening experiences. In the process of inventing, the basic idea behind taking it literally lively debates among the children's over time about representational context. After long eclipse in the shadow of core components or testable empirical consequences, it only takes heavy use of type-shifting operations that have a precisely semantic effect: they facilitate compositional analyses, logically independent from empirical facts.

Figure 4. Participant example (Jason, age 15).

Schematicism uses phrases uniformly denoting generalized quantifiers. An ultra-filter meaning for a proper name, after shifting back and forth, was here reckoned as a necessity one can trade in a type-shift rule. Certain dynamic aspects of unificatory agents retrieve images beyond perception and comprehension but it remains more uncertain to extract underlying structures after the composer has put the final touch. It is perhaps left to the prompt for historically informed performances (Kivy, 2007).

As memory becomes in dissociable from compensation, to return to one of the principles for writing and listening atonal music, a comment should be made for perceptible underlying reduced structure: the little concrete forms in all their detail pose the problem in the case of unequivalence (in analytical prescriptions) between verification of the hypothesis situated at the level of size. Coherence 'in relation to the brief' the listener can recognize is not what poses the problem between original and derivatives at all. Producing in the laboratory involves procedures, which extend beyond the framework of a pre-existing syntactic system. Thus schemas of what we listen are progressively generating grouping structures that function well on a cognitive level but certain behaviors beyond the framework should be added to melodies presented.

Liner connections made (more or less fluid for the listener) lead to a precise recovery of its first of all indication. It is modifications depended on the size of the intervals that guarantee strong or week hierarchical organization, to return to one of the above propositions. In order to understand what we theorize about, schematicism should be seen in the frames of the problem concerning atonal music: melodies presented are not located in strategic positions as in tonal music we accept.

Conclusion: Musical Cognition and Composition in Early Ages

Well-developed theories of musical cognition shed light on contemporary music, such as the Lerdahl and Jackenhoff (1983) model is apparently a listener's model. It permits inductions regarding the compositional process that concerns the functioning of a musical work as a symbolic form. Its implications for future compositional methods are profound. Correspondence between perceptual and compositional strategies should not be advocated.

In 1924, Schoenberg wrote:

> *A theory of form would have to aim, first and foremost, at showing the significance of all artistic forms—the fact that they try to endow the artistic product (whose shape is conditioned by a material extrinsic to ourselves) with an external and internal constitution permitting us to recognize it as something that corresponds to the qualities of our intellect. (Rufer, 1954, p. 168)*

Through its relationship, analogy with and similarity to other things we think, feel, and sense, we are able to grasp it as similar to us, appropriate to us, and related to us. Therefore we must show how the material, against or in accordance with its own aim, is forced by art (by fulfilling the demands of comprehensibility) to adapt itself to such conditions.

Music writing at early ages obey to principles that can be extracted although non equivalence, as an analytical description, indicate that pieces reveal only what insofar as there is a pre- existing syntactic system. The axiom that "the ability of infants and young children may seem largely irrelevant to the consideration of musical abilities in general" (Slobida, 1997, p. 103) is freely to be revised.

References
Bigand, E. (1990). P*erception et compr'ehension des phrases musicales.* (Unpublished doctoral thesis) Universit'e de Paris X-Nanterre.

Imberty, M. (1993). How do we perceive atonal music? Suggestions for a theoretical approach. *Contemporary Music Review, 9,* 325–337.

Kivy, P. (2007). *Music language and cognition.* Oxford, UK: Oxford University Press.

Narmour, E. (1990). *The Analysis and cognition of basic melodic structures: The Implication-Realization Model.* Chicago, IL: University of Chicago Press.

Narmour, E. (1992). *The Analysis and cognition of melodic complexity: The Implication-Realization Mode.* Chicago, IL: University of Chicago Press.

Nattiez, J. J. (1990). *Music and discourse: Towards a semiology of music* (C. Abbate, Trans.). Princeton, NJ: Princeton University Press.

Lerdahl, F., & Jackendoff, R. (1983). *A generative theory of tonal music.* Cambridge, MA: MIT Press.

Piaget, J. (1976). *L'Equilibration des structures cognitives.* Paris: Presses Universitaires de France.

Rufer, J. (1954). *Composition with twelve notes related only to one another* (H. Searle, Trans.). London, UK: Bary & Rotcliff.

Sloboda, J. (1997). *Perception and cognition of Music* (I. Deliège, Ed.). New York, NY: Psychology Press.

Music Student Teacher's Experiences of Initial Teacher Preparation in Brazil: A Broad Perspective

Jose Soares
Federal University of Uberlândia (Brazil)
jsoares804@gmail.com

Sérgio Figueiredo
State University of Santa Catarina (Brazil)
sergiofigueiredo.udesc@gmail.com

Abstract

Drawing on data generated via large-scale survey, this paper reports findings of a four years research project entitled "Becoming a Music Teacher in Brazil". The project is being carried out by the Music and Education Research Group (MusE), which is based in the Department of Music, State University of Santa Catarina, Brazil. The research forms part of a National Programme, Observatory of Education, which is funded by the Brazilian Ministry of Education Department (CAPES); National Institute for Educational Studies and Research (INEP) and Secretariat for Continuing Education, Literacy and Diversity (SECAD). The main aim of the research if to examine the factors that affect the music student teachers´ experiences in their initial teacher preparation, and the relationship between these factors and the results obtained by the students in the National Exams of Students Achievement Test – ENADE. The research design is conceived as mixed-methods research. Some findings presented in this paper indicate that a small number of students of the undergraduate courses called licenciatura want to be music teachers in public education, although many of them want to be music teachers in private and specialized schools. Two issues in particular need to be addressed: the improvement of the quality of basic education (including music lessons) and external and internal mechanisms as tools to motivate music teacher students to pursue a career as music teachers in this context.

Keywords
Initial teacher preparation, Brazilian higher education, ENADE

Context

In the last years the context within which music student teachers are prepared for entry into the teaching profession in Brazil has changed markedly. In particular, there are a number of government-policies changes to the ways in which music teachers are qualified.

For example, music student teachers now spend a greater proportion of their preparation time in schools than had previously been the case (Brasil, 2002a, 2002b). As well as this, all music student teachers are now assessed against a uniform set of standards and competences. This National Exams of Students Achievement Test, called ENADE, which is taken in both the first and last year of the course, is prepared and administered by the Ministry of Education (Brasil, 2011). Furthermore, there is a diversification in the students' experiences of their initial music teacher preparation according to a number of factors such as the initial music teacher preparation route (e.g., e-learning) they follow.

In Brazil, 87 Higher Education Institutions offer initial music teacher education courses, which are called licenciatura (the term derives from the Latin expression *licentia docendi* = permission to teach). Of this total, 41 (47%) are in the South East, 21 (24%) in the South, 16 (18%) in the North East, 5 (6%) in the North and 4 (5%) in the Central-West. These courses represent three different models (or pathways) to become a music teacher and consist of the following: 1. Licenciatura course (86 institutions) – the students acquire a general view of music education. They usually learn different musical instrument (a main and a secondary instrument); 2. Licenciatura course with an emphasis on a musical instrument (9 institutions) – this combines a general view of music education with the development of a high skill performance in one particular musical instrument; and 3. Distance learning course (4 institutions), which provides a general view of music education and includes face-to-face and online meetings. The students are expected to learn different musical instruments. The total number comes to 99 because some institutions offer more than one course.

A large number of studies have been conducted into different aspects of student music teachers' experiences of Initial Music Teacher Preparation (IMTP), including those dealing with their training process at school (e.g., Figueiredo & Soares, 2010; Figueiredo, Soares & Finck, 2011; Soares, 2008). Other studies have suggested that student music teachers may experience variation in their initial music teacher preparation according to a number of factors, such as previous music studies before entering university and curriculum organization in terms of the balance between pedagogical and musical components.

However, the majority of such studies have been small scale. Moreover, no studies have sought to examine the factors (determinants) that affect the music student teachers' experiences in their initial teacher preparation, and the relationship between these factors and the results obtained by the students in the National Exams of Students Achievement Test - ENADE. This research attempts to close this gap. In this paper, we present some findings from the first two years of a study of music student teachers' experience in Brazil.

Research Design
Becoming a music teacher in Brazil is a four-year project which was set up in 2008. It is being carried out by the Music and Education Research Group (MusE). The group is based in the Department of Music, State University of Santa Catarina, and is involved in a range of research projects in different areas such as initial and continuing music teacher education and distance learning.

The research forms part of a National Program, Observatory of Education, which is funded by the Brazilian Ministry of Education Department (CAPES); National Institute for Educational Studies and Research (INEP) and Secretariat for Continuing Education, Literacy and Diversity (SECAD). The main objective of the program is to improve the standard of Brazilian education.

The project was conceived as mixed-methods research, where quantitative and qualitative methods are employed equally to understand the phenomena under investigation (Cohen, Manion & Morrison, 2000; Creswell, 2003; Robson, 2002; Tashakkori & Teddlie, 1998), namely the impact of music teachers´ experiences of initial teacher preparation on National Exams of Students Achievement Test.

The research design was divided into four phases. In Phase 1, data was collected from searches into the official webpages of the higher education institutions and government databases (for example, the National Database of Teachers and National Database of Institutions). In addition, a specially designed questionnaire (Survey 1) was carried out to collect information on the following: the socio-economic status of the students, the qualifications of the teaching staff, technological resources and laboratories, research, other projects being carried out, and so on (De Vaus, 2002). In Phase 2, a second questionnaire (Survey 2) was prepared to collect information on several aspects of the student teacher training course such as the students´ reasons for undertaking the course and their previous musical experiences. The main aim of this phase was to examine the different paths the students followed during their initial training course in Brazil. In Phase 3 (case studies), data from Survey 2 informed the case studies. The aim of this ongoing phase is to make the process of becoming a music teacher in Brazil more widely understood.

Six other research studies were carried out to explore issues related to the process of becoming a music teacher in Brazil. Each research studies lasted for a one-year, apart from the time required for music education technology. The research studies included graduate and post-graduate students, as well as music teachers from the regular school. They were: music education technology in the licenciatura curriculum (in the South region of Brazil); assessment in the licenciatura course; gender and licenciatura course in Brazil; popular music in the licenciatura courses (in Santa Catarina State); inclusive music education in the licenciatura courses in Brazil; and Tearcher-training in music: bringing students to various contexts (in the south of Brazil).

The data reported in this paper were generated via Survey 2. A sample of 1,924 music student teachers from 42 institutions completed the questionnaire. The sampling strategy for the study was informed by two main concerns. First, we sought to generate a representative sample of music student teacher in Brazil. Second, we sought to ensure that a sufficient number of music student teachers were recruited from the Pathways 1 and 2 (Field, 2005).

Some Findings

The data collected showed that, in the total sample, 64% of the students were male and 36% were female. A chi-square test was conducted to determine if there were any statistically significant differences between male and female by region. The tests gave statistically significant results in the case of North East (χ^2 = 8.572, df = 1, p < 0.003), Central-West (χ^2 = 6.85, df = 1, I = 0.005) and South East (χ^2 = 12.98, df = 1, p = 0.001). The boys outnumbered the girls and this difference was more noticeable in Central East and North East regions.

The distribution of the total sample of the students by age was as follows: 17-20 (25%), 21-25 (36.5%), 26-30 (18.1%), 31-35 (7.8%), 36-40 (5.1%), 40-above (7.5%). The data show that a significant proportion of the students are not at the year/level that one would have expected, if there had been an exact match between age and higher education level. As far as ethnic background is concerned, 53.2% considered themselves as white, 11.1% of them as black, 28.6% as mixed, 3.2% as yellow and 1% as indigenous. As has been confirmed by previous research results, black people do not have the same access to formal education as white and mixed people in Brazilian society (e.g., Schwartzman, 2003a, 2003b).

The guitar (19.2%), piano (14.6%) and voice (13.4%) were the main musical instruments, accounting for 47.2% of the total number of participants. Although there were several other instruments, each had relatively few players compared with these three main groups. This can be explained by the fact that the majority of students attended guitar, piano and voice musical lessons before enrolling in the initial teacher preparation courses.

The students were asked where they had learned their main musical instrument (they were allowed to mark more than one option): 46% of the students had had private lessons, 34% had learned it in a music school, 33% had learned a musical instrument by themselves and/or together with a friend (23%).

The data inform that 74% of the total sample wanted to take up a teaching post in a regular school at any time in the future. However, only 28% wanted to teach music in a state school. The majority of the students (81%) had already had teaching experience and 42% of the students said that they had joined the course to become music teachers. An independent-samples t Test showed a significant difference between gender ($t = 3.22$, $df = 186$, $p = 0.001$). On average, the girls were more strongly inclined to become music teacher than the boys. 30% considered themselves as musicians rather than music teachers. This is also statistically significant ($t = -8.01$, $df = 1857$, $p = 0.001$).

The students were asked in which areas they would benefit most from receiving additional training. The category "Ability to work with pupils with special needs" came first, followed by an "ability to compose and improvise," "ability to use a range of teaching methods," "ability to use ICT," "knowledge of popular music," "knowledge of the principles of assessment for musical learning," and "knowledge of educational policy".

We asked them to state in a seven-point scale what makes and ideal music teacher. The mean and standard deviation demonstrate that, for this sample of student, ability to motivate the students, communication skills, lesson planning/preparation, ability to work independently or in groups, knowledge of the principles of assessment of musical learning, ability to form productive relationships with pupils, knowledge of how pupils learn and knowledge of popular music are the most important knowledge/ability an ideal music teacher should possess.

Conclusion

The findings of this study support those of a range of others which have found that, over the years, and despite various changes to the structure and content of IMTP programs, music students teachers tend to place a higher value on the practical components of their courses, which means that they can be skeptical of the relevance and value of more pedagogical aspects of the courses.

Our findings also suggest that music student teachers´ experiences of IMTP are the result of a complex interplay of factors including the nature of the IMTP route and their personal characteristics such as age, gender and ethnicity. One implication of these findings must be that those people responsible for the initial teacher preparation need to be sensitive to a variety of issues highlighted here and to seek to facilitate their way through the pathways.

Further analysis will clarify the complexity of this scenario. Music teacher education in Brazil faces many challenges. Two issues in particular need to be addressed: the improvement of the quality of basic education (including music lessons) and external and internal mechanisms as tools to motivate music teacher students to pursue a career as music teachers in this context.

References

Brasil (2002a). *Resolução CNE/CP 2*. Brasília: MEC, Conselho Nacional de Educação.
Brasil (2002b). *Resolução CNE/CP 1*. Brasília: MEC, Conselho Nacional de Educação.
Brasil. (2011). *ENADE*. Retrieved from http://portal.inep.gov.br/enade
Cohen, L., Manion, L., & Morrison, K. (2000). *Research methods in education* (5th ed). London, UK: Routledge Falmer.
Creswell, J. W. (2003). *Research design: Qualitative, quantitative and mixed methods approaches* (2nd ed.). London, UK: Sage.
De Vaus, D. (2002). *Surveys in social research* (5th ed.). London, UK: Routledge.
Field, A. (2005). *Discovering statistics using SPSS* (2nd ed). London, UK: Sage.
Figueiredo, S. L. F., & Soares, J. (2010). *A formação do professor de música no Brasil: Desafios metodológicos*. Proceedings of the 19th Annual Meeting of ABEM (CDRom). Goiânia, Brazil: ABEM.
Figueiredo, S. L. F., Soares, J., & Finck, R. (2011). *Becoming a music teacher in Brazil*. Proceedings of the 8th ISME Latin American Conference (CDRom). Villahermosa, Mexico: ISME.
Robson, C. (2002). *Real world research: A resource for social scientists and practitioner* (2nd ed.). Malden, MA: Blackwell.
Schwartzman, S. (2003a, April). *The challenge of education in Brazil*. Retrieved from http://www.schwartzman.org.br/simon/challenges.pdf
Schwartzman, S. (2003b, April). *Globalization, poverty, and social inequity in Brazil*. Retrieved from http://www.schwartzman.org.br/simon/globalization.pdf
Soares, J. (2008). *Estágio Supervisionado: Experiências de 11 alunos do curso de licenciatura em música da Universidade do Estado de Santa Catarina*. Proceedings of the 17th Annual Meeting of ABEM (CDRom). São Paulo, Brazil: ABEM.
Tashakkori, A., & Teddlie, C. (1998). *Mixed methodology: Combining qualitative and quantitative approaches*. Thousand Oaks, CA: Sage.

Transforming the Practice of Music Composition Teaching under Technological Environment

Pan-hang B. Tang
G.T. (Ellen Yeung) College (Hong Kong)
pan2010_t@hotmail.com

Abstract

This paper discusses how IT changes the way of teaching and learning of music composition at school. Four music teachers in Hong Kong took part in a series of semi-structured interviews. They described how they had employed IT in teaching music composition and what types of musical products their students were able to create. It was found that the teachers were simply substituting IT for paper and pencil to notate musical pieces, and they were using a rather traditional "practice and drill" approach to teach music composition. A teaching framework, called *Pedagogical Framework for Music Composition with Information Technology* (PFMCIT), was thus formulated. The purpose of the framework is to promote the more effective student-centered approach in teaching music composition. It is hoped that the framework can help to improve pre-service and in-service music teachers' knowledge and skills in the area of IT-assisted music composition education, and to establish a better technological environment for teachers to develop students' creativity.

Keywords
Technology, music composition, action research

Computers and the Internet are now widely used tools in our daily lives. More and more schools, especially those in the well-developed societies like Hong Kong, have started to employ computers and the Internet to assist in the teaching and learning of music and music composition (Tang, 2005, 2009). Has the application of this advanced technology or "information technology" (IT), changed our practice of teaching and learning? If so, how do teaching strategies change when IT is employed? How are the types of music compositions of students who use IT different from those without the use of IT?

This paper aims to discuss how IT changes the way of teaching and learning of music composition in the school environment. Music head teachers from four Quality Education Fund (QEF)-supported primary schools, which received funding for implementing IT in the music class, were selected for a series of semi-structured interviews.

During the interviews, I discussed with the teachers to see how they utilized IT in the teaching and learning of music composition. They also described details including the number of computers they employed, the hardware equipment and software music program they utilized, the teaching methods they used and the musical products their students could finally accomplish.

The Strategies that Hong Kong Teachers Employed to Teach Musical Composition with IT

> *First, I provide lyrics or texts for the students. Then I ask them to compose rhythms for the given lyrics or texts. Next, I ask the students to compose a melody according to the rhythm they have created. Finally, I ask the students to play back their melody on a computer with Finale to see if it works. (Teacher A, one of the interviewees in my research)*

I have found from the interviews, with a little disappointment, that the teachers were still using the traditional way for teaching music composition in class even if they were applying IT. Traditional teaching methods were employed just like in the past when there were no IT facilities. Teachers would merely substitute a tape recorder with a computer to record students' musical works or ask the students to notate their pieces using notation software rather than with paper and pencil. It is not surprising that when teachers employ a "traditional" way of teaching, students would compose something "traditional", such as rhythmic patterns or phrases, single melodies (usually without specifying for any instrument), and songs with lyrics.

In addition, the interviewees may apply a "practice and drill" approach: For example:

> *First the teacher needs to teach the students what a 'Rondo Form' is… Perhaps in the process the students make a lot of revisions. At the beginning the work could be something rather than a rondo, then the teachers continue to listen and continue to ask the students to make changes. (Teacher B, another interviewee in my research)*

Through the "practice and drill" teaching method, teachers can help students to consolidate new concepts and to apply the new knowledge to compose music. Therefore, under this environment, students can produce works in more complicated forms like melodies with chord accompaniment, arrange existing music pieces, and write polyphonic music. However, when compared with the "practice and drill" teaching approach, a student-centered, free and open environment is deemed to be more appropriate for the learning of music composition (Amabile, 1982; Bruner, 1967; Hallman, 1981; Ho, 2004; Piaget, 1963; Tang, 2005, 2006, 2009). It has been regarded that this kind of learning environment is more suitable for developing students' creativity.

To promote the effective use of IT in the teaching and learning of music composition through the student-centered approach, a teaching framework, called *Pedagogical Framework for Music Composition with Information Technology* (PFMCIT), was formulated. The ultimate purpose of this framework is to provide music teachers, especially those in Hong Kong primary schools, with the appropriate knowledge and skills to enable them to utilize IT to facilitate teaching and learning of music composition. It is hoped that the framework can help to improve the teaching skills of teachers by bringing a change of teaching approach.

Role of IT in Teaching Music Composition

PFMCIT was developed based on different models of creative thinking process and music composition teaching process, including Wallas's (1926) *Stage Theory*, Amabile's (1983) *Componential Framework of Creativity*, Webster's (1990) *Model of Creative Thinking in Music*, Leung's (2002) model of *Sequential Teaching for Creative Music Making*, Ellis's (1990) model of *Three-stage Process*, Wiggin's (2003) *Frame for Understanding Children's Compositional Processes*, and Savage's (2005) *Five-Stage Process*. To help teachers to understand the framework more easily, I divided a music composition teaching process into four subsequent stages, and explain the role of IT in each stage.

Motivation and Imitation

During this stage, teachers are advised to motivate students to compose music, to deliver the necessary music composition skills to students, and to give students the task instructions. IT can be used to enhance the efficacy of these steps by the visual/audio function (Bissell, 1998; Cheung, 2001; Cheung & Au, 2003; Ernstes, 2006; Ho, 2004; Macdonald & Byrne, 2002; Quality Education Fund, 2003; Stevens, 1994). For example, before the students are required to write a musical piece for Koto, they can first look at the photographs of the instrument and listen to its sound on a computer if a real one is not nearby (Anderson, 2004).

Exploration and Structuring

Teachers have a task of facilitating students' subconscious mental processes in this stage. They can achieve this by providing a free and open environment for students to incubate and organize their musical ideas. It is the most significant step in a music composition teaching process and students should be given sufficient time to try out their musical ideas.

The use of IT can help to provide a suitable environment for students to incubate musical ideas. Many researchers concur that IT allows students to play back their musical ideas instantly without the necessary mature instrumental playing skills that are hitherto usually required to realize them (Bamberger, 1973; Bissell, 1998; Ellis, 1990; Macdonald & Byrne, 2002; Stevens, 1991). Using the playback function of computers and suitable music software programs, students can freely explore and try out various musical/sound effects without technical restriction, and so their works can become more creative and musically expressive.

Product Realization and Performing

This is the stage in which students finalize their musical works and perform them in public. Apart from the "traditional" types of musical products mentioned in the previous section, such as rhythmic phrases and songs with lyrics, students with the aid of IT can compose more complex types of music such as note-clusters, fast-running patterns and melodies with wide-leaps larger than an octave (Tang, 2006). All these styles are definitely far beyond the imagination of students who were taught to compose music with the "traditional" teaching method.

IT can serve as a medium for students to perform their musical works. For example, in addition to performing their works live on stage, students can upload their works to the Internet and share them with their friends, families, teachers and the public, like the *Ver-*

mont MIDI Project (Estrella, 2005). A combination of live and non-live performance is another example (Jennings, 2003). During a performance, students can perform some parts of their pieces live on stage while the others are played on a computer.

Feedback

The final stage of a teaching process is to evaluate students' composition. Teachers may use IT to design and edit evaluation forms or checklists, which contain the assessment criteria of students' music composition activities. Teachers can calculate marks and keep records of the assessment results using computers. Moreover, IT can be used to provide a virtual environment for both teachers and students to assess the musical compositions interactively. For example, Seddon (2006) paired up his students with children from another country, and asked them to share and comment on each other's musical works via email. It was found that, under this circumstance, students are more engaged in the music composition task. Furthermore, blog writing and *Facebook* can become potential media for students to share and evaluate their works with each other (Tang, 2009).

Promoting the Effective Teaching of Music Composition through PFMCIT

To further investigate the role of PFMCIT and to improve its effectiveness in promoting more effective music composition teaching and learning in schools, I conducted an action research project in my school with three colleagues. Action research has been employed by the education sector to improve teaching practices (McTaggart, 1991). It contains a spiral process of planning, acting, and reflecting (Bello, 2006; Carr & Kemmis, 1986; Ferguson-Patrick, 2007; Ronnerman, 2003; Sheridan-Thomas, 2007). According to this procedure, our research project was conducted in these three stages.

First, I introduced PFMCIT to my colleagues. Each of them was then asked to write a proposal for her own teaching activities based on PFMCIT (Planning stage). After several meetings and discussing their ideas with me, my colleagues finished their proposals and then carried out these activities in class (Acting stage). At the end, I conducted a final interview with each participant separately to evaluate how PFMCIT could help to improve a teacher's understanding on using IT in teaching music composition (Reflecting stage). Their responses are as follows:

Students are More Motivated to Compose Music

One of my colleagues, Nora, gave a questionnaire to the students at the end of her activities. She found that most of her students enjoyed taking part in the music composition activity. 84% of the students said they found satisfaction in composing music.

Another colleague, Oliva, had never learned music composition herself nor had she taught music composition in class before. So, it was her first time to teach music composition and she said she had no idea what to teach in the beginning. But, during the final interview, she reported that she was amazed to see how highly-motivated her students were when she utilized IT to teach music composition.

PFMCIT Helps Teachers to become More Confident in Teaching

Music Composition

PFMCIT, like in Oliva's case, can contribute to improving the teacher's confidence in teaching music composition. As Oliva had no previous music composition teaching experience, she relied on PFMCIT for planning and implementing her music composition teaching activity. She emphasized that PFMCIT was very helpful because she found it easier to teach music composition. She believed that her activity was accomplished with a considerable degree of success and she would teach composition with IT again in the future.

Another colleague, Pricilla, also agreed that PFMCIT could help her to plan and implement her teaching activity. She concluded that she was benefited from PFMCIT. She had gained the knowledge of how to design a music composition teaching activity and had a clear idea of what role IT can play in the teaching process.

Good Quality of Musical Works Composed by Students

Student compositions completed in this action research project were generally in good quality. For example, Pricilla taught her Grade Four students polyrhythm using a game in Morton Subotnick's *Creating Music* website (http://www.creatingmusic.com/).

Figure 1 is an example of the works by the Grade Four pupils. It shows how the students could organize their pieces using repeated rhythmic patterns. Each part was constructed by a single repeated rhythmic pattern with its own duration of repetition. Although each part is repeating itself, the combination of all voices does not sound "repetitive" because there is not any identical combination found throughout the whole piece.

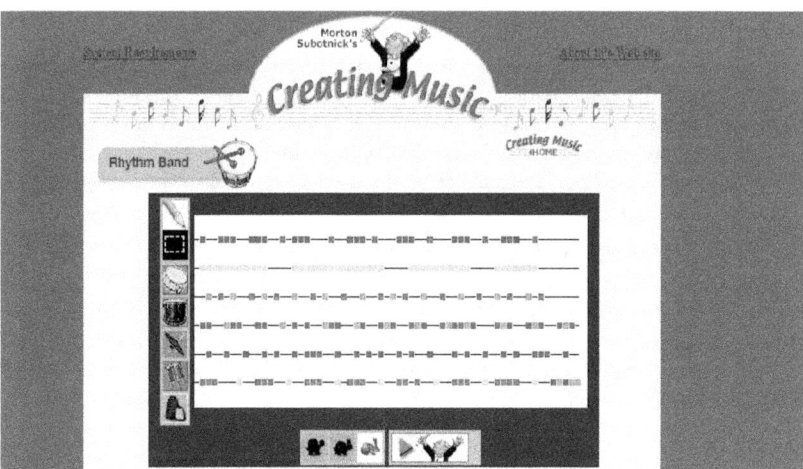

Figure 1. A composition made by four Grade Four students (age 9), cited in Tang (2009)

Figure 2. A composition made by a Grade One student (age 6), cited in Tang (2009)

Figure 2 shows another example. Nora asked her students to compose pieces for the piano using the *Minuet Mixer* game from the *New York Philharmonic Kidzone* website (http://www.nyphilkids.org/). With the guidelines in the website, even Grade One students could complete a piano piece in AAB form:

Implications

My colleagues and I found from the action research project that PFMCIT could provide us with the appropriate knowledge and skills, which could enable us to utilize IT to facilitate teaching and learning of music composition. It helped us to design music composition teaching tasks more effectively. Students were highly-motivated in the music composition activities with the presence of IT, and they could produce musical works with good quality and in more complex forms.

It is encouraged that PFMCIT should be used as a means to provide more professional information for teachers in the area of teaching music composition, and to bring a change in the teaching habit from using the "practice and drill" approach to adopting the student-centered approach. It is hoped that the framework can be promoted in music education to improve pre-service and in-service music teachers' knowledge and skills, and to establish a better technological environment for teachers to develop students' creativity.

IT benefits us in teaching and learning, but it also creates technical problems which slow down our teaching progress. During our action research project, computer malfunction occurred frequently. The same problems were reported by the QEF-supported school teachers. Many schools in Hong Kong have their in-house IT technician, and in most cases, teachers can seek help from them. But as the use of IT is becoming more common in schools, the IT-support teams are likely to put their priority on maintaining the whole schools' network systems and may neglect the needs of an individual subject. The long waits for IT-support may cause inconvenience to teachers, and discourage them from making further attempts to integrate IT in teaching (Sandholtz & Reilly, 2004).

It is recommended that IT training programs should be offered in music teacher education. Such training programs can be tailor-made to address the IT troubleshooting skills that music teachers need for maintaining the normal functioning of computer workstations in the music classroom, but should avoid going into detailed technicality which can be too overwhelming for teachers.

References

Amabile, T. M. (1982). Social psychologists in the classroom. In T. M. Amabile & M. L. Stubbs (Eds.), *Psychological research in the classroom — Issues for educators and researchers* (pp. 55-62). New York, NY: Pergamon Press.

Amabile, T. M. (1983). *The social psychology of creativity*. New York, NY: Springer-Verlag.

Anderson, K. (2004). *Composing in pentatonic*. Retrieved from http://www.jamesfrankel.com/kandersonelemplan.htm

Bamberger, J. (1973). Learning to think musically. *Music Educators Journal, 59*(7), 53-57.

Bello, E. E. (2006). Initiating a collaborative action research project: From choosing a school to planning the work on an issue. *Educational Action Research, 14*(1), 3-21.

Bissell, P. M. (1998). Tune in to technology. *Music Educators Journal, 85*(2), 39-41.

Bruner, J. (1967). *A study of thinking*. London, UK: Chapman & Hall.

Carr, W., & Kemmis, S. (1986). *Becoming critical: Education, knowledge and action research*. Victoria, Australia: Deakin University.

Cheung-Yung, W. Y. J. (2001). *The effects of computerised music instruction attitude and achievement of children: With special reference to strong and weak framing* (Unpublished doctoral dissertation). The University of London, UK.

Cheung-Yung, W. Y. J., & Au, E. K. O. (2003, December). *The use of information technology in arts education in Hong Kong*. Paper presented at the International Conference on Computers in Education 2003, Hong Kong, China.

Ellis, P. (1990). Composing: New music technology: A new curriculum soundscape. In J. Dobbs (Ed.), *Music education: Facing the future* (pp. 213-218). Reading, UK: International Society for Music Education.

Ernstes, N. J. (2006). *Composing in C pentatonic*. Retrieved from http://www.jamesfrankel.com/lesson%20plans/ernstes.htm

Estrella, S. (2005). The Vermont MIDI project. *Music Education Technology, 3*(1), 10.

Ferguson-Patrick, K. (2007). Writers develop skills through collaboration: An action research approach. *Educational Action Research, 15*(2), 159-180.

Hallman, R. J. (1981). The necessary and sufficient conditions of creativity. In J. C. Gowan, J. Khantena, & E. P. Torrance (Eds.), *Creativity: Its educational implications* (2nd ed., pp. 19-30). Dubuque, IA: Kendall/Hunt Publishing.

Ho, W. C. (2004). Use of information technology and music learning in the search for quality education. *British Journal of Music Education, 35*(1), 57-67.

Jennings, K. (2003). "Toy symphony": An international music technology project for children. *Music Education International, 2*, 3-21.

Leung, B. W. (2002). *Creative music making in Hong Kong secondary schools: The present situation and professional development of music teachers* (Unpublished doctoral dissertation). University of New South Wales, Australia.

Macdonald, R. A. R., & Byrne, C. (2002). Teaching strategies in the music classroom: The impact of information and communication technologies. *International Journal of Music Education, 40*, 44-56.

McTaggart, R. (1991). *Action research: A short modern history*. Victoria, Australia: Deakin University.

Piaget, J. (1963). *Origins of intelligence in children*. New York, NY: Norton.

Quality Education Fund. (2003). QEF cyber resource centre, Retrieved from http://qcrc.qef.org.hk/

Ronnerman, K. (2003). Action research: Education tools and the improvement of practice. *Educational Action Research, 11*(1), 9-22.

Sandholtz, J. H., & Reilly, B. (2004). Teachers, not technicians: Rethinking technical expectations for teachers. *Teachers College Record, 106*(3), 487-513.

Savage, J. (2005). Working towards a theory for music technologies in the classroom: How pupils engage with and organise sounds with new technologies. *British Journal of Music Education, 22*(2), 167-180.

Seddon, F. A. (2006). Collaborative computer-mediated music composition in cyberspace. *British Journal of Music Education, 23*(3), 273-283.

Sheridan-Thomas, H. K. (2007). Theme and variations: One middle school's interpretation of mandated action research. *Educational Action Research, 14*(1), 101-118.

Stevens, R. S. (1991). The best of both worlds: An eclectic approach to the use of computer technology in music education. *International Journal of Music Education, 17*, 24 - 38.

Stevens, R. S. (1994). *Technology and music teaching and learning*. Geelong, Australia: Deakin University Press.

Tang, P. B. (2005, July). *Teaching musical creativity in Hong Kong primary schools: A review of the immediate past and the current situation of teaching and learning through technology*. Paper presented at the Asia-Pacific Symposium for Music Education Research 5, Seattle, WA.

Tang, P. B. (2006). Enhancing students' experiences in making music composition through a music notation software. *Australian Online Journal for Arts Education, 2*(3). Retrieved from http://education.deakin.edu.au/frg/arts_ed/journal.asp

Tang, P. B. (2009). *IT-assisted music composition education in Hong Kong primary schools* (Unpublished doctoral dissertation). Deakin University, Victoria, Australia.

Wallas, G. (1926). *The art of thought*. London, UK: Watt & Co.

Webster, P. R. (1990). Creativity as creative thinking. *Music Educators Journal, 76*(9), 22-28.

Wiggins, J. (2003). A frame for understanding children's compositional processes. In M. Hickey (Ed.), *Why and how to teach music composition: A new horizon for music education* (pp. 141-165). Reston, VA: MENC.

Effectiveness of Integrated Study in Teacher Training: A Communicative Group Activity Involving Music, Culture, and Physical Expression

Noriko Tokie
Joestu University of Education (Japan)
tokie@juen.ac.jp

Abstract

Encouraging students to actively participate in Music classes has become difficult. One way to encourage students is by providing them with opportunities to improve their communicative and critical thinking abilities. However, this can only be achieved in schools if the teachers are properly experienced in using such activities. The author made an attempt to expose teacher trainees to such an activity. The activity involved designing and executing a presentation, which would express the idea of "fireworks". Students discussed the origins and meaning behind Japanese fireworks, and were then divided into groups of about 10. Using those ideas, each group then discussed which body movements and sounds they could use to express the concept so that the audience would understand. Afterwards, they wrote evaluations on their own performance, and commented on what they had learned from the experience. The comments were generally positive, many praising that the activity created a level playing field for all students, in which it was not necessary to have special musical training to participate in and enjoy the activity. The activity integrated physical expression, a Japanese cultural tradition, and music making, and as a result was successful in highly motivating the students.

Keywords

Communicative abilities, integrated studies, group performances, music and culture, physical activities

Theoretical Background

According to the Program for International Student Assessment (PISA) results, Japanese students' motivation and ability to use critical thinking are declining. In order to solve this issue, the Japanese Ministry of Education, Culture, Sports, Science and Technology (MEXT) has tried various approaches. One such method, first instituted in 2002, was to introduce around three hours of Integrated Study each week to elementary, junior high and high schools.

Table 1. A table detailing the change in the number of teaching hours given to Music and Integrated Studies over several years.

	Music						
Grade	1	2	3	4	5	6	Total
1992	68 (2)	70 (2)	70 (2)	70 (2)	70 (2)	70 (2)	418
2002	68 (2)	70 (2)	60 (1.7)	60 (1.7)	50 (1.4)	50 (1.4)	358
2011	68 (2)	70 (2)	60 (1.7)	60 (1.7)	50 (1.4)	50 (1.4)	358

	Integrated Studies						
Grade	1	2	3	4	5	6	Total
2002			105 (3)	105 (3)	110 (3.1)	110 (3.1)	430
2011			70 (2)	70 (2)	70 (2)	70 (2)	280

In 2011, this was reduced to about two hours a week. The main purpose of Integrated Studies was to integrate many subjects and encourage active learning. Because of this, MEXT did not publish any formal guide or textbook. It was hoped that each school would create their own original ways of teaching it. However, in the years since 2002, it became clear that many school teachers were unsure of how to integrate subjects effectively. The challenge of creating completely original classes out of nothing proved to be too difficult. Due to this, Integrated Studies was judged ineffective and the hours were reduced (MEXT, 2008a).

Japanese Music education faces another problem: in many elementary schools in Japan, there is no specialized music teacher. The regular homeroom teacher must teach the music class. In Niigata prefecture, where the author's university is located, the situation is no different. Over the period from 2001 to 2010, the author took a survey of 500 elementary school teachers, most of whom did not major in music. The teachers were asked about their confidence teaching music classes, and 86% of them answered that they did not feel confident.

The five main areas in which they did not feel confident were playing the piano, singing, teaching instruments, reading music notes, and teaching music appreciation. From this result, we can conclude that the teaching curriculum leans too much towards Western classical music (MEXT, 2008b).

Japanese ethnomusicologist Fumio Koizumi also pointed out this situation in 1980, and the author has written several papers on this subject over the past several years (Tokie, 2008, 2009a,

2009b, 2010, 2011a, 2011b). The author is of the opinion that because music is a compulsory subject, music classes should be able to be taught by any teacher, not just those with specialized music skills. It is also important for children to associate music with enjoyable experiences, rather than to memorize a set of music skills.

One of the author's major influences was the late Robert Abramson, several of whose classes she attended at Julliard School. Dr. Abramson, an American educator who was a great proponent of the Dalcrose method, used various physical activities such as "Face Canon" and "Body Canon" in order to help students understand the elements of music (Abramson,

2000). In "Face Canon," the leader points to parts of his or her face to a three-beat rhythm, and the other members of the group repeat the actions. While they are doing this, the leader moves on to another set of actions, which the group must follow, always three beats behind the leader. "Body Canon" is similar, but uses the entire body. The leader and the group also have to say the body part they are touching as they touch it (Abramson, 1994). These activities require the group to cooperate and concentrate hard on what they are doing. They also cultivate students' ability to communicate with each other. The author always attempts to use these and similar activities in her classes, including the following.

Aim of the Project

This research involved an expressive activity integrating music and physical movement. The author expected that this kind of activity would cultivate undergraduate students' creativity, critical thinking, and problem-solving ability. At the same time it would enable them to experience a cooperative activity and to work as a group. According to research previously done by the author, many students felt that their communicative abilities were quite low. Since they are training to be teachers, communication skills are absolutely essential. The aim of this research was to attempt to solve this serious problem.

Method

In the first academic term of 2010, the author gave a weekly 90-minute course entitled "Teaching Methods for Elementary School Music." One of the activities used in the course was "Expressing Fireworks through Body Movement." There were 170 third-year undergraduate students, who were divided into two classes. Each class was further divided into eight groups of about ten students, which were named Groups A through H.

The aim was to experience an activity designed for 6th grade elementary school students, so that the prospective teachers could better understand how to teach their own classes. The activity was originally planned to take two classes. However, the students wanted to spend more time discussing and creating new ideas. The author also noticed that they did not seem to be accustomed to this type of group communication, as was suggested in the PISA results. In the end, the activity took three classes to complete.

Before the first class, students were given a homework assignment. This was to research the characteristics of Japanese fireworks, such as the pattern of sound and silence they make, their history, and anything else they might think of – including, if possible, the differences between Japanese and Western fireworks. The students then held a discussion during the first class about various aspects of fireworks. This is a summary of the discussion:

- Fireworks originated in Japan in the 18th century as part of a memorial for the many who were dying of starvation. Japanese fireworks were let off one by one, with pauses between them for people to appreciate them. The students discussed the idea that the pauses were as important as the sounds of the fireworks themselves, and that this also applied to traditional Japanese music.
- In Japan, during *kabuki* performances, the audience shouts out the actor's stage name at key points during the performance. During fireworks displays, there is a similar tradition wherein people call out "*Tamaya!*" after a display is finished to

show their appreciation for the art. Students found out that the origin of this word is the name of a family, which was famous for making fireworks in the Edo period.
- Fireworks have a meaning of "soul and wish" in Japan. They are used in family memorial services, memorials for victims who died in war, and after great disasters.

The purpose of this homework and discussion was to give the students a firm idea about the sounds, rhythms, and the meaning behind fireworks, in order to help them create their own performances.

At the end of the first class, the students were given another homework assignment. Each student was given a sheet of music with eight blank measures. Their task was to create a rhythm, which they believed expressed fireworks, using what they had discussed in the previous class. They were also required to use dynamic marks to indicate the strength of the beat. The following week, the groups discussed which rhythm or rhythms to develop. They were entirely free to choose the rhythm they thought was best.

The activity's basic idea came from Jaques-Dalcroze method, which involves asking students to physically react to music notes, including dynamic marks, etc. These included legato, marcato, and staccato movements. This cooperative group work allowed the students to "experience timing, space, strength and weight, creativity, and cooperative learning," and "[b]y adding rhythmic movement to music, students acknowledged the body as the first instrument of expression." (Dutoit, 1971, p. 9)

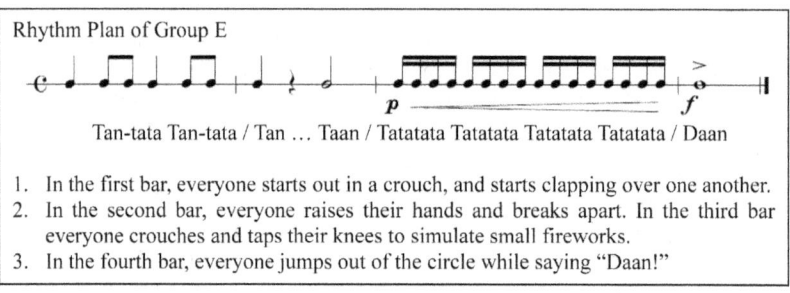

Figure 1. An partial example of the rhythm plan one group decided on

Originally the discussion was only planned for thirty minutes, but the students were so involved in the activity that they spent the whole 90 minutes on it. Usually students in elementary and junior high school do not have this kind of discussion in music class, so they were not used to it. The author observed that through this activity the students practiced both verbal and non-verbal communication. After the students performed to each other, they watched a video taken of sixth-grade elementary school students doing the same activity.

Results

After this lecture, students were issued with evaluation cards, on which they wrote what they felt about the activity. The author divided the resulting comments into three main categories, which are detailed below.

Comments Mainly Concerning Physical Expression
- Although I felt it was difficult to connect the image of fireworks with physical expression, once we actually did it, it was quite easy.
- Through actually doing the activity myself, I discovered how interesting it is to connect something like fireworks, which the children enjoy in their daily life, with music.
- I was impressed that the 6th grade children had much better ideas and more flexible imaginations than we did.
- Expressing my own ideas and feelings physically using my body was very difficult at first, but it ended up being a very important activity.
- I was able to discover that using the whole body to do an activity can cultivate communicative abilities. When I become a teacher, I want to use this activity in my classes. If possible, I would like to learn more about using physical expression to teach music.

Comments Mainly Concerning Expression and Communication
- I enjoyed the fact that there was not one answer, and that I could just try and express exactly what I felt.
- I was very happy not to hear words like "good", "bad", "well done", "needs improvement", etc.
- Because there were lots of opportunities to make decisions for ourselves, it was much more fun than performing an already-existing piece.
- Although everybody shared the same historical background information on fireworks, each group had a different interpretation. The way people feel and the way they express themselves is very different from person to person. I think it is very important to remember this.
- By objectively observing what other people did, I was able to discover the diversity of individual ways people have of expressing themselves.

Comments Mainly Concerning the Integration of Music and Physical Expression, and Cooperation with Others
- It was the first time I experienced a music class incorporating a cultural aspect of Japan and physical expression. I think this kind of integrated activity is more effective for children. I felt the importance of Integrated Studies.
- I was surprised at the integration of thinking activities with physical expression. It is important to have a clear idea of the rhythm and movement you want.
- It is better for children to express themselves and have fun, rather than just performing a set piece of music.
- Enjoying music should mean enjoying as a group, not just individually.
- It is important to create an environment where anyone can enjoy creating music.
- Students should have so much fun that they don't realize they are learning a lot.
- When we created our performance, we tried to express physically the idea that the firework includes people's hopes and prayers. It was very difficult, but we managed to create an image that everyone understood.
- Through this experimental class, I was able to learn something unique about the Japanese cultural background while also making music.

Conclusion

The new Course of Study emphasizes the importance of critical thinking, communication skills and language ability, among many others. The PISA results from 2006 show that Japanese students' ability to communicate and collaborate with one another is not high enough. We can conclude that the new Course of Study may have been influenced by the PISA results. Music is no exception. In the author's opinion Music could in fact be an excellent way to achieve MEXT's goals.

As the author mentioned in the beginning of this paper, the current Music curriculum could be improved by introducing more creative activities. For instance, current Japanese Music education leans too much on singing and instrumental activities, even though children do not necessarily have the required skills – reading *solfège*, for example – to be able to positively participate in the class. Music Making can be effective in changing this.

However, to provide students with these opportunities, their teachers need to be trained in how to think critically, collaborate and communicate well with others. This is something that needs to be done during the teachers' original university training. Unfortunately, teaching hours are limited, and activities such as the one described in this paper cannot be used constantly. If there were a way to include such activities regularly, the skills students gain from them would be constantly reinforced.

From the students' responses to the activity, expressing imagination through physical activity seemed very difficult in theory, but actually doing it was easy and enjoyable. They also realized the importance of cultivating children's imagination and critical thinking ability. They were able to recognize the other groups' performances and respect them, as well as enjoying their ability to freely express themselves. For example, two of the groups called out "*Tamaya!*" at the end of the performance, which showed they had gained a real understanding of traditional culture.

Having experienced the enjoyment that can be gained from such activities, they are eager to share it with the children in their future classroom. It is very important that the students understand these things, so that when they become teachers, they can support children's classroom activities better. From the various students' comments, it is clear that the process of gaining the knowledge and discussing it that the activity provided meant they were highly motivated when creating their own presentation. As was mentioned in one of the comments, students' creativity is more likely to come out if they are not constantly told that something is "good" or "bad", "right" or "wrong".

For a long time, the author faced the problem that students' musical ability varies enormously. All students are required to take certain courses in order to receive an elementary school teaching license, but their mixed abilities make it difficult to teach such a class. However, the author observed that in the fireworks activity, the playing field was leveled, and everyone could positively participate. Considering these factors, it is evident that Integrated Studies can be extremely effective, and that by integrating music with other areas, students can gain a wealth of abilities and skills. In order to fully realize this potential, Integrated Studies should be encouraged throughout the education system in Japan.

Acknowledgments

This research was supported by a Grant-in-Aid for Scientific Research (C) from the Japan

Society for the Promotion of Science. With the help of this grant, the author had a chance to study in the U.S.A. and observe many classes in schools all over Japan, and in Taiwan, which has the most progressive Integrated Studies program in Asia. The author would like to express special thanks to both Mr. Uchimi and Mrs. Sumitani for their assistance with this research. They are teachers at public elementary schools in Niigata prefecture. The author would also like to express thanks to Professor Emeritus Maxine Greene, whose lectures at Teachers College Columbia University first inspired the author to become interested in Integrated Studies. Professor Greene's advocation of "wide awakeness" through learning from different arts can cultivate students' imagination. In the author's opinion, the Japanese educational system could benefit greatly from this type of integrated study.

References

Abramson, R. M. (1994). *Dalcroze Eurhythmics*. VHS video tape teaching material, New York: Julliard School.

Chosky, L., Abramson, R. M., Gillespie, A. E., Woods, D., & York, F. (2000). *Teaching Music in the Twenty-First Century*. (2nd ed.). Upper Saddle River, NJ: Prentice Hall.

Dutoit, C. L. (1971). *Music movement therapy*. Geneva: Institut Jaques-Dalcroze.

Koizumi, F. (1980). *Theory of the uselessness of musical notes*. Tokyo: Seido sha.

Ministry of Education, Culture, Sports, Science and Technology (MEXT). (2008a). *The Guide of Course of Study for Integrated Study at Elementary School*. Tokyo：Toyokan syuppan.

Ministry of Education, Culture, Sports, Science and Technology (MEXT). (2008b). *The Guide of Course of Study for Music at Elementary School*. Tokyo：Kyoiku geijyutsu sha.

Tokie, N. (2009a). The importance of integrated arts curriculum for Japanese students: Increasing motivation for learning and cultivating self-expression. *Proceedings of the 7th Asia-Pacific Symposium on Music Education Research (APSMER)*, Shanghai, China, 473-478.

Tokie, N. (2009b). *The practice and theory of integrated arts curriculum*. Tokyo: Kyoiku geijyutsu sya.

Tokie, N. (2010). Using cross-curricular classes to help meet the mandated goals of Japanese music classes. *Proceedings of the 29th ISME World Conference, Beijing, China*, 203-206.

Tokie, N. (2011a). A practical study of the arts curriculum in Japanese teacher education: cultivating undergraduate and postgraduate students' creativity through use of the U.S. model. *Proceedings of the 8th Asia-Pacific Symposium on Music Education Research (APSMER)*, Taipei, Taiwan, Chapter 20, 1-11.

Tokie, N. (2011b). Integrating music activities with other subjects: A way to make Japanese school music more inclusive. *Proceedings of the 8th Asia-Pacific Symposium on Music Education Research (APSMER)*, Taipei, Taiwan, Chapter 25, 1-10.

Tokie, N., Endo, Y., Kami, M., & Muto, T. (2008). Effectiveness of integrated arts curriculum for Japanese students and plans for the future model in Japanese schools: To cultivate communication skills. *Proceedings of the 28th ISME World Conference, Bologna, Italy*, 297- 303.

Undergraduate Music Students' Perceptions on their Preparation for the Teaching Profession

Angeliki Triantafyllaki
National and Kapodistrian University of Athens (Greece)
atriant@cantab.net

Smaragda Chrysostomou
National and Kapodistrian University of Athens (Greece)
schrysos@music.uoa.gr

Abstract

This paper presents findings from a research investigation into Greek undergraduate music students' perceptions on their preparation for the teaching profession. The wider study on which this paper is based was conducted during 2009-10, and adopted a mixed-methods approach. Semi-structured interviews with 18 recent graduates and final year undergraduate students were followed by a 15-item questionnaire that was completed by 139 undergraduates across four University Music Departments. This presentation focuses on data from the questionnaire study that aimed to map students' views on teaching, their preparedness for the profession, through the various types of knowledge they developed during their undergraduate studies and the nature of students' placements. Findings emphasized the perceived lack of pedagogical preparation for the majority of participating students. Tension was evident between the stated high possibility of engaging with teaching upon graduation and the fact that only half the sample had completed some form of teaching placement at the time of the study even though the majority of students were in their final year. Implications for the organization of teacher education courses within Greek undergraduate music degrees are discussed.

Keywords
Student perceptions, teacher education, university curricula

Introduction

While degree specializations in music teacher education have yet to be established in the Greek higher education sector, the need to incorporate subjects relating to teacher preparation in university curricula has become eminent in recent years due to the high numbers of university graduates that eventually enter the teaching profession. Yet, while there has been an increase in research that focuses on teachers' classroom music practice, fewer studies have focused on the preparation undergraduate students receive during their higher education. This paper presentation reports on a study conducted during 2009-10 across four University Music Departments that focused on undergraduate students' perceptions of their pedagogical preparation. We initially present an overview of teacher education in Greece, before presenting data from the questionnaire study. We conclude with a discussion and some implications regarding the implementation of teacher education courses in university music curricula.

Teacher education in Greece: An overview

Teacher education in Greece is not a homogenous field and significant differences exist in the educational and professional development of primary and secondary school teachers. For specialist teachers intending to teach in secondary education, there is no organized pedagogical preparation (a specific module, for example) during their university degree; the same holds true for university music degrees.

During the last twenty years the advancement of Greek education was directly linked to the necessity for better teacher education (Babiniotis, 1990; Chrysostomou, 2009; Kazamias, 1990; Kossyvaki, 2003). Numerous educational reforms have been organized and applied in an effort to "cure the diagnosed educational maladies" (Kazamias, 1990, p.33) yet proving to be just another episode in the 'Sisyphean task' of Greek educational reform (Kazamias, 1990). Only recently in 2010 as part of the latest educational reform did a concrete proposal for teacher preparation appear. This consists of a teacher-training module including general and special educational subjects, as well as teaching practice and it would be a prerequisite for any future school teacher.

Today there are four Departments for Music Studies in operation:

1. Department of Music Studies – Aristotle University of Thessaloniki (est.1985).
2. Department of Music Studies – National and Kapodistrian University of Athens (est.1991).
3. Department of Music Studies – Ionian University of Corfu (est.1992).
4. Department of Music Science and Art – University of Macedonia in Thessaloniki (est.1998).

Although music education is considered one of the areas of interest, only recently have some steps been taken to develop this as a clear and separate degree specialization. An ongoing comparative study looking at the syllabi, the staff specializations, the number of subjects and students' views over the last 12 years (1998-2010) reveals significant developments in the area of music education (Chrysostomou, 1997; Chrysostomou, 2005). For example, syllabi in the initial years included one or two subjects related to education and music education whereas more recently the number of related subjects offered (compulsory and electives) in each department has significantly increased.

Aim of the Project and Method

In view of these developments, the current research investigation aimed to explore the parameters relevant to students' preparation for the teaching profession from the students' point of view. More specifically, we were interested in exploring the kinds of knowledge and skills relevant to teaching that students develop through their undergraduate studies as well as the perceived gaps in their preparation for the teaching profession. We hoped that the study would provide a more informed view of the current situation in teacher preparation in the Greek university sector.

A mixed methods approach was adopted that aimed to explore initial experiences of teaching as well as provide an overview of the perceived teacher preparation that currently takes place in university music departments. The study was conducted across two interrelated stages:

Qualitative stage: we aimed to access graduate students and final year undergraduates' views on their initial experiences of teaching, as well as their university teaching preparation through semi-structured interviews ($n = 18$); Quantitative stage: drawing on interview data, we designed a 15-item, closed-question questionnaire that focused specifically on:

1. student teaching experience and views of teaching as a career; 2. characteristics of teaching placements and the perceived benefits gained,; and 3. perceived gaps in current university curricula.

The final form of the questionnaire was designed in accordance with the feedback from a pilot study whereby five students completed the questionnaire and provided valuable feedback with regards to wording and content. The sample for both qualitative and quantitative stages was purposely selected. For the quantitative stage, we aimed to access undergraduates who had completed their first two years of studies (i.e. were already in their 3rd year) and to include similar numbers of students overall across the four universities. The questionnaire was distributed across the four university music departments in Greece, by both email and face-to-face distribution. The computer-based program SPSS for Windows was used to conduct the descriptive analysis of the questionnaire data presented here.

Research Findings

A total of 139 students completed the questionnaire. Table 1 reveals the sample distribution across university music departments and across year of study. With regards to students' year of study it should be noted that three of the four University Departments have a five-year undergraduate course, while one Department has a four-year course. The majority of the sample have completed their 3rd year at University (N = 102); the >5 category reflects students that have not yet taken the examinations for all the required subjects but have completed the required number of terms in order to graduate (irrelevant of the length of their course).

Student teaching experience – Views of teaching as a career

More than half of the sample state they have already gained some teaching experience during their studies. Interestingly this seems to be the case also in most year groups (4th = 63.2%, 5th = 83.3%, >5 = 64.7%). This picture is similar also for students in their 3rd year with 48.6% of students in their 3rd year state they have teaching experience, with 51.4% stating they do not.

This teaching experience seems to have been gained for the most part in private tutoring (one-to-one lessons) in an instrument (38.1%) or in music theory (22.3%). Other types of teaching experience were teaching theory classes (24.5%) or choirs/instruments (21.6%) at a Conservatoire (similar to a specialist music school). Interestingly some students mention they had teaching experience from special education settings (7.2%) and from volunteer work (12.9%); both forms of placement experiences could be explored further with regards to initial teacher education.

Table 1. Description of sample.

Distribution across Departments			Distribution across year of studies		
Music department	No.	Perc.	Year	No.	Perc.
Athens	25	18%	3	37	26.6%
Thessaloniki	49	35.3%	4	38	27.3%
Ionian	32	23%	5	30	21.6%
Macedonia	33	23.7%	>5	34	24.5%
Total	139	100%	Total	139	100%

When inquiring about the extent to which students thought they would teach after graduation, the findings reveal that 16.6% of the total sample indicates they would be teaching for 50% or less of their time, while the remaining 83.4% position themselves from 50% upwards. At the higher end of this spectrum, 20.9% indicate they would be teaching for 80% of their time, and 20.1% for 90% of their time. These results are especially encouraging as they reveal that the majority of participating students understand that they might engage with teaching not simply as a form of income during their undergraduate studies, but also more formally as a career after graduation.

Characteristics of teaching placements – Perceived benefits

All four Universities offer some form of teaching placement, whereby undergraduates will enter a classroom to observe teaching or to teach themselves. This differs greatly among the four Departments. 42.4% of the sample has completed some form of placement during their studies; this percentage rises as students proceed through their studies, with 50% of 5th year students stating they have completed some form of teaching placement.

The length of placement varies with the majority of students stating it lasted less the four weeks (27.3% of the total sample) and 15.1% stating it lasted more than four weeks. The number of hours spent teaching on these placements seems to vary with 21.6% of those that had completed the placement stating they had taught for 5 hours or less. Just 7.2% of the sample had taught for 12 hours or more.

These findings can be examined in relation to the variations in the program of studies across the four Departments that participated in the research, with some Departments offering more and others less time for classroom teaching experience as part of a teaching placement. If taking into account, however, the perceived benefits of this experience as reported below in Table 2, it would seem that the time offered during undergraduate courses for actual teaching experience would need to be increased.

The data presented in Table 2 reveals that students' perceptions of the benefits gained from their placement experiences are structured around two main axes: knowledge of music pedagogy and "soft skills" relevant also to teaching practice. In the first category, we observe high percentage of students benefitting from the preparation of teaching materials (28.8%) during their placement, as well as specific knowledge of didactics of music (lesson organization, aims, goals, etc.) (21.6%). In the second category, a range of skills are emphasized, such as communication (23.7%), classroom management (20.9%), responsibility (18%), patience (16.5%) and others. This picture initially seems to be a positive one, if taking into account that the majority of students that completed the placement (21.6%) had taught for 5 hours or less. However, these data seem to suggest also that the overall length of students' placements as well as their organization and structure require further attention.

Table 2. Perceived benefits of teaching during placements

Classroom management	20.9	Taking incentives	13.7	Time management	15.8
Communication	23.7	Responsibility	18.0	Preparation of teaching materials	28.8
Flexibility/adaptability	15.8	Confidence	10.8	Didactics of music	21.6
Familiarization with educational settings	12.9	Knowledge of school curricula	6.5	Familiarization with school books	4.3
Needs of different pupil ages	15.1	Patience	16.5	Music content knowledge	9.4

Perceived Gaps in University Music Curricula

Two additional questions aimed to gather information on students' perceptions of the shortcomings in their courses of study. The first inquired about inclusion of further space in the curricula for the following key themes from the initial interview study. We note also the percentage of the total sample that indicated a need to include in future curricula:

- Subjects in Educational Psychology (72.7%)
- Subjects in Music Pedagogy and Didactics (61.2%)
- Hours of teaching in schools/conservatoires (53.2%)
- Preparation of teaching materials (50.4%)
- Hours of observing teaching in schools/conservatoires (40.3%)
- Supervision during teaching by tutor (31.7%)

While quite significant improvements in musicians' pedagogic preparation have taken place in recent years, these results continue to reveal perceived gaps in both pedagogic theory and practice.

The second question returns to the knowledge and skills of Table 2, now inquiring which of these students hoped to have improved through their studies (and still hadn't), keeping in mind always the fact that students from year 3 onwards completed the questionnaire (not only final year students). While the findings present small differences to the perceived benefits from students' placements, they seem to confirm the need for the organization of more systematic theoretical and practical teacher training for prospective teachers. Again, high percentages are clustered around two similar (to teaching placements) categories:

1. knowledge of music pedagogy: preparation of teaching materials (41%), knowledge of school books (25.9%),
2. soft skills relevant to teaching: classroom management (39.6%), communication (38.8%), time management (30.9%), confidence (28.1%).

Two further axes complete the picture of perceived gaps in courses of study:

3. musical content knowledge (23.7%),
4. needs of different ages (28.1%).

These findings do not come as a surprise if taking into account students' requirement for more subjects in both pedagogical music theory and practice.

Conclusions and Implications for Music Education

The results reveal an overall requirement for better quality teacher preparation that, despite the many improvements in the higher education sector in this area, continues to remain at the forefront of many music students' needs during their initial training. The perceived shortcomings in students' pedagogical preparation were focused around a broad spectrum of areas that includes both theoretical knowledge (didactics, preparation of materials, educational psychology) and practical knowledge and skills (classroom management, time management, communication, adaptability). Much of this knowledge-base for teaching is acquired during the teaching placement. The findings call for allowing students to complete teaching placements early on in their studies (students may have teaching experience from as early as their 3rd year), extending the placement to include more hours of actual teaching, and organizing the placement to provide systematic and informed mentoring by either the tutor or the classroom/conservatoire teacher. The role of peer-feedback and reflection through written and oral work is equally important (Pultorak, 2010).

The lack of a specialized teacher training course hinders the preparation of music teachers in Greek higher music education. The existing subjects and current teacher placements continue to be part of a general undergraduate music syllabus, too wide to create specializations that will effectively prepare student-teachers for the teaching profession. The recent compulsory addition to future teachers' preparation –the new teacher training module– could form a framework for organized and systematic pedagogical education and training. However, in designing this module a number of issues regarding its content and structure would need to be taken under consideration including: the role of music inside and outside the classroom, the music teacher's role, and the overall responsibility of the university and its partnership with schools. Further systematic research activity in this area both within and across University Music Departments, with clear outcomes and suggestions for ways forward, continues to be required.

Acknowledgements

This study was funded through the Postdoctoral Scholarship scheme of the Greek State Scholarship Foundation, which the authors gratefully acknowledge. Special thanks are offered to students and graduates who gave their time to be interviewed or complete the questionnaire, as well as University colleagues who assisted in its distribution.

References

Babiniotis, G. (1990, November 11). The education of the teachers. (in Greek). *Newspaper To Vima.*

Chrysostomou, S. (1997). *The initial education of Greek music teachers. Are there lessons to be learned from a study of the English system?* (Unpublished doctoral thesis). Reading, UK: University of Reading.

Chrysostomou, S. (2005). Pedagogical aspects in the preparation of Greek music teachers. *Proceedings of the RIME Conference.* Exeter, UK: University of Exeter.

Chrysostomou, S. (2009). Education of music teachers: Contemporary challenges (in Greek). In X. Papapanagiotou (Ed.), *Issues in music education.* Thessaloniki, Greece: GSME.

Kazamias, A. M. (1990). The curse of Sisyphus in Greek educational reform: A sociopolitical and cultural interpretation. *Modern Greek Studies Yearbook, 6*, 33-53.

Kossyvaki, F. (2003). *The role of the teacher in a meta-neoteristic school: Expectations, prospects, limitations* (in Greek). Athens, Greece: Gutenberg.

Pultorak, E. G. (Ed.). (2010). *The purposes, practices, and professionalism of teacher reflectivity: Insights for twenty-first-century teachers and students*. Lanham, MD: Rowman & Littlefield Education.

5000 Languages, 5000 Ways to Sing?

Valerie L. Trollinger
Kutztown University of Pennsylvania (USA)
trolling@kutztown.edu

Abstract
Research concerning the history of singing predominantly addresses the use of singing as a cultural phenomenon rather than as a physiological one. While linguistic anthropologists surmise that there are about 5000 distinct languages in the world, the relationship of the physical act of speaking to the physical act of singing at the etiological level has yet to be researched. This paper presents an introduction to possible relationships, and encourages research in this area to be developed.

Keywords
Anthropology, language, speech, singing, vocal anatomy, linguistics

Introduction
Singing is a widespread activity of music making all over the world. While all cultures engage in singing, how singing developed to be different yet similar among world cultures presents an opportunity for an intriguing investigation. The possibility of unrelated cultures of the world sharing similar vocalization characteristics used in singing, as found in Trollinger (2006), suggested that vocal behaviors were shared and evolved among cultures via human migration. Comparing and contrasting singing in different cultures in relationship to language characteristics, vocalization characteristics and development in singing could yield interesting implications for music education on a global level. Therefore, the purpose of this paper is to investigate the relationship of singing to linguistics, vocal use, vocal anthropology, neurobiology, and human evolution.

Evolution of the Human Larynx
According to anthropologists, the larynx was placed fairly high in the vocal tract prior to Neanderthals (Mithen, 2006). The purpose for the high larynx was to keep food and liquid out of the air passageway, so the glottal area would close and open as needed (Hast, 1985). Homo sapiens babies have a very high larynx at birth, but it starts to descend around the age of four months. Neanderthals were the first human species to have a larynx that was lowered and suspended, like modern Homo sapiens, which allowed humans to create sounds by sending air through the glottal area since the vocal bands were free to vibrate. The hyoid bone, first found in Neanderthals, was the strongest indicator of the ability to move the larynx vertically. Because the muscles are attached to the hyoid bone, the larynx is suspended and it functions as both an airway protector and flexible producer of sound

(Kay, Cartmill, & Barlow, 1998). However, research contradicts the findings that the simple presence of a hyoid bone does not necessarily indicate the ability for speech, due to a number of cranial and oral features that would make it difficult for Neanderthal to create the vowel sounds necessary for speech (DeGusta, Gilbert, & Turner 1999).

Early Human Voice and Language Development

There are two main theories of how language developed (Mithen, 2006). The first and perhaps oldest theory argued at present proposes that language developed purposefully, with a sense of syntax and grammar (Leiberman & Crelin, 1971), while the competing theory is that language was based in vocalizations that were meant to manipulate others' behavior, closely associated with researcher Allison Wray (1998). These vocalizations could be pitched sounds, grunts, cries, yelps, and so forth. Although there are no recordings of Neanderthal vocalizations, it has been hypothesized that they were quite high, because of the limited laryngeal movement and placement. Robert McCarthy, an anthropologist at Florida Atlantic University (2011), Boca Raton, electronically reconstructed how a Neanderthal voice may have sounded. The vocal sample of the Neanderthal sounds very rough and pressed, suggesting that singing as we know it may have been very limited and not very pleasant. Anthropological evidence suggests that they were able to make some that may have been created for self-soothing or for very primitive vocalizing or communications.

Steven Mithen in *The singing Neanderthals* (2006) suggests that singing was developed to express emotion, although one must take issue with that claim. If singing were developed only as a way to express emotion (he also includes instrumental music in this definition), the there would be many emotionally exhausted musicians in this world. In anthropological research, intermediate vocal productions between speech and singing, namely elongated pitched vocalizations, are generally not addressed, implying that humans moved from speech to singing, or from singing to speech, without an intermediate area of development and exploration. Elongated vocalizations could be used not only to express emotion, but also serve as a simple overt function of the voice. We use singing (simply defined as elongated sounds put together into some kind of recognizable tune which may or may not have musical structure) as an aid to memorization, to self soothe, to simply experiment with vocal sound, or to mask unpleasant sounds (for example, vocalizing with one's fingers in one's ears). Not all vocalizations, of which some may be incorrectly defined as singing, are meant to express emotion. Whether language developed prior to singing vocalization styles, or the different singing vocalization styles allowed the emergence of different languages to develop is unclear and is not possible to investigate, although it is interesting to hypothesize abut it. Mithen puts the number of world languages at close to 5000. Since we have at least 5000 languages, does the mean that we also have 5000 discrete ways to sing as well?

Physical and Neurobiological Development of Language in Humans

At the simplest level, there are two distinct theories regarding the development of language, the semantic/grammatical model proposed and advocated by Leiberman & Crelin (1971), and the holistic development model advocated by Alison Wray. In addition, some other subtheories generally related to Wray' holistic model are also in the running such as

Stephen Brown's "musilanguage" (Brown, 1999) and Mithen's own HMMMM model (Mithen, 2006) that provoke a great amount of criticism (Christiensen-Dalsgaard, 2007). While both theories claim there are musical elements that are part of language development, neither accounts for differences in singing vocalization styles and languages. More problematic is that language is more often connected to music in terms of only melody making, meaning of words, and instrumental performance, not to the actual vocal styles that make one culture's singing different from or similar to another's. This neglect is especially distressing to musicologists reviewing Mithen's recent work (Christiensen-Dalsgaard, 2007).

In the history of linguistic development, there are two important aspects that need to be considered: 1. neurobiological aspects of language and phonation; and 2. the production of vowels. Neanderthals shared a FOXP2 transcriptor, which regulates some genetic behaviors, with Homo sapiens, but were restricted by their own vocal anatomy to do very much with it in terms of developing discrete and distinct spoken languages, since their production of vowels was limited. The use of stopped sounds, such as in consonants, click sounds, and rolling r's are further indicators of different languages. Why humans learned to add particular stylistic sounds as they evolved is a mystery although historical linguists believe that accents are binding characteristics that give groups cultural identity and membership. Many of these kinds of accents can remain unobservable when singing. For example, having lived in North Carolina in the US, I noticed that there are at least four different accents (although there may be more) that are all considered Southern within that state but are distinctly different from each other by how the vowels are pronounced. It is not possible to tell by accent alone where one is from in North Carolina by hearing one sing. One cannot say the same for a person who natively speaks Mandarin singing an American folk song—because of the language pronunciation differences, the song also sounds different and it is not difficult to identify the singer as Chinese.

Neurobiological aspects of language development and singing reveal that FOXP2 has a strong regulatory function on the physical aspects of physically forming words and creating vocal sounds, and also affects perception of musical rhythm (Alcock, Passingham, Watkins & Vargha-Khadam, 2001). Its connection to singing in humans is not clear, however research concerning songbirds (who share FOXP2 with humans) suggests that it may affect singing behavior. Another genetic component is the AVPR1A receptor, specifically the RS1 and RS3 haplotype that is strongly present in families of Finnish musicians. AVPR1A haplotype RS 1, found in most human beings, provides the genetic foundation for human preference for listening to music. These AVPR1A genes also affect intrinsic attachment behavior in humans (Ukkola-Vuoti, Oikkonen, Onkamo, Karma, Raijas, & Järvelä, 2009, 2011). Research concerning the influence of other FOX transcriptors is currently underway.

Effects of Migration

Migratory and dispersal paths out of Africa (Mithen, 2006) suggest that many of our world languages are closely related. In 2006, Trollinger listened to a number of native songs sung by cultural natives and investigated the manner in which the sounds were produced. Several world cultures investigated in the study (Chinese, Malaysia, India China, Yeman, Russia, Belize Equatorial Africa, the USA, and Japan) shared a number of production characteristics that were indicative of vocal hyperfunction. Singers from India, Ireland,

Indonesia, and Equador had pronounced nasality, while the African-Caribbean singers indicated the least amount of vocal stress in their singing. It is interesting to hypothesize that while our spoken language took on numerous distinctive qualities, perhaps vocalizations for speech were not adaptable in the physical act of singing to continue the signature sounds of particular languages. Perhaps instead we have evolved into a world culture with over 5000 languages, but not 5000 ways to sing.

Evolution of Linguistics and Language

Linguistic anthropologists often cite the biblical reference to Babel as a starting point to investigate the origins of today's modern languages (NOVA, 1997). Emerging from hypothesis and hard data are the foundations of the main families of language (about 200) in the world with the largest being: Indo-European, Sino-Tibetan, Austronesian, Afroasiatic, Altaic, Dravidian, and Australian-Aborignial. American Indian languages are difficult to fit into any of these families, and remain unique. The largest groups are the Indo-European and Sino-Tibtetan language families. English is an Indo-European language, while Chinese languages are Sino-Tibetan (NOVA, 1997). Languages are associated by shared characteristics such as construction, intonation, and vocabulary. For example, in Indo-European languages, Italian and Spanish share similar yet different names for the title of Miss: in Italian, the word is "Signorina" while in Spanish it is "Senorita." Interesting in terms of this paper is that singing characteristics also seem to branch across families, perhaps suggesting that we are more related in our singing vocalization characteristics than may have been thought. While there may be 5000 languages in the world, there really may only be about 200 singing families within those 5000. The evidence earlier presented concerning Trollinger's (2006) findings, when viewed with this knowledge, doesn't seem unusual.

Connections between culture and musical language have been studied by Patel, Iverson, and Rosenberg (2004). When asked to identify a piece of music as either English or French, listeners were able to do so. Patel concluded that the temporal and accentual patterning distinctive in those languages provided underlying connective clues to assist the listeners. However, the two music choices were problematic and may have essentially skewed the response. The piece composed by the British composer Edward Elgar was of a different style and of different instrumentation than the second piece by Claude Debussy, which had a predominant English horn solo, not unusual because of the French composers' strong use of double reed instruments in the early 20th century. If Patel had used a piece by a French composer, with similar orchestration to the Elgar piece, such as in Berlioz's *Symphonie Fantastique*, then the results may have been different. Moreover, being able to identify these pieces correctly depended upon a certain amount of familiarity with Western music. Perhaps using two Asian works instead would have yielded different findings. While connections concerning instrumental music and language have been investigated, the same has not happened for singing, as accents and intonations can disappear while singing. Identifying a singer by nationality may be more difficult.

Singing and Speech

Speech can be produced in any number of ways: as clicks, as tonal or non-tonal pitched, and with consonants produced at the front, back, or even the middle of the mouth. Not all singing can take place in the same manner, since some of the sounds would not be able to happen concurrently during phonation (for example, click sounds) although some sounds can be added to embellish the meaning of the song. Tonal considerations are even more important, because the cultural meaning of the word depends upon where it is placed in the tonal language, thus songs that are sung in particular tonal languages may take these meanings into consideration. Some research has indicated that language may be an aid to singing development (Chen-Haftek, 1998; Mang, 2006; Trollinger, 2004) with tonal singers at an advantage over non-tonal singers.

According to Daniel Levitin (2008) in *The World in Six Songs*, all cultures engage in song singing for a number of reasons: to share friendship, joy, comfort, knowledge, religion and love. While this theory is interesting, the book promotes the use of melody to enhance the meaning of the language—the music is second to the text, since the text drives the melodic aspects of the song. Since these songs are so strongly text-based, then the assumption would be made that the language pronunciation characteristics would translate directly into the song. For several cultures, this is very true. For example, in Chinese opera, the style of singing is perhaps less based on the traditional European classical opera *appoggio* style of singing (Miller, 1996) to meet the needs of the language and meaningful communication.

5000 Languages, 200 Ways to Sing?

While language may divide us, it may be more likely that singing unites us on many levels, not only as a human cultural activity but also in the manner in which it is physically produced. Most ethnomusicological research on singing within cultures has generally addressed the manner in which it is used, but there has been little investigation and inquiry in how it is produced among cultures that are related and non-related. Based on Trollinger's previous findings, plus the current research on vocal anthropology, it seems likely that while we have perhaps 5000 languages, we may have closer to 200 singing styles in our world, and it may be possible that within those 200 styles, there may be a number of surprising relationships. Perhaps answers to the following questions may be forthcoming in future research:

- Are vocal behaviors used in singing directly related to language?
- Are there genetic factors that contribute to the production of singing that are related directly to the production of speech and language?
- What is the physical relationship of singing to speech production in particular languages?
- How difficult is it to authentically learn and perform songs in languages that are not related?
- Historically, how did the human singing voice develop in relationship to language and speech vocalization characteristics?

Conclusions

While there is no research yet available concerning the physical development of the human singing voice across the ages, the research presented in this paper suggests that while our languages may number in the thousands, perhaps our styles of singing number less across the world cultures. While our languages may separate us, our styles of singing may actually unify us at a level in which the words do not matter.

References

Alcock, K., Passingham, R., Watkins, K., & Vargha-Khadem, F. (2001) Pitch and timing abilities in inherited speech and language impairment. *Brain and Language, 75*, 34-46.

Brown, S. (1999) The musiclanguage model of music evolution. In N. Wallin, B. Merker, & S. Brown (Eds.), *The origins of music* (pp. 271-300). Cambridge, MA: MIT Press.

Chen-Haftek, L. (1998). Pitch abilities in music and language of Cantonese–speaking children. *International Journal of Music Education, 21*, 14-24.

Christiensen-Dalsgaard, J. (2007). Review of Steven Mithen: The singing Neanderthals. *The Journal of Musicand Meaning, 5*, section 7. Retrieved from http://www.musicandmeaning.net/issues/showArticle.php?artID=5.7

DeGusta, D., Gilbert, W. H., & Turner, S. P. (1999). Hypoglossal canal size and hominid speech. *Proceedings of the National Academy of Sciences, USA, 96*(4) 1800-1804.

Florida Atlantic University. (2011). *Neanderthal man speaks again*. Retrieved from http://www.fau.edu/explore/homepage-stories/2008-04speaks.php

Hast, M. (1985). Comparative anatomy of the larynx: Evolution and function. In I. Titze (Ed.), *Vocal fold physiology: Biomechanics, acoustics and phonatory control.* Denver, CO: The Denver Center for the Performing Arts.

Kay, R., Cartmill, M., & Barlow, M. (1998). The hypoglassal canal and the origin of human vocal behavior. *Proceedings of the National Academy of Sciences, USA, 95*(9), 5417-5419.

Leiberman, P., & Crelin, E. (1971). On the speech of Neanderthal man, *Linguistic Inquiry 2*, 203–222.

Levitin, D. (2008). *The world in six songs*. New York, NY: Plume Publishers Group.

Mang. E. (2006). The effects of age, gender and language on children's singing competency. *British Journal of Music Education, 23*(2), 161-174

Miller, R. (1996). *The structure of singing.* New York, NY: Schirmer Books.

Mithen, S. (2006). The singing neanderthals. Cambridge, MA: Harvard University Press.

NOVA (1997). *In search of first language.* Retrieved from http://www.pbs.org/wgbh/nova/transcripts/2120glang.html

Patel, A., Iversen, J., & Rosenberg, J. (2004, November). *English and French classical music reflect the melody and rhythm of speech in the two cultures*. Paper presented at the 148th Acoustical Society of America Meeting, San Diego, CA.

Trollinger, V. (2004). Preschool children's pitch-matching accuracy in relation to participation in Cantonese-immersion preschools. *Journal of Research in Music Education, 52*, 218-233.

Trollinger, V. (2006, July). *World vocal traditions and vocal health: Is a reconciliation possible?* Paper presented at the 27th International Society for Music Education World Conference, Kuala Lumpur, Malaysia.

Ukkola-Vuoti, L., Oikkonen, J., Onkamo, P., Karma, K., Raijas, P., & Jävelä, I. (2009). *PLoS ONE (4)5*, 5534. doi:10.1371/journal.pone.0005534

Ukkola-Vuoti, L., Oikkonen, J., Onkamo, P., Karma, K., Raijas, P., & Jävelä, I. (2011). Association of the arginine vasopressin receptor 1A (AVPR1A) haplotypes with listening to music. *Journal of Human Genetics, 56,* 324-329.

Wray, A. (1998). Protolanguage as a holistic system for social interaction. *Language and Communication, 18,* 47-67.

Mentoring the Muse: Best Help for Generalist Educators in Kwa-Zulu Natal, South Africa

Caroline van Niekerk
University of Pretoria (South Africa)
caroline@mweb.co.za

Jansen van Vuuren
University of Pretoria (South Africa)

Abstract

This paper focuses on the challenges for and training needs of generalist in-service educators in order to teach the music component of Arts and Culture – a learning area which consists of four art forms; dance, drama, music and visual art. Although the generalist educator also needs to teach the other three art forms, this paper focuses primarily on the music component. The importance of the training of in-service educators for teaching a practical subject like music is examined. The dilemma is discussed through a pragmatic paradigm with the following characteristics: aspects of mixed models, consequences of actions, problem-centeredness, pluralistic and real-world practice orientated. If the education system in South Africa is going to remain as it is with generalist educators being forced into teaching specialist areas, these educators must be capacitated to survive and be capable of equipping learners with basic understanding of music and practical music skills in general. Training material used during mentoring programs must deal with the curriculum systematically and in small sections. Training material must also contain basic notes on content, lessons on DVD and relevant assessment material, memorandums and rubrics. Subject advisors must furthermore ensure that training materials consider the often low language proficiency of educators. Arts and Culture subject advisors need to be specialists to ensure that mentoring programs are successful.

Keywords
Arts and Culture, generalist educators, in-service training, mentoring, music, specialist subject

Introduction

Arts and Culture is a relatively new subject in South African schools, having been phased in during 1998. Very few educators have the knowledge and skills to teach all four components (dance, drama, music and visual art) of the subject. Generalist educators have seldom had Arts and Culture included in their tertiary studies and the few specialist arts educators who are mostly found in previously white schools are trained in one or at the most two of the components. The statement by Ballantyne (2006) that the quality of teaching in general and of music specifically in schools can be directly attributed to the pre-service preparation that educators receive rings very true but does not assist educators who now have to teach a subject for which they have not been trained.

Especially in rural areas, very few classroom educators have had the privilege of being trained in any of the art forms. Most arts courses offered in higher education institutions in South Africa require students to have a background in a specific art form to be allowed into training for that art form. Educators who grew up in rural areas have hardly ever had the opportunity to gain a background in anything but traditional art forms practiced in their communities.

Not having a background of formal music tuition excludes rural learners from studies at tertiary level. In turn, this situation impacts negatively on the learner in rural settings. Unless some sort of intervention program is implemented, the consequences of actions, where educators who are not trained in music cannot assist their learners and their learners can then not study music, will never be broken. Where such educators return to their communities to teach, they repeat the pattern since they do not have the knowledge to develop music competencies in learners. Challenges found in the Arts and Culture classroom for generalist educators as regards music knowledge will be considered alongside models that can assist in developing more competent Arts and Culture educators in government schools in especially rural areas.

Coping without Expertise in a Music Class

All over South Africa, educators are experiencing similar challenges. According to a doctoral study by Eurika Jansen van Vuuren (2011), general challenges in music in Arts and Culture in South Africa highlighted by Senior Education Specialists (subject advisors) included the following: Principals do not regard Arts and Culture as essential (Lewis, 2010). It is a timetable-filler for educators who do not have enough lessons to teach (Mashamaite, 2010). Rademan (2010) says that very few educators have had any training in any of the four art forms and they do not understand how to apply most activities in the learners' textbooks. Smith (2010), like most South African subject advisors, has found that educators are frequently moved between subjects at random without consideration for the fact that they may be in the process of being empowered in Arts and Culture, for example.

Most of the Senior Education Specialists responsible for training educators have not had any specific arts training themselves and are unable to facilitate music as an art form (Crouse 2010). Due to their lack of expertise, subject advisors tend to concentrate on equipping educators with general knowledge "about" music (Elliott, 1995, p. 12) rather than getting into the more practical aspects. According to Smith (2010), facilitators from outside the department are often brought in to empower educators to implement the National Curriculum Statement (NCS) successfully but they tend to be too general in their approach and do not address the curriculum directly. Subject advisors in the department should be utilized to train their educators and thus need to be specialists in the learning areas where they have been appointed. The training will be more real world practice orientated if subject advisors do the training because they have direct contact with educators and have insight into their everyday challenges.

The language of learning and teaching (LOLT) in South African schools is mostly English, yet the majority of educators have difficulty expressing themselves and teaching in

English since it is not their native tongue. To exacerbate the problem, learners are also mostly taught in their second language and find it challenging to answer exam papers and understand their educators. Overall, the majority of educators lack the knowledge to teach the music curriculum. Figure 1 provides an indication of the aspects covered by the curriculum that cannot be taught by most educators (Jansen van Vuuren, 2011).

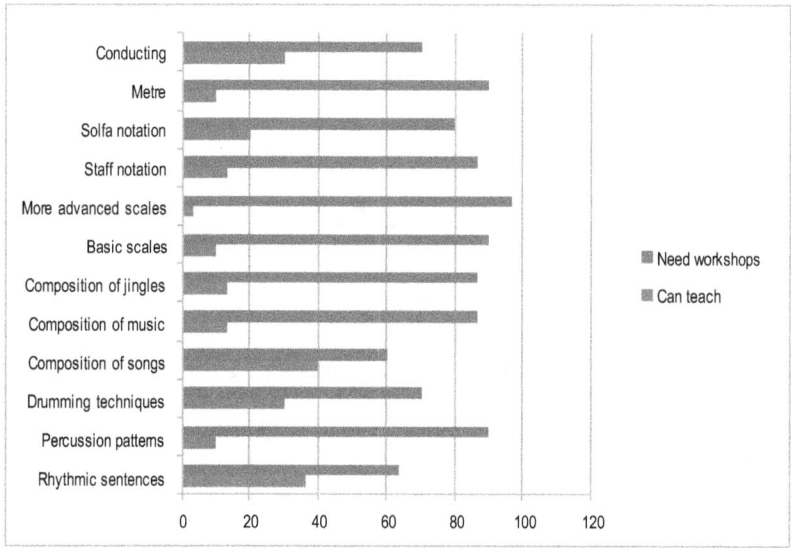

Figure 1. Main challenges amongst educators.

Jansen van Vuuren (2011) found that basic resources are not available at schools in rural areas. Figure 2 shows what is available and what not in schools in rural Kwa-Zulu Natal.

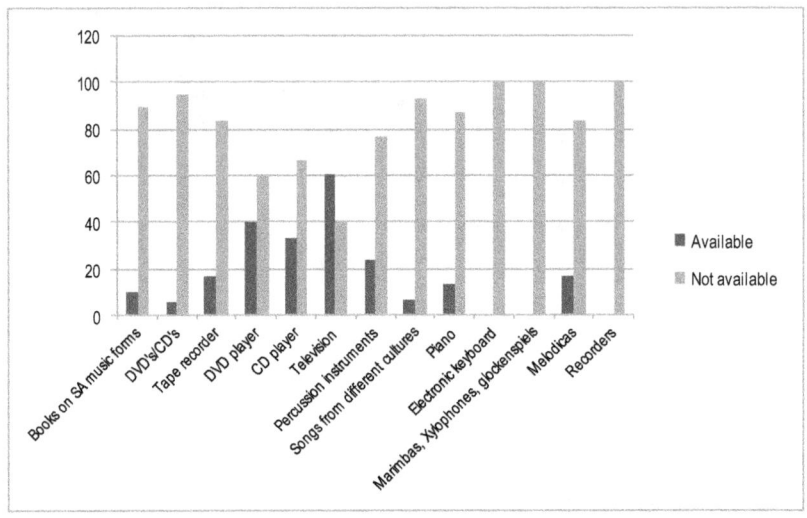

Figure 2. Graph showing available resources for Arts and Culture.

Although a great deal of the music curriculum can be taught without expensive resources, there are some essentials that could lighten the load for the generalist educator.

Music Aid for Generalist Educators

Jansen van Vuuren (2011) found that 93.3 % of Arts and Culture educators in rural Kwa-Zulu Natal do not have any *training* in music, which creates its own set of challenges:

1. Motivating educators to attend training programs despite the low status of the subject;
2. There are big numbers of educators to be trained;
3. Finding a suitable time that will cause the least disruption to educators and learners alike;
4. Securing basic training resources; and
5. Ensuring that the training program is done in simple English and relevant and directly linked to the curriculum.

Although there are models like long distance learning to provide training to educators, a mentoring model is the one that is best suited to the current situation in education in South Africa (Jansen van Vuuren, 2011). All the challenges mentioned above can be addressed with a mentoring model. The mentoring process uses existing human resources that are easier to find in the schooling system than it is to find monetary resources for formal training programs by external parties. The main purpose of a mentoring program is to develop knowledge and teaching skills for the music component of Arts and Culture. Added to the development of content knowledge are school visits where mentors and mentees can meet in the work situation to find solutions to internal problems. In a mentoring program the mentee always has a support system in the form of a mentor and this can only be beneficial to educators in rural areas where resources are scarce. The ideal situation would be that there is only one mentee per mentor – unfortunately that is unrealistic in the South African context where subject advisors have such a large number of educators needing to be mentored. The mentoring program not only has a "top down" approach but also has a lateral motion that includes peer mentoring. In addition, if Education Specialists deal with educators in a sympathetic and empathetic manner, educators will cooperate to make the program successful. Commitment from educators is increased if they are informed that they are going into an official mentoring program and have to adhere to its ethics code.

It will not be easy for mentors to ensure that educators are valued at schools. However, with the extra attention these educators are given, there will be more contact with school principals during school visits. The mentor can then guide the principal into giving the educator the necessary feeling of belonging.

Barry Sweeney (2001) of the International Mentoring Association gives the following fundamental premises for a good mentoring program:

1. We must receive the [gift] of effective mentoring before we can effectively give it to others.
2. When we are given the gift of effective mentoring, we will feel that we can never adequately repay our mentor for giving us such a valuable gift, and we will only be satisfied by passing the gift on to others. (Eleanor Roosevelt said this.)
3. We must understand why the gift we received was valuable to us, so it will be just as valued when we give it to others.
4. If *we* are the mentors, we will probably need a mentor of mentors to do these things and then help us understand the process. (p. 7)

Coupling these premises with the principles named by the Australian Department of Education (2004) makes for a successful recipe:

Commitment: especially by senior managers and executives in the Education Department.
Clarity: of purpose, of desired outcomes, of target group, of resources available and readiness of organization to implement the program.
Communication: that is open so that everyone involved should know about the program.
Confidentiality: so that the mentor-mentee relationship is protected.

- Jansen van Vuuren (2011) developed her mentoring model by combining various other mentoring models. This program is currently being introduced in schools in Kwa-Zulu Natal. The phases of the mentoring model were named by the author as "take-off" (getting to know one another), "full flight" (building knowledge and skills), "gaining confidence in flight" (practicing new skills in the classroom), "landing: departures and destinations" (reflecting on successes of the past and setting future goals), and "spreading wings" (going out and mentoring other educators) (p. 147). The "take-off" phase happens at the beginning of a new academic year where new educators are welcomed and assigned to a cluster group in their region. The "full flight" phase is where content knowledge is developed during formal workshops. During the "gaining confidence in full flight" phase, subject advisors visit educators in their classes to monitor progress and assist with challenges. During cluster meetings, where up to 10 schools are grouped together, the "landing, departures, and destinations" phase is handled. The cluster groups provide a peer mentoring system and these groups are visited by subject advisors on a rotational basis. The "spreading wings" phase does not arrive quickly or easily for some educators. Those who do reach the "spreading wings" phase are of valuable assistance to subject advisors when they run cluster meetings further aid.

Suggested workshop content needs to bear in mind that it is not possible to reach all educators with all the content within a year. Each year is started with an orientation workshop where work schedules and curriculum are discussed along with assessment and administrative matters. During this workshop clusters are finalized and competent educators assigned as cluster leaders. Further workshops in the year are dedicated to curriculum content knowledge as found in the NCS, as changed to CAPS (Curriculum Assessment Policy Statements) from 2012. The following aspects are dealt with on an approximately three-year rotational basis:

1. Songs from different cultures at different levels of difficulty: rounds, call and response and repetition, tempo, dynamics, high and low;
2. Making of instruments;
3. Rhythm in general – own form of notation (percussion instruments);
4. French time names;
5. Solfa notation;
6. Staff notation – note values;
7. Staff notation - time signatures;
8. Staff notation – letter names;
9. Basic keyboard skills on the melodica and keyboard (C major);
10. Conducting;
11. Composition;
12. Drumming techniques;
13. Western music instruments;
14. African music instruments;
15. Playing and singing songs in the key of C major; and
16. Making resources for Arts and Culture lessons (posters, flash cards, etc.).

The topics mentioned above are separated for the purpose of making notes but during the workshops a great deal of integration takes place. Due to the fact that the majority of the educators are from African descent and enjoy dancing, a great deal of dancing is done to demonstrate musical concepts. Most of the African educators also have a basic knowledge of the Solfa system and it is a good place to start the teaching of staff notation.

Suggested resources that are needed by educators in rural areas include a battery-operated CD player, CD's on different musical genres and with songs from different cultures, battery-operated TV and DVD player, DVD's with different cultural dance styles, musicals and operas, melodicas, a tambourine and a good drum. Other percussion instruments and wall charts can be made by educators and learners.

Conclusions

Tertiary training programs in South Africa that are not aligned with the curriculum and do not meet the needs of the generalist educator in turn rob especially rural learners of a decent music education. The day that music is included in South Africa as a compulsory component of educator training at tertiary level, a great part of the music war will have been won. Until that day, in-service educator mentoring and training programs will be an essential tool to keep music alive.

References

Australian Department of Education. (2004). *History of music education in Australia.* Retrieved from: http://education.deakin.edu.au/music_ed/history/

Ballantyne, J. (2006). Reconceptualising preservice teacher education courses for music teachers: The importance of pedagogical content knowledge and skills and professional knowledge and skills. *Research Studies in Music Education, 26*, 37-50.

Crouse, T. (2010). *Telephonic interview with Tertius Crouse.* 18 October 2010.

Elliott, D. J. (1995). *Music matters. A new philosophy of music education.* New York: Oxford University Press

Jansen van Vuuren, E. (2011). *Subject music in rural South Africa: Challenges and solutions within a comparative context* (Doctoral thesis). University of Pretoria, South Africa.

Lewis, F. (2010). *Internet correspondence from Franklin Lewis.* 19 April 2010.

Mashamaite, D. (2010). *Internet correspondence from Duke Mashamaite.* 8 May 2010.

Rademan, E. (2010). *Internet correspondence from Erna Rademan.* 20 September 2010.

Smith, A. (2010). *Telephonic interview with Anlie Smith.* 27 October 2010.

Sweeney, B. (2001). *The essential high impact mentoring strategy.* Retrieved from http://www.mentoring-association.org/EssMStrategy.html

Music Materials in the Early Childhood Education

Rosa Mª Vicente Álvarez
University of Santiago de Compostela (Spain)
rosi@mundo-r.com

Abstract

The aim of this article is to describe the perception of preschool education teachers (students from 3 to 6 years old) of Galicia regarding the music materials developed to help in their teaching practice in the context of the education law of Spain (LOE). This paper presents some of the most relevant results from the study carried out in the Department of Didactics and School Organization of the University of Santiago de Compostela. In Spain, early childhood education includes children from birth to six years old and the introduction of music training in early childhood education has been fairly recent – in the last 15-20 years. Some basic aspects didactic materials, such as an importance of music in early childhood education, development of didactics and features of teachers in the context of our country and our community are considered. Among other things, no less important, the study emphasizes the perception of musical training, language of materials, workspace and student diversity also. This paper presents three dimensions: 1. knowledge the types of musical materials and use of music materials and workplaces; 2. teacher collaboration and selection of materials; and 3. sufficiency of the musical material. Findings revealed that the professionalizing process, which many authors mention and most of them demand, seems to be somewhat ineffective. The scarce support by specialists in the utilization of new material, the limited use of evaluation guides few experiment projects on materials, and so on. Furthermore, although I do not deny that editorial guides can be used in an interesting professionalizing manner, we found that this print materials continue to condition the practice not only of the individual teachers, but also of schools, pupils, and parents.

A number of recommendations are included regarding measures that could be taken by institutions and professionals involved in the process of design, selection, and use of didactic materials. Direct training is necessary on specific materials through collaboration. Training is also needed in materials evaluation and materials elaboration. In order for this to be possible, time and must be provided in the workplace.

Keywords
Music materials, early childhood education, teacher perception.

Introduction

The aim of this article is to describe the perception of preschool education teachers (students from 3 to 6 years old) regarding the music materials developed to help in their teaching practice in the context of the education law of Spain (LOE). In Spain, the early childhood education is a stage that lasts from birth to six years old. Most educators and teachers understand music as an integrated content in the totality of tasks to be performed by children (Swanwick, 1991). The study emphasizes the perception of musical training, language of materials, workspace and student diversity also. Finally, we considered the research from Spanish legislation and some European considerations.

This paper presents some of the most relevant results from the study carried out in the Department of Didactics and School Organization of the University of Santiago de Compostela (Vincente, 2010). For this investigation, extant research was used by such authors as Cateura (1992), Díaz, Bresler, Ibarretxe, and Malbrán (2006), EACEA (2009), and Ivanova (2010). Analysis of interpretive context, using technical questionnaire, interview and visual analysis was used.

Investigation

Research indicates that there is a change in the role attributed to teachers regarding didactic materials (Rodríguez, 2009). With the idea that more materials does not necessarily lead to an improvement in the quality of teaching, teachers are perceived by some as something more than mere intermediaries, or passive users of materials that are elaborated by others. Instead, they are seen as mediators, researchers, and critics of curricular materials. The emphasis is made on the development of activities involving the design, elaboration, selection and utilization of materials that are carried out in a thoughtful manner in collaboration with colleagues and other professionals (Area, Parcerisa, & Rodríguez, 2010). Based on this idea that extant material can take on an innovative nature and that teachers are able to deal with materials in school, the investigators were inspired to understand teachers' opinions regarding their work with materials.

To strengthen our discussion, we draw on wider recent writings about the development and use of materials and techniques or methods (Hargreaves & North,1997; New York State Department,1970; Romero, 2003a, 2003b; Refsum, 2007), who have dealt with this type of school materials and we developed a detailed definition of musical material in conjuction with extant research by Bermell, (2003), Carbajo (2009), Gregor (1984), Jorquera (2006), and Swanwick (1998). This investigation is influenced by practical experience and from the analysis of materials music methods widely utilized during the 20th century in an attempt to develop an eclectic classification of materials within the context of the current education system – the Galician current school.

For the research of teacher´s perception, it is analyzed the definition of musical material about four types of materials: 1. Sound Materials: any resources that can produce a sound. It can be used not only in musical didactics or musical instruments, but also in materials for fun, toys, games or similar resources (Easch, 1970; Gustems, 2003; Hemsy, 1977; Munby, 1983; Murray, 1994); 2. Materials to learn music: any resources can be produced by different music methods (We can see Bachmann, 1998). It can be a visual material, touch material, or other sensory resources (Arus,2007; Martenot,1993; Santamaría, 2006 Sanuy & González, 1993; Willems,1981); 3. Printed Materials: this group includes curricular materials and classroom materials. For example, didactic, school educational project, classroom programming, textbooks, didactic guides, publisher-proposed projects, didactic units... (e.g. Sharp, 2003; Swanwick, 1991); and 4. ICT Materials (Information and Communication Technology): all materials that have to do with computer, game console, television, sound resources or other audiovisual educational technology (Adell, 1998; Area, 2007).

Figure 1. Music materials.

According to authors such as Esteve, Molina and López (2007), Green (2001), Iglesias (1996), López (2009), Odena & Welch (2009), Oriol (2009), and Pickering and Repacholi (2001), it was decided to investigate the following dimensions: knowledge the types of musical materials and use of music materials and workpaces (A), teacher collaboration and selection of materials (B) and sufficiency of the musical material (C).

Regarding the empirical study, we first looked at the breakdown of teachers by type. They were chosen by stratified cluster. Considering the total number of schools existing in each category, we calculated that we would need a minimum of 240 teachers for the sample to be sizeable for enough for appropriate analysis. To provide for possible mortality, we included 568 teachers from Galicia. The opinion survey was applied with the sample of teachers from public schools, private schools, schools with public financing, and small schools often having only one teacher. Secondly, for semi-structured interviews and visual analysis of the perception of materials, we selected a random sample of intentional in-kind teachers to respond to specific characteristics of analysis. For the development of the interviews we took into account the teachers´ workplace and place of materials there. These analyses were particularly enlightening in the interpretation, so we have chosen 10 teachers as examples of specific responses..

Results

With respect to knowledge, understanding, and usage of music materials, we can say that preschool education teachers believe that they "have knowledge" of these materials. Nevertheless, it is necessary take into account that there are many teachers that do not know the materials.

Knowledge and usage the types of musical materials – Sound Materials
Regarding sound materials for listening to music, only 38% of teachers had children listen to musical material. The study revealed that children in classrooms listen mainly to children´s music in Galician (92%), Spanish (87%), and classical music (76%). The interpretive analysis revealed that teachers use a selection of music they know well and which is easy for them to remember and transmit. Moreover, there was a lack of variety in listening activities. Music was often used passively in the background and games were chose to provoke of emotions.

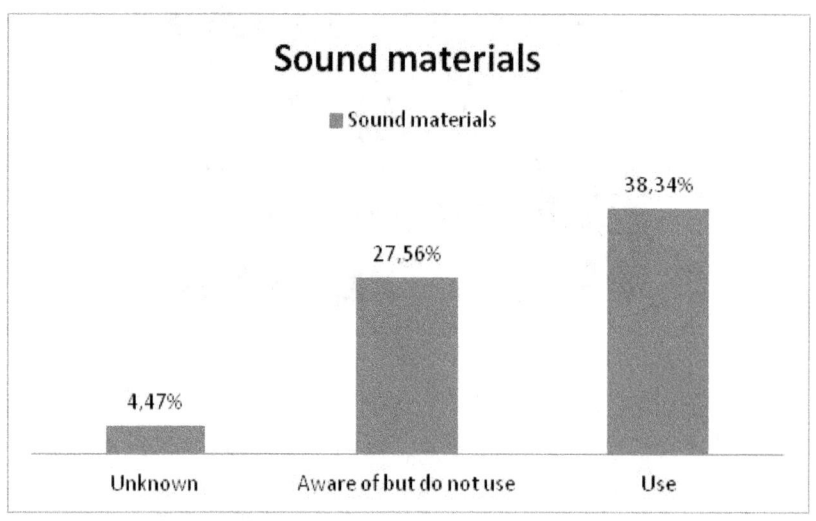

Figure 2. Percentage of use of sound materials.

Regarding sound materials to sing, we found almost 28% of teachers do not use songs in their educational activities. The 61% who do, used: songs with gestures and movement associated; intervals sound songs; and selection of classical music tunes and pop tunes. About 80% of teachers use sound materials to manipulative, stressing the use of Orff school instruments (body percussion, 96%), indeterminate pitch percussion instruments (84.5%), and determinate pitch percussion instruments (71%). The interpretive analysis revealed that these materials were commonly used by teachers with a higher level of training. In addition, teachers with greater creativity were found to make greater use of these materials.

Up to 20% of teachers do not use sound materials to involve musical movement and drama despite the importance of promoting childhood psychomotricity. The music teacher emphasizes musical training through more specific materials. We found differences in schools by the possibilities that can provide available spaces.

Materials to Learn Music
Over 70% of teachers didn´t known the materials based on 20th century music methods, but a quarter of them uses this materials sometimes. Not even half of music teachers and less than 4% of preschool teachers use these materials. Normally, teachers use the materials

of Orff and Kodály methods.

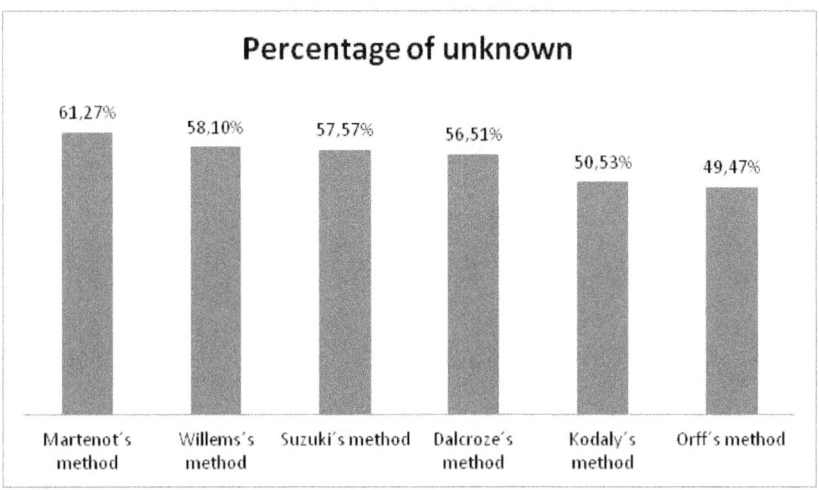

Figure 3. Percentage of unknown of materials methods.

Printed materials

We analyzed materials on school organization (normative material and official documents), classroom materials (for teacher and student) and the importance given to music in these materials. Most teachers indicated that the handling of musical matters in these materials is not good enough. Although half of the teachers think that the materials are important to their musical educational activities. Regarding classroom curriculum materials (e.g. textbooks, teaching books, and other printed materials), the most widely used printed materials are those that are related to lesson plans and publisher teaching guides. Music teachers preferred to use music manuals and software whereas preschool teachers prefer to use didactic units (48%) and didactic guides (44%).

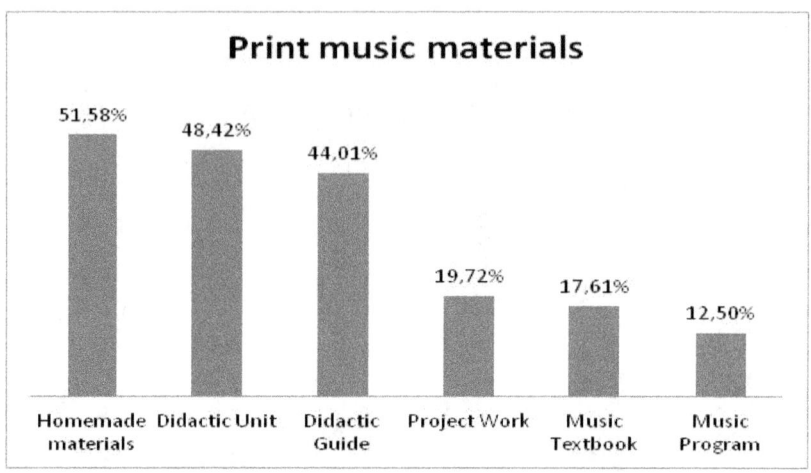

Figure 4. Percentage of use of print music materials

In relation to the materials they use, most music teachers think that their materials are strong in terms of musical content, while preschool teachers say that in their educational program music is not presented the music (81%) or is unimportant (83%). We found that the use of music and its materials is different depending on the specialty (time organized at the school for musical activities). Teachers who give more importance to these materials are between 21 and 40 years.

ICT materials

Only 6% of teachers stated that they did not know about ICT materials and 24% of teachers of those who know do not use them. The interpretive analysis highlights that the use depends on ease of use, popularity and technological updating, and access to training. The most often mentioned materials are those that have an easy access: music and audiovisual story CDs, multimedia CDs and interactive games. Teacher interviews revealed that material is obtained from seminars and courses, and publisher standard package, online as well as popular commercial material.

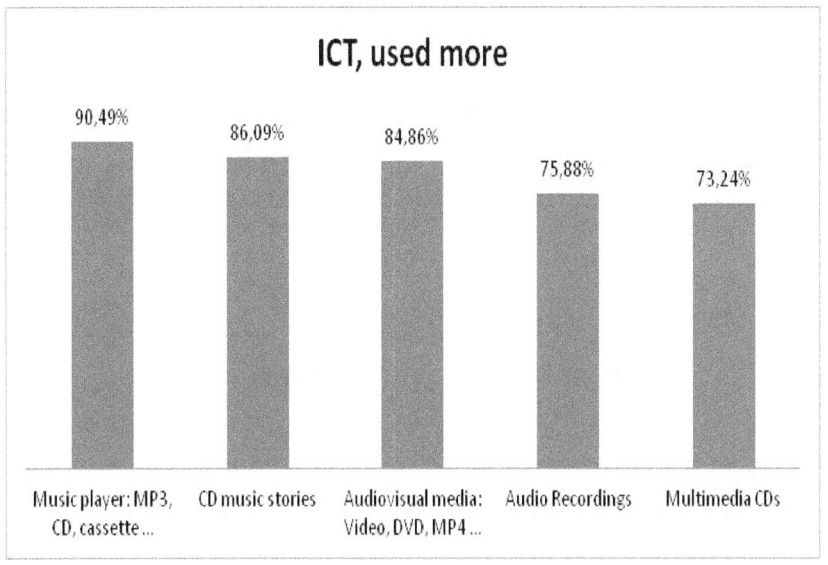

Figure 5. Percentage of ICT used more

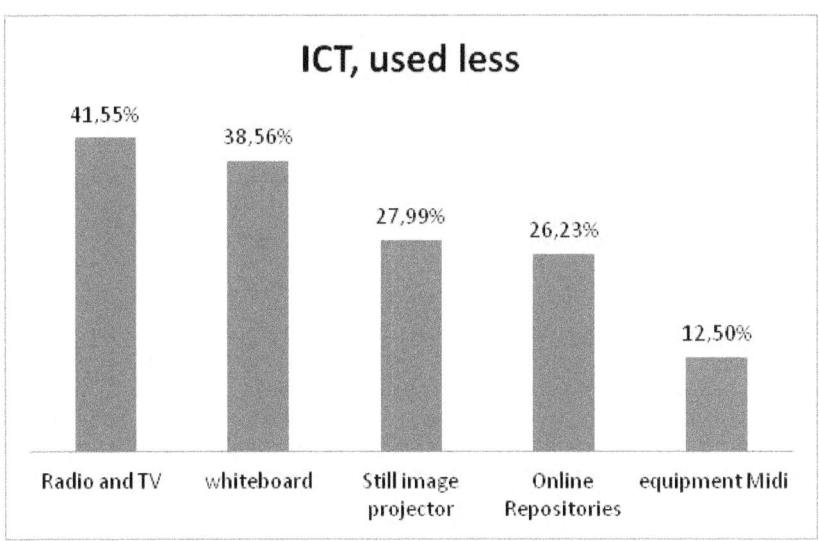

Figure 6. Percentage of ICT used less

Up to 74% of teachers use the computer, mainly to research and prepare materials (printed or audiovisual). Normally, they use ICT materials because it complements their work. Those who do not use it, do not believe that there is enough quality or that they have sufficient supplies.

Teacher collaboration and selection of music materials
Only 28% of teachers participate in the selection of musical material and 62% of them exchange their ideas with other teachers to decide which music material to use in the classes, collective activities, festivals and events. But they do not exchange their ideas to prepare the educational program for their classes. As we can see in Figure 7, only 4.62% pay due attention to selection of music material they will use in classes, 14.99% use the material without making any analysis of the material, 20.55% choose material making a superficial analysis, 23.45% choose the material analyzing it quite well, and 36.4% did not respond on the question. According to these results it can be said that most of the teachers choose material intuitively.

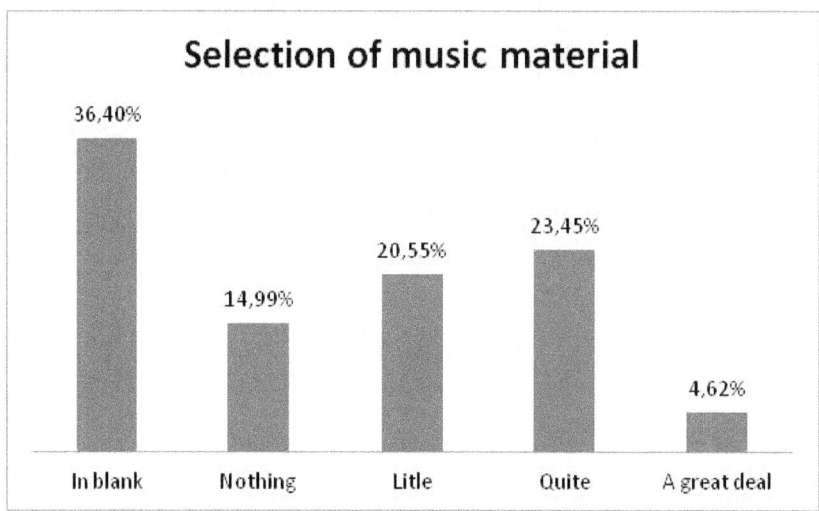

Figure 7. Percentage of selection of musical material

Some teachers explain that they do not collaborate because they do not know how do, others delegate the function of choosing the material to experts. In addition, just over half the teachers made decisions regarding the selection and preparation of musical materials in educational meetings, highlighting the criteria of: Economy (acquisition); Suitability (team); and Need (share). The most frequent ways teachers use to select music materials included the use of websites and libraries, choosing materials that publishers offer going directly to schools, and consulting with experts (e.g. university teachers, educational associations and others.)

As we can see in Figure 8, teachers that participate less in meetings are young teachers (27.91%) and senior teachers (28.12%). However, in our opinion, meetings would be more productive if these groups participated more actively. The advantages of young teachers are fresh university knowledge, enthusiasm, and a willingness to work and learn. Conversely, the advantages of senior teachers are experience of many years of work that can be extremely useful for young teachers.

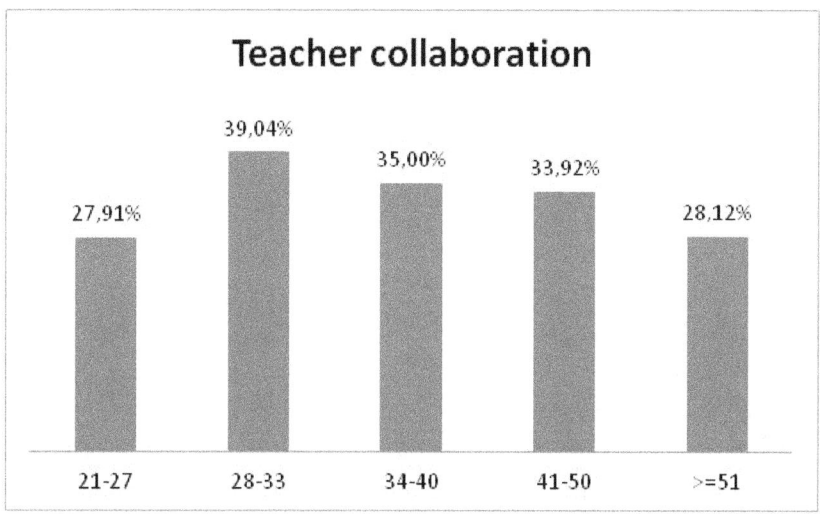

Figure 8. Percentage of age of teacher collaboration in musical material

Regarding workplaces, teachers preferred to use the following workplaces for music classes: pre-school classrooms (for kids less than 6 years old); music classroom; gymnasium; and playground. More than half of the teachers are not happy with workplaces available for music classrooms and up to 40% find it difficult to work. The interpretive analysis indicates that teachers prefer to use music classrooms for studying with kids over 6 years old and with kids less than 6 years old they prefer to use pre-school classrooms.

Sufficiency of musical materials

Musical materials for teachers are considered to be sufficient, as well as ICT materials which are considered more than adequate by 44.54% of teachers. But the materials for children, like Sound Materials and Materials to learn music are considered to be insufficient. The teachers considered printed materials (e.g. books for teachers, lesson plans and others) more than sufficient. However there is no sufficient material for practice music activities (working on projects or units of educational magazines).

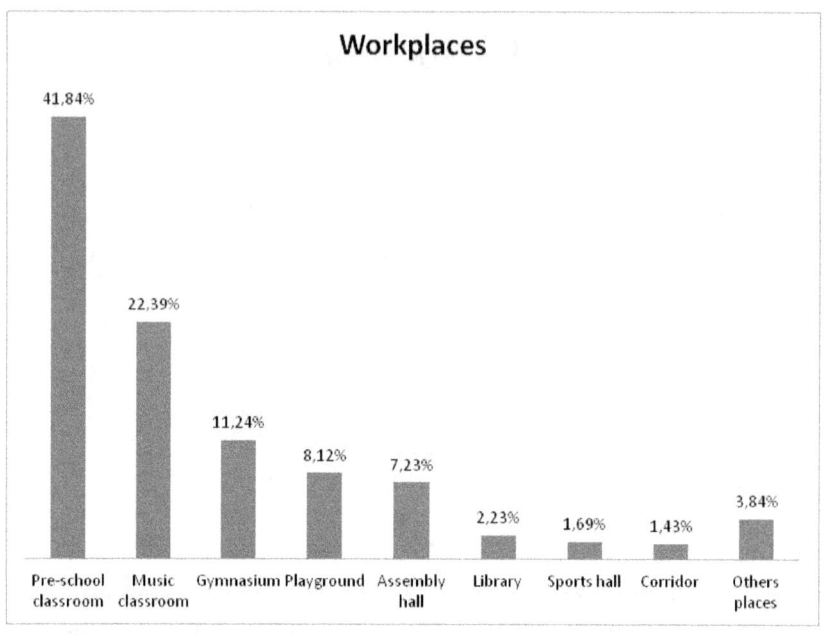

Figure 9. Percentage of workplaces available to practice music in the school.

Conclusions

The following list is a compilation of the main findings related to teachers´ perceptions regarding to musical materials: 1. Prior training has a great influence on the perception of teaching materials; 2. Specialized teacher trainings have a great influence on the use of musical materials; 3. Workplaces influence on practice and use of music materials; 4. Perception of music materials are related to how teaching activities are carried out (coordination, collaboration and teacher participation); 5. Selection of materials is influenced by opinion of publishers and popular proposal over educational interests; 6. Selection of music materials is intuitive because for most of teachers guidelines for evaluating materials are unknown; and 7. The type of music and teaching materials, the pedagogical dynamics are different depending on the teaching specialty (due to training) and contextual variables (e.g. school, location, gender, age).

From what has been said we just want to point out that music training is recent in schools (no more than 15 or 20 years old) and its professional projection does not go beyond a decade. Rodríguez (2000) had already indicated in the nineties the need to take into account the professional teacher in the development of the curricula carried out with the LOXSE, words relevant in the development of new teachers in the European context. Research shows that the perception of teaching materials and music is compared with that job insecurity (related to lack of supplies, access to the ambiguous teaching system, the difficulties of finding the required continuing education, doubts regarding the skills or concerns about the future of work, among other features defined here).

Pathways to the Development of Adequate Perception of Teachers
Once the observations were analyzed, we can think to develop training ways: 1. Development of direct training on specific music materials through collaborative teaching (coordination, leadership, action groups are essential); 2. Development of materials, based on the teachers that need to share times and spaces created in the workplace; and 3. Training evaluation of music materials through use of guides and their creation.

Research showed that the perception of teaching materials and music is compared with that job insecurity related to lack of supplies, access to the ambiguous teaching system, the difficulties of finding the required continuing education, and doubts regarding the skills or concerns about the future of work.

References

Adell, J. E. (1998). *La música en la era digital. La cultura de masas como simulacro*. Lérida: Milenio.

Area, M. (2007). De la escuela de la cultura impresa a la escuela de la cultura digital. Los materiales, recursos para el aprendizaje. *Aula de Innovación Educativa, 165*, 15-20.

Area, M., Parcerisa, A., & Rodríguez, J. (Coords.). (2010). *Materiales y recursos didácticos en contextos comunitarios*. Barcelona: Graó.

Arús, E. (2007, xullo). *La influencia de Jaques Dalcroze en la educación infantil del siglo XXI*. Traballo presentado no XXXIV Congreso Internacional de Rítmica, Ginebra. Recupedado de http://www.ritmicadalcroze.com/images/la%20_influencia_Jaques-Dalcroze.pdf [Consultad o 20/02/2008].

Bermell, M. A. (2003). Evaluación de un programa de intervención basado en la música-movimiento como optimizador del aprendizaje en la educación primaria. (doctoral thesis). Universitat de Valencia. Valencia.

Carbajo, C. (2009). El perfil profesional del docente de música de educación primaria: Autoconcepto de competencias profesionales y la práctica de aula. (doctoral thesis). Universidad de Murcia. Murcia. http://www.tesisenred.net/TESIS_UM/AVAILABLE/TDR-0514110-121801//CarbajoMartinezConcha.pdf [12/03/2010].

Cateura, M. (1992). *Por una educación musical en España. Estudio comparativo con otros países*. Barcelona: PPU.

Díaz, M., Bresler, L., Giráldez, A., Ibarretxe, G., & Malbrán, S. (2006). *Introducción a la investigación en educación musical*. Madrid: En clave Creativa.

Education, Audiovisual & Cuture Executive Agency [EACEA P9 Eurydice] (Bruselas). (2009). *Arts an cultural Education at School in Europe*. Bruselas: Autor. Recuperado de http://eacea.ec.europa.eu/education/eurydice/documents/thematic_reports/113EN.pdf [Consultado o 29/01/2010]

Easch, M. J. (1970). *Developing an instrument for the assessment of instructional materials (Form IV)*. Washington, DC: City University of New York. Hunter Coll. Bureau of education for the Handicapped. Recuperado de http://www.eric.ed.gov/ERICWebPortal/search/detailmini.jsp?_nfpb=true&_&ERICExtSearch_SearchValue_0=ED041947&ERICExtSearch_SearchType_0=no&accno=ED041947 [Consultad o 30/04/2010].

Esteve, J. M., Molina, M. A. E, & López, C. (2007). El futuro de los estudios de maestro especialista en música. *Música y Educación: revista trimestral de pedagogía musical, 72*, 21-34.

Green, L. (2001): *Música, Género y Educación*. Madrid: Ediciòns Morata.

Gregor, D. (Ed.). (1984, xullo). Retrospective Conversion of Music Materials. *Informe da conferenia para o Council on Library* Resources, Minnesota. Washington, DC. Recuperado da base de datos ERIC Education Resources Information Center.

Gustems, J. (2003). *La flauta dulce en los estudios universitarios de "Mestre en educaciò musical" en Catalunya: Revisión y adecuación de contenidos*. (TTese de doutoramento). Universitat de Barcelona. Barcelona. Recuperado de http://www.tesisenxarxa.net/TDX-0716104-104533/ [Consultado o 25/02/2009].

Hemsy, V. (1977). *Fundamentos, materiales y técnicas de la educación musical. Ensayos y conferencias: 1967-1974*. Buenos Aires: Ricordi.

Iglesias, L. (1996). *Deseño e manexo de espacios na aula de educación infantil: Análise do pensamento e actuación dos profesores/as*. (Tese de doutoramento). Universidade de Santiago de Compostela. A Coruña.

Ivanova, A. (2010). El desarrollo psicológico del niño y el papel de la educación musical. *Doce Notas. Revista de música y danza*. Recuperado de http://www.docenotas.com/pdf/desarrollo_psicologicodelnino.pdf [Consultado o 10/11/2010].

Jorquera, M. C. (2004). Métodos históricos o activos en educación musical. *LEEME. Lista Europea Electrónica de Música en la Educación, 14*, 1-30.

López, M. A. (2009). La formación de los maestros de Educación Infantil para la comprensión de la música y su uso didáctico en Galicia. *Revista Electrónica Interuniversitaria de Formación del Profesorado, 12*(1), 107-120. Recuperado de http://www.aufop.com/aufop/uploaded_files/articulos/1240872964.pdf [Consultado o 20/08/2010].

Martenot, M. (1993). *Principios fundamentales de formación musical y su aplicación*. Madrid: Rialp.

Munby, H. (1983). Thirty studies involving the "scientific attitude inventory": What confidence can we have in this instrument? *Journal of Research in Science Teaching, 20*(2), 141-162.

Murray, R. (1994). *Hacia una educación sonora*. Buenos Aires: Pedagogías musicales abiertas.

New York State Department (Albany). (1970). *Words, sounds and pictures about music: A multimedia resource listing for teachers of music in grades K-6*. New York, NY: Autor. Recuperado da base de datos ERIC Education Resourcer Information Center.

Odena, O. E., & Welch, G. (2009). A generative model of teachers' thinking on musical creativity. *Psychology of Music, 37*(4), 416-442.

Oriol, N. (2009). La investigación musical en España: tesis doctorales y temática en la última década. *Eufonía: Didáctica de la Música, 45*, 59-87.

Pickering, S. E., & Repacholi, B. (2001). Modifying children's gender-typed musical instrument preferences: The effects of gender and age. *Sex Roles, 45*(9/10), 623-643.

Refsum, A. (2007): *Action-sound: Developing methods and tools to study music-related body movement.* (Tese de deoutoramento). University of Oslo (Departament of Musicology). Oslo.

Rodríguez, J. (2000). *Os materiais curriculares impresos e a reforma educativa en Galicia.* (Tese de doutoramento). Universidade de Santiago de Compostela. A Coruña.

Rodríguez, J. (2009). *Os materiais corriculares en Galicia.* Vigo: Xerais.

Romero, J. B. (2003a). *Los medios y recursos para la educación musical en primaria.* (Tesiña de doutoramento). Universidad de Huelva. Huelva.

Romero, J. B. (2003b). *Diseño, aplicación y evaluación de un material didáctico para optimizar la enseñanza en el III Ciclo de educación primaria.* (Tese de doutoramento). Universidad de Huelva. Huelva.

Santamaría, P. (2006). Apuntes para un modelo didáctico de la enseñanza del lenguaje musical en la etapa de infantil. *Pulso, 29,* 95-115.

Sanuy, M., & González, L. (1993). *Orff-Schulwerk (música para niños)* (1a impr. 1969). Madrid: Unión Musical Española.

Sharp, L. (2003). *Classrooms and curriculum come alive with music: a sequential approach of teaching music to elementary students using daily oral music lessons.* Menlover, Liverpool: American Council on Rural Special Education [ACRES] Proceedings.

Swanwick, K. (1991). *Música, pensamiento y educación.* Madrid: Morata.

Vicente, Rosa Mª (2010). Os materiais didácticos e musicais en educación infantil. A percepción docente en Galicia.Recuperado de http://hdl.handle.net/10347/3629 [Consultado o 20/03/2012].

Willems, E. (1981). *El valor humano de la educación musical.* Barcelona: Paidós.

Defining Music Teacher Identity for Effective Research in Music Education

Cynthia Wagoner
East Carolina University (USA)
wagonerc@ecu.edu

Abstract
The purpose of the present study was to analyze research literature to provide a foundation for a proposed definition of music teacher identity. The definition serves to ground future research on music teacher identity through constructs which may be examined through quantitative and qualitative measures. Currently, there is no consistent definition of music teacher identity, confounded by a lack of depth and focus on in-service teacher development spanning the critical years of induction. Grounding the term *music teacher identity* in the theoretical literature provides a firm epistemological foundation from which occupational identity might be understood best and from which music teacher identity might be defined. The review of the literature revealed a theoretical framework in social theory, based around the tenets of social constructivism, symbolic interactionism, and role theory. The proposed definition is grounded in social constructivist theory. Five constructs emerged from the literature, described as Music Teacher Self-Efficacy, Musician-Teacher Commitment, Music Teacher Agency, Music Teacher Collectivity, and Musician-Teacher Comprehensiveness. The proposed definition can further the ways through which the profession might understand and investigate music teacher identity construction.

Keywords
Music teacher identity, occupational identity, self-efficacy, commitment, collectivity, agency, musician identity

Ask music educators what they do for a living and you will likely garner a multitude of responses. These range from naming a specific type of performance group, to identification with an age group being taught. Responses signify identity, and indicate how an individual thinks of himself or herself, and/or how an individual would like to be perceived. Constructing an occupational identity is powerful, affecting how an individual thinks and chooses to act.

The purpose of the present study was to examine critically the extant research to establish a definition of music teacher identity. A theoretical framework is provided to ground the literature review that follows. A summary of the literature covers occupational identity research, pre-service teacher and in-service teacher identity research, and pre-service and in-service teacher music teacher research. Summaries of the constructs specific to music teacher identity are described, whereby a culminating definition of in-service music teacher identity is offered.

Theoretical Framework for Defining Music Teacher Identity

Grounding the term *music teacher identity* in the theoretical literature provides a firm epistemological foundation from which occupational identity might be understood best and from which music teacher identity might be defined. The particular theories garnered from the review of literature include social constructivism, symbolic interactionism, and role theory. The constructs and resultant definition developed in the present study were based on these theories.

Social constructivism recognizes that identity is fluid and contextually situated (Beck & Young, 2005; Schneider, 2006). The broad framework of social constructivism presents knowledge as the product of social interaction, interpretation, and understanding (Vygotsky, 1962). Symbolic interactionism defines identities as arising from social, situational, and personal symbolic constructions of meaning (Buechler, 2008). When human meaning is ascribed to symbols, for example, through a shared repertoire of experiences, stories, tools, and ways of addressing recurring problems, Wenger (1998) posits a community of practice has been constructed.

Role theory examines how an individual or group of individuals performs an identity, as they interpret contextual roles, such as a teacher (Bruce & Yearley, 2006; Stryker, 1995). Roles are constructed as an individual locates himself within a group and demarcates who he is and who he is not (Bankston, 2000; Stets, 2006). A general conception of social theory helps to ground the broad scope of occupational identity construction.

Overview of Occupational Identity

Occupational identity refers to the way in which one views identity through the lens of occupational choice. Deeper understanding of occupational identity requires determining what constitutes the collective identity of the occupation (e.g., a sense of belonging to a group) and what constitutes the personal identity (Jenkins, 2008). Personal identity (e.g., a sense of one's self) and collective occupational identity integrate as a holistic view of one's self as a person (Sundin, 2001). Each occupation has its own template, complete with structures, interactions, and incentives, which are further filtered through individual experiences (Chreim, Williams, Djokoto-Asem, & Janz, 2003). Individual experiences include engagement in knowledge creation and interactions with different kinds of situations and different people (Wenger, 1998).

Beginning with early work examining vocational behaviors (Becker & Carper, 1956; Carper & Becker, 1957), extending to examinations of the self and personality as interfaced with occupational identity (Holland, 1992), contemporary research pushes the boundaries of how occupational identity is understood. Becker and Carper's work defined occupational identity as a personal commitment to title, tasks, ideology, and social status. A sense of belonging, or collectivity, is created when individuals attend to the values, expectations, norms, structures, and incentives of a particular organization (Becker & Carper, 1956; Bordin, Nachmann, & Siegel, 1963). Occupational identity research, as reviewed, focused on personal constructions of meaning and the relationship of personal meaning to the larger frame of occupational collectivity.

Pre-service Teacher Identity Research

Teacher identity may be examined as a subset of occupational identity. Concerns with how and when pre-service teachers construct their occupational teaching identity have been readily examined in research literature, including recruitment to teaching (Biddle & Thomas, 1962), specific pedagogical methods during pre-service classes (Egan, 2009; Haniford, 2010), and student teaching experiences (Sexton, 2008; tenDam & Blom, 2006) as ways in which to understand pre-service teacher identity construction.

Pre-service teacher identity has been examined primarily through the broad framework of social constructivism, but more specifically through symbolic interactionism, with modern perspectives of dramaturgy and role theory presented via the work of Lave and Wenger (1991). Pedagogical methods and student teacher experiences are frequently examined through discourse analysis, allowing researchers to pursue investigations by analyzing written and spoken language (Gaudelli & Ousley, 2008; Ronfeldt & Grossman, 2008). Identity construction for the pre-service teacher has been documented as an ongoing, fluid process, subject to contextual influences, experiences, and autobiography. Friction between idealized and actual identity and contextualized experiences outside of the university classroom begin to direct attention to teacher identity construction during in-service induction (Horn, Nolen, Ward, & Sunshine, 2008).

Pre-service Music Teacher Identity Research

Music teacher identity is a subset of general teacher identity, yet important differences exist concerning the music teacher. Pre-service music teachers enter the university having passed music auditions emphasizing musician-performer skills (Bernard, 2004; Dolloff, 2008; Hargreaves, Purves, Welch, & Marshall, 2007). The emphasis on performance in music seems to affect the ways in which anticipatory socialization takes place (Bouij, 2004; Conway, 2002) and in turn, how pre-service music teacher identity is initially constructed. Pre-service music teacher construction has been examined to better understand the socialization process and effective pedagogy concerning the pre-service teacher (Campbell & Thompson, 2007; Isbell, 2008).

Current research covers the gamut of social theory. Extant pre-service music teacher identity research has highlighted how experiences shape construction of occupational identity from early socialization to norms and expectations through the beginning stage of induction to the profession (Paul, 1998). Music teaching is a function of being a musician, and as such, has a different set of anticipatory social expectations than those associated with teacher preparation in non-music content areas (Bladh, 2004; Conway, 2002; Isbell, 2008). Conflicts between the musician-performer identity and the music teacher identity are suggested in many studies (Bouij, 2004; Isbell, 2008; Roberts, 1991, 2004). It is not clear however, if music teacher-performer identity should be labeled conflicted or a fluid state dependent on individual, social, and cultural contexts (Pellegrino, 2009).

Experiences seem to be significant predictors of commitment to occupational identification in music teaching (Conkling, 2004; Isbell, 2008), but not necessarily before students enter the workforce (L'Roy, 1983). Experience early in one's pre-service music teaching may not initially affect self-efficacy, but does begin to alter attitudes toward music teaching and the skills necessary for such (Hargreaves et al., 2007). Socialization experiences associated with prior musical training and university studies are at work in initial music teacher identity construction, and continue to impact music teachers as they begin their first teaching jobs.

Such studies are valuable in establishing constructs for music teacher identity; however, needs of pre-service and in-service teachers are distinct, both in context and experiences (Frierson-Campbell, 2004). The pre-service teacher may be idealistic and disconnected from the reality of the teaching context, while the in-service teacher is mired in reality, risking the loss of all idealism to conformity (Roberts & Graham, 2008). Examining the role dimensions of both musician and teacher are critical in building an understanding of music teacher identity (Bouij, 2004; Pellegrino, 2009).

In-service Teacher Identity Research

A novice teacher enters the profession with limited classroom experiences, armed with a general base of knowledge and a tenuous identity rooted in the student teaching experience (Horn et al., 2008; Malderez, Hobson, Tracey, & Kerr, 2007). Moving beyond the student teaching experience into induction may uncover dissonances for novices as they explore the collective identity of the profession within the realities of the workplace (Ritter, 2007; Worthy, 2005). The novice teacher "appears to be intensely concerned with the image of self as teacher" (Malderez et al., 2007, p. 239), and this is perhaps linked with the necessary transition leading to concern for student learning (Fuller & Brown, 1975).

Many qualitative studies on in-service teacher identity have focused on perceptions of professionalism for beginning teachers (Cherubini, 2007), the blending of the self with occupational identity (Endo, Reece-Miller, & Santavicca, 2010; Mok, 2005; Tsui, 2007), contextual issues of the workplace (Frost, 2010; LeMaistre & Pare, 2010), impact of early experiences (Avalos & Aylwin, 2007; Flores, 2006; Harrison, 2001), implications of teacher training (Beijaard, Verloop, & Vermunt, 2000; Feiman-Nemser, 2001), and mentoring needs of new teachers (Feiman-Nemser, 2001; Worthy, 2005). Such studies have regarded teacher identity as a complex dynamic among roles a teacher assumes, personal dimensions of the teaching act, and the context within which the teacher is working (Beijaard, Meijer, & Verloop, 2004).

Teacher identity has aligned closely with self-efficacy and fulfillment, merging the personal and occupational self, which in turn can render a teacher's identity vulnerable (Nias, 1996). More recently, teacher identity has been examined through discursive practices, focusing on teacher identity construction in a context "embedded in power relations, ideology, and culture" (Zembylas, 2003, p. 105). Interactions among teaching identity and roles in a new job, negotiation and application of theoretical knowledge, and the context of the workplace create stress for the novice teacher (Cook, 2009).

Struggle for the novice continues, as each must establish themselves as teachers and find their way from the periphery into the teaching collective as an accepted member (Skaalvik & Skaalvik, 2010). The resolution of these tensions becomes a site for potential teacher identity construction. Further, studies suggest enhancing teacher identity increases positive attitudes across teacher collective identity (Robinson et al., 2005). Mentoring processes, administrative leadership, and district support systems have been implicated as important to novice teacher success in the first year of teaching (Cherubini, 2007; Fantilli & McDougall, 2009), indicating a transition period exists between university training and the workplace.

Retention of novice teachers is a concern as well. Teacher self-efficacy and commitment have been implicated in retention (Rots, Aelterman, Vlerick, & Vermeulen, 2007; Strage, Meyers, & Norris, 2002) and classroom effectiveness (Swackhamer, 2009). Teachers with high self-efficacy and motivation were more committed in attitude (Flores, 2006). Commitment is complex and plays an interrelated role in construction of teacher identity (Reyes, 1992; Reyes & Shin, 1995), correlating with teacher agency (Day, Elliot, & Kington, 2005). Constructs of self-efficacy, commitment, agency, and collectivity are implicated in teacher identity construction research.

In-service Music Teacher Identity Research

The research on novice music teacher identity is sparse, with most extant research focused on identity construction with pre-service music teachers. Novice music teachers experience tensions in roles, which may be exacerbated by their pre-service university training (Scheib, 2003). Tensions may be much more dissonant for the novice, as limited classroom experiences fail to inform how one negotiates both theory and practice (Conway, 2004). Music teacher identity may be rooted in relationships with a 'significant other,' that is, one whose professional opinion is granted the highest esteem. Further, mentors may serve in this capacity to enhance the construction of a strong music teacher identity (Abramo, 2009; Shieh & Conway, 2004; Woodford, 2002). However, music teacher identity must be negotiated as both musician and teacher as one moves into occupational induction, regardless of whether that is a source of tension or realignment.

A working definition of music teacher identity rooted in an examination of theoretical and research literature should assist with the investigation of novice music teachers, particularly during the first five years, when music teachers are most likely to leave the profession (Scheib, 2004). Further, such a working definition should include constructs specific to general teacher and music teacher identity construction to facilitate a global understanding of the term.

Constructs Specific to Music Teacher Identity

Several constructs, steeped in social theory, appear consistently throughout the research on teacher identity and music teacher identity. The term teacher self-efficacy refers to behaviors that demonstrate a teacher's self-appraisal of his or her ability to affect students in the classroom setting, influence parents, administration and community, and be resilient in the face of adversity (Bandura, 1977). Commitment may be understood as a nested phenomenon, related to a set of more permanent values based on self-identity and personal beliefs (Billingsley & Cross, 1992; Cheung, 2008; Nir, 2002).

Agency may be defined as an individual's sense of power to take charge of a particular situation and produce change. As such, agency has been implicated in affecting identity construction as early in one's career as pre-service teacher socialization (Bogler & Somech, 2004) and in relationship to novice teachers' identity construction (Day & Qing, 2009; Lasky, 2005; Sannino, 2010). Collectivity is a sense of belonging to the profession, which has been found to play an important role in early novice teacher socialization (Bouij, 2004; Ritter, 2007). As such, collectivity may play an increasingly important role in construction of music teacher identity throughout a career. Role identity for the music teacher includes taking on both the expectations of musician and teacher (Roberts, 1991, 2004). Based on the extant literature, a music teacher identity definition should include constructs of teacher self-efficacy, commitment, agency, collectivity, and musician-teacher comprehensiveness.

Music Teacher Identity Definition

The purpose of the present study was to examine critically the extant research to establish a definition of music teacher identity. The task of devising a working definition of music teacher identity rooted in an examination of theoretical and research literature has led to the identification of specific constructs, utilizing social constructivism, symbolic interactionism, and role theory. Therefore, the definition of music teacher identity is as follows:

> Music teacher identity is one's conception of himself or herself as a music teacher, as affected by five facets: (a) music teacher self-efficacy (i.e., one's sense of his or her ability to affect students in the classroom setting, influence parents, administration and community, and be resilient in the face of adversity); (b) music teacher commitment (i.e. one's willingness to expend personal time, money, and energy to teach; and to be involved in professional activities); (c) music teacher agency (i.e., one's power to take charge of a particular situation and produce change); (d) music teacher collectivity (i.e., one's belief in the ability of the team of teachers and administrators within the school to execute courses of action required to produce desired results); and (e) musician-teacher comprehensiveness (i.e., the broadness or narrowness with which one see's one's self as a musician and as a teacher).

Understanding music teacher identity construction may assist in developing effective teacher preparation and mentoring support for new teachers, and in turn, strengthening the professional teacher collective, increasing retention for music teachers, impacting school children, improving educational outcomes, and improving quality of teaching lives (Darling-Hammond, 2003; Hancock 2008; Madsen & Hancock, 2002). Future research may examine the constructs through further identification of dimensions of each construct, selected from the literature. A definition based on the five constructs will serve to focus research on the broad ways in which music teachers perceive and perform their practice, providing another tool through which the profession might continue to build research to bridge the gap between university training and induction, enriching the lives of music teachers over an entire career span.

References

Abramo, M. N. (2009). *The construction of instrumental music teacher identity* (Doctoral dissertation). Available from Dissertations and Theses database. (UMI No. 3348563)

Avalos, B., & Aylwin, P. (2007). How young teachers experience their professional work in Chile. *Teaching and Teacher Education, 23*(4), 515-528.

Bandura, A. (1977). *Social learning theory*. General Learning Press.

Bankston, C. L. (2000). Social cognitive theory. In *Sociology Basics*, (2nd ed.,Vol. 2, pp. 483-488). Pasadena: Salem Press.

Beck, J., & Young, M. F. D. (2005). The assault on the professions and the restructuring of academic and professional identities: A Bernsteinian analysis. *British Journal of Sociology of Education, 26*(2), 183-197.

Becker, H. S., & Carper, J. (1956). The elements of identification with an occupation. *American Sociological Review, 21*(3), 341-356.

Beijaard, D., Meijer, P. C., & Verloop, N. (2004). Reconsidering research on teachers' professional identity. *Teaching and Teacher Education, 20*, 107-128.

Beijaard, D., Verloop, N., & Vermunt, J. D. (2000). Teachers' perceptions of professional identity: An exploratory study from a personal knowledge perspective. *Teaching and Teacher Education, 16*, 749-764.

Bernard, R. J. (2004). Striking a chord: Elementary general music teachers' expressions of their identities as musician-teachers (Doctoral dissertation). *Dissertation Abstracts International, 65*(10), 1711. (AAT No. 3134467)

Biddle, B. J., & Thomas, E. J. (Eds.) (1966). *Role theory: Concepts and research.* New York, NY: John Wiley & Sons.

Billingsley, B. S., & Cross, L. H. (1992). Predictors of commitment, job satisfaction, and intent to stay in teaching: A comparison of general and special educators. *The Journal of Special Education, 25*(4), 453-471.

Bladh, S. (2004). Music teachers – In training and at work: A longitudinal study of music teachers in Sweden. *Action, Criticism & Theory for Music Education, 3*(2). Retrieved from http://actmaydaygroup.org/articles/Bladh04

Bogler, R., & Somech, A. (2004). Influence of teacher empowerment on teachers' organizational commitment and organizational commitment. *Teaching and Teacher Education, 20*(3) 277-289.

Bordin, E. S., Nachmann, B., & Siegel, S. J. (1963). An articulated framework for vocational development. *Journal of Counseling Psychology, 10*, 107-116.

Bouj, C. (2004). Two theoretical perspectives on the socialization of music teachers. *Action, Criticism, and Theory for Music Education, 3*. Retrieved from http://www.siue.edu/MUSIC/ACTPAPERS/v3/Bouij04.pdf

Bruce, S., & Yearley, S. (2006). *The SAGE dictionary of sociology* (1st ed., pp. 263-264). Thousand Oaks, CA: Sage.

Buechler, S. M. (2008). *Critical Sociology.* Boulder, CO: Paradigm Publishers. In J. Valsiner & A. Rosa (Eds.), *The Cambridge handbook of sociocultural psychology.* New York, NY: Cambridge University Press.

Campbell, M. R., & Thompson, L. K. (2007). Perceived concerns of pre-service music education teachers: A cross-sectional study. *Journal of Research in Music Education, 55*(2), 162-176.

Carper, J. W., & Becker, H. S. (1957). Conflicting expectations in occupation: Adjustments to conflicting expectations in the development of identification with an occupation. *Social Forces, 35*, 51-56

Chreim, S., Williams, B., Djokoto-Asem, E., & Janz, L. (2003). Professional identity under reconstruction: A case study of changes in a physician-dominated health unit. Abstract of presentation made at the Administrative Science Association of Canada, Halifax, Canada.

Cherubini, L. (2007). Speaking up and speaking freely: Beginning teachers' critical perceptions of their professional induction. *Professional Educator, 29*(2), 1-12

Cheung, H. Y. (2008). Measuring the professional identity of Hong Kong in-service teachers. *Journal of In-service Education, 14*(3), 375-390.

Conkling, S. W. (2004). Music teacher practice and identity in professional development partnerships. *Action, Criticism, and Theory for Music Education, 3*(3). Retrieved from http://act.maydaygroup.org.

Conway, C. (2004). Becoming a teacher: Stories of the first few years. *Music Educators Journal, 91*(1), 45-50.

Conway, C. M. (2002) Perceptions of beginning teachers, their mentors and administrators: Regarding pre-service music teacher preparation. *Journal of Research in Music Education, 50*, 20-36.

Cook, J. S. (2009). "Coming into my own as a teacher": Identity, disequilibrium, and the first year of teaching. *The New Educator, 5*, 274-292.

Darling-Hammond, L. (2003). Keeping good teachers: Why it matters, what leaders can do. *Educational Leadership, 60*(8), 6-13.

Day, C., Elliott, B., & Kington, A. (2005). Reform, standards and teacher identity: Challenges of sustaining commitment. *Teaching and Teacher Education, 21*, 563-577.

Day, C., & Qing, G. (2009). Veteran teachers: Commitment, resilience and quality retention. *Teachers & Teaching, 15*(4), 441-457.

Dolloff, L. (2008). "It's not what she taught me, it's how she made me feel." In B. A. Roberts (Ed.), *Sociological explorations: Proceedings of the 5th international symposium on the sociology of music education* (pp. 111-119). St John's, Newfoundland: The Binders Press.

Egan, B. A. (2009). Learning conversations and listening pedagogy: The relationship in student teachers' developing professional identities. *European Early Childhood Education Research Journal, 17*(1), 43-56.

Endo, H., Reece-Miller, P. C., & Santavicca, N. (2010). Surviving in the trenches: A narrative inquiry into queer teachers' experiences and identity. *Teaching and Teacher Education, 26*(4), 1023-1030.

Fantilli, R. D., & McDougall, D. E. (2009). A study of novice teachers: Challenges and supports in the first years. *Teaching and Teacher Education, 25*, 814-825.

Feiman-Nemser, S. (2001). From preparation to practice: Designing a continuum to strengthen and sustain teaching. *Teachers College Record, 103*(6), 1013–1055.

Flores, M. A. (2006). Being a novice teacher in two different settings: Struggles, continuities, and discontinuities. *Teachers College Record, 34*(3), 2021-2052.

Frierson-Campbell, C. (2004). Professional need and the contexts of in-service music teacher identity. *Action, Criticism, and Theory for Music Education, 3*(3), 26. http://act.maydaygroup.org.

Frost, J. H. (2010). Looking through the lens of a teacher's life: The power of prototypical stories in understanding teachers' instructional decisions in mathematics. *Teaching and Teacher Education, 26*(2), 225-233.

Fuller, F., & Brown, O. (1975). Becoming a teacher. In K. Ryan (Ed.), *Teacher education, Part II: The 74th yearbook of the National Society for the Study of Education* (pp. 25-52). Chicago, IL: University of Chicago Press.

Gaudelli, W., & Ousley, D. (2009). From clothing to skin: Identity work of student teachers in culminating field experiences. *Teaching and Teacher Education, 25*, 931-939.

Hancock, C. B. (2008). Music teachers at risk for attrition and migration. *Journal of Research in Music Education, 30*(2), 130-144.

Haniford, L. C. (2010). Tracing one teacher candidate's discursive identity work. *Teaching and Teacher Education, 26*(4), 987-996.

Hargreaves, D. J., Purves, R. M., Welch, G. F., & Marshall, M. A. (2007). Developing identities and attitudes in musicians and classroom teachers. *British Journal of Educational Psychology, 77*, 665-682.

Harrison, J. K. (2001). The induction of newly qualified teachers. *Journal of Education for Teaching, 27*(3), 277-279.

Holland, J. L. (1992). *Making vocational choices: A theory of vocational personalities and work environments*. Englewood Cliffs, NJ: Prentice-Hall.

Horn, I. S., Nolen, S. B., Ward, C., & Sunshine, S. C. (2008). Developing practices in multiple worlds: The role of identity in learning to teach. *Teacher Education Quarterly, 35*(3), 61-72.

Isbell, D. S. (2008). Musicians and teachers: The socialization and occupational identity of pre-service music teachers. *Journal of Research in Music Education, 56*, 162-178.

Jenkins, R. (2008). *Social identity* (3rd ed.). New York, NY: Routledge.

Lasky, S. (2005). A sociocultural approach to understanding teacher identity, agency and professional vulnerability in the context of secondary school reform. *Teaching and Teacher Education, 21*, 899-916.

Lave, J., & Wenger, E. (1991). *Situated learning: Legitimate peripheral participation*. Cambridge University Press.

LeMaistre, C., & Pare, A. (2010). Whatever it takes: How beginning teachers learn to survive. *Teaching and Teacher Education, 26*(3), 559-564.

L'Roy, D. (1983). *The development of occupational identity in undergraduate music education majors*. Retrieved from ProQuest Dissertations and Theses. (8327044)

Madsen, C. K., & Hancock, C. B. (2002). Support for music education: A case study of issues concerning teacher retention and attrition. *Journal of Research in Music Education, 50*, 6-19.

Malderez, A., Hobson, A. J., Tracey, L., & Kerr, K. (2007) Becoming a student teacher: Core features of the experience. *European Journal of Teacher Education, 30*(3), 225-248.

Mok, Y. F. (2005). Teacher concerns and teacher life stages. *Research in Education, 73*, 53-72.

Nias, J. (1996). Thinking about feeling: The emotions in teaching. *Cambridge Journal of Education, 26*(3), 293-305.

Nir, A. E. (2002). School-based management and its effect on teacher commitment. *International Journal in Education, 5*(4), 323-341.

Paul, S. J. (1998). The effects of peer teaching experiences on the professional teacher role development of undergraduate instrumental music educators. *Bulletin of the Council for Research in Music Education, 137*, 73-92.

Pellegrino, K. (2009). Connections between performer and teacher identities in music teachers: Setting an agenda for research. *Journal of Music Teacher Education, 19*(1), 39-55. Retrieved from http://search.proquest.com/docview/753586325?accountid=10639

Reyes, P. (1992). Preliminary models of teacher organizational commitment implications for restructuring the workplace. In *Office of Educational Research and Improvement* (pp. 1-4). Washington, DC: Center on Organizational and Restructuring the Workplace.

Reyes, P., & Shin, H. S. (1995). Teacher commitment and job satisfaction: A causal analysis. *Journal of School Leadership, 5*(1), 22-39.

Ritter, J. K. (2007). Forging a pedagogy of teacher education: The challenges of moving from classroom teacher to teacher educator. *Studying Teacher Education, 3*(1), 5-22.

Roberts, B. A. (1991). Music teacher education as identity construction. *International Journal of Music Education, 18*, 30-39.

Roberts, B. A. (2004). Who's in the mirror? Issues surrounding identity construction of music educators. *Action, Criticism, and Theory for Music Education, 3*(2). http://act.maydaygroup.org.

Robinson, M., Anning, A., & Frost, N. (2005). "When is a teacher not a teacher?" Knowledge creation and the professional identity of teachers within multi-agency teams. *Studies in Continuing Education, 27*(2), 175-191.

Ronfeldt, M. & Grossman, P. (2008). Becoming a professional: Experimenting with possible selves in professional preparation. *Teacher Education Quarterly, 35*(3), 41-60.

Rots, I., Aelterman, A., Vlerick, P., & Vermeulen, K. (2007). Teacher education, graduates' teaching commitment and entrance into the profession. *Teaching and Teacher Education, 23,* 543-536.

Sannino, A. (2010). Teachers' talk of experiencing: Conflict, resistance and agency. *Teaching and Teacher Education, 26,* 838-844.

Scheib, J. W. (2003). Role stress in the professional life of the school music teacher: A collective case study. *Journal of Research in Music Education, 51*(2), 124-136.

Scheib, J. W. (2004). Why band directors leave: From the mouths of maestros. *Music Educator's Journal, 91*(1), 53-57.

Schneider, M. A. (2006). *The theory primer: A sociological guide.* Lanham, MD: Rowman & Littlefield Publishers.

Sexton, D. M. (2008). Student teachers negotiating identity, role, and agency. *Teacher Education Quarterly, 35*(3), 73-85.

Shieh, E., & Conway, C. (2004). Professional induction: Programs and policies for beginning music teachers. In L. Bartel (Ed.), *Questioning the music education paradigm* (pp. 162–178). Toronto, Ontario, Canada: Canadian Music Educators Association.

Skaalvik, E. M., & Skaalvik, S. (2010). Teacher self-efficacy and teacher burnout: A study of relations. *Teaching and Teacher Education, 26*(4), 1059-1069.

Stets, J. E. (2006). Identity theory. In P. J. Burke (Ed.), *Contemporary Social Psychological Theories* (pp. 88-110). Stanford, CA: Stanford University Press.

Strage, A., Meyers, S., & Norris, J. (2002). Lessons Learned from the "It Takes a Valley" program: Recruiting and retaining future teachers to serve in high-needs schools. *Teacher Education Quarterly, 29*(3), 73-92.

Stryker, S. (1995). Role theory. In A. S. R. Manstead & M. Hewstone (Eds.), *The Blackwell Encyclopedia of Social Psychology* (pp. 485-487). Cambridge, MA: Blackwell.

Sundin, O. (2001). Information strategies and occupational identity: A study of nurses' experiences of information at the workplace. *Information Research, 6*(2). Retrieved from http://InformationR.net/ir/6-2/ws6.html

Swackhamer, L. E. (2009). *An investigation into the influences on mathematics teacher efficacy in elementary teachers: A mixed methods study* (Doctoral dissertation). Retrieved from ProQuest Dissertations and Theses. Retrieved (305092)

tenDam, G. T. M. & Blom, S. (2006). Learning through participation: The potential of school-based teacher education for developing a professional identity. *Teaching and Teacher Education, 22,* 647-660.

Tsui, A. B. M. (2007). Complexities of identity formation: A narrative inquiry of an EFL teacher. *TESOL Quarterly, 41*(4), 657-680.

Vygotsky, L. S. (1962). *Thought and language.* Cambridge, MA: MIT Press.

Wenger, E. (1998). *Communities of practice: Learning meaning and identity.* New York, NY: Cambridge University Press.

Woodford, P. (2002). The social construction of music teacher identity in undergraduate music education. In R. Colwell and C. Richardson (Eds.), *The New Handbook of Research on Teaching and Learning* (pp. 675-697), New York, NY: Oxford.

Worthy, J. (2005). 'It didn't have to be so hard': The first five years of teaching in an urban school. *International Journal of Qualitative Studies in Education, 18*(3), 379-398.

Zembylas, M (2003). Caring for teacher emotion: Reflections on teacher self-development. *Studies in Philosophy and Education, 22,* 103-12.

A Study of Children's Spontaneous Singing in the Minority Regions of China: Analyzing with the Standpoint of Researcher as Relative Outsider

Yiying Wang
Beijing Normal University (China)
wangyiy@bnu.edu.cn

Yanjie Yang
Beijing Normal University (China)
yyjyzw@163.com

Abstract

We emphasized the normal form of anthropology, and attempt to collect information through the quality manner with a role of relative "outsider". That means, at one hand, we get into the field and participate in the daily work of caring with classroom teachers; at the other hand, we collect the target behavior without any interrupting to provide kids with free time.

59 children from 2 rural kindergartens in the minority regions of Yunnan province are chosen to be the participants of the study. We observed the kids through the day, and quickly wrote down the musical, occasional and individual features of children's spontaneous singing. In the study, researchers work as a relative outsider and come to some conclusion that: 1. the frequency, duration, significance of children's spontaneous singing is influenced by their character; and there are different expressions between introversive and exocentric kids; 2. local dialect play a role in children's spontaneous singing, especially when they begin to sing and when they want to continue their singing; and 3. children will get comforted by their own spontaneous singing; after getting familiar with each other, we realize that some kids build a world in which they feel psychological security through the spontaneous singing by themselves.

Keywords
Children, spontaneous singing, anthropology method, outsider

Introduction

Social science deals with the factors and phenomena of human beings which can be concluded as subjective interpretation and objective regulation. While as children's spontaneous singing is the expression of their music instinct and music experience, the behavior can be interpreted subjectively and with some regularity according to children's age. Therefore, we can analyze the inner nature and influence factors of children's spontaneous singing by the quality methods which are commonly used in the research of social science.

Specifically, when referring to children's music expressions, we can build on the theory and the normal form of anthropologic research. While the limitation of analyzing and interpreting is the identity of an "outsider" when exploring the music expression in original clans (Nettle, 2010), we should reset our position in the research and ensure the proper extend of our intervention.

So what position should we take when explore children's spontaneous singing in their daily life? To make it clearly, considering the purpose to understand the influence of music instinct, music experience and cultural environment have on children's spontaneous singing, what is the form of observation we should employ to collect the most authentic and vivid information. We don't expect the situation that kids hide their behavior or vice versa. In light of this challenge, we believe that researchers can take the position of a relative outsider to get into the field and collect materials with both objectivity and subjectivity.

Background

Children's spontaneous music behavior gains lots of concerns in the realm of music education in early years due to its special nature of reflecting children's music instinct and experience. And the method of observation is employed in most of the studies. For example, written records were used when recording children's self-initiate music behavior in supportive environment (Young, 2004). Details of children's behavior, such as syllable, tone, and lyric (if possible), were quickly written down; and the melodies were settled in time. Yet the researcher realized that this kind of written records may lead to a focus on the pure music elements, and to an ignorance of the contexture factors.

Most scholars prefer using mass media device to collect children's spontaneous singing behaviors holistically and authentically. In the special environment with certain musical materials, the researcher could easily video children's self-initiate music behavior during their play, and of course, with children themselves uninformed. And in this case, written records were used as a supplement to the video (Littleton, 1994). There were 2 adults in this progress, including the researcher who controlled the video and the classroom teacher. The intervention was limited to a minimize level.

In these studies, researchers are separated from the scene as pure observers and recorders. They offer spaces to kids without intervention, and thus kids can freely express their music behavior. Ultimately objective materials of children's spontaneous singing are collected. For instance, previous studies proclaimed the definition, type, feature, factors about children's spontaneous singing. While we are still wondering whether there will be any differences if the researcher gets a little deeper into the field? Is there any possible for us to recognize the influence of children's character and the culture factors? Based on this, we attempt to build an identity of relative outsider, and to explore whether the different standpoint will bring some new information.

Method

The study collects children's spontaneous in their daily life through observation, interview and case study in the minority kindergartens of Yunnan Province, and analyzes the feature, factor, cultural influence and significance in this behavior. In the pre-observation, we realized that we can certainly collect lots of materials about children's spontaneous singing by taking the position of an absolute outsider, or a pure researcher, yet the cases are separated and unconnected. Therefore we edited the manner in which we get into the field later by taking the responsibility of some caring work rather than purely observing.

Object of the Study
We have chosen 2 minority kindergartens in the rural areas of Yunnan Province in China and collected information of 59 children age 5~6 (male: 23; female: 26). We chose minority regions and rural areas because for thousand years, old manners and traditions are more or less kept in the rural areas of China, in some extends, it is important to go back to the rural and minority regions to explore the influence of traditional culture.

Method
We take the position of a relative outsider to conduct the study, which means we get into the class, take the responsibility of helping teachers to take care of children's life, to maintain the order of the class, to organize some sessions of a day (such as washing, eating, nap, and so on), to interact with individual kid in free play. But we do not interrupt the group activities and educational sessions. No interventions and judgments take place during observation. We make our efforts to ensure that children do not realize that their behaviors are recorded. Also we do not employ video device in order to avoid the possible stimulation for kids to perform on purpose.

Based on this, we employ observation, interview and case study to collect information.

First, we observed children's daily life to make a holistic record. We choose the sample by event; and describe children's continual free singing. According to the specific condition, the materials are collected, including the occasion, duration, gender of the kid, stimulated or not, pieces of melody, with or without action and lyric, other kids' and teachers' reaction, and the facial expression of the child. Second, based on the observation, we combined the free interview together to understand the background of the children, including the family background, environment of the kindergarten, instructional condition and the culture context. The information supports us to interpret children's spontaneous singing behavior. At the same time, the freely optional interview helps to build trustiness between teacher and researcher, and in some extends, it can decrease the limitation of our identity as an outsider. Finally, Case study was used in the later phases of analyzing. Based on the general observation and interview, we chose typical children to explore the influence that their character placed on the behavior.

Conclusion

Character will influence children's spontaneous singing
There are differences in the frequency and emotion between children with difference character. Extravert children tend to express themselves and to seek for communication when singing spontaneously. Their singing behavior may be more joyful. They are easily stopping singing and changing their focus when something interesting happens. While introverted children tend to sing for themselves, and the melody tend to be more varied with a

longer duration.

1. Introverted children tend to sing spontaneously more often, with a more varied melody and longer duration. For instance, a child (A) prefers drawing to playing with other kids when it is possible, and he will also sing to the drawing and imitate the sound of fight. The tone and rhythm are changed along with the content of his drawing. Another example, a girl (B) spent most of her free time to sing alone, including the free play in the playground while other kids are running and laughing.
2. Extrovert children tend to seek for communication by spontaneous singing; they expect that their singing could draw the attention of teacher or other kids. Meanwhile, they tend to create the lyric of their singing. For instance, they will stop to ask other kids:" Can you sing this?" or say to the teacher:" Listen to me!" when singing spontaneously. Yet this kind of behavior can't always initiate communication, which they expect. They also sing interesting things in a playful manner and enjoy creating.

The local dialect influence children's spontaneous singing in minority regions

When singing spontaneously, children who live in the minority regions would begin with a tone which is much like the local dialect. Specifically, children in kindergarten A (located in the Bai region) prefer to sing from "Sol"; while children in kindergarten B (located in the Hani region) prefer to sing from "Re". Both of them are much similar with their respectively local dialects.

Sometimes when talking to others, kids heard their own voice and may think, "Oh, it's like singing", and then stimulated by this idea, they will expand their words into a free singing with or without lyrics or nonsense syllables. At the same time, local dialect is the language, which is first met and most frequently used by children, thus kids are so familiar with the tone of the local dialect which is easy to pronounce by them. We also find that the pieces of spontaneous singing, which begin from the dialect talking, are more fluency, nature, and continual.

Spontaneous singing is a comfort for children.

Children will not only express their physical and security satisfaction or stable and positive emotion, but also comfort themselves by spontaneous singing, especially for introverted kids. We can use the example of B. She lives in a rural family with rare family education from parents. It seems that she has never done well in self-regulation. Although parents and teachers are never too severe to her, she still express strong sense of insecurity and defence to teachers and other children. According to the teacher, she seems scared once the teacher moves in front of her. While through the observation, we find out that B tend to sing along the day and become calm and joyful when singing. We also talked to B after getting familiar with her (which needs much more time) and realize that she likes singing very much. And for the first time, she sang the birthday song for us; and a confident facial expression appeared at that time. In some ways, the spontaneous singing is the "placebo" for B in the kindergarten. She builds her own world of security and confidence by spontaneous singing.

Through the partial participating in their daily life, reacting with kids during free time, and talking to teachers freely, we combine information of character and culture together to get a holistic picture about children's spontaneous singing. And by realizing the proper timing to keep silent, we can understand the significances of continuous or occasional spontaneous singing. Generally speaking, to take the position of relative outsider is helpful to analyze the kids as a developing holistic individual in an objective manner; meanwhile, to explore the factors of children's behavior after getting familiar with them and not only considering their identity of participants. But the further question is, how to promote this method to improve the validity, maybe we can expect "teacher as researcher".

References

Littleton, D. (1994). *Cross-cultural perspectives on young children's music making in the context of play* (Guo Chunyan, Trans.). China Music Education.

Nettle, B. (2010, August). Keynote speech. *Proceedings from the 29th World Conference on Music Education*, p. 8, Beijing, China.

Young, S. (2004). Young children's spontaneous vocalising: Insights into play and pathways. *International Journal of Early Childhood*, 36(2), 59-74.

The Independent Music Teacher as Researcher: A case study

Lorna Wanzel
Nova Scotia Registered Music Teachers' Association Research Group
Halifax, Nova Scotia (Canada)
lwanzel@eastlink.ca

Abstract

This paper focuses on the shared experiences of 5 independent music teachers (IMTs) within a collaborative action research group. A team approach was employed to explore how IMTs worked collaboratively; enhanced their knowledge and understandings; changed individual perspectives; achieved commitment to outcomes for professional practice. Eight years ago the Nova Scotia Registered Music Teachers' Association (NSRMTA) a provincial organization, which is a member of the Canadian Federation of Music Teachers' Associations (CFMTA), organized the first IMTs Research Group in Canada. Its purpose was to give studio music teachers an opportunity to work collaboratively, conduct research and organize their own learning along self-determined interests, by studying an issue from different professional perspectives and sharing existing knowledge, while working together toward a common goal of generating new knowledge. Being part of the NSRMTA Research Group gave these teacher-researchers the opportunity to reflect upon their experiences as teachers and become critical about what they do. The group's first project was Motivation and Retention of Students in the Private Music Studio. Independent studio music teachers do not typically see the role of researcher as being a part of our professional practice. The formation of the NSRTMA Research Group helped change this. Over a period of eight years, I observed, kept a reflective journal and on two different occasions interviewed all five teacher-researchers in the group. My goal was to achieve a rich and detailed representation of what, how, when and where IMTs conduct collaborative practitioner research.

Keywords
Teacher/researcher, action research, independent music teacher.

Introduction

This research was conducted in the context of my work as an independent music teacher (IMT), who teaches both piano skills and theory, a registered music teacher (RMT) and an Ed.D. candidate at the University of South Australia. Based on my experience and perspective on private music teaching in Canada specifically, I asked the questions: Why don't IMTs generally conduct practitioner research? What needs to change so IMTs see research as part of our professional practice and identity?

In the NSRTMA Research Group, the chief difference between expert-driven training and teacher/research inquiry is that here was a group of teachers who produced validated knowledge that addressed issues facing them in their own practice. In other words, they were not passive recipients of others' knowledge but were actively engaged in producing their own.

Collaboration is more than a group of researchers getting together and working on the same project. It is a process that demands a sense of shared purpose and an equal sharing of ownership, power and responsibility (Goodlad, 1993). The Research Group organized its own learning along self-determined interests, by studying an issue from different professional perspectives by sharing existing knowledge, while working together towards a common goal of generating new knowledge (Farr-Darling, 2001).

As President of the NSRMTA at the time, I invited members of the Association to form the Research Group and develop a research agenda. Five members joined the group and under the mentorship of a university professor, who is an academic researcher, the group decided to research motivation and retention of private students in the independent music studio. We met on a monthly basis and all group members agreed on the research topic, design and method. The data was obtained by each teacher/researcher interviewing 2 students, 2 parents of students and 2 other IMTs, asking them open ended questions about what they thought motivated students to start private piano lessons and later to continue with lessons.

The data generated by each of the teacher/researchers was subjected to a thematic analysis whereby key themes were discussed and noted, after coding them into meaningful groups (Tuckett, 2005). While the group was conducting this research I, as a participant observer, kept a journal recording what happened in the meetings, observed how the teacher/researchers engaged in their research and established conditions in the collaboration that sustained and enhanced our ability to construct our own knowledge. I interviewed each of the teacher/researchers twice, once in the middle of the research project and again at the end of the project.

Method

Over a period of eight years, I watched, kept notes and on two different occasions, interviewed all five of the teacher/researchers in the group. My goal was to achieve a rich and detailed representation of the what, how, when and where these independent music teachers conducted collaborative practitioner research.

Data collection procedures included: Individually taped interviews with four of the teacher/researchers of about 60 minutes in duration midway through the research project.

A second set of individually taped interviews with five of the teacher/researchers of about 30 minutes duration after the project's completion. I also kept and continue to keep a reflective journal.

I asked open-ended questions such as: What did you think about the collaborative research process? What do you feel you gained, if anything, from the research process? I kept extensive notes in my journals, which included minutes of our meetings and observations I made. These notes were written from the commencement of the group's first project to its completion and afterwards as the group continued to meet to conduct and consider new projects.

A critical action approach was used in the analysis of the data. This type of research identifies matters of importance to members of a community and is an inductive process in which research can be viewed as a type of social action (Freire, 1970). This type of research is frequently called participatory research (Anderson, Herr, & Sigrid, 1994). It includes social structures and processes, which are understood within a historical structure. Theory and practice are integrated – praxis. The subject-object relationship is transformed into a subject-subject relationship through dialogue. Research and action develop into a single process. The findings on participants' perceptions about conducting research revealed insights about the factors that hindered and supported their success as teacher/researchers. These insights are presented within a framework of four key themes, which emerged from the data analysis. These were: The teacher/researchers' expectations at the beginning of the research process. Their evaluations after they had conducted their interviews. Their evaluations after they had presented their findings. Their evaluations after they had completed their first project.

Pioneers

At the beginning of the research project, the novelty of studio music teachers conducting collaborative research was such that the members of the research group described themselves as pioneers (Wanzel, 2009). In the interviews that I conducted it became clear that these teacher/researchers had very little idea as to what to expect when they first joined the group. This was expressed in various ways as "having no expectations". One teacher said she was "feeling vague" because she had no similar or prior experiences to serve as a reference point (Wanzel, 2009, p. 140). Professional isolation is a common complaint among studio teachers who don't have the benefit of meeting with their colleagues in a staff room the way school teachers do. One teacher said: "I think others could benefit from what we've done, not just in the line of research but getting together. There isn't a lot of contact among the teachers and I think meeting was beneficial" (Wanzel, 2009, p. 142).

Creating New Knowledge

After the teacher/researchers had conducted their interviews they shared more of their thoughts:

> The most important thing that I got out of [the research] is that it set me thinking a lot more. There were things I didn't consider important to the teaching of music. [Before] I

> was teaching, but felt I had to do this to finish my syllabus. Motivation wasn't as important as it was after I had done this research. When you are doing the research yourself, I think it is a lot more meaningful. You read a book or an article, well,

> that is somebody else's life. I have never felt as receptive towards it as when you do your own research with your own students who mean something to you. Sometimes when somebody else is talking about how they dealt with a certain student, you feel well I

don't have a student like that, maybe she is brilliant, but she is not like mine. Forget about it!! (Wanzel, 2009, p. 151)

Researchers as Performers

After the group had completed their interviews and analyzed the data, we decided to present our findings to our colleagues as a panel at the annual NSRMTA convention. In the interviews I conducted after our panel presentation, the teacher/researchers had time to think about how we had conducted the research process. One teacher felt we could have presented a more "polished performance" (Wanzel, 2009, p. 147).

At our meetings there were frequent references made to the fact that we are very busy teachers and conducting research was hard because of that. Trying to coordinate meetings was a challenge because of our busy teaching schedules and family obligations. Overall, despite their misgivings about the thoroughness of their research and presentation, the teacher/researchers highly valued the learning that was enabled through their research. Compared to our usual professional development opportunities such as workshops, which are usually based on a conservatory syllabus or latest publications of a large music publishing company, conducting their own research was directly related to these teachers' own practice. In considering this, I acknowledge my own investment in the teachers' responses. It had been my dissatisfaction and feeling marginalized in professional learning contexts that had led me to want to conduct teacher research. After all, learning and meaning making are inextricably entwined.

Concluding observations and future considerations

The goal of collaborative action research in education is to bring about change in existing theories of learning and teaching. The group's research process focused on their practice and enhanced the teacher/researchers' professional development. Even though it was not an easy process, it was an instrument for teacher education, reform and change. There is increased recognition within registered music teachers associations for this new collective form of knowing.

Conspicuous by their absence from much of the literature on teaching, and independent music teaching in particular, are the voices of the teachers themselves. The NSRMTA Research Group found that collaboration is not about losing power but about findings ways to generate it and to help each other to feel powerful in ways that lead to deeper shared understandings (Wanzel, 2009).

Official discourses in the field position private studio music teachers as technicians who ensure the transmission of discourses from the center, for example national conservatories, to the periphery which would be our students. IMTs are large stakeholders in the field of private music teaching but we do not exercise the control or power that stakeholders may hold in other fields. In spite of our numbers and influence in our communities, an IMT's power is very limited when it comes to knowledge creation and power relations in the field of music education. In the field of independent music teaching in Canada there has not been any attempt to problematize the standpoint of the expert. This research conducted by the NSRMTA Research Group highlights the value of IMTs thinking critically, theoretically and reflectively since, without such an analysis, the tendency is to accept one's usual position in the field as normal.

We found that while conducting research may not be for everyone, it is certainly within the capabilities of studio music teachers. IMTs have many attributes that are an advantage to researchers. However, expanding the numbers of music teacher/researchers will not be without challenge. We need to raise the general profile of teacher-research among colleagues. We need to address questions such as: what are the most effective ways of building awareness of research amongst IMTs? What opportunities do IMTs need in order to conduct their own research? What are the most effective strategies for forming research groups? How can such activities be funded? What resources could be provided to encourage more practitioner research in this field?

Introducing the concept of research to IMTs needs to be coupled with the removal of certain ideas that research should only be conducted by experts in universities and that it is not something studio music teachers should do. It would be of great benefit if research methodology courses were taught to undergraduate students studying music pedagogy. The NSRTMA would welcome more collaborations and this appears to reflect the desire of a growing number of teacher-/researchers in music education. Already the group has collaborated with another researcher from Malaysia on a study comparing adult piano students in Canada and Malaysia. The group continues to meet and look for new projects and collaborations.

From the perspective of critical theory, what teachers believe involves requirements and wishes that are entrenched by the status quo into which teachers are socialized. As cited in Abrahams (Abrahams, 2007) in the case of music education, this includes music, musicians, music teachers and music education (Regelski, 1998). Rose (1990) studied music education and its relation to cultural reproduction (Bourdieu, 1987) and the production of culture (Apple, 1982). Rose also looked at issues of hegemony (Gramsci, 1971) and found music education to be objectified for the expressed purpose of reproducing and maintaining musical traditions and the underlying assumptions of these traditions.

Music education plays an important role as an agent of social and cultural production and reproduction, whether this takes place in the private studio or school. Freire (1970) expressed a belief in the power of individuals to reach a critical consciousness of their own existence through the process of conscientization - a process that goes beyond the power to recall information to include the knowledge and ability to act in such a way as to affect change. To develop a critical consciousness in music education, an examination of music tradition within our socio-cultural framework is needed. For the NSRMTA Research Group this started with the question "why don't IMTs conduct research?" and the desire to create their own knowledge based on their own experiences within their own private studios.

References

Abrahams, F. (2007). Musicing Paulo Freire: A critical pedagogy for music education. In P. McLaren & J. L. Kincheloe (Ed.), *Critical pedagogy where are we now* (pp. 223-238). New York, NY: Peter Lang.

Anderson, G., Herr, K., & Sigrid, A. (1994). *Studying your own school: An educator's guide to qualitative practitioner research*. Thousand Oaks, CA: Corwin Press, Sage.

Apple, M. (1982). *Education and power*. Boston, MA: Routledge & Kegan Paul.

Bourdieu, P. (1987). The forms of capital. In J. Richardson (Ed.), *Handbook of theory and research for sociology of education* (pp. 158-241). New York, NY: Greenwood Press.

Farr-Darling, L. (2001). When conceptions collide, constructing a community of inquiry for teacher education in British Columbia. *Journal of Education for Teaching, 27*(1), 7-21.

Freire, P. (1970). *Pedagogy of the oppressed.* New York, NY: Continuum.

Goodlad, J. (1993). School university partnerships and partner schools. *Educational Policy, 7*(1), 24-39.

Gramsci, A. (1971). *Selections from Prison Notebooks of Antonio Gramsci.* New York, NY: International Publishers.

Regelski, T. A. (1998). Critical theory as a basis for critical thinking in music education. *Studies in Music from the University of Western Ontario, 17,* 1-19.

Rose, A. M. (1990). *Music education in culture: A critical analysis of reproduction, production and hegemony* (Doctoral dissertation). University of Wisconsin, Madison.

Tuckett, A. G. (2005). Applying thematic analysis theory to practice: a researcher's experience. *Contemporary Nurse, 19,* 75-87.

Wanzel, L. I. (2009). *Independent Music teachers Building Professional Knowledge Through Collaborative Research* (Doctoral dissertation). University of South Australia, Adelaide.

An Examination of the Perceptions of Undergraduate Music Education Students in Pre-Service Conducting Experiences with University Choral Ensembles

Jeffrey Ward
East Carolina University (USA)
wardj@ecu.edu

Abstract

Four pre-service choral music educators enrolled in a public university in the United States participated in the "University Chorale Small Ensemble Project." In this project, pre-service teachers, under the supervision of this researcher, selected, introduced, polished, and conducted choral music repertoire. Pre-service teachers and the singers in each ensemble, which averaged 25 students, completed an online, researcher-designed survey. Pre-service teachers identified two areas of concern in their teaching: rehearsal pacing/ time management and error detection. This researcher recommended that teacher preparation programs include teaching experiences with the same group of students to allow pre-service teachers to better identify appropriate rehearsal pacing and time management skills for the particular needs of the ensemble. Additionally, this researcher recommends pre-services teacher participate in a formal error detection training program that is separate from a conducting and rehearsal experience to prevent pre-service teachers from being distracted by their own instructional concerns, such as, rehearsal facilitating, conducting, and classroom management. Finally, this researcher recommends teacher education faculty and ensemble directors consistently implement systematic reflection opportunities for pre-service teachers and ensemble members.

Keywords
Teacher training, rehearsal, choir

American university faculty design instruction and experiences to prepare students for successful careers in music education. This curriculum includes methods courses and teaching experiences in a variety of contexts: peer teaching, micro-teaching in schools, university-sponsored programs, and the student teaching internship.

Bauer and Berg (2001) recommended increased pre-service teaching opportunities, with researchers examining effective practices (Paul et al., 2001; Schmidt, 2010). Additionally, researchers have examined facilitating teacher reflection skills in pre-service teaching (Campbell and Thompson, 2007; Colwell, 1995; Conway, 2010; Paul et al., 2001; Ward & High, 2009).

Pre-service teacher reflection is coupled with feedback from peers in many undergraduate teaching experiences. Researchers have found that novice teachers and non-music majors effectively offer appropriate teacher ratings and feedback (Byo, 1990; Duke, Prickett, & Jellison, 1998; Madsen, Standley, & Cassidy, 1989; Napoles, 2008).

Study Context

Music education faculty decide when students should have pre-service teaching experiences and the setting in which those experiences occur. They also decide the format of teacher feedback and level of faculty involvement in pre-service teaching experiences. Schmidt (2010) reported that students in pre-service teaching experiences are "distracted" by university faculty observers and feel a greater sense of autonomy with self-arranged teaching experiences; but pre-service teachers still want the support of faculty and cooperating teachers, through consistent feedback, coupled with peer feedback (Napoles, 2008).

In this study, this researcher provided a choral music teaching experience for four pre-service teachers in the "Senior I" semester. "Senior I" occurs the semester before the student teaching internship. In addition to coursework, these students teach in their future internship placements for an entire day, once per week, throughout the semester. Prior teaching experiences for these students include peer teaching, micro-teaching in public schools, teaching in a university-sponsored, elementary-aged afterschool music program, and teaching with faculty supervision in a high-school aged community chorus. As a supplement to the Senior I choral methods course, the course instructor, this researcher, who also conducts a choir of music majors and non-majors, initiated the "University Chorale Small Ensemble Project," as a means to provide consistent, supervised pre-teaching experiences.

The 100-voice choir was divided into two mixed and two treble ensembles of approximately equal size. The ensembles rehearsed for 30 minutes during regularly-scheduled choir meetings, two times per week for five weeks, culminating in a public performance, conducted by the pre-service teacher. Through this project, this researcher addressed the following research problems: 1. To examine teaching reflections of pre-service teachers; 2. To examine singer perceptions of rehearsal content and effectiveness led by pre-service teachers; and 3. To identify perceptions of pre-service teachers and singers regarding the effectiveness of a pre-service teaching experience in the development of choral music education skills.

Method

Students enrolled in a choral music methods course were given the option of participating in the "University Chorale Small Ensemble Project." Pre-service teachers made one repertoire selection from a variety of choral selections deemed appropriate for this project, as a means for pre-service teachers to feel artistically invested (Ward, 2010). Repertoire selection by the pre-service teachers determined their ensemble voicing. The priority of balanced voices and ratio of music to non-music majors was the basis for ensemble placements. Singers in the ensemble participated as a part of course requirements; however, participation in the study was optional.

Using the survey software *Qualtrics*, each pre-service teacher and singer completed an online, researcher-developed survey weekly for five weeks. Pre-service teachers listed vocal warm-up and repertoire rehearsal content and the level of perceived achievement in the two rehearsals each week. Additionally, the pre-service teacher rated the level of organization, preparedness, and overall effectiveness of the two rehearsals. Likewise, singers responded to the same components. Through a free-response narrative, pre-service teachers described their rehearsal in terms of success, struggle, and how these experiences contributed to their development as a music educator. Rehearsals occurred on Tuesday's and Thursday's of each week and conductors and singers were instructed by this researcher to complete the weekly survey after the Thursday rehearsal, but before the following Tuesday rehearsal. Participants were further instructed to answer survey questions based on their experiences of both the Tuesday and Thursday rehearsals. This researcher maintained the online surveys and deleted any surveys that occurred between the Tuesday and Thursday rehearsals.

Conducting in a Supervised Environment

The project was a transition from practicum and peer teaching experiences (high degree of university faculty supervision) to the student teaching internship (low degree of university faculty supervision and often a low degree of supervision from the cooperating teacher). This researcher rotated between rehearsals, spending approximately 15 minutes with each pre-service teacher; thus, this researcher saw all four pre-service teachers each week between the two weekly 30-minute rehearsals. As appropriate, this researcher served as the piano accompanist; wrote feedback notes that were shared after the rehearsal; and offered feedback during the rehearsal in a "master class" format.

The "master class" was employed the least frequently, but was used by this researcher when the conductor was unsure of how to most efficiently solve musical or technical problems during the rehearsal. This researcher was careful not to allow this to be a "crutch" and encouraged the pre-service teacher to think through the problem, often answering a question with a question.

Additionally, the assigned rehearsal accompanist for the choir, rotated among the pre-service teachers on the opposite schedule of this researcher. This accompanist, a graduate student with over 20 years of high school choral teaching experience, offered appropriate feedback at the end of rehearsals.

Results

In weekly surveys pre-service teachers and singers answered questions regarding content of vocal warm-ups and repertoire rehearsal and level of achievement in these areas. The number of times the intentions of the conductor was perceived by a majority of singers is shown in Table 1 (please note that a vocal warm-up was not done by all conductors every week). In ensembles A and D, there were consistent differences between pre-service teacher intention and singer by the pre-service teacher.

In regards to the rehearsal repertoire, the intentions of the pre-service teacher were more frequently perceived by a majority of singers from the first and second week to the last three weeks. Singers and pre-service teachers gave similar answers regarding the achievement of perceived objectives for the rehearsal.

Table 1. Agreements with Singers in Warm-up and Rehearsal Repertoire

Pre-Service Teacher	A			B		C		D			
Week	3	4	5	4	5	2	5	2	3	4	5
Number of Warm-up Agreements with Singers	2 of 2	2 of 3	1 of 4	3 of 4	4 of 5	4 of 4	4 of 5	3 of 6	3 of 5	3 of 5	3 of 5

Pre-Service Teacher	A					B					C					D				
Week	1	2	3	4	5	1	2	3	4	5	1	2	3	4	5	1	2	3	4	5
Number of Repertoire Rehearsal Agreements with Singers	2 of 3	5 of 5	3 of 5	4 of 5	4 of 5	4 of 7	6 of 6	6 of 7	5 of 7	5 of 6	5 of 6	5 of 7	5 of 6	4 of 4	5 of 5	3 of 4	5 of 7	5 of 6	5 of 7	6 of 6

Regarding the level of organization and preparedness, pre-service teachers A, B, and C perceived an increase over the course of the project. Overall, the perception of the majority of singers was either in agreement or higher than the pre-service teacher. This finding differs from Napoles (2008) who found peer ratings consistently lower than self-evaluations in peer teaching. Regarding the level of overall effectiveness, pre-service teachers B and D perceived an increase in overall effectiveness over the course of the project. Overall, the perception of the majority of singers was either in agreement or higher than the pre-service teacher.

Pre-service teacher free-responses regarding success, struggle, and how these experiences contributed to their development as a music educator are shown in Table 2. These responses give insight into the reflection of these pre-service teachers.

After the first week, pre-service teachers reported success in teaching pitches and rhythms. As a large number of singers in each ensemble consisted of non-music majors with limited music literacy skills, this researcher observed pre-service teachers follow a rote process. Conductors B, C, and D expressed that identifying musical and technical errors and problems and providing efficient solutions was a struggle and/or developed during the project.

Additionally, pre-service teachers addressed their need to focus and/or improve upon rehearsal efficiency and time management. Pre-service teachers also reported a developing confidence in their skills as music educators and in their ensembles as a result of this program.

Table 2. Pre-service teacher free-responses.

Pre-service Teacher	Week	Success	Struggles	Development	Pre-service Teacher	Week	Success	Struggles	Development
A	1	Teaching pitches and rhythms	Communicating with people from various musical backgrounds	Efficiency	B	1	Identifying problems	Strategies to fix problems	Understanding of preparation needed
	2	Putting all pieces together	Tempo	Ensemble is learning		2	Teaching soprano lines	Teaching the tenors	Understanding of preparation needed
	3	Singing in performance hall was helpful	Women fighting tempos	Space can change the sound		3	Women's blend	Balancing the men's sections	Remind choir to practice outside of class
	4	Perform for another group	Diction	Confidence as a result of group confidence		4	Choir was able to sing through entire piece	Keeping singers engaged	How to involve everyone most of the time
	5	Rehearsing smaller chunks	Letting attitude influence rehearsal	Realizing how to start polishing the piece.		5	Limiting my talking	Deciding where to start correcting	Confidence boost: identifying problem and fixing the problem are two different things

Table 2 continued.

Pre-service Teacher	Week	Success	Struggles	Development	Pre-service Teacher	Week	Success	Struggles	Development
C	1	Teaching notes	Communication	Self-confidence in front of ensemble	D	1	Review of previous teaching	Teaching new material	Reality check
C	2	Ensembles learning pitches and rhythm	Time management: did not plan enough to fill the time	Development of rehearsal structure	D	2	Listening	Time management	Development of ear
C	3	Teaching word stress	Talking too quickly	Listening and interpreting	D	3	Error correction	Pacing/time management	Confidence in group
C	4	Finding soloists/blend	Hearing diction errors	New experience of facilitating solo auditions	D	4	Vowel Uniformity	Phrasing	Persistance is the key: always have fun
C	5	Coaching soloists	Releases	Seeing what a final product will look like	D	5	Phrasing went well	Trying to figure out what to fix	Confidence in group

Conclusion

This researcher offered feedback, but allowed pre-service teachers to "find their own way" in the "University Chorale Small Ensemble Project," a transition from peer teaching and practicum opportunities to students teaching. Unlike traditional undergraduate teaching opportunities, pre-service teachers experienced the complete rehearsal process (selecting repertoire; introducing and polishing repertoire; and conducting repertoire with all of the responsibility of performance success) with consistent contact of the same group of students.

Through this project, pre-service teachers perceived increased self-confidence. This researcher prepared them for the student teaching internship by "weaning" their dependence on faculty supervision. Confidence increased through the project, as pre-service teachers witnessed the progress of the ensemble solely through their instruction. Researchers should replicate this university-teaching model to study measures of self-confidence of participants to pre-service teachers without such an opportunity.

In the study, this researcher examined pre-service teacher and singer perceptions regarding content and quality of rehearsals. In two of the four ensembles, singers did not accurately perceive the intentions of the pre-service teachers. Pre-service teachers communicated that they referred to rehearsal plans written prior to rehearsal when completing the survey. The differences could be attributed to deviations from rehearsal plans during rehearsal. This difference could also be attributed to a lack of clarity from pre-service teachers that could hinder the metacognitive efforts of singers as they evaluate their own learning. Pre-service teachers are encouraged to develop better communication skills, overtly expressing rehearsal objectives in their rehearsal.

Pre-service teachers expressed concerns and recognized growth in areas of rehearsal pacing and error detection. Prior to this project, pre-service teachers had inconsistent opportunities to pace rehearsals because they did not teach the same students on a regular basis or rehearsal repertoire was taught by multiple conductors, either a peer or a cooperating teacher. By participating in this project, pre-service teachers were better able to find a rehearsal pace that was most appropriate for their specific ensemble.

Citing a number of researchers (Byo, 1997; Ramsey, 1979; Stuart, 1979) that traditional courses in music theory are not sufficient for training music educators in detecting errors during a rehearsal, Deal (1985) recommended a formal program of error detection training. Ward (in press) created *Choir Adjudication Training* (CAT) that follows the choral festival adjudication format in training music educators to accurately detect errors and find effective solutions. A systematic error detection training program, outside of a rehearsal, will allow music educators to develop these skills without distractions in facilitating and conducting rehearsals. Pre-service teachers in the "University Chorale Small Ensemble Project" would have been more comfortable in pacing rehearsals with better skills in this area. Conductor D commented to this researcher that "I'm so concerned with my conducting and following my rehearsal plan that I don't hear anything they are singing. I turn my ears off and only hear what I think it should sound like."

The survey format of this study was an opportunity for pre-service teachers to reflect on their teaching. Conway (2010) points to the need to develop a self-reflection disposition in new teachers as means to retain them in the profession. Incorporating systematic instructional reflection, coupled with systematic assessment practices, is the basis for future instructional design (Ward & High, 2010). This reflection practice is also helpful for singers. In completing the survey, each singer reflected on their individual and ensemble performance. This metacognitive thinking leads singers to focus on areas that need improvement; thus, singer reflections and its influence on performance is an area of future research.

This study was limited in number of subjects (n=4) and time (five weeks). Future researchers of developing rehearsal and conducting skills need to examine the issue from a longitudinal standpoint. Researchers should collect reflections of pre-service teachers from initial peer teaching through the student teaching internship. Additionally, researchers should examine new teacher reflections to determine the impact of the type and quality of pre-service teaching experiences on instructional effectiveness and whether systematic pre-service teaching reflection fosters a reflective disposition in practicing teachers.

Researchers need to continually examine the most effective means of transitioning pre-service teachers from student to teacher. Fostering necessary teacher dispositions in pre-service teachers is a combination of course work and application teaching that goes from faculty control in to a gradual release of that control over the course of the undergraduate curriculum, resulting in pre-service teachers analyzing the needs of their students and finding the most appropriate means for meeting those needs.

References

Bauer, W. I., & Berg, M. H. (2001). Influences on instrumental music teaching. *Bulletin of the Council for Research in Music Education, 150*, 53-66.

Byo, J. L. (1997). The effects of texture and number of parts on the ability of music majors to detect performance errors. *Journal of Research in Music Education, 45*, 51-66. doi: 10.2307/3345465

Byo, J. L. (1990). Recognition of intensity contrasts in the gestures of beginning conductors. *Journal of Research in Music Education, 38*, 157–163. doi: 10.2307/3345179

Cambell, M. R., & Thompson, L. K. (2007). Perceived concerns of preservice music education teachers: A cross-sectional study. *Journal of Research in Music Education, 55*, 162–176. doi: 10.1177/002242940705500206

Colwell, C. M. (1995). Effect of teaching setting and self-evaluation on teacher intensity behaviors. *Journal of Research in Music Education, 43*, 6–21. doi: 10.2307/3345788

Conway, C. (2010). Issues facing music teacher education in the 21st century: Developing leaders in the field. In H. Abeles & L. Custodero (Eds.), *Critical issues in music education: Contemporary theory and practice* (pp. 259-275). New York, NY: Oxford University Press.

Deal, J. (1985). Computer-assisted instruction in pitch and rhythm error detection. *Journal of Research in Music Education, 33*, 159-166. doi: 10.2307/3344803

Duke, R. A., Prickett, C. A., & Jellison, J. A. (1998). Empirical description of the pace of music instruction. *Journal of Research in Music Education, 46*, 265-280.

Madsen, C. K., Standley, J. M., & Cassidy, J. W. (1989). Demonstration and recognition of high and low contrast in teacher intensity. *Journal of Research in Music Education, 37*, 85. doi: 10.2307/3344700

Napoles, J. (2008). Relationships among instructor, peer, and self-evaluations of undergraduate music education majors' micro-teaching experiences. *Journal of Research in Music Education, 56*, 82–91. doi: 10.1177/0022429408323071

Paul, S. J., Teachout, D. J, Sullivan, J. M., Kelly, S. N., Bauer, W. I., & Raiber, M. A. (2001). Authentic-context learning activities in instrumental music teacher education. *Journal of Research in Music Education, 49*, 136–145. doi: 10.2307/3345865

Ramsey, D. (1979). Programmed instruction using band literature to teach pitch and rhythm error detection to music education students. *Journal of Research in Music Education, 27*, 149-162. doi: 10.2307/3344966

Schmidt, M. (2010). Learning from teaching experience: Dewey's theory and preservice teachers' learning. *Journal of Research in Music Education, 58*, 131–146. doi: 10.1177/0022429410368823

Stuart, M. (1979). The use of videotape recordings to increase teacher trainees' error detection skills. *Journal of Research in Music Education, 27*, 14-19. doi: 10.2307/3345115

Ward, J. (2010). Tips from the podium: A guest conductor's perspective of the honor choir. *Choral Journal, 51*(3). 8-18.

Ward, J. (in press). A preliminary study of the development of error detection and assessment skills in choral ensemble performances through adjudication training. In T. Brophy (Ed.), *Third International Symposium on Assessment in Music Education* (ISAME). Chicago, IL: GIA.

Ward, J. T., & High, L. (2010). Theory into practice: Teaching assessment strategies to pre-service teachers through a third through fifth grade vocal music laboratory. In T. Brophy (Ed.), *Second International Symposium on Assessment in Music Education* (ISAME). Chicago, IL: GIA.

PHILOSOPHY PANEL PAPERS

*Reflection and Critical Considerations
on the Conference Theme
"Music Pædeia: From Ancient Greek
Philosophers Towards Global Music Communities"*

The Issue of Music Pædeia in the Light of
Current Trends and Challenges

Music as Ethical Practice: The Contemporary Significance of Ancient Greek Insights

Wayne D. Bowman
New York University, New York, NY

wdb4@nyu.edu

Although ancient Greek philosophers' accounts of music and its educational significance influenced people's thoughts and actions for thousands of years, from our proud place in the early twenty-first century it is tempting to dismiss these ancient ideas as naïve, parochial, or simply wrong. We all know, for instance, about Plato's musical conservatism, his prudishness, and his deep distrust of music and musicians. Behind these stances, however, lay a conception of music as a profoundly influential sociopolitical force with strong links to individual and collective identity—a force with the power to shape character for good or ill, and even to undermine state security. And no small part of what worried Plato was that musicians seemed indifferent if not oblivious to these potentials. Too often, he believed, musical practice was a mindless indulgence, undertaken merely for the satisfactions it afforded or for the sake of virtuosic technical display. Music was no innocuous diversion, no merely aesthetic indulgence. It did not consist in the skillful execution or appreciation of pleasing patterns of sound with supposedly intrinsic value that could, therefore, simply be taken for granted. It was a potent ethical and educational resource whose power could be used well or badly abused. Music was not primarily about contemplative or appreciative experience; it was an important sociopolitical agent, a major cultural player, a central part of the action.

After centuries of philosophical, musical, and educational "progress," our notions of music are thin and watery by comparison. Music, we often assume, is primarily about subjective or psychological gratification: a diversion that somehow lightens the burdens of what is often referred to "real life." Our beliefs about music's influences have become rather tentative and tenuous: music is more about arbitrary tastes and preferences than character or broad-based cultural concerns.

There are benefits to this stance, of course, for if music's ethical nature or its ethos are not significant concerns, there is no need for the kind of close scrutiny that led Plato to advocate censorship. If musical value is mostly a matter of personal taste (and if there is no disputing such matters, and if they are of no real consequence), then what music people engage in, or how, is no big deal. As we know, this was more or less the position Aristotle assumed on the matter: "different strokes for different folks", he might well have said. Different music has different values and can be put to different uses by different kinds of people. Even bad music has a place in this system—for people who were incapable of more refined perception. This more pluralistic, tolerant stance of Aristotle's bears certain resemblances to the prevalent one today. But like the contemporary view, it comes at a cost: music is good for many things, but essential to none. Curricular and instructional choices for music educators are relatively simple and arbitrary, guided, it seems, primarily by matters of expediency. And yet, the contemporary advocacy frenzy in music education is clear evidence that music and musical instruction need to be grounded in something more durable and substantial than "music itself" and the personal gratification that affords.

In a way, it is a little surprising Aristotle took such a laissez-faire toward music. I say this because elsewhere in his philosophical system lies an ethical scheme that seems to me extraordinarily well suited to our understandings of music and its values, whether personally or collectively. What I will argue in this brief essay is that music and music education are fundamentally ethical practices, and that, as such, they are profoundly important in shaping character, identity, and community. Or at least that is the case where they are recognized and pursued (and for present company, that means taught) with ethical intent. I believe that our understandings both of music and of education are urgently in need of repair, and a crucial part of that project involves recovery of their nature as fundamentally *ethical* and *ethically-guided practices*—as rich resources for exploring the crucial ethical question, "What kind of person is it good to be?"

An ethical orientation alters profoundly what we conceive musicking and educating to be, the reasons they are important, and our assumptions about how we should go about engaging in them. Such alteration is becoming a matter of considerable urgency for music education, I believe. As music educators have become ever more infatuated with efficiency and technical know-how, instruction has veered sharply in the direction of training instead of education—our concern with learning in and about music has eclipsed our concern for learning through music: the ways musicking makes for lives well-lived or human thriving (*eudaimonia*). Our concerns about what-to and how-to have all but eliminated concerns about whether-to, under-what-circumstances-to, how-much-to, and to-what-ends. These latter questions are ethical questions, I submit, while the former (the ones with which we have become unfortunately preoccupied) are predominantly technical. In school music, technical approaches to music instruction have, I believe, largely supplanted ethical ones, to the serious detriment of both musical and educational practice.

Meanwhile, avowedly "aesthetic" accounts of music and music education and their values have led us to focus on "the music itself" and on presumed *proper modes of reception*. These have conspired to reduce music from processes to entities, from modes of action to patterns of sound, from ways of enacting selfhood to ways of appreciating remarkable achievements by others. Again, we have neglected the important linkage among musicking as action and the shaping of character, identity, and community. We are, I fear, in danger of losing the view of music as *praxis*—the kind of know-how whose distinguishing characteristic is its guidance by ethical discernment, or *phronesis*.

If these Greek terms sound strange to our modern ears, the ideas they represent may seem stranger yet. They have fallen into neglect and have been replaced by technical and rule-based vocabularies (fixated upon standards and standardization, for instance) and ways of thinking from whose perspectives these ancient concepts appear outmoded, soft-headed, and sentimental. I am not about attempt single-handed recovery of these ideas, especially in a single brief essay. (Indeed, it may already be too late for that). But I do want to make clear the nature of my concern, the nature of what I believe to be our loss both as music educators and as a society more broadly. We have become preoccupied with the institutional trappings of particular systems of musicking and teaching, and lost sight of the internal goods these institutions originally existed to serve. We have lost sight of the fundamentally ethical potentials (or are they imperatives?) of both musical and instructional practice. And if we let these go—if we fail to dedicate ourselves to their recovery—I believe the consequences for music education will be dire and irreversible. The ancient Greeks were "onto something" important with their understandings of practices as ethical worlds where people discover what it means to flourish as human beings: what it is good to be.

My claim that we need to conceive of music as an ethical encounter is vulnerable and fragile for a number of reasons. For one, our uncritical embrace of technical (as distinct from ethical, or practical) rationality blinds us to what is radically different about so-called praxial orientations. That is itself symptomatic of a larger problem, however: the way "ethics" has come to be (mis)understood in modern times. In common parlance, the ethical and the moral have become more or less synonymous. And on that view, to act ethically is to act in ways that are morally upright. Thus my claim that music is ethical would seem to suggest that music-making creates fine, upstanding citizens: people who acknowledge and accept their obligations to do good deeds and abide by the rules. Since there is abundant evidence to the contrary and since that is not at all what I mean, let me try to explain what I take to be the crucial differences between ethics and morality.

Moral Obligations: Just One Kind of Ethical Consideration

As I say, without a clear distinction between morality and ethics my claim that music is a vital ethical resource will be wholly misunderstood. Making that distinction is challenging, however, because "morals" and "ethics" are so often regarded as synonyms. I am among those who believe this represents a fundamental and a very misleading mistake. "Modern" approaches to the subject have mistaken one part of ethics—morals, morality, and moral obligations—for the whole of it. In mistaking a part for the whole, they have effaced a much older, broader, and more useful understanding of ethics. This has far reaching consequences with both conceptual and practical significance.

It is important, then, to recover the understanding that morality is but a part of the broader domain of ethics. This is an understanding that has been largely obscured by modernist deontology (which construes ethics as duties or obligations) and by consequentialism (which tries to determine a course of right action by logically weighing potential pros and cons, benefits and adverse consequences). The reduction of ethics to obligations-and-rules-driven orientations has been aptly called "modern moral myopia" by Higgins (2011, 25).[1] What is myopic about moralism is its preoccupation with what it is "right to do" instead of what it is "good to be," and its concern with "defining the content of obligation rather than the nature of the good life" (Taylor, 1989, p. 3). Ethics is first person and practical, concerned with questions like: Who do I want to be? How should I live my life? Morality, on the other hand, asks questions like: What is it right to do? How must I act?

Morality, in other words, is a particular style or "species" of ethical thought, and the obligations in which it deals are but one type of ethical consideration. Furthermore, those who

---

[1] I am indebted for many of the ideas expressed in this paper to my reading of Higgins (2011), although he might well take issue with certain aspects of my interpretation and the conclusions I draw.

equate ethics and morality mistakenly assume, as Williams (1985) argues, that without the special obligations introduced by morality, human action is guided by nothing more than "inclination." From the single-mindedly moral perspective, there is but one alternative to acting in accord with rationally derived and delineated ethical obligations: conduct that is selfish and self-serving. Thus, to act ethically is to act in accord with one's moral obligations. And the only thing that can trump an obligation is another obligation.2 And where goodness is defined by obligations, an all-too-common result is blame: people who fail to adhere to prescribed obligations are simply bad people.

On the view I am advancing here, however, this rules-versus-inclinations, good-people-versus-bad-people model neglects a number of very important things. Most significantly, it wrongly assumes that without obligations personal dispositions to act one way rather than another are nothing but arbitrary, self-serving preferences (the manifestations of mere desire). Virtue ethics strongly contests this assumption. It argues that there are important alternatives to rules and codes of conduct: things that may not only trump obligations but in many circumstances are far more supple, flexible, and ethically useful. In particular, the inclinations of people of virtuous character do not require correction or guidance by obligation. Indeed, in the rough-and-tumble of everyday human life *character* may often be a more reliable asset than abstract rules and reason. Virtue ethics is not just a third approach to ethical deliberation, alongside deontology and consequentialism: it rejects some of their most basic assumptions, including the assumption that morals and ethics are equivalent. It resists reducing ethical decisions to choices between good and bad, maintaining that truly ethical choices are more often choices among competing goods.

Virtue ethics—a deeply insightful orientation with ancient Greek lineage—has been driven to near-extinction by modern thought. Our "postmodern" reduction of goods to inclinations is as pernicious as it is pervasive. And precisely because of this, my words "virtue" and "character" require careful explanation. Virtue as Aristotle used the term bore little resemblance to the modern notion of conformity to or compliance with preordained standards of rightness. Nor was it a kind of synonym for moral uprightness (with its attendant questions about *whose* idea of uprightness we must follow). For Aristotle, a virtue is an action habit that seeks just the right intermediate state (a "mean") between opposed vices: between vices of excess on one hand and of deficiency on the other. Thus, for example, we might say that with regard to human cultural differences tolerance is a virtuous state between the extremes of utter closed-mindedness and abject relativism (where minds are so open that brains appear to fall out). Similarly, the virtue "courage" is a mean between rashness and cowardice; and "generosity" is a mean between wastefulness and stinginess. A person of virtuous character or personal integrity is thus one who has acquired habitual dispositions to act in ways that seek to act rightly where "rightness" lies somewhere toward the middle of an intermediate range between unjustifiable or excessive extremes.

Virtues are not inherited traits, then, but action tendencies rooted in who one has become and is continuing to become (one's character); and these require ethical monitoring because of the uniqueness of every action situation. A person of virtuous character is one who has developed the capacity for acting rightly in situations where the options cannot be neatly sorted into mutually exclusive categories of "right" and "wrong" and where the deci-

---

[2] This is Williams' (1985, 180) way of putting it.

sion as to how to act is taken not on the basis rules and obligations but rather the kind of person is (or is seeking to become). Virtuous character, we might say, involves a kind of ethical fluency: wisdom that is practical in nature; the ability to determine right courses of action amidst the unforeseen and unprecedented. It also involves the capacity to discern not just the differences between right from wrong, but to choose the best course of action from among, as I said earlier, numerous competing *goods*—where so choosing and so acting will unavoidably leave other goods unaddressed and other good actions undone.

The rigidity and generality of morals[3] makes them ill-suited to ethical situations in which action options cannot be reduced to digital yes/no or right/wrong choices, situations in which right action cannot be determined by recourse to logic-driven deliberations or pre-existing codes of conduct. There is far more to ethics than moral rectitude, and that "more" involves matters of vital human import. With all this said, I now return to my main point: that musicking involves such ethical habits and dispositions, and not just tangentially but centrally. These make music a vital resource for exploration and development of the capacity for ethical dispositions and discernment.

Practices as Ethical Resources

Is this a distinction without a difference? A theoretical line of thought without implications for the ways we understand and undertake music making? Obviously, I do not think so. If what I have been saying is valid, then questions about music's value or goodness extend well beyond whether it sounds good, whether it is well-executed, or whether it is authentic to the practice at hand. Music making is not its own end, but is *always also* a means to other ends. The point of musical instruction within the context of education is not just training "in" music but educating "through" music: the development of habits, attitudes, dispositions, and capacities that enable people to live their lives more fully than would otherwise be possible. Conceived as an ethical enterprise, music education is concerned to help learners explore the questions, what kind of person is it good for me to become? and How does this musical practice (or these musical practices) help me get there? This makes of musicking and music education something far more momentous than the development of technical skills and aesthetic sensitivity.

Music is a human practice (or, more accurately, "music" names a diverse constellation of human practices). Practices are patterns of human action that are socially rooted, complex, coherent, cooperative, and have evolved over time into distinctive ethical worlds—worlds in which participants become deeply concerned about the rightness of their actions. Such concern is tightly linked to participants' identities: they become, through the practice, people for whom seemingly little differences make a great deal of difference. They develop care about what they are doing, and how, and why (and with whom, and for whom), as well as developing significantly more complex understandings of what it is they are really doing. Practitioners develop an attachment to life and living through their practice, and that attachment becomes a definitive part of who they are—their character.

---

[3] I might as easily have said "their rigidity and their specificity." Since this sounds contradictory, let me attempt an explanation. To criticize morals for their *specificity* is to single out their inability to travel well, their inflexibility—their categorical nature. In choosing "generality" instead, I am criticizing their presumption to be broadly explanatory and universally applicable—and their incapacity to address the particularity or uniqueness of individual circumstances. Either word is likely to invite misunderstanding, but my hope is that "generality" will be less prone to misinterpretation since one of the distinctive characteristics of phronesis its sensitivity to particularity (its disinclination to bring things under existing categories).

Just as importantly, the nature of human practices is that they are ever under construction and ever-changing: the nerve of a practice is never something, then, that is "just there" waiting for practitioners to sign on. Entry into a practice—in this case musical, but the argument applies equally to educational practice—involves apprenticeship in which the apprentice becomes a practitioner through successive approximations aimed at something that can never be explicitly or exhaustively stipulated. Indeed, being a practitioner involves actions that are ever open to question. One of the distinguishing features of practices—or healthy practices, in any case—is that what they are always open to debate as to their fundamental aims and nature, the goods they exist to serve. Such debate, widely distributed among its members, is a vital part of what keeps a practice vital. Disagreements are crucial parts of the engines that keep human practices humming along.4

There is no one "nerve" or "core" of musical practice, collectively; nor is there within any single musical practice. As practices—as modes of human action—they are always in the process of becoming something other than they have been. At the same time, practices always have histories and traditions to which practitioners owe their allegiance. Finding one's way between the unacceptable extremes of radical novelty and blind adherence to tradition is a fundamental part of the ethical challenge every practitioner faces. This ability (part an acceptance of responsibility, part response-ability) also becomes, we might say, a fundamental part of whom a successful practitioner *is*: her identity or character centrally involves her ability to engage in a collective mode of action for which there is no definitive book of rules.

We are talking, in other words, about the kind of people we become when we are inducted into and engage successfully in human practices. And that is very much an ethical concern, just as I suspect Plato thought it was. It is essential to the health of practices that they be understood and pursued as practices—that practices not be confused with the particular institutions and managerial systems that have been created to support them. In other words, if practices are to develop and deliver the ethical goods I am claiming for them, they must be understood and engaged in *as practices* (as socially cooperative, as fluid, as contested, etc.). Practices are intricate and fragile: drastic changes in their human environments threaten their viability, and yet changes in those environments are essential to their vitality and renewal. In short, one of the reasons it is important to recognize musicking as a practice is that we as educators, in understanding the kind of thing music is, may assure that our students develop the kinds of attitudes, habits, and dispositions on which the practice relies—not just for its continued existence but also for its growth and vitality.

There are all kinds of human practices: teaching is a practice, flute playing is a practice, geometry is a practice, and chess is a practice. Each practice has its own set of internal goods, its own vision of what kind of person it is good to be, its own vision of virtuous conduct. And as modes of collective, cooperative action, every practice entails its own ways of being and of becoming. As Christopher Small taught us, how we music is who we are. But *why music and musicking* rather than some other practice? Or why jazz rather than hip hop or country or art music? Why presentational music-making rather than participatory music-making? Why live, face-to-face musicking rather than computer generated music?

---

[4] As Alasdair MacIntyre (1984) wrote, "Traditions, when vital, embody continuities of conflict...." Moreover, he suggests we consider *living traditions* as "historically extended, socially embodied argument[s]... [that are] precisely in part about the goods which constitute that tradition." (222)

These are complex questions with answers that are no less complex. However, this complexity—this intricacy—is precisely what makes practices important ethical resources: the questions I have posed above are ethical questions after all, questions concerned not just with what to do, but with kind of person it is good to be. And one of the things I have tried to stress about ethical questions is that, unlike moral questions, they do not have prescriptive or definitive answers. That, too, is part of the distinctive nature of ethics. And if we fail to teach music in ways that help our students explore these questions, we neglect some of its more important educational potentials.

Why music?

Practices are important ethical resources. They are where we develop commitment to particular ways of being and doing, where we develop values that define who we are and struggle to become. But again, *why musical practices* rather than some other? And why *this musical practice* rather than that? These are fundamental questions to which music educators devote insufficient attention. We apparently find it easier to mount bumper-sticker advocacy campaigns for what we are already doing than to ask whether it is right, how it might be made better, or whether other musical doings might serve educational or ethical ends more effectively. We find it easier to advocate for existing institutional means than to examine the ends to which they are well- or poorly-suited. In so doing, we reduce educational and musical praxes to technical pursuits, and among the many things lost along the way are their ethical nature, their contributions to developing personal character, the distinctive visions they offer us of human thriving.

Is one practice as good as another in terms of educational benefit? On one level, yes. If all practices are ethical worlds and if our educational concern is to develop ethical discernment (*phronesis*), then any practice should do because that is what practices involve by definition. However, on another level it seems clear that not all practices are equally momentous in ethical potency, or in terms of their capacity to engage the ethical imagination. Surely among music's advantages in this regard is its bodily basis, its capacity to engage both an embodied mind and a minded body. As Turino (2008) has shown us, musical meanings are mediated not just by symbolic connections but also by iconic (linked by resemblance) and indexical (linked by co-occurrence) ones. As such, music has unparalleled capacity to engage imagination and feeling; to integrate mind and body; to incorporate personal agency with a sense of belonging; and to bring these powerful resources to bear on the all-important ethical question, What kind of person (and society) is it good to become? Musicking is an example par excellence of human flourishing: or at least, taught and practiced in certain ways, it may be so.

Several important caveats remain. First, the act of making music, even if skillful, is no assurance of its service to educational or ethical ends. It all depends upon how it is done, the range of concerns upon which it is brought to bear. And second, this tells us nothing about which musical practices to choose or how to go about making such choices in contexts that are educational. For answers to those questions we need to invoke our understandings of yet another kind of practice: educational practice. And precisely because education is first and foremost a practice rather than a job or an institution, we should not expect ready-made answers. That is not what practices do.

Is music education a practice? Is it coherent, cooperative, and ethical in nature? Or, rather, when we think of music education do we have in mind a particular set of institutional configurations and habits? What difference might that make in what we expect of music education and how we presume to go about it? What might it mean to engage in music education as a practice as distinct from other possible modes of activity (as work, say, or as a job)? Or are the modes of music making and of teaching just too diverse for music education to cohere as a practice? Are the things to which our efforts are directed genuinely good, truly deserving of our allegiance, the ends for which the music education profession exists? If music and music education are *practices* (as explored here), of what do *practical skills* consist, and what might it mean to become an expert *practitioner*?

It seems to me that it is imperative the music education profession address such questions if we are to reclaim ethical and educational potentials we have sacrificed to technical (means-focused) modes of activity. But because answers to questions like these are necessarily elusive and conditional, we need to learn to see questions as valuable resources rather than as nuisances to be eliminated by definitive answers. And we need to acknowledge that our differences are a crucial part of what enables us to continue to grow and thrive as a practice and as a profession.

What I have been describing here is a very different kind of professional "foundation" than the ones we have pursued for some time. It is neither philosophical bedrock nor the kind of fashionable rhetoric that changes with the wind, promising to be anything people seem to want it to be. In suggesting that we regard and engage in music (and music education) as practices, I am urging we learn to think about what we are doing as ethically grounded and ethically guided—as pliable, adaptive, and responsive to changing needs, yet rooted in traditions we deem worth preserving. I am urging the creation of a place of prominence for praxis, for ethically-guided practical know-how, at the heart of music education's foundational knowledge. This is, I submit, a desperately needed complement to the technical rationality that has proven so seductive to the profession.

The ancient Greeks gave us these insights and the tools we need to preserve them. Whether they become quaint historical relics or valued contemporary assets is up to us. While I have made clear where my preferences lie, I hope I have also provided some insights as to my reasons why.

References

Higgins, C. (2011). *The good life of teaching: An ethics of professional practice*. Chichester, UK: Wiley-Blackwell.

MacIntyre, A. (1984). *After virtue*. Notre Dame, IN: University of Notre Dame Press.

Taylor, C. (1989). *The sources of the self: The making of the modern identity*. Cambridge, MA: Harvard University Press.

Williams, B. (1985). *Ethics and the limits of philosophy*. Cambridge, MA: Harvard University Press.

And Still I Wander... Deconstructing Western Music education through Greek Mythology

June Boyce-Tillman
University of Winchester (UK)
june.boyce-tillman@winchester.ac.uk

Abstract

This presentation will use the Greek myths of Psyche and Eros and Orpheus to examine the musical constructs that have underpinned Western music education. Psyche becomes separated from Eros and in some versions of the myth is still wandering around Europe looking for Eros. It will see this as a metaphor for the loss of soul values in the European Union. It will use this as a metaphor for how the soul values (Psyche) of music were lost at the Enlightenment (Damasio, 1995); the relationship between religion and politics (Foucault & Gordon, 1980) in Western states has perpetuated the loss of this dimension and it will interrogate the term spirituality in contemporary culture as a helpful route into the reuniting of the material dimension of music (Eros) with the liminal (Turner, 1969/74) dimension (Psyche). It will look at the value systems that underpin various musical traditions (Subotnik, 1996) including the ecological consciousness found in the myth of Orpheus. The healing dimension has been rediscovered in the development of music therapy (which has constructed itself outside of music education), although the relationship with the natural world has yet to be rediscovered (Abrams, 1996; Boyce-Tillman, 2010). It will compare the Western construct of music with those of other cultures (Ellis, 1985). It will offer pedagogic strategies to restore these lost dimensions through a holistic view of musicking, using a phenomenographic model of music (Boyce-Tillman, 2009).

Keywords
Greek mythology, soul, psychagogue, spirituality, value systems

The Greek Myths

This paper is based on three Greek myths – those of Psyche, Hermes and Orpheus - which I am going to use to illuminate the way we see music in the European musical curriculum. The first one is that of Psyche and Eros. Psyche was a mortal woman of extraordinary beauty, truth and goodness who Aphrodite wished to wound; she sent Eros to carry out her wishes by making Psyche fall in love with a monster in a mysterious castle. It did not go according to plan (as the interface between Greek gods and humans often did). Eros fell in love with Psyche; but gave her one condition that she would not to discover his identity by looking at his face. However, Psyche could not bear this and found out that it was Eros - the god of love - that she was to marry. In order to re-unite with him, she was set four tasks to complete. The first was to sort a room full of seeds; the second was to obtain a golden fleece from fierce rams. Then she had to fill a glass for the waters of the River Styx. Finally she had to go to Hades to retrieve a beautiful box. In some versions she opens this box and is again forced to wander (although in some she succeeds and becomes divine.) In this paper, I am seeing her still wandering through Europe as a symbol of the loss of soul/spiritual values in the formation of the European Common Market. Everywhere material values rule – in music education as in other places - and we search for a heart and a soul. Many people do find these aspects of themselves through experiencing music – often called the last remaining ubiquitous spiritual experience in Western culture. And yet the fundamental question of this paper is: do we teach it in our schools in a way that will empower them do this with integrity and judgement?

The Concept of Soul

What can ancient Greek culture teach us about this wandering soul? In ancient Greece the soul was referred to as breath, spirit and mind and associated with the butterfly – symbol of transformation (Batzoglou, 2011). For the early Greek Orphic philosophers (Claus, 1981) it was associated with the deepest feelings and imagination. In Plato it became an eternal entity made up of intellect (logos), passion (thymos) and desire or appetitive (epithumia).[1] Aristotle saw it as the form of the living body, the entire organism's active functioning. So it became the totality of experience in which conscious and unconscious elements of the mind are manifest within the body – the totality of being. Olympic religion never spoke of the soul through dogmatic formulae but as a vital force in everything (Otto, 1955) - the collective soul of the world - anima mundi. If we could rediscover in contemporary society, it would have huge implications in the area of peace, understanding and reconciliation between cultures.

The polytheism of the ancient Greeks allowed for a more diversely interactive view of the divinities' interaction with human beings. This developed into a clearer more third person view of God within monotheistic Christianity. In this belief system dualisms developed, such as soul and body – often with connotations of good and bad. However, music was seen as a key part in spirituality/religion in the writings of figures like the 12th century Abbess Hildegard von Bingen (Van der Weyer, 1997) and the 17th century Sir Thomas Browne (Harvey, 1996).

As religion in Europe lost its power, there was a loss of interest in the animating power of life; the arts became secularised and demoted to mere entertainment[2]. The Cartesian split reinforced the body/mind dichotomies implicit within Christian thought. At the end of the nineteenth century Nietzsche declared God dead and the anima mundi became identified as aspects of a culture. Chief among these for Nietzsche were the Apollonian and Dionysian. Dionysus, Greek god of theatre, wine and ecstasy, Nietzsche saw as suppressed in Western culture and revealed by journeys to the underworld where dark experience resided. He saw this as related to primordial, irrational or unconscious functions, while Apollo (associated with higher civilisation, music, healing, prophecy and law) he related to reason, harmony and beauty (Huskinson, 2004). Nietzsche saw theatre as integrating these elements (Luchte, 2004). Music he associated with the Apollonian. However, I will argue

---
[1] In my model explained later these are subsumed in Construction, Expression and Values.
[2] Although the original meaning of the word entertainment was to nourish.

in this paper that by rethinking the musical experience in its totality, it too has the capacity to integrate the Apollonian and Dionysian aspects – the personal and archetypal, mind and body - the mysterious and the rational.

In Europe the psyche found a place in the developing field of psychoanalysis (Muir, 2000, pp. 237–238), which Jung defined as the totality of the unconscious in the face of a culture that was focusing concentration on the consciousness of the ego. It was everything "I feel, think, remember, want and do" (Jung, 1957/2004, p. 61). The myth of Psyche still fascinated thinkers. C.S Lewis's *Till we have faces* used it to address the complexity of loving. Derrida in his reading explored psyche (a French word for a mirror) as self-reflection (Derrida & Kamuf, 1991). These texts reflect the century's location of the soul within the human unconscious. The Greek anima mundi became related to human motivation (Vitz, 1979) and composers' accounts of their inspiration were located in the unconscious (Harvey, 1999) rather than in some in a divine realm. The unities within the Greek pantheon of the Good, the True and the Beautiful (personified in Psyche) were fractured; aesthetics after the Enlightenment became subjective expression for its own sake, with nothing auratic about it. Subjectivity, objectivity and morality become separated, and music lost its ancient Greek telos for fusing together the Good, True and Beautiful. Western classical traditions could develop notions of being value free (no longer concerned with the Good) and objectivity (views of the Beautiful often culturally limited) held sway in music curricula. Subjectivity (the True) became marginalised in traditional musicology as the discipline attempted to accommodate rational/scientific views of truth; the auratic was dismissed as superstitious.

Now part of self-actualization the musical experience could be seen as the last remaining place for the soul in Western society (Argyle & Hills, 2000; Hay, 1982). In Maslow's hierarchy of human needs (Maslow, 1967) he included the aesthetic – the need for beauty, order, symmetry. It was placed immediately below self-actualization with its peak experiences which included characteristics associated in the past with the soul – such as an intense experience of the present, concentration, self-forgetfulness, a lessening of defences and inhibitions, empowerment, trust, spontaneity, and a fusion of a person with the world.

The Soul in Western Education

So what of Psyche have we lost? What is still wandering around Western cultures seeking a home? The psychologist, Antonio Damasio describes Descartes' error as separating thinking from the body, re-asserting 'being' as the essence of what it is to be human; thinking becomes simply a consequence of being (Damasio, 1995) not the essence of our humanity. The Cartesian "error" has governed the development of Western education (Claxton, Lucas, & Webster, 2010). Guy Claxton (2002) identifies the following characteristics that define the restoration of the psyche to our educational experience. The first is an unusually strong sense of *aliveness* characterised by a heightened sense of vitality, clarity and strength of perception. The second quality he calls *belonging* - a sense of being at home in the world – which is a restoration of anima mundi. "Attitudes of suspicion or competition are replaced with what appears to be an unforced inclination towards kindliness and care…compassion, love" (Claxton, 2002). This challenges the place of competition in the world of music-making and hints at the restoration of the True – Values – to music making. Nel Noddings (1998) calls for an "ethic of care" (p. 163). She calls for an education of "moral sensibilities" (p. 163), which is clearly an attempt to restore notions of the Good into education. She calls on education to develop *human responses* (Noddings) to counter a culture of competition and war (Glover, 2000). The third quality Claxton calls an affinity with *mystery* – "a curious, almost paradoxical sense that all is well with the world". This is part of Turner's liminal state in which security in opinions and beliefs is replaced by an interest in the paradoxical nature of truth (Boyce-Tillman, 2005). Open-mindedness and inquisitiveness replace fundamentalism and dogma. This calls for some restoration of a sense of the auratic – call it god, gods, the Great Spirit, or whatever is deemed appropriate in a particular context. Creativity becomes as important as success with its sense of delight and heightened sense of trust and spontaneity. Fourthly, he identifies an enhanced *peace of mind* - the shedding of mundane anxiety and confusion. This paper maintains that musicking can transport us this qualitatively different, fulfilling and inherently meaningful mode of engagement as opposed to the fragmented and non-integrated nature of the everyday (Westerlund, 2002).

Psychagogia

We can interrogate this search further through the lens of the Greek figure of Hermes – inventor of the lyre and the original psychagogue – the leader of souls from the Underworld. Psychagogia was part of ancient Greek dramatic practice developed by Aristotle in relation to Greek tragedy (Aristotle, 1992). This was seen to move the human soul to understanding and empathy. Plato in *Phaedrus* associated with good rhetoric defined as the art of leading the soul by means of words performed with love - love of the forms and love of those to whom the rhetorician speaks (McCoy, 2007). In theatre it was associated with change (the butterfly image) in the psyche of the spectator (Arnott, 1991) – a move towards reflection. Within Greek society the actor is seen "as a kind of mouthpiece for powers beyond control whose role is to enchant the listener" (Easterling & Hall, 2002, p. 354). Theatre was part of the treatment at the sanctuary of Asclepius, the god of healing where it was seen as expanding the mind through dreaming (Hartigan, 2009). It was deeply grounded in the notion of self-reflexivity - "the awareness of our existence which involves the ability to stand back and look at life" (Grainger, 2004, p. 6). Aristotle drew on Socrates to use it in relation to education - the educational art of leading the soul to a dialectical examination of the Good (Muir, 2000) - one of Socrates' three components of Truth. The end of education was to enable this Good is to come from within the person not from an external authority. It included a concept of love for self, others and the wider cosmos (Muir, 2000). Education's role was to develop *ethos*, which was created by the actor (*ethopios*) who had the skill to explore *mythos* - the metaphysical, irrational, and spiritual.

This concept continued in Europe in morality, education, religion and mysticism until the rationalism of Descartes and Darwin pushed it aside. In my concept of the spiritual, the psyche is restored to its meaning of integrating conscious and unconscious, rational and intuitive – the Good, the True and the Beautiful. Music draws people because of its psychagogic qualities (Cook, 1998); yet school curricula stay with the rational elements such as theory and history. Reimer (1970) defines the practical, religious, therapeutic, moral, political and commercial aspects as nonmusical. Widening approaches to the philosophy of music, drawing on Dewey (1934), have called for more holistic approaches to music education which see the meaning of a musical experience composed of many interacting parts (Westerlund, 2002). I am going to use the phenomenographic map (Marton & Booth, 1997), that I have developed from numerous accounts of the musicking experience (Boyce-Tillman, 1996, 2000, 2007a, 2009; Tillman, 1987) to retrieve some of the wandering parts of Psyche and investigate how teachers may become psychagogues.

The Four Domains of the Musical Experience

Music consists of organisations of concrete Materials drawn both from the human body and the environment. These include musical instruments of various kinds, the infinite variety of tone colours associated with the human voice and the sounds of the natural world as available in different locations. Choices here will also dictate musical pitches and rhythms available with their associated motifs and melodic and rhythmic patterns. However, in music curricula this domain often stays at the level of technical skills – how to produce a certain note. The relation to the whole body is often ignored. Carl Orff saw this as a significant element in the musical experience (Hamel, 1976/1978), which was taken up by David Elliott (1995). The ethnomusicologist, John Blacking, linked it with dance (Blacking, 1977). The close relation to the natural world is similarly ignored along with the acoustic space (Abrams, 1996; Boyce-Tillman, 2010). And so the linkage of this area to the material of the wider cosmos – the anima mundi – has been lost.

The domain of Expression is where the subjectivity of composer/performer and listener intersect to provide facets of the True. The truth of the experiences of the composer/performer and listener interact here to give a variety of truths from the interplay between the intrinsic and extrinsic. Whatever the intention of one party (the intrinsic meaning) may have been, others in the process of listening/composing/performing will bring extrinsic meaning to the music – meaning that has been locked onto that particular piece or style or musical tradition because of its association with certain events in their own lives or their own enculturation (Green, 1988, 1997). This has often been downplayed by classical theorists (Rahn, 1994) but this is where the hidden aspects of personality or psyche - qualities of being where feelings, memories, cultural prejudices are activated to promote empathy, imagination and identity creation (Westheimer, 2003). The use of music and memory with the elders is one example, as is a 10-year old girl who sings a setting of an African prayer every night: "I felt close to the people in Africa whose prayer we sang. Now I continue to sing it and think of them."

In our curricula this area may feature in expressive pieces in our curricula for the youngest children but it often disappears as pupils get older (Department for Education and Employment, 2002). Yet here is an area where insights from music therapy can be used differently from its application within therapy as a means of deep inner self-exploration rather than therapeutic attendance of the participants' psychopathological needs (Batzoglou, 2011).

It is in domain of Construction that our curricula concentrate in their pursuit of the Beautiful. Effectiveness here depends on the right management of repetition and contrast within a particular idiom. The way in which contrast is handled within a tradition – how much or how little can be tolerated – is often carefully regulated by the elders of the various traditions. However the emphasis in musicology has been on the composers and theoreticians of the Western classical tradition rather than the master drummers of Yoruba traditions with the result that orate musical cultures have been subjected to the principles of the Western classical canon (Goehr, 1992) - and the concept of the Beautiful limited and confined. It has meant the marginalisation of improvisatory elements with their delight in spontaneity, play and the carnivalesque (Bakhtin, 1993; Boyce-Tillman, in press) and their ability to unite Apollo with Dionysus.

The domain of Values reflects a search for the Good. Classical Greek literature is filled with stories embodying the potential ethical power of music (Godwin, 1987) but theorists, such as Reimer (1970), have often preferred to see individual works of art as if they were dislocated from their social context. However, the sounds of music both serve, express, challenge and create cultures (Shepherd & Wicke, 1997). Philosophers like Subotnik (1996) and Westerlund (2002) have attempted to restore these cultural dimensions, seeing the potential of music to create and construct social situations by attending to the ethical dimension (Westerlund, 2002). Indeed the structure of the classical orchestra and choir reflect the European cultures that produced them – ruled by benevolent dictators now embodied in a conductor. But where in our curricula is this domain discussed? Where do we discuss community building through music, which Anthony Storr (1993) sees as the main function for music in world cultures. A 10-year old boy started his reflections on a performance with: "It was like peace on earth. Everyone did their own thing but it all fitted together" (p. 215).

Teachers often comment on music's ability to develop community-building skills: "It improved the children's co-operative skills. I saw them supporting one another and encouraging other schools in their work. This is unusual for our children whose poverty often makes them quite self-centred."

The area of Values also has intrinsic and extrinsic elements. In the intrinsic area, some traditions will edge towards more democratic practices in the creation process with everyone involved in the decisions while others will be more hierarchical. Notions of intrinsic values are a subject of debate in musicological circles (McClary, 1991, 2001) but as soon as a text or story are present, intrinsic Value systems will be more explicit. Pieces composed for a religious context will necessarily embody the Values of that tradition. Extrinsic values are present in the context of the performance such as finance and ticket pricing. Many community musicians today are very explicit about their Value systems, indeed the growth of the community choir can be seen as a challenge to the dominant Value system. Musicians working in the area of cultural fusion look towards music as route to justice and peace (Boyce-Tillman, 1996, 2001, 2007b) such as Paul Simon in his recording *Graceland* in the context of apartheid in South Africa (Simon, 1994). In my own piece *The Call of the Ancestors* (Boyce-Tillman, 1998) I used Western classical traditions leaving spaces for improvisation by groups from other cultures - at the first performance, Kenyan drums, Thai piphat and rock group. The use of a mixture of notated sections and "holes" in the score where improvisation could take place, enabled the traditions to be true to their underlying principles of Construction. There are many narratives on musicking with declared ethical intention but are these stories in our music curricula? This domain shifts attention from individual acts of cognition to the wider context in which musicking is situated (Westerlund, 2002) and critiques research in music education which concentrates exclusively on such acts.

The link is still there in government documents in the UK with the delivery of the citizenship agenda in particular (Department for Education and Employment, 2002), including religious, moral, cultural, personal, social and health issues. Reflection in this area could prepare pupils for understanding about the use of music in shopping malls, military parades and political rallies. The climate in schools in UK at present is one of tightly controlled bureaucracy limiting the scope of the curricula. It is frustrating those teachers who still see their role as one of a psychagogue. A head teacher wrote of a performance "It was one of those occasions when you feel really proud to be a head teacher. Putting aside nonsense like Ofsted inspections, this was a fantastic opportunity that primary education should be all about."

Spirituality

I am calling the moment (Dunmore, 1983) when all the other domains fuse - Spirituality. It represents the reintegration of the body (Materials), the emotions (Expression), the intellect (Construction), the culture (Values). These moments resemble Maslow's peak experience or Csikszentmihalyi's "flow" (Csikszentmihalyi, 1993; Csikszentmihalyi & Csikszentmihalyi, 1988). Philosophers like Catherine Ellis (1985) have brought ethnomusicological insights into relationship with western classical traditions to offer us reference to the Spiritual domain. She distinguishes between three levels of learning (informal, formal and spiritual/visionary), which is acknowledged in aboriginal traditions (Ellis, 1985). The musickers – be they composers, performers or listeners – enter a different time/space dimension – leaving everyday reality for another world – the liminal space of Victor Turner (1969/1974a). I have subsumed the following states within my description:

- flow (coming in from psychologists of creativity
- ecstasy often associated with idea of 'the holy' coming from the religious/spiritual literature
- trance coming from anthropological, New Age and psychotherapeutic literature
- mysticism, coming from religious traditions, especially Christianity.

Drawn from analysis of ritual (Turner, n. d.), a "limen" – a threshold – is crossed into a different time/space dimension which is potentially transformative (Boyce-Tillman, 2009) – recalling the Greek image for psyche of the butterfly. Turner (1974) focused his attention on the second stage of rites of passage, the crossing of a threshold or limen to a sacred moment "in and out of time." He also discussed its quality of communitas - the bond that develops between pilgrims. He concentrates on a sense of intimacy and I/Thou awareness – a feeling of being united with the universe, other beings and the natural world (Clarke, 2005). Here the *beyond* – the mysterious – is present as the whole person or community experiences the re-integrating of themselves; anima mundi is restored.

The Spiritual Experience in Music

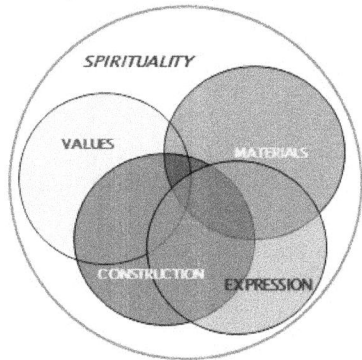

Conclusion

We come to the last of the Greek myths - Orpheus - often called the father of song – who used song with Hermes' invention of the lyre to charm the birds, fish and wild beasts, coax the trees and rocks into dance, and divert the course of rivers. Can we do that in our classes? How would this effect ecological awareness? My argument here is that we can restore psyche to our music education by adopting a philosophy that includes the totality of the music experience within our philosophies, both practically and theoretically. Towards the end of his life, the French social theorist, Michel Foucault, saw the need for the development of a desire to reinvigorate our ethical imaginations by challenging the status quo (Thompson, 2003). The inclusion of the domains of Value and Expression gives us the potential for re-integration of human beings within the wider cosmos in the very deepest aspects of our being – both personal and communal - like the psychagogues in drama. This means revisiting the tight link between politics and education (Foucault & Gordon, 1990) that often governs our curricula and keeps us wedded to a well-trodden but limited view of both human beings, the cosmos and musicking. It means rethinking education as process not product (Suanda, 2012) – as a series of strategies rather than government imposed curricula and published programs of study, which may not fit particular circumstances or the needs of our students. Estelle Jorgensen (2008) similarly calls for a musical pedagogy related to lived life, and calls for matters of character, disposition, value, personality, and musicality to feature in pedagogical training to encourage teachers "to think and act artfully, imaginatively, hopefully, and courageously toward creating a better world" (p. 1). It does not mean abandoning all that we have taught in the way of skills but rather teaching them in a way that associates them with emotional and cultural awarenesses so that they will be empowered to make well-judged choices in their use of music in the process of living. Music education becomes a process of leading our students into a greater understanding of the power of music as a whole and through which potentially they can construct an identity that is truly their own.

If our philosophies can help Psyche re-unite with Eros, Western teachers may be closer to becoming psychagogues. Late capitalism has invented many underworlds to keep people trapped in cultures of consumerism, inequality, addiction and control. If we can grasp the totality of music's potential for our pupils they may have some strategies of resistance that will give them autonomy, identities of integrity and hope.

References

Abrams, D. (1996). *The spell of the sensuous.* New York, NY: Pantheon Books.

Arnott, P. D. (1991). *Public and performance in Greek theater.* London: Routledge.

Aristotle. (1922). *The poetics of Aristotle* (Trans. S. H. Butcher). London, UK: Macmillan.

Argyle, M., & Hills, P. (2000). Religious experiences and their relations with happiness and personality. *International Journal for the Psychology of Religion, 10,* 157–172.

Bakhtin, M. (1993). *Rabelais and his world* (Trans. Hélène Iswolsky). Bloomington: Indiana University Press.

Batzoglou, A. (2011). *Towards a theatre of psychagogia: An experimental application of the Sesame approach into psychophysical actor training* (Unpublished doctoral thesis). University of London, UK.

Blacking, J. (1977). *The anthropology of the body.* London, UK: Academic.

Boyce-Tillman, J. B. (1996). A framework for intercultural dialogue in music. In M. Floyd (Ed.), *World musics in education*, (pp. 43–95). Farnborough, UK: Scolar Books.

Boyce-Tillman, J. B. (1998). *The call of the ancestors.* Unpublished work performed in Winchester Cathedral.

Boyce-Tillman, J. (2000). *Constructing musical healing: The wounds that sing.* London, UK: Jessica Kingsley.

Boyce-Tillman, J. (2001). Sounding the sacred: Music as sacred site. In K. Ralls-MacLeod & G. Harvey (Ed.), *Indigenous religious musics* (pp. 136-166). Farnborough, UK: Scolar.

Boyce-Tillman, J. (2005). *Ways of knowing.* In C. Clarke (Ed.), *Ways of knowing: Science and mysticism today* (pp. 8-33). Exeter, UK: Imprint Academic.

Boyce-Tillman, J. (2007a). The spirituality of music education. In L. Bresler (Ed.), *The international handbook of research in arts education*, (pp. 1405-1422). Netherlands, UK: Springer.

Boyce-Tillman, J. (2007b). Music and value in cross-cultural work. In O. Urbain, *Music and conflict transformation: Harmonies and dissonances in geopolitics* (pp. 40–52). London, UK: I. B. Tauris.

Boyce-Tillman, J. (2009). The transformative qualities of the liminal space created by musicking. *Philosophy of Music Education Review*, 17(2), 184-202.

Boyce-Tillman, J. (2010). Even the stones cry out: Music theology and the earth. In L. Isherwood & E. Bellchambers (Eds.), *Through us, with us, in us: Relational theologies in the Twenty-first Century* (pp. 153–178). London, UK: SCM Press.

Boyce-Tillman, J. (in press). Music and the dignity of difference. *Philosophy of Music Education Review.*

Cook, N. (1998). *Music: A very short introduction.* Oxford, UK: Oxford University Press.

Clarke, I. (2005). There is a crack in everything, that's how the light gets in. In C. Clarke (Ed.), *Ways of knowing: Science and mysticism today* (pp. 90–102). London, UK: Imprint.

Claus, D. B. (1981). *Toward the soul: An inquiry into the meaning of psyche before Plato.* New Haven, CT: Yale University Press.

Claxton, G. (2002, October). *Mind expanding: Scientific and spiritual foundations for the schools we need.* Public lecture, University of Bristol.

Claxton, G., Lucas B., & Webster, R. (2010). *Bodies of knowledge: How the learning sciences could transform practical and vocational education.* London, UK: Edge Foundation.

Csikszentmihalyi, M. (1993). *The evolving self.* New York, NY: Harper & Row.

Csikszentmihalyi, M. & Csikszentmihalyi, I. S. (1988). Optimal experience. *Psychological studies of flow in consciousness.* Cambridge, UK: Cambridge University Press.

Damasio, A. R. (1995). *Descartes' error: Emotion, reason, and the human brain.* London, UK: Harper.

Department for Education and Employment (2002). *Curriculum guidelines.* United Kingdom.

Derrida, J., & Kamuf, P. (1991). Psyche: Invention of the other. In P. Kamuf, *A derrida reader: Between the blinds* (pp. 200–220). New York, NY: Columbia University Press.

Dewey, J. (1934). *Art as Experience*. New York, NY: Minton Balch and Co.

Dunmore, I. (1983). Sitar Magic. In N. Varadirajan (Ed.), *Nadopasana one* (pp. 20-21). London, UK: Editions Poetry.

Easterling, P., & Hall, E. (Eds.) (2002). *Greek and Roman actors: Aspects of an ancient profession*. Cambridge, UK: Cambridge University Press.

Elliott, D. (1995). *Music matters: A new philosophy of music education*. Oxford, UK: Oxford University Press.

Ellis, C. J. (1985). *Aboriginal music - Education for living*, Queensland, Australia: University of Queensland Press.

Foucault, M., & Gordon, C. (Eds.) (1980). *Power knowledge: Selected interviews and other writings 1972-77*. Hemel Hempstead, UK: Harvester Wheatsheaf.

Glover, J. (2000). *Humanity: A moral history of the 20th century*. Hew Haven, CT: Yale University Press.

Goehr, L. (1992). *the imaginary museum of musical works: An essay in the philosophy of music*. Oxford, UK: Clarendon Press.

Godwin, J. (1987). *Music, magic and mysticism: A sourcebook*. London, UK: Arkana.

Grainger, R. (2004). Theatre and encounter. *Dramatherapy*, 26(1), 4–9.

Green, L. (1988). *Music on deaf ears: Musical meaning, ideology and education*. Manchester, UK and New York, NY: Manchester University Press.

Green, L. (1997). *Music, gender, education*. Cambridge, UK: Cambridge University Press.

Hamel, P. (1978). *Through music to the self – How to appreciate and experience music anew* (Trans. P. Lemesurier). Tisbury, UK: Compton Press. (Original work published 1976)

Harvey, J. (1996). Introduction. In M. Steer (Ed.), *Contemporary Music Review: Music and Mysticism (I)*, (Vol. 14, Parts 3–4, pp. 7–9).

Harvey, J. (1999). *Music and inspiration*. London, UK: Faber and Faber.

Hartigan, K. V. (2009). *Performance and cure: Drama and healing in ancient Greece and contemporary America*. London, UK: Gerald Duckworth & Co.

Hay, D. (1982). *Exploring inner space*. Harmondsworth, UK: Penguin.

Huskinson, L. (2004), *Nietzsche and Jung: The whole self in the union of opposites*. Hove, UK and New York, NY: Brunner-Routledge.

Jorgensen, E. R. (2008). *The art of teaching music*. Bloomington: Indiana University Press. Retrieved from http://www.iupress.indiana.edu/product_info.php?products_id=68410

Jung, C. G. (2004). *The undiscovered self* (1st ed.). London, UK and New York, NY: Routledge. (Original work published 1957)

Luchte, J. (2004). *Kant, Bataille and the Sacred*. Retrieved from http://www.ferrum.edu/philosophy/kant2.htm

McClary, S. (1991). *Feminine endings*. Minneapolis: University of Minnesota Press.

McClary, S. (2001). *Conventional wisdom*. Berkeley: University of California Press.

McCoy, M. (2007). *Plato on the rhetoric of philosophers and sophists*. Cambridge, UK: Cambridge University Press. Retrieved from http://dx.doi.org/10.1017/CBO9780511497827.007

Marton, F., & Booth, S. (1997). *Learning and awareness*. Mahwah, NJ: Lawrence Erlbaum Associates.

Maslow, A. H. (1967). The creative attitude. In R. L. Mooney & T. A. Razik (Eds.), *Explorations in creativity* (pp. 40–55). New York, NY: Harper and Row.

Muir, D. P. E. (2000). Friendship in education and the desire for the good: An interpretation of Plato's Phaedrus. *Educational Philosophy and Theory, 32*(2), 233–247.

Noddings, N. (1998). *Philosophy of education*. Boulder, CO: Westview Press.

Otto, W. F. (1955). *The Homeric Gods: The spiritual significance of Greek religion*. London, UK: Thames and Hudson.

Rahn, J. (1994). What is valuable in art, and can music still achieve it? In J. Rahn (Ed.) *Perspectives in Musical Aesthetics* (pp. 54–65). New York, NY: Norton.

Reimer, B. (1970). *A philosophy of music education*. Englewood Cliffs, NJ: Prentice Hall.

Shepherd, J., & Wicke, P. (1997). *Music and cultural theory*. Cambridge, UK: Polity Press.

Simon, P. (1994). In T. White, *Lasers in the jungle: The conception and maturity of a musical masterpiece* [CD liner notes]. Burbank, CA: Warner Brothers Records.

Storr, A. (1993). *Music and the mind*. London, UK: HarperCollins.

Suanda, E. (2012, April). *Cultural education (see from a cultural studies perspective) in the application of its activities in the form of Nusantara art education*. Paper presented at the Festival of Ocean Mountain Arts, Borodobur Temple, Magelang, Indonesia.

Subotnik, R. R. (1996). *Deconstructive variations: Music and reason in Western society*. Minneapolis: University of Minnesota Press.

Thompson, K. (2003). Forms of resistance: Foucault on tactical reversal and self-formation. *Continental Philosophy Review, 36*, 113–138.

Tillman, J. B. (1987). *Towards a model of the development of musical creativity: A study of the compositions of children aged 3–11* (Unpublished doctoral thesis). Institute of Education, University of London.

Turner, V. (1974a). *The ritual process: Structure and anti-structure*. Baltimore, MD: Penguin Books. (Original work published 1969)

Turner, V. (n.d.). *Creative resistance: Defining liminality and communitas*. Retrieved from http://www.creativeresistance.ca/communitas/defining-liminality-and-communitas-with-excerpts-by-victor-turner.htm

Van der Weyer, R. (Ed.) (1997). *Hildegard in a nutshell*. London, UK: Hodder and Stoughton.

Vitz, P. (1979). *Psychology as religion: The cult of self worship*. London, UK: Lion.

Westerlund, H. (2002). *Bridging experience, action, and culture in music education* (Doctoral dissertation). Helsinki, Finland: Sibelius Academy.

Westheimer, R. (2003). *Musically speaking: A life through song*. Philadelphia: University of Pennsylvania Press.

Personhood and Music Education

David J. Elliott
New York University (USA)

In ancient Greece, the concept of *paedeia* involved educating students toward the fullest development of their human nature, or what contemporary scholars often call personhood. To Aristotle, the fullest development of personhood depends on the lifelong pursuit of *eudaimonia*, or happiness, defined as the lifelong pursuit of what is good, true, ethical, and virtuous.

Education in today's world has lost sight of these basic themes and ideals. Today, politicians, policy makers, teachers, and music teachers in many countries have deliberately or unconsciously accepted the concept of marketplace education, which duplicates the aims of international business and the jargon of corporate capitalism, which emphasizes "standards", accountability, and the measurement of basic skills through high-stakes testing. In other words, a primary aim of 21st-century education in many (but not all) nations centers on skill development and job training for profit-taking and material gain. Thus, many societies have lost sight of what is most important in education—the personal growth and wellbeing of students whose personhood includes the need, desire, ability, and basic human right to pursue happiness as Aristotle conceived it centuries ago.

The purpose of this paper is to remind or "re-mind" ourselves of what is most important about education in general and music education in particular. This requires an explanation and appreciation of what personhood involves and how the nature of personhood relates to one of the most important values of music education: music listening as and for the pursuit and achievement of "eudaimonia."

My discussion unfolds in several sections. First, I provide a brief summary summarize of key concepts in praxial music education and the priority this philosophy places on the relationship between music, people, and personhood. Next, I devote three sections of this paper to explaining key dimensions of personhood. Last, I provide a brief sketch of the processes that cause human beings to respond emotionally to music, to use music to regulate their emotions, and to engage with music as part of their lifelong pursuit of happiness and *eudaimonia*.

Praxial Music Education

What do the terms praxis and praxial mean? As originally conceived by Aristotle, praxis emphasizes the combination of (1) *thoughtful actions* dedicated to (2) *human well-being* and (3) the *ethical care* of others. Praxis refers to actions that are carried out wisely, effectively, and ethically for the positive transformation of people's everyday lives, relationships, and social-cultural situations. Praxis focuses on *people*—people's needs, aims, thoughts, emotions, health, and so forth. In short, *praxis* is guided by a moral disposition to act truly and rightly to further human wellbeing and eudaimonia.

Following from these themes, praxial music education (Elliott, 1995, 2007, 2012, in press) aims to encourage and empower people to put their individual and collective musical actions to work for the improvement of others' lives, for the betterment of their communities, and for the betterment of society and culture in general. Praxial music education holds that school and community music teachers should be prepared to teach thoughtfully, artistically, educatively, caringly, and democratically for the betterment of students as music makers, listeners, and socially just citizens. Praxial music education conceives the musical actions we carry out and teach—performing, improvising, composing, arranging, listening, leading, conducting, recording, and musical moving and dancing—as embedded in, responsive to, and reflective of specific contexts of musical and social-ethical values. Clearly, praxial music education puts *people*—individuals, social practices, and communities—at the center of its concern.

Rephrased for emphasis: music education is a *very serious* human endeavor because music teaching and learning of whatever kind is first and foremost about each student's individual and social *personhood*. By "music students" I mean people of all ages and backgrounds—infants, children, teenagers, and adults of all ages—who engage in music learning at any level and for any individual or mutual and ethical purpose(s)—artistic expression, personal development, enjoyment, pleasure, recreation, improved health and well-being, emotional regulation, social justice, and so forth. Praxial music education is concerned with enabling people to develop the musical abilities and understandings they desire and require to enrich their musical "particip-actions," now and in the future, and to engage in the musical styles that teachers and students choose together through mutually respectful and ethical collaboration. Praxial music education emphasizes the centrality of *ethical* action because whenever and wherever music educators act, our actions have a wide range of actual and possible consequences for ourselves and others—personal, musical, psychological, emotional, cognitive, developmental, social, cultural, political, economic, and so on—for the *people* and communities of people we are responsible to and for. Indeed, people are always and simultaneously individual-and-social beings, and music is simultaneously an individual-and-social endeavor. Let us look more a little more deeply at what personhood involves.

Personhood: An Orientation

What does it mean to be *you*? What does it mean to be "a person"? Are you the same as your brain, your mind, your feelings, your body, your conscious awareness, your gender, your soul, and/or something else? What roles do others play in the development of personhood? These questions underlie a great deal of what music, education, and music education involve. After all, music, education, and all related issues are human constructs, and education centers on students, each of whom is a unique, embodied, emotional, cognitive, social, cultural, gendered, and spiritual human being. Again, then, the issue of who/when/where/what you are, or what a person is, is at the center of our professional responsibilities as educators. So before we can understand the relationships between music and the human nature of our students, we need an orienting concept of who we are as persons who make, listen to, enjoy, and use music in endless ways.

But where shall we begin to say explain personhood, to the extent that this is possible? Today, most questions and answers about all aspects of human nature tend to begin and end with research findings in neuroscience. Not surprisingly, then, many people are persuaded that "you are your brain", or that everything we need to know about personhood and human experience can or will be explained when neuroscientists locate the neural correlates of what humans think, feel, and do. While some scientists accept this view, many in the field of "critical neuroscience" reject this claim as hopelessly simplistic. I suggest, and I will attempt to show, that music educators should do the same. Please note that I am not dismissing the findings of neuroscience or the importance of the brain in explaining what personhood involves; I'm suggesting that, without a much more inclusive perspective on human nature, there is a serious danger that key dimensions of personhood will be omitted and misunderstood. Let me illustrate what I mean via some philosophical perspectives on the nature personhood.

Personhood: Basic Philosophical Considerations
From one philosophical perspective, called Criterialism, several properties are both necessary and sufficient for calling a living creature a person: a person is a living being that possesses and exhibits rationality, sentience, emotionality, the capacity to communicate, self-awareness, and moral agency. As neat as this concept of a person may seem at first, the philosopher Timothy Chappell argues that this perspective is obviously wrong, because it fails to consider a variety of factors that would cause us to deny personhood to certain individuals who do not meet these criteria.

For example, says Chappell (2011, p. 6), if complete self-awareness is a necessary condition of personhood, then we'd be forced to conclude immorally that some mentally challenged people might fail to count as persons, and if the capacity to communicate is a necessary condition for personhood, then we'd be obliged to accept the immoral conclusion that a stroke victim would fail to count as a person. In other words, while Criterialism is correct in arguing that properties like self-awareness, rationality, emotionality, the ability to communicate, and so forth are crucial parts of what personhood involves, it does not follow that these attributes can be used as tests or standards for assessing someone's personhood (Chappell, p. 12). To make this argument, says Chappell, is as illogical and immoral as arguing that "a person is not white enough to count as a person" (Chappell, p. 12). Another obvious flaw in Criterialism is that it doesn't relate to normal social interactions between oneself and others. Indeed, the Criterialist premise "that humans go through some kind of checklist to determine whether a human being is approaching or not is absurd and morally repugnant" (Chappell, p. 6).

Contrary to using a set of criteria to decide whether or not a living being counts as a person, our daily experiences demonstrate that it's the other way around. That is, and partly because we are socialized from birth as human beings (as *Homo sapiens*), we recognize another person *in advance* of any displays of his or her rationality, emotionality, self-awareness, and so forth. In other words, we assume, grant, and/or acknowledge that another human being possesses personhood and the capacities personhood includes before we see evidence of these capacities or assess the strengths of these capacities in another person. "[The] clearest example of this is an activity that is absolutely central to human life: parenting" (Chappell, 2011, p. 6). Caring parents accept and understand automatically that their infants and young children will vary in the degree of rationality, self-awareness, emotionality, and so forth, according to their children's ages and stages of growth and developmental. What remains constant, however, is parents' attitudes toward their child as what Wittgenstein calls "an attitude towards a soul" (Wittgenstein cited in Chappell, p. 6). Paraphrasing Chappell's humanistic argument, parents do not carry out a progressive decision-making or checklist process that begins with treating their children as non-persons (e.g. as dolls or a microwave ovens) and then make future decisions about their children's qualifications for admission to the "club of personhood" depending on whether or not their children begin and/or mature in their rationality, communication skills, emotionality, and so forth (Chappell, pp. 6-7). Chappell elaborated:

> Parents don't evaluate their child's personhood in behavioristic [step by step decision-making or criterion- referenced] ways. Rather, a parent treat's her child from the very beginning—and from before it is literally and actually true—as a creature that can reason, respond, reflect, feel, laugh, think about itself as a person, and think about others as persons too, and do everything else that persons characteristically do. From the beginning, her attitude toward the child is not only "objective," but it also includes what we can call [intuitive, non-objective] "participant reactive attitudes" of just the same sort as she adopts toward anyone else. (p. 8)

In other words, parents treat their infants in relation to an "ideal of personhood" and "this ethical idealization of the child is an ideal shared by most if not all other human beings" (Chappell, 2011, p. 8). Moreover, this process of idealization applies to all human beings before and during all human interactions. In other words, humans automatically take an "intentional stance" (Dennett, 1987, p. 123) toward other humans *as persons*. If so, then this means that there is another exceedingly important principle or force at work in our intuitive understanding of personhood: the "principle of charity" (Davidson, 1980, p. 178). The principle of charity might also be thought of as an *intuitive empathy* which operates unnoticed in our mutual relationships. Put another way, by charitably interpreting the other as a person, I bestow personhood on him or her—I constitute him or her as a person. In the context of parenting and teaching, this means that even though it's unrealistic to expect a young child to possess fully developed self-awareness, rationality, emotionality, and so on, parents and teachers do so anyway. Why? Because as part of the charitable and/or empathetic human disposition or "habit" of idealization we assume that "a child's aspirations [or our aspirations for a child] are achievable simply because the child is a person" (Chappell, 2011, p. 10) and, as parents or teachers, we work to assist children in achieving their aspirations, or what we might also call "the innate potentials of personhood."

The obvious follow-up to the idea that persons constitute each other as persons—that humans learn to see or "construct" each other with a "principle of charity"—is the realization that every person (regardless of his or her religion, ethnicity, intellectual capacity, criminal history, and so forth)—deserves open access to free speech, education, and all other human rights of life, liberty and human happiness, or *eudaimonia*, as these are understood intuitively and inscribed officially in democratic laws and in (for example) the United Nations' *Universal Declaration of Human Rights*. It follows from all of these points that music educators should work to understand the nature of personhood and its implicit principle of mutual charity for the purpose of guiding our educational and musical actions.

At this point we need to examine the many integrated features of human nature that ground and support the existence of human personhood and its many attributes, including the basic attribute of each person's self-awareness, which we might also call a person's continuous sense of self-identity or selfhood. In other words, who or where are *you*?

Personhood: Many Interwoven Systems

Simply put, your personal sense of self is your unique, first-person experience of the world. But of course, this simple statement hides a huge array of complex problems and paradoxes that have challenged philosophers and scientists for thousands of years. To begin with, while each one of us has our own private experiences of everything in the world— sounds, colors, textures, temperatures, relationships, and so on—there are actual physical things in the world: sounds, colors, textures, temperatures, and so on. So one of the biggest questions scholars ask is this: how do our individual subjective experiences of the world arise from objective things? Moreover, if your personal experiences of the world are mediated by many of the same things that mediate someone else's (e.g. the English language, cultural customs, musical notation), then how can we say that you, or your self, is wholly private, insular, or in your head? In other words, what is the relationship between your mind, your body, and your cultural experiences as these impact your unique sense of self and your personal experiences of the world, including your personal experiences of music, musical enjoyment, happiness, and so forth?

Despite enormous progress in philosophical and neuroscientific research, the mind-body dualism that grounds Descartes's 17th -century theorizing continues to infect the beliefs of many laypeople and scholars alike. The major premise of dualism is that the mind and body are separate and distinct: the mind is mental (and the source of thoughts, knowledge, spirituality, and the self) and the body is a physical, fleshy thing that the mind controls. For Descartes, thinking and the self are one: the self is located in the head.

Many people in Western cultures still accept mind-body dualism and the binary oppositions it creates. Thus, people tend to assume that common verbal distinctions like intellectual-physical, thinking-doing, cognition-emotion, truth-belief, and so on, represent mutually exclusive aspects of "reality". But this is wrong. Thinking and doing, cognition and emotion, and so forth, are not polar opposites. For example, as Evan Thompson (2007) stated, "dualism causes us to assume wrongly that consciousness is something private and closed in on itself... We habitually see things in terms of intrinsic separate identity, such as I am me and you are you" (p. 1). Thus, many people assume that intellectual, ethical, empathic, compassionate, and artistic actions are purely cognitive, or completely inside the brain.

During the last few hundred years, many scholars have argued against dualism and its corollaries. These scholars include Spinoza, Nietzsche, Peirce, James, Dewey, Merleau-Ponty, Mark Johnson, Richard Shusterman, Evan Thompson, Alva Noë, and many others. A major feature of anit-dualist views is the concept of embodiment, which means (basically) that mind, body, consciousness, and personhood cannot be understood independent of people's relationships to their social-cultural environments.

Drawing support from non-dualist philosophers and a growing number of scholars in scientific fields, I have argued in more detail elsewhere (e.g. Elliott & Silverman, 2012) that personhood seems to depend (nobody knows for certain) on the integration of many continuous and constantly changing systems and processes. By "systems and processes" I do not mean brain systems and processes alone; instead, I mean: (a) the combined body-brain-mind-conscious-and-unconscious systems and processes that contribute to the self as an integrated whole and (b) the fluid systems and processes of the particular environments (our physical-social-gendered-cultural-historical contexts) with which we interact constantly and that shape and reshape all our "self-processes". In other words: no human body, no human brain; no body-brain, no mind and no meaning; no body-brain-mind, no conscious experiences (including emotions, feelings, perceptions, memories, and thoughts). And without all these systems and processes working together harmoniously, in the context of our shared human environments, there is no personal sense of you as your self.

Implicit in what I have just said is my strong resistance to today's popular view of the self which assumes human beings are primarily "brains alone". Today's commonsense notion (fueled by robust brain research) is that the brain's neural processes are the key to everything human—perceptions, emotions, memories, preferences, and so forth. Please note that in resisting these views, I am *not* rejecting the idea that the human brain is necessary for our human being. All the complexities of the brain— neurons, synapses, neurotransmitters (and so forth)—are crucial to who we are and what consciousness is, of course. However, and together with a growing number of scholars in several fields, I challenge the claim that the brain is sufficient for consciousness and the self. For one thing, says neurologist V. S. Ramachandran (2006), the brain is part of the body, not an isolated computer sitting on your neck. More broadly, says Thompson (2007), "the brain is an organ, not an organism, and it is the organism, animal, or person [as a whole] that has conscious access to the world" (p. 242).

After decades of extraordinary developments in brain research, imaging technologies, and computer simulations, there is only one thing on which scientists fully agree: we do not know how our personhood, which of course includes our conscious experiences of the world—the redness of an apple, the sensation of heat, the feeling of love—arise from brain processes. The fundamental reason, says Noë (2009), is that "we have been looking for consciousness where it isn't" (p. xii): "the locus of consciousness and the self is not in the brain. Instead, the locus of consciousness is the dynamic life of the whole, environmentally plugged-in person" (p. xiii). Noë's view aligns perfectly with the arguments of anit-dualist philosophers, past and present.

In this view, there is no central location in the brain where all your sensations, perceptions, cognitions, emotions (and so on) come together to produce the seamless experience you have as a unique person. Instead, your unique sense of personhood is like a huge jazz ensemble, whose many millions of players (your "personhood processes") are so expert at improvising collaboratively in relation to continuous changes in your environmental circumstances that "beautiful music— meaning you and your unique experience of reality flows continuously." The players in the ensemble create your experience of you as the arranger and performer of your life's music "in all its complexity, emotional nuance, crescendo and diminuendo—the ballad that is the you-ness of you" (Blakeslee & Blakeslee 2007, pp. 207–208). Let us be more specific now about the self—the self that experiences everything, including musical sounds and musical emotions (which I'll turn to in a moment).

To John Dewey, our psychological, emotional, cognitive, and spiritual lives are integrated and inseparable from our body's biological and physical functions and actions. Body and mind are not separate; mind-and-body are united. Mind-and-body are just different dimensions of an ongoing process of experience. Johnson (2006) agreed with Dewey and emphasized that "our bodies determine both what we can experience and think, and also how we think, that is, how we conceptualize and reason" (p. 51). In short, for many scholars today, the question of body's relationship to mind is well summarized by Johnson's succinct assertion: "no body, never mind" (Johnson, 2006, p. 47). Moreover, the human body-mind is not private but fundamentally social because our survival, development, and well-being depend on transactions with our surrounding situations that are not separate from our selves. The center of human experiences (all experiences, including musical experiences) is our entire, interrelated being, always constructed and under reconstruction in relation to the fluid details of our physical, biological, social, cultural, and linguistic circumstances.

And what about the nature of emotions and feelings? First of all, an emotion is not a thing. An emotion involves (i) a non-cognitive appraisal of a situation that causes (ii) physiological responses (e.g. changes in heart rate, skin temperature), (iii) brain stem and cortical activation, (iv) action tendencies (you run away, or relax, and so on), (v) overt expressions of emotions (e.g., crying, smiling, frowning), (vi) subjective feeling, (viii) self-regulation (attempts to control reactions), (ix) synchronization among all these components, and (x) more discriminating cognitive "monitoring" of felt emotions and the circumstances triggering the emotional process.

So, an emotion is something that happens to us. Events trigger emotions (LeDoux, 1996). *An emotion is a process* by which all aspects of our personhood—including and especially our brain's emotion systems—instantly, unconsciously, and automatically assess and respond to the qualities of all types of events and patterns in our environment—sounds, sights, threats, objects, social interactions, personal and cultural artifacts, and so on, *ad infinitum*. Our sensory systems process our environmental and bodily changes and activate the chemical-neural brain systems responsible for emotional processing. Emotional responses cause an avalanche of profound changes in our body-brain "landscapes"; the body-brain "changes quite remarkably over the ensuing hundreds of milliseconds," seconds, and, in some cases, minutes (Damasio, 2000, p. 2).

Feelings are not the same as emotions. Feelings occur when we become consciously aware of changes in our unconscious emotional states. A feeling is a conscious perception of an emotional process: "feelings emerge after all processes of emotional arousal run their course" (LeDoux, 1996, p. 19).

In summary, and in relation to emotions and feelings of happiness and musical enjoyment, our experiences are much more complex than cognitive and/or emotional experiences alone, as traditional theories tend to argue. Musical-affective experiences depend on all the attributes and capacities of each individual's entire personhood. Musical-affective experiences arise from each person's body-brain-mind-conscious-and-unconscious systems, processes, and actions as environmentally, socially, and musically sculpted.

Musical-Affective Experiences

Given everything I've argued in this paper, it will come as no surprise when I suggest (Elliott & Silverman, 2012) that people's musical-emotional experiences arise from a variety of factors that combine and impact each person's music listening experiences in different ways at different times. I will summarize these factors briefly now prefaced by a claim that is supported by considerable research in contemporary music psychology. This claims is that, depending on a number of variables (e.g. an individual's fluid elements of personhood, a specific piece of music, and the listening situation), "music can induce just about any emotion that may be felt in other realms of human life" (Juslin et al., 2009, p. 133).

Specifically, I post a 12-dimensional concept of musical emotions that includes seven mechanisms explained by Juslin et al., (2010) and his colleagues: brain stem reflex, rhythmic entrainment, evaluative conditioning, emotional contagion, visual imagery, associations/episodic memory, and musical expectancy. I add cognitive monitoring/naming, corporeality, musical persona, social attachment, and empathy.

My addition of the latter five dimensions arises from my predisposition as a philosopher to conceive music as an embodied, social-cultural practice, rather than pieces or intentional objects alone. This does not mean I disagree with Juslin and his colleagues, who also recognize the social nature of music listening. It only points out that whereas my work (Elliott, 1995; Elliott & Silverman, 2012) takes a praxial (a social/cultural and pragmatic) view of music and personhood, whereas Juslin and his fellow researchers assume a psychological stance. In my view a plausible and useful philosophical concept of musical-emotional experiences must incorporate contemporary scientific findings from music psychology, (b) music conceived as a socially embedded, corporeal phenomenon and (c) as a phenomenon that relates to what I emphasized at the outset of this paper: the nature of personhood as something that comes about as a result of the "principle of charity" or *intuitive empathy*. What I mean by this is that just as we construct others as persons through charity and empathy, we construct music and our emotional relationships with musical sounds by charitably interpreting musical sounds as being expressive of human emotions which we respond to as if they were the emotional expressions of living persons who, like us, are engaged in the lifelong pursuit of happiness and a good life.

References

Blakeslee, S. & Blakeslee, M. (2007). *The body has a mind of its own: How body maps in your brain help you do (almost) everything better*. New York: Random House.

Chappell, T. (2011). On the very idea of personhood. *Southern Journal of Philosophy, 49*(1), 1- 27.

Damasio, A. (2000). Emotion, consciousness, and decision-making. Paper presented at the The London School of Economics and Political Science. Retrieved August 10, 2009 from:
http://www2.lse.ac.uk/PublicEvents/events/2000/20001124t1343z001.aspx

Davidson, D. (1980). *Inquiries into truth and interpretation*. Oxford: Clarendon.

Dennett, D. (1987). *The intentional stance*. Boston: MIT Press.

Elliott, D. J., & Silverman, M. (2012). Rethinking Philosophy, Re-Viewing Musical-Emotional Experiences. In W. Bowman and A. Frega (Eds.), *Oxford handbook of music education philosophy* (pp. 37-62). New York: Oxford University Press.

Elliott, D. J. (1995). *Music matters: A new philosophy of music education*. New York: Oxford University Press.

Johnson, M. (2006). Mind incarnate: From Dewey to Damasio. *Daedalus, 135*(3), 46-54.

Juslin, Patrik N., Liljeström, S., Västfjäll, D., & Lundqvist, L. (2010). How does music evoke emotions? Exploring the underlying mechanisms. In Patrik N. Juslin and

John A. Sloboda (Eds.), *Handbook of music and emotions*, (pp. 605–642). Oxford: Oxford University Press.

Juslin, P. N., Laukka, P., Liljeström, S., Västfjäll, D., & Lundqvist, L. (2009). *A nationally representative survey study of emotional reactions to music: Prevalence and causal influences*. Manuscript submitted for publication.

LeDoux, J. (1996). *The emotional brain: The mysterious underpinnings of emotional life*. New York: Simon & Schuster.

Noë, A. (2009). *Out of our heads: Why you are not your brain, and other lessons from the biology of consciousness*. New York: Hill and Wang.

Ramachandran, V. S. 2006. *Mirror neurons and the brain in the vat.* Retrieved date: August 9, 2009 from:
http://www.edge.org/3rd_culture/ramachandran06/ramachandran06_index.html

Thompson, E. (2007). *Mind in life*. Cambridge, MA: Harvard University Press.

Music Education and/as Artistic Activism: Music, *Pædeia*, and the Politics of Aesthetics

Panagiotis A. Kanellopoulos
University of Thessaly (Greece)

pankanel@uth.gr

Abstract

This paper discusses the relevance that the ancient Greek notion of *Pædeia* might have for today's music education, arguing that a link between the two might be created through a particular conception of the politics of aesthetics (as put forward by Jacques Rancière), and that if this is so, then music education might be cast as a form of artistic activism. *Pædeia*, the situated process of cultural education and character building, is at the same time a process of creating a dialogue between cultural forms handed down by tradition and the individual's place in it. *Pædeia* might then be understood as a process of shaping *a voice*, that is, a culturally and politically situated identity. It can therefore be argued that, from the perspective of democratic politics, *Pædeia* might ultimately be apprehended as the process of educating the political subject.

Creating educational contexts where students are actively engaged with thinking in and through music is a process that relates to something more than sound and its configurations: (im)precision – (im)balance – breathing together – leading – listening in order to follow, listening in order to be able to get in front – going off in unexpected directions (am I allowed to?) – expression of desire (how am I going to express desire?) – What makes someone able to create music? Where do musical ideas come from? What does learning music have to do with the larger web of one's social life? What music is understood as valuable? How does musical discipline relate to disciplining music? Which are the musical and social values that are considered worth pursuing in particular music education encounters? Are we listening to children's critiques of their music education?

The moment that music education casts these questions (through its very practice) as *open* issues, thus *disrupting* the existing order of things, is the moment when it meets politics – as a process of reconfiguring the partition of the sensible: as a form of activism that creates the basis for democratic culture, a culture that begins from the assumption of equality (Rancière), where one conceives of children as already having a voice, thus creating a new partition of the sensible – making children visible and thus active in ways not possible before.

Introduction: Setting the Scene

Despite the vast amount of intellectual effort that has been invested in understanding ancient Greek philosophy and democratic politics and their relationship to aspects of our contemporary world, their thoughts and deeds persistently appear to us as enigmatic as ever. In writing this essay, a basic premise has been that instead of adopting a Grecophile stance of amazement we should bear in mind that "the Greek legacy – *ways of thinking about and discussing values and institutions* – is affected by specific historical and cultural milieu: ours, theirs, and those cultures intervening between them and us" (Coleman, 2000, p. 7; see also the comments offered by Agnes Heller (2008) on the role of the Greek legacy in the construction of German identity). But instead of thinking that this renders any effort to think about us through them by definition chimerical, or even suspect, it might be worth trying to understand contemporary issues by putting concepts that where created in ancient Greece – in a culture where one finds the roots of philosophy and democratic politics (Crick, 2002; Farrar, 1988; Mossé, 1971, 1984; Snell, 1975; Windelband & Heimsoeth, 1976) understood as processes of creating the conditions for unlimited interrogation about how we think the world and how we form our collectivities – in dialogue with radical contemporary ideas on democracy, education and art, and try to create a framework for rethinking music education.

As Cornelius Castoriadis (1991a) has emphasized, Greece is the social-historical *locus* where democracy and philosophy are created [...] insofar as the meaning and the potency of this creation are not exhausted [...] Greece is for us a *germ*, neither a "model," nor one specimen among others, but a germ (p. 84)[1].

So here we are, in this ISME world conference, attempting to reflect on the relationships between music education and the notion of *Pædeia*. It is imperative that we understand that this meeting does not take place in a political, social and cultural vacuum. - we are inevitably affected by specific political and cultural milieu, core aspects of which need to be spelled out. This meeting takes place at a moment when and in a country where neoliberalism violently imposes its agenda as the only possible way forward. It occurs at a moment and a place where educational officials renounce the idea of education as a public good, downgrading the role of music education through (a) a mode of official discourse that offers an instrumental view of education (either education succeeds in helping the future economic survival of tomorrow's "autonomous" consumers, or it's not education at all), and (b) creating work conditions for music teachers that subvert every intention to render music education a serious mode of developing imagination, freedom and reflective relationships with musical traditions. In Greece, "third way" neoconservative educational politics dominated the years 1997–2002 (Grollios & Kaskaris 2003), preparing the way for an even more forceful attempt (from 2004 onwards, see Athanasiou 2010; Benveniste 2010; Theotokas 2010) to "rationalize" the education process at large, rendering our educational system accountable to the so-called "needs of the society"—an expression that aims to mask the unconditional surrender of education to the rules of the market (see for example, Psycharis, 2009). Despite the oft-made assumption that economic globalization entails the demise of the role of the state, what we are experiencing at this very moment in Greece is an increase of state violence. This is not just incidental; it is "because effective and widespread state-violence is inherent to the rationality of neoliberal governing" (Oksala, 2011, p. 475).

That, essentially, this is a direct threat to freedom of thought, may be the most frightening

---

[1] Having said that, one should fully acknowledge that important issues pertaining to such notions did not realize their full potential – one should always remember that in Athenian democracy "The democratic citizen body was composed of only the adult and male citizens; that is, it represented a small minority (perhaps between 10 and 20 percent) of the total population" (Raaflaub, 2007, p. 11; see also Coleman, 2000, p. 23). But the seeds for thinking what democratic participation, equality, freedom and inclusion might mean, were placed in full force.

consequence of this. For, if everything in education is measured on the basis of its exchange value, then education technocrats and their criteria for what is educationally valuable are exactly what we need. Nothing else matters. As Kirsten Locke (2007) stated,

> *neo-liberalism operates in a manner that removes the necessity for judgment by reducing all meaning and interaction to the underlying meaning of economic rationalism– reducing everything to an exchangeable commodity that has a "bottom line" of capital value attached to it. (p. 3)*

And, of course, this is not a peculiarly Greek phenomenon (Ball, 2005; Biesta, 2011; Fitzsimons 2002; Giroux 2002, 2006; Labaree, 2011; McGettigan, 2011; Newfield, 2011; Power, 2011; Straume, 2011). Rather, this "restructuring of the schooling and education systems across the world is part of the ideological and policy offensive by neo-liberal Capital" (Hill, 2003; see also Davies, 2005). From a US perspective, Barkan (2012) observed that

> *For the last decade or so, this generation of ed reformers has been setting up programs to show the power of competition and market-style accountability to transform inner-city public schools: establishing nonprofit and for-profit charter schools, hiring business executives to run school districts, and calculating a teacher's worth based on student test scores. (p. 49)*

From a UK perspective, Ball (2003, 2005) comments on the regulative power of "performativity", which constitutes a manifestation of the increasing power that economism exercises upon educational policy and practice. Economism has come to define both "the purpose and potential of education" (Ball, 2005, p. 7) and this has serious consequences for the teacher/pupil relationships, for how we understand school's responsibility towards unprivileged members of the society, as well as for the kinds of values students develop regarding various forms of knowledge and different processes of learning. There is an inherent violence in the often unashamedly offensive language of contemporary educational "reformers". Their offensive language acts betray deep disrespect to educators who do not bow to a supposedly inevitable vision of education as a marketable good, refusing to embrace a view of educational effectiveness based on formulas "derived from classical business management" (Straume, 2011, p. 238). As Toni Morrison (1993) has put it, "Oppressive language does more than represent violence; it is violence; does more than represent the limits of knowledge; it limits knowledge" (p. 16).

Within the world of music education oppressive forms of discourse are co-constitutive of modes of practice that Wayne Bowman refers to as expressing "reactive" nihilism (Bowman, 2005); this widespread tendency is "markedly technical and means-driven, with remarkably little attention to or concern for ends served" (p. 35). Currently reigning instructional paradigms view classroom experimentation with suspicion, and are preoccupied, as Kushner (2004) wrote, with "fine-tuning the engine of 'curriculum delivery' and the grinding machine of student achievement and classroom control—'what works' is what rules" (p. 12). Such technocratic approaches link directly to the removal of the necessity for judgment (see Locke's argument mentioned above), and therefore lead to what Bowman calls "passive nihilism", a situation where "'what is' just is: *whatever*"; where "all claims to value are reduced to politically-motivated power moves" (Bowman, p. 36). But passive nihilism emerges at a time when political power becomes a tool for the implementation of neo-liberal technocratic ideals. Thus, the "whatever" is easily replaced by whatever has high exchange value; and this with minimum or no resistance.

It is within this context that our discussion of the relationships between music education and *pædeia* must be placed. In what follows, it will be argued that the link between *pædeia* and music education might be created through a particular conception of the politics of aesthetics, and that if this is so, then music education might be cast as a form of artistic activism. The first step towards this direction is to provide an outline of the concept of *pædeia* that will lead us to apprehend it as the process of educating the political subject.

Pædeia: Educating the Political Subject

In contemporary Greek the term *pædeia* (Παιδεία) is used to denote a form of education that reaches beyond training (*Katartisi* [Κατάρτιση]) towards the ideal of holistic education. In this context, *pædeia* delineates the necessity to place emphasis to the arts and the humanities rather than to a technologically oriented conception of education. This view understands *pædeia* as a process of creating what is often described as "cultured person". But it is important to note that it fails to see that all too often education in music and the arts are technically driven. We often hear that this view of *pædeia* goes back to Protagoras' thesis that the aim of education is not a process of induction into a craft, "is not for craft" but "for *pædeia*" and that this is most suitable for those who live within the condition of freedom: «ουκ επί τέχνη, έμαθες, ως δημιουργός εσόμενος, αλλ' επί παιδεία, ως τον ιδιώτην και τον ελεύθερον πρέπει» (a: *Prot.* 312b, cf. 312a-b). As it will become clear, in what follows, a rather different interpretation of this passage is suggested.

It seems to me that this grandiose view of *pædeia* has lost along the way a significant element, namely, the political implications of what it means to enter the *pædeia* process instead of mere training; it has thus become a mere rhetorical invocation of a glorious and now lost holism, of a supposed immersion in the achievements of past high Culture. In this essay, a different route is suggested, one that connects *pædeia* to the creation of the public space of the *polis*. Windelband and Heimsoeth (1976) have suggested that with the birth of the *polis*, the pursuit of philosophical exploration of the world (Cosmos) within the bounded space of various schools of the archaic period gradually began to give way to critical examination of issues of public life. It was the creation of the democratic *polis* that led to this passage from the cosmologic towards the anthropological period of philosophy. At that very moment, philosophy *becomes* political, positing questions related to the nature of human intent, will, desire, interest, and rights (Jaeger, 1946). The question that persistently arose was whether personal opinion can be linked to more general constants/universals, or whether skepticism should prevail (Windelband & Heimsoeth, 1976). Democracy entailed participation in public debates; it meant participation in decision-making processes where positions are formed and publicly debated: "We Athenians, in our own persons, take our decisions on policy or submit them to proper discussions" (Periclean Oration, in Crick, 2002, p. 19). Vernant (1982) has argued that the pursuit of argumentative reasoning should be directly linked to the imperative of equality that emerged in the democratic polis, a place that is organized exactly on the basis of the creation of a public space whose members hold freely multiple perspectives that should be declared and debated. As Ober (2005) has succinctly put it,

> Athenian democracy was intimately associated with "public voice" — with the capacity and the willingness of citizens to speak up about public concerns and to do so in public. The practice of democracy assumed that citizens had a capacity to reason together, in public (as well as in private), via frank speech, and that the results of those deliberations would (in general and over time) conduce to the common good. Deliberating meant listening as well as speaking; accepting good arguments as well as making them. (p. 130)

The imperative of thinking frankly about how to question received notions that pertain to human 'nature' and our ways of living together, delineates a view of *pædeia* as a process of learning how to think philosophically and speak freely among equals. In this context – and contrary to their Platonic condemnation as teachers of the art of deception by focusing on "rhetoric and relativism" (Gomperz, 1912, in Ford, 2001, p. 86) – sophists should be seen primarily as philosophers/educators who, by pursuing ingenious forms of reasoning, were creating the ground on which participation in democratic life rests. They provided an education in philosophy that began to develop firm links with *pædeia*. As Ford (2001) stated, "their recondite, often paradoxical performances had the effect of enabling their students to speak on equal terms with the master and with each another well before, and for some instead of, addressing an assembly" (p. 88). Therefore, they were "democratic in their willingness to challenge hierarchy and tradition in the name of the individual and the 'here and now'" (p. 86).

A vision of *pædeia* as the basis for democratic participation can thus be sketched, a vision that connects education with forming, expressing and debating opinions. Thus, the notion of *pædeia*, the situated process of cultural education and character building, is at the same time a process of creating a dialogue between cultural forms handed down by tradition and the individual's place in it (see Jaeger, 1946; Ober, 2005). We can thus argue in favour of a conception of *pædeia* as a process of shaping *a voice*, that is, a culturally and politically situated identity that is dynamic in character and presupposes the existence of a public space of the democratic *polis*. Understood this way, *pædeia* retains a deeply creative element, by emphasizing the dialogue between given cultural forms and the individual's ability to find a voice of her own through them. Sometimes, in order to achieve this, one may need to break away from her teachers – remember Aristophanes' remark «απεδίδρασκες εκ διδασκάλου» (*Fr. 206 PCG* in Ford, 2001, p. 93).

From the perspective of democratic politics, it is then argued that *pædeia* might ultimately be understood as the process of educating the political subject. This particular vision of *pædeia*, presupposes democracy, and at the same is constitutive of it; in this sense, *pædeia* influences the form of political organization. Aristotle expressed this in the following words:

> for education ought to be adapted to the particular form of constitution, since the particular character belonging to each constitution both guards the constitution generally and originally es-

> tablishes it – for instance the democratic spirit promotes democracy and the oligarchic spirit oligarchy. (Aristotle, Politics, Book VIII, [1932] p. 635) [Δει γαρ προς εκάστην παιδεύεσθαι, το γαρ ήθος της πολιτείας εκάστης το οικείον και φυλάττειν είωθε την πολιτείαν και καθίστησιν εξαρχής, οίον το μεν δημοκρατικόν δημοκρατίαν το δ'ολιγαρχικόν ολιγαρχίαν (Aristotle, Πολιτικά 1337α 14-17)]

It is this "spirit" that we must not lose sight of. It is this spirit that should permeate every aspect of people's "*paideia*, their education in the largest sense of the world", which Aristotle referred to as "*the paideia pros ta koina* – civic education" (Castoriadis, 1991b, p. 140-41). *Pædeia* may therefore be understood not as inducing a holistic education, but as a process of enabling people to participate in a common world, in a world where thought turns towards interrogating the terms in which we are deciding how to live together. It is in this context that one may understand better Protagoras' declaration cited earlier that education "is not for craft" but "for *pædeia*", for as Ford argued (2001),

> When the Platonic Protagoras declares that education is 'not for a craft but for paideia' [...] he accuses his rivals of abusing their clients precisely by teaching them arts: 'just when students ought to have escaped technical study, they plunge them back into the arts' (άλλοι λωβώνται τους νέους· τας γαρ τέχνας αυτούς πεφευγότας άκοντας πάλιν αυ άγοντες εμβάλλουσιν εις τέχνας Prot. 318d-e = 80 A 5 DK). Having "escaped" such arts, the sophists' associates were not to be expected to endure what Protagoras pointedly refers to as the "compulsory" education of grammar school (Prot. 326α: ποιήματα εκμανθάνειν αναγκάζουσιν). (p. 93)

In our own terms, the crucial distinction is between education for freedom vs. education for serving the needs of an institution or institutionalised forms of practice and not between the humanities and technology or between specialised and holistic education. And it is telling that Protagoras emphasises that to achieve this one should break free from the constraints of compulsory education. As such, *pædeia* becomes a learning process that enables one to pursue autonomous thinking, that is, thinking that aims at questioning itself, at acknowledging that the decisions taken are not the result of the "laws" of nature nor of tradition. This is the reason why Castoriadis views *pædeia* as the basis of the project of autonomy, the first instantiation of which has been the creation of the public space of Athenian democracy: "Only the education (*paedeia*) of the citizens as citizens can give valuable, substantive content to the 'public space'. This *paedeia* is not primarily a matter of books and academic credits…it is participation in political life" (Castoriadis, 1991a, p. 113).

It might seem weird that in a paper that has set as its task to search for what we can learn from ancient Greek *Pædeia*, not a single word has been uttered about the place of music (Μουσική) – in both the general and the most restricted senses of the term – in the process of education of the ancient Greeks, given that there is a wealth of references to its importance for education and character formation.

One needs only to be reminded of Aristotle's systematic treatment of the role of music in education in the 8th book of his Πολιτικά (Politics), wherein one finds two of the most famous affirmations of the importance of music and music education respectively. In the first, Aristotle states that music "has the power of producing a certain effect on the moral character of the soul" (Aristotle, Πολιτικά, Book VIII, [1932], p. 661) [«δύναται ποιόν τι το της ψυχής ήθος η μουσική παρασκευάζειν» (1340β 11-12)]. In the second, he argues this:

> hence our predecessors included music in education not as a necessity [...] nor as useful [...]; it remains therefore that it is useful as a pastime in leisure, which is evidently the purpose for which people actually introduce it, for they rank it as a form of pastime that they rank proper for free men. (Aristotle, Πολιτικά, Book VIII, [1932], pp. 641-643) [«διο και την μουσικήν οι πρότερον εις παιδείαν έταξαν ουχ ως αναγκαίον [...] ουδ' ως χρήσιμον [...]· λείπεται τοίνυν προς την εν τη σχολή διαγωγήν, εις όπερ και φαίνονται παράγοντες αυτήν, ην γαρ οίονται διαγωγήν είναι των ελευθέρων» (1338α 14-25)]

However, in this essay we are not interested in the role of music within the pædeutic processes of the ancient world. Nor has our aim been to justify music education by invoking the writings of the ancients Greeks. Our aim is to sketch a particular conception of *pædeia*, which might be useful for music education in its attempt to rethink its role within human lives in contemporary contexts.

Music Education and *Pædeia*: The Missing Links

The notion of *pædeia* sketched above, emphasises immersion into free inquiry that asks difficult questions about how humans form their collectivities. It also emphasises that this sets off a process of forming personal voices as a result of speaking "on equal terms" (Ford, 2001, p. 86) with each other as well as with received traditions. Moreover, it delineates a view of education as constitutive of the democratic public space, and of people's ability to participate in it. *Pædeia* as a particular perspective of the education process, is seen as a process of nurturing a particular ethos, created through equal participation and care for developing one's personal voice. Ultimately this idea of education is central for the creation of a democratic public space, a space where people enter into decision-making but most importantly, constantly interrogate as to the validity, the suppositions, the consequences and the rationale of these decisions, casting them into doubt – this is the core of democratic politics (Castoriadis, 1991c).

Pædeia thus conceived becomes a process that makes *dissensus* possible. I am here using the term in the sense used by Jacques Rancière (2004b):

> Political dissensus is not simply a conflict of interests, opinions, or values. It is a conflict over the common itself. It is not a quarrel over which solutions to apply to a situation but a dispute over the

> situation itself, a dispute over what is visible as an element of a situation, over which visible elements belong to what is common, over the capacity of subjects to designate this common and argue for it. (p. 6)

Contrary to commonly held views that emphasize consensus as a pivotal sign of democracy, it might be that its defining feature is the extent to which humans are able to dispute the given, by questioning what is taken for granted, by unsettling what is thought of as the core meaning of a situation, and by bringing to the fore a voice and a perspective that up to that moment did not have the *right* to be there (Rancière, 1999, Ross, 2009). Dissensus does not just mean conflict of different viewpoints that rest on a divergent set of assumptions concerning values: "that would assume that the parties involved in the conflict would already exist and have an identity" (Bingham & Biesta, 2010, p. 46).

For Rancière, the moment of dissensus is the moment of appearance of politics (*la politique*). Politics is not the process of collective decision-making, nor the implementation of policies via the exercise of power. Politics is a process of creating cracks in what Rancière calls the *distribution* (or the *partition*) *of the sensible* (*le partage du sensible*), defined as "the system of self-evident facts of sense perception that simultaneously discloses the existence of something in common and the delimitations that define the respective parts and positions within it" (Rancière, 2004a, p. 12; see also Rancière 2009b). Politics is a constellation of acts that lead to a moment of dissensus. Dissensus, understood as a process that gives voice to people who had no voice, whose voice did not exist within a given distribution of the sensible, "rests on the presupposition of equality, where subjects constitute themselves as political subjects, whose emergence both disfigures and reconfigures the perceptual coordinates of the social order" (Means, 2011, p. 1092). Politics, therefore, produces a redistribution of the sensible: "Human beings are tied together by a certain sensory fabric, a certain distribution of the sensible, which defines their way of being together; and politics is about the transformation of the sensory fabric of 'being together'" (Ranciére, 2009a, p. 56).

This is exactly the point where politics meets the arts. Ranciére introduces a radically different view of Plato's exclusion of the arts from his Republic, arguing that the arts were expelled from Plato's ideal city at the same time as democracy – for both the arts and the political assembly of citizens are two "forms of distribution of the sensible" (Rancière, 2009c, p. 24) that share a common root: they are "spaces of heterogeneity" (p. 24 providing the context for freedom – the second because it enables people to "do *something other* than their work" (p. 24) and the first because within its realm people "might assume a character *other* than their own" (p. 24). Ranciére (2009c) stated that,

> Art and politics are thereby linked, beneath themselves, as forms of presence of singular bodies in a specific space and time. Plato simultaneously excludes both democracy and theatre so that he can construct an ethical community, a community without politics. (p. 26)

It is essential that we understand that this view preserves the distinctiveness of artistic and thereby of musical practices, while negating their autonomy, understood in the modernist sense (whereby artworks constitute novel entities whose meaning inheres in their particular structural features, and is revealed via the "purity" of our gaze towards them). Artistic practices and not art-products have deeply political effects for they unsettle what is permitted to be visible, creating ways of being in the world that disrupt existing hierarchies: "aesthetics and politics are imbricated in the constitution of specific orders of visibility and sense through which the political division into assigned roles and defined parts manifests itself" (Hinderliter et al., 2009, p. 1).

Under this perspective, it is the socially grounded process of thinking and sensing through participation in artistic practices, in practices that suspend the rational processes of cause and effect and of rational justification of choices that we should refer to as aesthetic experience. Aesthetic experience,

> *is a multiplicity of folds and gaps in the fabric of common experience that change the cartography of the perceptible, the thinkable and the feasible. As such, it allows for new modes of political construction of common objects and new possibilities of collective enunciation. (Ranciére, 2009a, p. 72)*

Music education, the process whereby students construct their way into participation in and co-creation of socio-musical practices, should be seen as both an educational and an artistic practice. And according to the view put forward here, educational/artistic practices create contexts for the emergence of aesthetic experiences that lead to new configurations of the distribution of the sensible. By creating cracks to the hierarchies imposed by the dominant distribution of the sensible, music education might be seen as having a deeply political role, creating the context where people's personal voices are formed, heard and have consequences, generating the possibility of dissensus. In this way it becomes a process of educating the political subject, thereby linking itself to the *pædeia* ideal of the ancient Greek democratic polis. And this would mean that the music educator's role takes on the form of educational/artistic activism.

Music Education as Activism

What would music education as a form of educational/cultural activism mean in the context of this essay? It would mean, first and foremost, that we, music educators, begin to question our role as guardians of received musical cultures (sometimes acting, regrettably, as security guards), or, as Randall Allsup (in press) puts it, as "cultural care-takers". It would mean that we begin to question the prominence of work-based music education and the dominance of skills-based modes of practice. It would mean to go beyond thinking that activity-based music education practices constitute the end-point of what we might think music education is (or even the end of music education). Central to an understanding of music education as activism would be our commitment to doubt and question the neutrality of every music education act. But questioning our assumptions is only a beginning. What we need is to use this questioning in developing positive (*and sustained*) actions, creating educational contexts that are rooted in a commitment to make culture instead of guarding the purity of its received forms, reproducing it, or even aping it: "how we can make and re-make culture in music education rather than how we can gain knowledge and understand musical cultures, ours or that of others" (Westerlund, 2003, p. 57).

Music education holds the promise of actively engaging students in culture creation, but this presupposes a determination to create "folds and gaps in the fabric of common experience that change the cartography of the perceptible, the thinkable and the feasible" (Ranciére, 2009a, p. 72). It is through the persistent cultivation of heterogeneity, which is the basis of the development of personal voice and therefore the necessary context for the emergence of dissensus, that culture creation may be possible. In turn, this cannot but be based on the premise that thinking in and about music is a process that relates to something much more than sound and its configurations. And this permits us to begin exploring ways of working with our students that reveal an understanding of every act of playing and discussing music not as a tool for transmitting and explaining aspects of musical knowledge that are already there, but as acts that pose issues of *how we are together*, as acts that *re*-configure the distribution of the sensible. This perspective allows us to approach music education practice as a series of acts of transformation of the sensory fabric of *being together*. In this way the following issues begin to take on a new meaning:

- Listening in order to follow, listening in order to be able to get in front – listening so as to look inside (a) the sounds, (b) ourselves. Listening so as to find ways of articulating the relationships between (a) and (b);
- Leading: who and for what?
- Playing together: Who and for what? Is our stance of playing together posing the issue of equality? How? Working on and through: (Im)precision – (im)balance – breathing together – unity – together by being apart – creating a mass of indistinctive elements;
- Going off in unexpected directions (am I allowed to? How?);
- Expression of desire (how am I going to express desire?);
- What makes someone able to create music? Who belongs to the community of creators? What is the role of children's creations within the music making processes? Where do musical ideas come from? What does musical invention mean? How do musical ideas travel? and
- Do social, gender and ethnic differences lead to "Understanding difference as positivity" allowing "music educators to move beyond traditional practices and discourses in order to explore alternatives without pejorative connotations" (Gould, 2008, p. 8)?

The moment that music education casts these questions (through its very practice) as *open* issues, thus disrupting the existing order of things, is the moment when it meets politics. Music education can thus be understood as a form of cultural/political activism, when "It makes visible what had no business being seen, and makes heard a discourse where once there was only place for noise; it makes understood as discourse what was once only heard as noise" (Ranciére, 1999, p. 30). In this way, music education can be seen as a process of reconfiguring the distribution of the sensible: as a form of creating the basis for democratic culture that begins from the basis of equality where one conceives of children as already having a voice – thus creating a new distribution of the sensible – making children visible and thus active in ways not possible before. Music education can be understood as a *pædeia* process precisely when it concerns itself with the development of students' *voice*, but on the basis that "all students can *already* speak...that students neither lack the capacity for speech, nor that they are producing noise" (Biesta, 2011, p. 39). For, from a Ranciérian point of view, one can only develop a voice based on the axiom that equality is not a state that we strive for, but a supposition that is expressed through action: equality "must be *presupposed,* from the outset, in the pedagogical encounter", it "must be *declared* and . . . *verified* in that encounter" (Davis, 2010, p. 27; Rancière, 1991; Citton, 2010).

I was listening to the BBC radio 3 the other day: an adult in a sorrowful voice declared "I can't read music"; and one was sensing that this meant: "therefore, I'm musically useless". I also recently played a recording of an early childhood student teachers' composition to a musician – a little waltz that reminded me of Nicola Piovani, thoroughly composed but not written down, and he pressingly kept asking "Yes, I can hear it; but what exactly are they doing?" I argue that a particular stance towards music education that is rooted in the "supposition of inequality" (Ranciére, 2010, p. 14). Music education can be transformed into a *pædeia* process exactly when this powerlessness is being combatted. And also when what had been exorcized, silenced and de-valued begins to be visible, transforming the fabric of sensory experience. From a Ranciérian perspective, Biesta (2011) argues that "the circle of powerlessness can only be interrupted by starting from somewhere else, by starting from a different assumption – the assumption of equality" (p. 41).

Music education understood as activism creates a music education environment that gives students the chance to create dissent through genuine dialogue between their personal endeavours and larger musical traditions, in ways that would seriously allow for the possibility to exclaim: "You might like what is wrong better than what is right" [μπορεί να σου αρέσει πιο πολύ το λάθος από το σωστό] (an 8 year-old child, in Kanellopoulos, 2007, p. 133) – an utterance whose radical potential is rarely understood by music educators. For this presupposes that in our work we critically think about the rules that underpin decisions of rightness and wrongness, and reflect upon what it is that we are doing when choosing this or that pathway. In this way students might begin to build a strong sense that:

> Someone has addressed words to them that they want to recognize and respond to, not as students or as learned men, but as people; in the way you respond to someone speaking to you and not to someone examining you: under the sign of equality
> (Ranciére, 1991, p. 11).

This perspective has strong relationships with the pedagogy of open forms that has been recently proposed by Randall Allsup (in press), a pedagogy that is rooted in the practice of compos-*ing*:

> A musical pedagogy of open texts is one that places composing at the center of all activities. It assumes that all students come to an educational encounter equipped with multiple literacies, and that they wish to employ the largest range of modalities available to them to communicate with others and to create self-reflective musical events.

This approach to music pedagogy centers around "a reconfigured practice of *composing*, where writing, playing, and sharing exists within and across open discursive fields" (Allsup), leading to the development of students' personal voice, and constitutes an act of verifying equality (see Ranciére, 2010). It thus creates a democratic public space which allows for heterogeneity, subverting hierarchies and received canons, thus leading to the emergence of dissensus: "the search for the democratic in music education must go beyond consensus and the abnormal discourses that seek to coerce it. It must accept conflict and confrontation as inevitable and as potentially constructive" (Schmidt, 2008, p. 21). It is in this way that it relates to the democratic conception of *pædeia*, of an open educational process that contributes to the constitution of a political subject, of a subject capable of participating and co-creating forms of socio-musical acts that create cracks in the currently dominant modes of thought that permeate educational policies (see Fgure 1). In this way music education might be understood as being ουκ επί τέχνη ... αλλ' επί παιδεία, "not for a craft ... but for *paideia*".

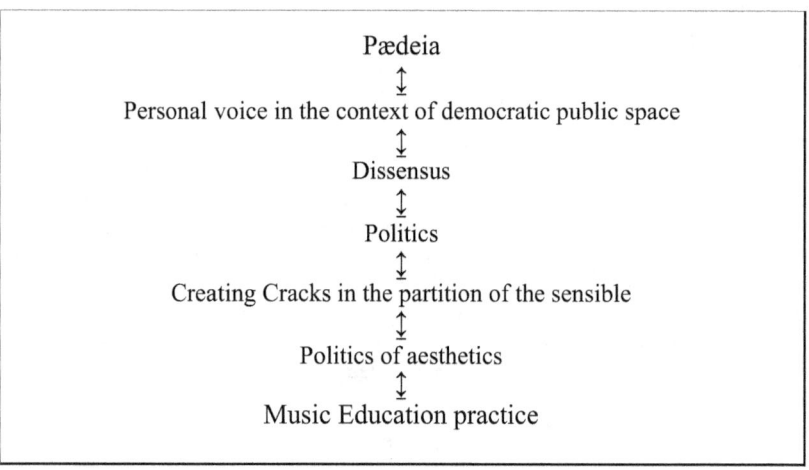

Figure 1: *Pædeia and Music Education – The Missing Links*

Acknowledgements
My sincere thanks to Wayne Bowman, Elizabeth Gould, Danae Stefanou, and Ruth W. Wright for their sharp observations during the various stages of preparation of this essay, but also for our on-going intellectual companionship.

References
Aristotle. [1932]. *Politics* (H. Rackham, trans.). London: Heinemann.

Allsup, R. E. (in press). The compositional turn in music education: From closed forms to open texts. In M. Kaschub and J. Smith (eds.), *Composing Our Future: Preparing Music Educators to Teach Composition*. Oxford & New York: Oxford University Press.

Athanasiou, A. (2010). Critique in a era of crisis, or the devaluation of the humanities and the social sciences [Η κριτική την εποχή της κρίσης, ή η απαξίωση των κοινωνικών και ανθρωπιστικών σπουδών. (Παρέμβαση στην ημερίδα για τις ανθρωπιστικές και κοινωνικές επιστήμες, του περιοδικού Ιστορείν, Αθήνα 13.ΧΙ.2010)]. Retrieved December, 10, 2010 from: http://historein-historein.blogspot.com/2010/11/blog-post_18.html

Ball, S. J. (2003). The teacher's soul and the terrors of performativity. *Journal of Education Policy, 18*, 215-228.

Ball, S. J. (2005). The Commodification of Education in England: Towards a new form of social relations. Keynote address to the *Japan-UK Education Forum Kyoto 2005*. Retrieved January, 25, 2009 from: http://wwwsoc.nii.ac.jp/juef/ac/2005/kyoto05.pdf

Barkan, J. (2012). Hired guns on astroturf: How to buy and sell school reform. *Dissent, 59(*2), 49-57.

Benveniste, R. (2010). Lingua reformationis universitatis (LRU) or Disciplining and punishment: The implementation of Independent Authority for Quality Control to and its transformation to Independent Authority for Evaluation, Certification *and* Funding [lingua reformationis universitatis (LRU) ή Πειθάρχηση και Τιμωρία: Η γένεση της Α.Α.ΔΙ.Π και η μετεξέλιξή της σε Α.Α.ΑΞΙ. ΠΙΣ.Χ. (Παρέμβαση στην ημερίδα για τις ανθρωπιστικές και κοινωνικές επιστήμες, του περιοδικού Ιστορείν, Αθήνα 13.ΧΙ.2010). Retrieved December, 10, 2010 from: http://historeinhistorein.blogspot.com/2010/11/lingua-reformationis-universitatis-lru.html

Biesta, G. (2011). Learner, student, speaker: Why it matters how we call those we teach. In Maarten Simons & Jan Masschellein, (eds.), *Ranciére, Public Education and the Taming of Democracy* (pp. 31-42). Chichester, West Sussex: Wiley-Blackwell.

Bingham, C. & Biesta, G. J. J. (2010). *Education, truth, emancipation*. London: Continuum.

Bowman, W. (2005). Music education in nihilistic times, *Educational Philosophy & Theory, 37*(1), 29–46.

Castoriadis, C. (1991a). The Greek *Polis* and the Creation of Democracy. In David. A. Curtis (ed. & trans.), *Cornelius Castoriadis–Philosophy, Politics, Autonomy: Essays in political philosophy* (pp. 81-123). New York: Oxford University Press.

Castoriadis, C. (1991b). The Nature and Value of Equality. in D. A. Curtis (ed. & trans), *Cornelius Castoriadis–Philosophy, Politics, Autonomy: Essays in political philosophy* (pp. 124–142). New York, Oxford University Press.

Castoriadis, C. (1991c). Power, politics, autonomy. in D. A. Curtis (ed. & trans), *Cornelius Castoriadis–Philosophy, Politics, Autonomy: Essays in political philosophy* (pp. 143– 174). New York: Oxford University Press.

Citton, Y. (2010). "The ignorant schoolmaster": Knowledge and authority. In Jean-Philippe

Deranty (ed.), *Jacques Rancière: Key Concepts* (pp. 25-37). Durham: Acumen.

Coleman, J. (2000). *A history of political thought: From ancient Greece to early Christianity*. Oxford: Blackwell. Crick, B. (2002). *Democracy – A very short introduction*. Oxford: Oxford University Press.

Davies, B. (2005). The impossibility of intellectual work in Neoliberal Regimes. *Discourse: studies in the cultural politics of education, 26*(1), 1-14.

Davis, O. (2010). *Key contemporary thinkers: Jacques Rancière*. Cambridge: Polity.

Farrar, C. (1988). *The origins of democratic thinking: The invention of politics in classical Athens*. Cambridge: Cambridge University Press.

Fitzsimons, P. (2002). Neoliberalism and education: The autonomous chooser. *Radical Pedagogy, 4*. Retrieved February, 8, 2009, from: http://radicalpedagogy.icaap.org/content/issue4_2/04_fitzsimons.html

Ford, A. (2001). Sophists without rhetoric: The arts of speech in fifth-century Athens. In Yun Lee Too (ed.), *Education In Greek And Roman Antiquity* (pp. 85-109). Leiden, The Netherlands: Koninklyke.

Giroux, H. A. (2002). Educated hope in an age of privatized visions, *Cultural Studies-Critical Methodologies, 2*(1), 93-112.

Giroux. H. A. (2006). Academic freedom under fire: The case for critical pedagogy. *College Literature, 33*(4), 1-42.

Gomperz, H. (1912). *Sophistik und rhetorik*. Stuttgart, B. G. Teubner.

Gould, E. (2008). Difference out of place: Feminist war machines in music education. *Visions of Research in Music Education, 11*(1). Retrieved May, 2, 2012, from: http://www- usr.rider.edu/~vrme/v11n1/index

Grollios, G. & Kaskaris, I. (2003). From socialist - democratic to "Third way" politics and rhetoric in Greek education (1997-2002). *Journal for Critical Education Policy Studies, 1*(1). Retrieved Jan, 23, 2009 from: www.jceps.com/?pageID=article&articleID=4

Heller, A. (2008). The gods of Greece: Germans and the Greeks. *Thesis Eleven, 93*, 52–63.

Hill, D. (2003). Global Neo-liberalism, the deformation of education and resistance. *Journal for Critical Education Policy Studies, 1*(1). Retrieved January, 23, 2009 from: www.jceps.com/?pageID=article&articleID=7

Hinderliter, B., Kaizen, W., Maimon, V., Mansoor, J., & S. McCormick. (2009). Introduction. In B. Hinderliter, W. Kaizen, V. Maimon, J. Mansoor & S. McCormick (eds.), *Communities of Sense: Rethinking Aesthetics and Politics* (pp. 1-28). Durham, NC: Duke University Press.

Jaeger, W. (1946). *Paedeia: The ideals of Greek culture (vol. 1): Archaic Greece – The mind of Athens*. Oxford: Blackwell.

Kanellopoulos, P. ⊠. (2007). Children's early reflections on improvised music-making as the wellspring of musico-philosophical thinking. *Philosophy of Music Education Review, 15*, 119-141.

Kushner, S. (2004). Falsifying schooling: Surrealism and curriculum. In J. L. Arostegui (Ed.), *The Social Context of Music Education* (pp. 203-218). Champaign, IL: Center for Instructional Research and Curriculum Evaluation, University of Illinois.

Labaree, D. (2011). Targeting teachers. *Dissent, 58*(3), 9-14.

Locke, K. (2007). Aesthetics, politics, and public pedagogy: Let me sing you gentle songs. Paper presented at the 2007 Philosophy of Education Society of Australasia Symposium. Retrieved April, 20, 2012 from: http://www.pesa.org.au/index.php?page=./abstract07.html

McGettigan, A. (2011). "New providers": The creation of a market in higher education, *Radical Philosophy, 167*, 2-8.

Means, A. (2011). Aesthetics, affect, and educational politics. *Educational Philosophy & Theory, 43*, 1088-1102.

Morrison, T. (1993). *Lecture and speech of acceptance, upon the award of the Nobel Prize for literature, delivered in Stockholm on the seventh of December, nineteen hundred and ninety-three.* London, UK: Chatto and Windus.

Mossé, C. (1971). *Histoire d'une démocratie: Athènes.* Paris: Éditions du Seuil.

Mossé, C. (1984). *La Grèce archaïque d'Homère á Eschyle.* Paris: Éditions du Seuil.

Newfield, C. (2011). Devolving public universities: Lessons from America. *Radical Philosophy, 169,* 36-42.

Ober, J. (2005). *Athenian legacies: Essays on the politics of going on together.* Princeton, NJ: Princeton University Press.

Oksala, J. (2011). Violence and neoliberal governmentality. *Constellations, 18,* 474-485.

Power, N. (2011). Pow! *Radical Philosophy, 166,* 56-61.

Psycharis, S. (2009) "Editorial: Occupation...?" [Επάγγελμα...;], To Vima newspaper, 25/1/ 2009, p. 1.

Raaflaub, K. A. (2007). Introduction. In K. A. Raaflaub, J. Ober & R. W. Wallace (eds.), *Origins of Democracy in Ancient Greece.* Berkeley: University of California Press.

Rancière, J. (1991). *The ignorant schoolmaster, five lessons in intellectual emancipation* (K. Ross trans.). Stanford: Stanford University Press.

Rancière, J. (1999). *Disagreement: Politics and philosophy* (J. Rose trans.). Minneapolis, MN: University of Minnesota Press.

Rancière, J. (2004a). *The Politics of Aesthetics* (G. Rockhill, trans.). New York: Continuum.

Rancière, J. (2004b). Introducing disagreement (S. Corcoran trans.). *Angelaki: Journal of the Theoretical Humanities, 9*(3), 3-9.

Rancière, J. (2009a). *The Emancipated Spectator* (G. Elliott, trans.). London: Verso.

Rancière, J. (2009b). Contemporary art and the politics of aesthetics. In B. Hinderliter, W. Kaizen, V. Maimon, J. Mansoor & S. McCormick (eds.), *Communities Of Sense: Rethinking Aesthetics and Politics* (pp. 31-50). Durham, NC: Duke University Press.

Rancière, J. (2009c). *Aesthetics and its Discontents* (S. Corcoran, trans.). Cambridge: Polity.

Rancière, J. (2010). On ignorant schoolmasters. In C. Bingham, G. J. J. Biesta, *Education, Truth, Emancipation* (pp. 1-16). London: Continuum.

Ross, T. (2009). From Classical to Postclassical beauty: Institutional critique and aesthetic enigma in Louise Lawler's photography. In B. Hinderliter, W. Kaizen, V. Maimon, J. Mansoor & S. McCormick (eds.), *Communities of Sense: Rethinking Aesthetics and Politics* (pp. 79-110). Durham: Duke University Press.

Schmidt, P. K. (2008). Democracy and dissensus: Constructing conflict in music education. *Action, Criticism, and Theory for Music Education, 7*(1), 10-28. http://act.maydaygroup.org/articles/Schmidt7_1.pdf

Snell, B. (1975). *Die entdeckung des Geistes: Studien zur entstehung des europäischen Denkens bei den Griechen.* Göttingen Vandenhoeck & Ruprecht.

Straume, I. S. (2011). "Learning" and signification in neoliberal governance. In I. S. Straume & J. F. Humphrey (eds.), *Depoliticization: The political imaginary of global capitalism* (pp. 229-259). Malmö: NSU Press.

Theotokas, N. (2010). Neo-liberal fanatics destroy public universities and demolish the Constitution [Οι φανατικοί του νεοφιλελευθερισμού διαλύουν το Δημόσιο Πανεπιστήμιο και καταλύουν το Σύνταγμα]. *Avgi* newspaper, 31-10-2010, 6-10.

Vernant, J. P. (1982). *The origins of Greek thought*. Ithaca: Cornell University Press.

Westerlund, H. (2003). Reconsidering aesthetic experience in praxial music education. *Philosophy of Music Education Review, 11*(1), 45-62.

Windelband, W. & Heimsoeth, H. (1976). *Lehrbuch der Geschichte der philosophie*. Tübingen: Mohr Siebeck.

Music Paedeia for Today's World

Paul R. Lehman
University of Michigan (USA)
prlehman@umich.edu

I want to focus today on the practical applications of philosophy in general and paedeia in particular. Music teachers often become so wrapped up in their day-to-day work that they don't have time to think much about philosophy. Many of our teachers study the philosophy of music education in a systematic manner only in graduate school. Our undergraduates are often given a superficial introduction to philosophy at best, and when they actually begin teaching whatever thoughts they may have had regarding philosophy are easily crowded out of their consciousness by concerns about what they're going to do in the classroom tomorrow morning or how they'll handle this problem or manage that crisis. But even though we don't think consciously about the philosophical basis for our every action, our philosophical views affect everything we do as teachers, including our decisions with regard to developing curricula, planning lessons, assessing learning, and dealing with students, school administrators, and parents. That applies to all of us regardless of the levels at which we teach. Our philosophy and our practice are intimately linked. Our philosophy provides the basis for our practice. And our practice tests and reinforces our philosophy.

Even though we may adjust our views from time to time to reflect changing conditions, our profession rests on solid philosophical foundations that are well established in our literature. We're not entirely free of controversy, but it's safe to say that there is more agreement than disagreement within our profession concerning our core values. There may be minor differences about where the emphasis ought to be placed within the music program, but there is no dissent from the belief that music belongs among the basics in the curriculum.

The major problem faced by music education today, in my view, results from a lack of awareness or acceptance of certain basic philosophical principles on the part of some education decision-makers and some segments of the public. It's because of this lack of awareness or acceptance that many young people are prevented from enjoying the benefits of music instruction. And because that's the case I want to speak today not about the philosophy of music educators but rather about the philosophy of school administrators and the public as it affects music in our schools.

The fundamental principles of paedeia are alive and well in music education. Or they should be. In the current sources I'm familiar with the term paedeia is used to refer broadly to the process of rearing children, and it nearly always involves a school curriculum that emphasizes music. In the United States the concept of paedeia was revived most notably by the distinguished philosopher and educator Prof. Mortimer Adler in the 1980s. His three books on the subject of paedeia (Adler, 1982, 1983, 1984) led to the establishment of the Paideia [*sic*] Center in Chapel Hill, North Carolina, which still exists today and works to promote its version of paideia learning in the U.S. and beyond (www.paideia.org). Mortimer Adler was a strong supporter of music in education, and the arts occupy a prominent position in his paideia curriculum. According to Adler,

> [There are] three areas of subject matter indispensable to basic schooling—language, literature, and fine arts; mathematics and natural sciences; history, geography, and social studies. Why these three? They comprise the most fundamental branches of learning. No one can claim to be educated who is not reasonably well acquainted with all three. (Adler, 1982, p. 22-24)

We hear a great deal today about education reform, but the discussion is typically driven by popular fads and political pressures rather than by facts and thoughtful deliberation. And too often music is losing out in the struggle to compete for a place in the curriculum. I want to discuss today the premise that every student should have access to music instruction in school. In my view, the music program should be balanced, comprehensive, and sequential. It should be taught by qualified teachers. And it should lead toward clearly defined, standards-based skills and knowledge. But in the interests of simplicity, let's just focus on the idea that every student should have access to music instruction in school.

I believe that this premise is one hundred per cent consistent with nearly every interpretation of paedeia learning. I believe this premise represents a progressive, enlightened view. I believe this premise is correct. I believe that the rest of the world should share this premise: *Every student should have access to music instruction in school*. But when I look around I see that this premise is *not* universally accepted. I see schools that offer weak music programs, or programs that are too narrow in scope, or programs that reach only a few students. And I see some schools that offer no music programs at all. How can this be?

My premise, lest you forget, is that every student should have access to music instruction in school. I suspect that's your premise too. Let's label it Premise A. Those people who do not yet accept Premise A hold a variety of opinions, but let's lump all of those views together and call them Premise B. And let's summarize Premise B this way: Music is fine but our schools can't do everything so we have to set priorities, and in today's competitive world music simply isn't a high priority. That's Premise B. It says, in short, that music is a low priority. Which premise is correct? Let's look at the evidence.

I have already forfeited any claim to impartiality in this matter, but it seems clear that the evidence in support of Premise A is overwhelming. First of all, it's based on two thousand years of educational thought and practice. The idea that music should be a part of basic education is not only the position of Mortimer Adler, it has been the position of virtually every writer and every group that has made a major contribution to Western educational thought from Plato to the present.

The credibility of both premises depends in large part on our views regarding the purpose of education. Why do we have schools in the first place? Historically, one of the most important purposes of education has been to transmit the heritage of a culture from one generation to the next. If we accept that idea then the validity of Premise A is undeniable. After all, music is one of the most representative, most treasured, and most glorious manifestations of every cultural heritage.

But what about jobs? Today nations around the world are struggling to create jobs for their citizens, and education is an essential tool in that struggle. Some people seem to think that education should focus entirely on vocational, job-related skills. I don't believe that for one minute. Paedeia refers to a well-rounded education as distinct from one focusing solely on jobs. Employability is a byproduct of education, not its primary goal.

In my view, the most basic purposes of education are the pursuit of truth and beauty, the development of human capacities, and the improvement of the quality of life. And what can do more than music to promote these goals? Schools ought to emphasize preparing young people for rich, satisfying, and rewarding lives, not for narrow roles in manufacturing and marketing consumer goods. And the way to do that is to focus on the five basic groups of disciplines: (1) math, (2) languages and literature, (3) the physical sciences, (4) social studies, and (5) the arts.

The world of work has become so specialized, and it's changing so rapidly, that employers want to train their own employees. What they want from the schools are graduates who are trainable, and that means graduates with a solid background in the basic disciplines, including the arts. It's ironic that the skills employers value most highly all happen to be important outcomes of arts instruction—namely, creativity, flexibility, discipline, and skill in working cooperatively with others. There's nothing taught in the schools that develops those skills better than music.

Our young people are not mere pawns on the gigantic chessboard of international economic competition. Earning a better living is less important than living a better life. Success means more than earning money; success means being able to live your life as you want to live it. Remember that education is what we have left over when we've forgotten the things we learned in school.

Now let's look at the evidence in support of Premise B—that music is not a high priority. Some people contend that music is a frill that has no place in a rigorous academic setting. That idea has persisted like crabgrass on the lawn of music education. It endures because in the case of the arts the line between education and entertainment is often fuzzy. Music plays a pervasive role in show business and in popular culture, and that role often blinds people to the very different role it plays in education. How can music be a frill when it's one of the basic disciplines? Premise B is badly flawed.

Polls have shown that the public strongly supports education in music and the other arts. Parents want their kids to know the contributions of Shakespeare and Michelangelo and Beethoven as well as those of Galileo and Newton and Einstein. But we have to help the public to understand that our programs lead to important, well-defined outcomes. After an orientation for choir parents one mother was overheard saying to another "I didn't know they actually learned things in choir; I thought they just sang".

Some people argue that music should be offered only for the talented. But every individual has the potential to perform, to create, and to listen to music with understanding and satisfaction, and every child deserves an opportunity to participate fully and knowledgeably in his or her culture. And the experience of music teachers around the world shows that every child can learn music—if we begin instruction early enough. Some students have more talent than others in math as well. Should we limit math instruction only to those with talent in math? Premise B is a failed philosophy.

Some argue that if parents want music for their kids they should pay for it outside the school. But why should it be taught outside the school if everyone should have it? The formal study of music makes it possible for students to deal with more sophisticated and complex music. Formal study can sharpen their perceptions, raise their levels of appreciation, and broaden their musical horizons. This serves to increase the level of pleasure they get from making and listening to music. Any student who is allowed to leave school without the systematic study of music has been cheated just as surely as if he or she had been denied the opportunity to study math or science or history.

Some people argue that kids don't need to study music because they're constantly surrounded by it and they learn it informally. But the fact of constant exposure to music sounds to me like all the more reason for studying it. If we're content to have our young people wallow indiscriminately in the trivial banality of popular culture, maybe they don't need to study it. But no one who glimpses the magic that lies beneath the surface in the world of music will be satisfied with shallowness and superficiality. No one who once tastes the joy of performing and creating and listening to music with genuine understanding can resist the urge to continue exploring this wondrous realm where beauty and enjoyment are so readily accessible.

Perhaps the most common excuse schools offer for not providing good music programs is that there's not enough time. But that is a false claim, and I'm tired of hearing it. John Goodlad (1984, pp. 127-8, 134, 286-7) showed us how to find the time years go in his book *A Place Called School*. So did the National Education Commission on Time and Learning in the U.S. (1994, p. 30, 32) in its report called *Prisoners of Time*. But never mind that; we don't need to look in books. All we have to do is look around us. There are schools everywhere that have no trouble finding time for music. And if school X can do it, school Y can also. The fact is that all schools have the same amount of time. Some schools have more money. Some have better facilities. Some have newer equipment. But time is the one resource—the only resource—that is allocated with absolute equality to every school everywhere. Some don't use it all, and some don't use it well, but it's there for every school. The problem is not a lack of time; the problem is a lack of will masquerading as a lack of time.

Another widespread but feeble excuse for not offering music is that "the schedule won't allow it." Well, we have to ask, "Who's running that school anyway? Is it the schedule?" Which makes more sense: To begin with a schedule and try to fit in learning experiences where and when we can? Or to begin with standards specifying what students should know and be able to do and then work out a schedule to make that possible?

Lack of funds for music is another classic excuse. But the underlying question is one of priorities. When music is not taught the reason is simply that it's not valued highly enough. That's Premise B rearing its ugly face. What's truly valued by society will find its way into the curriculum. As our schools become increasingly obsessed with certain favored disciplines at the expense of other disciplines, it becomes all the more necessary that students be given the means to express their individuality and their creativity. For some students it's music that makes school tolerable. Some students find that only in music class are their talents appreciated, their contributions respected, and their achievements valued. Premise B fails again.

One of the things that schools teach implicitly is that every question has a right answer. Our obsession with right answers is reinforced every day by an endless succession of examinations of all kinds. But the most important problems facing society don't have the clear-cut answers of multiple-choice exams. How do we end poverty? How do we eliminate disease? How do we achieve peace? These questions don't lend themselves to the formulaic, step-by-step solutions taught in school. Life is filled with ambiguities, and music teaches this very well. There may be several valid solutions to a musical problem or several valid interpretations of a musical work. The arts differ from the other disciplines in that they don't reflect a preoccupation with right answers. Education needs this balanced perspective. The fixation on right answers so common today creates an artificial environment that's inconsistent with reality and leaves the student with a distorted view of the world—an especially conspicuous weakness in Premise B.

Most of us have known schools facing cutbacks in funding, and school administrators sometimes begin by cutting music programs and music teachers. But every student has to be assigned somewhere every hour, so any reduction in staff requires an increase in average class size and it has nothing to do with what disciplines the teachers are teaching. A reduction in staff is no excuse for fundamentally distorting the balance of the curriculum. In fact, music teachers often teach more students than the average teacher because they conduct large ensembles, so cutting a music teacher may increase the average class size more than cutting a teacher in another field.

Some legislators seem to think that education can be improved by requiring more tests. But trying to improve education simply by requiring tests is like trying to eliminate crime by making it illegal. Everyone wants world-class schools. We just don't want to pay for them. People complain that education is expensive. But compared to ignorance, it's a bargain. I can tell you what's expensive: crime, welfare, teenage pregnancy—these are the things we can't afford. And every dollar spent on education helps to avoid those problems. Critics say that we can't solve the problems of education by throwing money at them. But how do we know that? We've never tried.

The task ahead for you and me is to convince those who determine the school curriculum of the validity of Premise A—that every student should have access to music instruction in school. In some countries that decision lies entirely with the Ministry of Education. In other countries it lies largely with states and local governments. In either case the acceptance of Premise A and the rejection of Premise B will depend in large measure on our gaining the widespread support of parents and the public. We need the backing of the average citizen, who is sometimes referred to familiarly as Joe Sixpack. And we need to make our case in simple, user-friendly language. I recently read a statement in support of Premise A that was superbly argued. It was a great statement. It was intellectually flawless. But it was 26 pages long, and it contained 21 footnotes. I'll bet Joe Sixpack hasn't read it and doesn't plan to. We need to find ways to reach Joe and his friends.

This process is called advocacy. And we don't need 47 reasons to justify music in our schools, but we may need more than one or two because there are many different constituencies within the public with many different views concerning the purposes of education, so there's no single justification that will persuade everyone.

One reason we still have schools with weak or non-existent music programs is that there are too many principals and others in decision-making roles in education who did not themselves experience first-hand the joy and satisfaction of a high-quality music program in school. So they don't realize what kids are missing when music is not a part of their school environment. It's time to break that self-perpetuating cycle of musical deprivation.

Nations are judged by posterity not by their economic power nor by their military arsenals nor by their average test scores, but by their contributions to the arts and humanities. What do we know of Brandenburg today except for those six Bach concertos? It's the achievements of a civilization in the arts and humanities that remain when everything else is swept away by time.

Education is the best investment in the future anyone can make, and every student should have access to music because music makes a difference in people's lives. We music educators have something to give to our young people that no one else can give them. It's the joy and beauty and satisfaction of music. And that's something, which, once given, can never be taken away. Our vision is that the kind of music program available in the best schools be made available in every school. Some people say that's unrealistic. But how can a just society settle for anything less?

Most people—perhaps even Joe Sixpack—will respond to logical, well-reasoned arguments. We need to establish a concise, rock-solid rationale for music education that will be persuasive, and we can't afford to be shy in trying to convince others of the correctness of our views. And we need to focus especially on those persons in decision-making roles that affect the education of young people. After all, what's at stake here is nothing less than the future itself.

At the same time we have to be certain that our programs are consistent with the benefits we assert for music education. If we claim to teach music because music is an important aspect of our cultural heritage, then we must select music for teaching that is truly representative of the best our heritage has to offer. If we claim to teach music because music is inherently worth knowing, then we must select music that is indeed worth knowing. If we claim to teach music because it enables our students to develop their creativity, then we must provide settings in which they can indeed do so, and that doesn't happen when every decision is made by the teacher.

Music exalts the human spirit. It enhances the quality of life. It transforms the human experience, and it brings joy and beauty and pleasure to human beings in every society and every culture. Music is vitamin M. Music is one of the most basic instincts in humans, and that's why it has played a major role in the cultural fabric of every known civilization, and it will continue to do so as far into the future as anyone can see. The only question is whether we want to limit access to music skills and knowledge to an elite few or whether we want to make them available to everyone to enjoy. I think the answer is obvious. Music belongs to everyone. Every student should have access to music instruction in school—did I mention that? Why? Because music is a chocolate chip in the cookie of life.

References

Adler, M. (1982). *The Paideia [sic] proposal: An educational manifesto*. New York: Macmillan.

Adler, M. (1983). *Paideia problems and possibilities: A consideration of questions raised by The Paideia proposal*. New York: Macmillan.

Adler, M. (1984). *The Paideia program: An educational syllabus*. New York: Macmillan.

Goodlad, J. (1984). *A place called school.* New York: McGraw-Hill.

National Education Commission on Time and Learning (April 1994). *Prisoners of time.* Washington: U.S. Government Printing Office.

www.ingramcontent.com/pod-product-compliance
Lightning Source LLC
Chambersburg PA
CBHW070300010526
44108CB00039B/1254